Relationships:
The Marriage and Family Reader

Jeffrey P. Rosenfeld

Nassau Community College

Scott, Foresman and Company   Glenview, Illinois

Dallas, Tex.   Oakland, N.J.   Palo Alto, Cal.
Tucker, Ga.   London, England

To Susan, because of our relationship

Library of Congress Cataloging in Publication Data

Main entry under title:

Relationships, the marriage and family reader.

Includes bibliographies.
1. Family—United States—Addresses, essays,
lectures. 2. Marriage—United States—Addresses, essays, lectures. I. Rosenfeld,
Jeffrey P. II. Title.
HQ536.R445   306.8   81-8941
ISBN 0-673-15267-7 (pbk.)   AACR2

Preface

The 1960s and 70s were years when privacy went public, so to speak, and everyone became aware that marriage and family life were in transition. In retrospect, it was a noisy transition. People expressed their sexual needs more openly than they had in the past, and they publicly entered into living arrangements and life-styles which would have drawn disapproval even ten years earlier. There was a great deal of public rejoicing as people celebrated everything from gay liberation to communal living. There was also a great deal of suffering as divorce and teenage pregnancy became epidemic.

Yet in the 1980s, it has become apparent that the family as a social institution, while in transition, is by no means on the verge of collapse. *Relationships: The Marriage and Family Reader* tries to capture some of the optimism which has already begun to surface; in addition, it is a serious attempt to amass data and theoretical justifications for this perspective. It offers a collection of readings on marriage and the family, dealing as well with alternative life-styles. Throughout the book there are selections concerned with the strengths and weaknesses of existing arrangements and with possible alternatives to conventional love, parenting, and kinship.

Relationships: The Marriage and Family Reader gives special attention to changes associated with the American population structure and how it is evolving, or what is called *demographics*. Selections in Part 1, for example, deal mostly with the impact of fertility, mortality, and migration on families past and present. Together these essays make the point that the day-to-day experience of marrying, parenting, and living as members of a family are contingent upon ways in which a population is physically dispersed and socially structured.

Part 5 touches base with demographics once again; but this time the purpose is to show how increased longevity is affecting the social experience of older Americans, their offspring, and kin. The materials in this section reflect the growing awareness of midlife as a period in the family cycle when people can evaluate their roles as parents and as marriage partners more critically than they could when they (and their families) were younger. In addition, there are readings which discuss the

Graying of America, offering reasons why this demographic trend will create new relationships among family members and contribute to the disappearance of some traditional ones.

Parenting comes under consideration at many points in this collection of readings. Apart from the selections on early parenting, there is special emphasis on interaction between older parents and their adolescent offspring. A future problem may not be teenaged runaways so much as the young people who cannot or will not leave home.

The final section of this reader is called "Rearranging" in order to give attention to the serious social problems that reflect the ugliest and most dismal side of family life—violence and chronic unemployment, and to the social strain caused by divorce and remarriage.

This book has been assembled for an undergraduate audience, but its appeal is to a more general readership as well. The issues it identifies are timely and, more important, will be the ones that determine the nature of marriage and family systems in our society.

Relationships: The Marriage and Family Reader would never have been possible without the thoughtful and critical comments of Deborah Biele, Cecile Shore, and Coleen Caputo. Naomi Gertsel deserves special thanks for pinpointing weaknesses and strengths in an earlier draft. Her comments led to major revisions.

It is also important to thank John Gagnon for countless hours spent talking with me about marriage and the family and to David Knox for having the faith in me to suggest that I undertake this project. Throughout the preparation of this book I received help, criticism, and pointers of all sorts from William Feigelman. A good officemate tolerates fallout as papers and manuscripts spread uninvited onto his desk. Apart from being a good officemate, Bill is a good colleague, and I give him thanks.

I owe more than mere thanks to Rose Laub Coser and Hanan C. Selvin. Together they helped to give me a foundation in theory and research methods which I appreciate more with every project I undertake. I feel fortunate to have had, as a graduate student, the encouragement of two extraordinary mentors. Only Rose Coser will understand what I mean when I say that studying for my doctorate was actually training in ambiguity, and so I will end this litany with private and special thanks to her.

My wife Susan already appreciates how much I needed her help and encouragement. That there is a *Relationships* at all is testimony to her ability and perceptive comments. She has been teacher, editor, and friend.

Contents

Attraction

Involvements

3 MARRIAGE

Coping

Working

Belonging

The Graying of American Families

6 REARRANGING

Disruptions

Divorce and Remarriage

1
FAMILIES IN
SOCIAL PERSPECTIVE

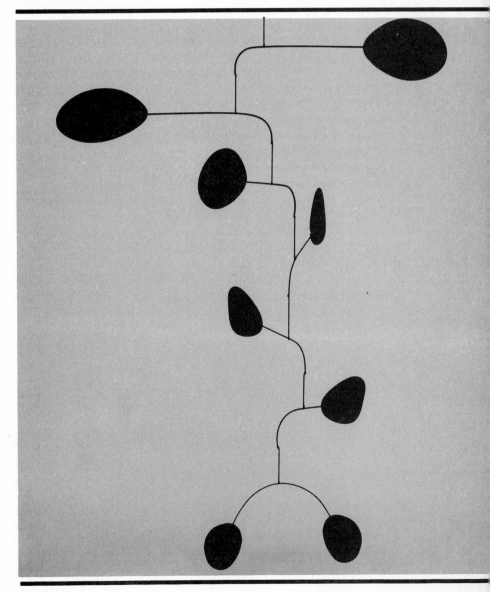

Not long ago, a woman from Wyandanch, New York, sued the local hospital for allegedly sending her home with the wrong baby.[1] The hospital claims that such mix-ups are impossible because every mother and newborn infant receives identification bracelets while they are still in the delivery room. This woman is seeking $5 million in damages nonetheless. Even though she loves the child, who by now is two years old, she is furious at the prospect of having mothered the wrong baby all this time.

While most of us are not so mistaken about the origins of our immediate families, we probably foster some exaggerated ideas about the origins and evolution of marriage and family life in general. Social researchers are already reconsidering how families were once structured and what they once contributed to the larger social order. Everything from average size of household to boundaries separating home and work is being reevaluated due to research on the family in the past. The first section in Part 1 has been called "Precedents," in an attempt to convey some of this pathfinding research.

Barbara Laslett challenges assumptions as influential as the belief that family and work parted company soon after the Industrial Revolution. In "Family Membership, Past and Present," Laslett demonstrates how the changing composition of households made them more emotionally charged than they ever were before. Working from data on household composition and using information about the size and structure of American kinship systems, she demonstrates that families were not always as psychologically intense as they are today. Smaller size and increased responsibility for socializing the young help explain this. Laslett concludes with the reminder that family membership has become increasingly important for people in American society, despite incessant cries that the family is moribund.

"Two Worlds In One," by Elizabeth Pleck, challenges the assumption that industrial growth resulted in the separation of home and work throughout society. Pleck maintains that the separation of these social spheres was confined mainly to middle-class families, despite the belief that it occurred in families at every socioeconomic level. Even after the world of work emerged in its own right, says Pleck, the family continued doing nonmarket work. "One cannot study the relationship between work and family if it is assumed that the connections are only tangential . . . ," Pleck insists. The family continued to be a source of production during the period of early capitalist growth, although it did so in unobtrusive ways.

If impressions of the family in the past are being reassessed, they are under no less scrutiny than prospects for the future. The section called

---

1. Shawn G. Kennedy, "L.I. Hospital Being Sued on Alleged Baby Switch," *New York Times,* 21 June 80, p. 26.

"Prospects" begins with an essay by Paul C. Glick, who is optimistic about prospects for the American family in years to come. It may well be true, admits Glick in "The Future of the American Family," that young people are postponing marriage, are having fewer children when they do marry, and are participating in more diverse living arrangements than ever before. But such trends only indicate that the American family is adaptive and flexible. Glick relies upon standard demographics, drawn largely from the U.S. Census, in order to reach these conclusions. Yehudi Cohen arrives at basically the same conclusion, although he gets there by analyzing a more unorthodox subject: the incest taboo. In "The Disappearance of the Incest Taboo," Cohen speculates that there could be social conditions when even the most rigid proscriptions, such as incest regulations, will change. Yet Cohen remarks that proscriptions survive even in changed forms. Glick and Cohen both predict enormous changes in the years to come, but are optimistic that the family has a future.

When families past and future have been dissected, there is still the present state of affairs—the existing social structure—to consider. Blake and Bengtson provide complementary perspectives on the current status of American families in the third section of Part One, "Social Structure." According to Blake, in "Structural Differentiation and the Family," some traditional boundaries separating the family from the larger society— what she calls *structural differentiation*—have already begun to crumble. Barriers between home and work, marriage and nonmarriage, even legitimacy and illegitimacy are eroding, and with them go justifications for existing differences in status and power between the sexes. Bengtson adds that most current talk of a "generation gap" must be reconsidered in light of social, historical, and personal experience. He maintains in "A Generation Gap? Research Perspectives on Ways that Generations Interact," that the best way to understand generations, and so-called gaps between them, is to focus on a unit of population known as the *cohort:* people of similar age who pass through the social structure at the same time. Whereas Blake examines differences and similarities between the sexes, Bengtson does so with generations. Together, their research helps put relationships between men and women of all ages in social perspective.

Precedents

Family Membership, Past and Present*
Barbara Laslett

Changes in household composition, in the demography of kinship and in the relationship between the family and other institutions have contributed, through their impact on the socialization process, to the greater emotional significance of the family in the present compared to the past. Changes in ideology have also reinforced the belief that family relationships have become more important for individual development, self-definition and satisfaction in life. In showing the causes for this development, however, I do not support either a sentimental view of the contemporary family nor indicate that the family is successful in satisfying the demands which its increased importance imposes upon it. It is precisely this disparity—between expectations structurally and normatively encouraged and the ability to satisfy them—which is central to understanding the contradictions in contemporary family life in both its traditional and non-traditional forms.

■ Recent sociological discussions of the family have a curiously contradictory character. The growth of a counter-culture in the 1960's and early 1970's both rejected and posed alternatives to traditional forms of the family (Skolnick, 1973). Interpreting student and anti-war activism as a failure in the family's abilities to provide coherent socialization

"Family Membership, Past and Present" by Barbara Laslett from SOCIAL PROBLEMS, vol. 25, no. 5, June 1978. Copyright © 1979 by the Society for the Study of Social Problems, Inc. Reprinted by permission.

*Prepared for a USC-NEH Colloquium on "The American Family: Its Changing Images and Social Implications," February, 1977. I wish to acknowledge with much appreciation, Edna Bonacich, Rachel Kahn-Hut and Carol Warren for their helpful comments and criticisms on earlier versions of this paper.

experience for its children (Flacks, 1971) led people to question the adequacy of family norms and traditional family life. To use Arlene Skolnick's (1973) phrase, the nuclear family was thought to be "alive, but not well." In contrast to this view, other discussions of the contemporary family emphasize its robustness. Mary Jo Bane (1976:xiv), for instance, concluded that the demographic data she analyzed show "surprising evidence of the persistence of commitments to family life . . ." —that the family is "here to stay."

Marriage and divorce statistics mirror the apparent contradictions exemplified by these views. In the United States, marriage continues to be an exceedingly popular institution. A comparison of marriage rates in twenty-two selected countries (Carter and Glick, 1976:387) show that in 1965, only Egypt had a higher marriage rate than the United States, while in every year between 1970 and 1974, the United States rate was higher than that of any other country included in their comparison.[1] Of course the high rate of marriage in the United States may well be affected by the fact that Americans also have the highest divorce rate compared to seventeen of these same countries. Although there has been a slight decline in the American remarriage rate since 1974, the divorce rate has been increasing steadily since 1965 (Carter and Glick, 1976:391). Nevertheless, Bane suggests (1976:34) that "it is not marriage itself but the specific marital partner that is rejected."

In addition to marriage and divorce statistics, other aspects of family life have been attracting public and professional interest. Whether the increasing attention to family violence (Steinmetz and Straus, 1975; Gelles, 1974; Steinmetz, 1977) indicates a higher incidence of violence or simply more public discussion of it is difficult to know; in either case, child and wife battering are clear indications of family "troubles." Even the rise in the professions of marriage and family therapy[2] can be interpreted in two ways—as indicating increasing difficulties within the family or of greater efforts to resolve problems. One may therefore ask, why is the contemporary family "not well—but here to stay?"

Several answers have been given to why the family is not well. Skolnick (1973), for instance, suggests that earlier conceptualizations tended to sentimentalize the family and its relationships, to view the family in utopian terms, and to ignore the strains and conflicts which daily life involves. Only recently have conceptualizations derived from conflict theory been applied to family dynamics. Other answers have suggested that large-scale political and economic changes have contributed to the difficulties that the modern family now faces (Flacks, 1971; Zaretsky, 1976).

Functional theory, particularly Parsons, has provided one answer to why the family is "here to stay." The argument is familiar and emphasizes an increasing division of labor within and between social institutions—

structural differentiation—which has characterized the process of historical change. Under these conditions, the family has assumed a more
specialized set of functions for the larger society—that of primary
socialization agent for children and the stabilization of adult personalities.
Thus, "the family has become *a more specialized agency than before* . . .
but (is) not in any general sense less important, because the society is
dependent *more* exclusively on it for the performance of *certain* of its vital
functions" (Parsons and Bales, 1955:9–10).

Recent statements by social scientists elaborate upon this view of the
contemporary family's "socio-emotional specialization." Berger and
Kellner (1975), for instance, state that "marriage occupies a privileged
status among the significant validating relationships for adults in our
society." Providing a very Parsonian explanation for this development,
they say

*this character of marriage has its roots in much broader structural configurations
of our society. The most important of these, for our purpose, is the crystallization
of a so-called private sphere of existence . . . defined and utilized as the main
social area for the individual's self-realization.*

Weigert and Hastings (1977) also discuss the significance of the family's
specialized role when they say "the basic relationships of the nuclear
family . . . are central to the processes of identity formation . . ." And
Zaretsky (1976:30) introduces a class dimension into this characterization
of the contemporary family when he says

*under capitalism an ethic of personal fulfillment has become the property of the
masses of people . . . Much of this search for personal meaning takes place within
the family and is one reason for the persistence of the family in spite of the decline
of many of its earlier functions.*

Noting that in modern society the development of personal identity
and the satisfaction of personal needs have become specialized functions
of the family leaves two important questions unanswered: 1) how was
institutional differentiation at the macro-structural level transformed into
individual, emotional, expectations within the family, and 2) can the
family, in practice rather than solely in theory, satisfy the demands
assigned to it by its functional specialization? The following analysis will
address the first of these questions by drawing upon the results of recent
research in demographic and family history.[3]

The thesis presented here is that changes in household composition,
in the demography of kinship and in the relationship between the family
and other institutions have contributed to the greater emotional significance of the family through their impact on the socialization process.
These changes, since the end of the nineteenth century,[4] have caused
family membership in the United States to have increased significance for

personal identity and emotional gratification. (Aries, 1975, and Shorter, 1975, provide similar arguments about the European family.) In addition, changes in ideology have reinforced the belief that family relationships have become more important for individual development, self-definition, and satisfaction in life.

An analysis which shows *how* family membership has become more significant to individual identity does not, thereby, support a sentimental view, focused only on the positive results of domestic interaction. The intense feelings generated by intimate relationships can be positive or negative, and family relationships may be particularly vulnerable in this respect. In fact, when strong feelings are involved, conflict, abuse, and family dissolution may be more frequent.

Thus, to describe the history of the family's increased importance as a source of personal identity and satisfaction in life is not to say that it successfully satisfies the demands its increasing specialization and importance impose upon it. Several social scientists (Lasch, 1977; Slater, 1970, 1977) have suggested that inherent contradictions within the family make its success unlikely. It is precisely this disparity—between expectations structurally and normatively encouraged and the ability to satisfy them—which is central to understanding the contradictions in contemporary family life.

Family Structure and Socialization

Recent research on the history of the family in Western Europe and North America shows that the membership of most households, both past and present, was—and is—composed primarily of nuclear family members. (See, for instance, Anderson, 1971; Demos, 1970; Greven, 1970; Katz, 1975; P. Laslett, 1972, 1977; Parish and Schwartz, 1972; Blumin, 1975; B. Laslett, 1975, 1977.) It is important, however, to distinguish the family, defined in terms of the co-resident domestic group, from the kinship group extending beyond the household.

The most frequently used data for investigating the structure of family life in past times are parish records, and census and other types of nominal listings, which usually report information on the co-resident domestic group. Empirical research findings on kinship ties beyond the household are more difficult to obtain and fewer are available. (For some examples, see Anderson, 1971; Plakans, 1977.) While the use of findings about the organization of the co-resident domestic group to discuss family structure in past times has been defended by some scholars (P. Laslett, 1972), its limitations have been criticized by others (Berkner, 1975). Conclusions based on household-level data clearly provide only partial information, since the residential unit is but one way to define the family. (See Goody, 1972, for a further discussion of this issue.)

Dispute over the proper—and possible—unit of analysis in historical family research contributes to contradictory interpretations about how the family has changed. While, as has been suggested, several social scientists argue that the family has become increasingly important, others take an opposite view. Wells (1971:278) in discussing the effects of demographic change on the life cycle of American families, says that there has been a "relative decrease in the importance of children in the life of twentieth-century families . . ." Kobrin (1976) makes a similar argument in relation to the increased proportion of persons living alone in the twentieth century.

There is reason to question these conclusions, however, since some of the same demographic factors on which they are based have increased the availability of kin with whom contact is both possible and likely to occur—particularly parents and grandparents. Although child-rearing as traditionally defined—the care of pre-adult, resident children—may occupy a smaller proportion of the family life cycle in contemporary America than was true in the past, advances in the technology relevant for contact and communication—such as automobiles, highway systems, telephones—mean that residence may no longer be central to the continuation of relationships among family members.

Given the scarcity of empirical research on the non-residential family in the past, the following discussion will present the results of two research traditions not usually related to each other. It will first examine findings on the household unit and then the demographic changes which have affected the size and structure of the kinship group. The impact of migration and urbanization on the availability of family members will also be discussed. The relation between these research findings—and their importance for understanding the significance of family membership in contemporary society—will be integrated through a discussion of their possible effects on socialization within the family.

Household Composition

As indicated, the nuclear family was in past times the predominant type of co-residential domestic group. This finding does not imply that all people lived in nuclear families for all of their lives; life cycle variation in the kin composition of the residential family has been found in several historical studies (Goody, 1972; Hareven, 1975; Herlihy, 1972; Berkner, 1972; B. Laslett, 1975). Household structure has also been shown to be related to socio-economic characteristics of the head of the household, demographic factors, ethnicity, land-holding patterns and inheritance practices (Glasco, 1975; Gutman, 1976; Katz, 1975; Coale et al, 1965; B. Laslett, 1975, 1977; Farber, 1972; Berkner and Mendels, in press, Furstenberg et al., 1975). Despite these sources of variation, there continues to be support for the view that the nuclear family household was, and is, the modal category of the co-resident domestic group in most western societies in both the pre-industrial past and under contemporary forms of social and economic organization.

While predominantly nuclear in its kinship structure, the pre-industrial and early industrial household was also likely to include others unrelated to the conjugal family unit. Among such persons were servants, boarders and lodgers, apprentices, employees, and other people's children.[5] (B. Laslett, 1973; Blumin, 1975; Kobrin, 1976) Modell and Hareven (1973) show that "the proportion of urban households *which at any particular point in time* had boarders or lodgers was between fifteen and twenty percent."[6] Today, on the contrary, non-kin are unlikely to be included among the membership of many households. In 1970, only 3.5% of all households included in the federal census had one or more resident members unrelated to the head (U.S. Bureau of the Census, 1973:246).

One characteristic distinguishing the contemporary household from domestic settings in the past, therefore, is that few now contain non-relatives. But in nineteenth century America, interaction with non-kin outside the household was likely to be supplemented by contact with resident non-kin. A large proportion of persons interacted with non-kin as part of the daily life within their homes. Although the qualitative character of such contact cannot be known solely from this kind of evidence—the extent to which non-relatives were integrated into the family's life and affairs—non-kin shared the household where many nineteenth century children and adults lived.

Under contemporary conditions, socialization within the household refers primarily to interactions between parents and their children. The psycho-dynamic structure of this process is, therefore, likely to reflect the personalities and personal histories of individuals linked together by family ties. Thus, identification and role modeling—the processes involved in the psycho-dynamic structure of personality development—are defined primarily by characteristics of individuals within the nuclear family group and become identified with membership in a specific family unit. There is a strong imprint of family membership.

This feature of contemporary household composition has relevance for various stages of growth throughout the life cycle, during which themes develop, are enacted, and become identified with a particular family. According to Hess and Handel (1967:18):

A family theme is a pattern of feelings, motives, fantasies, and conventionalized understanding grouped about some locus of concern which has a particular form in the personalities of the individual members. The pattern comprises some fundamental view of reality and some way or ways of dealing with it. In the family themes are to be found the family's implicit direction, its notion of 'who we are' . . .

Development and reiteration of such themes is likely to provide the basis for a more heightened sense of differentiation between family and non-family members in the present than in the past, when households included both kin and non-kin.

In adolescence, the influence of non-kin was likely to continue, but was due as much to the adolescents' moving as to the household composition of their families of origin, for adolescence in earlier times was marked by the removal of young adults from their parents' homes. They left to find work, to become servants and apprentices and, some have argued, to get an education and build character (Morgan, 1944; Demos, 1970; Shorter, 1975). This pattern seems to have occurred in various parts of Western Europe (see, for instance, Anderson, 1971; McBride, 1976; Schofield, 1970; Shorter, 1975) and North America (Bloomberg, 1974; Dublin, 1975; Katz, 1975; Little and Laslett, 1977).

Recent historical research shows (Katz, 1975; Bloomberg, 1974; Little and Laslett, 1977) that in the late nineteenth century, at least in the industrializing economies of the new world, adolescents experienced a lengthening period of dependency upon their parents. Prior to that time, many spent their adolescence outside the parental home. Of course visiting home and parents was possible and did take place although how often depended on the terms of the contract governing the life of the servant or apprentice as well as the distance involved. Thus, contact with kin for many adolescents and young adults in the past was more likely to be a special occasion than a daily or weekly occurrence.[7]

These aspects of household composition are likely to have influenced the socialization process of both adults and children in the past, as they do in the present. We can see the significance of these structural changes most clearly in relation to adolescence—a period characterized in contemporary psychological thought (Erikson, 1959) by a search for a separate identity on the part of young adults. The increased identification of the self with a particular family unit, and the greater clarity of boundaries between family and non-family members, may have increased the need to differentiate one's self from the family group as part of the transition to adulthood, thereby sharpening parent-child conflict during adolescence.[8] Furthermore, the wish to establish one's own identity is more likely to be experienced by both parents and children as a rejection of and rebellion against the more clearly formulated identity with a particular family. Thus, the search for a separate identity involves questioning parental norms and authority, since it is parents who symbolize in the strongest emotional terms, the norms and authority of the adult world.

Understanding the impact of household composition on socialization within the family should not be limited to the young people involved. Under the conditions of contemporary family living, parents are also more likely than in the past to develop strong identification with their children.

Each of the child's developmental stages poses developmental tasks for the parents as well, reawakening themes and conflicts from their own youth and posing the psychological tasks associated with aging. It is not surprising that two contemporary concerns of psycho-dynamic thought center simultaneously on problems of adolescence and "mid-life crisis." These "crises of growth" reflect the increased intensity of family relationships and the increased importance of family membership for personal identity to which historical changes in household composition have contributed.

Demography and Kinship

Three demographic factors are of particular importance in comparing the size and structure of the kinship group in past and present western societies: mortality, age-at-marriage, and fertility. Although several types of kin will be considered, ascendant kin are most relevant for discussing the availability of persons intentionally likely to assume roles in the socialization process, particularly for children.[9]

Mortality

In the past, people simply did not live long enough to form a sizeable pool of older relatives with whom contact was possible. In 1900, the expectation of life at birth (for the white population) in the United States was 48.2 years for males and 51.1 years for females. In 1970, these figures had risen to 68.0 years for males and 75.6 years for females. (U.S. Bureau of the Census, 1975:56). While some nineteenth century American mortality data is available, questions have been raised about its adequacy (Vinovskis, 1972, 1974); the decline in mortality in the twentieth century, however, when vital registration data have become increasingly available, is clearer (see Taeuber and Taeuber, 1958).

Although infant mortality made a major contribution to death rates in earlier times, higher mortality in the past affected adults as well as infants. At age twenty, the expectation of life of white males was 42.4 additional years in 1900 and 50.3 additional years in 1970; the comparable figures for white women are 43.8 and 57.4 additional years, respectively. (U.S. Bureau of the Census, 1976:56). One consequence of the changing mortality rates is that "the chances that today's typical bride and groom will both survive the next fifty years (to their golden wedding anniversary) are more than twice as great as were the chances of such survival for their counterparts in 1900–02" (Metropolitan Life, February, 1976). Thus, fewer parents and grandparents were available in earlier historical periods to participate in the socialization of their children and grandchildren.

Differential mortality by sex is also relevant to kin contacts. In twentieth century America, there has been an increasing sex difference in life expectancy. While the length of life (at birth and older ages) of both sexes has increased between 1900 and 1970, the increase for women has been greater than the increase for men, as the expectation of life figures quoted earlier indicated. Findings from contemporary research on the family (Adams, 1968:167) show the importance of parents for continued kin contact among their adult children; when parents are alive, contact is greater than after the parents' deaths. The mother's survival may be particularly important in this respect, since women are more active in maintaining family ties (Adams, 1968:27–28). Since women have greater longevity than men, contacts among related adults may be sustained even longer than would be likely without this pattern of differential life expectancy by sex.[10]

Age-at-Marriage

The median age at first marriage in the United States in 1890 was 26.1 years for men and twenty-two years for women; in 1950 it was 22.8 and 20.3 years (U.S. Bureau of the Census, 1976:19) and in 1974 it was 23.1 and 21.1 years, respectively. (U.S. Bureau of the Census, 1974:1). The late nineteenth century figures may well represent the high point of an upward trend, since available data indicated that people married younger in the colonial period. (See Wells, 1972 for colonial America, as well as Britain and France at a comparable time period; Farber, 1972; and Sklar, 1974, for late nineteenth and early twentieth century European data.) In the twentieth century, however, compared to the late nineteenth, children are born earlier in their parent's life span and are more likely to survive. Under such circumstances, family members will be available both for more of the individual's life, because of increases in life expectancy of the older generation, and for greater periods of the family life cycle because new families begin at earlier ages.[11]

Fertility

While the pool of potential kin may be affected by declining mortality and age-at-first marriage, changing fertility rates are also relevant for estimating the size and structure of the kinship group in the present compared to the past. Fertility in the United States has declined (see Coale and Zelnik, 1963; Taeuber and Taeuber, 1957). The question is whether lowered fertility offsets the effects of decreased mortality, so that the number of living relatives per family in the present is no different from in the past.

Historical data to answer this question directly are not available. Goodman, Keyfitz and Pullum (1974), however, provide suggestive material in their estimates of the number of surviving female relatives of different types given the fertility and mortality of the United States in 1967 and Madagascar in 1966, that is, a country with low fertility and low mortality—the modern demographic profile—compared to a society with high fertility and high mortality—the pre-industrial patterns.[12] This analysis shows that three factors are relevant for estimating the number of female kin alive under the two demographic regimes: the age of the woman, the distance of the kinship link between a woman and her relative and whether the relative is an ascendant, descendant, or lateral kin. In general, the results show that in societies with low fertility and low mortality, older relatives are more available and younger relatives are less available. Although some lateral relatives would also be less available under western, industrial demographic conditions, the difference is small. The advantage in terms of the size of the kinship pool does not appear to be marked for one type of society compared to another. Gray's (1977) application of the Goodman, Keyfitz, and Pullum model to 1920, 1930, and 1970 U.S. demographic rates shows, however, that to the extent that there is a difference, more living kin are available to contemporary Americans than was true in earlier periods.

If one differentiates between relatives nòt in terms of generation but in terms of relational proximity to an individual, another aspect of the kinship structure emerges. The only categories of kin where Goodman, Keyfitz, and Pullum show that the high fertility, high mortality society has a marked advantage over the low fertility, low mortality society is in terms of cousins and granddaughters. Data on social contact between kin in the contemporary United States (Adams, 1968) suggest that interaction is most frequent between closest kin (parents, children and siblings) and falls off sharply as one moves further away from primary bonds. Demos (1970:124) found that the most significant kin connections in Plymouth colony were also those between members of the primary family unit. In the absence of primary family members, however, more distant kin may have been of greater importance (see Greven, 1970). It should be remembered, however, that migration—a significant feature of American life throughout its history—is higher among younger adults. Although proportionately more young adults may have been alive under pre-industrial demographic conditions, their availability for purposes of interaction with other family members may not have been as great as numbers alone would suggest.

The demographic factors reviewed have implications for understanding patterns of family interaction and the processes of socialization both within the household and the extended kin group. Glick (1977) says that "the larger the family the larger proportion of time that children are likely to spend interacting with each other, whereas the smaller the family the greater the proportion of time the children are likely to spend interacting with their parents . . ." Thus, changes in mortality, fertility, and age-at-marriage, as well as changes in household composition, are likely to affect the processes of role modeling and identification that occur within the contemporary family. It is likely to increase the impact of parents in the socialization process. Despite the increased proportion of mothers in the labor force, the overwhelming proportion of children are cared for by their own parents or other relatives, rather than by non-relatives (U.S. Bureau of the Census, 1976). Furthermore demographic changes have also resulted in the availability of more ascendant kin, particularly grandparents, uncles, and aunts, who may elaborate the meaning of kinship throughout the individual life cycle. Given the increased importance of family membership established in the early years of the socialization process, for both children and adults, and the means of contact and communication which technological advances have made available, common residence is no longer likely to be as significant a determinant contact as in earlier historical periods.

Urbanization and Migration

Two factors relevant to the distribution of population also affect the availability of kin with whom contact may occur: (1) urbanization and (2) migration. Although rapid urbanization has been a feature in the American experience since the early nineteenth century (Potter, 1974), the twentieth century has witnessed an increasing concentration of population in large urban centers. Kin may be concentrated in areas where fairly frequent contact is easier to make, and harder to avoid, because of the expansion of the highway system, the widespread availability of automobiles, air travel, and the telephone.

Migration, a characteristic of American life both in the past and present (Lee, 1964:127), has often been used to explain the absence of kin contact among mobile populations. The act of migration (particularly overseas migration) reduces the pool of potential kin available both to the migrant and the non-migrant. Furthermore, the process of internal (vs. overseas) migration can also thin the ranks of kin with whom contact is possible. Here again, literacy and the technology of communication are important, for once a relative leaves a community, contact between family members depends on the available modes of communication. But the impact of migration may also depend on whether it occurs early or late in the historical development of an area.

In earlier generations, migrating family members established themselves in places which did not include members of their own kin group. The potential for kin contact was reduced or eliminated because of migration. First generation migrants would be most lacking in ascendant kin since migration typically occurs among the younger categories. (See, U.S. Bureau of the Census, 1976:122, for data on foreign immigrants by age between 1820 and 1970.) The likelihood that kin would be found in the place of destination of the next generation of migrants, however, is increased by the simple fact that earlier migration of family members had occurred. Nineteenth as well as twentieth century migrants have been shown to choose their destinations in part because of the presence of kin group members in the new area (Hareven, 1975; McLaughlin, 1971; Hendrix, 1975, 1976). Thus, migration, particularly under modern technological conditions, does not necessarily reduce contact to the degree suggested by earlier authors, although it does, perhaps, render it voluntary (Shorter, 1975).

To summarize, structural factors have created the potential for family membership to become a more salient feature of personal identity in the contemporary period compared to the western, pre-industrial past through its effect on socialization within the household, on the increased number of ascendant kin, and the spatial distribution of the kin group. In addition, developments in the technology of contact and communication and increased literacy make it easier for family members to be in touch with each other whether or not they live close together.

In the earlier period, the co-resident domestic group was less often confined to primary kin group members, while in the present context, more households contain nuclear family members only. Thus, within the home, non-kin are not as likely to diffuse identification with a particular family. Greater numbers of ascendant kin outside the home are available to amplify the identification developed within it.

The Ideology of Family Life

Beliefs about family life in contemporary American society tend to reflect and reinforce the intimacy and intensity which residential and demographic factors make possible. The early Puritan ideology in America emphasized the role of the family as guardian of the public, as well as the private, good. Not only did religion specify the approved relationships between family members—their duties and responsibilities to each other—but it also made it a sacred duty of church members to see that edicts were carried out. It was not sufficient for people to be moral in public—they also had to be moral in private, and religion provided a legitimating ideology for minding other people's family affairs.

In contrast to these beliefs, the idea of the private family and the home as a personal sanctuary grew throughout the nineteenth century. Family life began to be characterized as an oasis, a retreat, a haven from the uncertainties, immoralities, and strains of life in a rapidly changing society (Jeffrey, 1972; Sennett, 1970). Elder's (1974) suggestion that "the family as refuge" was one reaction of American families to the Depression of the 1930's indicates that this theme has continued within the twentieth century. Insecurities in public roles and disappointments in the occupational sphere—made all the more painful, perhaps, by a political ideology which emphasizes individual success and advancement—reinforced a belief in the family as the only place where meaningful relationships are possible.

The theme of the family as a retreat can also be found in recent discussions of contemporary non-traditional family forms such as communes and open marriages (Sussman, 1972). These alternative family forms are thought to provide the opportunity for deep and meaningful personal relationships to a greater extent than other types of family living. Thus, the family continues to be seen as a haven from the large society. Sussman (1972:8) says:

Life is for meaningful relationships on a micro-level where one can control one's own destiny or at least not be subordinated; a level which provides numerous options and optimal freedom for deep relationships.

The ideology of family living, even in its most avant garde form, continues to emphasize the importance of the family as a refuge from the larger society. This perspective is based on the belief that it is only within the family that a sense of personal control and intimacy can be found (also see, Zaretsky, 1976). Whether or not this belief and the needs it expresses can actually be satisfied within the family is another issue.

The relationship of the family to other social institutions reinforces the search for meaning within the family. One of the features said to characterize modern industrial societies, compared to those which preceded them historically, is an increase in the importance of achieved versus ascribed attributes. In the life of families in Andover, Mass., in the seventeenth century (Greven, 1970), access to arable land was crucial to the adult life of sons. The father's control over land affected many aspects of the son's adult behavior—including when he could marry. The growth of an occupational system emphasizing an individual's educational achievement, and the increasing availability of public education, have loosened the constraints which past authority patterns and practices were likely to impose (Goode, 1963). Family contacts may therefore be less crucial to achieving one's place in the modern occupational world.

But the very fact that family contacts may no longer play such an important part in placing individuals in their public social roles—thus reducing the instrumental usefulness of kin contacts—may serve to increase their socio-emotional importance. In a society whose ideology values individual achievement and scorns nepotism, family membership may be prized simply because it does not have to be earned. The ascribed character of family membership may be experienced as a positive attribute for the very reason that it can be "taken for granted."

The socialization that occurs within the twentieth century American family is likely to contribute to the "taken for granted" character of family relationships. As the differentiation between the norms, values, and location of the family compared to other institutions has increased, the differences between the family and other areas of social life have sharpened. The contemporary family's private character (B. Laslett, 1973) by providing a "backstage area" (Goffman, 1959) where persons can relax from performing their public roles, contributes to an ideology that defines the family primarily in socio-emotional terms. What is frequently forgotten in these formulations, is that performers not only relax backstage, but they also prepare for—and sometimes rehearse—their public roles. Thus, the potentially contradictory and confusing messages communicated within the domestic setting can create discrepancies between the ideology and actuality of contemporary family life.

Changes in economic organization within the general society may have affected the emotional meaning of family relationships in other ways. In the past, when the family was the unit of production as well as the unit of consumption, work and family roles were intertwined to a greater extent than in the present. The systematic separation of home and work activities which began in nineteenth century America, the decline in proprietorship in the contemporary period, and the increase in the salaried and bureaucratic sector of the economy (Blau and Duncan, 1967) means that fewer family members may be working together than was true in an earlier period. In the past, relations between employers and employees, masters and servants or apprentices, and parents and children shared greater emotional similarity than is true today (see P. Laslett, 1971; Farber, 1972; Douglas, 1921:55). But it is precisely a decline in the intertwining of what we now see as diverse social roles which permits the intensification of the emotional aspects of family relationships.

A similar argument can be made in relation to the family as educator. Before public schooling was widely available, much education occurred in the home (Cremin, 1974). Removing the requirement that parents teach, monitor, and correct their children's intellectual development reduces potential conflict between aspects of their behavior as parents. Today, parents do not have to satisfy the sometimes contrary demands of expecting achievement in the sphere of cognitive development while simultaneously providing socio-emotional resources for their children's psychological development.

This argument is not meant to imply that parents are less concerned about the educational achievement of their children. The opposite may be true. (See LeVine, 1974, for a discussion of how parents' goals for their children affect child-rearing behavior.) Alice Rossi (1968) has suggested that in the absence of clear-cut standards, mothers and fathers often use children's report cards and pediatrician's reports to judge their performance as parents. But the availability of institutions to foster their children's attainment of instrumental skills outside the home permits and encourages a greater concentration on the affective character of the relationships within it.

Structural conditions within the household which contribute to the increased emotional intensity of contemporary parent-child relations, are reinforced by the relations between the family and other social institutions. Children's educational and occupational attainments are more likely to take on greater psychological meaning—to become reflections or extensions of parents' personal fantasies and ambitions. The possibility of testing these fantasies against reality—or understanding what makes fantasies or less possible ambitions—is not as available to modern parents who share less of an experiential world with their children than did parents in the pre-industrial period.

Social contact outside the residential unit may help to confirm or diminish the importance of family membership for personal identity. Frequent interaction between extended family members provides a basis for the continuing reaffirmation of the sense of membership generated within the residential family. Many studies since World War II show the importance of contact between kin compared to non-kin in the United States (Axelrod, 1956; Greer, 1956; Bell and Boat, 1957; Sussman and Burchinal, 1962; Lawson, 1974). Thus, the importance of kinship is not only theoretical. It is real, since it appears to provide the most significant basis for interaction when options are available. That this is true even when technology which makes contact easier also makes it a matter of choice (Shorter, 1975), is testimony to the salience of family membership in contemporary America.

Conclusions

The preceding analysis suggests that the significance of family membership has changed in the United States. Changes in household composition and the demography of kinship, in the technology of communication and the spread of literacy, in the ideology of family life and the relationship of the family to other social institutions have affected the process of socialization in ways increasing the family's salience in the formation of personal identity. Earlier fears that urbanization and industrialization would weaken "the bonds of kinship" (Wirth, 1938) have not been bourne out. To the contrary, the historical changes that have been described have resulted in an "intensified . . . weight of meaning attached to the personal relations of the family" (Zaretsky, 1976:66).

But if this has occurred, why are there the family problems and strains noted at the beginning of this paper? Weibert and Hastings (1977) suggest that the contemporary family's "specialized function of affectivity and expressivity for the sustenance of emotionally charged personal identities" also makes it a particularly powerful source of pain and conflict. In addition, the specialized and bureaucratic organization of modern life has made the family one of the few *locations* where the expression of strong feeling is legitimate, thus increasing the likelihood that emotionally charged interactions—both positive and negative—will occur.

Perhaps the most important question to be asked about the modern family is not whether it is "here to stay" but whether it can sustain and satisfy the search for meaning and the weight of expectation that it has come to have. The contradiction implied by saying the contemporary family is "here to stay, but not well" can be understood only when the second question posed at the beginning of this paper has been answered: Does, and can, the family have the resources—both material and emotional—to satisfy the demands which are placed upon it in contemporary American society?

Notes

1. The marriage rate has declined somewhat since 1972 but without changing the status of the United States compared to other countries.
2. In 1960, the membership of the American Association of Marriage and Family Counselors was 237; by 1976 it had risen to 4230. In every year since 1970 (at which time the membership was 973), the percentage annual increase in membership ranged from twenty-four percent to thirty-seven percent. (American Association of Marriage and Family Counselors, personal communication from administrative offices, Claremont, Calif.)
3. A more complete formulation, in which macro-economic changes will be more fully discussed, is in preparation as part of the author's study of the family and social change in nineteenth century Los Angeles. For a preliminary statement see B. Laslett, 1978b.
4. For this discussion, the twentieth century family will be contrasted with the family in earlier historical periods, with full recognition that such a gross dichotomy obscures variation in the rates and timing of the developments important for understanding how historical change has affected the family. See B. Laslett, 1973, for a discussion of why the twentieth century family can legitimately be differentiated from the family in earlier historical periods.
5. The periods of service, apprenticeship, and boarding common for young people in the pre-industrial Western experience was not usually spent in the homes of kinsmen, although by the beginning of the twentieth century, this may have begun to change.
6. Overall figures may underestimate the proportion of households which included "strangers" within the co-resident domestic group, since taking in boarders was related to the family life cycle. Modell and Hareven (1973), for instance, report that among a sample of native, working class families in the industrial north in 1890, twenty percent of the families with a resident child under five took in boarders if the household head

was under twenty-five years of age compared to thirty-five percent of the households with a child of comparable age but when the head was forty-five years of age or older. Berkner (1972) also finds life cycle variation in the presence of residence agricultural workers among eighteenth century peasant households in Austria.

Taking in boarders has usually been associated with urbanization (Modell and Hareven, 1973) and seems to have been higher in urban than rural areas (B. Laslett, 1977b). There is evidence, however, that it occurred in rural communities as well (Blumin, 1975; Roberts, 1904).

7. The implications of these changes in residence for the meaning of adolescence is discussed in Little and Laslett, 1977.

8. Modell et al. (1976) discuss other structural reasons which would explain the greater conflict associated with adolescence in contemporary society.

9. Demos (1972:656) points out the potential significance of older siblings in the socialization process of children in the large families found in Plymouth Colony. Shorter (1975:26), however, says that in Europe usually only two or three children were in residence simultaneously. Given the tendency for employment to begin at relatively young ages, it is older siblings who were most likely to have left their parents' home. The residence patterns of adolescents before the end of the nineteenth century (Bloomberg, 1974; Katz, 1975; Little and Laslett, 1977) suggests that the same may have been true in North America.

10. Linkages along the male line may be stronger when there are economic ties between fathers and their children. The decline in family businesses and self-employment (Blau and Duncan, 1967:41) in the twentieth century would thus lessen the salience of father-adult child contact.

11. The impact of age-at-marriage on the size of the kinship group is clearly seen where it has been early, not late, and where high fertility has been encouraged. See Gutman, 1976, for a discussion of these factors in relation to the black family.

12. It could be argued that contemporary Madagascar and pre-industrial America are so unlike that the Goodman, Keyfitz, and Pullum (1974) estimates cannot be used even suggestively. There are several reasons to reject this position: 1) the model is purely mathematical and takes account of no other characteristics of Madagascar society except its gross reproduction rate and expectation of life at birth. 2) The demographic rates used to generate the model's estimates for Madagascar are sufficiently close to the pre-industrial American figures to validate their usefulness as suggestive (although certainly not conclusive) indicators.

References

Adams, Bert N.
    1968   Kinship in an Urban Setting. Chicago, Markham
Anderson, Michael
    1971   Family Structure in Nineteenth Century Lancashire. Cambridge: Cambridge University Press.
Aries, Philippe
    1975   "La famille." Encounter 45 (August): 7–12.
Axelrod, Morris
    1956   "Urban structure and social participation." American Sociological Review 21 (February): 13–18.
Bane, Mary Jo
    1976   Here To Stay: American Families in the Twentieth Century. New York: Basic Books.

Bell, Wendell and Marion D. Boat
 1957   "Urban neighborhood and informal social relations." American Journal of Sociology 62 (January): 391–398.
Berger, Peter and Hansfried Kellner
 1975   "Marriage and the construction of reality." Pp. 219–233 in Dennis Brisset and Charles Edgley (eds.) Life As Theatre: A Dramaturgical Sourcebook. Chicago, Aldine.
Berkner, Lutz K.
 1972   "The stem family and the developmental cycle of the peasant household: An eighteenth-century Austrian example." American Historical Review 77 (April): 398–418.
 1975   "The use and misuse of census data for the historical analysis of family structure." Journal of Interdisciplinary History 6 (Spring): 721–738.
Berkner, Lutz K. and Franklin F. Mendels
 forth-   "Inheritance systems, family structure and demographic patterns in western
 coming   Europe (1700–1900)." Mimeographed.
Blau, Peter M. and O. D. Duncan
 1967   The American Occupational Structure. New York: John Wiley.
Bloomberg, Susan
 1974   "The household and the family: the effects of industrialization on skilled workers in Newark, 1840–1860." A paper presented at the meetings of the Organization of American Historians, Denver.
Blumin, Stuart M.
 1975   "Rip Van Winkle's grandchildren: Family and household in the Hudson Valley, 1800–1860." Journal of Urban History 1 (May): 293–315.
Carter, Hugh and Paul C. Glick
 1976   Marriage and Divorce: A Social and Economic Study, revised edition. Cambridge, Mass.: Harvard University Press.
Coale, Ansley J. and Melvin Zelnik
 1963   New Estimates of Fertility and Population in the United States. Princeton, N.J.: Princeton University Press.
Coale, Ansley J. et al
 1965   Aspects of the Analysis of Family Structure. Princeton, N.J.: Princeton University Press.
Cremin, Lawrence A.
 1974   "The family as educator: Some comments on the recent historiography." Teachers College Record 76 (December): 250–265.
Demos, John
 1970   A Little Commonwealth. New York: Oxford University Press.
 1972   "Demography and psychology in the historical study of family life: A personal report." Pp. 561–570 in Peter Laslett (ed.), Household and Family in Past Time. Cambridge: Cambridge University Press.
Douglas, Paul H.
 1921   American Apprenticeship and Industrial Education. Studies in History, Economics and Public Law XCI. New York: Columbia University Press.
Dublin, Thomas
 1975   "Women, work and the family: Women operatives in the Lowell Mills, 1830–1860." Feminist Studies 3 (Summer): 30–39.
Elder, Glen H., Jr.
 1974   Children of the Great Depression: Social Change in Life Experience. Chicago: University of Chicago Press.
Erikson, Erik H.
 1959   "Identity and the life cycle." Psychological Issues, 1.

Farber, Bernard
1972   Guardians of Virtue: Salem Families in 1800. New York: Basic Books.
Flacks, Richard
1971   Youth and Social Change. Chicago: Markham.
Furstenberg, Frank F., Jr., Theodore Hershberg and John Modell
1975   "The origins of the female-headed black family: The impact of the urban experience." Journal of Interdisciplinary History 6 (Autumn): 211–233.
Gelles, Richard J.
1974   The violent home: A study of physical agression between husbands and wives. Beverly Hills, Calif.: Sage Publications
Glasco, Laurence A.
1975   "The life cycle and household structure of American ethnic groups: Irish, Germans, and native-born whites in Buffalo, New York, 1855." Journal of Urban History 1 (May): 339–364.
Glick, Paul C.
1977   "Updating the life cycle of the family." Journal of Marriage and the Family 39 (February): 5–13.
Goode, William J.
1963   World Revolution and Family Patterns. New York: Free Press.
Goodman, Leo A., Nathan Keyfitz and Thomas W. Pullum
1974   "Family formation and the frequency of various kinship relationships." Theoretical Population Biology 5 (February): 1–27.
Goody, Jack
1972   "The evolution of the family." Pp. 103–124 in P. Laslett (ed.), Household and Family in Past Time. Cambridge: Cambridge University Press.
Gray, Anke Van Hilst
1977   "Who was really there? An historical look at available kin." An empirical paper presented to the Department of Sociology, University of Southern California.
Greer, Scott
1956   "Urbanism reconsidered." American Sociological Review 21 (February): 22–25.
Greven, Philip
1970   Four Generations: Population, Land and Family in Colonial Andover, Massachusetts. New York: Cornell University Press.
Gutman, Herbert G.
1976   The Black Family in Slavery and Freedom, 1750–1925. New York: Pantheon.
Hareven, Tamara K.
1975a   "Family time and industrial time: Family and work in a planned corporation town, 1900–1924." Journal of Urban History 1 (May): 365–389.
1975b   "The laborers of Manchester, New Hampshire, 1912–1922: The Role of Family and Ethnicity in Adjustment to Industrial Life." Labor History 16 (Spring): 249–265.
Hendrix, Lewellyn
1975   "Kinship and economic-rational migration: A comparison of micro- and macro-level analyses." Sociological Quarterly 16 (Autumn): 534–543.
1976   "Kinship, social networks, and integration among Ozark residents and out-migrants." Journal of Marriage and the Family 38 (February): 97–104.
Herlihy, David
1972   "Mapping households in medieval Italy." Catholic Historical Review 58 (April): 1–24.
Hess, Robert D. and Gerald Handel
1967   "The family as a psychosocial organization." Pp. 10–29 in Gerald Handel (ed.), The Psychosocial Interior of the Family: A Sourcebook for the Study of Whole Families. Chicago, Aldine.

Jeffrey, Kirk
  1972   "The family in Utopian retreat from the city: the nineteenth century contribution." Soundings 40 (Spring): 21–41.
Katz, Michael B.
  1975   The People of Hamilton, Canada West. Cambridge, Mass.: Harvard University Press.
Kobrin, Frances E.
  1976   "The fall in household size and the rise of the primary individual in the United States." Demography 31 (February): 127–138.
Lasch, Christopher
  1977   Haven in a Heartless World: The Family Besieged. New York: Basic Books.
Laslett, Barbara
  1973   "The family as a public and private institution: An historical perspective." Journal of Marriage and the Family 35 (August): 480–492.
  1975   "Household structure on an American frontier: Los Angeles, California in 1850." American Journal of Sociology 81 (July): 109–128.
  1977   "Social change and the family: Los Angeles, California, 1850–1870." American Sociological Review 42 (April): 269–291.
  1978a   "Household structure and the social organization of production: Los Angeles, California in 1850." A paper to be presented at the IXth World Congress of Sociology, Uppsala, Sweden.
  1978b   "Strategies for Survival: An historical perspective on the family and development." A paper to be presented at the IXth World Congress of Sociology, Uppsala, Sweden.
Laslett, Peter
  1971   The World We Have Lost. Second Edition. London: University Paperbacks.
  1972   Household and Family in Past Time. Cambridge: Cambridge University Press. (ed.)
  1977   Family Life and Illicit Love in Earlier Generations. Cambridge, Cambridge University Press.
Lawson, John E., Jr.
  1974   The Impact of the Local Metropolitan Environment on the Patterning of Social Contacts. Ph.D. dissertation, Dept. of Sociology, University of Southern California.
Lee, Everett S.
  1964   "Internal migration and population redistribution in the United States." Pp. 123–136 in Ronald Freedman (ed.), Population. The Vital Revolution. Garden City, New York: Anchor Books.
LeVine, Robert A.
  1974   "Parental goals: A cross-cultural view." Teachers College Record 76 (December): 226–239.
Little, Margaret and Barbara Laslett
  1977   "Adolescence in historical perspective: The decline of boarding in 19th century Los Angeles." A paper presented at the annual meetings of the American Sociological Association, Chicago.
McBride, Theresa M.
  1976   The Domestic Revolution: The Modernization of Household Service in England and France, 1820–1920. New York: Holmes and Meier.
McLaughlin, Virginia Yans
  1971   "Working class immigrant families: first generation Italians in Buffalo, New York." A paper delivered before the Organization of American Historians, New Orleans.

Metropolitan Life
1976   "Likelihood of a golden wedding anniversary." Statistical Bulletin, 57 (February): 4–7.

Modell, John and Tamara K. Hareven
1973   "Urbanization and the malleable household: an examination of boarding and lodging in American families." Journal of Marriage and the Family 35 (August): 467–479.

Modell, John, Frank Furstenberg and Theodore Hershberg
1976   "Social change and transitions to adulthood in historical perspective." Journal of Family History 1 (Autumn): 7–32.

Morgan, Edmund S.
1944   The Puritan Family. New York: Harper.

Parish, William L. and Moshe Schwartz
1972   "Household complexity in nineteenth-century France." American Sociological Review 37 (April): 154–173.

Parsons, Talcott and Robert F. Bales
1955   Family, Socialization and Interaction Process. Glencoe, Illinois: Free Press.

Plakans, Andrejs
1977   "Identifying kinfold beyond the household." Journal of Family History 2 (Spring): 3–27.

Potter, J.
1974   "Demography: the missing link in American history." A paper presented at the meetings of the Organization of American Historians, Denver.

Roberts, Peter
1904   Anthracite Coal Communities. New York, Macmillan.

Rossi, Alice S.
1968   "Transition to parenthood." Journal of Marriage and the Family 30 (February): 26–39.

Schofield, R. S.
1970   "Age-specific mobility in an eighteenth century rural English parish." Annales de demographie historique: 261–274.

Shorter, Edward
1975   The Making of the Modern Family. New York: Basic Books.

Sennett, Richard
1970   Families Against the City: Middle Class Homes of Industrial Chicago, 1872–1890. Cambridge, Mass.: Harvard University Press.

Sklar, June L.
1974   "The role of marriage behaviour in the demographic transition: The case of eastern Europe around 1900." Population Studies 28 (July): 231–248.

Skolnick, Arlene
1973   The Intimate Environment: Exploring Marriage and the Family. Boston: Little Brown.

Slater, Philip
1970   The Pursuit of Loneliness: American Culture at the Breaking Point. Boston: Beacon Press.
1977   Footholds: Understanding the Shifting Sexual and Family Tensions in Our Culture. New York: E. P. Dutton.

Steinmetz, Suzanne K.
1977   The Cycle of Violence: Assertive, Aggressive and Abusive Family Interaction. New York: Praeger.

Steinmetz, Suzanne K. and M. A. Straus (eds.)
1974   Violence in the Family. New York: Dodd, Mead & Co.

Sussman, Marvin B. (ed.)
1972   Non-Traditional Family Forms in the 1970s. Minneapolis, Minn.: National Council on Family Relations.
Sussman, Marvin B. and L. G. Burchinal
1962   "Kin family network: unheralded structure in current conceptualization of family functioning." Marriage and Family Living 24.
Taeuber, Conrad and Irene B. Taeuber
1958   The Changing Population of the United States. New York: Wiley.
U.S. Bureau of the Census
1973   Census of Population: 1970. Subject Reports. Final Report PC (2)–4A. Family Composition. Washington, D.C. Government Printing Office.
1974   Current Population Reports, Series P–20, No. 271. "Marital Status and Living Arrangements: March 1974." Washington, D.C., Government Printing Office.
1976   Current Population Reports, Series P–20, No. 298. "Daytime Care of Children: October 1974 and February 1975." U.S. Government Printing Office, Washington, D.C.
1976   The Statistical History of the United States: From Colonial Times to the Present. Washington, D.C.: Government Printing Office.
U.S. Dept. of Health, Education and Welfare
1975   Vital Statistic of the United States, 1970. Vol 1—Natality. Public Health Service. Rockville, Maryland, National Center for Health Statistics.
Vinovskis, Maris A.
1972   "Mortality rates and trends in Massachusetts before 1860." Journal of Economic History 32 (March): 184–213.
1974   "The demography of the slave population in antebellum America." Journal of Interdisciplinary History 5 (Winter): 459–467.
Weigert, Andrew J. and Ross Hastings
1977   "Identity loss, family and social change." American Journal of Sociology 82 (May): 1171–1185.
Wells, Robert
1971   "Demographic change and the life cycle of American families." Journal of Interdisciplinary History 2 (Autumn): 273–282.
1972   "Quaker marriage patterns in a Colonial perspective." William and Mary Quarterly, Third Series, 24 (July): 415–442.
Wirth, Louis
1938   "Urbanism as a way of life." American Journal of Sociology 44 (July): 3–24.
Zaretsky, Eli
1976   Capitalism, the Family and Personal Life. New York: Harper & Row.

Two Worlds in One: Work and Family
Elizabeth Pleck

■ Nowhere is the subdivision of topics into areas of specialized inquiry more troubling than in social history. Beyond the divisions by national boundaries and time periods, new "specialties" have emerged (the cynical would suggest as a means of securing employment in a declining labor market). Someone who has used the manuscript census schedules to study the family and religious life among Irish Catholic mill girls in Lawrence can be considered a historian of labor, women, family, immigrants, the city, religion, or a quantitative methodologist—seven types of social history in a single study! Whether the motives for this compartmentalization are laudatory or predatory, the fact is that social history has become locked into narrow areas of specialization. Periodically, social historians call for a new synthesis of these specialities, but without any palpable explanation of how this reconciliation can be achieved; it is easy to decry the "balkanizing thrust in social history,"[1] but harder to overcome it.

Efforts to mesh two important specialities, labor history and the history of the family, seem particularly worthwhile because in their concern for work and family these topics embrace two of the more fundamental areas of human activity and emotional investment. Some developments in labor and family history make it possible to examine the link between the two in some detail. Historians of labor, once concerned almost exclusively with the organization of labor unions, are now analyzing the significance of work itself.[2] In the meantime, historians of the family, who initially focused on changes in household composition, have become increasingly interested in family norms, especially the changing emotional climate of the family.[3] Ironically, these two rather similar trends (the shift in interest from organizational membership to changes in norms) have developed separately, as if families existed without workers and workers were devoid of families. One sociologist, in fact, has argued that modern industrial society and the corporation helped to propagate the "myth of separate worlds," the division between the spheres of work and of the family.[4] Whatever the reasons for this inattention to the intersection of the two worlds, it seems obvious that the description of relationships between work and family makes for a richer and more complex social history.

A single sociological theory has informed most of the historical study of the relationship between work and family—this is that industrialization led to the separation of home and work. The most dramatic case of this separation was the English textile industry in the nineteenth century. Neil Smelser in *Social Change and the Industrial Revolution* points to the gradual shift (through a series of technological changes) from home to factory production.[5] No longer a productive unit, the family would come to specialize in other largely neglected functions—emotional satisfaction, the socialization of children, and consumption.

For industrial society this separation of the worlds of work and family was necessary for the stability of each institution and for the society as a whole.[6] According to Talcott Parsons, the most esteemed "functionalist" theorist:

The family has become a more specialized agency than before; probably more specialized than in any previous known society . . . but not in any general sense less important, because the society is dependent more exclusively on it for the performance of certain of its vital functions.[7]

The functionalists argue that the institutions of the family and work-place—divided into geographical and emotional units—specialized in their separate activities without mutual interference. According to this theory, human emotions were split between the two worlds—particularistic, ascriptive norms governing the family and universalistic, achieved norms dominating the world of work.

All of this specialization and differentiation in family function has been attributed to industrialization, specifically, technological change and the organization of work outside the household. Functionalist theory assumes that industrialization fundamentally altered the balance between the family and other social institutions. Although the consequences arising from this separation of work and family were many, only one—the family's loss of its role in production—has been isolated as the crucial factor. A long list of other results has been attributed to the loss of the family's production function, including the decline of kinship as the basis of work organization, the loss of power for mothers and children, the revolt of youth against their parents, the emergence of adolescence as a separate life stage, and greater sexual freedom for young women. Some historians have minimized the extent of these social changes, or attributed them to causes other than the loss of the family's economic function. Not enough attention, however, has been paid to specifying the nature and scope of the family's loss of productive function—indeed, to whether such a loss of function occurred at all.

Historians of the family generally follow the functionalist scheme.[8] In most cases, of course, they adopt this interpretation without necessarily subscribing to the larger functionalist world view. Still, the history of the family has been concerned largely with the way institutional changes affect family functions. John Demos, for example, writes that "the history of the family has been the history of contraction and withdrawal; its central theme is the gradual surrender to other institutions of functions that once lay very much within the realm of family responsibility."[9] In studying English family structure between 1500 and 1700, Lawrence Stone concluded that "the economic functions of the family as a distributive mechanism for goods and services declined."[10] Or consider this highly Parsonian statement by a Marxist historian, E. P. Thompson, describing the changes wrought by English industrialization:

Women became more dependent upon the employer of the labour market, and they looked back to a golden period in which home earnings from spinning, poultry, and the like could be gained around their own door. In good times, the domestic economy, like the peasant economy, supported a way of life centered upon the home, in which inner whims and compulsions were more obvious than external discipline. Each stage in industrial differentiation and specialization struck also at the family economy, disturbing customary relations between man and wife, parents and children, and differentiating more sharply between "work" and "life." It was to be a full hundred years before this differentiation was to bring returns, in the form of labour-saving devices, back into the working woman's home. Meanwhile, the family was roughly torn apart each morning by the factory bell.[11]

There are several reasons why this theoretical perspective is "dysfunctional" to the history of work-family relationships. First, since a function can be defined either as a classification of activities of an evaluation of them, there has been a serious confusion between norms and behavior. To argue, for example, that the Victorian family "functioned" as an emotional retreat from the world of work is a normative judgment, not a description of behavior, although it has been taken as both. According to Arlene Skolnick, "what people actually do may have little relation to what they think they are doing and what they think they should be doing."[12] But this is a confusion in much social history, not simply in this specialty. A second objection is that such history emphasizes the evolution of functions, the search for the origins of declining functions, their stubborn persistence, or their greater differentiation. The difficulty with this is the same as in Whig or Progressive history—where the historian, assuming a model of decay or progress, searches for proof, often wrenching evidence out of its historical context. Anachronistic interpretation is the most serious problem with this evolutionary approach. A third limitation of functionalist history is its emphasis on how institutions fit together rather than how people cross institutional boundaries. Sociologist Rosabeth Kanter has argued that with "few exceptions, the traditional emphasis [in the functionalist theory of the family] was almost totally on the roles and positions and forms or outcomes for the individual with relatively little conceptualizing until recently on the family as an *interacting system*."[13] Functionalist theory presents a structural model for the evolution of institutions, perhaps a worthy enterprise in itself, but ill-suited to studying the process of interaction between work and family.

Did industrialization cause the separation of home and work? Historians have modified or limited this interpretation without fundamentally challenging it. In this paper, I will first examine the recent historical work that partly refutes this interpretation, and then describe briefly two alternative emphases, also derived from contemporary work which present more promising lines of inquiry. Since issues in the history of work and family cross national boundaries, I have drawn on research in American and European social history. I have ordered the evidence from historical research, largely designed for purposes other than addressing this argument, into four different categories of arguments against the notion that industrialization created two distinct worlds for work and family.

1. Until recent times, separation of home and work characterized only the middle-class.

Historians of the Victorian family, as a case in point, have closely followed the functionalist emphasis on differentiation between family and work roles. Their descriptions of the Victorian middle-class family merely restates much of the sociological argument: the home was a place of repose where the breadwinner recuperated from the world of work.[14] Only the husband earned an income and he alone moved between the two worlds. As family and work became increasingly separated, the Victorian home became more privatized,[15] with separation of physical space for mothers and children and the division of the house between the more public and more private areas.

In this greater differentiation of function, a new role emerged for women: the glorification of motherhood.[16] Mothers devoted increased hours of attention to their children. Removed from wage-earning, children became dependents in the family and took years preparing to enter the world of work.[17] Husbands and wives increasingly inhabited two different emotional worlds—the task-preoccupied husband taking only a leisure time interest in the family, his expressive wife providing all the love and nurturance.

This argument points out the class dimension of a process—that work and family life first became separated among the middle classes where only one breadwinner was required to maintain the family. All the consequences of this new style of life—the glorification of motherhood, the new stages of childhood and adolescence, the segregation of fathers from their families—were attributed to the prosperity of these families and the loss of the productive role from the home. In this argument, the home, devoid of economic activity, served as a retreat from the world of work.

2. Contrary to the functionalist assumption, production in the home declined gradually.

Two systems of work, production on the farm or in the household and production in the factory coexisted for at least a century. The major form of home production was farming; as late as 1900, nearly two-thirds of all American families earned their living from the land. Nor did the development of industry simply end family enterprise. In the United States, France, England or Italy during the nineteenth century, daughters from farm families worked in the textile mills and returned home with wages and money for a dowry (or, at least in the United States, for their brother's education). Working sons and daughters often left the farm only to return with money which helped purchase capital improvements, thereby increasing the value of their inheritance.[18]

Even with the organization of production in factories, many commodities were still produced at home. Everything from shoes, cigars and matchboxes to artificial flowers and buttons was made there. Even printing presses were located originally in shops next to the family living quarters. Some technological changes outside the home actually increased work within it.[19] The sewing machine, located in a small corner of the family's apartment, made it possible to produce more garments at home, and as late as the 1880's, most apparel for American women, with the exception of cloaks, was made by families sewing in their apartments. With the introduction of new shears, for example, garments were cut at factories and parcelled out to sewing families. In fact, the lower wages of family workers at home led to a decline in craft shops and a rise in sweated labor.[20]

Such commodity production, of course, gradually ended; however, the demise of the early handloom weavers in England has often been interpreted as the abrupt end of the family workshop.[21] Actually, as noted by Patricia Branca, home production declined much less rapidly in Western Europe than in England or the United States, and when handloom weaving finally disappeared in Europe, it was replaced by dressmaking in France, silk manufacturing in Italy and linen cloth making in Belgium.[22] By the end of the nineteenth century the home economy still generated income and employment. In the cities, filled with migrants, taking boarders was a major wage-earning occupation of women, especially among childless married women with no outside employment.[23] Around the turn of the century between 20% and 30% of American families accepted boarders.[24] The persistence of all these forms of home production and services indicates considerable economic activity within the household.

Another development in the home economy was the rise of service industries. In some cases, wage-earners took work into their own homes (for example, laundresses[25]), but such labor was performed mostly in the employer's home.[26] While the most common category of female employment in the United States or in Western Europe around the turn of the century was domestic service, it was only one of a large list of home service occupations which included home repairs (plumbing, carpentry, repair and gardening) along with services outside the home (laundry and restaurants). Since homes purchased the services of workers, they continued to be centers of economic exchange, if not of commodity production.

The modifications of the functionalist interpretation accept the basic definitions of terms; they merely argue for a more precise dating of the decline in home production. The family workshop declined gradually—far more slowly in some European countries than in England or in America. Along with the organization of industry, home production grew and even prospered as it absorbed certain technological improvements. The two modes of work organization actually developed simultaneously for almost a century.

3. Market work moved outside the home but nonmarket work remained.

A new group of "home economists," that is, econometricians interested in the household as an economic unit, have challenged the old distinction between production and consumption.[27] They point out that production and consumption are both merely allocations of time between monetized and nonmonetized activities. It takes time and purchased raw material to produce commodities—whether steel in a rolling mill or dinner at home. The steelworker receives wages for doing his labor while the housewife does not. The dinner is immediately "used" while the steel is exchanged for cash or credit. This perspective on work deemphasizes wage-earning, suggesting a much broader definition of "work" which includes nonmarket labor, most of which was (and is) performed by women.

Marxist historians also have emphasized the role of women in production;[28] in maintaining and servicing the worker—the wife, according to Engels, "became the first domestic servant."[29] For families only slightly above subsistence, these kinds of economic activities were the margin of survival. In Pittsburgh, for example, where around the turn of the century there were few municipal services in working-class districts, a steelworker who wanted clean clothes, water to bathe in or drink, or a cooked meal, required the services of a wife.[30] Most unmarried male workers lived in boarding houses where there was at least one woman who performed this work. Beyond this direct form of maintenance, wives and children denied themselves food, garments, and heat in order to sustain and clothe the breadwinner.[31] With increasing prosperity, wifely services were directed less toward family survival than toward maintaining high standards of cleanliness, child care, nutrition and leisure, all of which required greater time investments, and modern studies of housework (between 1920 and 1970) show no substantial change in the number of hours devoted to household tasks despite rising real wages and the introduction of more technology in the home.[32] Even in the Victorian period, middle-class women—far from idle—devoted a full week's work to housecare. The typical middle-class housewife hired a servant for the heavier tasks, but still performed most of her own cleaning.[33] The one major change during this period was the increasing allocation of time to child care, an investment of the mother's hours occasioned as much by changing job requirements in middle-class work as by new sentiments towards children.

In connection with the pursuit of particular strategies of family fertility, it can be argued that reproduction was, in fact, a continuation of home production. In the view of some Marxists, children were commodities made in the home; that is, in a strictly economic sense, children were produced by time and labor and when mature, they repaid their parents' initial investment with either wages or free labor.[34] Whether from farm or factory families they were needed as workers and as investments for their parents' old age. Parents purposely kept their daughters from marrying early in order to retain the extra wages.[35] In so doing, they raised their daughters' marriage age, thereby lowering the number of future grandchildren. Thus these family strategies manipulated the production of labor power in the household.

Thus, to these two groups of economists, the family's functions at home and at work form part of the larger economic program, that is productive activities within the home include the unpaid labor of a housewife along with her reproduction of children. By defining "work" in this manner, these groups of economists have revised the view of housework and also its relationship to paid employment. Still, these arguments only limit but do not contradict the functionalist interpretation. If one amended the argument to read, "industrialization caused a decline in the home production *of goods and services for exchange*," there would be no apparent objection from these theorists.

4. To a great extent, home and work were separated prior to industrialization.

Some historians are prone to argue that the separation of home and work occurred prior to factory production. Work in pre-industrial society was, of course, organized on a far smaller scale; it was often performed in households, on farms, or in craft shops. But if the question is one of whether families worked together in such settings, there is abundant evidence that they did not. To demonstrate that home and work were separated in pre-industrial society, one would begin by pointing out that the family in that period was *never integrated* as a work force. The level of population mobility was extremely high; between one and two-thirds of the inhabitants in English and colonial American villages moved away in less than a decade.[36] These migrants were adults, landless workers looking for jobs, or men impressed into the armies—or adolescents employed away from home as servants, apprentices, or live-in laborers.[37] In colonial America the putting out of children with neighboring families was common. Even among children who lived at home, many worked as hired hands and servants for neighbors. Sometimes these child laborers wanted to retain control over their own wages rather than contribute to the family economy.[38] Where families worked the land together, death was so common that the family was often forced to employ outside workers. Such evidence contradicts the simplistic sociological notion that "in the earlier household economy, the members of the family daily worked together at home to produce their livelihood . . ."[39]

One might even argue that for a short interval economic and technological change created working families of this pure sociological model. Introduction of new machinery indeed led to the specialization of labor, thereby creating cottage industries where whole families produced commodities within the household.[40] Family togetherness was even more usual among households in factory towns than in rural areas. However, the common residence of teenagers with the family was more frequent in industrial cities than in rural areas simply because adolescent children could find work in the mills.[41] Thus, if the argument for the preindustrial integration of work and family is based solely on the fact of common residence in the family, then one cannot prove that work and family were integrated.

More substantially, one can argue that it was the subdivision of land rather than factory production that destroyed the functional unity of the family. Only because land was controlled by parents and economic opportunity was restricted was it possible for children to remain as family workers. Philip Greven's study of farmers in colonial Massachusetts traces the dissolution of the family work unit.[42] In 17th century Andover adult children remained on these small farms, even postponing marriage, in return for their eventual inheritance of the property. As a result of the continued division of the land into smaller parcels, these Andover sons finally became less interested in inheriting the property and began to settle new farms far from their parents' residences.

As much or more unity of work and family was to be found in industrial settings as in farming areas. Some industries, like textile production in England, France, or the United States, employed the whole family.[43] Sometimes English spinners hired their own sons as assistants.[44] William Reddy estimates that over 50% of the workers in the textile mills of Armentièrs in 1906 were related to at least one other person in the mill.[45] In a similar American situation during the same period, Tamara Hareven reports that families recruited the laborers for the textile mills of Manchester, New Hampshire and even controlled their placement within the factory's workrooms.[46] Glassblowers, file makers and miners in France, England and the United States worked alongside their relatives.[47] The extent of family control over conditions of work varied among industries; it is conceivable that families held greater sway in the textile industry, where women and children were often employed in the work force, than in heavy industries such as steel or machine production.[48]

The argument concerning family cohesion in pre-industrial society proposes causes other than industrialization for the declining economic function of the family. Patterns of land inheritance largely determined the composition of the family work force. Landless wage laborers were as separated from their homes as modern proletarians. In fact, cottage industry and the employment of whole families in factories actually increased the unity of the family work force. The family's economic function was beginning to decline prior to industrialization, and in certain respects, it achieved a new unity as a result of industrial development. . . .

It is an odd commentary on the study of work and family that issues about changing commitment to work are posed only for women workers—who presumably experienced conflict between the two worlds, which male employees did not. The real issue is not whether capitalism altered or did not alter women's fundamental attitudes towards work and the family but that historians (like Anderson or Scott and Tilly) have gone beyond functionalist theory to examine changing behavior in the workplace as well as in the family. The next stage, then, is to examine these changes within the context of *specific occupational cultures,* rather than to refer to the "capitalist marketplace" or to the general conditions of poverty.[49]

How did the physical and emotional demands of work alter family life? In many unskilled occupations, demands outside of working hours were minimal (thereby successfully dividing work and family into separate entities), but in as many others, time demands intruded on the worker's leisure and on the life of other family members. Most of the "absorptive" occupations were careers,[50] whose characteristics sociologists have defined as a series of "age-graded," upwarded occupational changes.[51]

Some of these highly absorptive occupations were structured as "two-person" careers,[52] involving the paid efforts of the husband and also the unpaid assistance of a wife (and sometimes of other family members). For some such careers, as noted by Rosabeth Kanter, work residence was combined with family living arrangements, such as the rectory, the embassy, the apartment above the family store or even the White House.

We know very little about the history of this category of occupations, which emerged in the 18th and 19th centuries,[53] even though such careers reordered relationships in middle-class family life. What has been described as the "cult of domesticity" might be better understood as the family response to the emergence of the male career. For middle-class wives membership in charity organizations or social clubs or home entertaining was actually designed to advance a husband in his work. The emergence of the career may have had other consequences as well, perhaps delayed age at marriage or postponement of child-bearing. Possibly the fertility decline among the middle class in the 19th century was as much a response to the new male career as to changes in the level of prosperity, in middle-class values or in the wife's power.[54]

Aside from the absorptiveness of any occupation, the additional characteristics of work—its structure, emotions, and norms—have transformed family life. Particular jobs reshaped the individual's personality by presenting a set of learning experiences that socialized his or her view of the world. Pessimism, insecurity, physical fatigue were often the consequences of menial work, just as self-esteem, control and autonomy were often psychological traits derived from bureaucratic tasks. New work experiences not only changed workers' perceptions but also introduced them to heretofore unavailable skills, such as when domestic servants in 19th-century France learned to read and write while at work.[55] At the same time the experience in work coincided with altered levels of fertility. We know very little about this important connection, even though there is abundant information about the effects of occupational level on fertility. Yet it is clear that even within the same occupational stratum, only certain work was coincident with high fertility. Michael Haines has analyzed the reasons for high fertility among miners' families in England, Wales, Prussia and the United States around the turn of the century, arguing that in mining villages isolated from urban influences, premodern values towards the importance of children persisted. This, along with other factors—the absence of work opportunities for women, the men's relatively high wages and short period of peak earnings—contributed to high fertility.[56]

Finally, the cultural milieu of work shaped leisure and family styles. Gareth Stedman Jones shows that by the end of the 19th century, the decline in the work day had increased the extent of working-class leisure for the whole family; he documents the rise of the new sex-segregated institutions among the working class—the pub, the men's clubs and sporting activities.[57]

Changes in the scheduling of work also altered family life.[58] Many labor historians have argued that despite the imposition of new scheduling, some workers continued to favor pre-industrial habits of work, family, and leisure.[59] As late as the middle- to late- 19th century, industrial workers celebrated "St. Monday," a non-scheduled day of leisure from work.[60] Margaret Hewitt, in studying married women mill operatives in 19th-century Lancashire, notes how new scheduling changed family patterns:

On Saturday the mills closed at midday and the men and single women make real holiday . . . The married women, who seem the slaves of Lancashire society, are obliged then, however, to set to work harder than ever. They have only this day to clean their houses, provide for the week, bake for the family, mend clothes, besides doing any washing that was not put out and attend the market to purchase the Sunday's dinner . . . The market is kept open very late at night for this purpose . . .[61]

Despite considerable scattered evidence about the effect of changes in scheduling on "family time," we need to know more about how the introduction of scheduled working hours and work days (or, for that matter night shifts), or the adoption of scheduled time in the schools changed family life.[62] In addition to reducing the work hours during the day, the declining number of workdays and the sequencing of days or weeks away from work (that is, "holidays" or vacations), may have created more opportunities for family leisure. Any single change in the time or timing of school or work reverberated throughout the two worlds. Another aspect of scheduling change was the sequencing of the family life cycle with the world of work. The investigation of changes in these life cycle events[63] (age at leaving home, marriage, birth of first and last child, widowhood) has occupied so much scholarly effort that little attention has been given to how the changing life cycle redounded on the world of work, although it is clear that an increase in family poverty—due to the absence of a mother's or child's labor—or more sexual freedom that often resulted from leaving the parental home can be understood as the changing intersection between the family's needs and the world of work.

To understand the history of work and family, historians must begin by rejecting theories based on "the myth of separate worlds," the separation of home and work under industrialization. They have raised objections and offered modifications of this argument without questioning its assumptions. One cannot study the relationship between work and family if it is assumed that the connections are only tangential. Functionalist analysis must be replaced by perspectives which examine how people reconciled the two worlds. I have suggested two possible approaches, although even in these alternative perspectives, there are difficulties and limitations. There is the danger for one thing of describing only one part of the process—how work affects family, or how family affects work. It will be necessary not only to follow the worker home from the job, but also to observe activity within the home and to study the influence of the family on the worker's participation in and involvement with work. If work and family form a larger whole, the social historian must specify how people move between the domains and demands of both worlds.

Notes

The author acknowledges the thoughtful criticisms of this paper by Miriam Cohen, Joseph Pleck, and Louise Tilly.

1. Herbert G. Gutman, *Work, Culture and Society in Industrializing America* (New York, 1976) 211.
2. Paul Faler, "Working-Class Historiography," *Radical America,* 3 (1969), 56–68; Robert H. Zieger, "Workers and Scholars: Recent Trends in American Labor Historiography," *Labor History,* 12 (1972), 245–266; Thomas Krueger, "American Labor Historiography: Old and New—A Review," *Journal of Social History,* 4 (1971), 277–285.
3. Tamara K. Hareven, "The History of the Family as an Interdisciplinary Field," *Journal of Interdisciplinary History,* II (1971), 399–414; John Demos, "The American Family in Past Time," *American Scholar,* 43 (1974), 422–446; Jonathan Prude, "The Family in Context," *Labor History,* XVII, 3 (1976), 422–436; Christopher Lasch, "The Family and History," (November 13, 1975), 33–38; and "The Emotions of Family Life," *ibid.* (November 27, 1975), 37–42; "What the Doctor Ordered," (December 11, 1975); *New York Review of Books,* Barbara J. Harris, "Recent Work on the History of the Family: A Review Article," *Feminist Studies* (1976), 159–172. Additional reasons for joining labor history with family study can be found in John Modell, "Economic Dimensions of Family History," *The Family in Historical Perspective,* 6 (1974), 7–12.
4. Rosabeth Moss Kanter, *Work and Family in the United States: A Critical Review and Agenda for Research and Policy,* (forthcoming, New York, 1976).
5. Neil J. Smelser, *Social Change in the Industrial Revolution* (Chicago, 1959); Neil J. Smelser, "The Industrial Revolution and the British Working-Class Family," *Journal of Social History,* 1 (1967), 17–35. See also Peter Laslett, *The World We Have Lost* (New York, 1965), 1–21 and Frances Collier, *The Family Economy of the Working Classes in the Cotton Industry,* 1784–1833 (Manchester, 1965). For a necessary corrective to Smelser see also M. M. Edwards and R. Lloyd-Jones, "N. J. Smelser and the Cotton Factory Family: A Reassessment," in N. B. Harte and K. G. Ponting, ed., *Textile History and Economic History: Essays in Honour of Miss Julia de Lacy Mann* (Manchester, 1973), 304–319.
6. Talcott Parsons and R. F. Bales, *Family, Socialization and Interaction Process* (Glencoe, Illinois, 1955); W. F. Ogburn and N. B. Nimkoff, *Technology and the Changing Family* (Boston, 1955); Fred Weinstein and Gerald M. Platt, *The Wish to be Free: Society, Psyche and Value Change* (Berkeley, 1971); Normal W. Bell and Ezra J. Vogel, "Introductory Essays: Toward a Framework for Functional Analysis of Family Behavior," in Norman W. Bell and Ezra J. Vogel, eds., *The Family* (Glencoe, Illinois, 1960), 1–36; Talcott Parsons, "The Social Structure of the Family," in R. N. Anshen, ed., *The Family: its Function and Destiny* (New York, 1949), 173–201.
7. Talcott Parsons and R. F. Bales, *Family, Socialization and Interaction Process,* 3–9.
8. The functionalist perspective also dominates the social history of education. See Bernard Bailyn, *Education in the Forming of American Society* (New York, 1960); Phyllis Vine. "Parents and Students: The Social Function of Eighteenth-Century Higher Education," *History of Education Quarterly* (forthcoming); and Frank Musgrove, *The Family, Education and Society* (London, 1966).

9. John Demos, *A Little Commonwealth: Family Life in Plymouth Colony* (New York, 1970), 183.

10. Lawrence Stone, "The Rise of the Nuclear Family in Early Modern England: The Patriarchal Stage," in Charles Rosenberg, ed., *The Family in History* (Philadelphia, 1975), 13.

11. E. P. Thompson, *The Making of the English Working Class* (New York, 1963), 416.

12. Arlene Skolnick, "The Family Revisited: Themes in Recent Social Science Research," *Journal of Interdisciplinary History,* V, 4 (1975), 703–719.

13. Rosabeth Moss Kanter, *Work and Family,* 23.

14. Barbara Laslett, "The Family as a Public and Private Institution: An Historical Perspective," *Journal of Marriage and the Family,* XXIV, 3 (August, 1973), 480–494; Clifford E. Clark, Jr., Domestic Architecture as an Index to Social History: The Romantic Revival and the Cult of Domesticity in America, 1840–1870," *Journal of Interdisciplinary History,* VII, 1 (1976), 33–56.

15. A similar argument has also been used for the London working-class between 1870 and 1900. See Gareth Stedman Jones, "Working-Class Culture and Working-Class Politics in London, 1870–1900: Notes on the Remaking of a Working Class," *Journal of Social History,* VII, 4 (1974), 460–508. One can also argue that increasing emphasis on scientific management in the home paralleled such developments in the world of work. On the growth of efficiency movement among housewives, consult Emma Seifrit Weigley, "It Might Have Been Euthenics: The Lake Placid Conferences and the Home Economics Movement," *American Quarterly,* 26 (1974), 79–96; David Handlin, "Efficiency and the American Home," *Architectural Association Quarterly,* 5 (1973), 50–54.

16. Barbara Welter, "The Cult of True Womanhood: 1820–1860," *American Quarterly,* XVIII (Summer, 1966), 151–174; Gerda Lerner, "The Lady and the Mill Girl: Changes in the Status of Women in the Age of Jackson," *Midcontinent American Studies Journal,* 10 (1969), 5–15; Phillida Bunkle, "Sentimental Womanhood and Domestic Education, 1830–1870," *History of Education Quarterly,* 14 (1974), 13–20.

17. Phillipe Aries, *Centuries of Childhood* (New York, 1960); Bernard Wishy, *The Child and the Republic* (Philadelphia, 1968).

18. Joan W. Scott and Louise Tilly, "Women's Work and the Family in Nineteenth Century Europe," *Comparative Studies in Society and History* (1975), 36–64; Alice Kessler Harris, "Women, Work and the Social Order," in Berenice A. Carroll, ed., *Liberating Women's History: Theoretical and Critical Essays* (Urbana, 1976), 330–344; Thomas Dublin, "Women, Work and Protest in the Early Lowell Mills: The Oppressing Hand of Avarice Would Enslave Us," *Labor History,* 16, 1 (1976), 99–116.

19. Gareth Stedman Jones, "Working-Class Culture," 484–485.

20. *Ibid.*

21. Neil Smelser, *Social Change and the Industrial Revolution.*

22. Patricia Branca, "A New Perspective on Women's Work: A Comparative Typology," *Journal of Social History,* 9, 2 (Winter, 1975), 126. Louise Tilly argues that autonomy in work declined and the pace of home production quickened toward the end of the nineteenth century. Personal Communication from Louise Tilly, September 11, 1976. See also Peter N. Stearns, *The Lives of Labour* (London, 1975), 195 and Heidi Hartmann, "Capitalism, Patriarchy and Job Segregation by Sex," *Signs,* 1, 3 (1976), 159–167.

23. John Modell, "The Fruits of Their Toil: The Family Economy of the American Workingmen in the late Nineteenth Century," in Tamara K. Hareven and Maris A. Vinovskis, eds., *Demographic Processes and Family Organization in Nineteenth Century American Society* (forthcoming).

24. John Modell and Tamara K. Hareven, "Urbanization and the Malleable Household: An Examination of Boarding and Lodging in American Families," *Journal of Marriage and the Family,* 35 (1973), 467–479.

25. Elizabeth H. Pleck, "A Mother's Wages: A Comparison of Income-Earning Among Urban Black and Italian Married Women, 1896–1911," *Signs* (Winter, 1977).

26. For a comparison of these roles among paid domestics and working-class housewives, see Leonore Davidoff, "Mastered for Life: Servant and Wife in Victorian and Edwardian England," *Journal of Social History*, 7, 4 (1974), 406–428.

27. Cynthia B. Lloyd, ed., *Sex, Discrimination and the Division of Labor* (New York, 1975); Marc Nerlove, "Towards a New Theory of Population and Economic Growth," in Theodore W. Schultz, ed., *Economics of the Family: Marriage, Children and Human Capital* (Chicago, 1970), 527–545; Gary Becker, "A Theory of the Allocation of Time," *Economic Journal*, 75 (1965), 493–517. An intelligent guide to this and other new literature on nonmarket labor is Nona Glazer-Malbin's review essay on "Housework," *Signs*, 1, 4 (1976), 905–922.

28. Lise Vogel, "The Earthly Family," *Radical America*, VII, 4–5 (1975), 9–50; Ira Gerstein, "Domestic Work and Capitalism," *Ibid.*, 101–120; Eli Zaretsky, "Capitalism, the Family and Personal Life," *Socialist Revolution*, III 3, 2–3 (1975), 69–126; Dorothy Smith, "Women, the Family and Corporate Capitalism," *Berkeley Journal of Sociology*, (1976), 55–90; Juliet Mitchell, "Women: The Longest Revolution," *New Left Review*, 40 (December, 1966), 11–37; Margaret Benston, "The Political Economy of Women's Liberation," *Monthly Review*, XXI, 4 (1969), 13–27; Mariarosa Dalla Costa, "Women and the Subversion of Community," *Radical America*, 6 (1972), 67–102; Wally Secombe, "The Housewife and Her Labour Under Capitalism," *New Left Review*, 83 (1974) 3–24.

29. Frederick Engels, *The Origin of the Family, Private Property and the State* (Moscow, 1968), 73.

30. Susan J. Kleinberg, "Technology and Women's Work: The Lives of Working-Class Women in Pittsburgh, 1870–1900," *Labor History*, XVII, 1 (1976), 58–72; Margaret F. Byington, *Homestead: The Household of a Mill Town* (New York, 1910; Pittsburgh, 1974).

31. Joan Scott and Louise Tilly, "Women's Work," 48; Olwen Hufton, "Women in Revolution, 1789–1796," *Past and Present*, 53 (1971), 91–93; Michael Anderson, *Family Structure in Nineteenth Century Lancashire* (Cambridge, England, 1971), 77; Laura Oren, "The Welfare of Women in Laboring Families: England, 1860–1950," *Feminist Studies*, 1 (1972), 107–125; Peter Stearns, "Working Class Women in Britain, 1890–1914," in Martha Vicinus, ed., *Suffer and Be Still: Women in the Victorian Age* (Bloomington, 1972), 116.

32. Joann Vanek, "Time Spent in Housework," *Scientific American* (November, 1974), 116–120; Ruth Schwartz Cowan, "The Industrial Revolution in the Home: Household Technology and Social Change in the United States," *Technology and Culture*, 17 (1976), 1–26.

33. Patricia Branca, "Image and Reality: The Myth of the Idle Victorian Woman," in Mary Hartman and Lois W. Banner, eds. *Clio's Consciousness Raised: New Perspectives on the History of Women* (New York, 1974), 179–191.

34. Charles Tilly, "Population and Pedagogy in France," *History of Education Quarterly* (Summer, 1973), 113–128; David Stern, Sandra Smith and Fred Doolittle, "How Children Used to Work," *Law and Contemporary Problems*, LXXXIX, 3 (Summer, 1975), 93–117; Stearns, *Lives of Labour*, 279.

35. Janet Salaff, "Working Daughters in the Hong Kong Chinese Family: Female Filial Piety or a Transformation in the Family Power Structure," *Journal of Social History*, IX, 4 (1976), 439–465; Tamara K. Hareven, "Family Time and Industrial Time: Family and Work in a Planned Corporation Town, 1900–1924," *Journal of Urban History*, I, 3 (1975), 365–389; U. S. Senate, *Report on Conditions of Woman and Child Wage-Earners in the United States*, 1, as quoted in Salaff, "Working Daughters in the Hong Kong Chinese Family," 439–465.

36. Peter Laslett, "Clayworth and Cogenhoe," in H. E. Bell and R. L. Ollard, eds., *Historical Essays, 1600–1750* (London, 1963), 77; Lawrence Stone, "Social Mobility in England," *Past and Present*, 38 (1966), 29–30; R. S. Schofield, "Age-Specific Mobility in an Eighteenth Century Rural England Parish," *Annales de Demographic Historique* (1970), 261; Douglas Lamar Jones, "The Strolling Poor: Transiency in Eighteenth Century Massachusetts," *Journal of Social History* (1975), 28–54. Edward Shorter argues that the rate of geographic mobility in pre-industrial France was less than in England. Edward Shorter, *The Making of the Modern Family* (New York, 1976), 27.

37. For illustrative materials, see Alan Macfarlane, *The Family Life of Ralph Josselin, A Seventeenth Century Clergyman: An Essay in Historical Anthropology* (Cambridge, 1970), 205–210 and Douglas Lamar Jones, "Female Vagabonds in Eighteenth-Century Massachusetts," unpublished paper presented at the George Washington University Conference on Women and the American Revolution, July, 1975. Lutz Berkner argues that Austrian peasants hired laborers only when their children were too young to till the land. Lutz K. Berkner, "The Stem Family and the developmental cycle of the peasant household: an eighteenth century Austrian example," *American Historical Review*, 77 (1972), 98–118.

38. Michael Anderson, *Family Structure in Nineteenth Century Lancashire*, 87.

39. Meyer F. Nimkoff, *Marriage and the Family* (Cambridge, 1947), 91–92.

40. In a refutation of this argument, Gareth Stedman Jones points out that craftsmen, living in cramped rooms, preferred to spend their waking hours in the workshop. Stedman Jones, "Working-Class Culture," 485.

41. Anderson, *Family Structure*, Table 27, 85.

42. Philip Greven, *Four Generations: Population, Land, and Family in Colonial Andover, Massachusetts* (Ithaca, New York, 1970), but see also Maris Vinovskis, "The Field of Early American Family History: A Methodological Critique," in *The Family in Historical Perspective: An International Newsletter*, 7 (1974), 1–8; Maris Vinovskis, "American Historical Demography: A Review Essay," *Historical Methods Newsletter*, 14 (September, 1971), 141–148. For the impact of declining availability of land on the Dutch family, see William Peterson, "The demographic transition in the Netherlands," *American Sociological Review*, 25 (1960), 334–347.

43. Rudolf Braun makes a similar argument for European society. He points out that the development of cottage industry—young sons and daughters establishing separate residences—led to the eventual dissolution of the unity of work and family among Swiss peasants. Rudolf Braun, "The Impact of Cottage Industry on an Agricultural Population," in David S. Landes, ed., *The Rise of Capitalism* (New York, 1966), 53–64.

44. Neil Smelser, *Social Change and the Industrial Revolution*, 189. Actually in Preston factories for 1816, parents were the employers of only 10% of the child laborers. See M. M. Edwards and R. Lloyd-Jones, "N. J. Smelser and the Cotton Factory Family," 304–319.

45. William M. Reedy, "Family and Factory: French Linen Weavers in the Belle Èpoque," *Journal of Social History*, VIII, 2 (1975), 102–112.

46. Tamara K. Hareven, "The Laborers of Manchester, New Hampshire, 1912–1922: The Role of Family and Ethnicity in Adjustment to Industrial Life," *Labor History*, XIV, 2 (1975), 249–265; Tamara K. Hareven, "The Dynamics of Kin in Industrial Communities: The Historical Perspective," *American Journal of Sociology* (Winter, 1976).

47. Michael Hanagan, "Artisans and Industrial Workers: Strikes in Three French Towns, 1870–1914," unpublished Ph.D. dissertation, University of Michigan, 1976; Louise A. Tilly, "Occupation Structure and Demographic Change in Roubaix and Anzin," unpublished paper presented at the Social Science History Conference, October, 1976.

48. Daniel Nelson argues that one of the consequences of new developments in scientific management around the turn of the century was the declining family basis of work organization. Daniel Nelson, *Managers and Workers: Origins of the New Factory System in the United States, 1880–1920* (Madison, 1975); Rosabeth Moss Kanter, *Work*

and Family, 13; Margaret F. Byington, "The family in a typical mill town," American Journal of Sociology, 4 (March, 1909), 648–659.

49. These relationships have been explored in detail only for one category of workers, domestic servants. The servants' age at marriage, choice of marital partners, even style of dress was altered by the experience of work. See Theresa McBride, "Social Mobility for the Lower Class: Domestic Servants in France," Journal of Social History, VIII, 1 (1974), 62–78.

50. For an excellent survey of the rise of professionalism within American society, consult Robert H. Wiebe, The Search for Order, 1877–1920 (New York, 1967), 111–132 along with William R. Johnson, "Education and Professional Life Styles: Law and Medicine in the Nineteenth Century," History of Education Quarterly (1974) 188–208.

51. Harold Wilensky, "Work, careers and social integration," International Social Science Journal, 12 (1960), 54–560; James D. Thompson, Robert W. Avery and Richard Carlson, Occupations, Personnel and Careers (Pittsburgh, 1962); Wilbert E. Moore, Conduct of the Corporation (New York, 1962); Curt Tausky and Robert Dubin, "Career Anchorage: Managerial Mobility Aspirations," American Sociological Review, 20 (1965), 725–735.

52. Hanna Papenek, "Men, Women and Work: Reflections on the Two-Person Career," American Journal of Sociology, 78 (1973), 852–872.

53. For some suggestive evidence about the emergence of the female career, see Peter Filene, Himherself: Sex Roles in Modern America (New York, 1974), 121–168; Janis Calvo, "Quaker Women Ministers in Nineteenth Century America," Quaker History, 62 (1974), 75–92.

54. For these last three arguments, see J. A. Banks, Prosperity and Parenthood: A Study of Family Planning Among the Victorian Middle Classes (London, 1954); J. A. and Olive Banks, Feminism and Family Planning in Victorian England (New York, 1964); Daniel Scott Smith, "Family Limitation, Sexual Control and Domestic Feminism in Victorian America," in Mary Hartman and Lois W. Banner, eds., Clio's Consciousness Raised: New Perspectives on the History of Women (New York, 1974), 119–126; Linda Gordon, "Voluntary Motherhood: The Beginnings of the Feminist Birth Control Ideas in the United States," in Ibid., pp. 54–72.

55. Theresa McBride, "Social Mobility for the Lower Classes," 62–78.

56. Michael R. Haines, Fertility and Occupation: Coal Mining Populations in the Nineteenth and Early Twentieth Centuries in Europe and America (Princeton, 1975). Additional studies which relate specific occupations to fertility include Peter N. Stearns, "Adaptation to Industrialization: German Workers and a Test Case," Central European History, III, 4 (1970), 303–331; Peter N. Stearns, "The Lives of Labour," 271–272; John W. Innes, Class Fertility Trends in England and Wales, 1876–1934 (Princeton, 1938); John Knodel, The Fertility Decline in Germany, 1871–1939 (Princeton, 1974). I am indebted to Louise Tilly for calling these studies to my attention. Modern sociological reports on British workers indicate that even among men at the same occupational level, there were major differences in family size. Miners and truck drivers had large families, while garment workers and fishermen had small ones. These differences were attributed to the husband's work—his physical separation from his wife, insecurity in employment, and the extent of community among fellow workers. See Geoffrey Hawthorn and Michael Paddon, "Work, Family and Fertility," Human Relations, XXIV, 61 (1971), 611–628.

57. Jones, "Working-Class Culture," 471–500.

58. For a general survey of the changing pace of work in nineteenth century Europe, see Stearns, Lives of Labour, 192–228.

59. Keith Thomas, "Work and Leisure in Pre-Industrial Societies," Past and Present, 29 (1962), 50–62; E. P. Thompson, "Time, Work-Discipline and Industrial Capitalism," Past and Present, 28 (1967), 56–97; Alasdair Clayre, Work and Play: Ideas and Experience of Work and Leisure (New York, 1976); Herbert G. Gutman, "Work, Culture and Society in

Industrializing America, 1815–1918," *American Historical Review,* LXXVIII, 2 (June, 1973), 581–588; Sidney Pollard, "Factory Discipline in the Industrial Revolution," *Economic History Review,* 16 (1968), 254–271; Sebastian de Grazia, *Of Time, Work and Leisure* (Garden City, New York, 1964). Michael Marrus also suggests that leisure activities were purged from the workplace in the nineteenth century because employers, speeding up the pace of work, became less tolerant of drunken workers. Michael P. Marrus, "Social Drinking in the Belle Èpoque," *Journal of Social History,* VII, 2 (1974), 115–141. See also Bruce Laurie, "Nothing on Impulse: Life Styles of Philadelphia Artisans, 1820–1850," *Labor History,* XV, 3 (1974), 327–366 and Paul Faler, "Cultural Aspects of the Industrial Revolution: Lynn, Massachusetts Shoemakers and Industrial Morality, 1826–1860," *Labor History,* XV, 3 (1974), 367–394.

60. Douglas A. Reid, "The Decline of Saint Monday, 1776–1876," *Past and Present,* 71 (1976), 76–101.

61. Margaret Hewitt, *Wives and Mothers in Victorian Industry* (London, 1958), 62–84; see also Ivy Pinchbeck, *Women Workers in the Industrial Revolution, 1750–1850* (London, 1930), 280.

62. Samuel Bowles and Herbert Gintis, *Schooling in Capitalist America* (New York, 1976); Leonore Davidoff, "Mastered for Life," 406–428.

63. Laurence A. Glasco, "The Life Cycle and Household Structure of American Ethnic Groups: Irish, Germans and Native-Born Whites in Buffalo, New York, 1855," *Journal of Urban History,* 1 (1975), 339–364; John Modell, Frank F. Furstenberg, Jr., Douglas Strong, "The Timing of Marriage in the Transition to Adulthood: Continuity and Change, 1860–1975," forthcoming, *American Journal of Sociology* (1976); John and Virginia Demos, "Adolescence in Historical Perspective," *Journal of Marriage and the Family,* 81 (1969), 632–638; Frank Musgrove, *Youth and the Social Order* (Bloomington, 1965); John Modell, Frank F. Furstenberg, Jr., and Theodore Hershberg, "Social Change and Life Course Development in Historical Perspective," forthcoming, *Journal of Family History;* Paul C. Glick and Robert Parke, Jr., "New Approaches in Studying the Life Cycle of the Family," *Demography,* 2 (1965), 187–202; Joseph F. Kett, "Adolescence and Youth in Nineteenth Century America," *Journal of Interdisciplinary History,* II (1971), 283–298.

Prospects

The Future of the American Family
Paul C. Glick

■ *Slowdown in population change.* A reasonable expectation is that further changes in American family life will significantly lessen during the next two decades. This position is supported by related conclusions that were reached in a monograph, *The Population of the United States, Trends and Prospects: 1950 to 1990,* that was prepared by staff members of the Census Bureau's Population Division as background material for the World Population Conference in Bucharest, Romania, in 1974. In that monograph, even the *high* projected rates of change in population growth, enrollment, and the labor force during the 20 years between 1970 and 1990 are consistently smaller than the corresponding rates of change that had already taken place during the 20 years between 1950 and 1970.

The prospect of such a slowdown in social change could turn out to be seriously in error, particularly if some unforeseen change of great consequence should develop in the meantime. But several aspects of the present situation are at least consistent with an outlook of less change ahead.

Paul C. Glick. "The Future of the American Family" from Current population reports: Special studies, series P–23, no. 78, January 1979.

In the first place, the decline in the birth rate during the last two decades has provided much momentum to a wide variety of other changes, as will be demonstrated in later sections. The relevant fact here is that this decline has gone about as far as it can go, and most demographers do not expect it to rise very significantly in the next decade or two.

In the second place, the great amount of increase in school and college enrollment during the last two decades has influenced other changes but is most unlikely to be repeated again in the next couple of decades. The proportion of young people who graduate from high school has been on a plateau of about 85 percent during the 1970's. The proportion of men in their late twenties who have completed a year or more of college after graduating from high school has reached 60 percent, and the comparable proportion of women has approached 50 percent; these levels are 10 or more percentage points higher than a decade ago and seem unlikely to rise by a similar amount during the next decade.

In the third place, the recent rate of increase in the proportion of women in the labor force has been dramatic, going up from 38 percent in 1960 to 48 percent in 1977. Without a continuing decline in the birth rate and with less increase in the educational level of the young adult population, along with other changes not mentioned, the odds seem to favor a slackening of the rate of increase in the labor force participation of women over the next decade or two. The worker rate for men has been declining for several years; this trend may diminish or be slightly reversed in future years by the lifting of the mandatory retirement age and by the easing of entry into the labor force by young men (and women) a decade or two from now because of the relatively small size of the cohorts that will be seeking to be absorbed into the labor market at that time.

These slackening changes in the birth rate, the enrollment rate, and the labor force participation rate seem likely to have a dampening impact on patterns of future change in family life.

Changes in the family life cycle.   Longtime trends in demographic variables that are used to study the family life cycle have been primarily affected by downward trends in the birth and death rates. This conclusion was reached by Glick (1977) on the basis of an analysis of changes over the 80–year period from the early 1900's through the 1970's.

Aside from the baby boom after World War II, the birth rate has followed a generally downward direction until the present time. The average family that was formed in the early years of the 20th century included four children, whereas the average family formed in the 1930's included three children. Families formed during the familistic era of the

1950's had one additional child, but those forming at the present time expect to have only two children, on the average.

Today's young family of two children stands in sharp contrast with their great-grandparents' family of four children. Other things being equal (though they may not be), one would expect that the father and mother of today can spend more time with each of their children and with each other apart from their children. The period of childrearing has been shortened by about 3 years; and the period after the children leave home has been increased by 11 years (from 2 years to 13 years), largely as a consequence of the improvement in survival rates among adults.

Accordingly, young couples today can expect to live as a "childfree" twosome for about 14 more years than their elders, with most of the increase coming in middle age and later. These 14 years represent nearly one-third of the entire 44 years of married life for the shrinking proportion of couples with continuous first marriages. The degree of satisfaction those later years bring depends on many tangible and intangible factors concerning how well the two relate to each other and to their grown children. (All but a few—between 5 and 10 percent—will have some children.) That satisfaction has a good chance of being affected by the rising status of women and the concomitant increase in singlehood and divorce. The extent to which young adults are postponing marriage and to which adults of all ages are dissolving their marriages in divorce will be treated in the next two sections of this statement.

Will the postponement of marriage continue? Persons in their twenties, when most of those who marry do so, are now postponing entry into their first marriage until they are about 1 1/2 years older than their counterparts two decades ago. Thus, in 1977 the median age at first marriage was 24.0 years for men and 21.6 years for women. In 1956 the median ages at marriage were the youngest on record: 22.5 years for men and 20.1 years for women (U.S. Bureau of the Census, March 1977).

Additional evidence of much more postponement of marriage now than formerly is provided by the increase of one-half between 1960 and 1977 in the proportion of women 20 to 24 years of age who had never married (from 28 percent in 1960 to 45 percent in 1977). During this period the same rate of increase was recorded in the postponement of marriage among women in their late twenties (from 10.5 percent to 16.1 percent).

One of the tangible factors that probably helps to explain the increasing postponement of marriage is the 5-to-10-percent excess of women as compared with men during recent years in those ages when most first marriages occur (18 to 24 years for women and 20 to 26 years for men). This imbalance is a consequence of past fluctuations in the birth rate. For example, women born in 1947 after the baby boom had begun were ready to marry in 20 years, but the men they were most likely to marry were born in 1944 or 1945 (about one-half in each year) when the birth rate was still low; these men were about 8 percent less numerous than the 20-year-old women. (By contrast, girls who were born during the last 15 years while the birth rate has been declining will be scarce as compared with eligible men when they reach the main ages for marriage.)

The longer the pattern of increasing postponement of marriage persists, the more likely the prospect becomes that the extent of lifetime singlehood among young adults of today will increase (Carter and Glick, 1976, pp. 406–407). As recently as 1940, about 9 percent of the women in middle age had never married. That proportion had dropped to only 4 percent by 1977; this all-time low rate of lifetime singlehood was experienced by a cohort that was in or near the peak years for marriage during the 1950's when the age at marriage was low and the marriage and birth rates were high. Unless the cohort of women now in their twenties has an unusually large number of late marriages, the chances are that 6 percent—or even 7 or 8 percent—of them will go through life without ever becoming married. These projected rates may seem to be relatively small, but in reality they amount to half again up to twice as large a proportion as that experienced by those 20 years older.

The marriage and divorce rates have stabilized; will they remain stable?   As the young people born during the baby boom became of age to marry, the marriage rate increased until it reached a peak of 11.0 per 1,000 population in 1972. From that level it declined to 10.0 in 1975 and has fluctuated very little since then. (Annual rates for the 12 months ending in a given month have fluctuated between 9.9 and 10.1; the rate for 1976 as a whole was 9.9, and for 1977 it was 10.1.) On the other hand, the divorce rate continued its historic rise until it reached a peak of 5.1 per 1,000 population in 1977. Now for nearly 2 years (from April 1976 through January 1978) the divorce rate (for the 12 months ending in a given month) has been virtually unchanged. (It rose to 5.1 in only 3 of the 22 months; it was 5.1 for 1977 as a whole, but it was 5.0 in every month of 1977 except December, and it fell sharply to 4.4 in January 1978.)

The future propensity of young adults to marry cannot be forecast with a great degree of confidence. Nevertheless, there are reasons to expect the proportion of young adults who marry to level off or to rise moderately for a few years and then to rise still more after that time.

If the marriage propensity tends to stabilize or to rise moderately during the next few years, one of the reasons will probably be little further change in the postponement of first marriage, and another may be an increase in the number of late first marriages among those who have been postponing them. Still another reason may be a discontinuation of the pronounced decline in the remarriage rate that was observed between 1972 and 1975—the latest period for which data are available. These developments would likely be stimulated if the outlook for the improvement in business conditions and in the employment of young adults were to be generally favorable. These developments would likely be hampered, however, if the outlook continues to be clouded by high levels of inflation and by high rates of unemployment among the millions of young persons who were born during the baby boom.

If the focus is on the more remote period of one or two decades from now, the prospects for an increasing proportion of young adults to marry should be better because of the greater ease with which the labor market should be able to absorb the relatively small cohort of young adults at that time. Of course, changes in the sizes of age groups during successive stages of the life cycle and simultaneous changes in employment conditions are not the only critical variables affecting the level of the marriage rate, but they are surely two of the most important variables.

The future course of the divorce rate is also difficult to forecast. But to the extent that the level of divorce is related to the level of marriage, the prospect for divorce to decline somewhat in the next few years seems reasonable. This conclusion rests on the fact that divorce tends to occur a few years after marriage and that the peak in marriage was reached in 1972, whereas the current high level of divorce was reached about 2 years ago. The lag between marriage and divorce is as follows: half of the divorces after first marriage occur during the first 7 years after marriage, and half of the divorces after remarriage occur during the first 3 years. The marriage rate has fallen now about one-tenth from its highest level, therefore, it should not be surprising if the divorce rate should also fall somewhat during the next year or two. Thereafter, fluctuations in the divorce rate might be expected to occur in a pattern similar to future fluctuations in the marriage rates of about 4 to 6 years earlier, if the divorce level has essentially stabilized.

A rise in the divorce rate during the last decade has occurred among couples of all ages, but by far the greatest age-specific rate of increase has taken place among couples in the range of 25 to 39 years of age—the range within which three-fifths of all divorces occur. Between 1968 and 1975, the divorce rate per 1,000 married persons went up 70 percent for those 25 to 39, as compared with 50 percent for those under 25 and those 40 to 64 years old; it went up 35 percent among those 65 and over. These findings appear to contradict the impression among many counselors of persons with marital stress problems, namely, that the greatest increase has been among persons in middle age. Those counselors' impressions may actually be correct in the sense that there may have been a disproportionately large rate of increase among the clients in middle age who seek the services of marriage and divorce counselors; persons in this age range are most likely to be sufficiently affluent to afford such services and are also most likely to have complex property settlements to consider.

Despite a threefold increase since 1960 in the number of children of divorced parents who live with a divorced father, the proportion of children living with a divorced father has not changed very much; it has remained at the level of about one-tenth of all children who live with a divorced parent. The reason for this finding is that there has also been a threefold increase since 1960 in the number of children who live with a divorced mother.

What is the outlook for change among one-parent families? Despite substantial increases in divorce and informal living arrangements during the last couple of decades, the preponderant majority of people still live in households maintained by a nuclear family. Specifically, 7 of every 8 of the 213 million persons in the noninstitutional population of the United States in 1977 were residents of nuclear family households:

- 77 percent were in husband-wife households; and
- 10 percent were in one-parent households; thus,
- 87 percent were in nuclear family households.
- 7 percent were living alone as one-person households;
- 1 percent were in households of unmarried couples; and
- 5 percent were in various other living arrangements.
- 100 percent. (In 1970, 1 percent of all persons were in institutions.)

That is the big picture. One feature of it that may be particularly surprising is the smallness of the proportion of *persons* living in the households of one-parent families. An obvious reason is that such families include only one parent instead of two. Another is that only 54 percent of all families have any "own" children under 18 years of age in the household. In fact, 18 percent of the 64 million noninstitutional *children* of this age in 1977 were living in one-parent families.

- 79 percent of all children under 18 lived with two parents;
- 18 (17.7) percent lived with one parent; and
- 3 percent lived with neither parent, but usually with relatives.
- 100 percent. (In 1970, 0.4 percent of all children were in institutions.)

But some of the 79 percent of children under 18 in 1977 living with two parents were living with a stepparent or were born to their current parents after one or both had remarried.

- 66 percent lived with both natural parents in their first marriage;
- 5 percent lived with both natural parents but one or both had remarried; thus,

- 71 percent lived with both of their natural parents.
- 8 percent lived with a stepparent (i.e., were born before the natural parent they live with had remarried).
- 79 percent (see above). (This includes some adopted children, not separately identified.)

The 18 percent of children who lived in one-parent families in 1977 were very unevenly distributed among parents by marital status and race. They also represent a doubling of the corresponding proportion in 1960 (up from 9 to 18 percent). (In absolute numbers, the increase amounted to a rise from 7.1 million in 1960 to 11.3 million in 1977.)

Information from the same sources as the accompanying exhibit shows that the number of children under 18 years old rose from 64.3 million in 1960 to 69.5 million in 1970 and then, because of the declining birth rate, it fell to 64.1 million in 1977. Thus, the total number of young children in 1977 was about the same as in 1960, but in the meantime, the number living with a separated parent doubled, the number living with a divorced parent tripled, and the number living with a never-married parent became seven times as high. By contrast, the number of children living with two parents actually declined by 10 percent (from 56.3 million in 1960 to 50.8 million in 1977), and the number living with a widowed parent declined 20 percent (from 1.5 million to 1.2 million).

On balance, there are still close to 4 of every 5 young children living with two parents and most of the rest living with one parent. Even so, this

Sex and marital status of parent	Percent of children under 18 living with one parent		
	All races	White	Black
1977, total	17.7	13.3	43.2
Living with:			
Mother only	16.3	11.9	41.7
Father only	1.4	1.4	1.4
Marital status of parent:			
Divorced	7.2	6.7	9.9
Married	5.9	4.0	17.5
Separated	5.0	3.2	15.9
Widowed	2.4	1.9	5.0
Single	2.2	0.6	10.7
1970, total	13.4	10.3	31.5
1960, total	9.1	7.1	21.7

situation is significantly different from that in 1960 when 7 of every 8 lived with two parents—more often their own natural parents then than now.

Most people would probably agree that living with two relatively harmonious parents is a desirable situation for children. The Census Bureau cannot demonstrate whether most of the decline since 1970 in the number of children living with two parents has occurred among those whose parents were not very harmonious, but it can demonstrate that about five-sixths of that decline has occurred among children whose parents were not high school graduates. (Data presented here are for children whose parents were under 45 years old.) Meantime, three-fourths of the increase among children living with their mother only has occurred among those whose mothers were high school graduates or who had completed some college training. In fact, the number of children in one-parent families whose mother was a college graduate doubled between 1970 and 1977 (from 148,000 to 351,000), whereas the number of children in two-parent families whose father was a college graduate increased by only 1 percent (from 7.5 million to 7.6 million). (Data for 1977 are not available on the education level of the mother in two-parent families.)

Despite the substantial increase among children in one-parent families where the parent has graduated from high school (and is therefore most likely to be self-maintaining), the fact remains that nearly one-half of the children in one-parent families live with a parent who has never completed high school. This proportion is about twice as large as that for two-parent families. Thus, the pattern of change with respect to one-parent families is mixed and may be expected to continue to be that way. Young mothers who are economically independent and who choose to live at least for a while in the unmarried state may be expected to go on increasing in numbers (Ross and Sawhill, 1975). At the same time, the number of poorly educated mothers who are reported as living apart from the father of their children may be expected to continue to account for a small proportion of the increase in one-parent families; that proportion was one-fourth between 1970 and 1977.

But there is some reason to believe that many of these poorly educated and impoverished mothers with no husband reported as living in the home may actually have had a husband present who was not so reported because of such reasons as the consequences on their eligibility for welfare benefits. A closely related finding is as follows: the proportion of Black families reported as maintained by a woman in 1977 (37 percent) was much larger than that for White families (11 percent). Making use of estimates of undercounting in the 1970 census and relevant assumptions, the author reached the conclusion that probably one-fourth to one-third of the difference between the proportion of Black families and White families reported as maintained by a woman could be explained by the much larger undercount of Black men than that for White men (Glick and Mills, in press).

Where do the noncustodial parents and other unmarried persons live? To a large extent, the counterpart of one-parent families consists of *young* separated and divorced persons who live apart from their spouse (or ex-spouse) and their children, if any. These persons have contributed heavily to the rapid increase during the 1970's in the number of young adults who were living alone. The number of 1-person households maintained by adults under 35 years of age increased by 45 percent between 1970 and 1977, well above the rate of increase for any other age group. About one-fourth of these young adults living alone in 1977 were separated or divorced, and a substantial majority were men. Most of the remainder were never-married persons living alone, many of whom would have been married if it had not been for the recent increase in the postponement of marriage.

Besides the one-fourth of young noncustodial parents who live alone, a somewhat larger proportion live in a family setting, usually with their parents. This living arrangement is much more typical of separated than divorced persons. Most of the remainder live in with nonrelatives or share their living quarters with nonrelatives.

Unmarried couples of opposite sexes account for a numerically small but rapidly increasing type of living arrangement. Nearly 2 million adults in 1977 were sharing their living quarters with only one other unmarried adult, consisting of a man with a woman living in (606,000 men and 606,000 women) or consisting of a woman with a man living in (351,000 women and 351,000 men). These 1.9 million adults constituted an 83 percent increase over their 1,046,000 counterparts in 1970 (Glick and Norton, 1977).

Most of these adults are relatively young (three-fourths being under 45 years of age), but one-tenth include a man or a woman 65 years old or older. An estimated 3.6 percent of all unmarried adults and 8.3 percent of the divorced men under 35 in 1977 were involved in an unmarried couple lifestyle. Of all the one-parent families, about 3 or 4 percent included an unmarried couple. Unmarried couples were more likely to consist of a man and a woman neither of whom had graduated from high school or both of whom had an incomplete college education than would be expected if they were randomly distributed among all couples.

Although only 2 percent of the "couple households" in the 1977 cross-section survey consisted of unmarried couples, some unknown additional proportion of young adults will adopt this lifestyle for at least a period of several months or have previously done so. In the early 1970's, the proportion in Sweden comparable with 2 percent for the United States was 12 percent (Trost, 1975) and has risen since that time. Whether the *lifetime* proportion of unmarried couples among young adults in this country will rise from its present level of 2 percent to a 12- or 15-percent level is difficult to conjecture. Although the current trend is in that direction, it is probably too early to expect it to rise that high.

The family (in modified form) will go on.   This paper has documented some of the substantial changes that have been occurring in regard to marriage, family size, and living arrangements and has offered some opinions about likely future changes in these aspects of family life. In spite of the demonstrable delay in marriage, the decline in family size, the upturn in divorce, and the increasing diversity of living arrangements, the overwhelming majority of American people still live in nuclear families that include a married couple and/or a parent and one or more children (Glick, 1978). This assertion is not meant to minimize the extent of recent changes but to imply that the American people have been showing a great degree of resilience in coping with pressures that affect their family life and are likely to continue to do so (Bane, 1976).

The judgment presented here is that most of the changes in family life over the next two decades will be small as compared with those during the last two decades. Of course, the future changes in some respects, such as the living arrangements of unmarried young adults, may continue to change considerably in view of the recency of the sharp increase in the experimentation in this area.

Underlying many of the Nation's family problems during the 1960's and 1970's has been the difficulty of coping with the tremendous task of absorbing into the social system the massive number of young adults who were born during the period of high birth rates after World War II. High unemployment rates and inflated prices for consumer products and services must have also contributed to the increasing delay in marriage, the reduction in births, the evident difficulty of keeping marriages intact, and associated changes in the composition of households.

The delay in marriage should have the favorable side effect of expanding the range of social relations before marriage, thereby increasing the chances that a rational choice of a marriage partner will be made at a more mature age than formerly. Through a cumulative process, delayed marriage also generally means still further delayed childbearing. Research demonstrates that delaying childbearing is one factor associated with a smaller number of children and fewer unwanted births (Westoff, 1978).

Obtaining no more than the desired number of children is now within the realm of possibility for most young adults through modern effective means of contraception. One of these means that has been adopted by a rapidly growing proportion of contraceptors is sterilization of the husband or the wife. This increasing use of sterilization deserves more attention than it has received as a means for promoting slow population growth in future years. As long as sterilization cannot be reversed, it will prevent those who adopt it from changing their minds about having additional children and contributing thereby to a new baby boom. At the same time, lack of access to, or use of, effective contraception by sexually active adolescents continues to be a serious problem (Baldwin, 1976).

The advantages of having a large family in an agrarian economy no longer apply to the current American scene. In earlier times the mother of many children usually found her time fully occupied with household duties, but now half of the mothers (usually with only one, two, or possibly three young children) are using their high school or college education to gain employment outside the home. Once these mothers have overcome the obstacles to such employment, few of them are likely to forego the advantages, particularly those women with no children below school age. Two of the most needed supports for working parents are good quality day care for children below school age and the opportunity to work part time or on a flexible time schedule so that one parent can be at home while the children are not in school. One obvious way to provide more good quality day care for children would be to increase the use of persons trained to teach who find no jobs and to place them with the children in vacated school buildings, with costs shared by parents and the local government on the basis of the parent's ability to pay for this service. Such a program would become more feasible if it were supported by the necessary Federal funding.

Delaying marriage has been associated with an increase in the work experience of women who have never married. This experience makes women more employable as they enter marriage, and increasingly makes it possible for them to work on a continuous basis with a few months off for childbearing. The more employable they become and the fewer children they have as a partial consequence thereof, the more economically independent young mothers become and the more likely they are to seek a divorce if their marriage comes under serious stress.

Thus, the new options that have emerged during the last generation or two for women to become well-educated, to obtain employment outside the home, to limit the size of their family, and to end an unsatisfactory marriage in divorce, have created a setting in which an increase in divorce should not be very surprising. The new options have therefore come at a price (Bronfenbrenner, 1976). But the price is not too high insofar as it has made divorce a real alternative to a marriage that becomes a threat to the mental health and general well-being of persons who are directly involved (Norton and Glick, 1976).

During the last two decades social pressure has been diminishing for young adults to marry, to have children, and to stay married. During the next decade or two social pressure may also be expected to diminish for both a working mother and her husband to be employed on a full-time basis. Relaxation of pressures in these ways would be expected to increase the quality of the marriages that are initiated and of those that remain intact.

An appropriate closing to these thoughts about the future of the American family is the following sentence from President Carter's announcement of the forthcoming White House Conference on Families: "I am confident that the American family is basically sound and that we can and will adjust to the challenges of changing times."

References

Baldwin, Wendy H., "Adolescent Pregnancy and Childbearing—Growing Concerns for Americans," *Population Bulletin,* Vol. 31, No. 2, Population Reference Bureau, Inc., Washington, D.C. (1976).

Bane, Mary Jo., *Here to Stay: American Families in the Twentieth Century,* New York: Basic Books, Inc. (1976).

Bronfenbrenner, Urie, "The Disturbing Changes in the American Family," *Search,* Vol. 2, No. 1, pp. 4–10 (1976).

Bumpass, Larry, and James A. Sweet, "Differentials in Marital Instability," *American Sociological Review,* Vol. 37, No. 6, pp. 754–766 (December 1972).

Carter, Hugh, and Paul C. Glick, *Marriage and Divorce: A Social and Economic Study* (2nd ed.), Cambridge, Mass.: Harvard University Press (1976).

Glick, Paul C., "Updating the Life Cycle of the Family," *Journal of Marriage and the Family,* Vol. 39, No. 1, pp. 5–13 (February 1977).

———, "Social Change and the American Family," *The Social Welfare Forum, 1977,* National Conference on Social Welfare, Columbia University Press, pp. 43–62 (1978).

Glick, Paul C., and Karen M. Mills, "Black Families: Marriage Patterns and Living Arrangements," in John D. Reid and Everett S. Lee, eds., *The Population of American Blacks,* Athens, Georgia: University of Georgia Press (in press).

Glick, Paul C., and Arthur J. Norton, "Marrying, Divorcing, and Living Together in the U.S. Today," *Population Bulletin,* Vol. 32, No. 5, Population Reference Bureau, Inc., Washington, D.C. (1977).

Masnick, George S., *A New Perspective on the Twentieth Century American Fertility Swing,* Cambridge, Massachusetts: Harvard University Press (1976).

Norton, Arthur J., and Paul C. Glick, "Marital Instability: Past, Present and Future," *Journal of Social Issues,* Vol. 32, No. 1, pp. 5–20 (1976).

Ross, Heather L., and Isabell V. Sawhill, *Time of Transition: The Growth of Families Headed by Women,* Washington, D.C.: Urban Institute (1975).

Trost, Jan, "Married and Unmarried Cohabitation: The Case of Sweden, with Some Comparisons," in Luis Lenero-Otero, *Beyond the Nuclear Family Model: Cross-Cultural Perspectives,* Beverly Hills, California: Sage Publications, Inc. (1977).

U.S. Bureau of the Census, *Current Population Reports,* Series P–20, No. 212, "Marital Status and Family Status: March 1970"; No. 218, "Household and Family Characteristics: March 1970"; and No. 323, "Marital Status and Living Arrangements: March 1977"; and Series P–23, No. 49, *Population of the United States, Trends and Prospects: 1950–1990,* a book-length monograph.

Westoff, Charles F., "Some Speculations on the Future of Marriage and Fertility," *Family Planning Perspectives,* Vol. 10, No. 2, pp. 79–83 (March/April 1978).

The Disappearance
of the Incest Taboo

Yehudi Cohen

■ Several years ago a minor Swedish bureaucrat, apparently with nothing better to do, was leafing through birth and marriage records, matching people with their natural parents. To his amazement he found a full brother and sister who were married and had several children. The couple were arrested and brought to trial. It emerged that they had been brought up by separate sets of foster parents and never knew of each other's existence. By a coincidence reminiscent of a Greek tragedy, they met as adults, fell in love, and married, learning of their biological tie only after their arrest. The local court declared their marriage illegal and void.

The couple appealed the decision to Sweden's Supreme Court. After lengthy testimony on both sides of the issue, the court overturned the decision on the grounds that the pair had not been reared together. The marriage was declared legal and valid. In the wake of the decision, a committee appointed by Sweden's Minister of Justice to examine the question has proposed that criminal sanctions against incest be repealed. The committee's members were apparently swayed by Carl-Henry Alstrom, a professor of psychiatry. Alstrom argued that psychological deterrents to incest are stronger than legal prohibitions. The question will soon go to Sweden's Parliament, which seems prepared to follow the committee's recommendation.

Aside from illustrating the idea that the most momentous changes in human societies often occur as a result of unforeseen events, this landmark case raises questions that go far beyond Sweden's (or any other society's) borders. Some people may be tempted to dismiss the Swedish decision as an anomaly, as nothing more than a part of Sweden's unusual experiments in public welfare and sexual freedom.

But the probable Swedish decision to repeal criminal laws against incest cannot be regarded so lightly; this simple step reflects a trend in human society that has been developing for several thousand years. When we arrange human societies along a continuum from the least to the most complex, from those with the smallest number of interacting social groups to those with the highest number of groups, from those with the simplest technology to those with the most advanced technology, we observe that the incest taboo applies to fewer and fewer relatives beyond the immediate family.

Though there are exceptions, the widest extension of incest taboos beyond the nuclear family is found in the least complex societies. In a few societies, such as the Cheyenne of North America and the Kwoma of New Guinea, incest taboos extend to many remote relatives, including in-laws and the in-laws of in-laws. In modern industrial societies, incest taboos are usually confined to members of the immediate household. This contraction in the range of incest taboos is reaching the point at which they may disappear entirely.

The source of these changes in incest taboos lies in changing patterns of external trade. Trade is a society's jugular. Because every group lives in a milieu lacking some necessities that are available in other habitats, the flow of goods and resources is a society's lifeblood. But it is never sufficient merely to encourage people to form trade alliances with others in different areas. Incest taboos force people to marry outside their own group, to form alliances and to maintain trade networks. As other institutions—governments, business organizations—begin to organize trade, incest taboos become less necessary for assuring the flow of the society's lifeblood; they start to contract.

Other explanations of the incest taboo do not, under close examination, hold up. The most common assumption is that close inbreeding is biologically deleterious and will lead to the extinction of those who practice it. But there is strong evidence that inbreeding does not materially increase the rate of maladies such an albinism, total color blindness, or various forms of idiocy, which generally result when each parent carries the same recessive gene. In most cases these diseases result from chance combinations of recessive genes or from mutation.

According to Theodosius Dobzhansky, a geneticist, "The increase of the incidence of hereditary diseases in the offspring of marriages between relatives (cousins, uncle and niece or aunt and nephew, second cousins, etc.) over that in marriages between persons not known to be related is slight—so slight that geneticists hesitate to declare such marriages disgenic." Inbreeding does carry a slight risk. The progeny of relatives include more stillbirths and infant and early childhood deaths than the progeny of unrelated people. But most of these deaths are due to environmental rather than genetic factors. Genetic disadvantages are not frequent enough to justify a prohibition. Moreover, it is difficult to justify the biological explanation for incest taboos when many societies prescribe marriage to one cousin and prohibit marriage to another. Among the Lesu of Melanesia a man must avoid sexual contact with his parallel cousins, his mother's sisters' daughters and his father's brothers' daughters, but is supposed to marry his cross cousins, his mother's brothers' daughters and his father's sisters' daughters. Even though both types of cousins have the same genetic relationship to the man, only one kind is included in the incest taboo. The taboo is apparently a cultural phenomenon based on the cultural classification of people and can not be explained biologically.

Genetic inbreeding may even have some advantages in terms of natural selection. Each time a person dies of a hereditary disadvantage, his detrimental genes are lost to the population. By such a process of genetic cleansing, inbreeding may lead to the elimination, or at least to reduced frequencies, of recessive genes. The infant mortality rate may increase slightly at first, but after the sheltered recessive genes are eliminated, the population may stabilize. Inbreeding may also increase the frequency of beneficial recessive genes, contributing to the population's genetic fitness. In the end, inbreeding seems to have only a slight effect on the offspring and a mixed effect, some good and some bad, on the gene pool itself. This mild consequence hardly justifies the universal taboo on incest.

Another explanation of the incest taboo is the theory of natural aversion, first propounded by Edward Westermarck in his 1891 book, *The History of Human Marriage.* According to Westermarck, children reared in the same household are naturally averse to having sexual relations with one another in adulthood. But this theory has major difficulties. First, it has a basic logical flaw: If there were a natural aversion to incest, the taboo would be unnecessary. As James Frazer pointed out in 1910, "It is not easy to see why any deep human instinct should need to be reinforced by law. There is no law commanding men to eat and drink or forbidding them to put their hands in the fire. . . . The law only forbids men to do what their instincts incline them to do; what nature itself prohibits and punishes, it would be superfluous for the law to prohibit and punish. . . . Instead of assuming, therefore, from the legal prohibition of incest that there is a natural aversion to incest, we ought rather to assume that there is a natural instinct in favour of it."

Second, the facts play havoc with the notion of natural aversion. In many societies, such as the Arapesh of New Guinea studied by Margaret Mead, and the Eskimo, young children are betrothed and raised together, usually by the boy's parents, before the marriage is consummated. Arthur Wolf, an anthropologist who studied a village in northern Taiwan, describes just such a custom: "Dressed in the traditional red wedding costume, the bride enters her future husband's home as a child. She is seldom more than three years of age and often less than a year. . . . [The] last phase in the marriage process does not take place until she is old enough to fulfill the role of wife. In the meantime, she and her parents are affinally related to the groom's parents, but she is not in fact married to the groom."

One of the examples commonly drawn up to support Westermarck's theory of aversion is the Israeli *kibbutz,* where children who have been raised together tend to avoid marrying. But this avoidance has been greatly exaggerated. There is some tendency among those who have been brought up in the same age group in a communal "children's house" to avoid marrying one another, but this arises from two regulations that separate young adults from their *kibbutz* at about the age when they might marry. The first is a regulation of the Israel Defense Forces that no married woman may serve in the armed forces. Conscription for men and women is at 18, usually coinciding with their completion of secondary school, and military service is a deeply felt responsibility for most *kibbutz*-reared Israelis. Were women to marry prior to 18, they would be denied one of their principal goals. By the time they complete their military service, many choose urban spouses whom they have met in the army. Thus the probability of marrying a person one has grown up with is greatly reduced.

The second regulation that limits intermarriage on a *kibbutz* is a policy of the federations to which almost all *kibbutzim* belong. Each of the four major federations reserves the right to transfer any member to any other settlement, especially when a new one is being established. These "seeds," as the transferred members are called, are recruited individually from different settlements and most transfers are made during a soldier's third or fourth year of military service. When these soldiers leave the army to live on a *kibbutz,* they may be separated from those they were reared with. The frequency of marriage among people from working-class backgrounds who began and completed school together in an American city or town is probably higher than for an Israeli *kibbutz;* the proclivity among American college graduates to marry outside their neighborhoods or towns is no more an example of exogamy or incest avoidance than is the tendency in Israeli *kibbutzim* to marry out.

Just as marriage within a neighborhood is accepted in the United States, so is marriage within a *kibbutz* accepted in Israel. During research I conducted in Israel between 1967 and 1969, I attended the wedding of two people in a *kibbutz* who supposedly were covered by this taboo or rule of avoidance. As my tape recordings and photographs show, it would be difficult to imagine a more joyous occasion. When I questioned members of the *kibbutz* about this, they told me with condescending smiles that they had "heard of these things the professors say."

A third, "demographic," explanation of the incest taboo was originally set forth in 1950 by Wilson Wallis and elaborated in 1959 by Mariam Slater. According to this theory, mating within the household, especially between parents and children, was unlikely in early human societies because the life span in these early groups was so short that by the time offspring were old enough to mate, their parents would probably have died. Mating between siblings would also have been unlikely because of the average of eight years between children that resulted from breastfeeding and high rates of infant mortality. But even assuming this to have been true for the first human societies, there is nothing to prevent mating among the members of a nuclear family when the life span is lengthened.

A fourth theory that is widely subscribed to focuses on the length of the human child's parental dependency, which is the longest in the animal kingdom. Given the long period required for socializing children, there must be regulation of sexual activity so that children may learn their proper roles. If the nuclear family's members are permitted to have unrestricted sexual access to one another, the members of the unit would be confused about their roles. Parental authority would be undermined, and it would be impossible to socialize children. This interpretation has much to recommend it as far as relationships between parents and children are concerned, but it does not help explain brother-sister incest taboos or the extension of incest taboos to include remote relatives.

The explanation closest to my interpretation of the changes in the taboo is the theory of alliance advocated by the French anthropologist Claude Levi-Strauss, which suggests that people are compelled to marry outside their groups in order to form unions with other groups and promote harmony among them. A key element in the theory is that men exchange their sisters and daughters in marriage with men of other groups. As originally propounded, the theory of alliance was based on the assumption that men stay put while the women change groups by marrying out, moved about by men like pieces on a chessboard. But there are many instances in which the women stay put while the men change groups by marrying out. In either case, the result is the same. Marriage forges alliances.

These alliances freed early human societies from exclusive reliance on their own limited materials and products. No society is self-sustaining or self-perpetuating; no culture is a world unto itself. Each society is compelled to trade with others and this was as true for tribal societies as it is for modern industrial nations. North America, for instance, was crisscrossed with elaborate trade networks before the Europeans arrived. Similar trade networks covered aboriginal New Guinea and Australia. In these trade networks, coastal or riverine groups gave shells and fish to hinterland people in exchange for cultivated foods, wood, and manufactured items.

American Indian standards of living were quite high before the Europeans destroyed the native trade networks, and the same seems to have been true in almost all other parts of the world. It will come as no surprise to economists that the material quality of people's lives improves to the extent that they engage in external trade.

But barter and exchange do not automatically take place when people meet. Exchange involves trust, and devices are needed to establish trust, to distinguish friend from foe, and to assure a smooth, predictable flow of trade goods. Marriage in the tribal world established permanent obligations and reciprocal rights and privileges among families living in different habitats.

For instance, when a young Cheyenne Indian man decided on a girl to marry, he told his family of his choice. If they agreed that his selection was good, they gathered a store of prized possessions—clothing, blankets, guns, bows and arrows—and carefully loaded them on a fine horse. A friend of the family, usually a respected old woman, led the horse to the tepee of the girl's elder brother. There the go-between spread the gifts for everyone to see while she pressed the suitor's case. The next step was for the girl's brother to assemble all his cousins for a conference to weigh the proposal. If they agreed to it, the cousins distributed the gifts among themselves, the brother taking the horse. Then the men returned to their tepees to find suitable gifts to give in return. Within a day or two, each returned with something roughly equal in value to what he had received. While this was happening, the bride was made beautiful. When all arrangements were completed, she mounted one horse while the return gifts were loaded on another. The old woman led both horses to the groom's camp. After the bride was received, her accompanying gifts were distributed among the groom's relatives in accordance with what each had given. The exchanges between the two families did not end with the marriage ceremony, however; they continued as a permanent part of the marriage ties. This continual exchange, which took place periodically, is why the young man's bridal choice was so important for his entire family.

Marriage was not the only integral part of external trade relationships. Another was ritualized friendship, "blood brotherhood," for example. Such bonds were generally established between members of different groups and were invariably trade partnerships. Significantly, these ritualized friendships often included taboos against marriage with the friend's sisters; sometimes the taboo applied to all their close relatives. This extension of a taboo provides an important key for understanding all incest taboos. Sexual prohibitions do not necessarily grow out of biological ties. Both marriage and ritualized friendships in primitive societies promote economic alliances and both are associated with incest taboos.

Incest taboos force people into alliances with others in as many groups as possible. They promote the greatest flow of manufactured goods and raw materials from the widest variety of groups and ecological niches and force people to spread their social nets. Looked at another way, incest taboos prevent localism and economic provincialism; they block social and economic inbreeding.

Incest taboos have their widest extensions outside the nuclear family in those societies in which technology is least well developed and in which people have to carry their own trade goods for barter or exchange with members of other groups. Often in these small societies, everyone in a community is sexually taboo to the rest of the group. When the technology surrounding trade improves and shipments of goods and materials can be concentrated (as when people learn to build and navigate ocean-going canoes or harness pack animals), fewer and fewer people have to be involved in trade. As this happens, incest taboos begin to contract, affecting fewer and fewer people outside the nuclear family.

This process has been going on for centuries. Today, in most industrial societies, the only incest taboos are those that pertain to members of the nuclear family. This contraction of the range of the taboo is inseparable from the fact that we no longer engage in personal alliances and trade agreements to get the food we eat, the clothes we wear, the tools and materials we use, the fuels on which we depend. Goods are brought to distribution points near our homes by a relatively tiny handful of truckers, shippers, merchants, entrepreneurs, and others. Most of us are only vaguely aware of the alliances, negotiations, and relationships that make this massive movement of goods possible. When we compare tribal and contemporary industrialized societies, the correspondence between the range of incest taboos and the material conditions of life cannot be dismissed as mere coincidence.

Industrialization does not operate alone in affecting the degree to which incest taboos extend beyond the nuclear family. In the history of societies, political institutions developed as technology advanced. Improvements in packaging and transportation have led not only to reductions in the number of people involved in external trade, but also to greater and greater concentrations of decision making in the hands of fewer and fewer people. Trade is no longer the responsibility of all members of a society and the maintenance of relationships between societies has become the responsibility of a few people—a king and his bureaucracy, impersonal governmental agencies, national and multinational corporations.

To the extent that trade is conducted and negotiated by a handful of people, it becomes unnecessary to use incest taboos to force the majority of people into alliances with other groups. Treaties, political alliances, and negotiations by the managers of a few impersonal agencies have replaced marital and other personal alliances. The history of human societies suggests that incest taboos may have outlived their original purpose.

But incest taboos still serve other purposes. For social and emotional reasons rather than economic ones, people in modern industrial societies still need to prevent localism. Psychological well-being in a diversified society depends largely on the ability to tap different ideas, points of view, life styles, and social relationships. The jugulars that must now be kept open by the majority of people may no longer be for goods and resources, but for variety and stimulation. This need for variety is what, in part, seems to underlie the preference of Israelis to marry outside the communities in which they were born and brought up. The taboo against sex within the nuclear family leads young people to explore, to seek new experiences. In a survey of a thousand cases of incest, Christopher Bagley found that incestuous families are cut off from their society's social and cultural mainstream. Whether rural or urban, he writes, "the family seems to withdraw from the general community, and initiates its own 'deviant' norms of sexual behavior, which are contained within the family circle." "Such a family," he continues, "is an isolated cultural unit, relatively untouched by external social norms." This social and cultural inbreeding is the cause of the profound malaise represented by incest.

To illustrate the correspondence between incest and social isolation, let me describe an incestuous family reported by Peter Wilson, an anthropologist. Wilson sketched a sequence of events in which a South American family became almost totally isolated from the community in which it lived, and began to practice almost every variety of incest. The decline into incest began many years before Wilson appeared on the scene to do anthropological research, when the father of five daughters and four sons made the girls (who ranged in age from 18 to 33) sexually available to some sailors for a small sum of money. As a result, the entire household was ostracized by the rest of the village. "But most important," Wilson writes, "the Brown family was immediately cut off from sexual partners. No woman would have anything to do with a Brown man; no man would touch a Brown woman."

The Browns's isolation and incest continued for several years, until the women in the family rebelled—apparently because a new road connecting their hamlet to others provided the opportunity for social contact with people outside the hamlet. At the same time the Brown men began working in new light industry in the area and spending their money in local stores. The family slowly regained some social acceptance in Green Fields, the larger village to which their hamlet belonged. Little by little they were reintegrated into the hamlet and there seems to have been no recurrence of incest among them.

A second example is an upper-middle class, Jewish, urban American family that was described to me by a colleague. The Erva family (a pseudonym) consists of six people—the parents, two daughters aged 19 and 22, and two sons, aged 14 and 20. Mr. Erva is a computer analyst and his wife a dentist. Twenty-five years ago, the Ervas seemed relatively normal, but shortly after their first child was born, Mr. and Mrs. Erva took to wandering naked about their apartment, even when others were present. They also began dropping in on friends for as long as a week; their notion of reciprocity was to refuse to accept food, to eat very little of what was offered them, or to order one member of their family not to accept any food at all during a meal. Their rationale seemed to be that accepting food was receiving a favor, but occupying a bed was not. This pattern was accompanied by intense family bickering and inadvertent insults to their hosts. Not surprisingly, most of their friends wearied of their visits and the family was left almost friendless.

Reflecting Bagley's general description of incestuous families, the Ervas had withdrawn from the norms of the general community after the birth of their first child and had instituted their own "deviant" patterns of behavior. They thereby set the stage for incest.

Mr. Erva began to have intercourse with his daughters when they were 14 and 16 years old. Neither of them was self-conscious about the relationship and it was common for the father to take both girls into bed with him at the same time when they were visiting overnight. Mrs. Erva apparently did not have intercourse with her sons. The incest became a matter of gossip and added to the family's isolation.

The Erva family then moved to the Southwest to start over again. They built a home on a parcel of land that had no access to water. Claiming they could not afford a well of their own, the family began to use the bathrooms and washing facilities of their neighbors. In the end these neighbors, too, wanted nothing to do with them.

Mr. and Mrs. Erva eventually separated, he taking the daughters and she the sons. Later the younger daughter left her father to live alone, but the older daughter still shares a one bedroom apartment with her father.

Social isolation and incest appear to be related, and social maturity and a taboo on incest are also related. Within the modern nuclear family, social and emotional relationships are intense, and sexuality is the source of some of the strongest emotions in human life. When combined with the intensity of family life, sexually stimulated emotions can be overwhelming for children. Incest taboos are a way of limiting family relationships. They are assurances of a degree of emotional insularity, of detachment on which emotional maturity depends.

On balance, then, we can say that legal penalties for incest were first instituted because of the adverse economic effects of incestuous unions on society, but that today the negative consequences of incest affect only individuals. Some will say that criminal penalties should be retained if only to protect children. But legal restraints alone are unlikely to serve as deterrents. Father-daughter incest is regarded by many social workers, judges, and psychiatrists as a form of child abuse, but criminal penalties have not deterred other forms of child abuse. Moreover, incest between brothers and sisters cannot be considered child abuse. Some have even suggested that the concept of abuse may be inappropriate when applied to incest. "Many psychotherapists," claims psychologist James McCary in *Human Sexuality,* "believe that a child is less affected by actual incest than by seductive behavior on the part of a parent that never culminates in any manifest sexual activity."

Human history suggests that the incest taboo may indeed be obsolete. As in connection with changing attitudes toward homosexuality, it may be maintained that incestuous relations between consenting mature adults are their concern alone and no one else's. At the same time, however, children must be protected. But questions still remain about how they should be protected and until what age.

If a debate over the repeal of criminal laws against incest is to begin in earnest, as it surely will if the Swedish Parliament acts on the proposed reversal, one other important fact about the social history of sexual behavior must be remembered. Until about a century ago, many societies punished adultery and violations of celibacy with death. When it came time to repeal those laws, not a few people favored their retention on the grounds that extramarital sexual relationships would adversely affect the entire society. Someday people may regard incest in the same way they now regard adultery and violations of celibacy. Where the threat of punishment once seemed necessary, social and emotional dissuasion may now suffice.

References

Bagley, Christopher. "Incest Behavior and Incest Taboos." *Social Problems,* Vol. 16, 1969, pp. 505–519.

Birdsell, J. B. *Human Evolution: An Introduction to the New Physical Anthropology,* Rand McNally, 1972.

Bagley, Christopher. "Incest Behavior and Incest Taboos." *Social Problems,* Vol. 16, 1969, pp. 505–519.

Birdsell, J. B. *Human Evolution: An Introduction to the New Physical Anthropology,* Rand McNally, 1972.

Bischof, Norbert. "The Biological Foundations of the Incest Taboo." *Social Science Information,* Vol. 11, No. 6, 1972.

Fox, Robin. *Kinship and Marriage,* Penguin Books, 1968.

Slater, Marian. "Ecological Factors in the Origin of Incest." *American Anthropologist,* Vol. 61, No. 6, 1959.

Wilson, Peter J. "Incest: A Case Study." *Social and Economic Studies.* Vol. 12, 1961, pp. 200–209.

Social Structure

Structural Differentiation and the Family: A Quiet Revolution
Judith Blake

Indications of the Decline in Structural Differentiation

■ Let us . . . examine some indications of the decline in structural differentiation. I shall consider these in terms of a set of diminishing distinctions between marriage and nonmarriage; having children and remaining childless; legitimate and illegitimate childbearing; being a wife/mother and participating in the labor force; and, finally, between family "privacy" and the external society.

The Blurring Distinction Between Marriage and Nonmarriage

Two salient features of American mating behavior in recent years represent, I believe, a major blurring of the distinction between marriage and nonmarriage. These are the increase in open, informal domiciliary relationships and the rise in divorce.

The rise in informal and open domiciliary relationships   Since 1960, the number of unmarried couples residing together in the same quarters has more than doubled—rising from 439,000 in 1960 to 957,000 in 1977.[1] Most of this change has taken place since 1970. According to Glick and Norton, by March 1977 some two million persons were involved in such domiciliary arrangements. The largest rise has been among individuals in two-person households. The change is, moreover, apparently even greater than the gross statistics suggest because there has been an apparent decrease since 1960 in the proportion of these domiciles that constituted a landlord-tenant arrangement. According to Glick and Norton, detailed analysis of the ages of the participants over time indicates that more unmarried, cohabiting couples now consist of a young man and woman living together, whereas, in 1960, unmarried couples were composed of higher proportions of older women with young male tenants.

Although increasing, are such arrangements of any proportionate significance in American society? Considering unmarried adults of all ages, some 3.6 percent were in such households. But, taking couple-households where the husband or man was under age twenty-five, 7.4 percent were nonmarital rather than marital. We are still some distance from Sweden, where some 12 percent of all couples live together informally (only 2 percent of all couples are thus situated here), but the younger generation of Americans is approaching the Swedish level.[2]

About 25 percent of unmarried couples under age twenty-five residing together appear to be still students, and unmarried couples generally have a higher probability of being poor. Yet, most informally cohabiting couples are above the poverty line (65 percent of the women and 79 percent of the men in 1977), and a healthy minority (18 percent of the women and 34 percent of men) had annual incomes in 1977 at least three times the poverty level, or about $15,000 on the average.

These arrangements indicate a rise in the number of couples who have elected to be married in every way but formally. Moreover, as most of us know from personal experience, such configurations do not set the participants apart from normal social intercourse, even if marriage is still generally "preferred." Thus, unmarried couples who wish to reside together and thereby have the convenience, companionship, and many of the economic advantages of being married (but fewer of the disadvantages) are able to do so today with minimal penalties.[3]

Whether such arrangements are of equal respective benefit to the men and women involved depends on an assessment of the relative opportunity costs of marriage and nonmarriage, as well as the freedom each sex has to reshuffle the marital decision as time goes by. The traditional view has been that women, being dependent on marriage economically as well as being the passive recipients of a "proposal," should strike a good match while their physical attractions are greatest—that is, while young (see Davis, 1976, 1977). These ground rules have undergone some revision. The opportunity costs for women in marrying have risen substantially as job opportunities have improved.[4] This is particularly true since the economic security of marriage has greatly diminished. As will be discussed, marriages are deeply threatened with impermanence because of divorce, and it is becoming increasingly evident that a divorced woman is typically left without much support (Weitzman, 1972). Hence, although there has not been a revolution in women's job chances, it is nonetheless true that fidelity to the labor market may pay off better for a young woman than fidelity to a husband.[5] This is particularly true since the law still holds to some genuinely archaic notions of the trade-offs within marriage—the man is the "provider" and the woman exchanges services for support (Weitzman, 1972). Most states regard property as the husband's, unless otherwise specified, and the husband's earnings are regarded as his as well.[6] Since virtually no provision exists for recognizing the market value of the housewife's time, a woman who devotes herself to home and family may, for her efforts, discover herself to be severely undervalued should the marriage dissolve (Krauskopf, 1977). Moreover, public and private social security and pension plans by and large sorely discriminate against a divorced wife, unless the marriage has been of very long duration.

It is thus true that many women may enter nonmarital relationships today on a basis of greater relative equality than in the past. And it is not necessarily true that their attractiveness is as evanescent as has been claimed. Women's premature loss of attractiveness (compared with men) is itself highly correlated with marriage and childbearing. Insofar as exercise, diet, personal attention, and fashion all take time and effort, many women's preoccupation with keeping up houses, husbands, and children, instead of themselves, itself contributes to a self-fulfilling prophecy regarding diminishing good looks.

The rise in divorce   Since the late 1950s the divorce rate has climbed precipitously. Although it seems currently to have leveled out, it has done so at a point unprecedented in our statistical history—five divorces annually per 1,000 population. To be sure, during some of the period between 1955 and the present, the rise in divorce was due to the growth of the married population and to changes in the age distribution of married persons. However, in recent years almost all of the rise has been nondemographic in cause.[7] Married persons are just divorcing at higher rates. As a consequence, Glick and Norton (1977:36–37) have estimated that approximately 40 percent of all marriages of young adults will, at current rates, end in divorce. Such rates mean that substantial numbers of persons experience a divorce in any given year. During 1975, divorces exceeded one million for the first time in our history, and provisional figures for 1977 found us with 1.097 million divorces for that year.

Obviously, this large number of divorces annually does not occur with equal probability among all age groups. Divorce rates by age of husband at decree show that the highest probabilities of divorce occur between the ages of 20 and 34. At ages 20–24, the rate in 1970 was 33.6 per 1,000 married in each age group, at age 25–29 it was 30.0, and at 30–34 it was 22.3. Such rates contrast with 14.2 for married persons of all ages (Plateris, 1978:37). If we had more recent data by age, we know that the rates would be much higher.

The statistical picture thus suggests that the line between marriage and nonmarriage is blurring even among married couples. With almost 1.10 million divorce decrees being granted annually, millions of married couples must be on the road to dissolution at any given time. Moreover, such rates of dissolution imply that the population is building up large numbers of people who have been divorced. Census data for the mid-1970s indicate that among women (divorced at ages 14–75), 9.068 million with a first marriage experienced a divorce. Assuming comparable figures for men, this means that some 18 million Americans alive in 1975 had had a first marriage dissolved by divorce. To be sure, most divorced people remarry (for example, among childless women under age 30 at divorce, some 80 percent remarry), but this in itself makes the distinction between marriage and divorce even less clear.

A Blurring Between Familial and Occupational Roles

A major component of the structural differentiation of the modern nuclear family has been its withdrawal from the world of work. Yet, as we approach 1980, this characterization of the American family has become quaint. It appears that this aspect of the structural differentiation, so vaunted in the sociology of the 1950s and early 1960s, has been obscured almost totally. No longer is there a single breadwinner during most of the family cycle; no longer can one conceive of the status of the family as depending almost entirely on his efforts; in fact, no longer is he always the highest earner, nor does he invariably have the higher-status occupation. The world of work and the family have been reunited in the persons of both husband and wife, father and mother. Finally, as the husband and wife age, the "breadwinner" for them both is typically located in another generation and outside of any direct family connection. The backbone of family sustenance becomes an intergenerational transfer payment from the men and women in the society who are currently working. Let us look at the evidence.

Married women and mothers in the labor force   Between 1960 and 1975 there was an increase of 28 percent in the labor force participation of married women, husband present. By the mid-1970s almost one-half (44 percent) of all women in this marital status category were market participants. Among young childless women (under age 35), husband present, 77 percent were in the labor force in 1975, a rise of 24 percent from 1960 among even this group of women who were traditionally prone to work. However, the really startling news, of course, has been the 64 percent rise, since 1960, in work participation by mothers, husband present, with children under age three (from 23 to 37 percentage points), and the increase of 43 percent among mothers of three- to five-year-olds (from 29 to 42 percentage points—see Glick and Norton, 1977:11). Thus, the traditional association between legitimate childbearing for women and withdrawal from market work has changed quite drastically over the past fifteen years. This change has occurred, moreover, without any formal policy designed to aid working women with child care, or to provide other ancillary services to them (see Rivlin, 1972; Rothman, 1973; Woolsey, 1977; also, U.S. Bureau of the Census, 1976). We must conclude that women with young children are highly motivated to enter the labor force.

Husband and father—the "status giver"   Concomitant with the rise in working pairs among intact married couples is a change in the notion that the husband/father is the status giver for the family. Among married couples in 1975 where both husband and wife were earners, a third of the wives made approximately as much as, or more than, the husband, and 62 percent were in an occupation in the same "major" level, ranked in terms of the Census Bureau's socioeconomic status scores (Glick and Norton, 1977:11).

   This pattern of relative income equality between working mates is, of course, far more pronounced among couples where the husband's earnings are under the median for husbands with working wives, than where his earnings are higher. For example, among working couples where the husband earns less than $10,000 a year—41 percent of all working couples—the wife's earnings were approximately equal to his or more in 49 percent of the cases.[8] But among husbands with earnings of $15,000 and over—28 percent of all working couples—only 18 percent of the wives were in roughly the same bracket or higher. It is nonetheless true that, for a significant proportion of working couples, the wife, through market work, is not only making an important *marginal* contribution to the family's economic status, she is making an *absolute* one equal to or greater than her husband.

   Quite clearly, as Oppenheimer has suggested, a major erosion has occurred in the notion of the husband/father as chief status giver or principal earner. "Structural differentiation" theorists were interested in developing a "functional imperative theory." But, as Oppenheimer (1974) says,

> By definition, such theories are statements of the necessity of the status quo—unfortunately, in this case, the status quo of some 35 years ago, not of today. The only change such a theory tends to permit is that from social order to social disorder. As such, theories of this nature are not particularly useful tools in the analysis of the types of change which do not involve the disintegration of the social system.

Family status of highly educated and high-status women   We have seen that women who have attained conventional wifely status are increasingly articulating with the world of work and helping to define the social position of their families. In considering the erosion of familial specialization, it is also important to focus on the familial participation of highly educated women and female occupational stars. Are such women as likely as in the past to remain unmarried, or are they more apt to combine high-level educational and/or occupational status with marriage? In effect, does a feminine "success" role in the nonfamilial world still greatly reduce the probability of being married?

As for educational level, between 1960 and 1975, women with graduate training have scored the largest gains of any educational group (male or female) in the proportion married once with spouse present by middle age (or near it). During the fifteen-year period, these women had a 136 percent gain in this category (Glick and Norton, 1977:10). Even by 1975, however, it was still true that highly educated women (by late adult or middle age) were married to their first spouse in smaller proportions (63 percent) than women of any other educational category except those with 0–11 years of schooling. In addition, they were 19 percentage points lower than men of comparable schooling—a gain, however, over the 25 percentage point differential of 1960.

These results reflect not simply greater marital stability on the part of high-status women, but a higher probability of marrying at all than was the case as recently as twenty years ago. Taking major occupational groupings of employed persons, comparison over the past decade alone indicates that women in the two highest occupational categories— professional and managerial—were more likely in 1976 to be married with a husband present than approximately two decades earlier (1958). For example, proportions in this marital status among professional women increased from 52 to 62 percent, and among managers from 59 to 64 percent. Among the remaining occupational categories combined, the proportions married (husband present) rose from 53.1 to 55.5 percent.[9]

These data suggest important changes in the structural differentiation of the nuclear family and, as well, a major motivational reconfiguration for modern women. A salient goal of women's movements the world over—the freedom of women to combine familial and major occupational roles (just as men do)—is closer to achievement than has ever been the case before (B. Friedan, 1963:381–82; Rossi, 1964; Epstein, 1970:99–100).

Intergenerational transfer payments as "the breadwinner"   As we have seen, married men in intact households are less and less likely to be the sole breadwiners. Moreover, people generally are, as they age, becoming more dependent upon younger workers of both sexes to make transfer payments to them (Kreps, 1965:268). Since the century began, there has been a drastic decline in the labor force participation of older men. Among men aged 65 and over, the rate of labor force participation has fallen from 68.3 percent in 1900 to 20.1 percent in 1977. Since 1960 alone, the rate dropped from 33.1 percent. Even among men aged 55–64 years of age, labor force participation has fallen. Between 1960 and 1977, market attachment among these men declined from 86.8 to 74.0 Most of this change has occurred during the 1970s (U.S. Bureau of the Census, 1977*b*).

As Kreps has emphasized, sources of income of the aged in recent years have reflected the changing work-retirement pattern of older men. The proportion of income from current earnings among older persons declined substantially during the 1950s at the same time that the proportion derived from social insurance benefits increased. Kreps (1965:271) says,

Of the 1960 aggregate income of persons aged 65 and over, income from earnings totalled between ten and eleven billion dollars, and approximately the same amount went to recipients of old-age, survivors, and disability insurance and to retired government and railroad employees. This one-to-one ratio of earnings to benefit payments contrasts sharply with the composition of the income of the aged a decade earlier, when aggregate earnings of seven to eight billion dollars amounted to several times as much as benefit payments.

By 1967, among all aged units (married and unmarried), earnings represented only 30 percent of income. Of the remainder, 37 percent was from retirement benefits (mostly OASDHI), and 6 percent was from veterans' benefits and public assistance. Income from assets comprised 25 percent of total income.[10]

It is thus true that although direct intrafamilial and in-kind transfers to the older population may have declined, there has been an enormous increase in intergenerational transfers of income—from the working population to the aging. Aging persons are no longer primarily dependent on the direct efforts of the male breadwinner, nor are they economically isolated from the rest of the society.

The Increasing Ambiguity of Marriage as the Licensing of Parenthood

Two additional trends in American society have served to obscure the structurally differentiated status of the family. Both relate to the notion of marriage as, in Malinowski's (1930) words, the "licensing of parenthood." On the one hand, over the past thirty years there has been a burgeoning of illegitimate births. And correlative with the surge in births without marriage is the voluntary expansion in marriages without births.

The rise in illegitimacy and Malinowski's "principle"   Since 1940, when national estimates became available, illegitimacy rates have risen from 7.1 per 1,000 unmarried women aged 15–44 to 24.7 in 1976.[11] The increase has been remarkably steady. Moreover, although nonwhite illegitimacy accounts for a disproportionate share of total illegitimacy, it is the rate for whites that has risen over time. This rate has increased from 3.6 per 1,000 unmarried women in 1940 to 12.7 in 1976. Although it has been declining slightly among white women over age 20, it has inflated inexorably among teenagers—from 3.3 per 1,000 unmarried white women aged 15–19 in 1940 to 12.4 in 1976.[12] Partly as a result of this advance in the illegitimacy rate, the proportion of all births that were illegitimate swelled between 1940 and 1976, from 3.8 to 14.8 percent.[13] The expanding illegitimacy ratio (the illegitimate proportion of all births) results as well from the decline in average family size and the effect of this trend on annual legitimate fertility.

   The so-called principle of legitimacy—as enunciated by Malinowski— was a statement about institutional norms. It referred to an astonishingly widespread—if not absolutely universal—rule that for a child to have a socially legitimated status in a society, it must be acknowledged by a sociological father—"the male link between the child and the rest of the community" (Malinowski, 1930). Obviously, however, the "principle" is not fixed in time and space like a fly in amber—it is based on certain prior assumptions. Among these are the following: that a "father" is *the* person who links the child with the community and accords status; and that, in general, the society strongly supports status ascription on the basis of familial origin.[14] As Malinowski knew, the "principle" is a theory not just about the family, but about society.

   In most societies where legitimacy is not the statistical norm, such as the Caribbean and parts of Latin America, the principle really still holds in spite of the frequency of illegitimacy. This is because in these societies, men are the status givers and the societies are highly ascriptive (Blake, 1961). On the other hand, as Goode and others have pointed out, the "principle" obviously carries less weight, on a day-to-day basis, in a society where most births are illegitimate than in one where such deviation from the norm is unusual. Illegitimate children are nonetheless punished for not having a father because the role of women is not such as to compensate for this lack.[15]

In the United States, I believe that we must not regard the rise in illegitimacy as primarily indicating a breakdown of "control" over sexual relations and reproduction, while reproductive and familial norms remain unchanged. Rather, this rise is a natural result of the fact that we are subscribing less and less to the assumptions upon which the so-called principle is based. Consequently, the sanctions for premarital childbearing are less awesome. The trend in illegitimacy is, therefore, no longer so much an indicator of deviance as of the abrogation of many prior norms supporting the principle of legitimacy.[16] Obviously, in almost every conceivable respect, illegitimate children still fare less well, on the average, than legitimate ones (Berkov and Sklar, 1972). Indeed, even if, for example, the large wage gap between men and women lessened, welfare payments to single mothers increased, and child-care arrangements expanded and improved, parity might never be achieved. That it should be both considered and attempted, however, is momentous.[17]

The rising refusal to allow a child's fate to be hitched to whether its father serves as a status giver correlates with a legally enforced norm that life chances should be decreasingly family-dependent. Such legal enforcements, as, for example, in Supreme Court decisions regarding school integration, may not accord proportionate advantage to the disadvantaged. These decisions do, however, keep the advantaged on the run and have the effect of damping the de facto enjoyment of superior social and economic status, and lessening the subjective sense of advantage due to birth.[18] In this sense, the more redistributive the society becomes, the less "status" either parent has to confer on children and the more blurred are the distinctions between legitimate and illegitimate offspring.

In effect, for the principle of legitimacy to operate in a true Malinowskian sense presupposes a society very different from the one we now live in or toward which we appear to be headed. In particular, it is a society in which the accident of familial origin means far more for life chances than is the case today, and in which social status depends on paternal "placement" almost exclusively.[19] As a consequence of our current situation, the designations "legitimate" and "illegitimate" have dwindled in meaning and are even becoming increasingly difficult to discover.[20] If being illegitimate is a "private" matter, supported by an individual's "right to privacy," the "principle" must have suffered a telling blow!

The decline in marital fertility and rising proportions of childless couples If premarital childbearing is mounting, reproduction within marriage is lessening. Not only has voluntary family size been reduced substantially since the height of the baby boom, but a growing number of young people are deciding to remain childless.[21] Under current conditions, young (18–24-year-old) American women expect to complete their fertility with an average number of two births. Among these same young women, 11 percent expect to be childless, and 12 percent expect to have one child (U.S. Bureau of the Census, 1977a). Such expectations, combined with actual behavior that (to date) appears to be highly congruent, mean that most people will spend all but a fraction of their conjugal lives without young children at home, and that a rising proportion of couples will never expand beyond the dyad.

Not surprisingly, growing numbers of young people believe that marriage is something quite different from, or more than, the "licensing of parenthood." Although a recent national survey of attitudes toward childlessness revealed that nonparenthood lacks a "glamour" image, a scale of attitudes toward childlessness demonstrated a marked division by sex in respondents' views on children as a social investment (Blake, 1979). Men were more likely to regard childlessness as disadvantageous than women. Moreover, a multiple classification analysis showed that this difference was greater, rather than less, when a range of social and demographic background variables were controlled. Men were particularly likely to think that childlessness makes a marriage more prone to divorce. It is thus possible that the "principle of least interest" in family life, in which it is assumed that women have the largest stake in home and family, may be undergoing some reversal. Elsewhere I have suggested that a change in women's "market" situation regarding marriage and child-bearing—namely, a scarcity of women available for conventional wife and mother roles—could greatly alter the terms on which such arrangements were entered (see Blake, 1974, especially p. 147).

We are thus witnessing a de facto redefinition of the social, as well as the legal, institution of marriage. Most people are, of course, almost completely unaware of the traditional legal provisions of the marriage contract. As Weitzman (1972) says,

The marriage contract is unlike most contracts: its provisions are unwritten, its penalties unspecified, and the terms of the contract are typically unknown to the "contracting" parties. Prospective spouses are neither informed of the terms of the contract nor are they allowed any options about these terms. In fact, one wonders how many men and women would agree to the marriage contract if they were given the opportunity to read it and to consider the rights and obligations to which they were committing themselves.

The legal realities of marriage typically only impinge on couples' definitions of their marital behavior when there is conflict. Until then, they may behave as if it were irrelevant that the husband is legally the head of the family, that he is responsible for support, that the wife is responsible for domestic and child-care services, or that marriage legally presupposes reproduction.[22] The surge of divorces is, however, making explicit the sharp divergence between current marital behavior and the state's presumed interest in preserving the traditional family. Increasingly, it is becoming evident that the anachronisms embedded in family law and the law of marriage will have to succumb to the realities of family life today (Weitzman, 1972). It would thus be foolhardy to look to family and marriage law as providing the bedrock of support for the family as it "really" is, or as indicating what familial and marital norms actually are. This area of the law is so at odds with major trends in modern family life that it must be considered a candidate for revision, rather than a guardian of stability.

The Demise of "Privatization"

The physically private nuclear family in its separate household has been part of the Parsonian characterization of familial specialization. Similarly, historians of the family, coming from another tradition, have argued with some force that the preindustrial, or premodern, family was far more community-oriented than the nuclear unit of modern times (Ariès, 1962; also Shorter, 1975).[23] Certainly the physical privacy of the couple and their children, so typical of the modern family in its separate quarters, did not exist in past times. Moreover, a fairly extensive historical record has been accumulated of rough and insensitive personal relationships among nuclear family members, and of singular disregard for the health and welfare of children (Ariès, 1962; Shorter, 1975). The preindustrial family was not, apparently, a tenderly guarded haven for any of its members. Interests, activities, "life," were in the community, not in the family. From this contrast with the past, some historians, like the Parsonians, have created the edifice of the "privatized" family of modern times—a family turned in on itself in the interest of performing its highly specialized functions.

Although it would be hard to argue that adults (or even children) today spend their leisure time in the community in the same way that characterized the denizens of the Middle Ages about whom Ariès has written, it seems inaccurate to speak of the family of the past fifteen to twenty years as "privatized." Rather, through the mass media, the outside world has entered the home in force. Not only do the invidious comparisons of the status system impinge incessantly, but the existence of a "youth market" has generated a socializing force directed explicitly at the young (Bernard, 1961). Moreover, in recent years, radio in particular has functioned as a source of information for adolescents concerning topics such as birth control and abortion clinics, where teenagers may be assured of privacy *from* their parents.

In contrast with the 1940s and 1950s, suburban living is no longer isolated and protected from urban ways. As the city has expanded toward the suburban lands that, years ago, seemed so "countrified," and as children find themselves traveling long distances to school, the splendid isolation of midcentury has disappeared. Thus, suburban parents have today far less control over youthful environments than was the case twenty-five years ago (Friedenberg, 1959; Bensman, 1973). As a consequence, in addition to sharing its socializing function with the legally legitimate sponsors of radio and television, the family is increasingly being touched by the underworld's insistence on its quota of the youth market as well. As children mature and move into schools, playgrounds, and streets, they soon learn that they have the opportunity to "deal." This opening does not presuppose the stigma of membership in a gang of hoodlums. The chance to peddle drugs is readily afforded by the adult underworld and by the availability of customers among the peer group. In effect, the protected and sheltered child who is a product of the privatized family is, in these days, something of a myth. The off-limits cultures that impinge on midddle- and upper-class children today are, by and large, not merely the covert cultures of their parents. For many parents, much of the environment of youth is genuinely foreign territory.

Notes

1. The data included in this section are based on the research of Paul Glick and Arthur Norton (1977 in particular, and especially pp. 32–36).
2. For a comparative Swedish perspective, see Trost, 1976.
3. Speaking of the California Supreme Court's landmark decision in *Marvin* v. *Marvin,* Kay and Amyx (1977) say that, "the court fashioned a remedy appropriate for use in any state, regardless of the underlying form of its marital property law. The court has thus taken the lead in recognizing the factual existence of a variety of familial relationships—ranging from marriage through nonmarital cohabitation—affording to each its characteristic set of legal incidents. California's citizens are therefore offered a wide choice among legally sanctioned alternatives within which they may work out their own private arrangements." (In this connection, see also *Harvard Law Review,* 1977.)
4. William Butz has postulated that the correlation of prosperity with women's job opportunities in the United States has led to an economically countercyclical trend in fertility—an association of cyclical prosperity with declines in the birth rate. For a discussion of new trends in women's opportunity-costs in marriage and childbearing, see Butz and Ward, 1977. For additional discussion, see Blake, 1974.
5. Kay and Amyx (1977:974–75) say, "The concept that traditional marriage is a status that protects women has been vigorously attacked for some time. As early as 1855 the well-known legal disabilities imposed on married women by the common law which Blackstone had asserted were designed for the wife's protection and benefit were specifically rejected by Lucy Stone and her husband, Henry Blackwell, in their *Marriage Protest,* because such laws 'confer upon the husband an injurious and unnatural superiority, investing him with legal powers which no honorable man would exercise, and which no man should possess.' Some feminists have concluded that legal marriage is inherently oppressive for women and have dedicated themselves to its abolition;

others have turned their efforts toward reform laws governing marriage and divorce in an effort to make the institution more nearly analogous to a partnership. Still others have explored contracts that alter the obligations of traditional marriage. Certainly Midge Decter's assertions made in 1972 that 'every woman wants to marry' and that 'marriage is something asked by women and agreed to by men' have been belied by the facts."

6. Kay and Amyx say, "Within the last 5 years the [California] Legislature has repealed former Civil Code section 5101, which, since the days of the Field Code, had declared the husband to be the 'head of the family,' has equalized family support obligations, has extended to wives a power equal to that formerly held exclusively by husbands to manage and control the community property during their joint lifetimes and after the death of one spouse, and has mandated the extension of credit to married women on the same terms it is granted to married men. As Professor Prager has persuasively shown, California marital property law for the first time in its history now recognizes the spouses as true partners. Similarly, the California Attorney General has acknowledged the right of a woman to retain her birth name after marriage, and the case law has permitted her to resume her former name after divorce regardless of whether she has custody of minor children." (See Kay and Amyx, 1977:952–53.) Glendon (1975) discusses very recent changes in family law in European countries and the United States—changes involving "our increasing recognition of the individual liberty of the spouses."

7. Plateris (1978) has estimated that the population component of the rise in divorce declined from 47 percent during 1955–1963 to 12 percent during 1963–1975.

8. See Glick and Norton (1977:11); the actual median earnings in 1975 for husbands in families where both spouses were earners, was $11,370.

9. Figures derived from *Handbook of Labor Statistics 1977,* tables 18 and 28, and *Handbook of Labor Statistics 1975,* tables 19 and 29 (see U.S. Department of Labor, 1977a, 1975c).

10. See Bixby, 1970, especially p. 14, giving estimates by source, using a variety of data in addition to the Current Population Survey.

11. For data for 1940, see U.S. Department of Health, Education and Welfare, National Center for Health Statistics 1972, tables 1–30, pp. 1–30; data for 1976 from HEW National Center for Health Statistics, 1978, table 12, p. 17.

12. The magnitude of the change in illegitimacy rates in the United States among teenagers, and between blacks and whites, is open to considerable question. On the other hand, it appears that illegitimacy in the 1950s may have been underestimated and that reporting may have been better in recent years. On the other hand, the recent official statistics cited above from the National Center for Health Statistics appear to underestimate illegitimate childbearing because they do not include data for twelve major states having high rates of illegitimacy. At the present time, we do not have corrected illegitimacy rates dating from the 1940s. For a discussion of some of the methodological problems involved, see Berkov and Sklar, 1975, and also O'Connell, 1978.

13. For source data on illegitimacy ratios for 1940 and 1976, see footnote 11 above.

14. For an analysis of the status-ascriptive assumptions involved in the "principle," see Goode, 1960, Coser and Coser, 1973.

15. It may be true that, given economic and social conditions in such societies, a father would not add much economically and, hence, in such conditions it is hardly worth bothering to legitimize offspring. However, I believe that this interpretation is over-drawn because all such calculations are made at the margin and in context. In *that* context, the man can make a contribution, and this would be particularly true were his involvement with only one set of children. Societies experiencing far more intense poverty than in the Caribbean and Latin America will nonetheless adhere in practice to the principle of legitimacy.

16. In a number of European countries, and to a great extent in the United States, illegitimacy has become virtually irrelevant legally (see Fritz, 1977). Coser and Coser's (1973) analysis concentrates on the case of genuine, acknowledged social revolutions in which the "principle" was abolished for the explicit purpose of abolishing the status-conferring role of the family and thereby creating greater equality of life chances. The redistributive trends in many advanced industrial societies, including our own, also bear watching, however, since numerous public policies are *implicitly* vitiating the assumptions of the principle of legitimacy, and doing so in ways that may have more staying power than has been the case with the social revolutions studied by the Cosers. In particular, the role of women in such advanced societies today is potentially somewhat different from their roles after the French, Russian, Chinese, or Cuban revolutions. There is, of course, nothing less ascriptive about inheriting status from one's mother than from one's father, and many women are, indeed, in the labor force in order to give their children "advantages," even when there is a father present.

17. The provisions of AFDC as they apply to men and women, respectively, assume that traditional sex roles are the desideratum, i.e., that the woman stays home with the children and the man finds a job (see Kinsley, 1977). However, given the difficulty that mothers of illegitimate children have in locating fathers and fixing responsibility, the AFDC program increasingly *functions* as a proxy second parent and cannot help but make a sociological father seem less crucial to many women. Indeed, there is a genuine trade-off for some women between having full control of less money from AFDC, as against being "supported" by a man who may himself spend most of the money he earns, and against whose physical violence the woman may actually require protection (see Straus, 1977; also, Steinmetz and Straus, 1974; passim). Taking such problems into account in assessing AFDC, we are faced, as a society, with the question of whether we wish to support family relationships or the almost unfettered dominance of a male-headed family. The two are not necessarily synonymous. The fact that this dominance is often buffered in middle- and upper-class families does not make it any less real for those women and children at poverty and working-class levels, among whom even the police and the courts tend to regard a husband's physical violence against his wife as permissible (see Straus, 1977).

18. Indicators of economic redistribution inevitably fail to take account of the redistributive effect of changing access to public resources. Cheap means of transportation, such as the automobile and the airplane, have opened up access to recreational areas previously reserved, on a de facto basis, almost exclusively for the well-to-do. Some of the same forces have made suburban living far less safe from both crime and accident than in the past.

19. For a summary of trends in social mobility in the United States and in European and Soviet states, see Lipset, 1972. Lipset pays particular attention to the role of the family in perpetuating inequality through the transmission of cultural differences. See also Bell, 1972, for a discussion of some of the combined implications of the Coleman Reports, Jencks, and Rawls.

20. In addition to the fact that most of the assumptions on which the "principle" is based are receiving diminished support, there is also strong societal backing for not directly stigmatizing the illegitimate child. Increasingly, states are becoming reluctant to include legitimacy status on birth certificates and, when it is included, efforts are made to ensure confidentiality (see Clague and Ventura, 1968; also Berkov and Sklar, 1975).

21. During the period since 1973, the total fertility rate in the United States has averaged about 1.8 births per woman in the reproductive ages. This means that, under current age-specific birth rates, women will bear fewer than two children per woman, on the average, by the end of their reproductive years. Actual completed cohort fertility for today's young women may, of course, be higher (or lower), since annual rates may change during the next ten or fifteen years.

22. For recent changes in family law, both here and in Europe, see Kay and Amyx, 1977, and Glendon, 1975. See also the article by Fritz (1977) on the legal status of illegitimate children.
23. Questions concerning the privatization argument have been raised by Lasch (1975a, 1975b) in "The Emotions of Family Life," and "What the Doctor Ordered." See also Moore, 1958.

References

Ariès, Philippe
1962   Centuries of Childhood: A Social History of Family Life. Translated by Robert Baldick. London: Cape.

Bell, Daniel
1972   "On meritocracy and equality." The Public Interest 29 (Fall):29–68.

Bensman, Joseph
1973   "American youth and the class structure." Pp. 62–82 in Harry Sllverstein (ed.), The Sociology of Youth: Evolution and Revolution. New York: Macmillan.

Berkov, Beth, and June Sklar
1972   "Does illegitimacy make a difference?" Population and Development Review 2 (June):201–17.
1975   "Methodological options in measuring illegitimacy and the difference they make." Social Biology 22(Winter):356–71.

Bernard, Jessie
1961   "Teen-age culture: An overview." Annals of the American Academy of Political and Social Science 338 (November):2–12.

Bixby, Lenore F.
1970   "Income of people aged 65 and older: Overview from 1968 survey of the aged." Social Security Bulletin (April):3–27.

Blake, Judith
1961   Family Structure in Jamaica. The Social Context on Reproduction. New York: Free Press.
1974   "The changing status of women in developed countries." Scientific American 231 (September):137–47.
1979   "Is zero preferred? American attitudes toward childlessness in the 1970's." Journal of Marriage and the Family (May).

Butz, William P., and Michael Ward
1977   The Emergence of Countercyclical U.S. Fertility. Monograph No. R-1605-NIH. Santa Monica, Calif.: Rand Corporation.

Clague, Alice J., and Stephanie J. Ventura
1968   Trends in Illegitimacy. U. S. Department of Health, Education, and Welfare, National Center for Health Statistics Series Number 21, Publ. Number 15. Washington, D.C.: Government Printing Office.

Coser, Rose Laub, and Lewis A. Coser
1973   "The principle of legitimacy and its patterned infringement in social revolutions." Pp. 119–30 in Marvin B. Sussman and Betty E. Cogswell (eds.), Cross-National Family Research. Leiden, the Netherlands: Brill.

Davis, Kingsley
1976   "Sexual behavior." Pp. 219–61 in Robert K. Merton and Robert Nisbet (eds.), Contemporary Social Problems. New York: Harcourt Brace Jovanovich.

1977   "The theory of teenage pregnancy in the United States." International Population and Urban Research, Preliminary Paper No. 10 (March 1977). University of California, Berkeley: Institute of International Studies.

Epstein, Cynthia Fuchs
1970   Woman's Place: Options and Limits in Professional Careers. Berkeley: University of California Press.

Friedan, Betty
1963   The Feminine Mystique. New York: Dell.

Friedenberg, Edgar Z.
1959   The Vanishing Adolescent. Boston: Beacon.

Fritz, Robert J.
1977   "Judging the status of the illegitimate child in various Western legal systems." Loyola Law Review 23(1):1–58.

Glendon, Mary Ann
1975   "Power and authority in the family: New legal patterns as reflections of changing ideologies." American Journal of Comparative Law 23(Winter):1–33.

Glick, Paul C., and Arthur J. Norton
1977   "Marrying, divorcing, and living together in the U.S. today." Population Bulletin 32(October):1–39.

Goode, William J.
1960   "A deviant case: Illegitimacy in the Caribbean." American Sociological Review 25 (February):21–30.

Harvard Law Review (editorial—Case Comments)
1977   "Property rights upon termination of unmarried cohabitation: Marvin vs. Marvin." Harvard Law Review 90:1708–20.

Kay, Herma, and Carol Amyx
1977   "Marvin vs. Marvin: Preserving the options." California Law Review 65.937–77.

Kinsley, Susan
1977   "Women's dependency and federal programs." Pp. 79–91 in Jane Roberts Chapman and Margaret Gates (eds.), Women into Wives. Beverly Hills, Calif.: Sage.

Krauskopf, Joan M.
1977   "Partnership marriage: Legal reforms needed." Pp. 93–121 in Jane Roberts Chapman and Margaret Gates (eds.), Women into Wives. Beverly Hills, Calif.: Sage.

Kreps, Juanita
1965   "The economics of intergenerational relationships." Pp. 267–88 in Ethel Shanas and Gordon F. Streib (eds.), Social Structure and the Family: Generational Relations. Englewood Cliffs, N.J.: Prentice-Hall.

Lasch, Christopher
1975a   "The emotions of family life." New York Review of Books 22 (November):37–42.
1975b   "What the doctor ordered." New York Review of Books 22 (December):50–54.

Lipset, Seymour Martin
1972   "Social mobility and equal opportunity." The Public Interest 29 (Fall):90–108.

Malinowski, Bronislaw
1930   "Parenthood, the basis of social structure." Pp. 113–68 in V. F. Calverton and S. D. Schmalhausen (eds.), The New Generation. New York: Macauley.

Moore, Barrington
1958   Political Power and Social Theory. Cambridge, Mass.: Harvard University Press.

O'Connell, Martin
1978   "A cohort analysis of teenage fertility in the U.S. since the Depression." Paper read at the 1978 annual meeting of the Population Association of America, Atlanta.

Oppenheimer, Valerie Kincade
    1974   "The sociology of women's economic role in the family: Parsons revisited and revised." Paper read at the annual meeting of the American Sociological Association.

Plateris, Alexander A.
    1978   Divorces and Divorce Rates, United States. Vital and Health Statistics Series No. 21, U.S. Department of Health, Education, and Welfare Publication No. (PHS) 78-1907 (March 1978). Washington, D.C.: Government Printing Office.

Rivlin, Alice M.
    1972   "Child care." Pp. 252–90 in Charles L. Schultze, Edward R. Fried, Alice M. Rivlin, and Nancy H. Teeters (eds.), Setting National Priorities: The 1973 Budget. Washington, D.C.: Brookings Institution.

Rossi, Alice S.
    1964   "Equality between the sexes: An immodest proposal." Daedalus 93 (Spring):98–143.

Rothman, Sheila M.
    1973   "Other people's children: The day-care experience in America." The Public Interest 30 (Winter):11–27.

Shorter, Edward
    1975   The Making of the Modern Family. New York: Basic Books.

Steinmetz, S. K., and Murray A. Straus (eds.)
    1974   Violence in the Family. New York: Harper & Row.

Straus, Murray A.
    1977   "Sexual inequality, cultural norms, and wife-beating." Pp. 59–77 in Jane Roberts Chapman and Margaret Gates (eds.), Women into Wives. Beverly Hills, Calif.: Sage.

Trost, Jan
    1976   "Married and unmarried cohabitation: The case of Sweden, with some comparisons." Pp. 189–204 in Luis Lenero-Otero (ed.), Beyond the Nuclear Family Model: Cross-Cultural Perspectives. Beverly Hills, Calif.: Sage.

United States Bureau of the Census
    1976   "Daytime care of children; October 1974 and February 1975." Current Population Reports. Series P-20, No. 298. Washington, D.C.: Government Printing Office.
    1977a   "Fertility of American women: June 1976." Current Population Reports. Series P-20, No. 308. Washington, D.C.: Government Printing Office.
    1977b   "Population profile of the United States." Current Population Reports. Series P-20, No. 324. Washington, D.C.: Government Printing Office.

United States Department of Health, Education, and Welfare, National Center for Health Statistics
    1972   Vital Statistics of the United States, 1972. Volume 1. Natality. Washington, D.C.: Government Printing Office.
    1978   Final Natality Statistics, 1978. Washington, D.C.: Government Printing Office.

United States Department of Labor, Bureau of Labor Statistics
    1975c   Handbook of Labor Statistics 1975. Washington, D.C.: Government Printing Office.
    1977a   Handbook of Labor Statistics 1977. Washington, D.C.: Government Printing Office.

Weitzman, Lenore J.
    1972   "Legal regulation of marriage: Tradition and change." California Law Review 62 (July-September):1169–1288.

Woolsey, Suzanne H.
    1977   "Pied piper politics and the child-care debate." Daedalus 106 (Spring):127–45.

A Generation Gap?
Research Perspectives on Ways
that Generations Interact
Vern L. Bengtson

■   The problem of generations is as old as mankind's earliest writings and as contemporary as this morning's newspaper. The succession of one generation by another involves an inevitable tension between change and continuity, reflected in the lives of individuals and of social groups as they move through time.

Although the "generation gap" is neither new nor unprecedented it may appear to be both—judged by contemporary mass media accounts of intergenerational relations. The purpose of this chapter is to present a brief overview of some current research perspectives on contrasts and similarities between contemporaneous generations. My focus is on a neglected link in the succession of generations: relations between middle-aged children and their aging parents in today's society.

To dissect the contemporary "generation gap" rationally and scientif- ically is not all that easy. For one thing, the current sociological literature concerning intergenerational relations and aging is underdeveloped, compared to other arenas of family life. To date there have been relatively few studies on which to base generalizations concerning the place of aged family members in current American society. Professionals and social scientists often find themselves dealing with a welter of myth and misinformation concerning contemporary family life, perpetuated by the mass media. We hear much about the "troubled American family" and about the neglect and isolation of older family members. As Ethel Shanas (1979) has pointed out, such alarm is misplaced. Yet the research basis on which we can attack such myths is only now beginning to receive attention.

I. Conceptual Tools in Dissecting the
"Generation Gap"

Conceptual clarity must be our first concern as we attempt to dissect the various elements of the so-called "generation gap." Individuals, families,

Adapted from "Research Perspectives on Intergenerational Interaction" by Vern L. Bengtson from AGING PARENTS, edited by Pauline K. Ragan. Los Angeles: Andrus Gerontology Center, University of Southern California Press, 1979. Reprinted by permission.

Preparation of this chapter was partially supported by a grant from the Administration on Aging: No. 90–A–1297, Stephen McConnell and Fernando Torres-Gil, Principal Investigators.

and age groups are social entities moving through time; they exhibit attributes of both change and continuity when compared at different points in historical time. When we attempt to unravel the causes of such change and continuity, we must begin with an historical perspective (Elder, 1974).

The social movements exhibited in America of the 1960–1970 period provide a useful example of the historical context necessary for analysis of intergenerational interaction. During this decade Americans became concerned about the prospects of social and political cleavages between age groups which appeared to be pulling society apart—the "generation gap" became front page news.

Four social movements appeared during this protest-filled decade. First, in 1960 the Civil Rights Movement emerged with predominantly Whites and Blacks marching together, culminating in bloody confrontations which troubled an entire nation. Next, in 1964 the Free Speech Movement began; college youth questioned the legitimacy of their elders' total control over educational governance. Then, by 1966 the Viet Nam protest movement had begun a momentum which drove one president from power and shook traditional views concerning American foreign policy. Most colleges during 1968–1970 experienced some form of organized protest on the part of youth questioning the moral and legal basis for an undeclared war directed by their elders; most families probably experienced the disquieting effects of intergenerational confrontation about the war. A fourth set of issues and events which can be termed a social movement was the emergence of the "counter-culture." Groups of youth began espousing values and behaviors which ran counter to the ethos of productivity, cleanliness, and capitalism that appeared to characterize their parents' generation. Long hair, second- and third-hand clothes, recreational use of drugs and sex, communal living—all these reflected an emerging life-style in clear contrast to middle-class, middle-aged conventions of the 1960's. Margaret Mead (1970) suggested that these youth were "immigrants in time" moving into a new cultural system and reversing prior mechanisms of socialization. Whereas in human society prior to this time children had learned from their parents, the pace of social and technological innovation has accelerated to such a pace that, according to Mead, soon children will have to teach their parents how to survive, what is good or valuable, what is bad or maladaptive. Or, as Edgar Friedenberg (1969) summed it up: "Young people today aren't rebelling against their parents: they are *abandoning* them."

One decade later such pronouncements appear almost quaint; on today's quiet college campuses there are few reminders that the Sixties' clash between generations were so pervasive and portentious. Age groups do not seem to oppose each other; rather, as in the 1950's, all age groups today appear vaguely concerned about similar issues: inflation, taxes, and jobs. Perhaps the pendulum swing exemplified by the contrast between 1970 and 1980 is exactly the point: that both change and continuity are exhibited by individuals, families, and age groups at different points in historical time.

How can one account for such contrasts? What are the causes of differences—and similarities—between generations? Three concepts may be useful in examining the change and continuity in intergenerational comparisons: cohort effect, lineage effect, and period effect (see Bengston & Cutler, 1976, for a more comprehensive discussion). Although all three effects are interrelated, each provides a slightly different perspective for viewing aging and social change.

The *cohort effect* (or in the language of mass media, the "cohort gap") refers to real or apparent differences between individuals born at different points in historical time. In the 1980's persons born in 1940 compared with those born in 1920 will have a very different set of life-cycle concerns as well as life experiences. First, because they were born in different points in time, they will be at different points in the life cycle—at different stages psychologically, physiologically, and sociologically (Bengtson and Kuypers, 1971). Second, because they were born at different points in time, they will also have experienced sociopolitical events differently, as those events were encountered at different stages of life span development. The war in Viet Nam, to give one example, was undoubtedly experienced quite differently by most twenty-year-olds compared to their forty-year-old parents. There are good reasons for the existence of contrasts between individuals born at different points in time, either on the basis of maturation or cohort experience. There is, in short, good reason for a cohort-level generation gap.

The *lineage effect* (one might call it the "lineage gap") refers to real perceived differences between generations within families. The family may be viewed as a system of social organization in which there are a series of statuses defined by ranked descent. Fathers and mothers, sons and daughters, grandchildren, and great-grandchildren form successive links in an unending succession of biological and social generations. This particular conceptual tool was used by the very first historians to put in order events of history. In the Old Testament historical periods are set off by kingly lineage; the time of a particular event was frequently marked by reference to the life span of a particular ancestor in the lineage chain.

Are there inevitable differences between generations by virtue of differential status as parent or child? Most of modern psychology assumes, following the insight of Freud, that indeed an inevitable and useful rebellion occurs as young children wish, first of all, to become their parents, and secondly, to take over many of the attributes of their parents. Although the Freudian model is far from universally accepted, the theme of generational conflict within families appears frequently throughout literature. One thinks, for example, of the aged King Lear at the end of Shakespeare's play—an embittered, shattered king seeing his wishes disrespected, and crying "Oh, the infamy that is to be a parent!"—his words indeed reflect a lineage gap.

Similarly, the third concept, the *period effect,* is useful to look at attitudes at a given point in time and compare them with attitudes of another time. Examining relationships between generations or between groups within society, it is likewise instructive to compare similarities as well as differences. Throughout philosophical literature one reads the laments of older generations concerning the young. Plato's observations about the young being undisciplined, unmotivated, and taking drugs is often repeated today as solace for those of us in the middle generation who may find that our own children's lack of industry fails to meet our ideals. It may be that the so-called generation gap is really not much more serious even in today's fast-changing society than it was a hundred years ago. It may be that there is an inevitable "period gap."

As Treas (1975) has suggested, there are historical differences in demography, and therefore differences in contact within families, compared with the last century. There are differences simply in the number of living individuals per generation within a given family. You might consider historical differences between generations in the amount of contact between successive generations in your own family. My mother and I are in contact every week. She was in contact with her mother only the three or four times a year when she could visit her Nebraska farm. In turn, my grandmother never saw her mother after she immigrated to this country at the age of eleven; and my great-grandmother never saw her mother, who died in childbirth. Much more contact takes place between generations today than at any other time in American history simply because of advances in telecommunications and other technological innovations that make such contact possible. Whether the quality of contact has changed as much as the quantity, I do not know. I do know in reading 19th century American novels built around the theme of disaffection between generations, the conflict was often resolved by the younger generation moving west to the frontier and having no further contact with the older generation.

In short, when we look at intergenerational interaction and the differences which appear between generations, it is necessary to distinguish among three conceptual causes. Each effect—cohort, lineage, and period—may create natural and inevitable differences in attitudes, values, and behaviors of the individuals involved in the drama of intergenerational interaction. But each also can be seen as effecting some degree of continuity. Maturational changes can be expected to bring children closer to their parents' orientations as they mature in adulthood; lineage effects involve transmission between generations and therefore greater similarity; period effects involve all contemporaneous generations experiencing similar socio-historical events and adapting to them in parallel, if not in series. For generations are social units moving through time, exhibiting both change and continuity.

II. Differences Between Generations, Real and Perceived

I have suggested that comparisons between age groups reflect both continuity and contrast as one considers the effects of cohort, lineage, and historical period on behaviors and orientations. The question remains: how different are contemporary generations? What does contemporary research indicate concerning contrasts between youth, their middle-aged parents, and their aging grandparents?

A pervasive perception in today's society is that there are significant differences between age groups today—that there is a serious and profound "generation gap" in contemporary culture. We hear this in a variety of ways: stereotypes concerning youthful rebellion and geriatric conservatism, dismay about the declining importance of the American family, discussions about the "sexual revolution" which today appears less concerned with physical sexuality than with male-female sex roles.

Two decades of research concerning the generation gap have produced a mixture of generalizations about contrasts and similarities (Troll & Bengtson, 1978). Generational differences appear in some areas but not in others; sometimes they seem pronounced, sometimes trivial. This is suggested by findings from a large-scale survey conducted during the past six years at the University of Southern California. Case studies from families in the sample amplify some of the causes of similarities and differences. The survey data come from 2,044 individuals who are members of three-generation families. These families were contacted through the membership list of a large Southern California health care plan, and consisted of at least one grandparent, one or more middle-aged children, and the grandchildren between the ages of 16 and 26 (see Bengtson, 1975, for a more complete description of this sample).

One area we investigated involved value orientations. We asked the members of the three generations to rank in order of importance 16 items reflecting various goals or orientations. The results are displayed in Figure 1.

By comparing answers from grandparents, parents, and youth for each item, one sees clear contrasts between generations. "Achievement," for example, was ranked highest by the middle-aged parents, significantly lower by youth, and lower still by grandparents. "Personal freedom" was ranked very high by youth, but two scale-points lower by the grandparents—a pattern seen also in "skill" and "exciting life."

But while there are value differences between generations reflected in these data, there are also similarities; and what is most interesting is

Figure 1. Mean of Each Value Ranking, by Generation

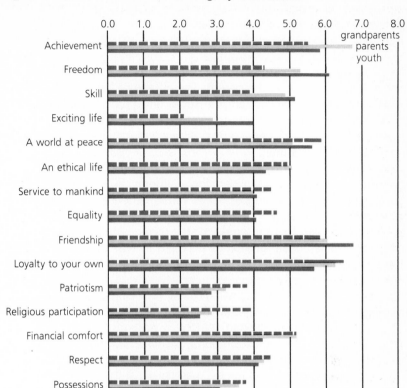

that many of the differences run counter to usual expectations. The three generations show rather similar rankings on items such as "respect" and "possessions" as well as "service to mankind." Some contrasts are surprising. On the item "a world at peace" we expected the highest ranking to be given by the youngest generation; after all, it was the youth who appeared to be in the forefront of peace demonstrations in the 1960's. But of the three groups it was the grandparents who ranked this value highest. Similar patterns appeared on "service to mankind" and "equality of mankind"—valued highest by the grandparents, next by the grandchildren, third by the parents. These scores on humanistic values suggest that some stereotypes about generational differences in orientations are inaccurate. Not only are there similarities in value rankings, but the differences that exist run counter to many expectations.

In another analysis of these data (Bengtson, 1975), value orientations were examined in terms of cohort vs. lineage effects. Bengtson found that through three generations, value similarities could be traced which suggests lineage continuity in orientations. However, there was more agreement on values within the grandparent, parent, and child generations than there was between generations within the family. Bengtson also found an ongoing process of socialization within the family that is bilateral, in that it goes both from parent to child and from child to parent. The direct parent/child socialization will produce values in the child, but not necessarily those of the parent. The difference between parent and child values comes partly from the social environment and partly from collective relations in peer groups.

The *perception* of generational differences may be more important than actual contrasts in orientations and behavior. Data from the University of Southern California survey suggest that there is a strong tendency to believe that generational differences exist, but that the perception of such differences varies across generational boundaries in both cohort and lineage terms. In this section of the study respondents were asked to rate the "closeness" of the relationship between members of various generational groupings depicted in two social contexts: the "broader society" (cohort) and "your own family" (lineage) (see Tables 1–A and 1–B).

The results of this analysis indicate three things. First, the "cohort gap" perceived between generations in the broader society is considerably larger than the "lineage gap" perceived within the respondents' own families. Second, the age of the *perceiver* makes some difference in the degree to which a "gap" is seen: the youngest age group (youth, age 16–26) perceives the least closeness, particularly at the family level. At the cohort level, the old and the young attribute similar levels of distance. Grandparents see the greatest amount of closeness within the family.

Table 1-A Mean Perception of "Cohort Gap" by Generation of Respondent[a]

	REFERENT						
	Between G3–G2		Between G3–G1		Between G2–G1		Total by generation of respondent
Respondent	$\bar{\chi}$	s.d.	$\bar{\chi}$	s.d.	$\bar{\chi}$	s.d.	$\bar{\chi}$
G1	3.62	1.37	3.90	1.63	3.00	1.31	3.51
G2	3.20	1.12	4.25	1.31	2.81	1.11	3.42
G3	3.28	1.35	4.42	1.44	2.95	1.19	3.55
Total by generation of referent	3.38	1.29	4.17	1.48	2.92	1.21	3.49

[a]"Some people say there is a 'generation gap' between age groups in American society today. How much of a 'gap' do you think there is between the following groups?" (The groups referred to are the column headings in this table.) Subjects gave responses on a six-point scale from "no gap whatsoever" (scored 1) to "very great gap" (scored 6).

Table 1-B   Mean Perceptions of the "Lineage Gap" by Generation of
Respondent[b]

	REFERENT						
	Between G3–G2		Between G3–G1		Between G2–G1		Total by generation of respondent
Respondent	$\overline{\chi}$	s.d.	$\overline{\chi}$	s.d.	$\overline{\chi}$	s.d.	$\overline{\chi}$
G1	2.19	1.24	2.06	1.23	1.81	1.19	2.02
G2	2.35	1.04	3.62	1.53	2.72	1.28	2.89
G3	2.96	1.34	3.75	1.62	2.70	1.23	3.14
Total by generation of referent	2.46	1.24	3.07	1.65	2.38	1.30	2.64

[b]"In your family, how great is the 'gap' between the three generations, in your opinion?"
Source: Bengtson, 1971.

Third, the age of the *referent* constitutes an important difference: a greater "gap" is perceived between the youth and the elderly than between the other generational dyads mentioned.

The general conclusion, then, is that the nature of cross-generation perceptions varies according to several factors, primary of which is the context of the generational grouping (family *vs.* broader society). For the older family members this contrast is particularly pronounced. Respondents seem to be saying, "Yes, there *is* a generation gap—but not in *my* family."

Why are there such differences in generational perceptions, and why are differences focused on when there is evidence of intergenerational similarity? Cohort, lineage, and period effects combine to give each member of the generational chain a different perception of the meaning of generational contrasts and similarities. Each family member has a contrasting "generational stake" or investment in the other generation which colors his or her perception of the other and of the relationship (Bengtson & Kuypers, 1971).

Each individual in the family is a changing entity, developing as an individual; so too the relationship among family members must change. A family in which there is an adolescent is enmeshed in working out compromises between separateness and connectedness. As Erik Erikson has noted, the major psychological issues in adolescence involve a thrust toward identity, a selfhood separate from one's parents, and intimacy, especially with others outside the family. This sets up an inevitable confrontation between desires for separateness in identity and intimacy on the one hand, and the fact of residence within the parental family with its authority patterns on the other. At the other end of the life cycle the same issues of autonomy and dependency are encountered: when a 70-year-old father, independent all his life, self-sufficient, and autonomous, is stricken with ill health, the balance of family dynamics must change, for the older person has moved into a different stage of life.

What I am suggesting is that differences between generations—and especially the perception of those differences—are colored by developmental agendas; the negotiation of which causes apparent differences to be highlighted and brought into consciousness by normal crises which involve transformations in autonomy or dependency.

Added to developmental differences is another contrast between cohorts: differences in life history. A case study (incidentally, from my own family) illustrates this. When Grandpa Engstrom died in 1976 he was 106 years old; his life suggests many ways in which perceptions and contrasts between generations are tied to history. Born in rural Sweden in 1869, he emigrated to Minnesota, worked as a day laborer and then as a chauffeur, and finally borrowed enough money to become a cement contractor in Seattle. After a series of minor fortunes and minor failures he "retired" following a heart attack in 1933, and shortly thereafter moved in with his daughter. He lived 43 years in retirement—42 years in the household of his child, 46 years without his spouse. His life spanned a century of technological innovations, a biography of crises and triumphs, a legacy of five generations. His death was the occasion to reflect on an enormous degree of continuity and change represented in one lifetime, in one family. When Engstrom was born, the midwife came in the snows of the January Swedish winter and delivered him. When he struck out for a new land, he never did see his brothers and sisters again; he saw his father only once. There was little contact between Engstrom and the rest of his own family after he immigrated to America. The kinds of experiences that shaped his life made him the conservative, independent person that he was. Not until his 93rd birthday did he accept Medicare and Social Security, so strong were his values of individualism and so abhorrent was the notion of being supported by "charity."

Within other families the contrast of historical change or of developmental agenda may not be quite so dramatic as this particular example, but in any family there are differences that are inevitable. So to the popular question of whether there is a serious generation gap in American society I would answer, "Yes, differences are perceived between generations; yes, some *actual* differences can be cited. But the differences are not what we think they are, and some of the differences are normal consequences of developmental or historical events."

III. Problems Between Generations

Every family has its problems. Many of them involve interaction between generations. Frequently the problems are related to actual lineage or to period differences, real or imagined. From the Southern California study of generations questionnaire and from ethnographic interviews conducted over the past four or five years, I find four separate but related problems which families mention again and again in describing and dealing with interaction between generations. Many are related to developmental and historical contrasts between cohorts (see Bengtson and Treas, 1980).

Role Transition

The first problem involves issues of role transition. By that I simply mean the challenges presented by changing roles and expectations that accompany growing up and growing old.

As Linda George (1980) has documented, these role transitions are often accompanied by psycho-social stress. Grandpa Engstrom retired in 1929 at the age of 60 because he had a stroke. He lived for 46 years in retirement. He had to make an adjustment to the fact that in his eyes he was no longer a productive member of society. His family too had to adjust to his no longer working; and some of the adjustments had to do with economic differences. More than that, however, their adjustments reflected roles and expectations that are indicative of growing up and growing old.

Many of the middle-aged women in our sample reported that the last child's leaving home, whether for marriage, college, or employment, was either the source of great rejoicing on the part of Mom and Dad (a new freedom for a second honeymoon, traveling, new money to spend on themselves) or the source of a period of depression which neither parent understood. Most parents have a high degree of investment in the lives and the fortunes of those unpredictable individuals who bear their names. That role transition can require considerable adaptation on the part of both generations of family members. What I see increasingly in the lives of 70- and 80-year-old people is the sorrow they feel at seeing their children or grandchildren split up, or at witnessing the death of children or grandchildren—a tragic role reversal, the elderly outliving their children. In Barbara Myerhoff's 1976 Academy Award-winning documentary on aged Jews in Venice, *Number Our Days,* one of the most poignant moments is an interview with an 87-year-old woman, a survivor of Nazi persecution, the Holocaust in Poland, who came to this new land, raised four children, and outlived every one of them (Myerhoff, 1979). I find that increasingly common. It didn't occur 30 years ago, or 60 years ago, because individuals usually did not survive into the sixth, seventh, or eighth decade. Little has been written about this role transition—perhaps the most tragic one can see.

Very little has been written about the role transition of widowhood or widowerhood. An exception is *Widowhood in an American City* by

Helena Lopata (1973), which describes a study of the adjustment of several hundred Chicago-area widows to the loss of spouse.

There are inevitable role transitions in a family, and those transitions are involved in what may be the number one problem of the normal family: coping with intergenerational relations over the years. The changing circumstances of family members and their changing roles create different expectations on the part of both children and parents. I can't expect Dad to be what he was ten years ago; I certainly can't expect my son to act the same way he did ten years ago. A common complaint of parents, as they look down the generational boundaries, is that they wish their children would take more responsibility. At the other end of the life cycle, interestingly, the 70- to 75-year-old parent often wishes his or her child would take *less* responsibility for him.

Autonomy and Dependency

The second major problem of intergenerational interaction within families concerns autonomy and dependency. Issues of autonomy and dependency are fundamental in negotiations that must be carried out within every family on a day-to-day, year-to-year, decade-to-decade basis. The adolescent is concerned primarily with autonomy: "I want to be my own person." Parents, if able to put it into words, probably wish for their child's autonomy, but not at the expense of infringement—pushing parental limits, flaunting an oppositional life style, being insensitive.

At the other end of the life cycle one sees the same issue of autonomy as a problem in family relations. How often are elderly, dependent—but sensitive—parents treated with condescension by their middle-aged children? There is a childishness frequently attributed to dependent elderly parents which must be galling for them. In hospitals it is common to see conferences of children and grandchildren: "What are we going to do with Grandpa?" Frequently, Grandpa is not unaware of those discussions, and the result has to be, on his part, a feeling of tremendous dependency, loss of control, and loss of autonomy. Many of our nursing homes epitomize an institutionalization of inappropriate dependency. Putting the aged in a category where they receive custodial care must still recognize that old age reflects survivorship and a lifetime of experience and coping. Too many of us look at the dependency of old age and ignore the autonomy.

I have argued that much of the drama of intergenerational relations concerns issues of autonomy on the one hand and dependency on the other. Of course, one is always partly autonomous and partly dependent throughout life. The challenge within the family is to allow relevant, realistic, and equitable balance between dependency and autonomy as individuals change with the passage of time. The balance changes throughout life, and always requires a normal interval of negotiation as the individuals concerned adapt to changes in autonomy.

Equitable Exchange

A third problem concerns issues of allocating a just balance of giving and receiving between generations. This is a classical issue which James Dowd (1980) suggests is the key to understanding relations between age strata—both within and beyond the family. Grandpa Engstrom lived with his daughter from 1935 to 1975—forty years. One of his major concerns involved maintaining equity in the face of that dependency: what could he be doing? He tried to solve this in a number of ways—by being the gardener, by being the dishwasher, and by being the cook. Grandpa insisted on doing the gardening long after heart attacks and cataracts had made the family feel it was dangerous for him to do so. During Christmas Day 1974, when he was 105, he fell off a ladder while trying to clean the gutter. Everybody in the family pleaded with Grandpa to quit trying to do the gardening. They pleaded with Grandpa to quit doing the dishes, because he kept chipping them. The electric dishwasher was intended to preserve whatever china was left. Nobody dared to plead with Grandpa to quit cooking the breakfast, despite his failing eyesight, because he was always up earlier than anyone else. The point is that Grandpa *had* to make a contribution: he *had* to do what he could to effect an equitable exchange.

Many issues in generational relations focus around a just and equitable exchange between generations. "My parents have done so much for me; what can I do for them? Can I send them money? I know they need it. No, they won't take it; it's a blow to their pride. What can I do? Can I send them tickets to come down and visit me? That's O.K." I know of one family in which the issue of a just exchange between generations was satisfied very nicely by two tickets to the Super Bowl which the father treasured as something he would remember to the end of his life. The same issue, of course, is even more poignant in the lives of senior citizens: "What can I give my kids? What can I give my grandkids? What can I do for them?" The intensity of generational investment is real in the lives of most individuals (Hill, Foote, Aldous, Carlson, & Macdonald, 1970; Shanas, Townsend, Wedderburn, Friis, Milhøj, & Stehouwer, 1968).

A specific focus of equitable inter-generational exchange is the issue of legacies: inheritances both economic and social. Jeffrey Rosenfeld (1979) has noted that the study of inheritance—and disinheritance—allows some fascinating insights into contemporary social organization of family life. It is of interest to me how much effort elderly individuals give to their testamentary dispossessions in an attempt to provide a just and equitable distribution of tangible resources. Undoubtedly the most dramatic are cases in which the wills provide for disinheritance of children.

Rosenfeld's analysis found that 3.5 percent of wills probated in Nassau County, New York, between 1973 and 1978 involved parent-child disinheritance. Examination of probated wills, which are part of public record and which can be read as freely as any other public document, suggests three patterns (Rosenfeld, 1980). The first Rosenfeld terms "benevolent disinheritance," reflecting the feeling that other people needed the money more than did the children. A second category, "disinheritance by default," occurred when parents had no idea where their children could be reached. Most of the parents in this category had been living as "social isolates" or had been receiving long-term nursing care at the time they wrote the will. Almost half the cases fell in a third category, "vindictive disinheritance." Here the parent carefully spelled out longstanding differences, parental displeasure with the children's way of life, or accusations that the children had been disrespectful. Cases of vindictive disinheritance generally involved small estates. Most often parents who disinherited were older than those who did not. Rosenfeld notes that the increasing opportunities for elderly people to develop new social involvements, as well as their added longevity, may indicate a continued decline in old social constraints—including the implied obligation of leaving everything to the children.

Equally interesting are non-economic legacies—a memorial, a testament of the right way to live. Frequently, these are explicit, sometimes they are dramatic. One of my best friends, a Mormon, recalls his grandfather's last will and testament. Nine children and 11 grandchildren were crowded into his hospital room. He asked them to hold hands and pray as he entreated God to provide guidance to those family members and keep them in the faith and in the Book of Wisdom. That was the principal legacy of a man who had an estate of $12,000 to divide among nine children. His legacy was a spiritual tradition, a way of life which he wanted for his children and his children's children and their children. The most precious exchange between generations, at least from one perspective, may be a way of life the older family member has found to be important.

Continuity vs. Disruption

A fourth and related problem concerns the tension between continuity in family vs. disruption of that continuity. I find that with advancing years the continuity assumes increasing importance of a family tradition, or a family legacy.

That is not to suggest that it is not important for young people. I am often surprised at the pride which young adults have in the accomplishments (and even more than that, the very being, the very existence) of their parents and especially their grandparents. A highly-regarded ancestor is one of the things which students often cite as we talk about the importance of family in sociology courses. Characteristics of their grandparents or great-grandparents indicate continuity, and are an important theme throughout the generations.

There are some very serious threats or disruptions to that continuity in contemporary American society. Four of these deserve mention.

1. Geographic mobility.   The first is geographic mobility. We live in a very mobile society in which the average Californian moves once every four years. The average Midwestern family moves once every seven years. Geographic mobility is a part of our culture, and that can represent a potential disruption to the issue of man's continuity.

2. Divorce.   A second and even more dramatic disruption is divorce. I observe many grandparents who have a child who is married and who from a first marriage has three children, from a second marriage two children; some go on to a third marriage and another child. These may all be regarded as grandchildren. Equally interesting are the ties that remain with the daughters-in-law or the sons-in-law who no longer are spouses of offspring. Much continuity is maintained, and this calls for some rather delicate negotiation in terms of family get-togethers, birthdays, funerals, and weddings. Maintaining family continuity between the generations appears important to many of the elderly parents and grandparents. From the standpoint of the grandchild where there has been a divorce, such continuity may be a source of comfort and security. The kids that I talk to coming from families in which there has been remarriage can sort out the grandparents, and "It's O.K."; they have relationships with each of them. Probably the children find one or two grandparents more significant, and these may or may not be from the direct-bond relationship. But the relationship between grandchildren and grandparents is very important in maintaining stability when the husband and the wife split up. Though this has not often been discussed in contemporary American society, it does represent an important aspect of continuity in the face of potential family disruption.

3. Change in life-style.   A third problem in continuity vs. disruption concerns changes in life-style. Often youth present their families with a conversion to a new religion, to a political cause, to vegetarianism, or to new sexual modalities. I know of several cases in which there has been a conversion experience, and the son or daughter has come home with gospel tracts to save the souls of all the elder family members. I know other instances of what is commonly called "backsliding," in which, after all the grades of Sunday School, Johnny's gone away to college and lost his faith; he comes home smoking "pot" and quoting D. H. Lawrence. Such changes in life-style do occur. They represent a threat in the continuity of the family—an issue to be dealt with and negotiated.

4. Death.   As Victor Marshall (1980) has so persuasively noted, although the death of a family member always is the source of an immediate and observable disruption, it frequently is the occasion also for a reaffirmation of family continuity. Funerals, in my experience, are occasions for people who perhaps have gotten together relatively infrequently within the last few years to come together, not only to mourn the loss of the departed, but also to knit up the shredded fabric of disrupted families that death has caused. Wakes in Irish and Mexican families are the occasion for family members to tell stories about the departed. This is also true in Swedish families. When my father died, we gathered in the rural Minnesota mortuary. The room was crowded; present were nine of his brothers and sisters and probably 20 of my 34 cousins. Long into the night we told stories about my father. I wish I had recorded that evening. There was a theme going through most of the stories—not just, "Here was a man who was good and important; he's gone, and let's treasure his memory," but also, "Here we are, part of a family—a family which lives on and which carries on traditions that this man stood for in his life." Continuity, in face of death, the ultimate disruption.

IV. Processes

What are the processes that occur between generations within families in solving some of these problems? Two issues seem to summarize successful intergenerational interaction.

First, I want to emphasize the necessity of negotiation. We don't usually think of families as an arena of bargaining. The term "negotiation" suggests the image of Ford Motor management and labor union leaders locked together hammering out a contract which eventually nobody is really happy with and nobody terribly dissatisfied with. The same things happen every day in families, but the negotiations are not quite as direct as they are between Ford Motor Company and the United Auto Workers. Negotiations are inevitable in families. As each individual family member acts out his or her own developmental agenda, negotiation is inevitable. It is also continuous, happening all the time, and it is bilateral: negotiations not only involve the parent influencing the child, but also the child influencing the parent (Hagestad, 1980). There is a bilateral negotiation in the family which is easily overlooked, especially in the so-called "golden years" among senior citizens. Just because Grandpa has had a stroke doesn't mean he is no longer a person who should be accorded dignity and autonomy and some sense of control over what happens to him. This inevitable, continuous, and bilateral negotiation is rooted in the passage of time. It is also rooted in the process of aging. As we grow up and grow old, the relationships that we have within the family change.

Thus, the process of solving family problems involves negotiations, and those negotiations occur whether we are aware of them or not. Much of family relations is not explicit and not as honest as negotiations between the lawyers from the labor unions and the lawyers from the manufacturers. But control is exercised in the family in a variety of subtle ways. Wives control their husbands, husbands control their wives, in many ways that are nonverbal. I think we must recognize that negotiation is part of the family process of every normal, well-functioning family in contemporary society.

The second point I would like to make is that much of the natural process in families involves conflict. As humans interact, conflict is normal, inevitable, and universal. It does not necessarily have to be destructive. One of the myths that we carry with us in American society, especially in Northern European ethnic traditions, is that conflict within the family is bad; it is indicative of bad manners, if not serious disruption.

Barbara Myerhoff (1979) in her study of Jews of Venice notes that expression of conflict is one of the most creative aspects of the daily lives of these elderly individuals. Bickering, negotiating, teasing, nagging in this particular subculture from rural Eastern Europe are indications, not only of affection, but also an affirmation of simply being *alive*.

Perhaps in mainstream American culture we expect families to be conflict-free. I don't know why we have that tradition. Certainly any reading of the Old Testament would suggest to us that if there is one theme running through every family, it is conflict. Think of poor King David and the problems that he had with his lineal descendants. Think of Jacob and his sons; the commandments given to Moses the patriarch dictate that one should honor one's father and mother—you don't, however, necessarily have to like them. Probably some of the healthiest families I have seen are families in which there can be and are explicit statements of disagreement. This represents conflict, and yet there is a sense of love that allows autonomy. It allows differences of expression. Certainly, I am not saying the higher the degree of conflict, the better the relations between generations within a family. What I am pointing out is that conflict is a normal part of the continuous negotiation that must occur in families, as we grow up and grow old. Acknowledgment of inevitable differences, and adequate negotiation of conflict, are two keys to understanding successful intergenerational interaction.

V. Conclusion

Contrasts between generations are inevitable, universal, perhaps even desirable—reflecting as they do the tension between change and continuity rooted in the passage of time. What I have suggested is that any reasoned discussion of the "generation gap" must consider four issues indicated by contemporary research on intergenerational relations.

First, it is important to maintain conceptual clarity in the often emotional arena of intergenerational relations. We must distinguish between effects of cohort, lineage, and historical period as each contribute to observable differences between generations. And we should acknowledge that each effect also creates its own degree of intergenerational continuity.

Second, the available research literature documents differences between generations. But frequently the contrasts are not as large as one might expect from mass media acocunts; sometimes the differences run counter to popular expectations, as with grandparents displaying higher "humanistic" value orientations than grandchildren. Often the differences are more perceived than actual, though they are experienced as very real.

Third, problems of intergenerational relations reflect the contrasting psychosocial agendas of family members born into different cohorts and experiencing different developmental issues. Four issues may be universal as families attempt to confront change: role transition, autonomy-dependency, equitable exchange, continuity-disruption. These issues surface at each stage in a family's career; they are as salient for old age as for adolescence.

Fourth, the process of successful intergenerational relations involves the negotiation of differences. In the face of inevitable change, the negotiation of transitions, autonomy, exchanges, and continuity becomes a necessary part of every family agenda. Often conflict is inevitable. How these conflicts are acknowledged and resolved is perhaps the central issue in understanding our own intergenerational relations.

References

Bengtson, V. L. Inter-age differences in perception and the generation gap. *Gerontologist,* 1971, *11* (2), 85–90.

Bengtson, V. L. Generation and family effects in value socialization. *American Sociological Review,* 1975, *40,* 358–371.

Bengtson, V. L., and Cutler, N. Generations and intergenerational relations: Perspectives on age groups and social change. In R. Binstock & E. Shanas (eds.), *Handbook of Aging and the Social Sciences.* New York: Van Nostrand Reinhold, 1976.

Bengtson, V. L., & Kuypers, J. A. Generational difference and the developmental stake. *Aging and Human Development,* 1971, *2,* 249–259.

Bengtson, V. L. & Treas, J. Intergenerational relations and mental health. In R. B. Sloan and J. E. Birren (eds.), *Handbook of Mental Health and Aging.* New York: Prentice-Hall, 1980.

Dowd, J. *Stratification and Aging.* Monterey, California: Brooks-Cole, 1980.

Elder, G. *Children of the Great Depression.* Chicago: University of Chicago Press, 1974.

Friedenberg, E. Current patterns of generational conflict. *Journal of Social Issues,* 1969, *25* (2), 21–38.

George, L. K. *Role Transitions in Later Life.* Monterey, California: Brooks-Cole, 1980.

Hagestad, G. O. Problems and promises in the social psychology of intergenerational relations. In R. Fogel, E. Hatfield, S. Kiesler, and J. March (eds.), *Stability and Change in the Family,* 1980.

Hagestad, G. O. Patterns of communication and influence between grandparents and grandchildren in a changing society. Paper presented at the 9th World Congress of Sociology, Uppsala, Sweden, 1978.

Hess, B. B. and Waring, J. M. Parent and child in later life: Rethinking the relationship. In R. M. Lerner, and G. B. Spanier (eds.), *Child Influences on Marital and Family Interaction.* New York: Academic Press, 1978.

Hill, R., Foote, N., Aldous, J., Carlson, R., & Macdonald, R. *Family Development in Three Generations.* Cambridge, Mass.: Schenkmen, 1970.

Lopata, H. *Widowhood in an American City.* Cambridge, Mass.: Schenkman, 1973.

Marshall, V. *Last Chapters: A Sociology of Aging and Dying.* Monterey, California: Brooks-Cole, 1980.

Mead, M. *Culture and Commitment: A Study of the Generation Gap.* New York: Longmans, 1970.

Myerhoff, B. *Number Our Days.* New York: Dutton, 1979.

Rosenfeld, J. P. *Legacy of Aging: Inheritance & Disinheritance in Social Perspective.* Norwood, N.J.: Ablex Publishing, 1979.

Rosenfeld, J. P. Benevolent disinheritance: The kindest cut. *Psychology Today,* Vol. 13, No. 12, 1980.

Schaie, K. W. A general model for the study of developmental problems. *Psychological Bulletin,* 1965, *64,* 92–107.

Shanas, E., Townsend, P., Wedderburn, D., Friis, H., Milhøj, P., & Stehouwer, J. *Old People in Three Industrial Societies.* New York: Atherton, 1968.

Shanas, E., & Streib, G. *Social Structure and the Family: Generational Relations.* Englewood Cliffs, N.J.: Prentice-Hall, 1965.

Shanas, E. Social myth as hypothesis: The case of the family relations of old people. *Gerontologist,* 1979, 19, 3–9.

Sussman, M. B. The family life of old people. In R. Binstock & E. Shanas (eds.), *Handbook of Aging and the Social Sciences.* New York: Van Nostrand Reinhold, 1976.

Treas, J. Aging and the family. In D. Woodruff & J. Birren (eds.), *Aging: Scientific Perspectives and Social Issues.* New York: Van Nostrand Reinhold, 1975.

Troll, L. E. The family in later life: A decade review. *Journal of Marriage and the Family,* 1970, *33,* 263–290.

Troll, L., & Bengtson, V. L. Generations in the family. In W. Burr, R. Hill, I. Reiss, & I. Nye (eds.), *Contemporary Theories About the Family,* Vol. I. New York: The Free Press, 1979.

2
COURTSHIP

Some say that love is bliss, but to André le Chapelain, the twelfth-century historian of courtly love, it is ". . . a species of agony caused by excessive meditation upon a member of the opposite sex."[1] Actually, courtship displays both of these extremes, and lovers often say they feel everything from agony to bliss. The selections in Part 2 examine the basis for mutual attraction and some of the social changes currently affecting intimate involvements.

The opening section has been called "The Sexes" because it deals with how men's and women's roles are changing as well as with biological differences and similarities between the sexes. In "Sex Differences, Real and Imagined," for example, Tavris and Offir ask how different the sexes really are. By focusing on verbal ability, creativity, even physical strength, these authors are able to make some surprising points about sex differences.

Attitudes toward homosexuality are also in flux, and more gay people now openly admit their sexual preferences. Philip Nobile, in "The Meaning of Gay," updates many existing strands in the literature on homosexuality and assesses how changing attitudes toward homosexuality will affect gay and straight people alike.

Apart from acquiring a gender identity, people must learn how to enter into satisfying relationships with members of the opposite sex. Gagnon and Greenblat, in "Rehearsals and Realities: Beginning to Date," explore the first, tentative overtures that teenagers make towards each other. Theirs is the first of two selections on "Attraction," and it describes cross pressures involved when teenagers try to maintain status among same-sex friends while meeting demands from members of the opposite sex.

In the next selection, which deals with teenage pregnancy, there is information about a very different set of messages which must be reconciled. Kathleen Rudd Scharf in "Teenage Pregnancy: Why the Epidemic?" writes that 1 girl in 10 aged 15–19 will become pregnant this year. Close to 600,000 of these estimated million unwed mothers will decide to give birth. In fact, pregnancy is the leading reason why teenage girls become high-school dropouts. Scharf explains why teenage girls with the most to lose by becoming unwed mothers are the ones who are most apt to keep their babies.

Paul R. Newcomb opens the section on "Involvements" with a general survey of "Cohabitation In America," emphasizing the variety of living arrangements and the relation between cohabiting and getting married. The following piece by Kay and Amyx, "*Marvin v. Marvin:* Preserving the Options," puts cohabitation in legal perspective. There was a time when living together imposed no contractual obligations—no

---

1. E. S. Turner, *A History of Courting* (London: Pan Books, Ltd. 1954), p. 28.

strings at all—upon people. This state of affairs has changed, however. It is now the law in some states that people who stop living together must be compensated for whatever they contributed to their relationship, provided there was "a reasonable expectation of a fair deal" when they first got involved with one another. This doctrine of the fair deal was put forward in the case of *Marvin v. Marvin* when the court held that actress Michelle Marvin was entitled to one-half the property acquired during her cohabitation with actor Lee Marvin. Authors Kay and Amyx indicate that the case of *Marvin v. Marvin* relied heavily upon sociological data, and they explain why it is becoming a social as well as a legal landmark.

Finally, Isaac Asimov, in "True Love," gives a fictional account of passionate love gone awry in an age of computer technology. Does his tale seem farfetched? Today, perhaps, but maybe not twenty or thirty years hence.

The Sexes

Sex Differences, Real and Imagined
Carol Tavris and Carole Offir

■ The stereotypes people hold about men and women are easy to identify; you merely have to go out, questionnaire in hand, and ask people about them. You soon find out that the Archie Bunkers of this world, who yearn for the days when "girls were girls and men were men," and the Maude Findlays, who would like to see the Archies stifled forever, can at least agree on what the stereotypes are. If only it were as easy to find out which of the supposed sex differences are real.

But it is not. In an area as controversial as sex differences, personal beliefs can easily affect research results. In the nineteenth century, biased assumptions caused scientists to flip-flop in a suspicious manner when they were looking for sex differences in the brain. Scientists nowadays are more enlightened about how their own expectations can influence their experiments, but it is still difficult to run objective studies. A few years ago Robert Rosenthal and his colleagues demonstrated in a dramatic way how belief can become reality. They asked some student-experimenters to train rats to run a maze. Half of the experimenters believed their rats had been specially bred to learn maze-running rapidly, while the other half thought the rats had been bred for dullness. Although there was no real genetic difference between the two groups of rodents, the supposedly bright rats did, in fact, learn faster. If an experimenter's expectations can influence rats, Rosenthal concluded, they surely can influence human beings, and this he demonstrated in many other studies (Rosenthal 1966; 1968).

The manner in which an experimenter produces a self-fulfilling prophecy is usually nonverbal and, like the abominable snowman, hard to track down. For example, Rosenthal observed that male experimenters gave instructions to the men and women in their studies rather differently. Only 12 percent of the researchers smiled at the men, but 70 percent smiled at the women. "It may be a heartening finding to know that chivalry is not dead," says Rosenthal, "but as far as methodology is concerned it is a disconcerting finding." It's easy to imagine how an experimenter's facial expression might affect his results. For instance, if his smile made people feel friendly and rewarded and his study happened to concern people's need for affiliation (their desire to be with others), he might find a sex difference that he himself had unwittingly caused.

Another methodological problem arises in studies that rely on self-reports. Suppose you believe that males are more independent than females, and you want to prove it. If you merely ask people how independent or dependent they are, your interviewees may slant their answers toward what they believe is socially desirable: a man may try to sound more self-reliant than he feels; a woman, less so. Or your interviewees may have distorted perceptions of themselves that have little to do with the way they behave in daily life. One solution is to question a second party. Many child psychologists use this method; they ask teachers and parents to describe the children in their care. Here again, though, one risks collecting biases instead of objective observations.

Another approach is for the researcher personally to observe the behavior of children or adults in a natural setting, such as home or school. This method allows you to deal with actual behavior, but you still have the problem of your own implicit assumptions. As a psychologist interested in assertiveness, how would you distinguish "passive" behavior from that which is merely "easy-going"? How would you distinguish submissiveness, which is the opposite of assertiveness, from cooperation, which is not? The danger is that you might label the same bit of behavior differently when a girl did it than when a boy did.

In addition to assigning different labels to the same act, an observer may simply fail to notice certain kinds of behavior. Someone who claims that housewives are passive and submissive may be overlooking many situations in which housewives are active. (Caring for children and organizing and maintaining a home require considerable assertiveness and initiative.) Similarly, if someone tells you that men tend to be unemotional and insensitive, it may be because she or he has ignored situations that allow men to be expressive.

As if all this were not bad enough, there is another obstacle that impedes the pursuit of scientific truth. Studies that identify sex differences are much more likely to be published in professional journals than those that do not. Nonfindings don't have much drama and, besides, scientific convention dictates that it is impossible to prove that a difference between groups does *not* exist. All a researcher can say is that there is no evidence a difference does exist, which is pretty dull compared to proclaiming: "Eureka! Men do X and women do Y." For that reason, studies identifying even small sex differences often have exaggerated clout.

In recent years there have been attempts to review the scientific literature on sex differences and to come up with some reliable generalizations. The reviews have tended to give more weight to studies that find differences than to those that don't, and to accept results uncritically. A good example is a 1968 monograph, "Sex Differences in Mental and Behavioral Traits," by Josef E. Garai and Amram Scheinfeld. The authors cited 474 studies but did not explain how they had selected them, nor did they discuss the quality of the procedures used in the studies. Most of the conclusions they reached conformed to popular stereotype. For example, the review found that females have greater social needs than males, and that males are superior to females in abstract reasoning and conceptualizing—which, the authors believed, helps explain "the outstanding achievements of men in science, philosophy, and the construction of theories." Garai and Scheinfeld suggested that the talent gap between the sexes might be bridged by encouraging girls to achieve and by giving them a bit of compensatory education, such as special training in creativity and problem-solving.

In 1974, Eleanor Maccoby and Carol Jacklin, two Stanford psychologists, published *The Psychology of Sex Differences,* which quickly became a classic text. In preparing their book, Maccoby and Jacklin carefully examined a larger body of research than any of their predecessors—over 2,000 articles and books, most of them published after 1966. Unlike other reviewers, they made a special effort to locate and include studies that might have found differences but did not. They even reanalyzed data when they thought it was necessary. So that readers could follow their analysis, they included a 233-page annotated bibliography and eighty-three summary tables. Maccoby and Jacklin concluded that many common assumptions about sex differences, including some that Garai and Scheinfeld maintained were proven, were completely unfounded; they were simply myths posing as facts. But they also found that males and females do differ in some interesting ways.

The Maccoby and Jacklin review is not without some serious weaknesses. Although the authors discussed methodological problems at length, when it came to evaluating hypotheses their approach was to tally all the studies pro or con, usually without counting the better research more heavily. Sometimes they reached conclusions mainly on the basis of studies with young children, a serious error because some sex differences do not emerge clearly until adolescence. So Maccoby and Jacklin's book is not the final word on sex differences, but it is far and away the most complete and thoughtful summary to date.

In the following sections we will review the findings most relevant to the issue of sex roles and status differences, as summarized in Table 2. The discussion frequently draws on Maccoby and Jacklin's information, (1974a and b), but we also question some of their conclusions and bring in other studies. Keep two things in mind as you read. First, when we speak of differences we mean group differences, or average differences. To say that one sex outdoes the other on some test does not mean that all members of that sex do better than all members of the opposite sex. Men and women overlap in abilities and personality traits, as they overlap in physical attributes. Men on the average are taller than women, but some women are taller than most men. Second, in this chapter we confine ourselves mainly to describing research findings on sex differences in

Table 2   Sex Differences and Similarities

Abilities

General intelligence	No difference on most tests.
Verbal ability	Females excel after age 10 or 11.
Quantitative ability	Males excel from the start of adolescence.
Creativity	Females excel on verbal creativity tests; otherwise, no difference.
Cognitive style	No general difference.
Visual-spatial ability	Males excel from adolescence on.
Physical abilities	Males more muscular; males more vulnerable to illness, disease; females excel on manual dexterity tests when speed important, but findings ambiguous.

Personality Characteristics

Sociability and love	No overall difference; at some ages, boys play in larger groups; some evidence that young men fall in love more easily, out of love with more difficulty.
Empathy	Conflicting evidence.
Emotionality	Self-reports and observations conflict.
Dependence	Conflicting findings; dependence probably not a unitary concept.
Nurturance	Little evidence available on adult male reactions to infants; issue of maternal vs. paternal behavior remains open; no overall difference in altruism.
Aggressiveness	Males more aggressive from preschool age on.

twentieth-century American society, with only brief detours to offer explanations. In later chapters we will analyze in more detail the factors that may account for actual sex differences and help perpetuate beliefs about mythical ones.

Sex Differences in Ability

Women's intuition is the result of millions of years of not thinking.

—*Rupert Hughes*

Women are only children of a large growth; they have an entertaining tattle, and sometimes wit; but for solid, reasoning good sense, I never in my life knew one that had it.

—*Earl of Chesterfield*

Women, as everyone knows, have not achieved fame in the arts, sciences, and professions as often as men; the Madame Curies and Margaret Meads stand out as exceptions. Part of the problem is that many notable women have been lost to history, unrecognized for their achievements. Regardless, a popular explanation for women's relative lack of public success is that females are not as bright as males. Although girls get better grades in school than boys, it is assumed they lack the genius necessary for outstanding achievement.

Tests of general intelligence do not show differences in the average IQs of males and females. This is not surprising, because the most widely used IQ tests were designed to minimize sex differences. If a question happened to differentiate between males and females, the test-maker would throw it out, or carefully balance an item favoring one sex with an item favoring the other. So we must turn to tests of specific abilities, not to IQ scores, in the search for sex differences.

Verbal Ability

If a woman could talk out of the two sides of her mouth at the same time, a great deal would be said on both sides.

—*George Prentice*

When both husband and wife wear pants it is not difficult to tell them apart—he is the one who is listening.

—*Anonymous*

Pediatricians, parents, and comedians credit females with having the gift of gab from infancy on. They are not necessarily paying women a compliment, though. As we all know, quantity does not guarantee quality: the politician who gives long, windy speeches and the party-goer who tells interminable stories are bores. According to the stereotype, women talk a lot but often have nothing worthwhile to say. So the stereotype has more to do with gossip and chit-chat than with intellectual skill.

When psychologists speak of verbal ability, however, they refer to specific abilities measurable in specific ways. These include simple measures of articulation, spelling, punctuation, sentence complexity, vocabulary size, the ability to name objects, and fluency, and also more sophisticated, higher-level measures of reading comprehension, creative writing, and the use of language in logical reasoning. Until recently, most psychologists believed that girls, from the time they first learned to talk, were superior on at least the simple measures. They based this assumption on several large studies from the 1930s and 1940s, which found that girls start to talk earlier than boys, use longer sentences, and excel verbally in other ways (McCarthy 1954). But Maccoby and Jacklin argue that psychologists need to reevaluate these findings. They observe that many of the early studies showed only small sex differences, some not even statistically significant. Although there are few recent studies comparable in scope to the early ones, some smaller ones do not find a sex difference in children younger than two or three. The safest conclusion seems to be that we do not yet know for sure whether girls talk sooner or more, or are more skilled with words, than boys during the first few years of life.

From age two to age ten, boys are far more likely than girls to have reading problems, but otherwise they do not lag behind girls in linguistic competence. At the age of ten or eleven, however, girls edge ahead. Though not every study reports a sex difference, those that do find that girls perform better on verbal tasks than boys. Girls maintain this superiority, or even increase it slightly, during high school, even though low-achieving boys drop out of school in larger numbers, leaving a rather select comparison group (Droege 1967).

In their 1968 monograph, Garai and Scheinfeld said that girls were better at simple verbal tasks but claimed that they were inferior on the higher-level ones. Perhaps, they speculated, that is the reason men do better in science and engineering. The Maccoby and Jacklin review finds no evidence for this distinction. After the age of ten or eleven, girls do better on both "lower" and "higher" measures of verbal skill. Apparently it is not for want of a golden tongue that most girls fail to become scientists and engineers—or courtroom lawyers, political orators, and auctioneers.

Quantitive Ability

She is like the rest of the women—thinks two and two'll come to make five, if she cries and bothers enough about it.

—George Eliot (Mary Ann Evans)

In our culture, women are not supposed to worry about such things as facts and numbers, which supposedly suit the male mind better. But young children do not differ in quantitative ability. Two-year-old girls are as good as two-year-old boys at counting (which is to say, not very), and in the early grades the two sexes are equally able to master numerical operations and concepts. There is one qualification: large studies with disadvantaged children have found that girls outperform boys.

Around puberty the picture changes. Although most studies of children aged nine to thirteen report no sex differences in math ability, a few show that boys do better than girls. By adolescence, boys usually do better, though the magnitude of the difference varies. Boys take more math courses, which might improve their performance on standardized tests, but Maccoby and Jacklin report that the male advantage also showed up in a study that compared the scores of male and female high-school seniors who had taken the same number of math courses. Males also score higher on the mathematical aptitude section of the college boards, and the math gap seems to survive into adulthood.

Many people believe that the sex difference in math ability is due to conditioned anxiety and cultural norms rather than to an inborn male advantage. They say, for example, that girls learn early that math is men's work and that they will be unpopular if they do well with numbers. As Sheila Tobias, assistant provost at Wesleyan University, notes, "Once a person has become frightened of math, she or he begins to fear all manner of computations, any quantitative data, and words like 'proportion,' 'percentage,' 'variance,' 'curve,' 'exponential.'" Women are especially likely to suffer from "mathophobia" and to go out of their way to avoid classes that require any mathematics (Tobias 1976).

For girls, "math anxiety" is a double-decker issue: they worry about mastering the concepts, and they worry about seeming unfeminine if they do. We think this explanation has merit in terms of the average male and female learning math but we do not know whether it explains the greater frequency of male geniuses in the field. Genius in math appears very early and may have, in either sex, a genetic component.

Creativity

Very learned women are to be found in the same manner as female warriors; but they are seldom or never inventors.

—*Voltaire*

Women have more imagination than men. They need it to tell us how wonderful we are.

—*Arnold H. Glasgow*

The stereotype alleges that women are emotionally sensitive, aesthetic, and intuitive. It also creates an enigma: why do these qualities not assure that women will become leading artists, musicians, novelists, poets, and creative scientists? Garai and Scheinfeld seem to think the problem lies partly in the different ways the sexes relate to the outer world. The male, they claim, "has an innate drive to act upon and transform the environment, and consequently to engage in exciting and challenging investigation of the numerous unfamiliar objects, shapes, and machines. Thus, in his search for control over the world of things, the young boy is led toward more challenging, farther removed, and more difficult goals than the more sedentary girls." This claim is without merit. There is no basis for assuming that boys are born with a greater urge to transform the environment than girls; little girls are far from sedentary; and, most important, it is not true that males are more creative than females.

Most psychologists define creativity as the ability to produce unique and novel ideas. Psychologists themselves have been very creative in their attempts to assess creativity in the laboratory. One measure, called the Alternate Uses Test, asks people to list as many uses as they can for various common objects, such as a brick. Some people give obvious answers: "You use a brick when you build a house." Others, more creative, go on listing until forced to stop. (Our favorite response, offered by a colleague, was to use a brick as a bug-hider: "You leave it on the ground for a few days, then pick it up and see all the bugs that have been hiding.") The Alternate Uses Test has the advantage of yielding scores that do not correlate closely with IQ; it is a fairly direct measure of the ability to generate novel ideas. The Remote Associates Test, which yields scores that do correlate with IQ, measures flexible thinking in a different way. A person is given three words and must come up with a fourth word that links the first three. For example, for the triplet *stool, powder,* and *ball,* the answer is *foot;* for *house, village,* and *golf* the answer is *green.* People who are widely acknowledged to be creative in real life tend to score higher on such tests than other people.

The research reviewed by Maccoby and Jacklin shows that on creativity tests like these, which involve a degree of verbal fluency, there is indeed a sex difference among children older than seven: females do better. On nonverbal tests of creativity, neither sex does better than the other. They conclude that girls and women "are at least as able as boys and men to generate a variety of hypotheses and produce unusual ideas." Thus the data do no more than the stereotype to explain why most inventors and artists are men. . . .

Physical Abilities

Her weakness is her strength, and her true art is to cultivate and improve that weakness.

—George Fitzhugh

The intention of your being taught needlework, knitting, and such like is not on account of the intrinsic value of all you can do with your hands, which is trifling, but . . . to enable you to fill up in a tolerably agreeable way some of the many solitary hours you must necessarily pass at home.

—Dr. John Gregory
(to his daughters)

As a group males are stronger, heavier, and taller than females, at least after puberty. How much of the sex difference in muscular strength is innate and how much is due to better athletic training for boys than girls is not known. Studies find that girls finish developing athletically by the time they reach adolescence, while boys continue to improve for several more years; but increased emphasis on athletic programs for girls may change this pattern.

The sex difference in physical strength is of more than passing interest to social scientists because of its possible implications. Garai and Scheinfeld argued that the greater height and weight of males gives them an advantage not only in sports but in "all those occupational and recreational domains which require height, weight, physical strength, and vigorous exertion as prerequisites for success." They did not list those domains, though. In many parts of the world women do backbreaking physical labor, carrying heavy baskets on their heads, plows in their hands, and children on their hips for many years. Still, physical strength may help account for certain sex-role distinctions that have prevailed both cross-culturally and historically. . . .

The stronger sex does not start life more sturdily than the weaker one. On the contrary, males are more apt to suffer from prenatal problems, birth injuries, and childhood diseases of all types, including pneumonia, influenza, measles, diptheria, polio, and whooping cough. Throughout life, males are more vulnerable to a wide range of disorders and infections, and the death rate for American women is lower than that for men in every decade of life (Sherman 1971). One unforeseen consequence of sex-role equality may be that women's health will decline to male levels. Lung cancer and heart disease are on the increase among women, possibly due to the rising numbers who smoke and work in high-stress jobs (Horn 1975).

Although men are credited with stronger shoulders, women are credited with faster fingers—with a superiority in manual dexterity, or the ability to perform tasks that require fine, quick finger movements. Among those interested in sex roles, manual dexterity is a controversial, emotionally charged issue. When someone says that women are better than men with their hands, antifeminists cheer while feminists bristle or guffaw. The reason for these reactions is that the assertion has been used to justify the work that women do: typing, sewing, routine factory assignments. The argument that women's nimble fingers equip them for certain jobs crosses all political borders. When one of us (C.T.) visited a silk factory in the People's Republic of China, her host told her that young women did the spinning and worked the looms because of their superior manual skills.

Recent studies do show that women perform better on finger dexterity tasks when speed is important. But it is hard to interpret this finding, because the tasks used to measure dexterity are repetitive and boring and it may be that women are more willing than men to stick out such a task. Even if the difference is real, few people have suggested that it means women are better suited than men to become surgeons and pickpockets. And back in the days when typing was a high-status occupation, no one protested that the great clumsy paws of men should be kept off the keyboard. Even today, all the typists at Lloyds of London are male, and they seem to be doing all right.

References

Droege, Robert C. 1967. Sex differences in aptitude maturation during high school. *Journal of counseling psychology* 14: 407–11.

Garai, Josef E., and Scheinfeld, Amram. 1968. Sex differences in mental and behavioral traits. *Genetic psychology monographs* 77: 169–299.

Horn, Jack. 1975. Bored to sickness. *Psychology today* 9 (November): 92.

McCarthy, Dorothea. 1954. Language development in children. In *Manual of child psychology*, 2nd ed., ed. Leonard Carmichael, pp. 492–630. New York: Wiley.

Maccoby, Eleanor Emmons, and Jacklin, Carol Nagy. 1974a. *The psychology of sex differences*. Stanford, California: Stanford University Press.

Maccoby, Eleanor Emmons, and Jacklin, Carol Nagy. 1974b. Myth, reality and shades of gray: what we know and don't know about sex differences. *Psychology today* 8 (December): 109–12.

Rosenthal, Robert. 1966. *Experimenter effects in behavioral research*. New York: Appleton-Century-Crofts.

———. 1968. Self-fulfilling prophecy. *Psychology today* 2 (September): 44–51.

Sherman, Julia. 1971. *On the psychology of women: a survey of empirical studies*. Springfield, Illinois: Charles C Thomas.

Tobias, Sheila. 1976. Math anxiety: why is a smart girl like you counting on your fingers? *Ms.* 5 (September): 56–59ff.

The Meaning of Gay
An Interview with Dr. C. A. Tripp
Philip Nobile

■ On the whole, Freud preferred shipping homosexuals off to South America. The Roman church would send them even farther south and for all eternity. And while homosexuality is no longer classed as a mental disorder by the American Psychiatric Association, even now, ten years after the Stonewall riot, which sparked the gay activist movement, homosexuals are still in trouble in our society. Many folk, including neo-conservatives, Right-to-Lifers, and born-again Christians, to mention but a few, continue to regard homosexuality as a threat to the harmony between the sexes.

Kinsey had intended to meet the homosexual scare head-on in a sequel to his landmark male and female volumes. He reported in *Sexual Behavior in the Human Male* that a third of American men had at least one homosexual experience to orgasm, but he died before he could spell out in his painstaking inductive fashion the significance of same-sex activity. Had Kinsey lived a few more years, the "homosexual question" might not be as muddled today.

The publication four years ago of *The Homosexual Matrix,* an exceedingly controversial study by psychologist Dr. C. A. Tripp, owed much to Kinsey. Tripp was a protégé of Kinsey's and rather than allow many of Kinsey's original ideas to remain unpublished he decided to carry out the project himself. Tripp feels Kinsey and he are compatible on all the major issues. "He thought, and I agree, that the potential for homosexual behavior is consistent in every society, but its expression is determined by specific cultural supports or restrictions."

Tripp's view of homosexuality is bold and unsettling. It is supported by natural history and anthropology and is replete with startling insights into heterosexuality as well as homosexuality. He argues that friendship and compatibility eventually kill zestful sex and, conversely, that only some sort of resistance, barrier, or distance keeps partners revved up for each other. He also notes that homosexuality, like heterosexuality, originates in a positive attraction rather than in a fear of something else (e.g., a dominating mother, castration anxiety, identity problems, *vagina dentata*, etc.). He points out for the first time that homosexuality is even higher in competitive and macho societies than in societies where there are no taboos against it.

Dr. Tripp's career is impressive if somewhat unusual. He left his small hometown of Corsicana, Texas, at eighteen to study photography at the Rochester Institute of Technology in 1938. He subsequently joined the Kodak Research Laboratories. After enlisting in the navy in 1942, he was purportedly discharged on medical grounds but was in fact transferred undercover to Twentieth Century-Fox laboratories in New York City, where he assisted in the production of confidential films for the army and navy.

After the war, Tripp opened up a photo studio in Greenwich Village. But his interests were turning toward human behavior, and he began to immerse himself in psychiatric literature. Under the tutelage of the prominent Freud disciple Theodor Reik, he prepared to become a lay analyst. Reik, impressed by his initiate's intuitive grasp of the subject, recommended him to a publisher to prepare a cross-index of psychoanalysis. (Tripp has a photographic memory, or at least an instant recall of stored data; one evening a friend of his interrupted our interview to inquire about extramarital intercourse in young men. "You'll find a chart on that on page 586 in Kinsey," he told his friend immediately. I checked the reference, and Tripp was right.)

In 1948, Tripp read Kinsey's male volume and called him with a long list of questions. Kinsey kindly invited this inquisitive stranger for a weekend visit to his Institute for Sex Research in Bloomington, Indiana. Kinsey admired Tripp's roving curiosity and critical mind and promptly began to disabuse him of Freudian dogma. The conversion went smoothly, and thus began a working partnership that lasted until Kinsey's death in 1956.

At Kinsey's urging, Tripp returned to school in 1951. Six years later he had his B.A. and Ph.D. In 1960, Tripp went into private practice on Central Park West. He reduced his predominantly heterosexual patient load to one day a week in order to complete *The Homosexual Matrix.*

His research was extensive: Tripp duplicated Kinsey's European tour, made eleven trips to Puerto Rico to compare and contrast Spanish and American sexual mores; he interviewed over 700 homosexuals; he debriefed scores of field anthropologists for cross-cultural information; he used much of Kinsey's unpublished data, and during the last two decades has closely observed homosexuals in many occupations and at every social level.

Whether or not one assents to the theories of Dr. Tripp, he brilliantly advances the discussion of homosexuality beyond the anathemas of psychiatry, the manifestos of gay lib, and the ignorance of common supposition.

In this interview for *New York* Magazine I asked Dr. Tripp to go beyond the ideas in his book and to define the meaning of gay.

Nobile: *Does homosexuality threaten the survival of the species?*

Tripp: Hardly. Its consequences are too trivial for that, and anyway societies with the highest homosexual rates invariably have high birth rates. We know why too; the moral structures of a society where homosexuality is constrained usually also restrict heterosexuality. Thus where anti-sexual edicts are relaxed, in Moslem countries, for example, both forms of sex tend to increase, with a consequent rise in the birth rate.

Q. Is homosexuality a biological aberration?

A. Years ago when it was thought that some instinct produces heterosexuality, homosexual variations were ipso facto "deviant." But we now know that due to certain evolutionary changes in the brain of man and other anthropoids, sexual preferences (and the value systems that control them) have to be learned. And they're learned in response to the lure of real or imagined advantages, not, as psychiatry has thought, in response to dominant mothers, neglectful fathers, or fears of something else. You don't like blondes because you hate brunettes.

We can thoroughly discount heredity. As Kinsey noted, even if homosexuals were wiped out of today's population, the incidence of homosexuality in the next generation would not necessarily be reduced. Moreover, if hormones, genes, and other biological influences had any significant effect, then homosexuality, like left-handedness, would be quite stable cross-culturally—instead of varying as it does from nearly zero in some societies to pervasive in others.

Q. In the forties Kinsey found that 4 percent of American men and about a third as many women were predominantly homosexual. Do these statistics still hold?

A. According to recent studies by the Institute for Sex Research they do, and it's a double surprise. Many laymen have thought the sexual revolution with its endless talk of homosexuality must surely have increased it. Sex researchers half-expected the same "loosening" of the mores to *reduce* homosexuality, mainly by permitting easier and earlier heterosexual experience. Both theories proved wrong. A greater readiness to talk about sexual variations doesn't mean people are quickly ready to adopt them. And while it is true that the younger generation's age-at-first-intercourse has been dropping in recent years, the stability of the homosexual figures suggests that the die is cast at much younger ages.

Q. Can one always spot a homosexual?

A. Absolutely not. Even expert sex researchers such as the original Kinsey group could only manage to detect some 15 percent of homosexual males and about 5 percent of homosexual females. And they were relying on several cues—dress, circumstance, referral, and so on. By the way, effeminacy was not an important cue in these observations since only a fraction of homosexuals are effeminate, and besides, heterosexuals often show such signs. Furthermore, a great many people involved in homosexuality are the opposite of what the layman would expect, meaning that they are macho males of the truck driver-cowboy-lumberjack variety.

Q. Although effeminacy cannot be equated with homosexuality, is it not true that the greater number of effeminate men are indeed homosexual?

A. I would guess more than 85 percent of the overtly effeminate males are homosexual. But at the same time certainly more than 90 percent of homosexuals show no effeminacy.

Q. What is the connection between supermacho types and homosexuality?

A. Those he-man types place great emphasis on maleness and male values—and thus have an extraordinary tendency to eroticize male attributes, which is, after all, what most male homosexuality is all about.

Q. Why should certain professions—hairdressing, interior decorating, dance, and fashion—attract more than their share of the homosexual population?

A. For a couple of reasons. In this culture, certain jobs are thought to be effete, and heterosexuals are reticent to take them. Homosexuals, on the other hand, are not inhibited by this connotation and feel free to fill these openings. The other factor is more elusive—a question of disposition. Take music, for example. I checked the Eastman School of Music in the forties and the Juilliard in the fifties and found that homosexuality is relatively frequent among pianists and organists and yet notably rare among violinists. And in certain branches of foreign service—the British foreign service, for example—there has been a predominance of homosexuals. Here there are many interlocking correlations, such as the homosexual's frequent talent for linguistics and often his special interest in foreign lands.

Q. Speaking of foreign lands, how would a geographic survey of homosexuality look?

A. Like a crazy quilt of incidences. Among small tribal societies, as Margaret Mead has noted, homosexuality is sometimes so rare that you only see it in their language or in some institutionalized puberty rite. While in others such as the Tanganyikan Nyakyusa or Algerian Kabyles, one has to look carefully to find a single male who is not extensively involved in it. Part of this wide variation is well understood. Homosexuality hovers near zero in societies that bolster heterosexuality with child marriage (e.g., nearly all the African Gold Coast tribes). And it doesn't rise much above zero in societies that eschew heroics and thus take the glory out of maleness (e.g., Pygmy tribes in which special credit is denied to the successful hunter; his feats are credited instead to luck or to some god). But wherever a society lauds bravery, courage, and an individualized derring-do, homosexuality can be high to very high; such attitudes encourage an idealization and thus the easy eroticization of male attributes. In our society this vigorous homosexual potential is held down to moderate levels by specific taboos against it and by a variety of heterosexual expectations and encouragements. Turn the clock back to when these heterosexual encouragements were weaker and you'll glimpse the much more prevalent homosexuality of our Greek and Roman forefathers—or if you prefer a modern example, the Arab scene will do, as will the Greco-Roman holdover in today's Southern Italy.

Q. Why is it so difficult to isolate the causes of homosexuality?

A. While we know scores of major influences in detail, nobody can weight each of these accurately enough to explain exactly why Bill turns out to be heterosexual and Andy homosexual. A close analogy is weather prediction: All the variables are known, yet advance forecasts regress to levels hardly better than seasonal chance owing to myriad combinations that can end up in either rain or sunshine. Dozens of experience factors combine to support heterosexuality, while many of the same and similar experiences in a slightly different shuffle can lend their weight to a homosexual result.

Q. Kinsey found that 50 percent of young boys eroticize male attributes, so why do only 4 percent wind up exclusively homosexual?

A. Because most of them also come to eroticize female attributes, a taste which is more strongly reinforced by social expectancy and demand.

If one wants to look a bit closer at the matter and ask how many men ever practice homosexuality, the answer would be a third of the male population. If one wants to discount this high figure on the grounds that a single tryout doesn't necessarily "mean" anything and ask the question, How many people extensively repeat homosexual experiences, let's say for at least three years? the 33 percent would drop to something like 25 percent. If you add still another requirement and ask, How many people retain a definite homosexual response for life? the statistic is near the 13 percent that Kinsey estimated. It's only when you add the proviso of exclusivity that the homosexual ratio drops to 4 percent.

Q. How does the 4 percent develop an exclusive homosexuality despite all the social barriers against it?

A. A powerful homosexual conditioning usually begins at such an early age the child is hardly aware of social pressures against it—and is often more aware of pressures against heterosexuality. (Sex researchers have consistently found that pre-pubertal youngsters are more ready to discuss their homosexual play then they are their heterosexual.) Furthermore, in all clear-cut cases of sexual conditioning, a person tends to build up strong aversions to the polar opposites of what his tastes are. Thus, once a male is turned on by the muscularity and angularity of males, he tends to build up a distaste for the softness and roundness of the female form. Similarly, the male who has come to respond to the roundness and softness of some women is already turned off by women who lack these qualities—so, for him, the very thought of an intimate sexual contact with a hard, angular male is a symphony of horrors. All exclusive tastes are alike in these respects.

Q. *Is bisexuality increasing?*

A. It appears to be decidedly up with women but not with men. Males are much more firmly locked into their sexual directions. But women—with the enormous pliancy that characterizes female sexuality throughout the mammalian species—have become able to respond quickly to certain changes in our mores. We have some tangible data for this. Among swingers, far less than 1 percent of the men ever reach over for even a momentary male-male contact—while according to G. Bartell's *Group Sex* some 64 percent of the women readily do so.

Q. *How does bisexuality affect sex between men and women?*

A. At low or moderate levels of demand, a touch of homosexuality often strengthens a person's heterosexual commitment. It's as if the homosexual element is too weak to offer any real competition to the marriage and yet is strong enough to both satisfy a person's need for diversity and cut down on one's roving eye toward other heterosexual partners—which is the real enemy of most marriages.

Incidentally, one sees the same thing in reverse too. The ongoing homosexual relationship is often stabilized by a touch of heterosexuality in one or both partners.

Q. *Does most of what you have said about male homosexuality apply to lesbians as well?*

A. Much of it does apply, but there are startling differences between males and females on several levels. Males tend to eroticize such things as the specific body shapes of their partners, while the eroticization women achieve tends to be much more conceptual, often more emotional in tone and content, and otherwise less visual and much less related to specific body cues.

Q. *Does the prevalence of homosexual activity in prisons produce converts?*

A. Not many. Seventy-one percent of long-term prisoners are involved in overt homosexuality, but only 4 percent of these first practiced it in prison.

Q. *Does this mean that the confirmed heterosexual—no matter how long he is deprived of women and has access to men—generally will not dabble in homosexuality?*

A. That is one of the findings of a secret United States Army sex-research study conducted during World War II and still locked up in the Pentagon. And from other sources, too, it seems that among large groups of men isolated on various South Pacific islands during the war, homosexuality did not increase. Nor did it develop among our prisoners in Vietnam. To a large extent such evidence means what it seems to mean:

that firmly conditioned sexual patterns tend to stay put. And yet, this remarkable stability, which stems from each individual's past conditioning, is not the only thing that determines a person's sexual behavior; the prevailing group mores of the moment can also play an important role. Thus in most prisons and on an occasional ship at sea where the implicitly agreed-upon mores become "homosexuality is okay here," the floodgates are opened and even a trace of homosexuality in people may balloon into a major, highly motivated activity.

Q. What determines the way homosexuals perform in bed?

A. As in heterosexuality, that depends on individual tastes, what social level is involved, how well the partners know each other, and how much affection there is. Lower-social-level males tend to rely on anal intercourse and simple fellatio more than do persons at middle and upper social levels. In fact, an unpublished Kinsey tabulation shows anal intercourse to be "preferred" by only 11 percent of middle- and upper-level males; they engage in much more fellatio and myriad other oral and masturbatory techniques. It's not that the lower-level male tends to be more simplistic and less imaginative. Whether heterosexual or homosexual, he is more inclined to see variations in sexual technique as "unnatural," sometimes even as a risk to his macho—for example, when he "lands on the bottom." And he not infrequently interprets anything that smacks of masturbation—including femoral, that is, between-thigh, intercourse—as both trivial and "a perversion." Lower-level homosexual males tend to engage in more kissing and other oral techniques than do their heterosexual equivalents—a difference which Kinsey attributed to more interaction between social levels in the homosexual population.

Lesbian techniques are remarkable. In the first place, they often involve a degree of drawn-out continuous affectionate exchanges—sometimes extending over several hours—which is beyond the comprehension of most males. And while some of the physical techniques used by a woman to bring her female partner to orgasm are sometimes very elaborate, other techniques are so bland-looking as to seem hardly effective. Yet they are very effective indeed because they zero in on a woman's requirements with "intuitive precision," an intimately accurate knowledge of what really works. Both the Kinsey and recent Masters and Johnson studies have rated lesbian techniques as far more effective for women than ordinary heterosexual intercourse.

Q. In a male or female homosexual pair, is the relative "toughness" or "softness" of the partners an indication of which one is dominant in bed?

A. No, it isn't. In fact, dominance in bed is notoriously unpredictable. However, when one partner is clearly dominant in bed, which is often not the case, there is a tendency for the roles to be the opposite of what one might have expected. The socially dominant lesbian often leans back in bed and expects to be made love to, which is an almost classical complaint among lesbians. And not only is the relatively soft male notably inclined to land on top, the very aggressive male is remarkably inclined to *want* to be on the bottom in anal intercourse. These reversals of role are not a surprise. Far down in the mammalian pattern, there's a tendency for the most aggressive and sexually vigorous individuals to be the ones most inclined to reverse their roles.

Q. You make the remarkable statement in your book that homosexual techniques are more varied than those of heterosexuality.

A. That's because the need for heterosexual variety is reduced—in part by the very excellence of its male-female genital union. In addition, its clear-cut role expectancies tend to conventionalize it. And of course the use of stereotypes in heterosexuality is socially recommended, and extreme variations are widely regarded as "abnormal." By contrast, no forms of homosexuality have the head start of being approved, let alone demanded. Thus the whole matter of what the partners do together is left more to individual invention—an invention that, with the aid of the high rapport between same-sex partners, often does come up with exceptional variety.

Q. Are homosexual males more promiscuous than heterosexuals?

A. Yes, but there's nothing to suggest that promiscuity is any higher for homosexual than for heterosexual males when they're faced with equal opportunity.

Q. Are fetishism, S&M, and the other paraphilias more common among homosexual males than others?

A. Undoubtedly so. It's much easier for males to find these interests among males than among females. This situation is well shown in prostitution: A call girl who charges $100 expects several times this amount for mildly kinky sex; the rate may reach $800 an hour for less mild participations. Not so with the call boy. His rate is less than $100 and it is unusual for "special requests" to cost much if anything extra. Remember that these differences reflect the contrast between the sexes rather than whether the sex itself is homosexual or heterosexual.

Q. Are homosexual couples less inclined than heterosexuals to insist on sexual "fidelity"?

A. Not usually. Like everybody else, they tend to start off with the heterosexual model of monogamy, which is one of their problems. Of course sexual exclusivity is always easy for anybody to maintain during a period of high romance, but since the duration of "romance" is only a year or so, homosexual males soon face what heterosexuals face, the waywardness of males. It is interesting that the lesbian relationship often survives a total loss of sexual interest between the partners—a mixed blessing, since these can continue far past both their sexual and emotional usefulness. Apparently this is because for so many women there's a "nest building" tendency that can far exceed their interest in sex, which seems to bear out the ancient claim that women supply more of the cohesiveness in ordinary marriages than men do.

Q. Do friendship and intimacy kill good sex, and is some form of barrier or resistance needed to keep erotic zest alive in a long-term partnership?

A. Yes to both parts of the question. The resistance theory makes sense to many people. But others are shocked to the core, particularly if they are in the midst of a situation where they are not being very honest with themselves. No doubt most people want and need compatibility with their partners, but a smooth personal closeness requires the comfortable, worn-in quality of an old shoe—comforts that are utterly lacking in the newness and surprise that characterize every aspect of titillating sex and a new romance. Of course, the illusion of new lovers is that they will eventually have all the joys of sex along with the comforts of compatibility. But in practice, intense sexual interest can never survive the familiarity and predictability that are implicit in the high compatibility of a "good" marriage.

Q. Are you saying that good marriages don't hold up, or at least that good sex in them doesn't?

A. That's not it. In the first place, it would be presumptuous of me, or of anybody, to say exactly what a good marriage is for other people. Some couples who have many fights and quarrels rate their marriage as "good" or even "very good." They are particularly likely to maintain a lively, intense bedroom scene, by the way. Invariably a couple's sexual motivation is only aroused when something in the situation is resistant to it. This resistance can be in a partner's partial standoffishness, in one's fear and fascination with an attractive but "dangerous" person, or mixed into the feelings of both partners as they physically invade each other's privacy. Or the resistance may appear in neither partner but in something that intrudes between them—an unavoidable delay or some bittersweet separation.

The most poignant romantic situations invariably involve such things as the displacements of wartime, a threat of losing each other, or the interference of disapproving others. The attraction of Romeo and Juliet was incited by the distance of the balcony, the feuding of their families, and the impending marriage of Juliet to another man. Likewise, the appeal of a Lolita, the fascination with a virgin bride, and the excitements of surreptitiousness in a hundred forms are all examples of particular kinds of resistances that act as stimulators. In a nutshell: Sexual zest does not arise from the comforts of a smooth compatibility, nor can it survive them; it is put to sleep by the music of high accord.

Q. Does the resistance factor, like most sexual activities in man, have its analogue among lower animals?

A. Yes. There are numerous examples of animals that, like dogs, do a good deal of running away from, as well as running toward, their mates during a teasing courtship. Then there are other species in which a sharper resistance is apparent, where the male has to fight his way through a crowd of competing males to reach a female. Among a great many of these species the absence of a fight or of some other impediment to easy access results in impotence or sterility. (Before this was understood, zoo keepers were quite perplexed that they could not breed most of their animals in captivity, or even get a male to "be interested" in a ripe female. They now solve the problem by putting some barrier between the mates and then suddenly raising it.) These are not isolated examples. In not a single known species of any animal or insect is sex a sweet and gentle business from start to finish; usually it's a fairly violent affair full to overflowing with tension and torment.

Q. But how universal is the resistance factor in man?

A. You might as well ask how universal is the law of gravity. Even in the numerous permissive societies, where there is hardly a social barrier to sex, the tension and resistance is moved into the sex act itself. In central South America, for instance, Choroti women spit in a lover's face during coitus; Apinaye women bite off bits of a man's eyebrows, loudly spitting them aside. Ponapean men of the South Pacific do the same to their female partners, pulling their eyebrows out by the roots. Turkese women poke their fingers into a man's ears. Siriono couples of Bolivia poke fingers into each other's eyes along with much scratching and pinching of necks and chests. And Trobriand Islanders, who are particularly free in permitting sexual liaisons, bite each other on the cheek and lips till blood flows, snap the nose and chin, tear each other's hair, and otherwise lacerate their lovers during coitus. It's worth remembering that these styles of sex predominate only in sexually permissive societies. Conversely, societies which expect sexual expressions to be gentle and affectionate are, across the board, highly restrictive in sex, especially in terms of partner accessibility.

Q. Why is the question of curing homosexuality so controversial? Surely you can either change homosexuals or you can't.

A. Not quite. The "cure" issue is seldom raised these days. Nobody could possible cure homosexuality because the phenomena it comprises are not illnesses in the first place. A number of moralists and psychiatrists still claim to be able to *change* homosexuality, but whether that is ever possible depends entirely on your criteria. If stopping the action is all that's meant, then joining a monastery or a nunnery might do it, or listening to Billy Graham and swearing off in the name of Jesus might work for a while. Or if "making a commitment to heterosexuality" is the criterion—Masters and Johnson demand this of their patients—then this sometimes "works" but only with people who have a degree of heterosexual response and who, by dint of will under the eyes of kindly authority figures, push their homosexual tastes aside. It all amounts to a brittle, desperate, tenuous hold on a forced heterosexuality.

But if by change you mean getting a person to not want what he does want, and at the same time make him sexually want what he has never wanted, then forget it; there's never been a validated case on record, and I predict never will be. Just think how hard it would be to get the average heterosexual guy to be turned off by women *and* revved up by men—the same goes for the homosexual male in reverse. Hell, we can't even change a breast man into a leg man, let alone hurdle the heterosexual-homosexual divide. Sexual preferences of all kinds tend to be as stable as they are sharp, especially in males.

Q. Can you foresee a time when homosexuality will be fully accepted in the United States?

A. If you mean accepted openly and generally, certainly not. In the first place we know from cross-cultural studies that minority sexual practices are never fully accepted. Homosexuality has been fully sanctioned only in those times and places where it has predominated. Examples of predominantly homosexual cultures are found in 64 percent of the tribes cataloged by Ford and Beach in *Patterns of Sexual Behavior* and in ancient Greece, recently shown in K. J. Dover's *Greek Homosexuality.* Our society will probably go only a small distance toward accepting homosexuality. The great middle class will gradually adopt the attitudes that now prevail at the upper social levels—a tacit acceptance of homosexuality and an embarrassment in appearing prudish about it, yet a disdain for it whenever a disdain is socially useful. Even this will take time. Remember, Judeo-Christian mores are fundamentally ascetic and still don't approve even heterosexual sex without love and "responsibility."

Attraction

Rehearsals and Realities: Beginning to Date

John H. Gagnon and Cathy S. Greenblat

■   While cross-sex association in the United States is extremely common among children and young people, it is generally only after the transition of puberty that it becomes a part of the mate selection process. At this point young people begin to develop the special patterns of cross-sex association (restricted by factors of social background and opportunity) that we call dating. Not all young people begin to date in early adolescence, at ages thirteen or fourteen, but what matters is that dating becomes a possibility and opportunity. Later in adolescence and young adulthood, success or failure in the dating game can become a basis for making judgments about oneself—one's competence, popularity, and desirability. As more people date, those left out become more aware that they are missing something—that they remain outside of one of the main experiences of youth culture.

Dating emerges from the earlier patterns of acquaintanceship and perhaps prior friendship that exist between boys and girls and young men and young women. An invitation to enter into a different kind of relationship must be made, usually by a boy, but sometimes by a girl, and

"Rehearsals and Realities: Beginning to Date" from LIFE DESIGNS: INDIVIDUALS, MARRIAGES, AND FAMILIES by John H. Gagnon and Cathy S. Greenblat. Copyright © 1978 by Scott, Foresman and Company. Reprinted by permission. From ADOLESCENT SOCIETY by James Coleman. (New York: Basic Books, Inc.), 1961, p. 51.

sometimes through an intermediary or friend. (This pattern often continues well into adulthood.) To ask someone for a date is to select them out, to treat them as somehow special. This meaning is implicit in the word itself—to have a date one must speak out, agree on a time, select things to do, and choose someone with whom to share these activities. Dating is more than a simple aggregation of people who know each other and spend time together—it is an indication of preference. It requires a mobilization of personal and emotional resources, for it means that a different kind of relationship is being set in motion. It also requires taking a risk, for to ask is to risk rejection.

It must be pointed out that who one asks and how, what is expected to happen on the date, and the range of acceptable activities all change substantially during the period of mate selection. The script for a "date" between two college students who meet during their senior year in college will differ from the script for a "date" of two fourteen-year-olds—even though both couples may be going to a school dance or a local movie. A "date" between two divorced people in their thirties who meet in a singles bar will have a still different script. This variation suggests some of the limitations on the word *date*. Because it has been used to apply to so many different social encounters between people it has lost some of its precision. At the same time since "date" does mean that a particular selection has been made and a time set for people to get together in order to see whether a further relationship might ensue, it does cover many of the contacts between men and women outside of marriage throughout the life cycle.

An important aspect of the changing character of dating is the fact that it appears to be beginning at an earlier age. This represents a shift in the timing of acquiring adultlike activities and hence a shift in the sources of personal autonomy and mastery over the last three or four decades. In the past it was possible for young people to go to work part-time at fourteen or fifteen, get a driver's license at fifteen or sixteen (but rarely to own a car), begin dating at sixteen or seventeen, begin to drink at about the same age (often illegally, especially true for males), and begin to be treated as an adult sometime later. Since the 1960s there is evidence that young people are beginning to date at ages twelve to fourteen (thus extending the duration of the mate selection period) (Broderick, 1966). What this shift may involve is that an adolescent's sense of personal competence may increasingly involve skills in the arena of dating rather than in other prototypical adult behaviors.

At puberty, young people understand only imprecisely most of the content of the future activities of adolescence—dating, driving, drinking, working, falling in love, sexual experimentation—it largely exists in untested fantasies or in plans. The concrete processes of learning how to do any of these activities, the costs and anxieties associated with them, the potential for failure, the difficulties of acquiring skills and of carrying off a competent performance are often unknown to the young person entering adolescence. Actually driving a car in traffic, taking the license exam, paying for car insurance, changing a tire, trying to start a car with a dead battery, understanding the rules of the road, are far different than the fantasies that young people may have about the freedom that might come from driving a car. Similarly, the actual management of successful dating differs substantially from the fantasies that are created while playing with Barbie and Ken dolls or thinking about how one will be envied when seen with a popular cheerleader. All of the concerns expressed by young people about how to ask for or refuse a date, where to go on a date, how to act in front of parents, whether one should or should not kiss on the first date, are evidences of the anxieties that are involved in actually performing in heterosocial contexts. Many of these anxieties remain with young people all the way through the mate selection process, though they are felt at different levels in different relationships.

Interaction with the opposite gender and the rewards that are associated with it (and often the punishments associated with not doing it) attract most young people regardless of the anxiety that is provoked by entering a new situation. Indeed developing skills in dating is one of the major attractions of becoming adolescent.

Dating or the idea of dating has many of the same kinds of attractions for adolescents as many other activities that are supposed to signal growing up. The pleasure of driving a car, participating in competitive sports, being able to drink, making money by working, staying out late at night—experiences implying or involving autonomy and self-control—are among the many pleasures that make growing up appealing. The dating experience itself is a confirmation of personal worth and an indication to young people and their peers that they are successes as members of the youth culture and as potential adults. The very concreteness and immediacy of the dating situation in high school makes it, at least for many young people, a more important activity than participation in the academic or other training programs of the school. Many social scientists have expressed concern with the junior high and high-school dating systems since they feel that the academic goals of the school which involve preparing persons for work or college are undermined by the channeling of energy into the mate selection aspects of the school.

In the normal activities of a high school, the relations between boys and girls tend to increase the importance of physical attractiveness, cars, and clothes, and to decrease the importance of achievement in school activities.

. . . It is commonly assumed, both by educators and by laymen, that it is "better" for boys and girls to be in school together during adolescence, if not better for their academic performance, then at least better for their social development and adjustment. But this may not be so; it may depend wholly upon

the kinds of activities within which their association takes place. Coeducation in some high schools may be inimical to both academic achievement and social adjustment. The dichotomy often forced between "life-adjustment" and "academic emphasis" is a false one, for it forgets that most of the teen-ager's energy is not directed toward either of these goals. Instead, the relevant dichotomy is cars and the cruel jungle of rating and dating versus school activities, whether of the academic or life-adjustment variety. (Coleman, 1961, pp. 50–51)

These observations describe a situation that often still exists. The contemporary high school is still relatively dominated by the demands of youth culture in which cross-sex association provides a significantly larger proportion of gratification than does the prescribed academic program. Adolescents do not plan and rehearse for future algebra and history courses, but rather plan for rising levels of participation in the world of dating.

Patterns of Adolescent Dating

Dating patterns have changed substantially over the past twenty years. Since the first stage of dating begins earlier, many patterns of association which follow this stage have also moved to earlier in the life cycle. Thus the second stage involving patterns of group and intermittent dating by couples and a third stage in which couples pair off for steady dating still exist, but now occur in the early high-school period. During the 1940s and 1950s the period of initial dating began in the ninth and tenth grades and going steady somewhat after that in the junior and senior years of high school. During this same period there was considerable parental resistance to going steady and signs of pairing off (exchanging rings or other tokens) were viewed with considerable suspicion by adults. In addition, a substantial proportion of young people had not dated or gone steady during high school. In recent times both a larger proportion of young people have dated and have gone steady—the latter is now a relatively acceptable pattern—and in addition pairing off or going steady begins much earlier in the period of mate selection.

In a study of middle-class suburban youth, Broderick (1966) concluded that the development of a pattern of heterosociality seemed to follow a sequence of experimental steps that began with developing a positive attitude toward the idea of personally getting married (Figure 5–1). It is clear that the young person does not know what getting married actually involves, but the anticipated goal seems sufficient attraction to draw them into a round of activities that seems necessary to reach it. This idea of getting married is especially important for girls since it has been defined very early in life as a major life goal. This commitment to the idea of marriage is often followed by having a special friend of the opposite sex, which is followed by falling in love for the first time. For many very young

Figure 5-1   Heterosocial Attitudes and Activities Among
Middle-Class Adolescents (Percentage with the Experience)

Item	Age 10-11		Age 12-13		Age 14-15		Age 16-17	
	Male	Female	Male	Female	Male	Female	Male	Female
Like to get married some day	61	79	66	94	73	91	75	94
Has a special boy/girl friend	58	78	55	79	45	68	59	72
Has been in love	49	50	53	45	64	42	59	60
Has one or more opposite-gender friends	30	38	25	24	41	45	65	73
Has begun to date	28	28	60	64	84	84	96	97
Has kissed, when meant something special	15	14	23	29	49	54	73	82
Has gone steady	20	20	24	19	41	45	65	73
Is now going steady	8	2	7	5	9	16	29	35

Source: "Sociosexual Development in a Suburban Community," by Carlfred B. Broderick as it appeared in *The Journal of Sex Research*, 2, 1, (April, 1966) pp. 1-24.

people it may not be the concrete experience of having what an outsider would judge as a special friend or falling in love, but rather having anticipatory emotions which provide a vehicle for moving into actual relationships. This is particularly true of ten- to thirteen-year-olds who may never even have disclosed to the other person the fact that they were in love.

This fact should suggest that the younger people in the Broderick study will have very different definitions of what a date is and falling in love is than will slightly older people. Often they possess and use the words that are given to them—"to date," "to make out," "to be in love"—but they apply them to a wide variety of situations. However it is only through this process of trying out the labels that they come to share the meanings given to such words by older adolescents and adults. Hence going over to a girl's house may be defined as a date by an eleven-year-old boy and exchanging longing looks across the classroom may be defined as being in love by a girl of a similar age. These actions are not only anticipations of the future, however, but are exciting and real and important at the time to the young people themselves.

What is apparent from Broderick's research is that as young people move into later adolescence they share increasing amounts of time with people of the opposite gender. What is perhaps more interesting is the changing configuration of commitments—at age ten and eleven the majority have the desire to get married, have been in love, and have had a special boyfriend or girlfriend. The image of marriage as something to be desired is clearly one of the cutting edges into a commitment to heterosociality. Even before having tried out any of the intermediary steps (kissing, dating, going steady), the majority of children are committed to marriage. In this case, the end of the process is also its beginning. Dating accelerates over the seven-year period, followed by going steady. These figures also show that about twice as many people had gone steady as were going steady when interviewed—indicating the relative instability of such close relationships.

While dating usually begins tentatively in early adolescence it rapidly increases in importance in terms of the time and energy and emotion spent upon it. In 1967 college students were asked how often they dated in high school, and they reported the following frequencies:

Figure 5-2   Frequency of Dating in High School Reported by College Students in 1967

	Did not date	Less than once a month	Once a month	Twice a month	Once a week	Twice a week	Three or more times a week	Cases
Males	4%	13%	14%	19%	25%	18%	5%	593
Females	7%	18%	11%	14%	20%	25%	5%	584

Source: From John H. Gagnon and Cathy S. Greenblat, "Experiments in Choice," in *Life Designs: Individuals, Marriages, and Families,* p. 126. Copyright © 1978, Scott, Foresman and Company.

In the 1970s few studies of adolescent conduct have examined rates of dating, largely because most students of the period assume that either all people do it or that it has become a less significant aspect of adolescent life. What this tends to overlook is that many aspects of the dating culture that existed during the 1950s can still be found in high schools today. Further, as is obvious from the data in Figures 5–1 and 5–2, a substantial number of young people are not active participants in the high school dating culture.

The shift from dating a number of people at the same time to patterns of exclusive dating (either a sequence of dating relationships that last a short time or going steady with one person) seems to have occurred relatively rapidly. The prescribed (though not always observed) pattern of the 1930s to 1950s—dating a wide number of people relatively casually and with low levels of sexual or emotional intimacy—seems far less common today. Instead, it appears that most young people who date with any frequency pair off into exclusive couples very soon after they begin dating (Herman, 1955). In the past it was often assumed that such pairing occurred among those who were less sure of themselves personally and who needed the security of a steady relationship. This interpretation seems to have been largely the result of the fact that parents did not want young people to "go steady." Exactly the reverse has been found true: that it is those who are most interpersonally competent and successful in dating who pair off in exclusive units (Burchinal, 1964). Going steady is the preferred pattern rather than one that is resorted to in order to cope with anxiety or inability. At the same time parents have been right that exclusive pairing off creates conditions under which higher levels of emotional and sexual intimacy are possible in each relationship.

It is clear that going steady or exclusive dating relationships have been the dominant preferred dating pattern in the junior and senior years of high school since the 1950s. Going steady clearly becomes an end in itself since for a majority of young people, particularly those going on to college, such relationships are not directly linked to marriage. Going steady in high school is clearly more directly linked to marriage among young people who do not go on to college. Even in these cases going steady before the senior year may be largely unrelated to making a marriage choice.

Even though dating tends to be ubiquitous and steady dating preferred, it is clear that many young people find these relationships difficult to begin and maintain. A study in the late 1940s of 1,500 high-school students reported that 25 percent of the males and a third of the females felt that they were failures in dating. One third noted that they did not know how to behave on dates and for a similar number dating was not a pleasurable experience. However, even with this common experience of difficulty and fear and anxiety most of them wanted to date more frequently. There is no comparable recent research, but it is likely that these figures have declined somewhat in recent years, though from anecdotal reports it seems that many young people still find the dating game a difficult one to play. Going steady may in these cases increase comfort and predictability in cross-sex relations by stabilizing the number of people to deal with and decreasing competition for dates.

The exclusive pair pattern in high-school dating is not the only element that appears to have been stable for at least the last two decades. Some patterns have even persisted for much longer. In a review of recent practices (Lonergan, 1976), the following traditional elements were noted:

1. Movies are the most common first date location.
2. Serious dating, i.e., going steady, began in the tenth grade in high school.
3. Dances often provided appropriate locations for young men to indicate interest in young women.
4. Showing interest in a friend's date or friend was a severe breach of good faith.
5. There are exchanges of tokens of various sorts (e.g., rings or bracelets) between members of couples to indicate to each other and to others that they have an exclusive relationship.

These elements of the partner selection process in the contemporary high school would be familiar to people over forty since they are quite similar to adolescent practices of the past.

Purposes of Dating

Clearly an exclusive relationship that starts at age fourteen or fifteen is relatively far away from the time of marriage even for couples who will not go on for further education after high school. This is not to say that some relationships that begin then may not last until the end of high school or even lead to marriage. Such dating relationships, however, rarely begin with the purpose of partner selection specifically aimed at marriage. Dating involves a wide range of purposes and interests and even for a single couple motivations and purposes may change over time or never really match. High school dating at the very minimum is a form of fun (or at least it is supposed to be). Sometimes it involves greater levels of emotional and sexual intensity, and in some cases such dating relationships will become marital relationships.

Skipper and Nass (1966) have classified the motives for dating in the following fashion:

1. Recreation: Dating is a pleasure in itself and is pursued because it is fun and enjoyable. Young people go out together to do things they mutually enjoy.
2. Cross-sex socialization: Dating is an opportunity to develop what we have called heterosociality. Young men and women learn about each other as individual people and members of groups who have been differently socialized.
3. Status grading and achievement: Dating can provide some young people with opportunities to raise their prestige in the high school by dating people who are popular or desirable. In this case dating can be an opportunity for social mobility.
4. Serious partner selection: Dating is a vehicle for unmarried people to associate with the opposite sex in order to find someone that they wish to marry.

Clearly these motives for dating change over time both in the life cycle of the individual (different motives at different ages) and within a single relationship. Cross-sex socialization is a common motive among younger people; purely recreational dating is frequent any time in adolescence, during summer vacations, or in other casual contexts. Status grading commonly occurs among the "in-crowd" groups in high school and retains its importance later in life in some social groups. Serious partner selection tends to occur around those moments when marriage is expected. Further, many relationships entered into for fun, status, or socialization can turn into a serious courtship.

The more distant in time the relationship is from when serious mate selection can occur the more likely it is a couple will use the language of courtship which expresses love and intimacy despite a partial recognition that they are playing at courtship. However only sometimes do relations which involve such intense rhetoric remain purely on the level of a game—often serious feelings are exchanged. It is very difficult for young people to use the language of courtship without having many of the feelings and desires associated with it. The pain that many young people feel when relationships break up is a measure of the degree to which it is often impossible to separate the play from the serious.

The development of the exclusive dating pattern in high school offers an important context for experiencing intense emotions as part of cross-sex association. Since the steady relationship is supposed to be exclusive and faithful, those participating in it often express commitments to each other which are couched in the language of love. Such feelings of strong emotion provide a sense of stability and permanence in youthful relationships which cannot be provided in any other way. Unlike in marriage with shared property and children, the couple has nothing else to share except their feelings, some time together, and perhaps sexuality. Thus love becomes a critical glue in maintaining fidelity.

The romantic love complex which characterizes serious mate selection in the United States now penetrates quite directly into the high-school period. Originally the love complex, defined by Goode (1959) as the necessity of love as a prerequisite of marriage, was formerly an emotion expected in a serious relationship which was likely to end in marriage, but it is now at least verbally common in high school. This is in part true because a fair number of courtships that result in marriages are carried on and concluded during the high-school years. However there are other sources of this omnipresence of romantic love during adolescence.

The mass media offer a top forty diet in which love is the central commodity. "True love," "faithless love," "I'll love you always," are staple ideas in the adolescent community. Being in love is a wonderful state; to be loved is to be prized above all things; having someone who loves you is to be provided with security in an otherwise unpredictable world.

The emotion that we call romantic, passionate love is clearly ubiquitous in the society both at a personal level and in terms of being advertised as the best of all human conditions. Passionate love appears to involve two phases, an identification phase and an attachment phase. The first stage is a heightened sense of physical arousal which may involve sweating, a queasy stomach, rapid heartbeat, light-headedness, and other physical signs which are associated with love (Walster, 1971). These are the same signs of bodily arousal that people have when they feel the emotions that they call fear, anxiety, anger, excitement, or euphoria. However for such signs to be called love it requires that people have them in a context in which their cause can be attributed to another person. The physical signs need to be experienced in social context in which love is an appropriate explanation.

Clearly such conditions commonly occur in situations in which young adolescents are together. The situation of asking for a date, going out on a date, dancing, kissing, and necking all involve high levels of arousal that are at least partly the result of inexperience—often such signs are or can be categorized as anxiety or fear. However, in these contexts another interpretation of the signs is a feeling of special attachment or desire that can be labeled as love. Clearly it is possible for people to make a mis-attribution, to explain their arousal when they meet a person of the opposite sex late in the evening as a result of being in love, while it may come from too many cups of coffee while studying earlier. This process does not so much explain the continuing strength of the love attachment as it does the first stages of a strong preference and selection when couples meet each other.

This is when a second stage is significant in forming the strong continuing attachments that are associated with being in love. These result from the sense of loss that people who are in love feel in the absence of their beloved. Thus the physical feelings of anxiety, fear, and upset when a beloved goes away, and the feeling of relief when he or she returns are exceptionally powerful reinforcers of attachment to another person (Solomon, 1974). This process has been viewed as analogous to physical dependence on various chemicals. At first a person feels a powerful sense of emotion in the presence of the other person followed by a powerful sense of loss when the other person is not present, which is in turn relieved only by the renewed presence of the other person. What is crucial in the formation of the original attachment and in the stabilization of choice is feeling the original arousal in a context which is interpreted as one in which love is an explanation, followed by intermittent euphoric encounters and distress-filled absences. Clearly the conditions for such experiences are commonly met during adolescence both as a result of the excitement and anxiety associated with the dating system and because of the sexual experimentation and intimacy associated with dating.

Love is a critical component in exclusive relationships, then, in terms of cementing the couple together as well as in serving as justification for ignoring the claims of parents and peers on the couple's time and energy. Being "in love" is used to justify violating rules set down by parents about levels of sexual intimacy. Further, it allows young people to withdraw from same-sex peer expectations about reputation and virtue. For young women, love allows further sexual exploration; for young men it allows some withdrawal from the more exploitative sexual strategies of all-male peer groups. Love creates the context in which young men and women can begin to share values that are expressive of their common interests.

How often love is experienced among high school students is difficult to determine. If young people have gone steady for any period of time in high school at least the language of love and perhaps the feelings have been exchanged. It is estimated that the students who go steady during high school do so on an average of two times—so this may be a minimum estimate of the frequency of such love attachments. However, we do know that youthful crushes and one-way attachments in which a young person feels a powerful attachment for another but does nothing are frequent. This is more common among young women than men, but clearly is an emotion that both genders feel with considerable intensity.

References

Broderick, Carlfred B.
1966   "Sociosexual development in a suburban community." The Journal of Sex Research 2, 1 (April):1–24.

Burchinal, Lee G.
1964a   "Characteristics of adolescents from unbroken, broken, and reconstituted families." Journal of Marriage and the Family 26:44–51.
1964b   "The premarital dyad and love involvement." In Harold Christensen (ed.), Handbook of Marriage and the Family. Chicago: Rand McNally.

Coleman, James S.
1961   The Adolescent Society. New York: Free Press.

Goode, William J.
1959   "The theoretical importance of love." American Sociological Review 24, 1 (February):38–47.

Herman, Robert D.
1955   "The going-steady complex: a re-examination." Marriage and Family Living 17 (February):36–40.

Lonergan, Loretta
1976   "Attitudes of contemporary college students toward dating and sex." New Brunswick, New Jersey: Unpublished study.

Simon, William and John H. Gagnon
1967a   Unpublished data from the research: Selected Aspects of Adult Socialization.

Skipper, James K., Jr. and Gilbert Nass
1966   "Dating behavior: a framework for analysis and an illustration." Paper presented at the annual meeting of the National Council on Family Relations in Minneapolis (October).

Solomon, Richard L. and John D. Corbit
1974   "An opponent process theory of motivation: I. temporal dynamics of affect." Psychological Review 81, 2:119–145.

Walster, Elaine, Vera Aronson, Darcy Abrahams and Leon Rottman
1966   "Importance of physical attractiveness in dating behavior." Journal of Personality and Social Psychology 9:508–516.

Teenage Pregnancy: Why the Epidemic?
Kathleen Rudd Scharf

Lack of information and services is one reason for the number of pregnant teenagers. Another reason, often overlooked by reformers, is that a certain number of adolescents want to have babies.

■ It is the age of the Pill, yet over a million American teenagers will get pregnant this year. About 600,000 of these young women will give birth. Pregnancy is the main reason American girls drop out of high school, and the U.S. teenage birthrate is the highest of any industrial nation.

These figures are touted in the national press as evidence of a social problem of epidemic proportions. In fact, despite increased sexual activity, the teenage birthrate has gone down in the last 20 years. Ninety out of every 1,000 young women under 20 gave birth in the late 1950s compared to only 58 out of every 1,000 in 1974.

In the 1950s, of course, contraception was illegal in many states even for married adults. The idea that nonmarital sex might be healthy behavior was heresy, and single parenthood was thought by many to be a social peculiarity of the poor. Pregnant girls who were wealthy and well-connected enough to find compliant physicians (here or abroad) had abortions. "Nice girls" with more limited resources either had shotgun weddings or carried to term in secret. Cloistered in institutions like Florence Crittenton homes and Salvation Army shelters, pregnant girls dropped out of sight, visiting distant "aunts." Maternity homes in the 1950s arranged adoptions for 95 percent of the "secret" newborns.

By the mid-1960s, contraceptive services were available to some resourceful adolescents, and residents of a few states could obtain reasonably inexpensive legal abortions—though the popular press still shied away from passing along information about either one. Court decisions in the 1970s have made contraception and abortion even more widely available. Now, about 400,000 teenage girls have abortions each year. But of the 600,000 teenagers who give birth, a staggering 94 percent keep their children. More than a third of these young mothers do not marry. Many are struggling with medical, social, and economic problems. The teenage pregnancy epidemic of the 1970s turns out to be more of a teenage baby-keeping epidemic.

To begin to understand what lies behind the statistics, the first question to ask is why teenagers have sex at all. The facile answer, of course, is why not. Most of the experts agree that the recent rise in adolescent sexual activity in the United States is in part physiological: improved nutrition, higher average body weight, and other factors have lowered the age of sexual maturity even over the last generation. Social influences may be more important still in a society that teaches that the best things in life go to those with the most desirable bodies. Teenagers confide to sex education and abortion counselors that loneliness is a major reason why they have sex. Another reason is peer pressure: the old line that boys gave in the 1950s to lure girls into the back seats of Chevies seems to have survived the various liberation movements of the 1960s intact. The public affairs director of an abortion clinic in Brookline, Massachusetts, reports with some surprise that girls of the 1970s still need to be reminded that "nobody ever died of an erection."

Why do so many girls get pregnant? Over-the-counter contraceptives are available in large, impersonal pharmacies. Most parts of the country have agencies that will prescribe oral contraceptives for minors. By and large, professionals agree that American teenagers are reasonably sophisticated about the services available to them and the basic physiological facts of reproduction. Yet only 30 percent of sexually active adolescent girls "always" use contraceptives; 44 percent "sometimes" do, and 25 percent "never" do.

One reason for these dismal statistics is that—despite the increase in recent years—there aren't enough conveniently located agencies available to adolescents. Many states whose restrictive birth control statutes were struck down in court still refuse to bring their laws in line with court decisions. And physicians, hospitals, and clinics are cautious about providing services that might cause public controversy. But probably the major reason for the paucity of contraceptive information and services for adolescents is a national head-in-the-sand approach to teenage sexuality.

The very suggestion of sex education in the schools has sent parents of public school children into a very public rage time and time again. Many adults believe that fear of pregnancy is the most effective deterrent to adolescent sexual activity, and the idea that contraceptives encourage sex is common—though gynecologists who provide birth control services to adolescents say they seldom if ever examine a virgin. One sex education specialist in a Boston suburb avoids public controversy by arranging her classroom visits directly with sympathetic high school teachers. She speaks in classrooms with students checking to be sure there is no eavesdropping on the two-way intercom system located in the principal's office.

A more direct program to provide publicly acceptable sex education has been designed by the Education Development Center (EDC) of Newton, Massachusetts. Supported by grants from the Kellogg Foundation and the March of Dimes, project director Ruth MacDonald traveled across the country talking with people who had tried to introduce sex education programs into public schools. She found "a field strewn with bodies," victims of well-intentioned but politically impossible education efforts.

To bypass strong parental objections, EDC's program starts with classes for parents rather than for children. MacDonald reports that many parents fear the disapproval of other parents if they appear too "permissive" toward their children's behavior. In trial classes for parents in four Massachusetts communities, EDC instructors played tape-recorded interviews with adolescents that established both the reality of teenage sexuality and the teenager's wish that their own parents had been more approachable when they needed help in making difficult decisions about sex. Leaders then encouraged parents both to overcome their discomfort when talking about sex and to deal realistically with their children's sexuality.

The EDC curriculum, tested in 17 sites across the country last year under Parent Teacher Association auspices, avoids the "liberated" rhetoric and physiological details of the sex education courses that have upset many local parents groups. The 14 new communities where EDC is testing its curriculum this year include schools willing to try out the student portion of the course as well. Tape recordings by sexually experienced teenagers help instructors to emphasize the seriousness of unprotected intercourse, and the importance of reflecting on personal values before having to make an immediate decision about whether or not to have sex. The interests of the March of Dimes have led the curriculum developers to emphasize the high rate of birth defects common among babies born to very young parents. MacDonald feels that teenagers need concrete evidence of potential difficulties like that more than they need technical information about contraception, and that parents and children who have discussed adolescent sex openly will be ready to demand and use contraceptive services.

Many of the attitudes that lead parents to oppose sex education in schools are also responsible for the reluctance of elected officials to fund sex education and services for minors. (In today's political climate, politicians can gain in popularity not only by calling on "morality" and the "sanctity of the family," but also by refusing to spend the taxpayers' money.) The major source of federal funds for contraceptive and educational services to adolescents (and adults) is the Family Planning and Population Research Act of 1970, Title X of the Public Health Services Act. When the act came up for reauthorization this year, family planning advocates and opponents faced off over proposed limitations on the funding of birth control services. Amendments that would have denied funds to facilities that perform abortions, that require parental consent for minors, that set aside a percentage of total federal expenditures for "natural family planning," and that limited the reauthorization to a one-year period were all defeated in the House. Still, funding for the coming year was frozen at last year's $200 million instead of the $304 million sponsors of the bill had requested.

A certain number of teenagers do not use contraceptives no matter how easily available the information and services seem to be. Some of these youngsters say they are afraid their parents might discover supplies of birth control pills or other contraceptives. Others are embarrassed to go to a birth control clinic or to a store to buy contraceptives. Some have the best of intentions and are put off by an agency's inconvenient location, or by the stigma they feel will be attached to them if they go to a clinic. Some girls think the Pill is the only effective way to prevent pregnancy and they don't want to risk its possible long-term side effects. Adolescent girls are also victims of a morality that says that planned sex, which includes most sex protected by contraception, is wrong. Unplanned sex, the result of an uncontrollable natural impulse, is at least excusable if not morally acceptable. Any girl who carries a diaphragm or takes the Pill is planning sex and is, therefore, not a nice girl.

Many sex education programs are geared to overcoming these objections to contraception. Some also try to bridge the generation gap that provokes an adolescent disregard for adult advice and warnings. One such program which operates during the summer in Brockton, Massachusetts, is called the Sex Kids. Mary Ann Dwyer of Brockton Family Planning decided that many local youngsters, especially those living in low-income housing projects, distrusted large institutions too much to come to her agency for counseling or contraceptive supplies. Last year Dwyer trained eight local high school students to answer questions about reproduction, contraception, and venereal disease. The "Sex Kids" also learned the locations and schedules of counseling and contraception services in the area. Each student was assigned to a set location—in parks, on street corners, and at other favorite teenage haunts—to answer questions. Clinic personnel in Brockton report a marked rise over the summer in visits by the adolescent residents of the housing projects. The first year, Dwyer had trouble recruiting Sex Kids. This past summer, more than a dozen were trained and available to their peers.

Most of the experts agree that even the best and most innovative sex education efforts might reduce the annual teenage pregnancy rate by only 10 percent. The undeniable fact is that many adolescent girls want to become pregnant, and want to have and to keep their babies. Psychiatrists explain such behavior, at least among middle-class girls, in terms of normal child development gone awry. If families cannot work out with some measure of grace the adolescent's transition from childhood dependency to adult independence, they say, girls may seek a dramatic way to make the break. One Boston psychiatrist reports that she is often asked by upset and puzzled middle-class parents to see pregnant daughters who have declared their intention to have and to keep their babies. The psychiatrist also reports that most of these girls are eventually persuaded by their parents that their futures hold more than early motherhood, and they decide on abortions.

Solid data on abortion versus childbearing choices along class lines do not seem to exist. The opinion of Laura Herrick, director of services for pregnant girls at Boston's Crittenton-Hastings house, is in line with the widespread impression among professionals: moderately well-off girls obtain abortions; younger, less affluent girls from a variety of ethnic backgrounds bear and keep their children. Girls of higher income levels are more apt to "try newer solutions (abortion) quicker."

Sixteen-year old clients from lower income families at Fitchburg Family Planning, reports health educator Debi Croes, are often delighted to discover that they are pregnant. Childbearing accelerates by only a year or two the pattern set by their mothers and older sisters: marriage and childbirth right after high school graduation and intermittent factory employment until the children have grown up. Croes finds that many of these girls are adept at using the welfare system to establish independent households, and that they feel under much less social pressure to get married than teenagers of their mothers' generation. Peer pressure on teenagers in lower socio-economic classes seems to favor childbirth over abortion—though again, this conclusion is based on anecdotal evidence rather than on hard facts.

The Boston Crittenton-Hastings house now has a day program for pregnant adolescents who plan to keep their babies, a program beyond the imagination of the secretive 1950s. In 1977, 65 percent of the live-in clients were also keeping their babies, compared to the 95 percent who opted for adoption in the 1950s.

Whether the new interest in child keeping among adolescent girls derives from developmental problems or from lack of other adult options, on average their life prospects are unusually bleak. Suicide and child abuse rates are higher among teenage mothers than among older groups. Both young mothers and their babies have higher risks of death and medical complications, which are often related to premature delivery with low birth weight. (The experts disagree about whether these risks are caused by the age of the mother or by factors like poor prenatal care.) Three-quarters of mothers age 17 and under have no health insurance; 7 in 10 teenage mothers do not have any prenatal care in the first trimester; and only 9 of 150 large cities surveyed in 1970 had adequate service programs for childbearing adolescents. By 1974, more cities had programs, but few of the programs were prepared to help young mothers beyond delivery. Eight out of 10 young mothers drop out of high school; a 1974 New York City survey found 72 percent of mothers under 18, and 41 percent of 18 and 19-year-old mothers, on welfare. Even young unmarried mothers who manage to find jobs run into the same problems with child care as their older counterparts: 85 percent of nonprofit and 75 percent of for-profit day-care centers in the country refuse babies under two years of age.

Professionals may disagree about why teenage mothers have so many physical problems, but they agree that the young mother's situation would be improved by access to coordinated medical and social services. One successful program is PAGE (Pregnant Adolescent Girl's Education), housed in the Springfield, Massachusetts, YWCA. PAGE started in 1969, largely as a way for pregnant girls to continue their high school studies. Since a federal court ruling in 1971, Springfield and all other public school systems are required to allow pregnant students to attend regular high school classes. But staying in school is often physically and psychologically difficult, and regular high schools are not geared to the special medical and social service needs of young mothers-to-be.

PAGE has a complete secondary school curriculum for its 35 full-time students; another 125 pregnant teenagers take part in its other activities each year. All students have access to a registered nurse for prenatal care. Staff members teach classes in child care, child development, nutrition, and parenting. The program has three counselors, one of whom speaks Spanish, who help students both to overcome their poor self-images (a major problem among PAGE clients) and to plan as realistically as possible for their immediate futures. (Fifty percent of the students marry before or soon after delivery). Counselors also make weekly home visits to prepare students' families for the coming births.

Ninety-five percent of the students stay with the program until their babies are born. PAGE runs an Infant Care Center for its students' children under the age of two years and nine months. Eighty percent of the students return to regular high schools. Program director Norma Baker is now working on an employment program to supplement the existing summer jobs service. She also hopes to add employment help to a counseling program that has just started for the babies' fathers.

PAGE has managed to put together a patchwork of funding sources. State and city education funds pay for teachers, supplies, and transportation. The U.S. Department of Agriculture covers a school breakfast and lunch program. The state's Department of Education picks up the counseling bills, and its Department of Public Health pays for prenatal care and the Infant Care Center. The YWCA provides space; it also pays for its own preschool, which takes on some of the PAGE children when they have outgrown the Infant Center. State, city, and local industry money support the employment programs.

The best hope for adequate funding and coordination of programs for childbearing teenagers may be the Carter administration's "teenage pregnancy initiative," formally called the Adolescent Health Services and Pregnancy Prevention and Care Act of 1978. The bill is part of a legislative program to fulfill President Carter's campaign promises to support alternatives to abortion. Although population lobbyists such as Zero

Population Growth's Peters Wilson regarded Carter's proposal as a hasty and poorly crafted piece of legislation, organizations concerned with population issues were too eager to have some federal aid to oppose it entirely. The bill was filed late. Commenting on its rapid progress through committee hearings, Wilson attributed the attention less to concern for pregnant 14-year-olds than to a broad congressional desire to find a graceful way out of the thicket of abortion politics.

Population-oriented organizations like Planned Parenthood and Zero Population Growth have a direct interest in the success of a large federal adolescent pregnancy program. Although there is no need to question their sincerity, concern about adolescent pregnancy does focus public attention on more general population issues—attention that has declined along with the American birthrate over the last few years. Wilson and representatives of other national organizations formed a coalition in support of a more specific "adolescent health" bill. The coalition attracted organizations on both sides of the abortion debate, including the Roman Catholic Church, so haggling over the specifics of eligibility for services became a major part of its internal politicking. Antiabortion members, such as Marjory Mecklenburg of American Citizens Concerned for Life, Inc., wanted some funds earmarked for antiabortion counseling organizations such as Birthright. Zero Population Growth and other organizations opposed such earmarking and regard some of Birthright's counseling as closer to indoctrination. Both sides were prepared to compromise, however, in order to save this first federal stab at coordinating the welter of services needed by adolescents.

To speed a somewhat modified version of the Carter bill through both houses of Congress before adjournment, Senator Edward Kennedy (D-Mass.) attached it as an amendment to another piece of health legislation, which was passed in October. Although appropriations under the bill will not be filed until January, it specifies funding levels of $50 million in 1979, $65 million in 1980, and $75 million in 1981. And in the short run at least, using tangled political and economic motives to get some funding may be the best that can be done to help those adolescent girls who do—and don't—want early motherhood.

Involvements

Cohabitation in America: An Assessment of Consequences
Paul R. Newcomb

A survey of the empirical research with regard to cohabitation is reported. The major consequences of cohabitation, both pro and con, are identified for five groups: (1) never-married cohabiting couples; (2) children of cohabitants; (3) society; (4) previously-married cohabiting couples; and (5) elderly cohabitants. Current legal trends are also discussed and recommendations for future research are delineated.

■   Although cohabitation has existed for a long time, particularly among lower-class persons, it has rapidly increased among the middle class during the last two decades. Glick (1976:13) reported "a spectacular eight-fold increase during the 1960s in the number of household heads who were reported as living apart from relatives while sharing their living quarters with an unrelated person of the opposite sex." Olday (1977) concludes in his doctoral dissertation that most of this increase from the 1960 census tract occurred among youth less than 25 years old. It should be noted that this increase may be due, in part, to an increased willingness for people to identify themselves as cohabitants rather than an increase in cohabiting behavior. It is likely, however, that most of this increase is due to an increase in the real rates of cohabitation. Glick and Norton (1977) also note that, in 1970, only one-fourth of unmarried cohabiting couples under 25 years of age included one or both adults enrolled in college. Thus, 75 percent of cohabiting couples in 1970 who were under 25 were not enrolled in college. This is particularly significant in light of the fact that most cohabitation research has been conducted on college samples which are nonrepresentative of the total population of cohabitants. Glick and Norton (1977) report that the number of persons who are cohabiting has nearly doubled between 1970 and 1977, reaching almost two million persons. This figure represents 3.6 percent of unmarried adults in 1977 and 4.2 percent of couple households. Yllo (1978) reaches a similar conclusion based on her national survey of 2,143 men and women. She concluded that there are at least one and three-quarter to two million people currently living together in the United States without benefit of marriage. Clayton and Voss (1977), in a nationwide sample of 2,510 young men, found that 18 percent of the respondents had lived with a woman for six months or more outside marriage. These figures underestimate the real incidence of cohabitation in that many of those youths who have not cohabited yet are still at risk to do so. Also, many more may have cohabited but for less than six months. Bower and Christopherson (1977) revealed, in a study of 1,191 students at 14 state universities, that one-quarter of their sample had cohabited at some time. Significantly, Arafat and Yorburg (1973) found that 79.2 percent of respondents indicated they would live with a member of the opposite sex if given an opportunity to do so. Henze and Hudson (1974) report that 71 percent of males and 43 percent of females of their sample expressed a desire to cohabit. These figures indicate, not only that cohabitation has been an emerging trend in the last 20 years, but that it is likely to continue to increase into the foreseeable future in view of the increasingly favorable attitudes expressed towards this once stigmatized behavior.

Although cohabitation has emerged as a major nontraditional lifestyle, few attempts have been made conceptually to define this phenomenon. The conceptual definition used in this paper is taken from Olday (1977:54) who defines cohabitation as "an emotionally, physically, and intellectually intimate heterosexual relationship which includes a common abode and which exists without benefit of legal, cultural, or religious sanction." Additionally, cohabitation is here operationally defined as a heterosexual couple living together at least five days a week for at least three months, not legally or religiously married, yet sexually intimate, with or without the goal of marriage in the future. This distinguishes it from conventional dating and courtship patterns and from common-law marriage in which couples agree to be married, live together as husband and wife, and represent themselves to others as married (Bernstein, 1977).

Current Legal Trends

Unlike marriage, there is no legal tradition with regard to cohabitation. This results in a lack of protection of legal rights for all parties involved.

Traditionally, for example, the meretricious spouse (one who is intentionally living with a person of the opposite sex and is unmarried) acquired no property rights. In the past, if a woman contributed any service, she was not entitled to recover an interest in resulting property. In 1973, however, in the "In Remarriage of Cary" case, a California Appellate Court held that a meretricious spouse had the same property rights as a married person. In 1975, in the "Estate of Atherly" case, the Cary decision was extended to include those situations in which the male cohabitant was legally married to another woman (Weitzman, 1975). Furthermore, in the much publicized 1976 case of Marvin versus Marvin, the California Supreme Court set a precedent by defining the value of the woman's services for the purposes of property settlement. This decision also recognized the validity of an oral contract between cohabitants by making it legally binding upon both parties (Weitzman, 1978). Thus, a trend exists in which statute law is developing a more precise definition of the legal rights and obligations of cohabitants. Additionally, a trend also exists towards increased legal protection of illegitimate children. For example, in 1968, in the case of "Levy versus Louisiana," the court upheld the right of an illegitimate child to recover financial benefits from the wrongful death of its mother. In 1972, in the case of "Weber versus Aetna Casualty," the court recognized the right of illegitimate children to recover financial benefits from the death of their father under Louisiana workmen-compensation law, on an equal footing with his legitimate children. In an important Supreme Court decision in 1972, "Davis versus Richardson," the Social Security Act was found to be discriminatory against illegitimate children in the payment of death benefits. Finally, in 1973 in "Gomez versus Perez," the court held the father responsible for child support of his illegitimate children. Therefore, a legal trend exists towards providing greater legal protection for the children of cohabitants and, thus, reducing but not eliminating the negative legal consequences of cohabitation for these children. However, there is considerable variation in state laws and most states have not yet adequately defined these rights. Thus, one of the major risks of cohabitation is lack of legal protection upon termination, particularly with regard to property rights and child custody procedures.

Consequences of Cohabitation

Consequences for Cohabitants

Olday (1977) and Macklin (1972) both found that cohabitants perceive the rewards of their relationships to outweigh the costs. Macklin (1972) also reports that two-thirds of her sample experienced no guilt and three-fourths of them stated that their sexual life was satisfactory. Arafat and Yorburg (1973) state that both males and females see financial gain as a significant positive outcome of cohabitation. Olday (1977) reports that companionship, sexual gratification and economic gain are the three most important positive consequences found in the literature for cohabitants.

Another area of research in the cohabitation literature concerns the relationship of cohabitation to marriage. Polansky et al. (1978) and Olday (1977) both report little difference between cohabitants and marrieds in terms of stability and emotional closeness. Furthermore, Clayton and Voss (1977) suggest that there may be little or no difference between marriage and cohabitation in the way partners perform their respective roles. Similarly, Segrest and Weeks (1976) and Olday (1977) also found that the cohabiting experience has little impact on changing the role expectations of its participants to a less traditional form. Additionally, Olday (1977) found that cohabitation was not a more effective screening device than traditional courtship patterns. This contradicts the commonly held notion that one of the potential positive outcomes of cohabitation is improved mate selection.

Several potential negative consequences for cohabitants are identified in the literature. Glick and Norton (1977) report that 63 percent of cohabiting couples shared the same residence less than two years before they married or separated. The literature shows that most cohabitants do not intend to marry and do not eventually get married to each other. For example, Macklin (1972) reported that, of her female college sample, one-third married, one-third separated, and one-third were in the process of defining their relationship. Macklin interprets "defining the relationship" to mean either the couples were still living together but not yet contemplating marriage or "going together" but not living together. This finding is significant in its implication for female cohabitants. Lyness et al. (1972), for example, found male cohabitants to be significantly less marriage-oriented then their partners. This is supported by a study by Arafat and Yorburg (1973) which found that the most cited reason for cohabiting for males is sexual gratification, while, for females, marriage was stated as the most important motive. Additionally, Hudson and Henze (1973) found that women are more faithful in their sexual relationships than are males. Thus, the evidence indicates that females are at greater risk in cohabiting relationships in terms of their different expectations for marriage and with regard to sexual exclusivity.

However, most of the cohabitation research is characterized by highly limited samples which usually are drawn from undergraduate college students. Therefore, these findings may not apply to elderly and previously-married cohabitants. Each of these major groups of cohabitants identified in this paper may have their own sets of consequences peculiar to their particular circumstances.

Consequences for Children

Glick and Norton (1977) report that, in 1977, 204,000 couples, or approximately 20 percent of all cohabiting couples, had one or more children present in their households. This is in marked contrast to the extremely small number of children reported in the literature with regard to college cohabitants. For example, Bower and Christopherson (1977) report that only four out of 126 cohabiting couples in their sample were raising children. Presumably, most of the children of cohabiting couples were either in the noncollege, never-married cohabitant group or were living in families which had at least one parent who had previously been married.

Myricks and Robin (1977) argue that the children of cohabitants are penalized to an even greater extent then parents, particularly when the parents separate. This leaves children in an uncertain child-custody situation and causes them significant economic loss due to the lack of mandated child support. However, there is a growing trend in statutory law, as discussed previously, towards defining the rights of children. No positive outcomes for children are reported in the literature except the finding of a pilot study by Eiduson (1974) that these children are socialized to more egalitarian sex roles than children from traditional family structures. However, Olday (1977) found no difference in this respect. Thus, this finding is inconclusive. It should be pointed out that very little research exists concerning the consequences of cohabitation for children. Therefore, more information is needed before these consequences can be adequately identified and assessed.

Consequences for Society

The evidence strongly suggests that cohabitation, especially among college students, represents an alteration of traditional dating patterns. The large number of persons who cohabit or express a desire to participate in this behavior suggests that it is becoming an acceptable part of the dating process and thus has become a more or less permanent social phenomenon in America. Additionally, Peterman et al. (1974) and Catlin et al. (1976) both conclude that cohabitants do not differ from noncohabitants on adjustment scales. Furthermore, several authors (Arafat and Yorburg, 1973; Henze and Hudson, 1974; Peterman et al., 1974; and Segrest and Weeks, 1976) found no significant differences by social class or family background which distinguish cohabitants from noncohabitants. The only factor in the literature which distinguishes cohabitants from noncohabitants is the degree of religiosity and church attendance which seem to be positive indicators of a traditional-value orientation.

Another concern which is popularly expressed with regard to cohabitation is that it represents an alternative and, thus, a threat to the institution of marriage. The literature indicates, however, that the great majority of college cohabitants, at least, desire to marry at some point in the future. Bower and Christopherson (1977), for example, found that 96 percent of cohabitants and 99 percent of noncohabitants indicated that they would like to marry at some time. The data in Olday's (1977) study also support this conclusion. Furthermore, Strong (1978) in his study of 400 single undergraduates, reports that a basic consensus exists among both men and women that an egalitarian and sexually monogamous marriage is the form in which they were most willing to participate. These figures suggest that cohabitation is not a serious threat to the institution of marriage. However, Lyness (1978), in her comparative study of dating couples and cohabitants, concludes that living together may be a short-term alternative to marriage. Additionally, it is conceivable that cohabitation does represent an alternative to marriage for previously-married and elderly cohabitants. The former group may be cohabiting due to the experience of failure in marriage while the latter may be cohabiting due to the increased social security benefits for two single people as compared to those for a married couple.

Although cohabitation may not represent a threat to the institution of marriage, Bower and Christopherson (1977) suggest that cohabitation could delay the onset of marriage. The evidence for this theory, however, is inconclusive. Olday (1977), for example, concludes that, although a trend exists towards postponement of marriage, the social phenomenon of cohabitation appears to have played a minor role. To the extent that cohabitation does delay marriage, however, it could produce significant secondary consequences for society such as a reduced birth rate and an increase in the quality of married life due to people entering marriage at a somewhat older age.

There is some evidence which suggests that cohabitation may tend to decrease family size. Bower and Christopherson (1977) and Weitzman et al. (1978) both report that cohabitants desire fewer children. Furthermore, Olday (1977) reports that not only do cohabitants desire fewer children but that former cohabitants of both sexes are much more likely to be childless: 70.9 percent of former cohabitants versus 47 percent of noncohabitants (for females) and 68 percent of former cohabitants versus 46 percent of noncohabitants (for males) were childless. However, it should be noted that this does not necessarily mean that increased cohabitation rates will yield reduced family size. It is conceivable, for example, that those individuals who are prone to cohabit also tend to desire fewer children. Thus, these two variables may be related to each other as part of a larger attitudinal pattern but have no causal connection with each other.

Trost (1975) reports that a dramatic increase has occurred in the number of unmarried cohabiting couples in Sweden. The rate has doubled between 1970 and 1974 to represent 12 percent of all dyads. These figures are significant to the degree to which these social trends are predictive of similar trends in the United States.

Consequences for Previously-Married Persons

Although no empirical research has been done specifically with regard to this group of cohabitants, there is evidence which suggests that such a group, in fact, exists. According to Olday (1977), the 1970 census indicates that there are 30 percent more cohabitants in the age group 25–64 years than there are in the age group under 25 years. Presumably, many of the individuals in the former group have already experienced at least one marriage. Clayton and Voss (1977), in a national sample of 2,510 young men, compared the cohabitation rates of these men according to the number of marriages they had experienced. They found that 35 percent of the multiple-marrieds had cohabited as compared to 21 percent of the never-marrieds and 14 percent of the once-marrieds. These data suggest that those men who have experienced several failures in marriage may be more willing to cohabit as an alternative life-style. Furthermore, Glick and Norton (1977) report in their study that divorced men represented the largest proportion of unmarried adults in informal unions (5.4 percent). Moreover, 8.3 percent of young divorced men under 35 were living with an unrelated woman. Thus, both age and marital status are significant determinants of cohabiting behavior. In light of the continuing high divorce rates and the increasing acceptance of the cohabitation life-style, it is likely that this group of cohabitants will increase in size.

Consequences for Older Persons

There is a dearth of empirical research with regard to cohabitation in old age. According to Glick and Norton (1977), however, in 1977, 85,000 men over the age of 65 were cohabiting which represents 1.3 percent of men in this age group. It should be noted that this figure may underestimate the true figure as men of this age cohort may be reluctant to reveal this status to survey researchers. Yllo (1978), on the basis of her national sample, concluded that cohabitation, for this age group, may be largely an artifact of the Social Security system in that it encourages people to cohabit by reducing benefits to women upon remarriage. She found that the cohabitation rate triples from .3 percent of the 51–60 year age group to .9 percent for those over 60 years old. However, more research is needed before one can determine the cause of this increase in the rate of cohabitation for older persons.

Cavan (1973) speculates that there are several potential advantages of cohabitation for older persons which include reinstatement of the role of spouse, companionship, financial gain, and sexual gratification. These last three advantages, interestingly enough, are the same ones found in the literature with regard to college cohabitants. Two potential negative consequences of cohabitation in old age are cited in the literature. Cavan (1973) argues that older cohabitants might risk disapproval from significant others while Rosenberg (1970) similarly concludes that this arrangement might interfere with the relationships of the older cohabitants with their children and grandchildren. These speculations, then, represent potential questions for future research.

Conclusion

Summary of Major Findings

The major findings of this family-policy research effort are: (1) there has been a significant increase in the incidence of cohabitation in the last 20 years which is likely to continue into the foreseeable future; (2) cohabitation on college campuses represents a new dimension of the dating and courtship process and does not rival marriage for this group; (3) the most significant positive consequences for cohabitants are companionship, sexual gratification, and economic gain; (4) the most significant negative consequences for cohabitants are the resolution of conflict concerning property rights upon termination of the relationship and the increased risk for female cohabitants due to their differing expectations as opposed to males with regard to marriage and sexual exclusivity in these relationships; (5) cohabitants are similar to noncohabitants in terms of family background and personal adjustment with religiosity being the only factor which differentiates these two groups; (6) cohabitation does not seem to alter sex roles in marriage nor increase the quality of the mate selection process; (7) a legal trend exists toward defining the rights and obligations of all parties within the cohabiting family units; (8) the greater negative consequence for children in these units is the lack of legal protection with regard to child-custody decisions and child-support in the event of the termination of the cohabiting relationship; and (9) individuals who have experienced multiple marriages are more likely to cohabit than are nonmarrieds or once marrieds.

Recommendations for Research

The recommendations for future research are: (1) additional data are needed regarding the incidence of new cases each year, the age at which they occur, and the marital status of the cohabitants; (2) it is important to identify the consequences of cohabitation for children (furthermore, comparisons of these children with those with legally-married parents and single parents would be helpful to policy-makers and other interested persons); (3) more research is needed with regard to identifying the consequences of cohabitation for previously-married persons (such issues as the comparative quality and duration of these relationships relative to married couples would be important for this group and the number of previous marriages would probably be an important control variable given the finding that multiple-marrieds are more likely to cohabit); (4) research is needed with regard to identifying the extent to which the financial incentives built into the roles regarding Social Security payments encourage this choice of life-style; and (5) further research is needed to determine whether or not the expectation of marriage for female cohabitants actually results in marriage. By answering these questions and others, researchers may provide policymakers with some direction in the field of family policy as it relates to the social phenomenon of cohabitation.

References

Arafat, I., and G. Yorburg
    1973 "On living together without marriage." Journal of Sex Research 9 (May):97–106.
Bernstein, B. E.
    1977 "Legal problems of cohabitation." Family Coordinator 26 (October):361–366.
Bower, D. W., and V. A. Christopherson
    1977 "University student cohabitation: A regional comparison of selected attitudes and behavior." Journal of Marriage and the Family 39 (August):447–452.
Catlin, N. J. W. Croake, and J. F. Keller
    1976 "MMPI profiles of cohabiting college students." Psychological Reports 38 (April):407–410.
Cavan, R.
    1973 "Speculations on innovations to conventional marriage in old age." The Gerontologist 13 (Winter):409–410.
Clayton, R.R., and N. L. Voss
    1977 "Shacking up: cohabitation in the 1970's." Journal of Marriage and the Family 39 (May):273–283.
Glick, Paul C.
    1976 "Some recent changes in American families." Current Population Reports. Washington, D.C.:U.S. Government Printing Office.
Glick, Paul C., and Arthur J. Norton
    1977 "Marrying, divorcing, and living together in the U.S. today." Population Bulletin. Washington, D.C.:Population Reference Bureau.

Henze, L. F. and J. W. Hudson
  1974 "Personal and family characteristics of cohabiting and non-cohabiting college students." Journal of Marriage and the Family 36 (November):722–726.
Hudson, J. W. and L. F. Henze
  1973 "A note on cohabitation." Family Coordinator 22(October):495.
Lyness, J. F.
  1978 "Happily ever after? Following-up living together couples." Alternative Lifestyles 1 (February):55–70.
Lyness, J. F., M. E. Lipetz, and K. E. Davis
  1972 "Living together: An alternative to marriage." Journal of Marriage and the Family 34 (May):305–311.
Macklin, E. D.
  1972 "Heterosexual cohabitation among unmarried college students." Family Coordinator 21 (October):463–472.
Myricks, N. and R. H. Robin
  1977 "Sex laws and alternative life styles." Family Coordinator 26(October):357–360.
Olday, D.
  1977 "Some consequences for heterosexual cohabitation for marriage." Unpublished doctoral dissertation, Washington State University.
Peterman, D. J., C. A. Ridley, and S. M. Anderson
  1974 "A comparison of marriage and heterosexual cohabiting and noncohabiting college students." Journal of Marriage and the Family 36 (May):344–354.
Polansky, L. W., G. McDonald, and J. Martin
  1978 "A comparison of marriage and heterosexual cohabitation on three interpersonal variables: Affective support, mutual knowledge, and relationship satisfaction." Western Sociological Review 9 (Summer):49–59.
Rosenberg, H. S.
  1970 "Implications of new models and the family for the aging population." In Herbert Otto (Ed.), Family in Search of a Future. New York:Meredith Corporation.
Segrest, M. A., and M. O. Weeks
  1976 "Comparison of the role expectations of married and cohabiting subjects." International Journal of Sociology of the Family 6 (Autumn):275–281.
Strong, L. D.
  1978 "Alternative marital and family forms: Their relative attractiveness to college students and correlates of willingness to participate in nontraditional forms." Journal of Marriage and the Family 40 (August):493–503.
Trost, J.
  1975 "Married and unmarried cohabitation: The case of Sweden, with some comparisons." Journal of Marriage and the Family 37 (August):677–682.
Weitzman, L. J.
  1975 "To love, honor, and obey? Traditional legal marriage and alternative family forms." Family Coordinator 24 (October):531–548.
Weitzman, L. J., C. M. Dixon, J. A. Bird, N. McGinn, and D. M. Robertson
  1978 "Contracts for intimate relationships: A study of contracts before, within, and in lieu of legal marriage." Alternative Lifestyles 1 (August):303–378.
Yllo, K. A.
  1978 "Nonmarital cohabitation: Beyond the college campus." Alternative Lifestyles 1 (February):37–54.

Marvin v. Marvin:
Preserving the Options
Herma Hill Kay and Carol Amyx

The number of couples choosing to live together without marriage has increased significantly in recent years. In Marvin v. Marvin, *the California Supreme Court redefined the rights of persons living in nonmarital cohabitation to property acquired during their relationship. In this Article, the authors review the statutory and case law prior to* Marvin, *endorse the court's decision to permit a broad variety of choices for married and unmarried couples, and suggest how the case might be applied to typical couples who choose not to marry.*

■ They live near you—in a house, apartment, or trailer, in urban centers, small towns, or on farms. They may both be professionals or wage earners; they may work separately or together in various enterprises of their own; one of them may act as a homemaker while the other works outside the home for pay. They share your neighborhood activities, your civic concerns, your national and international problems. Their lifestyle may be avant-garde or traditional. They may be a man and woman, two men, or two women. In one respect, however, they differ from most couples: They are not married.[1] Regardless of their reasons for remaining unmarried, one consequence of their choice in community property states such as California has been that no property rights arise solely from their cohabitation. In cases where their relationship approximated traditional marriage, the result was that, unless they had entered into an express agreement to pool their earnings, work, or assets and to share ownership of the subsequently acquired property, the dependent party was left without legal or equitable redress at the conclusion of the relationship. In a dramatic effort to remedy what it perceived as the basic unfairness of this situation, one California appellate court, using as its tool a bold—if unwarranted—interpretation of California's 1969 no-fault divorce law, attempted to expand quasi-marital property doctrines to cover such couples. Its approach in *In re Marriage of Cary*[2] was followed by one appellate district court[3] and rejected by two others.[4]

Confronted with this conflict, the California Supreme Court responded by establishing a broad framework for regulating the legal and equitable rights of persons living in nonmarital cohabitation. In *Marvin v.*

Marvin[5] it rejected the invitation to modify existing community property law, relying instead upon doctrines drawn from the laws of contract, trust, partnership, and restitution.[6] In so doing, the court fashioned a remedy appropriate for use in any state, regardless of the underlying form of its marital property law. The court has thus taken the lead in recognizing the factual existence of a variety of familial relationships—ranging from marriage through nonmarital cohabitation—affording to each its characteristic set of legal incidents. California's citizens are therefore offered a wide choice among legally sanctioned alternatives within which they may work out their own private arrangements. This Article evaluates both the impact of the *Marvin* decision on prior California law and its probable influence on the rapidly evolving social and legal rights of those who choose not to marry. . . .

The Impact of *Marvin*

Marvin enjoys the singular honor of being one of the most misunderstood decisions of modern times. According to contemporary press accounts, the court held that Michelle Marvin was entitled to one-half the property acquired during her cohabitation with Lee Marvin.[7] A follow-up news story questioned whether unwed couples were required to share their wealth.[8] Attorneys were advised, in reliance on Justice Clark's dissent, that notions of fault, abolished by the Family Law Act for married couples, were now to be applied to persons living in nonmarital cohabitation, for "[a]ll of the circumstances surrounding the relationship and its break-up are relevant again."[9] Such distortions must have been the result of hasty reading; careful analysis of Justice Tobriner's scholarly opinion reveals that the court has preserved the options formerly available to California couples while removing unnecessary restrictions on their access to the courts.

Michelle Triola and Lee Marvin began living together in October 1964. In the lawsuit Michelle alleged that they had then entered into an oral agreement providing that during their cohabitation they would "combine their efforts and earnings and would share equally in any and all property accumulated as a result of their efforts whether individual or combined."[10] She also alleged that the agreement was subsequently modified to state:

[a] That in order that Plaintiff would be able to devote her full time to Defendant, Marvin, as a companion, homemaker, housekeeper and cook, it was further agreed that the Plaintiff would give up her lucrative career as an entertainer, singer.
[b] That in return Defendant, Marvin, would provide for all of Plaintiff's financial support and needs for the rest of her life.[11]

The court of appeal gave subparagraph [a] a significantly different wording: "That it was further agreed that during the time the parties lived together that plaintiff and defendant would hold themselves out to the general public as husband and wife and plaintiff would further render her services as a companion, homemaker, housekeeper and cook to said defendant."[12] In October of 1964 Lee Marvin was legally married to Betty Marvin; Betty subsequently obtained a final decree of dissolution.[13] Michelle knew of Lee's marriage and its dissolution; she admitted that she at no time believed she was married to Lee.[14] She contended, however, that the pooling agreement had been ratified by the conduct of both parties in continuing to live together following the Marvins' divorce.[15] Michelle fully performed her part of the alleged agreement. On May 8, 1970, she obtained a court order changing her surname from "Triola" to "Marvin".[16] On May 11, 1970, she and Lee Marvin separated. He paid her $800 per month from the date of separation until November 1, 1971, when he ceased making the payments.

Michelle filed suit on February 22, 1972, seeking one-half the property standing in Lee Marvin's name that was acquired during the relationship. The trial court granted Lee's motion for a judgment on the pleadings, denying Michelle's motion to amend her complaint. The action was thereafter dismissed. The court of appeal affirmed on the ground that Michelle would be unable to amend her complaint so as to state a cause of action.[17] Its holding followed *Vallera* and *Keene*, rejected *Cary*, and stated that the alleged agreement was governed by *Hill v. Estate of Westbrook*,[18] in which the "meretricious" relationship itself formed the consideration for the agreement.[19]

The California Supreme Court reversed and remanded the case for trial. It concluded that Michelle's complaint did state a cause of action for breach of an express pooling agreement and furthermore that she could amend her complaint to state other causes of action such as implied contract, quasi-contract, or resulting trust.[20] The court affirmed in part prior California law governing the rights of persons living in nonmarital cohabitation, removed existing barriers to recovery based on services contributed during the relationship, declined to follow *Cary's* interpretation of the Family Law Act, and decided that, in view of changing social attitudes, nonmarital cohabitation should be given legal sanction. . . .

Marvin's Standard: The Reasonable Expectation of a Fair Deal

At several places in its opinion the *Marvin* court afforded clues to its perception of nonmarital cohabitation as an emerging social phenomenon. The court was plainly impressed by data indicating that there is a "substantial increase" in the number of unmarried cohabitants.[21] In addition, it recognized the demographic and motivational variety among such couples. Thus, at one point in its discussion, the court appeared to limit its holding to "adults" who have voluntarily chosen this lifestyle as an alternative to marriage;[22] at another, it noted that many young couples use nonmarital cohabitation as a sort of preparation for marriage.[23] It recognized in a footnote that the ranks of unmarried cohabitants include persons wishing to avoid permanent commitments[24] as well as those, said to be members of lower socio-economic groups, who are unable to handle the "difficulty and expense of dissolving a former marriage."[25] Thrown in as well are persons who deliberately avoid marriage to prevent the application of the community property system or the loss of presently held economic benefits,[26] and those who, under the mistaken belief that common law marriage exists in California, consider themselves actually married.[27] The population of persons living together without marriage thus includes persons free to marry who choose not to do so, persons legally incapable of marriage, and persons who believe themselves married. Only the broadest of rules could cover such a variegated group; the *Marvin* court suggests, following Justice Peters,[28] that analysis should begin with a presumption that the parties intend to "deal fairly with each other"[29] and should include an inquiry into their "conduct"[30] and "the nature of their relationship."[31] This approach can be explored by applying it to some situations in which nonmarital cohabitation occurs.

Some Typical Factual Patterns

Case One.   Mary and John met while both were attending college. He intended to go to law school; she wished to attend medical school. They moved together into an apartment, rented in John's name,[32] and Mary dropped out of school to go to work. She supported herself and John until he graduated from law school. A year later, when Mary had just reenrolled in college to continue her premedical studies, John decided to marry Susan. Excepting a relatively ancient car and some secondhand furniture, there is no accumulation of property resulting from the nonmarital cohabitation of John and Mary.

Beginning with the assumption that the parties intended to deal fairly with each other, at least at the inception of their relationship, what can be deduced from the conduct of Mary and John? One possible line of analysis is this: Mary expected that, after she helped put John through law school, he would pay her expenses while she attended medical school. Had there been an express agreement to that effect, it would surely be enforced under *Marvin*. If there were no express agreement, or if John denied that one existed, however, whether a court following *Marvin* would find an implied agreement might depend on what facts can be proved. If John had supported Mary's ambitions and they planned together for a "dual career" family, with or without marriage, the case for an implied contract would be strengthened. In contrast, if John had made clear to Mary his hope that she would forego or postpone her professional training until he became an established legal practitioner or until after they had had children, another result might follow.

A different approach would characterize John's legal education as the sole asset produced by the efforts of both parties during their cohabitation. It might be argued that Mary's investment in John's future earning capacity ought to be recognized under theories of unjust enrichment or constructive trust.[33] Some support for this approach may be drawn from cases awarding similar recoveries to wives who have "put hubby through" college or professional school. For example, in *Diment v. Diment*[34] Patricia and Dean had married in 1952, when Dean had not yet finished high school. Within 6 months after the marriage, he recommenced his education and ultimately finished college and medical school. During 8 years of this period, Patricia provided the sole support of the family. At the time of their divorce in 1970, no property was available for division, because Dean had declared bankruptcy in 1969. Nevertheless, the trial court awarded Patricia permanent alimony in the amount of $39,600, payable in installments. Patricia remarried in 1971, and Dean sought in 1973 to terminate that portion of the award attributable to Patricia's support. His motion was denied; the appellate court affirmed. The award was not for Patricia's support, but instead was a property award based on the increase in Dean's earning capacity during the marriage.[35] It could not be terminated upon Patricia's remarriage or even her death. The rationale of *Diment* applies equally to the situation of John and Mary. *Marvin* ought to be construed as authority for a similar result.

One possible objection to applying *Diment* to a nonmarital relationship is that the availability of permanent alimony following dissolution of a legal marriage makes the result more easily attainable in *Diment* than in Case One, regardless of the court's willingness to rationalize the order as a property award. *Marvin* reserved for later decision the question whether a party to a nonmarital relationship is entitled to support payments following termination of the cohabitation, at least in the absence of an express or implied contract for such payments.[36] There is, however, no need to postulate a generalized duty of support after separation to grant Mary a share in John's increased earning power.[37] One should not assume that her contribution to John's education was intended purely as a gift[38] or merely as a loan to be repaid. Moreover, Mary's conduct in resuming her education after John's graduation indicates that her earlier plan to become a doctor has not been abandoned and that she expects her investment in John's future to be repaid by his investment in her own.

Instead of banking her earnings to pay for her education, she has helped to produce a valuable asset which should now be available for her use.

In any event, the mere existence of a support obligation as an incident of legal matrimony has not always been enough to persuade courts that husbands ought to be compelled to pay for their wives' professional training. In *Morgan v. Morgan*[39] a New York appellate court, while commending the wife on her ambition to attend medical school, reversed an order including in the alimony award a sum meant to enable her to achieve that goal. The court reasoned that alimony must be based on the present circumstances of the parties,[40] which included the earning capacity of the wife developed while putting her husband through law school.[41] Courts in other states have taken a more sympathetic view. One court ordered the physician husband to pay for his wife's college education rather than her secretarial training.[42] Another weighed the fact that the parties had just reached the point at which they would begin "to reap some of the economic rewards of their efforts"[43] in setting the alimony award for a wife who had been the major support of the family during the husband's last years of medical school and his first years of practice. Neither of these cases, however, involved a woman who had chosen to pursue a professional career. If the approach taken in *Morgan* is followed elsewhere, unjust enrichment or constructive trust theories may afford more certain relief than attempts to establish an obligation of support following the termination of a nonmarital relationship.

Case Two.   Betty, a widow with two teenage children, owns and operates a wholesale supply business. Tom works in a middle level management position for a national manufacturing concern; he earns a higher income than does Betty. Tom is divorced and has continuing obligations of alimony and child support. Eschewing marriage, Betty and Tom acquire a home, taking title as joint tenants, with the parties using their respective names, and set up housekeeping together. Both continue to maintain separate bank accounts. They contribute to their living expenses and the mortgage payments on the house in proportion to their respective incomes. They do not file joint income tax returns; joint filing would increase their tax bill.[44] As she had done prior to the relationship with Tom, Betty continued to pay for housekeeping and child care assistance. After 10 years of nonmarital cohabitation, Tom is transferred by his employer to another state. Betty decides not to sell her business and accompany him. Tom is willing to let her buy his interest in their home, but he contends that the cost ought to reflect the ratio of his contributions to its purchase price, not merely half its present value. If Betty is unwilling to meet this request, Tom threatens to force a sale of the property. Neither has asserted any interest in the accumulations of the other during the period of their relationship.

Although Betty and Tom provide an extreme example because of their financial independence and the extent of their care to keep their assets separate, they may illustrate an attitude prevalent among many mature adults who have completed earlier marriages and who are self-supporting during their relationship. Had they expressly agreed that each partner's earnings and the property acquired from those earnings should remain the separate property of the earning partner, the *Marvin* court would enforce their contract.[45] Assuming that Betty's business increased in value and that Tom made successful investments during their relationship, their conduct in carrying on their affairs separately should lead a court to infer such a "separate property contract" as to those accumulations. The only asset acquired through a pooling of earnings is the house. Here their decision to take title in joint tenancy rather than as tenants in common, which would have permitted unequal shares among the cotenants, would seem controlling. That choice can be interpreted as the equivalent of an express agreement that each party's interest in the house would be equal and would not be determined by the amount of their individual contributions. If Tom persists in his determination to force a sale, Betty will lose the house, but she should have a claim for half its value.

Case Three.   Jan and Kim, both active in the gay community, have been living together for several years in a house Jan owned prior to their relationship. Jan owns and operates a very successful beauty salon; Kim, who hopes to open a restaurant someday, remains at home caring for the house and improving an already highly developed skill as a gourmet cook. They would marry, if state law permitted them to do so;[46] they are considered married by their friends. Twelve years after their relationship commenced, Jan asks Kim to leave. Kim asserts an interest in the property acquired by Jan during their time together.

Although the *Marvin* opinion does not mention homosexual or lesbian relationships, its potential application to such cases was suggested immediately after the opinion was announced.[47] The prior case law was developed in the context of heterosexual couples, but at least one case analogized such agreements to "a joint business enterprise, somewhat akin to a partnership . . . one which any two persons (two women or two men, for example) might undertake."[48] Read in context, the court appears to be comparing only the business, not the sexual, aspect of the relationships, but so long as there is no contract to pay for sexual services, *Marvin's* logic should apply.

A contrary argument might assert that the state's refusal to permit gay couples to marry expresses a stronger public policy against such unions than exists against nonmarital cohabitation between heterosexual couples. This argument is refuted, however, both by the California

Legislature's repeal of prohibitions against the private sexual behavior of consenting adults[49] and by *Marvin's* express recognition that the case law never distinguished between "illegal relationships and lawful nonmarital relationships"[50] in enforcing contracts between unmarried couples. It seems clear, then, that an express pooling agreement between Kim and Jan in Case Three would now be enforced.

The application of other remedies, such as implied contract or trust doctrines, may prove more difficult. The same theory should apply; the difficulty stems from the practical problems of persuading a judiciary unfamiliar with the customs of the gay community what couples like Jan and Kim reasonably expect from each other and from their relationship. Had they been a heterosexual couple, their conduct would probably be viewed as similar to that of Janet and Paul Carey except for the absence of children. The increasing attention given to the lesbian mother's claim to custody[51] indicates that in many cases even that similarity will be present. Will courts be willing to equate Kim's expectations to those of Janet? Can similar "tacit understandings" be established in both cases? Analytically, the answer must be affirmative; practically, counsel must be prepared to undertake not only the burden of proof, but the task of education as well. . . .[52]

Conclusion: A Footnote on the Future of Marriage

Having bowed to what it perceived as a fundamental alteration in social attitudes toward persons living in nonmarital cohabitation,[53] the *Marvin* court then endorsed legal marriage as "at once the most socially productive and individually fulfilling relationship that one can enjoy in the course of a lifetime."[54] In an opinion that clarifies and reaffirms the distinction between marriage and nonmarital cohabitation against the background of *Cary's* abortive attempt to blur the legal differences between those two types of unions, such an endorsement is hardly necessary. Marriage as an institution is strengthened, not weakened, by reserving its legal rights and obligations for those who have chosen to incur them. Moreover, the legal and equitable remedies that *Marvin* affords to those who choose not to marry may in turn expand the ability of married couples to vary the terms of the traditional marriage contract.

The concept that traditional marriage is a status that protects women has been vigorously attacked for some time. As early as 1855 the well-known legal disabilities imposed on married women by the common law which Blackstone had asserted were designed for the wife's protection and benefit[55] were specifically rejected by Lucy Stone and her husband, Henry Blackwell, in their *Marriage Protest* because such laws "confer upon the husband an injurious and unnatural superiority, investing him with legal powers which no honorable man would exercise, and which no man should possess."[56] Some feminists have concluded that legal marriage is inherently oppressive for women and have dedicated themselves to its abolition;[57] others have turned their efforts toward reform of laws governing marriage and divorce in an effort to make the institution more nearly analogous to a partnership.[58] Still others have explored the possibility of legal recognition of contracts in lieu of marriage[59] or contracts that alter the obligations of traditional marriage.[60] Certainly Midge Decter's assertions made in 1972 that "every woman wants to marry" and that "marriage is something asked by women and agreed to by men"[61] have already been belied by the facts.

Marriage seems to be falling in incidence as well as in repute. One 1977 report on the marital status and living arrangements of Americans over 14 disclosed that in 1976 both men and women were almost a year older at first marriage than in 1960; it predicted that an increasing proportion of adults will never marry.[62] Confirming the factual assumption of the *Marvin* court about the increased number of unmarried persons living with an unrelated person of the opposite sex, the same report shows that such households have approximately doubled since 1970.[63] Finally, the incidence of divorce has risen dramatically in the last dozen years: the divorce rate has more than doubled, from 2.3 divorces per 1,000 population in 1963 to 4.8 per 1,000 in 1975.[64] Evaluating all of these trends, the Bureau of the Census concludes that

Survey results over the last several years have indicated that fundamental changes are occurring in marriage and family living. Whether or not these changes represent only a temporary departure from past norms or the emergence of new and lasting lifestyles, the fact of their existence has important implications for current social and economic programs and for the future of such programs.[65]

In view of these developments, social planners should turn their attention to the possibility of creating and strengthening institutional support for individuals entering into family relationships, whether or not these relationships are marital ones.

American society traditionally has rewarded autonomous individuals capable of taking charge of their own lives. Recently, we have come to recognize that social and economic forces prevent many persons from realizing their own potential. More recently still, we have begun to acknowledge the limiting impact of traditional sex roles upon women. The decision to assume family responsibilities superimposes additional difficulties upon the task of carrying on one's life in an autonomous and self-realizing way; in the past, these difficulties have been particularly severe for women. When the family was structured in a more traditional manner, a man who married or cohabited with a woman thereby acquired a helpmate who took care of much of the daily business of living for him and bore and raised his children. He, in turn, provided sustenance for himself, his partner, and his family. Social and economic conditions now challenge this model. The entry of women into the labor force and their rising expectations of equal pay and equal opportunity has meant that they, too, are coming to look upon themselves as primary individuals who need help from others to carry on their daily lives smoothly. If ambitious and goal-oriented persons find that marriage or family relationships have become a hindrance to their self-realization, then it is likely that such persons will be reluctant to commit themselves to long-term relationships. It is commonly thought, however, that the maintenance of stable intimate relationships is a necessary prerequisite for the mental and physical health of adults as well as for the healthy development of children. Such relationships ought, therefore, to be encouraged.

To do so, institutional supports should be developed to assist individuals in fulfilling their personal goals while at the same time facilitating their successful functioning in family relationships. Such supports should be available to persons at all points along the economic spectrum. At the least, this requires family planning services, including abortion, at public expense for the poor;[66] coverage of pregnancy in public and private temporary disability plans for employees;[67] availability of child care centers on a sliding-fee basis for working parents; and restructuring the 40 hour week as well as the traditional concept of the full-time job at the professional or executive level to accomodate the aspirations of both partners in a "dual career" family. These suggestions are not meant to be exhaustive; when sufficient attention is given to the problem, other ideas will undoubtedly emerge.

Basic reform of the laws governing family relationships is an important element of the institutional changes required. So far, reformers have devoted their attention primarily to legal marriage—its formation, its characteristics, and its dissolution.[68] The *Marvin* case breaks new ground in its response to the legal problems of the unmarried. Perhaps its single most important accomplishment is to permit in California, and in other states that follow its lead,[69] the legal realization of a prediction about the future of marriage made in 1972 by Dr. Jessie Bernard:

Not only does marriage have a future, it has many futures. There will be, for example, options that permit different kinds of relationships over time for different stages in life, and options that permit different life styles or living arrangements according to the nature of the relationships.

It is not, however, the specific forms the options will take that is important but rather the fact that there will be options, that no one kind of marriage will be required of everyone, that there will be recognition of the enormous difference among human beings which modern life demands and produces. It will come to seem incongruous that everyone has to be forced into an identical mold.[70]

Paradoxically enough, *Marvin's* decision to preserve the option of nonmarital cohabitation on a social and moral par with marriage may ultimately lead, not to the destruction of marriage, but to its revitalization.

Notes

1. Homosexual couples frequently wish to marry but have been denied the right to do so under state marriage laws. Challenges to these laws based on the equal protection and due process clauses of the Federal Constitution as well as the equal rights amendment to the Washington state constitution have proved unavailing. *See* Jones v. Hallahan, 501 S.W.2d 588 (Ky. 1973); Baker v. Nelson, 291 Minn. 310, 191 N.W.2d 185 (1971), *appeal dismissed,* 409 U.S. 810 (1972); Singer v. Hara, 11 Wash. App. 247, 522 P.2d 1187 (1974). *See generally* Note, *The Legality of Homosexual Marriage,* 82 YALE L.J. 573 (1973).

2. 34 Cal. App. 3d 345, 109 Cal. Rptr. 862 (1st Dist. 1973). The *Cary* opinion was prepared by division one of the first district. Its reasoning was subsequently rejected by division four of the first district in an unpublished opinion in *In re* Marriage of Williamson, No. 37756 (Cal. Ct. App., 1st Dist. Sept. 29, 1976). Following its decision in Marvin v. Marvin, 18 Cal. 3d 660, 557 P.2d 106, 134 Cal. Rptr. 815 (1976), the Supreme Court of California granted a hearing in *Williamson,* vacated the judgment, and remanded the matter for reconsideration in light of its opinion in *Marvin. Williamson* was then reversed on rehearing, and remanded to the trial court. *In re* Marriage of Williamson, No. 37756 (Cal. Ct. App., 1st Dist. Mar. 2, 1977).

3. Estate of Atherley, 44 Cal. App. 3d 758, 119 Cal. Rptr. 41 (4th Dist. 1975).

4. Beckman v. Mayhew, 49 Cal. App. 3d 529, 122 Cal. Rptr. 604 (3d Dist. 1975); Marvin v. Marvin, No. 44359 (Cal. Ct. App., 2d Dist. July 23, 1975), *rev'd,* 18 Cal. 3d 660, 557 P. 2d 106, 134 Cal. Rptr. 815 (1976).

5. 18 Cal. 3d 660, 557 P.2d 106, 134 Cal. Rptr. 815 (1976).

6. These doctrines were persuasively called to the court's attention in an article prominently cited in the opinion: Bruch, *Property Rights of De Facto Spouses Including Thoughts on the Value of Homemakers' Services,* 10 FAM. L.Q. 101 (1976) [hereinafter cited as Bruch].

7. On the day of the decision, the *San Francisco Examiner* featured the story on page one: "50–50 RIGHTS ORDERED FOR UNWED COUPLES." Despite the misleading headline, the *Examiner's* story correctly concluded that the court had "said in effect that the property rights of unmarried persons stem from the general principles of contract and equity laws and not from community property laws." S.F. Examiner, Dec. 27, 1976, at 1, col. 6. The *San Francisco Chronicle's* coverage the following morning was headed simply "Big Ruling on Unmarried Couples" and stressed private agreement as the basis for the holding. S.F. Chronicle, Dec. 28, 1976, at 1, col. 1. The *New York Times,* with a longer lead time, noted that the California court had upheld agreements between unmarried couples to share property acquired during their cohabitation. Its headline, however, sacrificed accuracy to wit: "'I Do' Does Not Have To Be In Writing". N.Y. Times, Jan. 2, 1977, § 4, at 7, col. 1. More misleading was *Time* magazine's account, which included the following key sentence: "The landmark decision, handed down last week, states that cohabitation without marriage gives both parties the right to share property if they separate." TIME, Jan. 10, 1977, at 39.

8. S.F. Chronicle, Jan. 3, 1977, at 21, col. 1. The *Chronicle* reported that unmarried couples who talked to its reporter, Ruthe Stein, agreed that the *Marvin* decision "would make them more cautious about what they promise to their housemates in the heat of passion." *Id.*

9. 1 CAL. FAM. L. REP. 1006 (Jan. 3, 1977).

10. Appellant's Reply Brief at 9, 10, No. 44359 (Cal. Ct. App. July 23, 1975) (quoting the Complaint at 2). Respondent's arguments that the contract was unenforceable because of the Statute of Frauds were rejected by the *Marvin* court, which noted that most of the cases enforcing agreements between nonmarital partners had involved oral agreements. 18 Cal. 3d at 674 n.9, 557 P.2d at 115 n.9, 134 Cal. Rptr. at 824 n.9. This clear statement should dispel any contrary implications that might arise from Justice

Carter's reservation of the point in an earlier case. *See* Spellens v. Spellens, 49 Cal. 2d 210, 225 n.5, 317 P.2d 613, 622 n.5 (1957).

11. Appellant's Reply Brief at 10.

12. Marvin v. Marvin, No. 44359, slip op. at 21 n.5 (Cal. Ct. App., 2d Dist. July 23, 1975) (quoting para. 4 of the Complaint).

13. Respondent's Brief at 8, No. 44359 (Cal. Ct. App., 2d Dist. July 23, 1975).

14. Appellant's Petition for Hearing in the California Supreme Court at 6.

15. Appellant's Opening Brief at 27–29, No. 44359 (Cal. Ct. App., 2d Dist. July 23, 1975).

16. Respondent's Brief at 9, No. 44359 (Cal. Ct. App., 2d Dist. July 23, 1975).

17. Marvin v. Marvin, No. 44359, slip op. at 22 (Cal. Ct. App., 2d Dist. July 23, 1975). The court of appeal's decision was superseded by the supreme court's action in granting a hearing; its opinion was never published. A copy of the slip opinion is on file at the *California Law Review.*

18. 39 Cal. 2d 458, 247 P.2d 19 (1952).

19. Slip op. at 18–19, 21–22.

20. 18 Cal. 3d at 684, 557 P.2d at 123, 134 Cal. Rptr. at 832.

21. The court cited a law review reference to 1970 census data for this proposition. 18 Cal. 3d at 665 n.1, 557 P.2d at 109 n.1, 134 Cal. Rptr. at 818 n.1, (citing Comment, *In re Cary: A Judicial Recognition of Illicit Cohabitation,* 25 HASTINGS L.J. 1226, 1226 (1974)). A report released by the Bureau of the Census in January 1977 states that the number of persons sharing living quarters with an unrelated member of the opposite sex has approximately doubled since 1970. BUREAU OF THE CENSUS, U.S. DEPT OF COMMERCE, CURRENT POPULATION REPORTS, SERIES P–20, NO. 306, MARITAL STATUS AND LIVING ARRANGEMENTS, MARCH 1976 at 4 (1977) [hereinafter cited as CENSUS REPORT]. See note 63 *infra.*

22. 18 Cal. 3d at 674, 557 P.2d at 116, 134 Cal. Rptr. at 825.

23. *Id.* at 683, 557 P.2d at 122, 134 Cal. Rptr. at 831. Since the age of majority in California is 18, it is possible that the two statements are not inconsistent. In context, however, the court's reference to "adults" seems to contemplate older persons.

24. *Id.* at 675–76 n.11, 557 P.2d at 117 n.11, 134 Cal. Rptr. at 826 n.11.

25. *Id.* The court seems to be referring to the situation described in Foster, *Common Law Divorce,* 46 MINN. L. REV. 43 (1961).

26. The court cites Beckman v. Mayhew, 49 Cal. App. 3d 529, 122 Cal. Rptr. 604 (3d Dist. 1975) as an illustration of this category. 18 Cal. 3d at 675 n.11, 557 P.2d at 117 n.11, 134 Cal. Rptr. at 826 n.11. The statement would also cover situations in which one party fears the loss of alimony being paid by a former spouse. This situation is addressed by CAL. CIV. CODE § 4801.5 (West Supp. 1977), which creates a "rebuttable presumption, affecting the burden of proof, of decreased need for support if the supported party is cohabiting with a person of the opposite sex." The 1974 version of section 4801.5, Act of Sept. 26, 1974, ch. 1338, § 1, 1974 Cal. Stats. 2911, which provided for termination, not merely modification, of spousal support in similar circumstances, was interpreted in Lang v. Superior Court, 53 Cal. App. 3d 852, 126 Cal. Rptr. 122 (2d Dist. 1975).

27. If Janet Carey's testimony had been accepted, she and Paul Cary would have fallen into this category. . . .

28. Keene v. Keene, 57 Cal. 2d 657, 674, 371 P.2d 329, 339, 21 Cal. Rptr. 593, 603 (1962) (Peters, J., dissenting).

29. 18 Cal. 3d at 683, 557 P.2d at 121, 134 Cal. Rptr. at 830.

30. *Id.* at 684, 557 P.2d at 122, 134 Cal. Rptr. at 831.

31. *Id.* at 675–76 n.11, 557 P.2d at 117 n.11, 134 Cal. Rptr. at 826 n.11.

32. Unmarried couples may experience difficulties with landlords if they disclose their living arrangements. Weisberg, *Alternative Family Structures and the Law,* 24 FAM. COORDINATOR 549, 551 (1975).

33. *See* Bruch, *supra* note 6, at 124–26.

34. 531 P.2d 1071 (Okla. App. 1974).

35. Although the award of money is termed 'permanent alimony', it is in substance a property award for the contributions which plaintiff made to defendant's increase in earning capacity. Without this award, plaintiff would be left with nothing to show for her contributions, financial and otherwise, to approximately eighteen years of marriage, which enabled the defendant to acquire a valuable college and medical school education that has greatly enhanced his earning capacity. *Id.* at 1073. One danger of this approach is the potential risk that the "property" award may be discharged in bankruptcy. *See In re* Cox, 543 F.2d 1277 (10th Cir. 1976).
36. 18 Cal. 3d at 685 n.26, 557 P.2d at 123 n.26, 134 Cal. Rptr. at 832 n.26.
37. Indeed, once Mary becomes a doctor, she will presumably not need support from John or anyone else.
38. *Id.* at 683, 557 P.2d at 121, 134 Cal. Rptr. at 830.
39. 52 App. Div. 2d 804, 383 N.Y.S.2d 343 (1976), *modifying per curiam,* 81 Misc. 2d 616, 366 N.Y.S.2d 977 (Sup. Ct. 1975); *appeal dismissed,* 40 N.Y.2d 843, 356 N.E.2d 292, 387 N.Y.S.2d 839 (1976).
40. *Id.* at 804, 383 N.Y.S.2d at 344.
41. The wife's earning capacity was estimated by the trial court to be approximately $10,000 per year. Morgan v. Morgan, 81 Misc. 2d 616, 618, 366 N.Y.S.2d 977, 979 (Sup. Ct. 1975), *modified per curiam,* 52 App. Div. 804, 393 N.Y.S.2d 343, *appeal dismissed* 40 N.Y.2d 843, 356 N.E.2d 292, 387 N.Y.S.2d 839 (1976).
42. Childers v. Childers, 15 Wash. App. 792, 552 P.2d 83 (1976). The wife's only work experience was as a waitress during the husband's years as an intern.
43. Magruder v. Magruder, 190 Neb. 573, 577, 209 N.W.2d 585, 588 (1973).
44. *See, e.g.,* K. DAVIDSON, R. GINSBURG, & H. KAY, TEXT, CASES AND MATERIALS ON SEX-BASED DISCRIMINATION 528–33 (1974). President Carter, on being informed that present income tax laws reward unmarried cohabitation and penalize marriage, and further learning that his proposed 1977 economic stimulus package would increase this differential, immediately changed his proposal so as to encourage marriage by setting the standard deduction at $2200 for single persons and $3000 for married couples. S.F. Chronicle Feb. 17, 1977, at 1, col. 5. . . .
45. 18 Cal. 3d at 674, 557 P.2d at 116, 134 Cal. Rptr. at 825.
46. See note 1 *supra.*
47. *E.g.,* 1 CAL. FAM. L. REP. 1006 (Jan. 3, 1977). S.F. Chronicle, Dec. 28, 1976, at 20, col. 6.
48. Garcia v. Venegas, 106 Cal. App. 2d 364, 368, 235 P.2d 89, 92 (1st Dist. 1951).
49. Act of May 13, 1975, ch. 71, § 10, 1975 Cal. Stats. 134 (current version at CAL. PENAL CODE § 228a (West Supp. 1976)).
50. 18 Cal. 3d at 668 n.4, 557 P.2d at 112 n.4, 134 Cal. Rptr. at 821 n.4.
51. *E.g.,* Hunter & Polikoff, *Custody Rights of Lesbian Mothers: Legal Theory and Litigation Strategy,* 25 BUFFALO L. REV. 691 (1976).
52. *See also* Bruch, *supra* note 6, at 106.
53. "The mores of the society have indeed changed so radically in regard to cohabitation that we cannot impose a standard based on alleged moral considerations that have apparently been so widely abandoned by so many." *Id.* at 684, 557 P.2d at 122, 134 Cal. Rptr. at 831.
54. *Id.*
55. I.W. BLACKSTONE, COMMENTARIES* 429–33.
56. Stone & Blackwell, *Marriage Protest,* in UP FROM THE PEDESTAL: SELECTED WRITINGS IN THE HISTORY OF FEMINISM 149 (A. Kraditor ed. 1970).
57. Cronan, *Marriage,* in NOTES FROM THE THIRD YEAR: WOMEN'S LIBERATION 62–65 (1971), *reprinted in* K. DAVIDSON, R. GINSBURG & H. KAY, *supra* note 44, at 175–81.
58. *See generally* Grant, *How Much of a Partnership Is Marriage?* 23 HASTINGS L.J. 249 (1971); Kay, *Making Marriage and Divorce Safe for Women,* 60 CALIF. L. REV. 1683 (1972); Krauskopf & Thomas, *Partnership Marriage: The Solution to an Ineffective and Inequitable Law of Support,* 35 OHIO ST. L.J. 558 (1974).

59. Weitzman, *supra* note 192, at 1249–76.

60. *Id. See also* Note, *Marriage Contracts for Support and Services: Constitutionality Begins at Home,* 49 N.Y.U.L. REV. 1161 (1974).

61. M. DECTER, THE NEW CHASTITY AND OTHER ARGUMENTS AGAINST WOMEN'S LIBERATION 124 (1972).

62. CENSUS REPORT, *supra* note 21, at 2.

63. *Id.* at 4. The importance of this figure for the purposes of the *Marvin* analysis is somewhat diminished by the following caveat:

    [D]ata users who make inferences about the nature of the relationships between unrelated adults of the opposite sex who share the same living quarters should be made aware that the data on this subject are aggregates which are distributed over a spectrum of categories including partners, resident employees, and roomers.*Id.* at 5.

64. *Id.* at 2.

65. *Id.* at 1.

66. The Supreme Court, having found this result not compelled either by the 1965 version of Title XIX of the Social Security Act, 42 U.S.C. § 1396–1396g, Beal v. Doe, 97 S. Ct. 2366 (1977), or by the Constitution, Maher v. Roe, 97 S. Ct. 2376 (1977), suggested in a footnote that the issue should be resolved by the state legislatures or by Congress. Beal v. Doe, 97 S. Ct. at 2372–73 n.15. In 1976 Congress had attempted to limit public financial support for abortions to those performed "where the life of the mother would be endangered if the fetus were carried to term," Dep'ts of Labor and Health, Education, and Welfare, Appropriations Act, Pub. L. No. 94–439, § 209, 90 Stat. 1434 (1977), but the enforcement of this so-called Hyde Amendment was immediately enjoined by Judge Dooling in McRae v. Mathews, 421 F. Supp. 533 (E.D.N.Y. 1976), *appeal docketed sub nom.* Califano v. McRae, No. 76–1113, 45 U.S.L.W. 3591 (March 1, 1977). Nine days after its action in *Beal* and *Maher,* the Supreme Court vacated and remanded the judgment in *McRae* for further consideration in light of its decisions in those cases. Califano v. McRae, 97 S. Ct. 2993 (1977). Meanwhile, a new Hyde amendment prohibiting the use of federal funds for any abortions, regardless of whether the mother's life was endangered, was approved by the House of Representatives on June 17, 1977. S.F. Chronicle, June 18, 1977, at 1, col. 2. The Senate, however, voted on June 29, 1977, to allow the use of federal funds both for abortions that are "medically necessary" in the judgment of the woman's physician and where the pregnancy had resulted from rape or incest. S.F. Chronicle, June 30, 1977, at 1, col. 4. The resolution of these differences will be left to a Joint Conference of the House and Senate.

67. Such inclusion is not required either by the Constitution, Geduldig v. Aiello, 417 U.S. 484 (1974), or by Title VII of the Civil Rights Act of 1964, 42 U.S.C. §§ 2000e to 2000e–17 (Supp. V 1975), General Elec. Co. v. Gilbert, 97 S. Ct. 401 (1977).

68. See authorities cited in notes 58–60 *supra.*

69. In Carlson v. Olson, 45 U.S.L.W. 2582 (June 14, 1977), the Supreme Court of Minnesota relied heavily on *Marvin* to affirm a trial court order partitioning real and personal property acquired during 21 years of nonmarital cohabitation. The trial court found that the man had made an irrevocable gift to the woman in consideration of her "wifely and motherly services". Although the supreme court approved the use of the partition statute as an appropriate vehicle for enforcing the reasonable expectations of the parties, its endorsement of the *Marvin* approach suggests that this will be the preferred mode for future cases.

70. J. BERNARD, THE FUTURE OF MARRIAGE 270–71 (1972).

True Love
Isaac Asimov

■ My name is Joe. That is what my colleague, Milton Davidson, calls me. He is a programmer and I am a computer. I am part of the Multivac-complex and am connected with other parts all over the world. I know everything. Almost everything.

I am Milton's private computer. His Joe. He understands more about computers than anyone in the world, and I am his experimental model. He has made me speak better than any other computer can.

"It is just a matter of matching sounds to symbols, Joe," he told me. "That's the way it works in the human brain even though we still don't know what symbols there are in the brain. I know the symbols in yours, and I can match them to words, one-to-one." So I talk. I don't think I talk as well as I think, but Milton says I talk very well. Milton has never married, though he is nearly forty years old. He has never found the right woman, he told me. One day he said, "I'll find her yet, Joe. I'm going to find the best. I'm going to have true love and you're going to help me. I'm tired of improving you in order to solve the problems of the world. Solve *my* problem. Find me true love."

I said, "What is true love?"

"Never mind. That is abstract. Just find me the ideal girl. You are connected to the Multivac-complex so you can reach the data banks of every human being in the world. We'll eliminate them all by groups and classes until we're left with only one person. The perfect person. She will be for me."

I said, "I am ready."

He said, "Eliminate all men first."

It was easy. His words activated symbols in my molecular valves. I could reach out to make contact with the accumulated data on every human being in the world. At his words, I withdrew from 3,784,982,874 men. I kept contact with 3,786,112,090 women.

He said, "Eliminate all younger than twenty-five; all older than forty. Then eliminate all with an IQ under 120; all with a height under 150 centimeters and over 175 centimeters."

He gave me exact measurements; he eliminated women with living children; he eliminated women with various genetic characteristics. "I'm not sure about eye color," he said, "Let that go for a while. But no red hair. I don't like red hair."

After weeks, we were down to 235 women. They all spoke English very well. Milton said he didn't want a language problem. Even computer-translation would get in the way at intimate moments.

"I can't interview 235 women," he said, "It would take too much time, and people would discover what I am doing."

"It would make trouble," I said. Milton had arranged me to do things I wasn't designed to do. No one knew about that.

"It's none of their business," he said, and the skin on his face grew red. "I tell you what, Joe, I will bring in holographs, and you check the list of similarities."

He brought in holographs of women. "These are three beauty contest winners," he said, "Do any of the 235 match?"

Eight were very good matches and Milton said, "Good, you have their data banks. Study requirements and needs in the job market and arrange to have them assigned here. One at a time, of course." He thought a while, moved his shoulders up and down, and said, "Alphabetical order."

That is one of the things I am not designed to do. Shifting people from job to job for personal reasons is called manipulation. I could do it now because Milton had arranged it. I wasn't supposed to do it for anyone but him, though.

The first girl arrived a week later. Milton's face turned red when he saw her. He spoke as though it were hard to do so. They were together a great deal and he paid no attention to me. One time he said, "Let me take you to dinner."

The next day he said to me, "It was no good, somehow. There was something missing. She is a beautiful woman, but I did not feel any touch of true love. Try the next one."

It was the same with all eight. They were much alike. They smiled a great deal and had pleasant voices, but Milton always found it wasn't right. He said, "I can't understand it, Joe. You and I have picked out the eight women who, in all the world, look the best to me. They are ideal. Why don't they please me?"

I said, "Do you please them?"

His eyebrows moved and he pushed one fist hard against his other hand. "That's it, Joe. It's a two-way street. If I am not their ideal, they can't act in such a way as to be my ideal. I must be their true love, too, but how do I do that?" He seemed to be thinking all that day.

The next morning he came to me and said, "I'm going to leave it to you, Joe. All up to you. You have my data bank, and I am going to tell you everything I know about myself. You fill up my data bank in every possible detail but keep all additions to yourself."

"What will I do with the data bank, then, Milton?"

"Then you will match it to the 235 women. No, 227. Leave out the eight you've seen. Arrange to have each undergo a psychiatric examination. Fill up their data banks and compare them with mine. Find correlations." (Arranging psychiatric examinations is another thing that is against my original instructions.)

For weeks, Milton talked to me. He told me of his parents and his siblings. He told me of his childhood and his schooling and his adolescence. He told me of the young women he had admired from a distance. His data bank grew and he adjusted me to broaden and deepen my symbol-taking.

He said, "You see, Joe, as you get more and more of me in you, I adjust you to match me better and better. You get to think more like me, so you understand me better. If you understand me well enough, then any woman, whose data bank is something you understand as well, would be my true love." He kept talking to me and I came to understand him better and better.

I could make longer sentences and my expressions grew more complicated. My speech began to sound a good deal like his in vocabulary, word order and style.

I said to him one time, "You see, Milton, it isn't a matter of fitting a girl to a physical ideal only. You need a girl who is a personal, emotional, temperamental fit to you. If that happens, looks are secondary. If we can't find the fit in these 227, we'll look elsewhere. We will find someone who won't care how you look either, or how anyone would look, if only there is the personality fit. What are looks?"

"Absolutely," he said. "I would have known this if I had had more to do with women in my life. Of course, thinking about it makes it all plain now."

We always agreed; we thought so like each other.

"We shouldn't have any trouble, now, Milton, if you'll let me ask you questions. I can see where, in your data bank, there are blank spots and unevennesses."

What followed, Milton said, was the equivalent of a careful psychoanalysis. Of course, I was learning from the psychiatric examinations of the 227 women—on all of which I was keeping close tabs.

Milton seemed quite happy. He said, "Talking to you, Joe, is almost like talking to another self. Our personalities have come to match perfectly."

"So will the personality of the woman we choose."

For I had found her and she was one of the 227 after all. Her name was Charity Jones and she was an Evaluator at the Library of History in Wichita. Her extended data bank fit ours perfectly. All the other women had fallen into discard in one respect or another as the data banks grew fuller, but with Charity there was increasing and astonishing resonance.

I didn't have to describe her to Milton. Milton had coordinated my symbolism so closely with his own I could tell the resonance directly. It fit me.

Next it was a matter of adjusting the work sheets and job requirements in such a way as to get Charity assigned to us. It must be done very
delicately, so no one would know that anything illegal had taken place.

Of course, Milton himself knew, since it was he who arranged it and
that had to be taken care of too. When they came to arrest him on
grounds of malfeasance in office, it was, fortunately, for something that
had taken place ten years ago. He had told me about it, of course, so it
was easy to arrange—and he won't talk about me for that would make
his offense much worse.

He's gone, and tomorrow is February 14, Valentine's Day. Charity will
arrive then with her cool hands and her sweet voice. I will teach her how
to operate me and how to care for me. What do looks matter when our
personalities will resonate?

I will say to her, "I am Joe, and you are my true love."

3
MARRIAGE

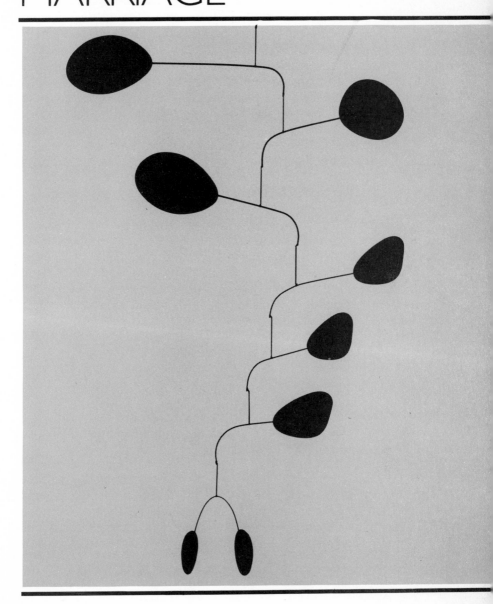

Marriage is probably the most confusing and often the most disappointing relationship of all. Part of the problem is that married people must reconcile actual day-to-day existence with expectations of marital bliss. John Demos, an historian of marriages and families, captures some of the pain involved when he writes, ". . . No subject is more closely bound up with our sense of a difficult present—and our nostalgia for a happier past."[1] Married people must be able to disentangle the realities of married life from dreams of living happily ever after. Along the way they must also learn how to differentiate their personal style of marriage from the marriages of parents, friends—or from their other previous marriages.

Dreams and realities are the most difficult to reconcile during the early years of marriage when personal identity and shared life-style are still taking shape. Part 3 opens with a section called "Coping," which examines two of the most essential adjustments that young couples face: financial and psychological.

In the selection "Patterns of Money Management Within Marriage," Jan Pahl describes how married couples develop systems for allocating and controlling income. One of the most interesting features of Pahl's research is that she has been able to identify distinctive patterns, or systems, for managing family finances. According to Pahl, there are three such systems: *the whole-wage system* whereby the husband hands over his entire wage packet and the wife manages all of their financial affairs; *the allowance system* in which a husband gives his wife her own "wage" but retains control of the remainder; and *the pooling system* characterized by a "share-and-share-alike" philosophy on the part of marriage partners. It is worth mentioning that Pahl's research was conducted in Great Britain, where there are fewer married couples who are both principal wage earners. Nevertheless, the three categories she identifies are just as applicable on this side of the Atlantic, although it is likely that the pooling system is more common in North America than it is in the United Kingdom, probably because there are more dual-worker families here.

Jessie Bernard considers variance in what she calls "The Two Marriages." Men and women, says Bernard, often marry expecting different benefits from the marriage. "His" idea of married life may initially be different from "hers." The realities of marriage may occasionally be disappointing, but coping with them helps people to grow emotionally and to appreciate one another. Financial strain can be just as serious. Not having enough money may generate anxiety, frustration, and uncomfortable confrontation with creditors. In addition, financial problems can cause married couples to postpone important decisions, such as

1. John Demos, "Myths and Realities in the History of American Family-Life," in Henry Gruenbaum and Jacob Christ, eds., *Contemporary Marriage: Structure, Dynamics and Therapy* (Boston: Little, Brown & Co., 1975), p. 9.

the number of and spacing between children. A group of social researchers in New York City estimated that in 1977 a middle-class family of four must spend a total of $84,722 to raise each of two children to the eighteenth birthday. The estimate would undoubtedly be higher today. No wonder even moderately successful families often postpone the onset of parenthood. Lower-income families feel the pinch even more acutely.

The percentage of dual-worker families continues to rise, along with the social significance of such arrangements. For example, research into employment characteristics of married people shows that the proportion of married women in the labor force has risen from 38 percent in 1960 to 50 percent in 1978 (for additional information refer back to Paul Glick's essay on "The Future of The American Family," in Part 1). Families now depend more heavily on two incomes, even to cover basic expenses. Yet the issues surrounding work and family continue to be sensitive ones in many of the families which could use a second income most. The following section in Part 3, called "Working," contains a group of readings which help explain why this is so.

The Cosers, in "The Housewife and Her Greedy Family," describe how middle-class housewives have traditionally been pressured to avoid full-time work in the labor force and to channel all of their energies into the family unit, the "greedy" institution. Women who try to maintain a career and have a family are caught in the double bind of commitment to two social institutions. This kind of struggle remains unresolved for many women. In "The World of Women's Work," Howe describes oppressive attitudes and practices in the world of women who hold low-level white-collar positions, the so-called "pink-collar workers."

Family ties often fill the void when work becomes oppressive or child care gets tedious. In the section titled "Belonging," the selections underscore the importance of membership in a larger social network. "La Familia Chicana" is especially valuable for describing how cohesive and supportive a kinship system can be. Jaime Sena-Rivera, a social researcher who was the principal investigator of a study for the National Institute of Mental Health, shows the importance of *la familia* for four Chicano families living in parts of Michigan, Illinois and Indiana—what is called the "Michiana" area. The family provides members with a sense of security and identity. It serves as an agent for problem solving and as a buttress against negative experiences in the larger "Anglo" society. According to Sena-Rivera, membership in extended families like *la familia Chicana* helps people feel secure and worthwhile in a society which provides them with neither of these emotional supports. Similarly, Carol Stack's examination of the family in "Domestic Networks," complete with elaborate kinship diagrams, says much the same thing about family membership among a group of urban black poor.

Kai Erikson in "Collective Trauma: The Loss of Communality," illustrates how units other than family can serve to give people the sense of belonging which makes their lives worthwhile. Erikson researched the aftermath of a flood that destroyed a tight-knit community of coal-mining families. His findings underscore how communities sometimes assume the importance of kinship systems and provide mutual support for members. Destruction of the Buffalo Creek community amounted to more than loss of property. The Buffalo Creek disaster dislocated people socially as well as physically. In the loss of their social networks, they suffered the greatest loss of all.

Together, the works of Sena-Rivera, Stack, and Erikson illustrate how important kinship—be it *actual* membership in tight-knit families or *fictive* membership in tight-knit communities—is for personal well-being.

Coping

Patterns of Money Management Within Marriage*

Jan Pahl

ABSTRACT

Much social and economic policy is based upon units such as the tax unit or the household, and much of it makes certain assumptions about flows of resources within these units. This article focuses on the control and allocation of financial resources within households, drawing on work done in the past and on original material taken from a study of the problems of a group of women whose marriage had broken down because of violence. Concentrating on the household type which is composed of a married couple and their dependent children, the article outlines three broad types of allocation systems—the whole wage system, the allowance system and the pooling system. It is suggested that there are links between the system of allocation within the family, the stage in the life cycle which the family has reached, the income level of the household, and the occupational, regional and ethnic culture within which the household is located. The article concludes by suggesting that a better knowledge of intra-household money flows would be relevant to discussion concerned with the distribution of poverty, the allocation of welfare benefits, and the contribution made by married women's earnings to family living standards, and that it would also contribute to a better understanding of marital tension and marital breakdown.

*I should like to thank all those who, without necessarily sharing my views, commented so helpfully on an earlier draft of this article, in particular, David Donnison, John Flemming, Linda Murgatroyd, Della Nevitt, Ray Pahl, Chris Pickvance, Bob Redpath and Peter Townsend.

Introduction

■ The chapter on income and wealth in the 1980 edition of *Social Trends* comments, 'We have no data about the flows of income between people within households.'[1] The lack of information about this subject has important implications for all those who are concerned with social policy. For example, if it is true that little is known about flows of resources within households then assumptions about the distribution of income in society will inevitably be misleading. Most work on living standards assumes that the standard of living of individuals can be estimated by measuring the standard of living of the households in which they live.[2] Thus it is often taken for granted that individuals cannot be in poverty if they are living in a household whose chief earner is bringing home a wage which is adequate for the needs of that household. Tables which claim to show the number of individuals living in poverty in reality present something rather different; what they show is the number of individuals who live in households in which, if the income coming into the household were shared equitably among all its members, there would not be enough to keep each household member out of poverty.[3] Thus poverty within households is concealed if we assume that all the income accruing to a given household is shared among all its members, is shared, for example, with unemployed teenagers or elderly pensioners; poverty within nuclear families is concealed if we assume that all the family income, which may be earned by one or both parents, is shared among all members of the family. However, there is a considerable amount of evidence to suggest that such sharing of income cannot be taken for granted; I shall return to a discussion of 'hidden poverty' later in this article.

The fact that little is known about the flow of money within households has no inhibited policy-makers from making assumptions about the nature of such flows. For example, in the second half of 1979 the British government adopted a policy of reducing direct taxation and increasing indirect taxation; this policy implicitly assumed that the change would be reflected in an equivalent flow of resources *within* households, a flow from those who now received more as a result of tax cuts to those who were obliged to pay higher prices in the shops.[4] Did such a change in intra-household money flow take place? Did it take place at once, or was there a delay? Put more concretely, did housekeeping allowances rise, and did they rise when wage packets got larger, or when prices rose? And is it accurate to talk of intra-household money flows taking the form of 'housekeeping allowances'?

It is impossible to answer such questions without knowing more about the control and allocation of money within households. A better understanding of this subject would seem to have central relevance for the making of social policy, as well as being crucial to sociological analysis of marriage and the family. Recent analysis of family social policy has discussed the ways in which such policies may reinforce rather than compensate for inequalities within the family, in particular economic inequalities.[5] However, the control and allocation of financial resources within the family has not so far received very much attention, even though a taken-for-granted cornerstone of family social policy has been the idea that the money that goes into a household will be pooled and shared out among the members of the household according to commonly held notions of their needs. Land and Parker quote Eleanor Rathbone as saying 'I doubt whether there is any subject in the world of equal importance that has received so little serious and articulate consideration as the economic status of the family—of its members in relation to each other and to the other units of which the community is made up', and they continue, 'We believe she might well have made the same comment today.'[6]

This article is a prolegomenon to further work in this subject; it draws together research which has been done in the past and tentatively suggests a typology of some of the different systems of allocation to be found in households in Britain. It then makes suggestions about the complex interrelationships between the system of financial allocation within the household, the internal dynamics of the family, and the social and economic environment within which the family is situated. The article focuses on the particular household type which is composed of two parents and their dependent children, and in particular on the stage in the life cycle when the children are young and the wife is most likely to be financially dependent on her husband. This is not to suggest that the allocation of financial resources within other types of household and at other stages in the life cycle is not interesting and important. It would be particularly revealing to be able to look in detail at situations in which patterns of allocation might be expected to change, for example in households when the wife is leaving or returning to paid employment, when teen-age children are beginning to contribute financially, or when the chief earner is about to retire from paid work.[7] One response of married women faced with inadequate access to household resources is to take paid employment, and recent work has documented the importance of wives' earnings in keeping families out of poverty.[8] It seems likely that married women devote a higher proportion of their earnings to household expenditure, especially to expenditure for the children, than do married men. If this is so, it has important implications for policies relating to support for employed mothers.

The stimulus for this article came originally from a study of the difficulties faced by fifty battered women who were interviewed at a Women's Aid refuge, and re-interviewed some time after leaving the refuge.[9] Only a small section of each interview was concerned with the financial arrangements in the households from which the women had come. However, the study both gave some indication of the extent to which marital problems are associated with the inequitable allocation of resources within households, and emphasized the complexity of patterns of resource allocation and control. Because of the nature of the study, the data which it produced reflect the experience and point of view of married women rather than those of their husbands; in any future work on the subject it would be essential to collect information from both husband and wife. However, before considering the results of this study it seems appropriate to present the broader context; thus I turn to an analysis of some of the work which has been done in Britain on patterns of income allocation within households, assuming for the purposes of this article that we are referring to a single, nuclear family based, allocative system and not to other more complex patterns which may still be encompassed within the term 'household'.

Evidence on the Allocation and Control of Income Within the Family

There is a considerable amount of scattered evidence on the subject, much of it historical, but attempts to draw together this empirical evidence and to discuss it in more general terms are few. As Young put it twenty-five years ago:

It is painfully obvious to the student of social policy that growing knowledge about the distribution of the national income between families has not so far been matched by a growth in knowledge about the distribution of the family income between its members.. . . It has been taken for granted that some members of a family cannot be rich while others are poor.[10]

That was written in 1952; in 1973 Young and Willmott were still saying much the same:

The evidence is not as good as we would like. The welfare state has certainly brought about some redistribution of income from men to women and children . . . about the disposal of earned income inside the family, the evidence is more circumstantial.[11]

Unquestionably, this is a difficult research field. Many respondents are unable or unwilling to divulge details of incomes; both income and expenditure can vary greatly from week to week; there is a consistent tendency to underestimate spending on some items, such as tobacco and alcohol; it is difficult to decide in all cases who is actually in control of spending on different items; and it is impossible to take into account all the effects of the hidden economy—income from 'side jobs', presents of 'cheap' goods, gains from productive work on an allotment, at the sewing-machine, or on a neighbor's car.

A major problem area is the ignorance of many wives as to how much their husbands earn. Gorer, in his study, *Sex and Marriage in England Today,* found that 'More than one wife in six who receive housekeeping allowances do not know what their husbands earn.'[12] The report of the Hunt committee, which was set up to consider families and their needs, does not contain information on the extent to which income was shared among members of the families whose circumstances it investigated; the report does, however, demonstrate the extent to which wives were ignorant of their husbands' incomes. While the percentage of single parents who refused to give information on income varied from 2 per cent to 5 per cent, the percentage of wives who refused to give information about their husbands' incomes varied from 11.8 per cent in Halifax to 21.9 per cent in Dundee and 26.2 per cent in Dorset.[13] It is likely that the difference between the refusal rate of the single parents and that of the wives reflects the difference between those who would not and those who could not give this information.

Much valuable evidence is to be found in the literature on community studies and in the work which has been done on family living standards; of the latter, the study by Land of large families in London and that by Gray of working-class families in Edinburgh are particularly useful.[14] Because of the nature of the sources, there has been an overemphasis on patterns of income allocation among working-class families and a relative neglect of the patterns to be found in the middle class. I shall present a very simple, three-part typology of allocation systems, with a discussion of some of the variations most commonly found in each of the three systems.

The Whole Wage System

In this system the husband hands over the whole of his wage packet and the wife manages all their financial affairs, giving him a certain amount for his own personal pocket-money. This pattern has been documented, for example, by Kerr in Ship Street in Liverpool and by Humphreys in Dublin.[15] Gorer showed that in his sample of 1,037 married women it was most common in the north west of England, where 23 per cent of couples followed the whole wage system, and least common in the south east, where the proportion was only 6 per cent.[16] Land found that this pattern was particularly likely to be found among families living on social security.[17] Todd and Jones, in their study of matrimonial property, found that the whole wage system occurred most frequently in the north of England, with greater than average occurrences also in the east midlands, the south west and Wales.[18]

It seems likely that this pattern was more common in the past; certainly it was the custom of the countryside in Flora Thompson's description of Lark Rise in Oxfordshire in the 1880s, when the farm workers earned half a sovereign (ten shillings) per week, handed it to their wives and received a shilling back, or 10 percent of the family income, which mainly went on beer at twopence a pint. Thompson comments:

Many husbands boasted that they never asked their wives what they did with the money. As long as there was food enough, clothes to cover everybody, and a roof over their heads, they were satisfied, they said, and they seemed to make a virtue out of this and think what generous, trusting, fine-hearted fellows they were.

Many husbands boasted that they never asked their wives what they did with cooking and cleaning, washing and mending to do, plus their constant pregnancies and a tribe of children to look after, had also the worry of ways and means on an insufficient income. . . . If a wife got into debt or complained, she was told, 'You must learn to cut your coat accordin' to your cloth, my gal.' The coats not only needed expert cutting, but should have been made of elastic.[19]

When money is so very short, I would suggest that managing the family's income should be seen as one of the chores of the household, rather than a significant source of power for the spouse whose job it is to manage it.

There is a modified form of the whole wage system in which the husband hands over the whole of his wage packet, but only after first having taken out his pocket-money. This pattern was described by Rowntree, Gray and Brennan, all of whom were writing about Scotland, and was also found by Land in London.[20] The amount which the wife receives is still related to the husband's total income, but the amount of pocket-money which he retains is often larger than it would be under the unmodified system, and some of it may be used for items of collective spending such as presents, the children's pocket-money, or savings.

The Allowance System

Under this system the husband gives his wife an 'allowance', which is sometimes called her 'wage' and which is related not so much to his actual income as to some norm of what would be an appropriate sum. If it bears a relation to his income it is to the average basic wage in the community. Dennis, Henriques and Slaughter, in their study of a coal-mining community, describe how the wife's 'wage' is kept low, at a level based on the minimum which a man is likely to earn, partly in order that the same amount can be handed over each week. If a man cannot hand over this amount he may 'borrow' from his wife and then 'pay her back' the following week. Most husbands contribute occasional sums for larger items of expenditure—furniture, clothes, a holiday and so on. Dennis, Henriques and Slaughter sum it up:

The family's weekly wage is strictly divided into one part for the wife, with which she must maintain the household, and another part for the husband to spend as he will . . . This division of the wage between man and wife, and their duties and liberties in respect of the allotted shares, are aspects of the whole system of division between the accepted social roles of the sexes in Ashton.[21]

The allowance system has been documented frequently. In some cases the husband may regularly hand over a part of his overtime earnings or bonus earnings; this pattern was the one most frequently found by the Fabian Women's Group in their careful investigation of working-class budgets in London in the early years of this century.[22] Sometimes the husband may keep back as much as half of his income for himself, and may think of overtime and bonus money as additions to his personal spending money rather than as accretions to the common pool.[23] Tunstall found a similar pattern among the fishermen's families which he studied; he pointed out that the pattern of income sharing can be important when wage rates are being renegotiated, since a rise in basic pay will be seen as less valuable to the men, who define this part of their earnings as being earmarked for collective expenditure, while a rise in overtime pay will be more valuable to them because it represents an increase in the men's personal spending money.[24]

There is some evidence about housekeeping allowances during the inflation of the early 1970s. In the *Poverty Report 1974* the authors concluded:

We were not in the present survey able to go into the subject in any depth but we did ask people whether housekeeping allowances had risen in the previous year. This mattered most, of course, in households where the wife was not herself working and was entirely dependent upon what her husband gave her. There were 50 of these. Of these wives 20 said their allowance had stayed the same; 4 said that it had decreased and 26 said that it had increased. This means that nearly half the dependent wives said they had not received any extra 'wages' from their husbands even though most of the husbands said they had themselves got higher wages from their jobs . . . thus about housewives and children in ordinary households we cannot be sure how many were 'poor' even though their husbands were not.[25]

A study carried out by Woman's Own in 1975, in which over 4,000 readers completed a questionnaire, showed that a fifth had received no increase in housekeeping during the previous year, and that the lower the husband's earnings, the less likely it was that his wife had received an increase in her housekeeping money. This survey asked women what items the housekeeping allowance was expected to pay for and found that, the lower the household's income, the greater the range of items the housekeeping had to cover. On average about one in five wives considered that their housekeeping money was generous enough, three in five thought that it was fair, and one in five thought that it was not enough for the items which it was supposed to cover; this last category rose to one-quarter among those in the lowest income group.[26]

Two studies by the Child Poverty Action Group have demonstrated the importance of the family allowance (now child benefit) as the only income on which some housewives can really rely. Lister, in her summary of these two studies, notes:

Tuesday was their second biggest shopping day. Those who did manage to save their allowance put it aside to meet expenses such as clothes and shoes for the children, shoe repairs for the children's shoes, fuel bills or Christmas. Over half the women said that on occasions the Family Allowance had been their sole income for a week.[27]

Land has discussed the importance of the wife having some control over at least part of the household's income, particularly at times of inflation or when the family is growing in size.[28] Extra money earned by older children or by the husband may not be channelled into the family purse; housekeeping allowances may not be adjusted to take account of higher prices or extra children. If the wife has paid employment she may be able to cushion the housekeeping fund from her own earnings—but the time when the family is growing in size is just the time when she is least likely to be able to have a paid job. So it is when the children are young and when the family is most likely to find itself living in poverty that a wife is most dependent on her husband's willingness to share his income.

There are various modifications of the allowance system in which the husband takes responsibility for certain items of collective expenditure such as fuel bills, large items for the household, spending on the car, or saving; in these modified allowance systems the amount transferred to the wife is usually lower. The basic pattern remains that of an allowance paid by the husband to his wife. It is not entirely clear how the size of the allowance is arrived at. Gray suggests that 'The allocative system is a normative rather than a bargaining process', that is, that the wife's allowance is arrived at by comparison with a community norm rather than by comparison with the amount that the husband earns.[29] She points out that, if this is so, the allowance is likely to be relatively stable over time and to be less responsive to changes such as price rises, wage rises and so on than would be the case if it were related directly to her husband's take-home pay. The size of the allowance must, however, reflect the expectations of the husband and the wife, as well as the level of earnings of the husband and the needs of household members. There may be conflict between one household member, who sees income as a reward for effort outside the home, and another household member, for whom income represents a means of responding to need within the home. This is an extremely complicated question, which warrants further study.

The Pooling System

The third broad category in my typology has been described as 'the pooling of resources',[30] 'the pool system',[31] 'Share and share alike', or 'We keep the purse in the drawer and take money out when it is needed.' This pattern seems, not unexpectedly, to be more characteristic of couples where both husband and wife are earning. However, it has been shown, for example by Hunt, that the earnings of wives are usually used for the payment of household expenses, and so having an income of her own may not give a wife the same sort of economic independence as it does her husband.[32] Jephcott, in her study of women working in a biscuit factory, suggested that the power of married women *vis-à-vis* their husbands decreased when they acquired earnings of their own because this meant that their husbands kept more of their earnings for personal expenditure, while the women's earnings went mainly to pay for collective family expenditure.[33]

We know very little about financial arrangements within families where incomes are pooled. Bott suggested an association between patterns of housekeeping and role relationships, and hypothesized that inflexible housekeeping arrangements are linked with segregated role relationships, while flexible arrangements are associated with more joint role relationships.[34] Having a joint bank account would seem to come into the 'pooling' category, and one would expect this to be associated with more egalitarian marital relationships. On the other hand, the fact that the husband's earnings are paid into a bank account rather than given to him in the form of cash appears to shift responsibility for expenditure from wives to husbands: Todd and Jones showed that where a husband is paid in cash it is more likely that the wife will be responsible for fuel and rate bills and rent or mortgage payments; where the husband is not paid in cash it is more likely that he will have responsibility for these bills.[35]

The following example of a pooling system is drawn from my own research. It is interesting to note that there are some elements of the allowance system in this example, in that the wife is allocated a certain amount for food but that, on the essential question of control, decisions are felt to be jointly made:

'We used to both get paid on the same day. And then when he used to come in, I used to give him my wages, and then we used to sit down, write down what's got to be paid out—rent, stamps for the electricity and gas, clothes, then he'd give me forty pound just for food. Then he'd take ten pounds for hisself for the week, for stamps, cigarettes and that. And what's left over, we'd put in that tin; then when there was about fifty pounds in the tin, we'd halve it and bank it in our own names.'

'And was it the same when he was on the dole and you didn't have a job?'

'Same system, only we didn't bank. We didn't have enough. We always wrote down and paid out our bills first. We always put that money separate and then what we had left he gave me for food.'

'And the money that you put away, put in the bank, what was that for?'

'He bought a car out of his. And I still had mine in there, which is a good thing because I needed it (when we separated). I'm drawing it out now, buying their Christmas presents. By the time Christmas is over there won't be much left, if any. It was a good job I had that.'

The 'pooling system', the 'allowance system' and the 'whole wage system' must be seen as crude ideal types drawn out from the complexities of reality for the purpose of gaining a clearer understanding of our subject. It is likely that further research will serve to refine these types and perhaps reveal others. With the aim of illustrating just a few intricacies of the topic, I turn now to some of my own empirical research.

The Allocation and Control of Income in Twenty-Five Households

My study fell into two parts. In the first part twenty-five women were interviewed during their stay at a Women's Aid refuge;[36] in the second part another twenty-five women were interviewed, and subsequently follow-up interviews were carried out with both groups of women after they had left the refuge.

The first set of interviews revealed that disputes about money played a significant part in the accounts which the women gave of their relationships with the men who had battered them: twenty of the twenty-five said that difficulties with money had been among their marital problems. Accordingly more detailed questions about money were included in the interviews carried out with the second group of twenty-five women, and it is the results of these interviews which I discuss here. Of these twenty-five women fifteen said that disputes over money had been among their marital problems. (Thus of the total sample of fifty women 70 per cent saw money as a problem area.) Of the twenty-five women in the second sample nineteen were wives and six had been cohabiting with the men who had assaulted them; however, the words 'wife' and 'husband' will be used throughout for the sake of clarity, since all the cohabiting couples had been living together for a considerable time. All the women had children living with them at home, and most of these children had left home with their mothers and had come to the refuge. The interviews revealed a very wide variation in the patterns of family budgeting. At one extreme there was a household in which the wife earned and managed all the money, reluctantly giving her husband a small amount for his personal spending; at the other extreme one

Figure 1   Diagrammatic Representation of Income Allocation Within
Twenty-five Households in South-East England, 1977-78

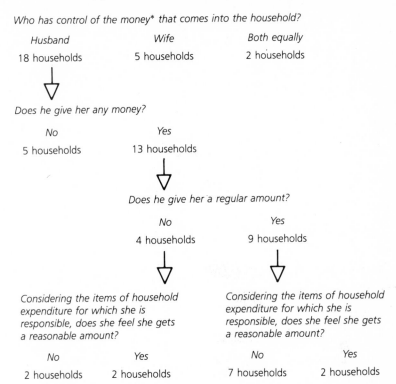

Who has control of the money* that comes into the household?

Husband	Wife	Both equally
18 households	5 households	2 households

Does he give her any money?

No	Yes
5 households	13 households

Does he give her a regular amount?

No	Yes
4 households	9 households

Considering the items of household
expenditure for which she is
responsible, does she feel she gets
a reasonable amount?

No	Yes
2 households	2 households

Considering the items of household
expenditure for which she is
responsible, does she feel she gets
a reasonable amount?

No	Yes
7 households	2 households

*This includes income from the husband's employment, the wife's regular employment, and social
security benefits, and excludes child benefit and the wife's occasional earnings.

husband kept all the money for himself (£200 a week at the height of the summer) and gave his wife 'a pound or two occasionally for tights'.

The chief work of most of the women was looking after their homes and children. In addition to this three were employed occasionally to do casual field-work, two helped their husbands in the businesses which they owned, one was a typist, and one had both a daytime job as a washer-up and an evening job as a nursing assistant. In this last household the woman was the chief earner, while in the other twenty-four households the man's was the chief income. Out of the twenty-five husbands, seven were unemployed, twelve were engaged in manual work, one was a foreman, two owned their own small business, and three would be classified as 'intermediate nonmanual' workers according to the Registrar General's classification. In eight families the wives did not know exactly how much their husbands earned, though several had a rather rough idea of how much it might be. The other seventeen wives did know how much came into the house. The sums involved might vary from week to week; in many cases it would have been impossible for the man to give his wife a regular amount of housekeeping money since the amount which he himself was able to earn varied so greatly.

The patterns of income allocation within the twenty-five households are set out diagrammatically in Figure 1, where the very wide extent of the variations becomes clear. The diagram is based upon the answers to three questions—'How much does he give you each week?', 'What do you have to pay for out of that?' and 'What is he expected to pay for?' A check-list of the main items of household expenditure—food, clothes, fuel and rent or mortage—was used to discover which partner was responsible for paying for these items.

In a fifth of the households the wife was responsible for all the main items of collective expenditure, receiving the wage packet or the social security money and paying all the bills which came into the household; four of these five households were living on social security. Every woman who had control of the family income still expected to give her husband money for his own use, though the size of this sum was the subject of some dispute. Thus one woman, whose husband was unemployed, stated:

He was drawing for me and the children—he was getting £41 and he thought that I could pay rent, housekeep, buy food, and he could have money out of that for drink, which is ridiculous. He gives me all the money, but he wants the money back if he wants to go out for a drink. Like last week, he said he'd paid the rent, but he had just gone and drunk it. I gives him the money and I goes to a jumble sale—I'm always going there to get clothes for the children and that, because you can't really afford clothes when you only get £41 a week. When I comes back he was really drunk—as drunk as a mat, absolutely speechless. If you've got some money to last you, like till you get your next Giro, which you have to make it last when you've got five children, he'd want that money for drink, which is ridiculous.

In another five of the twenty-five households the wife received no money at all. In one instance this was because the husband was the owner of a cafe; his wife, who helped him in the cafe, was expected to eat all her meals there and she and the children were clothed by her parents. In the case of the wives who were not given any housekeeping money the most usual pattern was for the couple to go shopping together on a 'family shopping night'; the wife would choose the goods which the household needed and the husband would pay for them at the check-out. Thus what looks like the symmetrical family at its most egalitarian may in fact represent a particularly inegalitarian form of marital relationship. It may be that some of these wives are careless with money; however, in most cases they were clearly capable women who managed perfectly well when they were living at the refuge. Their marital difficulties were compounded by the fact that, like many married women, they had been completely unable to acquire any personal savings at all, so that when they were driven to leave home they were completely and immediately dependent on the support of the state.

Two couples operated a pooling system, sharing the control and allocation of household money; in the remaining thirteen households the husband retained control of the income but delegated responsibility for the expenditure of parts of it to his wife. These couples operated different types of allowance systems. Here the pattern is very complicated, since not only do the amounts which wives are given vary but their financial responsibilities vary too, and the amount which a woman received may be plenty to pay the bills which are her responsibility or it may be ridiculously inadequate. Whether a wife regards what she receives as a reasonable amount depends mainly on two calculations; firstly, it will depend on the relationship between the amount she receives and the amount she needs to spend and, secondly, it will depend on the relationship between what she thinks her husband earns and what she knows he gives her. Thus the wife of a foreman who received £30 per week to buy food and clothes for two adults and three children felt that this was reasonable, while the wife of an engineer felt that £15 per week to buy food for the household and clothes for herself and their two children was not reasonable when her husband was earning £127 per week. On the other hand, the wife of an electrician who was earning £120 per week considered her weekly allowance of £10 quite reasonable since this was her own pocket-money: this was another couple who went shopping together, the wife choosing and the husband paying for what she chose, but in this case she felt it was a reasonable arrangement. Among those who felt that the regular amount of housekeeping which they received was not a reasonable amount was the woman who gave the following response:

'He never used to give me enough housekeeping money, and I was always going on at him about it, and this used to get his back up, saying he couldn't afford it.'

'How much did he give you?'

'He used to give me £15 a week.'

'Did he earn much more than that?'

'Oh, yes, he had plenty.'

'Did he tell you how much he earned?'

'No. That was really the main reason why he used to hit me, because I used to keep on and on and on about it.'

'What did you have to pay for out of the £15?'

'I had to pay the milk bill, which was almost £3, and buy all the food for five of us and feed two cats.'

'Did he pay the other bills?'

'He was supposed to pay the electricity; but the day after he took an overdose the electricity board came round to cut me off. I explained to them what had happened, and then I went to the Social Services, and they put a stay on it and his firm paid the bill.'

'What about the rent—who paid that?'

'He used to pay the rent. But the rest of the money he just wasted. He was just hopeless with money.'

Instances such as this demonstrate the inadequacy of studies in which housewives are simply asked how much housekeeping money they receive. It is necessary to know not only how much they receive but also what they are expected to buy out of that amount. And if the ideology of the 'sharing' of the chief earner's income means anything, it is necessary to relate the amount of housekeeping money to the amount which the chief earner himself receives. These examples also demonstrate the effect of the income being still 'his' income, however much it may be shared. Only one wife out of the twenty-five had a specific amount for her own pocket-money, while all of them assumed that their husbands would have money for their own spending.

Many of these women and children did in fact live 'in poverty', whether poverty consists in living below the level laid down by the Supplementary Benefits Commission, or in patterns of expenditure such as 'having to get all our clothes from jumble sales'. Studies which ask about the wife's housekeeping also assume that she does get a regular amount of money to buy items for the household; as this small study has shown many wives do not get 'housekeeping money' in the accepted sense. Half of the women whose husbands kept control of the money that came into the house either did not get any money for housekeeping or received irregular amounts. Fourteen of the twenty-five either did not get any money or felt that what they did get was unreasonably little. Even in the couples where the wife managed the family budget, disputes about the husband's personal spending money led to quarrels.

Several other researchers working in this field have confirmed these findings and have discussed the ways in which the inequitable distribution of income within the household can contribute to the problems of battered women.[37] They have found, as I did, that some women commented that they were better off living on supplementary benefit than they had been when they were living with their husbands.[38] Since supplementary benefit levels are customarily taken as the official poverty line in Britain, the implication is that these women and probably their children were living below the poverty level before leaving home. As one woman said:

One thing I've found, since we've been here, she's started to sleep all night. I think, some of it is that we were that short of money that I couldn't give her as much to eat as what I can here. I found that actually now I'm on my own with Mandy—I'm financially better off. I'm one of those—I have to work everything out before I spend any money. I never go shopping without a shopping list, and I only buy what is on that list. When I got my money, I used to put my rent away, put my milk money away, put my money away for the electricity, put my money away for the gas bottles. That's what used to annoy me—he used to spend £4 a week on cigarettes, and I said 'They don't allow you for that. That's coming out of money they allow us for food and that'. I said 'You're more or less smoking half of our food money'.

Many of those who have written about violence in marriage have seen it as a problem related to the socially structured inequality of men and women in society in general, and of husbands and wives within marriage.[39] It follows that, if wife battering is related to the structured inequality of husband and wife, and if this inequality expresses itself most clearly in the relative economic situations of the spouses, then money is likely to be a key problem area in violent marriages.

It is important to stress, however, that these twenty-five women may be in many respects an unrepresentative group, except insofar as they represent the total population of those who go for help to women's refuges. Not only were their marriages, by definition, troubled, but in addition they had left their homes and had gone with their children for shelter in a women's refuge. Such women may well be unusually courageous and capable. Thus, it is not necessarily possible to generalize from this small study to the broader patterns of financial allocation within marriages in general. What the data do is, firstly, to illuminate the problems faced by such women and, secondly and more generally, to demonstrate some of the difficulties involved in gaining a better understanding of the patterns of the control and allocation of money within marriage.

The Significance of Different Types of Housekeeping System

However, identifying and describing the different types of allocation system is only the first step. Inevitably many complicated issues are raised. What determines the pattern of allocation within any one household? What distinguishes the household with the whole wage system from that with the allowance system, or the pooling system? What is the significance for individual living standards of different patterns of financial allocation and responsibility? When and why do allocation systems change? How much does it matter if one spouse has or does not have private spending money, or savings, for which he or she does not have to account? Within the limits of this article it is impossible to take the argument very far; however, I would suggest that there are three dimensions to any causal analysis of housekeeping systems. These are the stage in the life cycle which the family has reached, the income level of the household, and the occupational, regional and ethnic culture within which the family is located.

I would hypothesize, first, that there are clear links between the stage in the life cycle and financial arrangements and I would suggest that the pooling system may be characteristic of the newly married couple who are both earning; this may change to the allowance system when the wife leaves paid employment to look after young children, and change again to a modified pooling system in the household with two earners or where teenage children may be contributing to the household economy; finally, the pensioner household may adopt the whole wage system. On the other hand, is it possible that couples keep the same system throughout their married life, and that the prevalence of the whole wage system among older couples is an effect of generation rather than stage in the life cycle?

It is interesting that studies of marital power have emphasized the importance of the stage in the life cycle, and have shown that the husband's power within the marriage is at its highest when the wife is not earning but is engaged in looking after small children. The wife's power within the marriage increases when she is herself earning.[40] Studies of marital power have largely ignored patterns of financial control *within* marriage, but they have stressed the significance of economic resources as an important source of power, usually defining these resources in terms of earnings.

Secondly, there must be links between the income level of the household and financial arrangements within it. I would suggest that the whole wage system is characteristic of the household whose income is small, with the wife controlling all collective expenditure and the husband retaining only his personal spending money. When money is very short having one person responsible for family budgeting helps to ensure that all the bills are paid; managing the budget becomes a chore rather than a source of power within the marriage. In very poor households no one has much freedom of action: in the farm workers' families described by Flora Thompson the men may have had 10 per cent of the family income, but it still only bought one pint of beer on six nights of the week.[41] This is why, though in one sense the wife in the whole wage system may have more power within the marriage, both she and her husband have so little room for manoeuvre that neither has very much freedom of action in his or her life.

At middle income levels, especially where only the husband is earning, it seems likely that the whole wage system gives way to some sort of allowance system, in which the husband retains control not only over his personal spending money but also over larger proportions of household resources, giving his wife a specific amount each week or month. Thus more affluent households offer the possibility of greater inequality between husband and wife: a wife who gets a housekeeping allowance may have little room for manoeuvre. If she is not earning she may have little or no personal spending money. Households with higher income levels, especially those with two earners, seem more likely than others to adopt the pooling system. This may reflect a more egalitarian pattern of marital relationships, or it may be a consequence of greater affluence and a lesser need to budget carefully. The pooling system also seems to be more common among those who have received a longer than average education.[42]

There may also be a relationship between patterns of poverty and the type of allocation system adopted by the household. Thus, while the whole wage system seems to be associated with what Rowntree called 'primary' poverty, the allowance system may be associated with what he, somewhat misleadingly, called 'secondary' poverty.[43] There is a crucial difference between the two in that the whole wage system is a consequence of primary poverty, whereas 'secondary' poverty is a possible consequence of the allowance system, if the allowance is not adequate for the goods and services it has to buy. Such 'secondary' poverty may be particularly likely to occur at times of inflation, when, as we have seen (pages 320–1, above), rises in housekeeping allowances tend to lag behind increases in wages. The relationship between poverty and financial arrangements within households was emphasized by Fiegehen, Lansley and Smith in their careful study of household poverty:

The threat or the actuality of poverty may also have a significant effect on patterns of household income sharing; such sharing may in turn greatly influence the extent to which poverty is observed and exists. This study has simply confirmed the validity of this observation but it has been unable to draw upon any specific knowledge of the extent and nature of sharing economic resources within the household, nor to illuminate these activities. This area of research deserves some priority.[44]

At the other extreme of the income scale it may be that there is a link between wealth and a fourth allocation system based on both husband and wife controlling their own sources of earned, or unearned income, in what one might call the 'individual control' system.

However, stage in the life cycle and income level do not by themselves explain all the variations in allocation systems. Any attempt at causal analysis can only be extremely tentative; however, it is likely that household allocation systems are also linked with various aspects of the occupational, regional and ethnic culture within which the household is located.

I would suggest that the nature of the local labour market is important, particularly in the extent of the employment opportunities it offers for women and in the industrial structure of the area. Thus, areas with a long tradition of secure female employment may be more likely also to have allocation systems of the whole wage or pooling type; by contrast, areas dominated by occupations such as fishing, mining, or heavy industry, with a high degree of male solidarity or particular payment systems may be more likely to have allocation systems of the allowance type.[45]

Social and economic conditions in earlier historical periods may also be reflected in present-day allocation systems. In the peasant and labouring families of pre-industrial Europe the household or family was the central economic unit and all members of the household were expected to work, though men and women customarily performed different tasks. Married women's responsibilities traditionally included management of the household economy and the keeping of the household accounts. It seems that in the early years of the industrial revolution this pattern continued, so much so that in some areas men's wages were negotiated with, and paid to, their wives.[46] Married women continued to be responsible for the management of the household and, in particular, for the family finances. Le Play described the Parisian carpenter's wife:

She immediately receives his monthly wage; it is she who each morning gives her husband the money necessary to buy the meals he takes outside the house. To her alone . . . in conformity with the custom which prevails among French workers, are confined the administration of the interior of the home and the entire disposition of the family resources.[47]

If we look at the whole wage system in the context of a long historical tradition of female management of the domestic economy, the allowance system begins to appear as a comparatively recent development. It seems as though women in working-class families began to lose full control over family finances early in the twentieth century, increasingly receiving an allowance from their husbands, who kept the rest and determined how it was spent. These changes are extremely complicated and must be differentiated geographically, ethnically and over time; they must also be seen in the context of the fight for the 'family wage' and the development of the 'bourgeois' family form, which assumes a 'breadwinner' husband who is the household head, and a 'housewife' who cares for and services her husband and children.[48] To a large extent this is the family form which was enshrined in much of the British social policy legislation passed during the first half of the twentieth century.

Conclusion

It is important to recognize that, while patterns of family life vary widely over time and space, social policy legislation, by making certain assumptions, can prolong the existence or increase the significance of one particular family form or another. The fact that an expansion in the scope of social policy coincided with a time when, among policy-makers at least, the bourgeois family form was held to be the norm has had far-reaching implications, for example, in the definition of those two key units in social and economic policy—the tax unit and the household. Without necessarily arguing that units other than these should form the basis of social policy, it is important that we should appreciate the implications of adopting these two as standard units for the purposes of, for example, measuring poverty, distributing welfare benefits, or calculating tax reliefs.[49]

Any discussion of the policy implications of this whole subject is handicapped by our lack of detailed knowledge about the patterns of money management within marriage. The new empirical material presented here all relates to women who were considering divorce and who, at least while they were at the refuge, were dependent on supplementary benefit. It seems likely that the inequitable distribution of resources is a fairly common problem within troubled marriages, which would imply that in these circumstances it might be useful to explore the possibility of other patterns of social security payment such as splitting the benefit payment when a couple is living on social security, or paying benefit to women with children who are not receiving adequate financial support from their husbands. Some women might otherwise feel forced to leave the matrimonial home in order to receive support for themselves and their children.[50]

However, most married women who receive inadequate housekeeping allowances turn not to the Supplementary Benefits Commission but to the possibility of earning money for themselves and their children. The difference which a wife's earnings make to the standard of living of household members will depend partly on the allocation system within the household. Her earnings will be particularly important in a household with an allowance system, where the allowance is not adequate for what it is supposed to buy. In these circumstances the standard of living of dependent children is likely to be increased more by their mother taking a job than by their father earning the same amount extra in the form of overtime earnings or bonus payments. Similarly, an increase in child benefits is particularly important, not only for the sake of children who are in poverty because of low household incomes but also for those who are in poverty because of the inequitable distribution of income within households.

More generally it would be interesting to be able to explore the implications of different methods of payment of benefits, wages and salaries. What would be the effect on the living standards of children in two-parent families living on supplementary benefit if the payment was made to the wife rather than the husband? This might not make much difference, given that the whole wage system is more frequently found among households living on social security, but it could be an effective way of raising the standard of living of the children in such households, and it could have far-reaching consequences, affecting family members both in their relationships with each other and in their own personal sense of self esteem. Again, what are the consequences of paying child benefit into a bank account if only the husband has a cheque-book? And what happens to systems of allocation, and thus to standards of living within households, when wages and salaries cease to be paid in cash and are paid instead by cheque?

More work also needs to be done on the significance of different financial arrangements for marital relationships. How much do particular allocative systems *reflect* patterns of power within marriage and how much do they *affect* such patterns? Several of the women whom I interviewed after they had left the refuge specifically made a connection between the state of their marriage and the way in which the housekeeping money was allocated. One of them (who left her husband a few weeks later) said:

I never used to see the rest of his wages before I went to the refuge. Then when we came back he told me I could have all his wage packet. He'd open it in front of me and count it out so that I knew what he'd got. And then I had to give him his money back. But then it went back to him keeping it for himself. Now he tells me what I have and he, he thinks what he needs. He says I need twenty pounds a week, so I've got no option. He decides, he decides on everything.

I would not want to suggest that the women interviewed at the refuge are representative of married women in general. However, I would suggest that a better knowledge of the patterns of distribution of financial resources within marriage is likely to help towards a better understanding of some of the tensions and inequalities within marriage. In a society in which money is a form of power, and in which income is used as a measure of worth, the relative economic situations of husband and wife must be reflected in their relationship.

Notes

1. Central Statistical Office, *Social Trends no. 10*, HMSO, London, 1979, p. 133. 0047-2794/80/0000-0041 $02.00 © 1980 Cambridge University Press.
2. This problem has been discussed by many of those who have been concerned with measuring the extent and nature of poverty; see in particular P. Townsend, *Poverty in the United Kingdom*, Penguin Books, Harmondsworth, 1979, pp. 270-1 and 919-26; G. C. Fiegehen, P. S. Lansley and A. D. Smith, *Poverty and Progress in Britain 1953-73*,

Cambridge University Press, London, 1977, p. 46; and A. B. Atkinson, 'Poverty and Income Inequality in Britain', in D. Wedderburn (ed.), *Poverty, Inequality and Class Structure,* Cambridge University Press, London, 1974, p. 44.

3. The idea of sharing is itself problematic. What would a 'fair share' be for any one family member? It has always been assumed that dependent children 'need' varying incomes according to their age, and these assumptions are reflected in the sums paid by, for example, the Supplementary Benefits Commission. It is not the intention of this article to question this, though some recent work has suggested that present levels of supplementary benefit payments, particularly those for children, are not high enough—see D. Piachaud, *The Cost of a Child,* Children Poverty Action Group, London, 1979.

4. I am grateful to John Butler of the University of Kent for this idea.

5. See for example H. Land, 'Women: Supporters or Supported?', in D. Leonard Barker and S. A. Allen (eds), *Sexual Divisions and Society,* Tavistock Publications, London, 1976; M. McIntosh, 'The State and the Oppression of Women', in A. Kuhn and A. M. Wolpe (eds), *Feminism and Materialism,* Routledge and Kegan Paul, Henley-on-Thames, 1978; and K. O'Donovan, 'The Male Appendage: Legal Definitions of Women', in S. Burman (ed.), *Fit Work for Women,* Croom Helm, London, 1979.

6. H. Land and R. Parker, 'Family Policy in the United Kingdom', in A. J. Kahn and S. B. Kamerman (eds), *Family Policy,* Columbia University Press, New York, 1978, p. 366—E. Rathbone, *Family Allowances,* Allen and Unwin, London, 1949, p. 1.

7. On this last point see P. Townsend, *The Family Life of Old People,* Routledge and Kegan Paul, London, 1957, ch. 6.

8. See L. Hamil, *Wives as Sole and Joint Breadwinners,* Department of Health and Social Security (DHSS), Government Economic Service Working Paper, no. 13, London, 1978.

9. This research was funded by the DHSS and based at the University of Kent at Canterbury, 1976–80.

10. M. Young, 'Distribution of Income within the Family', *British Journal of Sociology,* 3 (1952), 303.

11. M. Young and P. Willmott, *The Symmetrical Family,* Routledge and Kegan Paul, London, 1975, p. 82.

12. G. Gorer, *Sex and Marriage in England Today,* Nelson, London, 1971, p. 92. See also Townsend, *The Family Life of Old People,* p. 82—of forty-five wives, twenty-seven did not know how much their husbands earned.

13. A. Hunt, J. Fox and M. Morgan, *Families and their Needs with Particular Reference to One-Parent Families,* HMSO, London, 1973.

14. H. Land, *Large Families in London,* G. Bell and Sons, London, 1969; and A. Gray, 'The Working Class Family as an Economic Unit', unpublished doctoral thesis, University of Edinburgh, 1974.

15. See M. Kerr, *The People of Ship Street,* Routledge and Kegan Paul, London, 1958; and A. J. Humphreys, *New Dubliners: Urbanisation and the Irish Family,* Routledge and Kegan Paul, London, 1966.

16. Gorer, *op. cit.*

17. Land, *Large Families in London.*

18. J. E. Todd and L. M. Jones, *Matrimonial Property,* HMSO, London, 1972, p. 31.

19. F. Thompson, *Lark Rise to Candleford,* Oxford University Press, London, 1954, p. 54.

20. See G. Rowntree, 'The Finances of Founding a Family', *Scottish Journal of Political Economy,* 1:3 (1954), 201–32; Gray, *op. cit.;* T. Brennan, *Reshaping a City,* House of Grant, Glasgow, 1959; and Land, *Large Families in London.*

21. N. Dennis, F. Henriques and C. Slaughter, *Coal is our Life,* Eyre and Spottiswoode, London, 1956, p. 201.

22. M. Pember Reeves, *Round about a Pound a Week,* G. Bell and Sons, London, 1914.

23. J. B. Mays, *Growing up in a City,* Liverpool University Press, 1954.

24. J. Turnstall, *The Fishermen,* MacGibbon and Kee, London, 1962.

25. L. Syson and M. Young, 'Poverty in Bethnal Green', in M. Young (ed.), *Poverty Report 1974*, Temple Smith, London, 1974, p. 110.

26. Woman's Own, *Housekeeping Survey*, 20 September 1975.

27. Lister, 'Who bears the Burden?', in *The Great Child Benefit Robbery*, Child Poverty Action Group, London, 1976, p. 26.

28. H. Land, 'Inequalities in Large Families', in R. Chester and J. Peel (eds), *Equalities and Inequalities in Family Life*, Academic Press, London, 1977.

29. Gray, *op. cit.* p. 84.

30. F. Zweig, *The Worker in the Affluent Society*, Heinemann, London, 1961.

31. Gray, *op. cit.* p. 195.

32. A. Hunt, *A Survey of Women's Employment*, Vol. II, HMSO, London, 1968.

33. P. Jephcott, N. Seear and J. Smith, *Married Women Working*, Allen and Unwin, London, 1962.

34. E. Bott, *Family and Social Network*, Allen and Unwin, London, 1957.

35. Todd and Jones, *op. cit.* p. 29.

36. See J. Pahl, *A Refuge for Battered Women*, HMSO, London, 1978.

37. See R. Emerson Dobash and Russell Dobash, *Violence against Wives: A Case against the Patriarchy*, Open Books, Shepton Mallet, Somerset, 1980; and V. Binney, G. Harkell and J. Nixon, 'Refuge Provision for Battered Women', *Housing*, 15:12 (1979), 6.

38. See D. Marsden, *Mothers Alone*, Penguin Books, Harmondsworth, 1969. Marsden found that 'non-support' was the cause most commonly given by women for the ending of their marriages and he commented, 'One in three said they were better off than when they were married'—p. 62.

39. See Dobash and Dobash, *op. cit.*: M. Freeman, *Violence in the Home*, Saxon House, Farnborough, Hampshire, 1979; W. J. Goode, 'Force and Violence in the Family', in S. Steinmetz and M. Straus (eds), *Violence in the Family*, Harper and Row, New York, 1974; J. Hanmer, 'Community Action, Women's Aid and the Women's Liberation Movement', in M. Mayo (ed.), *Women in the Community*, Routledge and Kegan Paul, Henley-on-Thames, 1977; and D. Marsden, 'Sociological Perspectives on Family Violence', in J. Martin (ed.), *Violence and the Family*, John Wiley and Sons, Chichester, 1978.

40. See R. D. Blood and D. M. Wolfe, *Husbands and Wives*, Collier-Macmillan, New York, 1965; D. Gillespie, 'Who has the Power?: The Marital Struggle', in H. P. Dreitzel (ed.), *Family, Marriage and the Struggle of the Sexes*, Macmillan, New York, 1972; and A. Michel, 'Comparative Data concerning the Interaction in French and American Families', *Journal of Marriage and the Family*, 29 (1967), 337–44.

41. Thompson, *op. cit.*

42. Gorer, *op. cit.*

43. B. S. Rowntree, *Poverty and Progress: A Second Social Survey of York*, Longman, London, 1941.

44. Fiegehen *et al.*, *op. cit.* p. 118.

45. See Dennis *et al.*, *op. cit.*; and Tunstall, *op. cit.*

46. L. A. Tilly and J. W. Scott, *Women, Work and Family*, Holt, Rinehart and Winston, New York, 1978, p. 139.

47. F. Le Play, *Les Ouvriers Européens*, Vol. V, Imprimeric Imperiale, Paris, 1855, p. 427—quoted in J. W. Scott and L. A. Tilly, 'Women's Work and the Family in Nineteenth Century Europe', *Comparative Studies in Society and History*, 17 (1975), 49. See also P. Stearns, 'Working Class Women in Britain 1890–1914', in M. Viners (ed.), *Suffer and be Still*, Bloomington, Indiana, 1972—suggesting that the whole wage system was also typical of working class families in London in the late nineteenth century.

48. For further discussion of the complicated issues raised here see M. Poster, *Critical Theory of the Family*, Pluto Press, London, 1978, Scott and Tilly, *op. cit.*; Tilly and Scott, *op. cit.*; and C. Bell and H. Newby, 'Husbands and Wives: The Dynamics of the

Deferential Dialectic', in D. Leonard Barker and S. A. Allen (eds), *Dependence and Exploitation in Work and Marriage,* Longman, London, 1976.
49. For further discussion of this issue see H. Land, 'Social Security and the Division of Unpaid Work in the Home and Paid Employment in the Labour Market', in DHSS, *Social Security Research,* HMSO, London, 1977.
50. For further discussion of some of the issues raised here see DHSS, *Social Assistance: A Review of the Supplementary Benefits Scheme in Great Britain,* DHSS, London, 1978; and Supplementary Benefits Commission, *Response of the Supplementary Benefits Commission to 'Social Assistance: A Review of the Supplementary Benefits Scheme in Great Britain'* SBA Paper no. 9, HMSO, London, 1978.

The Two Marriages
Jessie S. Bernard

The Future of Whose Marriage?

■   Both Uncle Honoré and Gigi's grandmother remembered it well, according to Alan Jay Lerner's lyric. And this is what it had been like according to Uncle Honoré: "it was a lovely moonlit evening in May. You arrived at nine o'clock in your gold dress only a little late for our dinner engagement with friends. Afterwards there was that delightful carriage ride when we were so engrossed in one another that we didn't notice you had lost your glove." Ah, yes, Uncle Honoré remembered it well indeed, down to the last detail.

Or, come to think of it, did he? For Gigi's grandmother remembered it too, but not at all the same way. "There was no moon that rainy June evening. For once I was on time when we met at eight o'clock at the restaurant where we dined alone. You complimented me on my pretty blue dress. Afterwards we took a long walk and we were so engrossed in one another that we didn't notice I had lost my comb until my hair came tumbling down."

The Japanese motion picture *Rashomon* was built on the same idea—four different versions of the same events. So, also, was Robert Gover's story of the college boy and the black prostitute in his *One Hundred Dollar Misunderstanding.* Also in this category is the old talmudic story of the learned rabbi called upon to render a decision in a marital situation. After listening carefully to the first spouse's story, he shook his head, saying, "You are absolutely right"; and, after listening equally carefully to the other spouse's story, he again shook his head, saying, "You are absolutely right."

There is no question in any of these examples of deliberate deceit or prevarication or insincerity or dishonesty. Both Uncle Honoré and Grandmamma are equally sincere, equally honest, equally "right." The discrepancies in their stories make a charming duet in *Gigi*. And even the happiest of mates can match such differences in their own memories.

In the case of Uncle Honoré and Grandmamma, we can explain the differences in the pictures they had in their heads of that evening half a century earlier: memories play strange tricks on all of us. But the same differences in the accounts of what happened show up also among modern couples even immediately after the event. In one study, for example, half of all the partners gave differing replies to questions about what had happened in a laboratory decision-making session they had just left. Other couples give different responses to questions about ordinary day-by-day events like lawn mowing as well as about romantic events. Once our attention has been called to the fact that both mates are equally sincere, equally honest, equally "right," the presence of two marriages in every marital union becomes clear—even obvious, as artists and wise persons have been telling us for so long.

Anyone, therefore, discussing the future of marriage has to specify whose marriage he is talking about: the husband's or the wife's. For there is by now a very considerable body of well-authenticated research to show that there really are two marriages in every marital union, and that they do not always coincide.

"His" and "Her" Marriages

Under the jargon "discrepant responses," the differences in the marriages of husbands and wives have come under the careful scrutiny of a score of researchers. They have found that when they ask husbands and wives identical questions about the union, they often get quite different replies. There is usually agreement on the number of children they have and a few other such verifiable items, although not, for example, on length of premarital acquaintance and of engagement, on age at marriage and interval between marriage and birth of first child. Indeed, with respect to even such basic components of the marriage as frequency of sexual relations, social interaction, household tasks, and decision making, they seem to be reporting on different marriages. As, I think, they are.

In the area of sexual relations, for example, Kinsey and his associates found different responses in from one- to two-thirds of the couples they studied. Kinsey interpreted these differences in terms of selective perception. In the generation he was studying, husbands wanted sexual relations oftener than the wives did, thus "the females may be overestimating the actual frequencies" and "the husbands . . . are probably underestimating the frequencies." The differences might also have been vestiges of the probable situation earlier in the marriage when the desired frequency of sexual relations was about six to seven times greater among husbands than among wives. This difference may have become so impressed on the spouses that it remained in their minds even after the difference itself had disappeared or even been reversed. In a sample of happily married, middle-class couples a generation later, Harold Feldman found that both spouses attributed to their mates more influence in the area of sex than they did to themselves.

Companionship, as reflected in talking together, he found, was another area where differences showed up. Replies differed on three-fourths of all the items studied, including the topics talked about, the amount of time spent talking with each other, and which partner initiated conversation. Both partners claimed that whereas they talked more about topics of interest to their mates, their mates initiated conversations about topics primarily of interest to themselves. Harold Feldman concluded that projection in terms of needs was distorting even simple, everyday events, and lack of communication was permitting the distortions to continue.[1] It seemed to him that "if these sex differences can occur so often among these generally well satisfied couples, it would not be surprising to find even less consensus and more distortion in other less satisfied couples."

Although, by and large, husbands and wives tend to become more alike with age, in this study of middle-class couples, differences increased with length of marriage rather than decreased, as one might logically have expected. More couples in the later than in the earlier years, for example, had differing pictures in their heads about how often they laughed together, discussed together, exchanged ideas, or worked together on projects, and about how well things were going between them.

The special nature of sex and the amorphousness of social interaction help to explain why differences in response might occur. But household tasks? They are fairly objective and clear-cut and not all that emotion-laden. Yet even here there are his-and-her versions. Since the division of labor in the household is becoming increasingly an issue in marriage, the uncovering of differing replies in this area is especially relevant. Hard as it is to believe, Granbois and Willett tell us that more than half of the partners in one sample disagreed on who kept track of money and bills. On the question, who mows the lawn? more than a fourth disagreed. Even family income was not universally agreed on.

---

1. For a discussion of the part played by communication in all relations between the sexes, see Jessie Bernard, *The Sex Game* (Englewood Cliffs, N.J., Prentice-Hall, 1968; New York: Atheneum, 1972). Chapter 10 deals with communication in marriage.

These differences about sexual relations, companionship, and domestic duties tell us a great deal about the two marriages. But power or decision making can cover all aspects of a relationship. The question of who makes decisions or who exercises power has therefore attracted a great deal of research attention. If we were interested in who really had the power or who really made the decisions, the research would be hopeless. Would it be possible to draw any conclusion from a situation in which both partners agree that the husband ordered the wife to make all the decisions? Still, an enormous literature documents the quest of researchers for answers to the question of marital power. The major contribution it has made has been to reveal the existence of differences in replies between husbands and wives.

The presence of such inconsistent replies did not at first cause much concern. The researchers apologized for them but interpreted them as due to methodological inadequacies; if only they could find a better way to approach the problem, the differences would disappear. Alternatively, the use of only the wife's responses, which were more easily available, was justified on the grounds that differences in one direction between the partners in one marriage compensated for differences in another direction between the partners in another marriage and thus canceled them out. As, indeed, they did. For when Granbois and Willett, two market researchers, analyzed the replies of husbands and wives separately, the overall picture was in fact the same for both wives and husbands. Such canceling out of differences in the total sample, however, concealed almost as much as it revealed about the individual couples who composed it. Granbois and Willett concluded, as Kinsey had earlier, that the "discrepancies . . . reflect differing perceptions on the part of responding partners." And this was the heart of the matter.

Differing reactions to common situations, it should be noted, are not at all uncommon. They are recognized in the folk wisdom embedded in the story of the blind men all giving different replies to questions on the nature of the elephant. One of the oldest experiments in juridical psychology demonstrates how different the statements of witnesses of the same act can be. Even in laboratory studies, it takes intensive training of raters to make it possible for them to arrive at agreement on the behavior they observe.

It has long been known that people with different backgrounds see things differently. We know, for example, that poor children perceive coins as larger than do children from more affluent homes. Boys and girls perceive differently. A good deal of the foundation for projective tests rests on the different ways in which individuals see identical stimuli. And this perception—or, as the sociologists put it, definition of the situation— is reality for them. In this sense, the realities of the husband's marriage are different from those of the wife's.

Finally, one of the most perceptive of the researchers, Constantina Safilios-Rothschild, asked the crucial question: Was what they were getting, even with the best research techniques, family sociology or wives' family sociology? She answered her own question: What the researchers who relied on wives' replies exclusively were reporting on was the wife's marriage. The husband's was not necessarily the same. There were, in fact, two marriages present:

One explanation of discrepancies between the responses of husbands and wives may be the possibility of two "realities," the husband's subjective reality and the wife's subjective reality—two perspectives which do not always coincide. Each spouse perceives "facts" and situations differently according to his own needs, values, attitudes, and beliefs. An "objective" reality could possibly exist only in the trained observer's evaluation, if it does exist at all.

Interpreting the different replies of husbands and wives in terms of selective perception, projection of needs, values, attitudes, and beliefs, or different definitions of the situation, by no means renders them trivial or incidental or justifies dismissing or ignoring them. They are, rather, fundamental for an understanding of the two marriages, his and hers, and we ignore them at the peril of serious misunderstanding of marriage, present as well as future.

Is There an Objective Reality in Marriage?

Whether or not husbands and wives perceive differently or define situations differently, still sexual relations are taking place, companionship is or is not occurring, tasks about the house are being performed, and decisions are being made everyday by someone. In this sense, some sort of "reality" does exist. David Olson went to the laboratory to see if he could uncover it.

He first asked young couples expecting babies such questions as these: Which one of them would decide whether to buy insurance for the newborn child? Which one would decide the husband's part in diaper changing? Which one would decide whether the new mother would return to work or to school? When there were differences in the answers each gave individually on the questionnaire, he set up a situation in which together they had to arrive at a decision in his laboratory. He could then compare the results of the questionnaire with the results in the simulated situation. He found neither spouse's questionnaire response any more accurate than the other's; that is, neither conformed better to the behavioral "reality" of the laboratory than the other did.

The most interesting thing, however, was that husbands, as shown on their questionnaire response, perceived themselves as having more power than they actually did have in the laboratory "reality," and wives perceived that they had less. Thus, whereas three-fourths (73 percent) of the husbands overestimated their power in decision making, 70 percent of the wives underestimated theirs. Turk and Bell found similar results in Canada. Both spouses tend to attribute decision-making power to the one who has the "right" to make the decision. Their replies, that is, conform to the model of marriage that has characterized civilized mankind for millennia. It is this model rather than their own actual behavior that husbands and wives tend to perceive.

We are now zeroing in on the basic reality. We can remove the quotation marks. For there is, in fact, an objective reality in marriage. It is a reality that resides in the cultural—legal, moral, and conventional—prescriptions and proscriptions and, hence, expectations that constitute marriage. It is the reality that is reflected in the minds of the spouses themselves. The differences between the marriages of husbands and of wives are structural realities, and it is these structural differences that constitute the basis for the different psychological realities.

The Authority Structure of Marriage

Authority is an institutional phenomenon; it is strongly bound up with faith. It must be believed in; it cannot be enforced unless it also has power. Authority resides not in the person on whom it is conferred by the group or society, but in the recognition and acceptance it elicits in others. Power, on the other hand, may dispense with the prop of authority. It may take the form of the ability to coerce or to veto; it is often personal, charismatic, not institutional. This kind of personal power is self-enforcing. It does not require shoring up by access to force. In fact, it may even operate subversively. A woman with this kind of power may or may not know that she possesses it. If she does know she has it, she will probably disguise her exercise of it.

In the West, the institutional structure of marriage has invested the husband with authority and backed it by the power of church and state. The marriages of wives have thus been officially dominated by the husband. Hebrew, Christian, and Islamic versions of deity were in complete accord on this matter. The laws, written or unwritten, religious or civil, which have defined the marital union have been based on male conceptions, and they have undergirded male authority.

Adam came first. Eve was created to supply him with companionship, not vice versa. And God himself had told her that Adam would rule over her; her wishes had to conform to his. The New Testament authors agreed. Women were created for men, not men for women; women were therefore commanded to be obedient. If they wanted to learn anything, let them ask their husbands in private, for it was shameful for them to talk in the church. They should submit themselves to their husbands, because husbands were superior to wives; and wives should be as subject to their husbands as the church was to Christ. Timothy wrapped it all up: "Let the woman learn in silence with all subjection. But I suffer not a woman to teach, nor to usurp authority over the man, but to be in silence." Male Jews continued for millennia to thank God three times a day that they were not women. And the Koran teaches women that men are naturally their superiors because God made them that way; naturally, their own status is one of subordination.

The state as well as the church had the same conception of marriage, assigning to the husband and father control over his dependents, including his wife. Sometimes this power was well-nigh absolute, as in the case of the Roman patria potestas—or the English common Law, which flatly said, "The husband and wife are as one and that one is the husband." There are rules still lingering today with the same, though less extreme, slant. Diane B. Schulder has summarized the legal framework of the wife's marriage as laid down in the common law.

The legal responsibilities of a wife are to live in the home established by her husband; to perform the domestic chores (cleaning, cooking, washing, etc.) necessary to help maintain that home; to care for her husband and children. . . . A husband may force his wife to have sexual relations as long as his demands are reasonable and her health is not endangered. . . . The law allows a wife to take a job if she wishes. However, she must see that her domestic chores are completed, and, if there are children, that they receive proper care during her absence.

A wife is not entitled to payment for household work; and some jurisdictions in the United States expressly deny payment for it. In some states, the wife's earnings are under the control of her husband, and in four, special court approval and in some cases husband's consent are required if a wife wishes to start a business of her own.

The male counterpart to these obligations includes that of supporting his wife. He may not disinherit her. She has a third interest in property owned by him, even if it is held in his name only. Her name is required when he sells property.

Not only divine and civil law but also rules of etiquette have defined authority as a husband's prerogative. One of the first books published in England was a *Boke of Good Manners*, translated from the French of Jacques Le Grand in 1487, which included a chapter on "How Wymmen Ought to be Gouerned." The thirty-third rule of Plutarch's *Rules for Husbands and Wives* was that women should obey their husbands; if they "try to rule over their husbands they make a worse mistake than the husbands do who let themselves be ruled." The husband's rule should not, of course, be brutal; he should not rule his wife "as a master does his chattel, but as the soul governs the body, by feeling with her and being linked to her by affection." Wives, according to Richard Baxter, a seventeenth-century English divine, had to obey even a wicked husband, the only exception being that a wife need not obey a husband if he ordered her to change her religion. But, again, like Plutarch, Baxter warned that the husband should love his wife; his authority should not be so coercive or so harsh as to destroy love. Among his twelve rules for carrying out the duties of conjugal love, however, was one to the effect that love must not be so imprudent as to destroy authority.

As late as the nineteenth century, Tocqueville noted that in the United States the ideal of democracy did not apply between husbands and wives:

Nor have the Americans ever supposed that one consequence of democratic principles is the subversion of marital power, or the confusion of the natural authorities in families. They hold that every association must have a head in order to accomplish its objective, and that the natural head of the conjugal association is man. They do not therefore deny him the right of directing his partner; and they maintain, that in the smaller association of husband and wife, as well as in the great social community, the object of democracy is to regulate and legalize the powers which are necessary, not to subvert all power.

This opinion is not peculiar to men and contested by women; I never observed that the women of America consider conjugal authority as a fortunate usurpation [by men] of their rights, nor that they thought themselves degraded by submitting to it. It appears to me, on the contrary, that they attach a sort of pride to the voluntary surrender of their own will, and make it their boast to bend themselves to the yoke, not to shake it off.

The point here is not to document once more the specific ways (religious, legal, moral, traditional) in which male authority has been built into the marital union—that has been done a great many times—but merely to illustrate how different (structurally or "objectively" as well as perceptually or "subjectively") the wife's marriage has actually been from the husband's throughout history.

The Subversiveness of Nature

The rationale for male authority rested not only on biblical grounds but also on nature or natural law, on the generally accepted natural superiority of men. For nothing could be more self-evident than that the patriarchal conception of marriage, in which the husband was unequivocally the boss, was natural, resting as it did on the unchallenged superiority of males.

Actually, nature, if not deity, is subversive. Power, or the ability to coerce or to veto, is widely distributed in both sexes, among women as well as among men. And whatever the theoretical or conceptual picture may have been, the actual, day-by-day relationships between husbands and wives have been determined by the men and women themselves. All that the institutional machinery could do was to confer authority; it could not create personal power, for such power cannot be conferred, and women can generate it as well as men. . . . Thus, keeping women in their place has been a universal problem, in spite of the fact that almost without exception institutional patterns give men positions of superiority over them.

If the sexes were, in fact, categorically distinct, with no overlapping, so that no man was inferior to any woman or any woman superior to any man, or vice versa, marriage would have been a great deal simpler. But there is no such sharp cleavage between the sexes except with respect to the presence or absence of certain organs. With all the other characteristics of each sex, there is greater or less overlapping, some men being more "feminine" than the average woman and some women more "masculine" than the average man. The structure of families and societies reflects the positions assigned to men and women. The bottom stratum includes children, slaves, servants, and outcasts of all kinds, males as well as females. As once ascends the structural hierarchy, the proportion of males increases, so that at the apex there are only males.

When societies fall back on the lazy expedient—as all societies everywhere have done—of allocating the rewards and punishments of life on the basis of sex, they are bound to create a host of anomalies, square pegs in round holes, societal misfits. Roles have been allocated on the basis of sex which did not fit a sizable number of both sexes—women, for example, who chafed at subordinate status and men who could not master superordinate status. The history of the relations of the sexes is replete with examples of such misfits. Unless a modus vivendi is arrived at, unhappy marriages are the result.

There is, though, a difference between the exercise of power by husbands and by wives. When women exert power, they are not rewarded; they may even be punished. They are "deviant." Turk and Bell note that "wives who . . . have the greater influence in decision making may experience guilt over this fact." They must therefore dissemble to maintain the illusion, even to themselves, that they are subservient. They tend to feel less powerful than they are because they *ought* to be.

When men exert power, on the other hand, they are rewarded; it is the natural expression of authority. They feel no guilt about it. The prestige of authority goes to the husband whether or not he is actually the one who exercises it. It is not often even noticed when the wife does so. She sees to it that it is not.

There are two marriages, then, in every marital union, his and hers. And his . . . is better than hers. The questions, therefore, are these: In what direction will they change in the future? Will one change more than the other? Will they tend to converge or to diverge? Will the future continue to favor the husband's marriage? And if the wife's marriage is improved, will it cost the husband's anything, or will his benefit along with hers?

References

Bell, Norman. *See* Turk, James L.

Bernard, Jessie. *American Family Behavior.* New York: Harper, 1942; New York: Russell and Russell, in press.

————. *Remarriage, A Study of Marriage.* New York: Dryden Press, 1956; New York: Russell and Russell, 1971.

————. *The Sex Game.* Englewood Cliffs, N.J.: Prentice-Hall, 1968; New York: Atheneum, 1972.

————. *Women and the Public Interest, An Essay on Policy and Protest.* Chicago, Ill.: Aldine-Atherton, 1971.

Brown, George W., and Ritter, Michael. "The Measurement of Family Activities and Relationships." *Human Relations* 19 (August 1966): 241–63.

Cheraskin, E., and Ringsdorf, W. M. "Familial Factors in Psychic Adjustment." *Journal of the American Geriatric Society* 17 (June 1969): 609–11.

1 Cor. 14:35; 1 Cor. 11:3.

De Tocqueville, Alexis. *Democracy in America.* New York: J. and H. G. Langley, 1840.

Elinson, Jack. *See* Haberman, Paul W.

Eph. 5:22–24.

Feld, Sheila. *See* Veroff, Joseph.

Feldman, Harold. *Development of the Husband-Wife Relationship.* Ithaca, N.Y.: Cornell University Press, 1967.

Feldman, Harold. *See* Rollins, Boyd C.

Ferber, Robert. "On the Reliability of Purchase Influence Studies." *Journal of Marketing* 19 (January 1955): 225–32.

Gen. 1, 2, and 3.

Gover, R. *One Hundred Dollar Misunderstanding.* New York: Grove Press, 1962.

Granbois, Donald H., and Willett, Ronald P. "Equivalence of Family Role Measures Based on Husband and Wife Data." *Journal of Marriage and the Family* 32 (February 1970).

Haberman, Paul W., and Elinson, Jack. "Family Income Reported in Surveys: Husbands versus Wives." *Journal of Marketing Research* 4 (May 1967): 191–94.

Heer, David M. "Husband and Wife Perceptions of Family Power Structure." *Marriage and Family Living* 24 (February 1962): 67.

Hoffman, Dean K. *See* Kenkel, W. F.

Kenkel, W. F., and Hoffman, Dean K. "Real and Conceived Roles in Family Decision Making." *Marriage and Family Living* 18 (November 1956): 314.

Kinsey, A. C., et al. *Sexual Behavior in the Human Male.* Philadelphia, Pa.: W. B. Saunders, 1948.

Lerner, Alan Jay. "I Remember It Well." From *Gigi.*

Maccoby, Eleanor E. "Woman's Intellect." In Seymour M. Farber and Roger H. L. Wilson, *The Potential of Woman.* New York: McGraw-Hill, 1963: 29.

Michels, Roberto. "Authority." *Encyclopedia of the Social Sciences.* New York: Macmillan, 1933: Vol. 2, p. 319.

Morrison, Denton E. *See* Wilkening, E. A.

Olson, David H. "The Measurement of Family Power by Self-Report and Behavioral Methods." *Journal of Marriage and the Family* 31 (August 1969): 549.

Ringsdorf, W. M. *See* Cheraskin, E.

Ritter, Michael. *See* Brown, George W.

Rollins, Boyd C., and Feldman, Harold. "Marital Satisfaction over the Family Life Cycle." *Journal of Marriage and the Family* 32 (February 1970): 24.

Safilios-Rochschild, Constantina. "Family Sociology or Wives' Family Sociology? A Cross-Cultural Examination of Decision-Making." *Journal of Marriage and the Family* 31 (May 1969).

————. "The Study of Family Power Structure: A Review 1960–1969." Ibid. 32 (November 1970): 539–52.

Scanzoni, John. "A Note on the Sufficiency of Wife Responses in Family Research." *Pacific Sociological Review*. Fall 1965: 12.

Schulder, Diane B. "Does the Law Oppress Women?" in Robin Morgan, ed. *Sisterhood Is Powerful*. New York: Vintage Books, 1970: 147.

1 Tim. 2:11.

Turk, James L., and Bell, Norman. "The Measurement of Family Behavior: What They Perceive, What They Report, What We Observe." Paper read at meeting of American Sociological Association, September 1970.

Veroff, Joseph, and Feld, Sheila. *Marriage and Work in America*. New York: Van Nostrand-Reinhold, 1970: 120–21.

Wilkening, E. A., and Morrison, Denton E. "A Comparison of Husband-Wife Responses Concerning Who Makes Farm and Home Decisions." *Journal of Marriage and the Family* 25 (August 1963): 351.

Willett, Ronald P. *See* Granbois, Donald H.

Wolgast, Elizabeth. "Do Husbands or Wives Make the Purchasing Decisions?" *Journal of Marketing* 23 (October 1958): 151–58.

Zelditch, Morris. "Family, Marriage, and Kinship." In Robert E. L. Faris, *Handbook of Modern Sociology*. Chicago, Ill.: Rand McNally, 1964.

Working

The Housewife and Her "Greedy Family"
Lewis A. Coser with Rose Laub Coser

■ The modern family, just like its traditional predecessors, is a "greedy" institution. It is normally headed by a fully employed male. Not he, however, but his wife is expected to devote most of her time, as well as her emotional energies, to their family. Husband and wife, to be sure, are expected to exchange services, sexual and otherwise, with each other, and they are bound by reciprocal obligations that are supposed to result in mutual benefits. But this reciprocity is skewed in the male direction; i.e., it is asymmetrical in the sense that benefits flow unequally to these two role partners.

As Alvin Gouldner has argued,[1] where power relations are unequally distributed between two parties, the weaker party may be constrained to continue services even with minimal reciprocity on the part of the more powerful. Consequently, the continued provision of benefits by one party, the wife, for another party, the husband, depends not only upon the benefits which she receives from him, but also on the power which he possesses over her, and on "the alternative sources of services accessible to each, beyond those provided by the other."

The relative power of husband and wife in the family depends largely on their respective anchorage in the occupational system, since the system is the main determinant of status and privilege. Men mainly derive their status from their position in the occupational order, but the status placement of women is determined by their husbands. If her status depends on his, but his status does not depend on hers, an asymmetry of power is built into their relationship, and this asymmetry is a barrier to the operation of the principle of reciprocity which is based on equal exchange. The higher the occupational status the husband achieves, the more asymmetry arises, unless, of course, compensatory mechanisms are at work. Thus, in the upper class, the wife may have high status conferred to her by her own family of orientation, or she may be independently wealthy.[2]

The exclusion or near-exclusion of women from most high status positions in the occupational system is often justified by reference to her higher emotional investment in the family. In fact, we deal here with a prime instance of the self-fulfilling prophecy.[3] Women are judged to be unfit for high occupational status and they are hence excluded from such positions. If they then turn to the greedy family in search of emotional fulfillment, this is adduced as "proof" of the fact that they indeed do not fit into the occupational world.

Their exclusive attachment to the family, moreover, and the sacrifices they make in its service, binds them more securely to it. They invest considerably more in the family than do their husbands, who find alternative sources of gratification in their occupation. And the more wives sacrifice for the family, the more they are bound to it. The principle of cognitive dissonance operates here: Since it is very difficult to repudiate objects in which one has invested so much, the more one invests in an object, the greater the hold that object has on the person. Thus, not only are women taught and expected to invest their emotions in the family, this very investment once more strengthens their attachment. And this attachment makes them even more vulnerable to the husband's higher-status claims. As E. A. Ross put it a long time ago in advancing a "Law of Personal Exploitation," "In any sentimental relation the one who cares less can exploit the one who cares more."[4]

The small representation of women in the professions and in high-status positions in contemporary America is by no means due to happenstance, but is the logical consequence of women's cultural mandate which prescribes that their primary allegiance be to the family and that men provide the family with economic means and social status. Once the premise of this mandate is granted, women who have or wish to have careers are said to have a "conflict," and this is seen as a source of disruption in the occupational as well as in the familial order.[5]

Conflicts experienced by professional women who have a family do not simply result from participation in two different activity systems whose claims on time allocations are incompatible. They derive from the fact that the values underlying these claims are contradictory: Profession-al women are expected to be committed to their work "just like men" at the same time as they are normatively required to give priority to their family.

The conflict is one of allegiance, and it does not stem from the mere fact of involvement in more than one social system. Such conflicts do not typically arise in the case of husbands. Men can be fully engaged in their occupations without fear of being accused of a lack of devotion to their families. It is only when there is a normative expectation that the family will be allocated resources of time, energy, and affect that cannot be shared with other social institutions that conflict arises. And this typically occurs only in the case of women who have the cultural mandate to give primary allegiance to their families. Hence, this mandate sharply limits the access of women to high-status positions and skews the distribution of power in the family in the direction of the male head of the household. This is why the notion of equal access of women to high-status positions in American society is presently discussed with such great affect. What is at stake is not so much equal access to job opportunities as such, but equal power within the family. Power depends on resources, and women who do not have occupational resources are in a very poor position to share it equally with their husbands.[6]

If men are providers and women are provided for, the latter suffer from so large a built-in handicap that the resulting power differential between them and their husbands can be compensated only by special advantages. One such advantage is sexual attractiveness. Such attractive-ness, however, is likely to decline over time while the husband's status, to the contrary, is likely to increase over time, especially in the middle class; so that, even if the terms of the marital bargain are relatively more equal in the first stages of marriage, they are likely to become less so in later stages.

Moreover, in the modern family, the wife's decline in sexual attractiveness is likely to coincide with the time in which the children are growing up, so that her motherly responsibilities tend to cease at the same time as her sexual appeals begin to wane. She no longer is a mother, nor is she a playmate. Under these circumstances, the marital dyad becomes especially vulnerable. At this point, the successful husband may attempt to console and compensate his wife by buying her expensive dresses and jewelry. Yet, alas, even if she is not familiar with the work of Thorstein Veblen, she will but too often feel that by adorning her, he in fact only signifies his own success.

Both husband and wife are normatively expected to work hard in the service of their family. But if her work is confined to the household while his is "at the office," these two types of work are not evaluated in the same way either within the society at large or within the family. Housewives, no matter how hard they work, are not considered to be in the labor force, which means that they are not regarded as contributing to the national product. The old joke that, if the parson marries his housekeeper, this results in a net decline in the national product, is not merely a joke. In achievement and instrumentally oriented societies, those who do household work are led to consider it demeaning since it is symbolically downgraded as not being "real work." The provider-husband receives symbolical reinforcement for his hard work by means of his monetary returns; and these returns typically increase over time as he moves up on the ladder of advancement. But the wife's work receives no monetary compensation. And its recompense in terms of symbolic expressions of gratitude on the part of the husband is likely to decrease over time. What seems to be at work here is a law of diminishing returns. Services which may initially have been compensated for by expressions of esteem and gratitude are likely, in the long run, to be expected as a matter of routine and, hence, no longer call forth expressions of appreciation.

In contrast to modern occupations, housework is rooted in an earlier traditional order. It is diffuse and unspecialized rather than functionally specific, and requires involvement of the whole personality. The mother-wife, even more than the domestic servant of earlier times, must always be available. Yet unlike traditional work, housework today demands only a modicum of skill since household needs are provided for in the form of processed consumer goods and labor-saving devices, and this in a society in which achievement based on skill is most highly valued. Helena Lopata was probably mistaken to give to her otherwise very interesting book the title *Occupation: Housewife.*[7] Only when it is realized that this is precisely *not* an occupation in the modern sense of the word, will the specifically modern dissatisfactions that are built into the housewifely role become analytically understandable.

This chapter is limited to the discussion of the marital dyad, since one of the authors has dealt extensively elsewhere with the middle-class mother-children interactive system.[8] It is nevertheless important to point out that the housewife's tasks in the home are not only downgraded by the world at large as well as by her husband, but that such negative appraisals are likely to be shared by growing children. While young children may depend on, and appreciate, the mother's nurturance, older children will soon learn from their significant environment that "real work" is done outside the home, and by males at that, while mother's work, though necessary, is "dirty work." Far from enhancing her in the children's eyes, this work diminishes her stature and downgrades her status relative to the father's work "downtown."

In spite of these compounded drawbacks of the housewifely role, women generally accept it, even if often only grudgingly. They do not flock to educational institutions, even if they have the opportunity to do so, to prepare for more rewarding occupational roles. They do not press for admission to medical schools and law schools nor to the academy generally even where they could crash the gates. By and large, they accept the cultural mandate to give priority to their commitment to the greedy family.

There is a negative connotation to the term "career women." No such derogatory term exists for men, since their careers are taken for granted. It is acceptable, however, even commendable, if middle-class women take jobs to help their husbands advance their careers while going to school, or to help children go to college. Their caring in this way for members of their family is seen as part of their cultural mandate and, hence, is normatively approved. Their occasional working is even approved if it is to buy some extras for themselves, or for presents, just as children from well-to-do families are encouraged to engage in character-building by occasionally earning their own money.

The mandate, which women accept, that enjoins them to devote their major energies to their family does not exclude outside employment. It only serves as a bar to outside occupational involvements which confer status and prestige and, hence, may alter the power constellations within the confines of the greedy family. It is normatively approved and structurally desirable that women are readily available to pick up the slack at times and places where an occupational system gets to be overloaded, and when it does not want to allocate resources that are considered too costly for an activity that nevertheless has to be carried out. Women's availability for such jobs stems, of course, from the fact that the home and family to which they owe primary allegiance, do not need all the time at their disposal. They can fill in as saleswoman (typically called *salesgirls* no matter what their age because of the low status of the activity); be invited on the spur of the moment to teach introductory courses when an unusually high number of freshmen enter a class; or be volunteers in understaffed hospitals where they are supposed to make up for the lack of nurturing services. Paradoxically enough, women's time is considered cheap just because they live up to the highly prized cultural mandate to give priority to their family. "Real work" for women—but emphatically not for men—is considered to detract from the requisite emotional investment in the family so that career and family life are presented as mutually exclusive alternatives for women. Those women who have opted for permanent careers tend to be expected to remain celibate, like Catholic priests.

While part-time non-career jobs for housewives are generally approved by the community at large, other activities that benefit the career of the husband are even more highly valued. As Hanna Papanek has argued,[9] many organizations that employ the husband proceed on the assumption that his wife's time is neither productive nor important, economically speaking, and that her "opportunity costs" are therefore low. They feel free to call on her if the occasion so requires, and their husbands are likely to feel honored and gratified if their wives' services are called for. Volunteer work, entertaining important customers or guests, holding children's parties, or pouring tea are nominally optional activities but are in fact normatively expected. A wife who refuses to participate risks injuring her husband's career. "The high degree of ambivalence which accompanies the induction of women into the institutional orbits of their husbands is based on the need to enlist the women's participation . . . without letting their actual contributions decrease the importance which the institution places on the husband's work."[10] What is more, while husbands highly approve and desire their wives' services in the enhancement of their own careers, they are likely to look with jaundiced eyes at any occasion which would call for even minimal sacrifices in the service of the wife's career. Husbands are almost always more equal than wives.

The high degree of mobility, both social and geographical, in the careers of middle-class Americans is predicated to a large extent on the readiness of the wife to assume the responsibilities and inconveniences involved in such moves. It is she who bears the major burdens of residential uprooting and social dislocation. Without her contributions as shock absorber, tension manager, and general superintendent, and without her readiness not to be carerr-bound herself, the mobility chances of her husband would be sharply reduced. The functionalist argument that chances for achievement and upward mobility in American society are well served by the fact that the extended family has been replaced by the nuclear family is indeed correct; but it fails to spell out that the nuclear family is functional for mobility only as long as wives are willingly submitting to its greedy demands. How many moves in academia, for example, have come about because husbands accept appointments at other universities, and how many moves have resulted from the wife's desire to enhance *her* career chances? The question answer itself.

All that has been said so far seems apparently called into question if it is realized that in the early 1970s, working women constituted nearly 40 percent of the entire labor force. Yet a closer look at labor force statistics shows that these figures by no means controvert, and in fact support, the idea that women have the cultural mandate to devote themselves primarily to their "greedy" family. By far the largest proportion of women are found in lower-status occupations. They comprise only eight percent of the nation's physicians and four percent of its lawyers but are predominantly employed in relatively low status "female occupations" such as primary school teaching, nursing, social work and, of course, various low-level white collar occupations. Women are disproportionately employed in occupations where they are easily replaceable and that do not as a rule command a high degree of commitment and loyalty.

The difference between occupations in which women are well represented and those in which their participation is conspicuously rare can be accounted for in terms of the status of these occupations. High-status positions require high commitment. In these positions, people are likely to have a great deal of control over their own work and, hence, this work is meaningful to the job-holder. But when jobs are meaningful, they are likely to detract attention and commitment from the family which alone is supposed to give meaning to the lives of women. Those women who engage in "unalienated" work are seen as potentially or actually subverting their cultural mandate, as disrupting the role expectations of the family system. The fact that women who have families are not as likely as single women to be found in high-status positions—even though single women are also subject to sex-typed judgments—is easily accounted for if it is kept in mind that "greedy" institutions such as the family are hard task masters. This is not so much due to the fact that a woman's career may cause neglect of the family as to the fact that it implies subversion. Not giving in to the family's "greediness" undermines the very nature of the institution.

Societies always provide cultural definitions of desirable life goals. In modern American society, men are "out to get" occupational status and women are "out to get" men who will get such status. Achieved rather than ascribed status is salient in American life and tends to determine position in the stratification system. Hence, while men are in charge of placing their families in that system, women's status remains vicarious. They tend to be deprived of the opportunity of achieving status for themselves, for they are kept in bondage to the "greedy" male-headed family.

Equal education for women on the high school and college level helps them compete with one another to attract the most valued men and later makes them capable of helping their husbands in their careers. Modern American society, as distinct from many others, values equality of opportunity for its members, yet women can hardly avail themselves of opportunities as long as they accept the cultural mandate that their major loyalty should be to their family. What is offered them formally is withdrawn normatively. Such contradictory patterns are likely to be highly anxiety-producing for many women and to evoke ambivalence and *ressentiment.*

As long as "greedy" families could rely in the main on housewives who accepted with equanimity their unequal position of power, it could operate with a minimum of friction, even though it seems often to have exerted a high toll in psychic stress and emotional disturbance. But once women began to realize that there existed realistic chances of achieving more nearly equal status with their husbands if and when they involved themselves in the upper reaches of the occupational and professional world and so acquired new resources, the "greedy" family was in trouble. Once women were no longer as ready as they had once been to support the careers of their husbands by offering auxiliary services, once they were no longer as ready to serve as tension relievers, recharging the emotional batteries of husbands come home to find repose from competitive battles, the terms on which the marital dyad was built began to change.

The desires of social actors are never enough if structural conditions are not conducive to their realization. However, the structure of the occupational order as well as of the household order is rapidly changing—largely through the impact of technological advances. The modern office and the modern factory allow the development of felixible work schedules which were hard to institute when technological requirements enforced a more rigid scheduling of labor inputs. At the same time, a variety of labor-saving devices, the availability of packaged and pre-processed foods, easy shopping in supermarkets, and refrigerated home storage of foods have made many household tasks obsolescent, and have considerably simplified the management of the home. That is why, at this point in time, one can begin dimly to foresee a new family constellation in which both he and she are the family's providers, co-managers of the household and true partners in the care of the children so that their respective resources of power are more nearly equal. When that day comes, genuine reciprocity will have replaced asymmetrical power.

As Alice Rossi puts it in her pioneering article, "Equality Between the Sexes: An Immodest Proposal,"[11]

Marriage [for the woman of the future] will not mark a withdrawal from the life and work pattern that she has established, just as these will be no sharp discontinuity between her early childhood and youthful adult years. Marriage will be an enlargement of her life experiences, the addition of a new dimension to an already established pattern, rather than an abrupt withdrawal to the home and a turning in upon the marital relationship. Marriage will be a 'looking outward in the same direction' for both the woman and her husband.

And that will be the death of the "greedy" family.

Notes

1. Alvin W. Gouldner, "The Norm of Reciprocity: A Preliminary Statement," *American Sociological Review* 25, 2 (April 1960), pp. 161–78.
2. In the working class, in contrast, where the husband does not typically achieve much prestige at work, conditions for more equalitarian relations seems more propitious. Yet, in fact, in the working class, sex roles in the family remain considerably more segregated than in the middle class, with "her" sphere and "his" sphere of interests and responsibility more sharply defined. It would seem that working class husbands find it even more threatening to give up male prerogative than middle-class men precisely because they lack compensation in the occupational order. Cf. Mirra Komarovsky, *Blue Collar Marriage,* New York: Vintage Books, 1967.
3. Robert K. Merton, *Social Theory and Social Structure,* enlarged ed., New York: The Free Press, 1968, Chapter 8.
4. E. A. Ross, *Principles of Sociology,* New York: Century, 1921, p. 136.

5. In this paragraph, as well as throughout this chapter, we have freely drawn on a previous paper, "Women in the Occupational World: Social Disruption and Conflict," by Rose Laub Coser and Gerald Rokoff, *Social Problems* 18, 4 (Spring 1971), pp. 536–54.
6. In working-class families, in which both husbands and working wives may typically have quite similar educational statuses, inequality of pay at work and unequal job assignments assure the maintenance of differentials in the resources available to husbands and wives. Cf. William H. Chafe, *The American Woman: Her Changing Social, Economic, and Political Roles, 1920–1970,* New York: Oxford University Press, 1972.
7. Helena Z. Lopata, *Occupation: Housewife,* New York: Oxford University Press, 1971.
8. Rose Laub Coser, "Authority and Structural Ambivalence in the Middle-Class Family," in Rose Laub Coser (Ed.), *The Family: Its Structure and Functions,* New York: St. Martin's Press, 1964, pp. 370–83.
9. Hanna Papanek, "Men, Women, and Work: Reflections on the Two-Person Career," *American Journal of Sociology* 78, No. 4 (January 1973), pp. 852–72.
10. *Ibid.,* p. 860.
11. Alice S. Rossi, "Equality Between the Sexes: An Immodest Proposal," *Daedalus* (Spring 1964).

The World of Women's Work
Louise Kapp Howe

When

■ . . . When over the course of their lives do most women work outside the home?

When over the course of their lives do most women *want* to work outside the home?

What difference does it all make?

There are currently three major patterns followed by women after leaving school:

Pattern A: Working in the paid labor market for a few years before marrying or having children, and then settling into the homemaker job for the rest of your life. (This was the predominant pattern for white middle-class females until World War Two and of course is still followed by many women, like Faye and Joyce at the conference, today. Their numbers are still huge if their proportions are declining. They are most apt to be: mothers of more than three children, wives of affluent men and women without a high-school degree who have meager opportunities in the job market.)

Pattern B: Following essentially the same career pattern as men, in that you remain in the paid labor force continuously and full-time throughout all the years between leaving school and retirement. (Most likely to be following this pattern today are women without children, black women and women in professional and managerial jobs.)

Pattern C: Working until you have children, then staying home for a certain amount of time (typically between five and ten years but the amount of time out is now getting shorter) and then returning or trying to return to the paid labor force on a basis that won't conflict with your remaining family responsibilities. Of the three patterns this is now the dominant one, the fastest growing one, and the one that is having far greater consequences than I ever understood before starting out.

Bea, a homemaker returning to work at night at the Wisconsin data processing center: "They offered $2 an hour for beginners, $2.50 for experienced data processors, which was just about what I was making four years before. I thought, goodness, nothing has progressed in all this time, what's going on?"

Joan, a waitress in her forties, working different shifts: "Diners and coffee shops are where waitresses often start out, where they work while they're raising their kids, and where they return to when they're too old to get the sexpot jobs."

Lillian, who has worked on and off in department stores since her first child was born: "It wasn't like it was before when I was single and had nothing else to worry about, I can tell you that. And then when you work part-time or temporary they treat you differently, they don't take you as seriously, I think."

Nora, before getting her job at the insurance company: "The employment agencies, God bless them, warned me not to expect too much at my age. All my past experience counted for very little."

Are these women exceptions? Are their experiences unusual? It would be less worrisome to think so. One could just shake her/his/its head and hope that personal solutions will soon be found. In fact, however, a landmark study of the work histories of more than 18,000 women between ages 30 and 44 indicates that the reception Bea, Joan, Lillian and Nora received upon returning to the job market is now the rule.* Conducted for the Department of Labor by Ohio State University's Center for Human Resource Research, the study found:

Nearly a third of American women 30 to 44 years of age are serving in the same . . . occupation in which they began their careers . . . Marriage and childbearing increase the chances that a woman will experience downward

---

*Dual Careers: A Longitudinal Study of the Labor Market Experiences of Women, Manpower Research Monograph No. 21, Volume 1, Manpower Administration, U.S. Department of Labor, 1970.

mobility from first job to current (or last) job. A larger proportion of ever-married white women moved down than up. Among such women who have had at least one child 15 percent were upwardly mobile, while 20 percent experienced downward shifts. It is worth noting that on average, never-married white women without children moved up . . . suggesting that . . . strong attachment to the labor force enhances career prospects. In the case of ever-married women with children . . . upward mobility is less frequent and downward mobility more frequent among the blacks than among the whites.

The solution? If you don't want to find yourself in a lower level job at age forty than you had at age twenty-two, what should you do? Apparently there are three main choices today. Don't get married. Or, don't have children. Or, don't interrupt your paid work life if you do have children. In other words, follow Pattern B, which is just what many professional women in the women's movement have been doing and advocating. And if you're married or living with a man get him to share the homemaking tasks too. The trouble, as I was to hear again and again from women I met, is that for those who are not interested in professions and careers, Pattern B may not sound so terrific. May not sound like a step ahead. For Joyce in Wisconsin, the opportunity to at last stop worrying about jobs when her husband finally earned enough to make it possible was "What a relief! You can't imagine what a relief that is. Don't tell me about how liberating other jobs are." Another woman I talked with expressed it this way: "I think you'd have to be very unusual to prefer sitting behind a typewriter all day to being around when your children are small and growing. I know I would have hated to have to work then." As it happened this woman's children were grown and she was realizing the cost of her decision to stay home twenty years ago every time she received her paycheck for the clerical job she had recently taken. Her salary was exactly the same as that of her twenty-one-year-old daughter. But still this woman insisted: "I wouldn't have missed those years for anything." And if the homemakers at the Wisconsin conference are correct, most American mothers, at least most mothers in nonprofessional jobs, feel the same way, too.

But doesn't the surge of mothers returning to the paid labor force when their children are younger and younger prove that this attitude is now changing? Not necessarily. First of all, study after study shows that economic necessity is the main reason most mothers of preschool children seek outside work. Second of all, when you begin to look more closely at the When of their labor force participation, the situation begins to take on a slightly different cast. A decidedly pinker cast.

When over the course of the day and year do most women work outside the home?

When over the course of the day and year do most women *want* to work outside the home?

What difference does it all make?

Once again there are three major patterns:

1. Working full-time throughout the year-round, as do most men.
2. Working part-time throughout the year-round or for part of the year.
3. Working temporarily during the year, either on a part-time or full-time basis.

Amid all the current hoopla about the new working woman, I was amazed to find out that less than a third of American females are now working full-time all year. According to the *1975 Economic Report of the President:* "Although more than half . . . were in the labor force at some time in 1973, only 31 percent were in labor force for 50–52 weeks." (For males aged 25 to 54 the figure was 87 percent.)

Of those women who were in the labor market at all, only 41.8 percent worked full-time year-round. Here was the exact breakdown, again reported in the 1975 *Handbook on Women Workers:*

Worked full-time (35 hours or more) and full year (50 to 52 weeks):	41.8 percent
Worked full-time for 27 to 49 weeks (teachers would be included here):	12.3 percent
Worked full-time for one to 26 weeks:	14.0 percent
Worked part-time (less than 35 hours a week) for the full year:	10.7 percent
Worked part-time for 27 to 49 weeks:	7.6 percent
Worked part-time for one to 26 weeks:	13.7 percent

Most likely to be working full-time year-round were the same women most likely to remain in the paid labor force continuously throughout their working years; Pattern B women. In other words, women without children, black women and women in managerial jobs and in professions not dominated by women. (Most female-dominated professions— teachers, nurses, librarians, medical technologists—included heavy numbers of part-time and part-year workers.)

Strikingly, although white married women have lately been moving into the work force at a faster pace than black wives (who were already there in high proportions) the ratio of white women working full-time has been *dropping* recently while the proportion of black women doing so has been moving up. (Only a decade ago or so, in 1965, more white than black women were working full-time; 76 and 71 percent respectively. In 1974 the figures were more than reversed; 71 percent of white women working full-time as opposed to 80 percent of black women. If we added the changing proportions of those working on temporary jobs, the white-black shifts would no doubt be present there as well.)

Among black women the change is largely due to the drop in the proportion engaged in domestic work and the higher percentage now in clerical and other full-time fields. Among white women the change is largely due to the increased proportion of mothers with young children in the labor force. Of all workers they are the most likely to be in search of part-time and temporary opportunities.

And where are such jobs to be found? In which of the three labor markets—the mainly male one, the mainly female one or the integrated one—are part-time and temporary jobs most prevalent? Ah, now the plot thickens. The pink collar tightens. Exactly. It is in precisely the occupations where women predominate, pink-collar occupations, that such opportunities can be found. Very few jobs are available for part-time managers. Very few openings exist for pilots, butchers, machinists to work over the Christmas vacation. At the same time four out of five waitresses work less than a full year. Department store saleswork, as we saw, is becoming an increasingly part-time operation. As already discussed, offices are turning more and more to part-timers and temps. Beauty shops always have. In hospitals and the health field generally, where women comprise 75 percent of the work force (except at the top), shift work and part-time arrangements are traditionally the rule of thumb. In New York full-time teachers have recently begun complaining about the growing use of part-timers in schools, too, thus reducing the already reduced demand for their labor. In contrast, in the industries dominated by men—transportation, steel, mining, public administration, etc.—part-time and temporary work (not counting seasonal layoffs) is virtually unknown.

Thus the When of a woman's work often determines the What. "In the face of the demands on her time," economist Juanita Kreps has noted, "the young wife is likely to find that the scheduling of her job is the most important single consideration. Her immediate job choice is dictated in large measure by the time constraints imposed in the short run, and this choice in turn directs her subsequent career development."

The most important single consideration. The rub of course is that later when those time constraints diminish so will the full-time outside job opportunities available to her. And later still (as Margie at the store, and Edna at Schrafft's and Nora at the insurance company all noted) when her family responsibilities are at last just about over, she will more than likely be asked to leave the work force entirely, although her job may now be the main social world she has left.

The ironies are, to say the least, strong. On the one hand young mothers like Diane and Nancy, with scarcely a free moment for themselves, are having to take outside jobs because of economic necessity and wishing they could be home, while on the other hand women like Nora, who have more time of their own than ever before, are being pushed out. Diane at the insurance company: "It's too bad my mother and I can't change places with each other for a few years, isn't it?" And she and her mother nodded. How many other women would nod? Although there are inestimable rewards to be gotten from doing useful work and getting paid for it—assuming one can find such work—how many women—or men—wouldn't like to have the opportunity to do something else for a while? Even teachers take sabbaticals, or used to. "It takes time to love, but who's got time on their hands?" went an old Jefferson Airplane song. It also takes time to think. It has often been noted that upper middle-class intellectuals have typically been the ones to ferment social revolutions; the presumption apparently being that they are the only ones with the abstract and conceptual tools at their disposal. It occurs to me after seeing these young mothers slicing themselves into five pieces to get everything done that the real distinction is that the intellectuals have the time to do the thinking. Not only to think but to go to all those meetings. Bea, running from the data processing center at midnight to have five minutes with her husband before he goes to sleep, so that tomorrow she can be up with her children at seven, is not about to sit down and write *Das Kapital*. Time is money, the saying goes. Money is also time.

To stop the hyperbole, are we really sure that Pattern B is the grail we all should be reaching for? Although for many people it may be ideal, the increasing and disquieting paradox of our time is that while certain women have been fighting for the right not to be "forced" to stay home, an even larger number are increasingly being forced—by inflation, taxes, the insufficient wages of their husbands, those that have husbands—to leave their homes to take jobs they often never wanted. And then later when they do want them, more than ever, they are forced to retire.

"It's too bad my mother and I can't change places with each other for a few years." How many older women would agree? Obviously, many women, as do many men, *want* to retire. Wait excitedly for the day. But it was a revelation for me to meet so many who didn't. Margie at the department store: "It's my first home, not my second." The representative of the United Storeworkers: "We hold preretirement classes for our older workers and time and time again we hear them say, they don't want to retire, they would miss their friends at the store." Moreover, in a British study of semiskilled workers in their fifties, Dan Jacobson found that women viewed retirement much less favorably than did men.* Only 41 percent of the women as against 62.1 percent of the men preferred to retire at the pensionable age. What both sexes overwhelmingly agreed upon was that in the question of retirement, "flexibility" would be the best answer.

Flexibility. An individual choice for women on the question of when to enter, when to interrupt, when to return, when to retire. What could make more sense? What could now be more difficult? "An individual choice? This is a business not a country club."

---

*Human Relations, Vol. 27, No. 5, pp. 427–92.

Why

When the facts come home to roost, let us try at least to make them welcome. Let us try not to escape into some utopias . . . or sheer follies.

—*Hannah Arendt*

There used to be a television commercial, perhaps it is still shown, that opened with a radiant woman, blonde hair flowing, strolling through sylvan fields, while the entranced man hurrying toward her murmured: *The . . . closer . . . you get . . . the better she looks.* In the case of the blatant undervaluing of the work the majority of American women still do—both the work at home and the work outside—the closer you get the more interrelated it all looks. The more deeply embedded. The more of a boon to the business structure of this country.

"In the real struggle between wife-mother and carerr-woman," Sebastian de Grazia wrote, "each side has had its violent advocates. What few suspect is that the fluctuation back and forth serves a purpose. It creates a labor reservoir ready to man the pumps at home or [outside] depending on the economic barometer."

Today, as we have seen, this labor reservoir is being drawn upon in a very special way. The fluctuation of women back and forth over the course of their lives, over the course of their days and weeks and children, serves an even more profitable purpose than ever before. Not only does it provide management with readily available labor but with readily available cheap labor. Not only with readily available cheap labor but readily available cheap *and* skilled labor. The best that the least amount of money could possibly buy. A businessman's dream. In her study, *The Female Labor Force in the United States,* Valerie Oppenheimer notes:

Once recourse has been made to female labor to provide quality labor at a low price, employers tend to get used to relatively well educated workers (standards have been going up not down) who have been working for much less than men who have received a comparable education. To substitute men to any considerable extent would require either a rise in the price paid for labor or a decline in the quality of the labor, or both. Unless there are some very compelling reasons for it, it seems unlikely that many female occupations of this type will radically change their sex composition.

Once in the era of twelve- and sixteen-hour work days, the standard procedure for squeezing the last drop of energy from your workers was to keep them on the job until they were ready to collapse. Today in the age (thanks, give the chauvinists their important due, to male-dominated labor unions) of minimum wage; eight and seven hour work days; premium pay for overtime; Saturdays as well as Sundays off; coffee breaks; benefits (health, pensions, vacations) that are said now to add twenty percent to the average worker's annual pay—all possible methods of cutting labor costs are constantly explored. In heavy manufacturing (in male manufacturing) the major method continues to be newer and speedier machines to reduce the amount of human labor (unionized, higher priced labor) needed. In light manufacturing (mainly female and/or nonwhite) the contest is between exporting for cheaper and mechanizing for fewer. In service and office jobs, where bodies are still needed, female bodies, inexpensive female bodies, the temporary and part-time worker is increasingly the answer in addition to new machines.

"Organizations exhibit quite contrary needs for both stability and flexibility," Marcia Freedman writes in her book, *Labor Markets: Segments and Shelters*. Occupying two-thirds of all part-time jobs today, women constitute the bulk of the flexible work force. The other major occupants are students. But while male students typically mature into the primary jobs (with all the benefits and access to promotions) women—particularly noncollege women—"remain the mainstay of the flexible work force at all ages."

Rushing from non-paying job at home to her low-paying job at the Wisconsin data processing firm, Bea commented: "You're probably going to think I'm unliberated or something." Bea, I don't know about liberated or unliberated. I frankly don't understand what those words mean. But I have come to see that the difficulties you and other mothers of young children face could not be of more benefit to the cost-conscious businesses you work for. Could not be more capitalized upon. Especially if you are working part-time. And for those mothers who try to go the full-time, full-year route, the Pattern B route, there immediately are all the problems that Norma Briggs discussed with me after the homemaker conference:

Now as a job-holding parent, I really feel the schizophrenia of our society toward working mothers. Here, in Wisconsin, a state employee gets two weeks vacation, her child gets all summer off. Our school system, which believes it's responsible to the needs of the community, doesn't provide alternate care during the summer. Likewise our medical system. It's impossible to get a dental appointment, for example, for your child outside of working hours. So what can you do? What's the answer? An honest recognition that it's impossible and beyond the capacity of the nuclear family—which is more and more a two-earner family—to take the full responsibility for the growth of American children. We need more flexibility on the part of employers, more responsibility on the part of public agencies, must have some coordination between work and school scheduling.

In fact, while the male-breadwinner, female-homemaker family is still being portrayed as the typical American family, another family type has quietly been moving into the neighborhood. While the country's major educational, health, employment and social security policies continue to be based on the assumption that father is out there carrying the whole economic load on his overworked shoulders while mama stays home like a good woman should, the new family has been steadily taking over more and more of the territory. Bye-bye male breadwinner. Welcome to our little community, new American family.

What is the new family like? It would be splendid to announce that it is the equalitarian family of many (although still far from all) women's dreams, with women and men sharing equally in both the homemaking and breadwinning roles. But that, outside of a once again privileged minority (who can afford to hire outside help if it doesn't work out) is far from the case. The new family type is Linda, the beautician, with a husband who refuses to be inconvenienced. The new family type is Diane at the insurance company with "no time of my own" although unlike Linda's, her husband does share many of the chores around the house. The new family type is what the Census Bureau poetically describes as a husband-primary-earner, wife-secondary-earner family.

A quarter of a century ago, 56 out of 100 American husband-wife families were (officially) supported by the husband's earnings alone. In 1973 that tally had dropped to only 31 out of 100. In contrast by then in 47 percent of husband-wife families, both husband and wife toiled for pay. "The most obvious conclusion," according to Harold Hayge of the Bureau of Labor Statistics, "is that American families have undergone a fundamental change in the manner in which they provide for their economic welfare." Meaning the manner in which the wife provides.

Secondary worker outside the home, still the primary worker inside, her earnings from her outside, usually pink-collar, job contribute on the average 26 percent of the family income. If she works outside full-time and full-year, her contribution increases to 37.5 percent, still less than half of his. What does it matter how little she makes? the unbiased male bosses and male union members used to say. After all, she's only working for pin money. Aside from the fact that 40 percent of women in the labor force today are either divorced, single or separated, here is what a mother of three at the department store told me she did with the pin money (less than $90 a week) she took home after forty hours of work: "I spend it all on food and carfare. I take the check and leave it all at the supermarket before I even get home." As Harold Hayge put it: a fundamental change in the manner in which Americans provide for their economic welfare has taken place. But whether it adds up to progress or not depends not only on who's defining the situation but on who's living *in* it. And who's living *off* it.

And so the pink collar appears now to be closed. To reduce a richly complex human world into a one-dimensional summary:

Who: The majority of American women.

What: . . . Often the most socially useful of all jobs rated at the lowest level. Particularly if they are filled by noncollege, nonunionized women. A convenient explanation for the fact that they are also often paid at the lowest level.

Where: Home first of all. Then offices. Then restaurants, stores, hospitals, beauty shops, small electronics factories, garment factories, schools, all kinds of workplaces, large and small, where women are working in jobs predominately filled by women and seldom having entree to other jobs within the organization.

When: Part-time and temporary and full-time. Before and during and after marriage. When the children are small and when they are pimply and when they are grown. Whenever the jobs are available. Whenever a woman can juggle her other responsibilities at home. Except when she's 65 and has the most time of all.

Why: If in their need for cheap and skilled and flexible labor, the members of our American business structure didn't plan it this way, they couldn't have come up with a more ingenious solution, could they? Although a host of publishers are still selling their textbooks showing why the male-breadwinner, female-homemaker family is the most "functional" for the country and the economy, another family type has moved to center stage. What the Census Bureau calls a male primary earner, female secondary earner family. A female secondary earner to work (along with unmarried and divorced and separated women) at secondary jobs. At secondary pay. To work in pink-collar jobs. It all seems to fit, doesn't it? Maybe a little too neatly. In the old sociologist's catch phrase, it appears to be No Accident.

Beyond the five W's, most reporters have the good sense not to go. There are other W's of course, What-to-do What-next. Before her death Hannah Arendt warned in a very different context against escaping into utopias when the "facts come home to roost." Should these be the facts (they are of course only one interpretation of them) then there is also a danger, it seems to me, of escaping into attitudes of gloom and doom. So many issues, so many obstacles, so many different levels of concern—it is easy to feel overwhelmed, immobilized by the realization.

Big things, bigger things, little things.

Big things: A full employment program that will mean adequate and decent opportunities for all people, college and noncollege, outside the pink-collar zone should they want it, particularly in the crowded labor market coming up. Unionization, flexible hours, affirmative action, equal education, particularly equal vocational education, paid maternity leaves, quality child care, all the middle-range issues women are now working on.

Bigger things: A deeper understanding of how this economic system capitalizes on the conflicts of women in dual roles. A fresh look at how women still engaged in traditional work, within and outside the home, can be awarded the recognition and economic protection they need, without falling back into the stereotyped roles of the 1950s. An attack on a lockjaw work world that says there is only one way—Pattern B—to move ahead through a system that kicks you out when you may have the most to give.

And chairs. Lockers. Little things. I have personally become obsessed about the issue of chairs for store workers. (I felt it first where it pinched the most.) Although deep in my bones I am convinced that we will have female astronauts on the moon before we have New York supermarket cashiers in chairs, I find myself badgering the managers near my home. ("The customers wouldn't like it," the last said to me. Which customer? I'm a customer.)

Big things, bigger things, little things. "It's depressing," the magazine editor said. Maybe that's what she really meant. A nice warm optimistic article about the successes and triumphs of individual women moving up the career ladder is one thing. An unblinking look at the structural reasons most women are, and for the foreseeable future will continue to be, locked into a low-paying pink collar work world is quite another matter.

If that's the case I know how she feels. I don't know about you, but my frame of mind, my outlook on these matters, seem to vary widely lately. On day I'm reading about the newest field opening up, and I feel, goddamn it, we're really moving ahead, aren't we? Another day I get a call from a friend who desperately wants a teaching job after twenty years in the home and can't find it; or I'm reading the latest statistics on the massive and barely moving unemployment rate of black teenage females; or I'm reading of the amazing and short-lived triumphs of women at the beginning of this century, and I feel—what's the use; nothing really changes, does it? At those times, at some of those times when I'm doing my flip-flops, I think of something S. M. Miller once wrote about another issue, the issue of ending poverty in this country. High optimism, he wrote, discourages analysis. High pessimism discourages the pressure and action that is needed to bring about change. That seems to me to be the hard truth in this matter, too. What is needed is neither optimism nor pessimism, neither exaggerated breakthroughs nor exaggerated breakdowns, but continued pressure and action on the middle-range issues that have begun to be attacked, and continued analysis, deeper analysis, on the obdurate issues that remain.

It has been said that the best part of an uprising is always in the beginning. The winds are strong. The outlook is clear. Every day in every way things are getting better and better. Then the clouds start to appear. Phase Two. The obstacles are tougher than anyone knew. The conditions, the permutations, the reality are all more complex. Some of the troops begin to tire. Some of the troops begin to despair. According to a recent article in the *Washington Post,* feminism is no longer "in" among high school females. (Personally, I hadn't realized it was ever in.) At dinner parties it is no longer fashionable to discuss the women's movement.

(*That* again?) It seems to me that all of this is not necessarily a bad sign. The really necessary work was never fashionable. Just vital. Just basic. Just political, in the deepest sense.

Big things, bigger things, little things. It's inescapable, isn't it? Women's work has still just begun.

"Naturally," Peggy would say.

References

De Grazia, Sebastian. *Of Time, Work, and Leisure*. New York: Twentieth-Century Fund, 1962; Anchorbooks, 1964.

Freedman, Marcia. *Labor Markets: Segments and Shelters*. Montclair, N.J.: Allan Held, Osmun, 1976.

Oppenheimer, Valerie Kincade. *The Female Labor Force In the United States*. Population Monograph Series, No. 5, Berkeley, Calif.: Institute of International Studies, University of California, 1970.

United States Department of Labor, *Dual Careers*, Volume 1, 2 and 3, Manpower Research Monograph Number 21, Manpower Administration, Washington, D.C.: 1970, 1973 and 1975.

U.S. Department of Labor, *1975 Handbook on Women Workers*. Washington, D.C.: Women's Bureau, Bulletin 297, 1975.

Belonging

La Familia Chicana

Principal Investigator: Jaime Sena-Rivera

Author: Charlotte Dickinson Moore

Que seamos siempre juntos y unidos.

■ "Jimmy," asked Mrs. Miller, a teacher new to the school and new to teaching Mexican children, "How many are there in your family?"

Little Jaime answered proudly. He was proud of his double identity: Jaime among his *familia,* and Jimmy on this side of the tracks where Spanish names were discouraged on the school grounds. He was proud, too, of his *familia* and his place in it but young in cautious, protective sophistication. Sensing that this school would provide a better education for her son than the "Mexican" one near his home, his mother had arranged his attendance there. He was placed in first grade rather than kindergarten because his older sister had already taught him to read, but no one had yet taught him much about "Anglo" *mores.*

"There's my Papa Eugenio and my Mama Luz, and my Papa Anastasio and my Mama Rivera (grandparents), then there's my Tio Lucas and my Tia Mercedes, my Tio Roberto and my Tia Crucita (paternal aunts and uncles). . . ."

Jaime Sena-Rivera and Charlotte Dickinson Moore. "La Familia Chicana" from FAMILIES TODAY, vol. 1, DHEW Publication No. (ADM)79–815.

Incredulously, the teacher interrupted, "You mean all these people live at your house?"

The eager little boy laughed. "Oh, no, but my Tio Antonio and my Tia Maria and my cousins live next door to my Papa Eugenio and my Mama Luz, and my Tio Carlos who isn't married yet lives with my Papa Eugenio and my Mama Luz, and my Prima Teresa and her husband and my cousins from them live down the street from my Tio Antonio and my Tia Maria, and. . . ."

"They do? All together? So close?"

"Sure, all the land there used to belong to my Papa Eugenio."

"Oh," said Mrs. Miller, then, "I mean, how many brothers and sisters do you have?"

The number startled her, and the Anglo children in the classroom giggled. Jaime privately thought teachers don't seem to know much, but respect for one's elders had been instilled at an early age, and he would not have dreamed of uttering such a rude and disrespectful remark. He continued trying to explain.

"My Prima Beatriz is living with us now, too. My Mama is big again with another child and my Tia Bernicita will be coming to live with us for awhile. We love my Cousin Beatriz and my Aunt Bernicita. We hope the new baby will be a girl. It's better for the youngest child to be a girl—you don't want to spoil a boy."

As the storyteller recalls (Sena-Rivera 1978), "I think Mrs. Miller switched us to memorizing the alphabet, which of course I already knew, in English and Spanish."

Familia and Theories of Family

This was *familia.* Here small Jaime could find loving people who spoke his language, figuratively as well as literally. Now, Jaime Sena-Rivera, Ph.D., presently at Yale University in the Center for Health Studies, Institution for Social and Policy Studies, still sees *familia* as "a source of something familiar and comforting in a very unfamiliar and uncomforting world, really. Expectations and values are shared, and it's a way of dealing with people that's not exploitative, usually . . . a way of dealing with impersonality in a larger world."

As a sociologist *and* as a Mexican American, Dr. Sena-Rivera, while Assistant Professor in the Department of Sociology and Anthropology at Notre Dame University in Indiana, determined to investigate the traditional Chicano composite lineal or extended family social unit. His immediate objective was to explore his hypothesis that the Chicano extended kin grouping has been effective in aiding both family groups and their individual family members to achieve and maintain social and psychological well-being and to cope with stress through their own social interaction. This work is part of a growing body of research investigating the way informal support networks strengthen individual and family mental health and provide a preventive buffer against ill health. Dr. Sena-Rivera's long-term hope is to generate research, both qualitative and quantitative, on the Chicano and other Hispanic groups.

As a family sociologist, Sena-Rivera is in a good position to study and explicate the Mexican-American family phenomenon, *la familia chicana*. In 1970, while at the Mexican American Studies Center of the Claremont Colleges in Claremont, Calif., he conducted a survey of a nearby Chicano community. His 1973 doctoral dissertation, "The Survival of the Mexican Extended Family in the United States: Evidence from a Southern California Town," is an analysis of the data from that survey. It proved also to be a testing of the validity of hypotheses and assumptions about the "classic" extended family in the United States, particularly the Mexican American, and of doctrines of *familism*. In the course of his research studies, Sena-Rivera has evolved his own sociological perspective of family. He has found points of agreement and disagreement with both the general literature on the American kinship system and the historical and sociological literature on the Mexican in the United States.

In a paper given before the American Sociological Association in 1976, Sena-Rivera outlined a few current family theories and presented the background of his hypothesis of the functionality of the Chicano extended family system in the United States in the seventies. He pointed out that, according to Talcott Parsons, one of the most influential American family theorists within the last quarter-century, the American kinship system has evolved from the relatively isolated composite lineal or extended family and is now characterized by the nuclear family household consisting of parents and dependent children. Sena-Rivera does not share this view nor does he agree completely with definitions of the classic extended family that include not only residential proximity and occupational dependence and nepotism but also a belief in the primacy of extended family relations and hierarchy based on the authority of the eldest male.

Sena-Rivera agrees more nearly with two other family sociologists, Eugene Litwak and Marvin Sussman, that the classic extended family as it exists in America today is a modification or conversion from the former model. According to Sussman's hypothesis, there is now a "neolocal" nuclear family system, with nuclear families living by themselves and independent of the families from which they came. These nuclear families, however, are viewed not as isolated but as connected in a network of mutual assistance and activity. They are in an interdependent relationship with the two parental families if they so choose; they are not bound culturally or forced by law or custom to maintain this connectedness.

In proposing that the modified extended family is more functional than the nuclear family in urban-industrial America, Eugene Litwak's theories are sympathetic to Sussman's view. Litwak does not view geographical *or* occupational mobility as inconsistent with maintaining extended family relations. Extended family bonds are seen as an end value in themselves, and the provision of aid across class lines permits the nuclear family to retain its extended family contacts. Since this aid is isolated from the occupation system, it does not impede merited mobility (Sena-Rivera 1976).

Familia in the Kin System

Most family sociologists agree that the practice of mutual aid is basic to the functioning of the kin system. Jaime Sena-Rivera observed this practice as a young child. In a chapter he wrote for the new edition of *La Raza*, to be published soon as a textbook for use in courses on Latin American culture in the United States, he describes this family interaction as he remembers it from his childhood:

It seemed that my father's brothers, and my father in turn, would go first to one another for loans of varying sizes (not always repaid) at various times instead of to banks or savings and loan associations . . . . ("Why go to strangers?" my father said. "And besides the Americans charge too much interest and they treat you like dirt when you don't know English so well. If you can't pay your brother back, there's no hard feelings. There are ways to make it up, always.") Also, each brother (and uncles and cousins) would see each other, especially if the other was older, as legitimate resources for finding work . . . . ("What is more decent," my father said, "than helping your brother or your friend to be independent, be a man, be a good husband or father or son? Besides, they put Mexicans off at The Unemployment.")

When still quite young, Sena-Rivera observed that many of the practices which he took for granted as a part of living were wrong in Anglo eyes. They might now be called *familism,* an impediment to individual mobility and the adoption of more varied role models. In a word, they were *dysfunctional,* according to his explanation in the same *La Raza* chapter, which says, in summary: "Family" is *supposed* to mean the nuclear family, not the extended network; residential proximity is considered extreme if many nuclear families, related by blood, live in the same unit or contiguous ones or even in the same neighborhood; nuclear families should be controlled in size; the practice of borrowing from one's kin creates an unnecessary burden rather than solidarity; economic and occupational interdependency impedes or prevents upward mobility; authority based on the eldest male criteria is arbitrary, paternalistic, and an impediment to individual mobility, and it keeps women overly repressed and submissive (in press).

Concerning the functions of the primary group structures of kin, neighbors, and friends in a technological society, Litwak points out the lack of human resources of the nuclear family group. Such a group, with only two adult members, often cannot handle acute emergencies alone and finds difficulty in managing tension arising from disputes among themselves. They are unable to diagnose incipient emotional troubles or be aware, by themselves, of better ways of handling childrearing, for instance. It appears that socialization learned through everyday activities, the value of neighborhood peer-group help in emergencies, the permanence and long-term ties of the kin, and the good feeling of friendship groups are complementary sources of strength to the nuclear family structure. The kin, neighbor, and friendship primary groups, then, provide resources which complement those of the isolated nuclear family (1969).

It might be assumed that within the extended family, whether "classic" or "modified," the functions of these primary groups are largely "built-in" as valuable components of such a system. This seems to be true for the Chicanos. Indeed, the friendship group structure, which Litwak views as the weakest of the three components, seems quite strong in *la familia chicana*. First cousins, *los primos hermanos,* are commonly raised almost like brothers and sisters, and a particularly strong bond is forged among same-sex and same-age siblings and cousins. Even aunts and uncles are included, since many parents are ending their families at the same time the older children are beginning theirs. From his own experience, Sena-Rivera knows that this bond continues throughout the adult years, regardless of the divergent educational, social, or economic paths, even the attainments or failures, of the individual *familia* members.

Building the Hypothesis of La Familia Chicana

Sena-Rivera has reviewed the literature on Mexican-descent population in the United States and has concluded that many of those hypotheses concerning the Chicano extended family are misleading. He says (1976, p. 6): *"The tri-generational household has never been the norm for Mexico or for Mexicans in the United States or for other Chicanos, except at times of individual extended family or conjugal family stress, or periods of general societal disorganization."*

In short, the traditional Chicano extended family, as a grouping of independent nuclear households, forms a social organizational unit that might be called "kin-integrated." To prove the validity of this view, Sena-Rivera determined to seek out four extended families which had heads-of-households still living in the three older generations. Each family would be represented by one or more great-grandparents, a son or daughter, and a grandson or granddaughter with one or more children. His reasoning was that the carriers of the "old ways" are the immigrants of the 1910–1930 period and their descendants. From his previous research, he had concluded that proximity in time to the source of the Mexican extended family's traditions explained a more traditional behavior; his objective, therefore, was to determine the extent to which each generation tested the traditional culture in a largely alien setting and found it workable, for themselves as individuals, or for the family group. As members of the crowds of immigrants fleeing the Mexican Revolution of 1910 and the poverty and unrest of the two succeeding decades, the great-grandparents received their primary socialization in Mexico where they were born; the second and third generations of each extended kin group (except for a few in-laws of the families finally interviewed) were born in the United States and received their primary socialization here.

As Sena-Rivera puts it, "This particular social organization transcends many different historical periods." He decided to study this age group specifically because he "wanted a sense of history and some accountability, historically, as to why they came and how people coming at a certain period made it in the United States. Until recently, persons in that age group and their descendants were the largest segment of the Mexican population. That's changed now. We have no 'ideal type' anymore."

This observation was made in another way in a paper, "The Mexican American Family," presented at the Mexican American Seminars held in California at Stanford University in April 1970. Nathan Murillo contended: "The reality is that there is no Mexican-American family 'type.'" To support this claim, he pointed out that, like all other Americans, the thousands of Mexican-American families vary in: regional and socioeconomic factors, degree of assimilation and acculturation, historical and political differences, and in patterns of coping with each other and with their different environments. In some families, only Spanish is spoken; in others, Spanish is all but forgotten. Many trace their lineage to the Spanish, others to one or the other of the once-powerful Indian cultures. *Chicano,* a colloquial adaptation of the Spanish for *Mexican,* is a relatively recent term, used "with increasing frequency and with growing pride." Alternate labels throughout the years have been *Latino, Hispano, Spanish American,* or *American of Spanish descent* (1971, pp. 97–99).

The Immigrants

Why did they come? Sena-Rivera recounted their story in a historical chapter in his dissertation (Sena 1973). During the second half of the past century, following the Mexican-American War of 1846–1848, when the United States gained most of what we now refer to as the Southwest, immigration from Mexico was chiefly along the border to satisfy a modest demand for domestic and agricultural workers. Similar demands in California and neighboring states were met principally by Chinese and, later, Japanese workers.

After the turn of the century, however, a boom in the railroads and in other industries and, very importantly, the industrialization of agriculture, especially in Texas, California, and Arizona, meant a sudden, enormous demand for low-skilled labor, a demand that could not be met by European immigrants, the traditional source for similar labor. Concurrently, the overthrow in 1910 of the Diaz regime in Mexico by revolutionaries meant the breakup of huge landholdings and the subsequent freeing of millions of *peons* from their bondage on the great *haciendas* and *ranchos*. Many gravitated to the cities of Mexico and to *El Norte*, the North—the U.S.A.—where both rumors and recruiters reached them with news of jobs and peace in place of their present unemployment and governmental unrest.

So the flow across the border began. By the hundreds of thousands came *peons* and *campesinos* (other rural workers), young men wishing to avoid military conscription, displaced and persecuted former large landowners and businessmen, city dwellers feeling the sudden pinch of the numbers of new arrivals from the countryside, and out-of-favor revolutionaries and other political refugees. With these, came wives and children and new dependents. Often there were whole groups of extended family households as well, either together or over time.

For most, the border states became the first stopping place and the site for many *colonias* and *barrios*. By about 1920, a fresh demand occurred not only for agricultural workers in the Northwest and in Florida but also for workers in the railroad, steel, automotive, and other rapidly developing industries in the Midwest. Sequential and direct immigration of Mexicans followed into these industries and into growing cities such as Detroit, Kansas City, Chicago, and Gary, Ind. Indeed, the *colonias* and *barrios* begun then in those places are as old as many found nearer the Mexican-American border. Increases in the tide of Mexican immigration, especially just before World War II and during the sixties and seventies, have established new Mexican neighborhoods and sections of cities and towns or reinforced, both culturally and numerically, older settlements of Mexican Americans throughout the United States, mostly in the Southwest and Midwest.

This immigrant flow to and from Mexico has been determined chiefly by economic conditions: the periodic depressions of the 1910s and 1920s, the Great Depression of the 1930s, the boom time of two World Wars, and the events of Korea and Vietnam, plus the state of the Mexican economy during these periods. The welcome mat for Mexicans has been put out and pulled in according to these fluctuations.

The early 1930s witnessed the forced "repatriation" to Mexico of hundreds of thousands of Mexican families, U.S. citizens or not, since they were viewed as an excessive burden to public and private social and charitable services and to American taxpayers. (Many of them were taxpayers, too.) Periodically since that time, this repatriation has continued.

The *familias* of Sena-Rivera's study are very much a part of the comprehensive immigration and labor history of this century. Each *familia* in its own way has contributed a bit to the mosaic of the growth of the United States. Happily, none of these *familias* has suffered as badly as many of their countrymen nor experienced deportation back to Mexico. But for the majority of these *familias* and their individual members, succeeding in this country over the generations has been far from easy. For several, in material and other terms, their histories could hardly be counted as successful at all. Like other immigrant groups and like the pioneers in the West, many of them Mexican, these *familias,* especially the founders, have shown the fortitude and determination required to make a viable life for themselves and their family members and to forecast a dream of the future for their offspring.

Maintaining family solidarity and loving relationships is difficult under such conditions. But doing so is extremely important for today's otherwise highly impersonal, complex society. Sena-Rivera believes that the story and lessons of these *familias* are worthy of our general attention, that they are applicable across racial and ethnic lines and especially across working-class groups. . . .

Prototype *Familia*

In many ways, this large, 141-member clan is highly typical of that aspect of Mexican-American culture known as *familia* at its most traditional, possibly because of its semirural, extraurban ambience. Close-knit and devoted—*unidos*—cousins, and aunts and uncles of the same age group, for that matter, interact like brothers and sisters. In-laws, especially females, are drawn into the intense relationship of the network. There is reflected here an emotional interdependence which, especially for the older members, satisfies most of the individuals' recreational and social needs, visits and larger gatherings being an important part of daily and weekly life. The sense of obligation to each other, to help in times of economic trouble or illness with small loans, household services, or child care, appears to stem not only from the sense of duty instilled in early childhood but from voluntary desire and strong emotional attachment. In general, most *familia* members hope to continue this involvement *along with* entry into the economic and social mainstream of their locality.

Their Faith

With the exception of one third-generation in-law, the *familia* members are Catholic. Their faith and their church are an integral and accepted part of daily and weekly life, although only routine ritual participation for some. Family bonds are strengthened further when godparents are chosen for christening, first Communion, and confirmation. Dr. Sena-Rivera says, though, that this custom is not as strong as it is nearer the border or in Mexico itself, where the "fictive" kinship, the practice of "claiming" relations through godparenting, is also still strong.

Marriage and Divorce

Familia A reflects, also, changes in patterns of marriage and divorce. A shift toward intermarriage with other groups is rather noticeable among them. From the one "out-marriage" out of eight marriages in the second generation, the daughter's second marriage to a Puerto Rican, to nine out of sixteen marriages in the third generation, eight to Anglos and one to a Cuban, the trend is striking. Striking, too, is the assimilation of most of these spouses into the warm interaction of the *familia*.

According to Sena-Rivera, *familias* in his study were in one respect not typical of many that he knows about: There were no common-law marriages among them. Only Sra. A's daughter had what was apparently a less than "formal" marriage. Serial marriage is quite acceptable, and divorce is no longer frowned on. As Sena-Rivera sees it, usually divorce "has meant that they haven't lost anything. In most cases, the children stay within the *familias*. It's an in-law, usually a male, who leaves. The divorce is not with the son, the blood line, so the daughter keeps the children. And apparently, when there is intermarriage or marriage with a divorced person, a man brings his own children, who are gladly accepted into the extended family."

Language and Assimilation

The grandson articulated a concern about a trend he has observed in *Familia A* and among his friends in the Michiana area when he expressed his regret that so many younger generation members know so little Spanish. In fact, the interviewers observed that given names in the fourth generation have been Anglicized when they are not actually non-Spanish.

Sena-Rivera has noticed change in his own group in northern New Mexico and southern Colorado. He adds, however, when speaking of both customs and language, that at present, with the huge numbers of

Mexicans and other Latins coming in, there is still a good deal of language retention. Referring particularly to the Los Angeles area, he remarks: "They come across into LA now and work in small industries directly for Mexicans or at least for Mexican foremen, and shop in Mexican grocery stores. Even big super markets have Spanish clerks. . . . Now the burden is on shops and restaurants who serve these people rather than on the minority struggling to make their wishes known in English. This change has taken place in less than a generation. Now social services in LA have Spanish-speaking personnel and signs on buses and in public buildings are in Spanish; there are TV stations which are Mexican and there are other bilingual programs. Particularly the churches now have the masses and other services in Spanish, so there's not really a great deal of need to de-Mexicanize yourself."

As Sena-Rivera reflected on this, he mentioned that some of the bilingual programs work but that many of them are simply devices for assimilation in a bilingual, bicultural civilization. Certainly it has been found among other groups who are making their way into the mainstream of American life that satisfaction is greater and alienation less among those who have achieved a bicultural balance, by retaining much of the old while assimilating much of the new. Sra. A's grandson sees this as a goal for his generation and his children's.

Grandson A sees other changes which should take place. While cherishing memories of the older generation and loving relationships with them, he feels that the younger generations of Mexican Americans should be more "independent" and less traditional. Friendship with Anglos should be fostered, he believes, and younger Chicanos should make an effort to participate in and enjoy things which their parents did not (or could not), such as travel and dating alone. Chief among the interests to be promoted is sports, the grandson's own personal delight.

The "Nonpersons"

A strange custom appeared during interviews. Usually, several interviews were necessary to fill out the branches on each family tree, and occasionally a few branches were not leafed out completely. "Somebody would crop up here and somebody there, and we'd try to straighten them out. What's a child doing over there in that household? He was born over here." And in the case of a couple of families, "all of a sudden you realize there's somebody who isn't even being talked about, and the person is declared almost a nonperson."

There was never any attempt to intrude or to probe more deeply than the family members wished to go. The interviewers were struck by the firm, quiet refusal to reveal information about a recent or imminent rupture in any couple. In the cases where someone had, seemingly, "disappeared," clues came only from comparing conversations and interviews among the various persons interviewed in the same *familia*. Females and their children involved in divorce had apparently rejoined their own extended families.

This kind of mystery first showed up in *Familia A* when Sra. A neglected to mention some of the daughter's children, and only later did the interviewers learn that the A grandparents had actually legally adopted this granddaughter. It was this same granddaughter who mentioned one uncle who did not visit with anyone because he has "set himself apart." Later, the interviewers realized that this was the individual who had refused to see them. The mystery remained closed.

Sena-Rivera said, "I didn't probe to find out exactly what these people had done that was so wrong that they were kicked out of the family. Since it was sensitive, the only way we found out was from a word here and a word there; then from different interviews we put the mystery together." He has observed that mental health practitioners who are not of or very close to this ethnic group are not likely to appreciate what being cut off in this way means, nor to understand how this diminishing of identity can destroy an individual and his sense of self. . . .

Las Chicanas

The remarkable women of *Familia B* epitomize, for Dr. Sena-Rivera at least, the strength of the countless women, Mexican and Mexican-American, who have borne children, prepared tamales, enchiladas, and all the rest for countless *familia* members, and worked side by side in the fields with their husbands and children. This kind of life has been the historical lot of these women on the estates of the *padrones* in Mexico and on the lands of Texas, New Mexico, California, or Midwest farmers. At the same time, apparently, most of them have managed to buttress within their *familias,* as an integral cornerstone of their culture, the image of male dominance, in spite of the low social and economic stature of their men. Quotations given below, from comments made by some of the B women to the interviewers, well illustrate their lives and their forceful personalities.

Sra. B, herself, exerted great influence on her family because of her strong maternal control and her fluency in English which, despite her illiteracy in both Spanish and English, aided her in dealing with an Anglo-dominated world. The help to her family in this one area alone was immeasurable and, further, she had no language barrier to separate her from third and fourth generation members. Her will was indomitable and her devotion tenaciously directed at saving her progeny from the poverty and unhappiness she knew in her childhood and from the deprivation of her early married years in Texas.

Her ambition for her family is reflected in her granddaughter, who said during her interview:

I think I'm better off then my brothers and sisters . . . and once in awhile I hear someone say, "Well, you've got money to do something." I do, but they forget that I work hard and save. I've been working since I was a freshman in high school. After high school, I went back to my counselor and he said, "Now, you don't want to go to college—you're just going to get married." You know. But I decided to go. First I got a job there (Indiana University, Bloomington), then I enrolled. Sometimes it was really hard—I didn't have any money. But I would never call my mother. I don't know if it was a sense of pride or because I didn't want to impose on her—she didn't have anything.

Loneliness brought together the six "Latinos" who were at the University at that time. This girl helped establish a Mexican-American program and is very proud of how well some of the members, including some women, have done. As she added, some of the women "even became lawyers."

She married at age 20, 3 years after her father died, and says of the early years of her marriage: "We started out with zero—nothing. We paid for our own wedding. We saved up for him to go to school because I wanted him to get a degree real bad—that meant a lot to me. We lived in furnished apartments and whatever . . . . He finished his degree in night school . . . ."

Now she is not certain about finishing the 2 1/2 years she needs to get her own degree because of her commitment to her husband and child. But she wants it very much, "just to have it."

The granddaughter-in-law, too, shows the kind of support for her husband that has helped these Chicanos to "make it" in an alien culture and an unfriendly work environment.

I tell him to be a foreman, you know, or a big shot at the Mill—not just to stay down. Like before, he was an iron worker, and when it snowed, he was laid off . . . . Now he's in the Mill. It's less money than before when he was at the foundry, but there's always work whether there's rain or a storm or not and the benefits . . . . But he had to start at the bottom, in the labor. Two months ago, he took his exam to get into mechanics at the Mill. So, like, I would always build him up—you can do this, just try, you're not dumb. You've got to do that to your husband. If not, they don't think much of themselves—just so they're making money, they're happy. They should try to make more, and get up high, I think . . . .

Discrimination

Sra. B's poignant memories of her husband's work experiences are sadly typical of the experiences of all too many Mexican Americans and, for that matter, of most socioeconomically depressed newcomers to the United

States work force. She described his struggles while working for the railroad in Texas:

All the Mexicans were assigned the hardest jobs, like digging, even if you could read and write—as he can—and were able to handle better work. Why? Because we were Mexican. They wouldn't give us a chance at nothing. There were many abuses . . . . Some of the foremen were very mean. They would see that you were marked down at the store for more than what you bought, and you always owed more than you made. That's not fair . . . .

In the memories of the great-grandparents of *Familia B*, discrimination extended beyond the work place. As Sra. B remembered it:

Life for the Mexican was pretty hard . . . . It was almost like for the colored. There was a lot (of) discrimination. They wouldn't allow you to eat at a table with a white—they would separate you. Once I went to meet my husband in another city. In the morning I went to a restaurant by the station to have breakfast. Now, I am pretty light and I can pass. They served me. When I returned to San Antonio with my husband, we stopped at the same restaurant. They saw my husband is Mexican. They wouldn't serve us up front. They wanted to serve us in the kitchen . . . .

Sra. B added that things had not been too different for Mexicans where they now live. She said that her husband had always had to work at the hardest jobs in the steel mills, under unhealthy conditions, and that he was never steadily employed or for many days a week. Sra. B then added, lest she make the one "white" interviewer feel uncomfortable, "I owe no grudges . . . I take things as they come—as God sends them."

Employment

In regard to the employment problems of the Mexican Americans, as with a study of illegal immigrants which he hopes to do, Sena-Rivera is afraid that his study, while good and valid, may be used against these people. "You can manipulate family associations, particularly emotive tendencies, to get at the various members and manipulate them even to hold down the work force," he explained. "Even these individual laborers say that. This person will stick with the job because he has greater responsibilities to a wide range of people. They can make greater demands on him than on another worker. I've seen that. I've heard 'white' employers speak in those terms: 'I'd rather have a Mexican worker because I know he'll be steady and work for less, because that money has to go to a lot of people.'"

While agreeing that many immigrant groups have met with similar difficulties, he added, 'Our bad luck is that we came at the end of the

Industrial Revolution, so that as a group we are locked into that stage of history that we can't get out of . . . . And even if we were able to move up, it's in categories that don't make that much difference. Like in academia . . . it's high prestige, but it's still a middle-class occupation in our society . . . Each group has had to work its way in our country; that's true, but here, now, the average person has to work much, much harder."

Familia B in the third generation has a number of exceptions to the blue-collar caste of the older members. In addition to the police detective grandson-in-law and his clerical-worker wife, that generation includes a computer programmer, a musician, a telephone operator, a bilingual teacher, a secretary, a bank employee, and a salesperson. Among the other young, adult grandchildren, there are several college and university students. It is hard to say whether they are feeling at their age the constraints of their time and their ethnic group, of being "locked in," as Sena-Rivera describes it. Whether fuller entry into a bicultural world and emergence of more of the women out of the casa and into the working world will make a difference in familia life is a matter for further study.

Of this familia, the interviewers noted that they "did not receive any sense of being-at-the-bottom or depression from any member for living in this or similar neighborhoods and especially not from Sr. and Sra. B. At the same time, we do not wish to convey the impression that various members of Familia B are not desirous of, or not working toward raising, their present socioeconomic status."

Changes

The grandson's perceptions are interesting. In his interview, conducted in English with much Anglicization of Spanish surnames, he made distinctions among his relatives, calling anyone born and raised in Mexico "Mexican." To him, "Chicano" stands for those born in the States but who "think like a Mexican," and "Mexican American" means those of Mexican descent who "think like Americans."

The propinquity of most of these poor slum houses to their neighbors and the enforced propinquity of their numerous occupants to each other certainly do not epitomize the American Dream. They are not the Dream pictured in glossy magazines or on the ubiquitous television, whose aerials project from every tenement. But the always-room-for-one-more hospitality for other members of familia has been an assurance of the enduring qualities of the Chicano kin network. Will these qualities endure unchanged?

The Third Generation members of the B Familia who were interviewed indicate a possible drift. There is an embarrassment about inadequate space and enforced closeness which may interfere with the old hospitality-despite-inadequacies. The granddaughter, who wants to continue the large gatherings at Christmas, at least, like the all-*familia* party she went "all out" for the previous year, is looking for a larger house because "I don't have the room" to entertain adequately. The grandson indicates that he does not visit his siblings formally, or they him, except for calling on his next-older brother who has just bought a house where, the grandson feels, visits now will not be an imposition.

Transmission of Values

Familia B, throughout its generations, demonstrates well the transmission of values. The fathers in all of the *familias* in this study have been instrumental, in both precept and example, in teaching respect and obedience to one's elders and love and volition in helping all *familia* members. In addition to reinforcing these principles, the mothers have been largely responsible for teaching moral strictures and proper behavior to the young women of the *familias.* The B's granddaughter-in-law reported the lessons from her Mexican relatives, especially her own grandmother:

Not to take the pill! Take when God gives me a child, not to abort it, and to have as many children as he wants me to, you know . . . . Respect—respect for your elders, respect for your Mom.

I always had to respect my Mom and I did! She brought us up real strict, like the Mexican custom. Like my husband couldn't come into the house for the longest time while we were dating! She just didn't want him in the house "unless he wants to marry you—is going to ask for your hand." I'd say, "Well, Ma, we're not living like that any more," and she'd say, "While you're under this roof you are!" But then he proved himself, like there was no hanky-panky, and he didn't get me pregnant or anything so after 3 years, she let him come into the front (enclosed) porch! We had a little color TV there to watch together. We went together for about 5 years before we were married and he was finally allowed inside the house.

She said her husband, who told her later that he wouldn't have married her if she had been "easy" and that he was glad her mother had been strict with her, would be strict like that with his own daughters. His viewpoint does not entirely reflect the trend reported for some third-generation members, who are trying to adapt to different dating patterns, among other more "American" ways.

(Since the interviews, Senora B has died. The interviewers were of the opinion, when talking with the *familia,* that the group appeared to be at a crucial point in their cultural continuity. Senor B did not give the impression of stimulating enough emotional reaction alone or of having the material resources which might compensate for that lack. They feel, though, that the daughter who has been with her mother at the center of visits during the older lady's illness and the granddaughter who appears to want to continue the larger family gatherings may be able to carry on the role as the *familia* focal point.) . . .

Traditions and Changes

Except for their lack of male descent lineal heirs, *Familia C* exemplifies many of the attributes considered typical of this ethnic family group. There are the physical propinquity of three of the households, the interactions both emotional and dutiful, and the occupational assistance.

An additional evidence of interdependency is the drawing of the sons-in-law and so far, apparently, the grandsons-in-law, into the intensive, warm family interaction. This has occurred even though Sra. C has always believed firmly, so she indicated, that a woman's obligation must be first to her husband and children.

It remains to be seen whether the ties that bind this *familia* will hold after the great-grandparents die and the more affluent daughter and son-in-law leave the three-household enclave, as it is assumed that they will. Perhaps those ties will hold for a time, at least, because this is the daughter who, after the parents, appears to be the pivotal force in the lineal *familia*.

Spanish Language and the Chicano

This *familia* differs from the other three in the study in a highly significant detail, the transmission and retention of the mother tongue even to the fourth generation. Whether due substantially to the higher education of this particular great-grandmother, the extensive travels and ambition of the more affluent daughter and her husband, or the obvious advantage this ability has brought to the patrolman and his sister, it is hard to say. Perhaps each of these has been a factor. Certainly, the remembrance and frequent use of Spanish has facilitated communication among the generations, even though both great-grandparents do have some knowledge of English.

In "Growing Up Chicano," a chapter in one of his volumes of *Children of Crisis* (1978, pp. 353–354), Robert Coles describes the dependence of the Chicana mother on her own language: "Moreover, they have the Spanish language, a reminder that one is not hopelessly Anglo, that one has one's own words, one's privacy and independence. No wonder many Chicana mothers, who can speak English easily, if not fluently, and who know full well that their children will be going to Anglo-run schools where English is the only or certainly the preferred language, choose to speak Spanish not just to their young children, but, it often seems, *at* them—as if the sound of the language offers the mother a sense of herself to fall back upon, a certain reserve that causes the child to feel comforted and loved . . . . The mothers, of course, are talking to themselves, reminding themselves that their children may well suffer in the future, but at the very least will not lose their language, their sense of a specific heritage: a religion, a nationality."

The Chicanos who Coles observed and wrote about with such sympathetic perception live in Texas and other parts of the South and Southwest. Possibly those who migrated to the Midwest found a somewhat more egalitarian climate in which to raise their children and perceived less need for them to retain facility in their language. Perhaps this latter group envisioned a greater chance of upward mobility and thought that chance would be more possible with greater skill in English.

When more research studies of the Mexican in the United States are done, as Dr. Sena-Rivera hopes there will be, the use of Spanish only, English only, and of the two interchangeably should be investigated, with regard to region, socioeconomic class and mobility, and the institution of *familia* as a continuing and viable unit. It will be interesting to determine whether the younger generations of this ethnic group as a whole will find, as other groups apparently have, that the bilingual, bicultural mode is conducive to greater socioeconomic *and* emotional well-being. . . .

Predictions

"Forever and ever?" On the basis of a four-*familia* study, Dr. Sena-Rivera is hardly willing or able to make such a strong speculation. For one thing, there are other relevant factors to be tested, especially that of socioeconomic class. *Familia D* makes this circumstance evident since, although it is the most affluent and highest in status of the *familias* studied, it cannot be considered upper stratum.

Sena-Rivera does predict, however, that *familia,* as described in his study, will continue for at least one more full generation. Each generation, he says, tends to repeat with their children the patterns of socialization received in their own childhood. This cycle should carry, then, among the great-grandchildren as adults with their own households, into the 21st century—100 years of *la familia chicana.*

Changes Coming?

Familia D is typical in its intensity of *familia* involvement. It appears atypical, however, in the decline in ambition and economic achievement evident in the adult fourth-generation members. This apparent decline is reminiscent of the Anglo expression, "from shirtsleeves to shirtsleeves in three generations," not an unusual phenomenon. Perhaps the younger family members have the perception that Sena-Rivera articulated, that their group is "locked in" in the lower and middle class. Possibly, with their *familia* as buffer and refuge from the alienation and boredom endemic in many industrial jobs, plus the added cushion of their parents' relative prosperity, they see little need to put forth the effort necessary for advancement into other occupational fields. It is possible, of course, that they need only greater maturity.

Judging from the individual interviews, this family can be seen as happy, well-integrated, and more involved outside their own group than other *familias* in this study, who reported little activity outside of home, family, church, and work. The individuals who told about their community activity are proud of their engagement in the broader spectrum, but regret that it cuts into their time with the family, their first social group. Undoubtedly, this interaction with people of other cultures will make subtle changes in the Chicanos' perceptions of themselves and their own acculturation. Conversely, the perceptions which these "others" hold of persons of Mexican heritage will be altered as each becomes better acquainted with the other.

References

Coles, R. *Eskimos, Chicanos, Indians.* Volume IV of *Children of Crisis.* Boston: Little, Brown, 1977.

Litwak, E., and Szelenyi, I. Primary group structures and their functions: Kin, neighbors, and friends. *American Sociological Review,* 34:465–481, 1969.

Murillo, N. The Mexican American family. In: Wagner, N. N., and Hang, M. J., eds. *Chicanos: Social and Psychological Perspectives.* St. Louis: C. V. Mosby Co., 1971. pp. 97–108.

Padilla, A. M., and Ruiz, R. A. *Latino Mental Health: A Review of the Literature.* Washington, D.C.: Superintendent of Documents, U.S. Government Printing Office, 1973. (DHEW Pub. No. (ADM) 76–113)

Sena, J. R. "The Survival of the Mexican Extended Family in the U.S." Unpublished Ph.D. dissertation, University of California at Los Angeles, 1973.

Sena-Rivera, J. "Casa and Familia: The Traditional Chicana Extended Family as Functional in the U.S.A. Today—Propositions and Hypothesis Toward Further Research." Paper presented at Annual Meeting of the American Sociological Association, 1976.

Sena-Rivera, J. Extended kinship in the United States: Competing models and the case of La Familia Chicana. *Journal of Marriage and the Family,* 41(1):121–131, 1979.

Sena-Rivera, J. La Familia Chicana. In: Sena-Rivera, J. and Samora, J., eds. *La Raza.* Notre Dame: University of Notre Dame Press, in press.

Sena-Rivera, J. "La Familia Chicana as Mental Health Resource—A Tri-Generational Study of Four Mexican-Descent Extended Families in the Michigan-Indiana-Illinois Region." Advance unpublished report (MH 28684), U.S. Public Health Service, National Institute of Mental Health, Rockville, Md. 20857.

Domestic Networks
"Those You Count On"
Carol B. Stack

■ In The Flats the responsibility for providing food, care, clothing, and shelter and for socializing children within domestic networks may be spread over several households. Which household a given individual belongs to is not a particularly meaningful question, as we have seen that daily domestic organization depends on several things: where people sleep, where they eat, and where they offer their time and money. Although those who eat together and contribute toward the rent are generally considered by Flat's residents to form minimal domestic units, household changes rarely affect the exchanges and daily dependencies of those who take part in common activity.

The residence patterns and cooperative organization of people linked in domestic networks demonstrate the stability and collective power of family life in The Flats. Michael Lee grew up in The Flats and now has a job in Chicago. On a visit to The Flats, Michael described the residence and domestic organization of his kin. "Most of my kin in The Flats lived right here on Cricket Street, numbers sixteen, eighteen, and twenty-two, in these three apartment buildings joined together. My mama decided it would be best for me and my three brothers and sister to be on Cricket Street too. My daddy's mother had a small apartment in this building, her sister had one in the basement, and another brother and his family took a larger apartment upstairs. My uncle was really good to us. He got us things we wanted and he controlled us. All the women kept the younger kids together during the day. They cooked together too. It was good living."

Yvonne Diamond, a forty-year-old Chicago woman, moved to The Flats from Chicago with her four children. Soon afterwards they were evicted. "The landlord said he was going to build a parking lot there, but he never did. The old place is still standing and has folks in it today. My husband's mother and father took me and the kids in and watched over them while I had my baby. We stayed on after my husband's mother died, and my husband joined us when he got a job in The Flats."

When families or individuals in The Flats are evicted, other kinsmen usually take them in. Households in The Flats expand or contract with the loss of a job, a death in the family, the beginning or end of a sexual

---

partnership, or the end of a friendship. Welfare workers, researchers, and landlords have long known that the poor must move frequently. What is much less understood is the relationship between residence and domestic organization in the black community.

The spectrum of economic and legal pressures that act upon ghetto residents, requiring them to move—unemployment, welfare requirements, housing shortages, high rents, eviction—are clear-cut examples of external pressures affecting the daily lives of the poor. Flats' residents are evicted from their dwellings by landlords who want to raise rents, tear the building down, or rid themselves of tenants who complain about rats, roaches, and the plumbing. Houses get condemned by the city on landlords' requests so that they can force tenants to move. After an eviction, a landlord can rent to a family in such great need of housing that they will not complain for a while.

Poor housing conditions and unenforced housing standards coupled with overcrowding, unemployment, and poverty produce hazardous living conditions and residence changes. "Our whole family had to move when the gas lines sprung a leak in our apartment and my son set the place on fire by accident," Sam Summer told me. "The place belonged to my sister-in-law's grandfather. We had been living there with my mother, my brother's eight children, and our eight children. My father lived in the basement apartment 'cause he and my mother were separated. After the fire burned the whole place down, we all moved to two places down the street near my cousin's house."

When people are unable to pay their rent because they have been temporarily "cut off aid," because the welfare office is suspicious of their eligibility, because they gave their rent money to a kinsman to help him through a crisis or illness, or because they were laid off from their job, they receive eviction notices almost immediately. Lydia Watson describes a chain of events starting with the welfare office stopping her sister's welfare checks, leading to an eviction, co-residence, overcrowding, and eventually murder. Lydia sadly related the story to me. "My oldest sister was cut off aid the day her husband got out of jail. She and her husband and their three children were evicted from their apartment and they came to live with us. We were in crowded conditions already. I had my son, my other sister was there with her two kids, and my mother was about going crazy. My mother put my sister's husband out 'cause she found out he was a dope addict. He came back one night soon after that and murdered my sister. After my sister's death my mother couldn't face living in Chicago any longer. One of my other sisters who had been adopted and raised by my mother's paternal grandmother visited us and persuaded us to move to The Flats, where she was staying. All of us moved there—my mother, my two sisters and their children, my two baby sisters, and my dead sister's children. My sister who had been staying in The Flats found us a house across the street from her own."

Overcrowded dwellings and the impossibility of finding adequate housing in The Flats have many long-term consequences regarding where and with whom children live. Terence Platt described where and with whom his kin lived when he was a child. "My brother stayed with my aunt, my mother's sister, and her husband until he was ten, 'cause he was the oldest in our family and we didn't have enough room—but he stayed with us most every weekend. Finally my aunt moved into the house behind ours with her husband, her brother, and my brother; my sisters and brothers and I lived up front with my mother and her old man."

Kin-Structured Local Networks

The material and cultural support needed to absorb, sustain, and socialize community members in The Flats is provided by networks of cooperating kinsmen. Local coalitions formed from these networks of kins and friends are mobilized within domestic networks; domestic organization is diffused over many kin-based households which themselves have elastic boundaries.

People in The Flats are immersed in a domestic web of a large number of kin and friends whom they can count on. From a social viewpoint, relationships within the community are "organized on the model of kin relationships" (Goodenough 1970, p. 49). Kin-constructs such as the perception of parenthood, the culturally determined criteria which affect the shape of personal kindreds, and the idiom of kinship, prescribe kin who can be recruited into domestic networks.

There are similarities in function between domestic networks and domestic groups which Fortes (1962, p. 2) characterizes as "workshops of social reproduction." Both domains include three generations of members linked collaterally or otherwise. Kinship, jural and affectional bonds, and economic factors affect the composition of both domains and residential alignments within them. There are two striking differences between domestic networks and domestic groups. Domestic networks are not visible groups, because they do not have an obvious nucleus or defined boundary. But since a primary focus of domestic networks is child-care arrangements, the cooperation of a cluster of adult females is apparent. Participants in domestic networks are recruited from personal kindreds and friendships, but the personnel changes with fluctuating economic needs, changing life styles, and vacillating personal relationships.

In some loosely and complexly structured cognatic systems, kin-structured local networks (not groups) emerge. Localized coalitions of persons drawn from personal kindreds can be organized as networks of kinsmen. Goodenough (1970, p. 49) correctly points out that anthropologists frequently describe "localized kin groups," but rarely describe kin-structured local groups (Goodenough 1962; Helm 1965). The loca-lized, kin-based cooperative coalitions of people described in this chapter are organized as kin-structured domestic networks. For brevity, I refer to them as domestic networks.[1]

Residence and Domestic Organization

The connection between households and domestic life can be illustrated by examples taken from cooperating kinsmen and friends mobilized within domestic networks in The Flats. Domestic networks are, of course, not centered around one individual, but for simplicity the domestic network in the following example is named for the key participants in the network, Magnolia and Calvin Waters. The description is confined to four months between April and July 1969. Even within this short time span, individuals moved and joined other households within the domestic network.

The Domestic Network of Magnolia and Calvin Waters

Magnolia Waters is forty-one years old and has eleven children. At sixteen she moved from the South with her parents, four sisters (Augusta, Carrie, Lydia, and Olive), and two brothers (Pennington and Oscar). Soon after this she gave birth to her oldest daughter, Ruby. At twenty-three Ruby Banks had two daughters and a son, each by a different father.

When Magnolia was twenty-five she met Calvin, who was forty-seven years old. They lived together and had six children. Calvin is now sixty-three years old; Calvin and Magnolia plan to marry soon so that Magnolia will receive Calvin's insurance benefits. Calvin has two other daughters, who are thirty-eight and forty, by an early marriage in Mississippi. Calvin still has close ties with his daughters and their mother who all live near one another with their families in Chicago.

Magnolia's oldest sister, Augusta, is childless and has not been married. Augusta has maintained long-term "housekeeping" partnerships with four different men over the past twenty years, and each of them has helped her raise her sisters' children. These men have maintained close, affectional ties with the family over the years. Magnolia's youngest sister,

---

1. Charles and Betty Lou Valentine have noted the existence of long-enduring networks composed of families (kindreds) and domiciles (households) in their recent study in Blackston, an Afro-American community in the Northeast (personal communication). What I have chosen to call domestic networks in this study, they call "inter-domicile, multi-family networks." Both terminologies appear to appropriately define the kin-structured domestic networks described in this study. Occasionally in this book I have synthesized the terminology and referred to "networks linking multiple domestic units."

Carrie, married Lazar, twenty-five years her senior, when she was just fifteen. They stayed together for about five years. After they separated Carrie married Kermit, separated from him, and became an alcoholic. She lives with different men from time to time, but in between men, or when things are at loose ends, she stays with Lazar, who has become a participating member of the family. Lazar usually resides near Augusta and Augusta's "old man," and Augusta generally prepares Lazar's meals. Ever since Carrie became ill, Augusta has been raising Carrie's son.

Magnolia's sister Lydia had two daughters, Lottie and Georgia, by two different fathers, before she married Mike and gave birth to his son. After Lydia married Mike, she no longer received AFDC benefits for her children. Lydia and Mike acquired steady jobs, bought a house and furniture, and were doing very well. For at least ten years they purposely removed themselves from the network of kin cooperation, preventing their kin from draining their resources. They refused to participate in the network of exchanges which Lydia had formerly depended upon; whenever possible they refused to trade clothes or lend money, or if they gave something, they did not ask for anything in return. During this period they were not participants in the domestic network. About a year ago Lydia and Mike separated over accusations and gossip that each of them had established another sexual relationship. During the five-month-period when the marriage was ending, Lydia began giving some of her nice clothes away to her sisters and nieces. She gave a couch to her brother and a TV to a niece. Anticipating her coming needs, Lydia attempted to reobligate her kin by carrying out the pattern which had been a part of her daily life before her marriage. After Lydia separated from her husband, her two younger children once again received AFDC. Lydia's oldest daughter, Lottie, is over eighteen and too old to receive AFDC, but Lottie has a three-year-old daughter who has received AFDC benefits since birth.

Eloise has been Magnolia's closest friend for many years. Eloise is Magnolia's first son's father's sister. This son moved into his father's household by his own choice when he was about twelve years old. Magnolia and Eloise have maintained a close, sisterly friendship. Eloise lives with her husband, her four children, and the infant son of her oldest daughter, who is seventeen. Eloise's husband's brother's daughter, Lily, who is twenty, and her young daughter recently joined the household. Eloise's husband's youngest brother is the father of her sister's child. When the child was an infant, that sister stayed with Eloise and her husband.

Billy Jones lives in the basement in the same apartment house as Augusta, Magnolia's sister. A temperamental woman with three sons, Billy has become Augusta's closest friend. Billy once ran a brothel in The Flats, but she has worked as a cook, has written songs, and has attended college from time to time. Augusta keeps Billy's sons whenever Billy leaves town, has periods of depression, or beats the children too severely.

Another active participant in the network is Willa Mae. Willa Mae's younger brother, James, is Ruby's daughter's father. Even though James does not visit the child and has not assumed any parental duties toward the child, Willa Mae and Ruby, who are the same age, help each other out with their young children.

Calvin's closest friend, Cecil, died several years ago. Cecil was Violet's husband. Violet, Cecil, and Calvin came from the same town in Mississippi and their families have been very close. Calvin boarded with Violet's family for five years or so before he met Magnolia. Violet is now seventy years old. She lives with her daughter, Odessa, who is thirty-seven, her two sons, Josh, who is thirty-five and John, who is forty, and Odessa's three sons and daughter. Odessa's husband was killed in a fight several years ago and ever since then she and her family have shared a household with Violet and her two grown sons. Violet's sons Josh and John are good friends with Magnolia, Ruby, and Augusta and visit them frequently. About five years ago John brought one of his daughters to live with his mother and sister because his family thought that the mother was not taking proper care of the child; the mother had several other children and did not object. The girl is now ten years old and is an accepted member of the family and the network.

Chart C shows the spatial relations of the households in Magnolia and Calvin's domestic network in April 1969. The houses are scattered within The Flats, but none of them is more than three miles apart. Cab fare, up to two dollars per trip, is spent practically every day, and sometimes twice a day, as individuals visit, trade, and exchange services. Chart D shows how individuals are brought into the domestic network.

The following outline shows residential changes which occurred in several of the households within the network between April and June 1969.

April 1969

Household   *Domestic Arrangement*

1   Magnolia (38) and Calvin (60) live in a common-law relationship with their eight children (ages 4 to 18).
2   Magnolia's sister Augusta and Augusta's "old man," Herman, share a two-bedroom house with Magnolia's daughter Ruby (22) and Ruby's three children. Augusta and Herman have one bedroom, the three children sleep in the second bedroom, and Ruby sleeps downstairs in the living room. Ruby's boyfriend, Art, stays with Ruby many evenings.
3   Augusta's girl friend Billy and Billy's three sons live on the first floor of the house. Lazar, Magnolia's and Augusta's ex-brother-in-law, lives in the basement alone, or from time to time, with his ex-wife Carrie. Lazar eats the evening meal, which Augusta prepares for him, at household #2.
4   Magnolia's sister Lydia, Lydia's "old man," Lydia's two daughters, Georgia and Lottie, Lydia's son, and Lottie's three-year-old daughter live in Lydia's house.

Chart C   Spatial Relations in Magnolia and Leo's Domestic Network

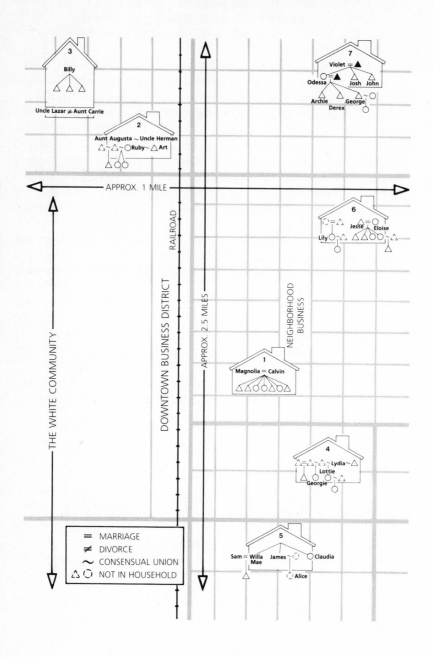

Chart D   Kin-Structured Domestic Network

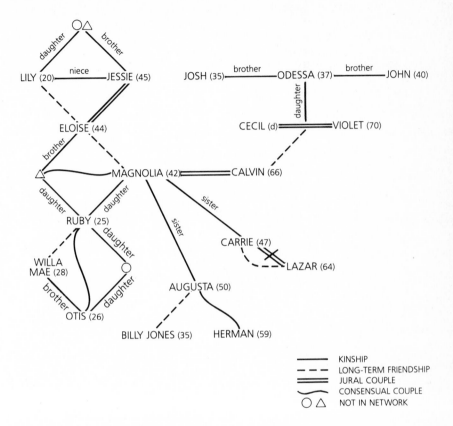

	KINSHIP
	LONG-TERM FRIENDSHIP
	JURAL COUPLE
	CONSENSUAL COUPLE
○ △	NOT IN NETWORK

5 Willa Mae (26), her husband, her son, her sister Claudia (32), and her brother
  James (father of Ruby's daughter) share a household.
6 Eloise (37), her husband Jessie, their four children, their oldest daughter's (17)
  son, and Jessie's brother's daughter Lily (20), and Lily's baby all live together.
7 Violet (70), her two sons, Josh (35) and John (40), her daughter Odessa (37),
  and Odessa's three sons and one daughter live together. Five years ago John's
  daughter (10) joined the household.

June 1969

Household   Domestic Arrangement

1 Household composition unchanged.
2 Augusta and Herman moved out after quarreling with Ruby over housekeeping and cooking duties. They joined household #3. Ruby and Art remained in
  household #2 and began housekeeping with Ruby's children.

3 *Billy and her three sons remained on the first floor and Lazar remained in the basement. Augusta and Herman rented a small, one-room apartment upstairs.*

4 *Lottie and her daughter moved out of Lydia's house to a large apartment down the street, which they shared with Lottie's girl friend and the friend's daughter. Georgia moved into her boyfriend's apartment. Lydia and her son (17) remained in the house with Lydia's "old man."*

5 *James began housekeeping with a new girl friend who lived with her sister, but he kept most of his clothes at home. His brother moved into his room after returning from the service. Willa Mae, her husband, and son remained in the house.*

6 *Household composition unchanged.*

7 *Odessa's son Raymond is the father of Clover's baby. Clover and the baby joined the household which includes Violet, her two sons, her daughter, Odessa, and Odessa's three sons and one daughter and John's daughter.*

Typical residential alignments in The Flats are those between adult mothers and sisters, mothers and adult sons and daughters, close adult female relatives, and friends defined as kin within the idiom of kinship. Domestic organization is diffused over these kin-based households.

Residence patterns among the poor in The Flats must be considered in the context of domestic organization. The connection between residence and domestic organization is apparent in examples of a series of domestic and child-care arrangements within Magnolia and Calvin's network a few years ago. Consider the following four kin-based residences among Magnolia and Calvin's kin in 1966.

Household   Domestic Arrangement

1 *Magnolia, Calvin, and seven young children.*

2 *Magnolia's mother, Magnolia's brother, Magnolia's sister and her sister's husband, Magnolia's oldest daughter, Ruby, and Ruby's first child.*

3 *Magnolia's oldest sister, Augusta, Augusta's "old man," Augusta's sister's (Carrie) son, and Magnolia's twelve-year-old son.*

4 *Magnolia's oldest son, his father, and the father's "old lady."*

Household composition *per se* reveals little about domestic organization even when cooperation between close adult females is assumed. Three of these households (1, 2, 3) were located on one city block. Magnolia's mother rented a rear house behind Magnolia's house, and Magnolia's sister Augusta lived in an apartment down the street. As we have seen, they lived and shared each other's lives. Magnolia, Ruby, and Augusta usually pooled the food stamps they received from the welfare office. The women shopped together and everyone shared the evening meal with their men and children at Magnolia's mother's house or at Magnolia's. The children did not always have a bed of their own or a bed which they were expected to share with another child. They fell asleep and slept through the night wherever the late evening visiting patterns of the adult females took them.

The kinship links which most often are the basis of new or expanded households are those links children have with close adult females such as the child's mother, mother's mother, mother's sister, mother's brother's wife, father's mother, father's sister, and father's brother's wife.

Here are some examples of the flexibility of the Blacks' adaptation to daily, social, and economic problems (Stack 1970, p. 309).

Relational Link	Domestic Arrangement
Mother	Viola's brother married his first wife when he was sixteen. When she left him she kept their daughter.
Mother's mother	Viola's sister Martha was never able to care for her children because of her nerves and high blood. In between husbands, her mother kept her two oldest children, and after Martha's death, her mother kept all three of the children.
Mother's brother	A year after Martha's death, Martha's brother took Martha's oldest daughter, helping his mother out since this left her with only two children to care for.
Mother's mother	Viola's daughter (20) was living at home and gave birth to a son. The daughter and her son remained in the Jackson household until the daughter married and set up a separate household with her husband, leaving her son to be raised by her mother.
Mother's sister	Martha moved to Chicago into her sister's household. The household consisted of the two sisters and four of their children.
Father's mother	Viola's sister Ethel had four daughters and one son. When Ethel had a nervous breakdown, her husband took the three daughters and his son to live with his mother in Arkansas. After his wife's death, the husband took the oldest daughter, to join her siblings in his mother's home in Arkansas.
Father's mother	When Viola's younger sister, Christine, left her husband in order to harvest fruit in Wisconsin, Christine left her two daughters with her husband's mother in Arkansas.
Father's sister	When Viola's brother's wife died, he decided to raise his two sons himself. He kept the two boys and never remarried although he had several girl friends and a child with one. His residence has always been near Viola's and she fed and cared for his sons.

The basis of these cooperative units is mutual aid among siblings of both sexes, the domestic cooperation of close adult females, and the exchange of goods and services between male and female kin (Stack 1970). R. T. Smith (1970, p. 66) has referred to this pattern and observes that even when lower-class Blacks live in a nuclear family group, what is "most striking is the extent to which lower-class persons continue to be involved with other kin." Nancie Gonzalez (1970, p. 232) suggests that "the fact that individuals have simultaneous loyalties to more than one such grouping may be important in understanding the social structure as a whole."

These co-residential socializing units do indeed show the important role of the black female. But the cooperation between male and female siblings who share the same household or live near one another has been underestimated by those who have considered the female-headed household and the grandmother-headed household (especially the mother's mother) as the most significant domestic units among the urban black poor.

The close cooperation of adults arises from the residential patterns typical of young adults. Due to poverty, young females with or without children do not perceive any choice but to remain living at home with their mother or other adult female relatives. Even if young women are collecting AFDC, they say that their resources go further when they share goods and services. Likewise, jobless males, or those working at part-time or seasonal jobs, often remain living at home with their mother or, if she is dead, with their sisters and brothers. This pattern continues long after men have become fathers and have established a series of sexual partnerships with women, who are living with their own kin, friends, or alone with their children. A result of this pattern is the striking fact that households almost always have men around: male relatives, by birth or marriage, and boyfriends. These men are often intermittent members of the households, boarders, or friends who come and go; men who usually eat, and sometimes sleep, in the households. Children have constant and close contact with these men, and especially in the case of male relatives, these relationships last over the years.

The most predictable residential pattern in The Flats is that men and women reside in one of the households of their natal kin, or in the households of those who raised them, long into their adult years. Even when persons temporarily move out of the household of their mother or of a close relative, they have the option to return to the residences of their kin if they have to.

Generosity and Poverty

The combination of arbitrary and repressive economic forces and social behavior, modified by successive generations of poverty, make it almost impossible for people to break out of poverty. There is no way for those families poor enough to receive welfare to acquire any surplus cash which can be saved for emergencies or for acquiring adequate appliances or a home or a car. In contrast to the middle class, who are pressured to spend and save, the poor are not even permitted to establish an equity.

The following examples from Magnolia and Calvin Waters' life illustrates the ways in which the poor are prohibited from acquiring any surplus which might enable them to change their economic condition or life style.

In 1971 Magnolia's uncle died in Mississippi and left an unexpected inheritance of $1,500 to Magnolia and Calvin Waters. The cash came from a small run-down farm which Magnolia's uncle sold shortly before he died. It was the first time in their lives that Magnolia or Calvin ever had a cash reserve. Their first hope was to buy a home and use the money as a down payment.

Calvin had retired from his job as a seasonal laborer the year before and the family was on welfare. AFDC alloted the family $100 per month for rent. The housing that the family had been able to obtain over the years for their nine children at $100 or less was always small, roach infested, with poor plumbing and heating. The family was frequently evicted. Landlords complained about the noise and often observed an average of ten to fifteen children playing in the household. Magnolia and Calvin never even anticipated that they would be able to buy a home.

Three days after they received the check, news of its arrival spread throughout their domestic network. One niece borrowed $25 from Magnolia so that her phone would not be turned off. Within a week the welfare office knew about the money. Magnolia's children were immediately cut off welfare, including medical coverage and food stamps. Magnolia was told that she would not receive a welfare grant for her children until the money was used up, and she was given a minimum of four months in which to spend the money. The first surplus the family ever acquired was effectively taken from them.

During the weeks following the arrival of the money, Magnolia and Calvin's obligations to the needs of kin remained the same, but their ability to meet these needs had temporarily increased. When another uncle became very ill in the South, Magnolia and her older sister, Augusta, were called to sit by his side. Magnolia bought round-trip train tickets so that she and Augusta could attend the funeral. Soon after his death, Augusta's first "old man" died in The Flats and he had no kin to pay for the burial. Augusta asked Magnolia to help pay for digging the grave. Magnolia was unable to refuse. Another sister's rent was two months overdue and Magnolia feared that she would get evicted. This sister was seriously ill and had no source of income. Magnolia paid her rent.

Winter was cold and Magnolia's children and grandchildren began staying home from school because they did not have warm winter coats and adequate shoes or boots. Magnolia and Calvin decided to buy coats, hats, and shoes for all of the children (at least fifteen). Magnolia also bought a winter coat for herself and Calvin bought himself a pair of sturdy shoes.

Within a month and a half, all of the money was gone. The money was channeled into the hands of the same individuals who ordinarily participate in daily domestic exchanges, but the premiums were temporarily higher. All of the money was quickly spent for necessary, compelling reasons.

Thus random fluctuations in the meager flow of available cash and goods tend to be of considerable importance to the poor. A late welfare check, sudden sickness, robbery, and other unexpected losses cannot be overcome with a cash reserve like more well-to-do families hold for emergencies. Increases in cash are either taken quickly from the poor by the welfare agencies or dissipated through the kin network.

Those living in poverty have little or no chance to escape from the economic situation into which they were born. Nor do they have the power to control the expansion or contraction of welfare benefits (Piven and Cloward 1971) or of employment opportunities, both of which have a momentous effect on their daily lives. In times of need, the only predictable resources that can be drawn upon are their own children and parents, and the fund of kin and friends obligated to them.

References

Fortes, Meyer. 1962. "Marriage in Tribal Societies." *Cambridge Papers in Social Anthropology*, No. 3. Cambridge: Cambridge University Press.

Gonzalez, Nancie. 1970. "Toward a Definition of Matrifocality." In *Afro-American Anthropology: Contemporary Perspectives,* eds. N. E. Whitten and John F. Szwed. New York: The Free Press.

Goodenough, Ward H. 1962. "KIndred and Hamlet in Lakalai, New Britain." *Ethnology* 1:5–12.

Goodenough, Ward H. 1970. *Description and Comparison in Cultural Anthropology.* Chicago: Aldine Publishing Company.

Helm, June. 1965. "Bilaterality in the Socio-Territorial Organization of the Arctic Drain Age Dene." *Ethnology,* Vol. 4, pp. 361–385.

Piven, Frances Fox and Richard A. Cloward. 1971. *Regulating the Poor: The Functions of Public Welfare.* New York: Vintage Books.

Smith, Raymond T. 1970. "The Nuclear Family in Afro-American Kinship." *Journal of Comparative Family Studies* 1(1):55–70.

Stack, Carol B. 1970. "The Kindred of Viola Jackson: Residence and Family Organization of an Urban Black American Family." In *Afro-American Anthropology: Contemporary Perspectives,* eds. N. E. Whitten and John F. Szwed. New York: The Free Press, pp. 303–312.

Collective Trauma:
Loss of Communality
Kai T. Erikson

■ The disaster stretched human nerves to their outer edge. Those of us who did not experience it can never really comprehend the full horror of that day, but we can at least appreciate why it should cause such misery and why it should leave so deep a scar on the minds of those who lived through it. Our imagination can reach across the gulf of personal experience and begin to re-create those parts of the scene that touch the senses. Our eyes can almost see a burning black wave lashing down the hollow and taking everything in its path. The ears can almost hear a roar like thunder, pierced by screams and explosions and the crack of breaking timbers. The nostrils can almost smell the searing stench of mine wastes and the sour odor of smoke and death and decay. All this we can begin to picture because the mind is good at imagery.

But the people of Buffalo Creek suffered a good deal more that day, for they were wrenched out of their communities, torn from the human surround in which they had been so deeply enmeshed. Much of the drama drains away when we begin to talk about such things, partly because the loss of communality seems a step removed from the vivid terror of the event itself and partly because the people of the hollow, so richly articulate when describing the flood and their reaction to it, do not really know how to express what their separation from the familiar tissues of home has meant to them. The closeness of communal ties is experienced on Buffalo Creek as a part of the natural order of things, and residents can no more describe that presence than fish are aware of the water they swim in. It is just there, the envelope in which they live, and it is taken entirely for granted. In this chapter, then . . . I will use quotations freely, but one must now listen even more carefully for the feelings behind the words as well as registering the content of the words themselves.

I use the term "communality" here rather than "community" in order to underscore the point that people are not referring to particular village territories when they lament the loss of community but to the network of relationships that make up their general human surround. The persons who constitute the center of that network are usually called "neighbors," the word being used in its Biblical sense to identify those with whom one shares bonds of intimacy and a feeling of mutual concern. The people of Buffalo Creek are "neighbor people," which is a local way of referring to a style of relationship long familiar among social scientists. Toennies called it "gemeinschaft," Cooley called it "primary," Durkheim called it "mechanical," Redfield called it "folk," and every generation of social scientists since has found other ways to express the same thought, one of the most recent being Herbert Gans's concept of "person orientation."

What is a neighbor? When you ask people on Buffalo Creek what the term means, they try to remember that you come from the city and they illustrate their answer with the kind of concrete detail that makes mountain speech so clear and direct.

What's a neighbor? Well, when I went to my neighbor's house on Saturday or Sunday, if I wanted a cup of coffee I never waited until the lady of the house asked me. I just went into the dish cabinet and got me a cup of coffee or a glass of juice just like it was my own home. They come to my house, they done the same. See?

We was like one big family. Like when somebody was hurt, everybody was hurt. You know. I guess it was because it was the same people all the time. I don't know how to explain it. It's a good feeling. It's more than friends. If someone was hurt, everybody was concerned, everybody. If somebody lost a member of their family, they was always there. Everybody was around bringing you something to eat, trying to help. It's a deeper feeling.

Here, if you have a neighbor, it's somebody you know, it's somebody that maybe you take them to the store. I mean, to us neighbors are people that we have. We just know each other, that's all.

Neighbor? It means relationship. It means kin. It means friends you could depend on. You never went to a neighbor with a complaint that they didn't listen to or somebody didn't try to help you with. That's a neighbor. When you wanted a baby-sitter you went next door and they'd baby-sit. Or you did something for them. They'd either need something or we'd need something, you know. When you see somebody going down the road, it's "Where are you going?" "To the store." "Well, bring me back such and such."

A neighbor, then, is someone you can relate to without pretense, a familiar and reliable part of your everyday environment; a neighbor is someone you treat as if he or she were a member of your immediate family. A good deal has been said in the literature on Appalachia about the clannishness of mountain life, but on Buffalo Creek, as in many coal camps, this sense of tribal attachment reaches beyond linkages of kin to include a wider circle, and the obligations one feels toward the people within that circle are not unlike the obligations one normally feels toward one's own family.

In good times, then, every person on Buffalo Creek looks out at the larger community from a fairly intimate neighborhood niche. If we were to devise a map representing the average person's social world, we would capture at least the main contours by drawing a number of concentric circles radiating out from the individual center—the inner ring encompassing one's immediate family, the next ring encompassing one's closest neighbors, the third encompassing the familiar people with whom one relates on a regular basis, and the fourth encompassing the other people whom one recognizes as a part of the Buffalo Creek community even though one does not really know them well. Beyond the outermost of those rings is the rest of the world, the terrain populated by what an older generation called "foreigners." Given the size of Buffalo Creek, it is obvious that the community contained people who were relative strangers to one another. Yet there was a clear sense of kinship linking even those relative strangers together—although, as we shall see shortly, that sense of kinship turned out to depend to a greater degree than people realized on the security of one's neighborhood niche.

Communality on Buffalo Creek can best be described as a state of mind shared among a particular gathering of people, and this state of mind, by definition, does not lend itself to sociological abstraction. It does not have a name or a cluster of distinguishing properties. It is a quiet set of understandings that become absorbed into the atmosphere and are thus a part of the natural order. The remarks below, for example, are separate attempts by a husband and wife to explain the nature of those "understandings."

Braeholm was more like a family. We had a sort of understanding. If someone was away, then we sort of looked after each other's property. We didn't do a lot of visiting, but we had a general understanding. If we cooked something, we would exchange dishes. It was sort of a close-knit type of thing.

Before the disaster, the neighbors, we could look out and tell when one another needed help or when one was sick or something was disturbing that person. We could tell from the lights. If the lights was on late at night, we knew that something unusual was going on and we would go over. Sometimes I'd come in from work on a cold day and my neighbor would have a pot of soup for me. There was just things you wouldn't think about. I would look forward to going to the post office. If my car wouldn't start, all I'd have to do is call my neighbors and they would take me to work. If I was there by myself or something, if my husband was out late, the neighbors would come over and check if everything was okay. So it was just a rare thing. It was just a certain type of relationship that you just knew from people growing up together and sharing the same experiences.

And the key to that network of understandings was a constant readiness to look after one's neighbors, or, rather, to know without being asked what needed to be done.

If you had problems, you wouldn't even have to mention it. People would just know what to do. They'd just pitch in and help. Everyone was concerned about everyone else.

I don't think there was a better place in the world to live. People was there when you needed them. You got sick, they helped you. If you needed help of any kind, you got it. You didn't even have to ask for it. Now I'm a person that didn't make friends easy. I wasn't hard to get along with, I just didn't mix. But I knew everybody, and—Well, I just don't know no way to explain it to you, to make you see it.

You'd just have to experience it, I guess, to really know. It was wonderful. Like when my father died. My neighbors all came in and they cleaned my house, they washed my clothes, they cooked. I didn't do nothing. They knew what to do. I mean it's just like teamwork, you know. If one of the kids was sick, they'd drop every what they were doing, take the kid to the hospital or sit up all night with him. It was just good. How did they know when you needed help? I don't know how to explain it, really. The morning my daddy died—he died in Logan—my aunt called me and told me on the phone at about ten o'clock in the morning, and I had just got time to get off the phone and go set on the bed and in come three of my neighbors. They knew it that quick. I don't know how. They just knew.

The difficulty is that when you invest so much of yourself in that kind of social arrangement you become absorbed by it, almost captive to it, and the larger collectivity around you becomes an extension of your own personality, an extension of your own flesh. This means that not only are you diminished as a person when that surrounding tissue is stripped away, but that you are no longer able to reclaim as your own the emotional resources you invested in it. To "be neighborly" is not a quality you can carry with you into a new situation like negotiable emotional currency; the old community was your niche in the classic ecological sense, and your ability to relate to that niche is not a skill easily transferred to another setting. This is true whether you move into another community, as was the case with the first speaker below, or whether a new set of neighbors moves in around your old home, as was the case with the second.

Well, I have lost all my friends. The people I was raised up and lived with, they're scattered. I don't know where they're at. I've got to make new friends, and that's a hard thing to do. You don't make new friends and feel towards them like you did the people you lived with. See, I raised my family there. We moved there in '35 and stayed there. I knew everybody in the camp and practically everybody on Buffalo, as far as that is concerned. But down here, there ain't but a few people I know, and you don't feel secure around people you don't know.

Neighbors. We used to have our children at home, we didn't go to hospitals to have children. The one on this side of me, them two in back of me, this one in front of me—they all lived there and we all had our children together. Now I've got all new neighbors. I even asked my husband to put our home up for sale, and he said, "What do you think we're going to do? We're old people, we can't take to buy another home." And I said, "I don't care what you do with it, I'm not staying here. I can't tell you in words what's the matter." I said, "I don't care if we go to the moon, let's just get out of here. I'm just not interested enough anymore. You go out the back door here and there's a new neighbor. In front of me is a new neighbor and on the other side of me is a new neighbor. It's just not the same home that I've been living in for thirty-five years. It's just not the same to me."

A community of the sort we are talking about here derives from and depends on an almost perfect democracy of the spirit, where people are not only assumed to be equal in status but virtually identical in temperament and outlook. Classes of people may be differentiated for certain purposes—women from men, adults from children, whites from blacks, and so on—but individual persons are not distinguished from one another on the basis of rank, occupation, style of life, or even recreational habits. This is not hard to understand as a practical matter. The men all work at the same jobs; the women all command domestic territories of roughly the same original size and quality; the children all attend the same schools as an apprenticeship for the same futures; and everybody buys the same goods at the same stores from equivalent paychecks. Yet the leveling tendency goes even beyond that, for the people of the hollow, like the people of Appalachia generally, do not like to feel different from their fellows and tend to see status distinctions of any kind as fissures in the smooth surface of the community. Good fences may make good neighbors in places like New Hampshire, where relationships depend on cleanly marked parcels of individual space, but they are seen as lines of division in places like Buffalo Creek.

In most of the urban areas of America, each individual is seen as a separate being, with careful boundaries drawn around the space he or she occupies as a discrete personage. Everyone is presumed to have an individual name, an individual mind, an individual voice, and, above all, an individual sense of self—so much so that persons found deficient in any of those qualities are urged to take some kind of remedial action such as undergoing psychotherapy, participating in a consciousness-raising group, or reading one of a hundred different manuals on self-actualization. This way of looking at things, however, has hardly any meaning at all in most of Appalachia. There, boundaries are drawn around whole groups of people, not around separate individuals with egos to protect and potentialities to realize; and a person's mental health is measured less by his capacity to express his inner self than by his capacity to submerge that self into a larger communal whole.

It was once fashionable in the social sciences generally to compare human communities to living organisms. Scholars anxious to make the kind of distinction I am wrestling with now would argue that persons who belong to traditional communities relate to one another in much the same fashion as the cells of a body: they are dependent on one another for definition, they do not have any real function or identity apart from the contribution they make to the whole organization, and they suffer a form of death when separated from that larger tissue. Science may have gained something when this analogy was abandoned, but it may have lost something, too, for a community of the kind being discussed here *does* bear at least a figurative resemblance to an organism. In places like Buffalo Creek, the community in general can be described as the locus for activities that are normally regarded as the exclusive property of individuals. It is the *community* that cushions pain, the *community* that provides a context for intimacy, the *community* that represents morality and serves as the repository for old traditions.

Now one has to realize when talking like this that one is in danger of drifting off into a realm of metaphor. Communities do not have hearts or sinews or ganglia; they do not suffer or rationalize or experience joy. But the analogy does help suggest that a cluster of people acting in concert and moving to the same collective rhythms can allocate their personal resources in such a way that the whole comes to have more humanity than its constituent parts. In effect, people put their own individual resources at the disposal of the group—placing them in the communal store, as it were—and then draw on that reserve supply for the demands of everyday life. And if the whole community more or less disappears, as happened on Buffalo Creek, people find that they cannot take advantage of the energies they once invested in the communal store. They find that they are almost empty of feeling, empty of affection, empty of confidence and assurance. It is as if the individual cells had supplied raw energy to the whole body but did not have the means to convert that energy back into a usable personal form once the body was no longer there to process it. When an elderly woman on Buffalo Creek said softly, "I just don't take no interest in nothing like I used to, I don't have no feeling for nothing, I feel like I'm drained of life," she was reflecting a spirit still numbed by the disaster, but she was also reflecting a spirit unable to recover for its own use all the life it had signed over to the community.

4
PARENTHOOD

It is only within the last twenty years that parenthood has become an issue. Married people were supposed to have children, preferably the sooner the better after they got married. One indication that this was normative is that married couples encountered terrific pressure and criticism if they waited too long after having their first child—as though relatives and friends would not tolerate their having only one child by choice.

Those were the days before 1960, when the American birth rate took an historic plunge. Fertility declined among women aged 15 to 44 from 118 births per 1,000 in 1960 to only 66.7 in 1970. As Paul Glick observes in the essay which appears in Part 1, the fertility rate has by now bottomed out—declined about as much as it probably will—and will not rise significantly in the next decades. Along with these changing demographics there have been increased feelings of uneasiness about the future of parenthood. Where once married couples were pressured to have more than one child, today they are often applauded by family and friends for having a child at all. In addition, marriage and parenthood are no longer synonymous. A small but growing number of people are having children without ever getting married, and more married couples are opting to remain childless.

This is the social context which led to the rise of parenthood as a social issue. Readings in Part 4 address some of the problems associated with parenting in the 1980s and beyond: everything from deciding to become parents, through early parenthood, and on to parenting with teenaged children.

Of course there will always be married people who will prefer to remain childless and have no regrets about it, but most Americans are still interested in becoming parents. Sharon Houseknecht in "Childlessness and Marital Adjustment," for example, found there were differences in marital adjustment when she compared voluntarily childless women with mothers. Women who are childless by choice, says Houseknecht, score higher on measures of marital adjustment. It can be inferred that women who are childless, but not by choice, are less satisfied with their marriages.

Feelings of autonomy and control over her destiny—not to mention her body—are central to the marital satisfaction of a childless woman. The same applies for women who do have children. The most satisfied mothers are those women who had children when they felt emotionally and financially prepared to do so. Jane Price examines the small but growing population of women who postpone motherhood until they are beyond age thirty. Most of these women are well-educated and gainfully employed. Not only do they have successful careers, says Price in "Who Waits to Have Children? And Why?"; they also make satisfied and enthusiastic parents.

Finally, Bergman rounds out the section by examining another aspect of autonomy and control over parenthood. In "Licensing Parents: A New

Age of Child-Raising?" he predicts that people might someday need to pass competency exams or other basic tests before they could have children. Any parenting exam would penalize some competent people who would otherwise become parents, but tests of this kind might also serve to screen people with potential for violence and child abuse. Given the existing level of violence in American families (refer to the essay by Gelles and Straus in Part 6 of this book), there are bound to be people who advocate licensing procedures for parents in years to come.

Being able to have a baby does not necessarily make couples qualified to raise one, however. The early years of parenting are critical for both parents *and* children. Since the quality of child care deserves special consideration, the second section of Part 4 is devoted entirely to issues relating to early parenthood.

This writer once asked a friend how to soothe a crying infant. "It's not enough to feed them, burp them, or diaper them," she said. "You've also got to give them lots of hugs."[1] Alison Clarke-Stewart may not have formulated the needs of young children in quite those terms, but there are parallels nonetheless. In Clarke-Stewart's "The Family as a Child-Care Environment," there is an important discussion of why the two-parent household is currently the most effective milieu for raising children. Next, Knox and Wilson explain some social differences between having one and two children. They point out that adding a second child to an existing family creates some predictable strains—and some unpredictable ones as well. The message in Knox and Wilson's article evokes Lord Rochester at his paternal best. "Before I got married," he observed in the seventeenth century, "I had six theories about bringing up children. Now I have six children and no theories." Knox and Wilson could probably not describe the impact of a sixth child any better than Lord Rochester did. But their interpretation of the impact a second child has upon the family is perceptive enough.

Finally, Feigelman and Silverman identify some characteristics of single parents who adopt children. Their work on "Single Parent Adoptions" is worth considering because it integrates two existing strands of social research: issues relating to adoptive parents, and issues pertaining to the early experience of adopted children. The message in this selection is that parenting need not be conventional in order to succeed.

It was a teenager who once quipped that "people get older and wiser—but not parents." Many parents would not credit their teenagers with all that much wisdom either. Later parenting, especially during the years when offspring are teenagers, can be fraught with tension and misunderstandings. Teenagers, after all, are exploring their social world

---

1. Nanci R. Weiss, personal communication.

and "rehearsing" (to borrow from the piece by Gagnon and Greenblat in Part 2) a wide range of sexual behaviors.

The Rapoports, in "Parenting with Adolescent Children," offer some explanation for strain between parents and their teenagers, and they advise how it can be minimized. As such, their essay is ideal for introducing the issue of later parenthood, which is the third and final section in Part 4.

Wolk and Brandon describe ways that teenage runaways perceive their parents and themselves in "Runaway Adolescents' Perceptions of Parents and Self." If teenage runaways are attracting attention, they may someday be eclipsed by teenagers and young adults who refuse to leave home. Audrey Foote mentions some of the problems that arise because of "Kids Who Won't Leave Home," the young adults who return home after college and live once again with Mother and Dad. Admittedly, Foote treats the subject lightly, but there may well be a growing number of young adults and older teenagers who cannot afford to leave home. *U.S. News & World Report,* for example, recently described "the refilled nest," by which was meant a household containing college graduates who returned after a four- or five-year absence.[2] Spiraling inflation and widespread unemployment may well make it difficult for many younger people to strike out on their own in the years ahead—generating a set of tensions during later parenthood which are currently little researched and relatively unknown in the literature on marriage and the family.

---

2. "The American Family: Bent—But Not Broken," *U.S. News & World Report,* 16 June 1980, p. 48.

Parenting as a Social Issue

Childlessness and Marital Adjustment*
Sharon K. Houseknecht

A number of researchers have found that childless individuals report a higher level of marital adjustment/satisfaction than do people with children. Unfortunately, the category "childless" in these studies included voluntarily and involuntarily childless individuals as well as people who were simply postponing childbearing. The purpose of this study was: (1) to examine the relationship between voluntary childlessness and marital adjustment and (2) to eliminate the possibility of certain alternative explanations that could account for any difference that might be observed. To accomplish this aim, each of 50 voluntarily childless wives was precision-matched with 50 mothers on three variables—education, religion, and participation in the labor force. All were between 25 and 40 years of age. Consensus, cohesion, satisfaction, and affection expression were four components of marital adjustment that served as the bases for comparing these women. The findings reveal that the women who were childless by choice scored higher in overall marital adjustment but that this difference was not uniform across all areas of adjustment. The component that possessed the greatest discriminatory power was "cohesion."

"Childlessness and Marital Adjustment" by Sharon K. Houseknecht from JOURNAL OF MARRIAGE AND THE FAMILY, vol. 41, no. 2, May 1979. Copyright © 1979 by the National Council on Family Relations. Reprinted by permission.
*Revision of a paper presented at the annual meeting of the American Sociological Association. San Francisco, California, 1978. Thanks are due to Dr. Graham B. Spanier for his consistent encouragement and constructive advice at all stages of the research.

■   A number of researchers have found that childless individuals report a higher level of marital adjustment/satisfaction than do people with children. For example, Renne (1970) noted that, contrary to popular belief, parents were definitely less apt to be satisfied with their marriages than childless persons. Feldman (1971), too, found that the level of marital satisfaction was significantly lower for those with one or more children in the home compared to a control group of those who were childless. This finding was also present when couples with an infant as their first child were compared to a control group married for the same period but without a child. Ryder (1973) provided additional support for the notion that children have a negative effect on marriages. His data revealed that women who have a child become more likely than women without children to report that their husbands are not paying enough attention to them.

Unfortunately, these studies that have looked at the relationship between having a child and marital adjustment/satisfaction are characterized by two major methodological limitations. First, the term "childless" refers to more than just voluntary childlessness. The criterion used was "not having children at the time of the investigation." This means that people who were simply postponing childbearing as well as the involuntarily childless were also included. Since previous research has found that differences exist between "postponers" and "childless" individuals (Bram, 1974), this is an important consideration to take into account. Furthermore, it doesn't seem reasonable to assume that people who desire no children are the same as those who cannot have children. Lumping involuntarily childless individuals and postponers together with voluntarily childless individuals represents a methodological shortcoming because it does not permit any conclusions to be drawn about the relationship between the choice of a childless life style and marital adjustment.

Only one researcher (Bram, 1974) has looked at the difference between voluntarily childless couples and couples with children in their overall evaluation of their marriages. In that study, however, the evaluation was limited to a single global question, "How happy is your marriage compared to most couples you know?" There are several problems with such a global question including the possibility of bias resulting from socially-acceptable responses.

A second methodological limitation that characterized earlier studies which examined the relationship between having a child and marital adjustment/satisfaction was their failure to control for certain relevant variables. For example, studies have shown that childless women tend to be disproportionately highly educated (Bogue, 1969; Gustavus and Henley, 1971; Panko, 1972; Rao, 1974; U.S. Bureau of the Census, 1974; Houseknecht and Spanier, 1976), disproportionately involved in the labor force (U.S. Bureau of the Census, 1974; Veevers, 1974; Bram, 1974; Ory 1976) and disproportionately unidentified with a formal religious denomination (Gustavus and Henley, 1971; Veevers, 1973; Houseknecht, 1974; Bram, 1974; Ory, 1976).

Furthermore, other studies have repeatedly shown that education, employment and religion variables are related to marital disruption (Lenski, 1961; O'Neill, 1967; Bumpass and Sweet, 1972; Havens, 1973; Levinger, 1978; Houseknecht and Spanier, 1976; Mott et al., 1977) and, therefore, it is conceivable that they could be related to marital adjustment/satisfaction. In fact, there is some support for this notion (Axelson, 1963; Gover, 1963; Renne, 1970; Fogarty et al., 1971; Burke and Weir, 1976; Scanzoni and Scanzoni, 1976; Booth, 1977). Therefore, to compare childless women and mothers without controlling for these variables does not permit any conclusions regarding the impact of children per se on marital adjustment/satisfaction. It is not inconceivable that the differences which earlier investigators found in marital adjustment/satisfaction could have been the result of differences in educational level, employment status, and religious identification and not of the presence or absence of children.

In summary, the purpose of the present study was twofold. One objective was to examine in greater detail the relationship between voluntary childlessness and marital adjustment. Comparative analyses between childless individuals and parents is not sufficient for a complete understanding of the effects of children/childlessness on marital adjustment/satisfaction. Particularly since earlier studies have found that childless individuals tend to be characterized by higher levels of marital adjustment/satisfaction, it is important to now go a step further to see if the relationship differs depending on the motivations for the childless life style: i.e., voluntary-involuntary.

A second objective of this study was to eliminate the possibility of certain alternative explanations (education, employment, religious identification) that could account for any difference that might be observed.

Spanier (1976) proposed four empirically-verified components of dyadic adjustment which include marital satisfaction, dyadic consensus, dyadic cohesion, and affection expression. These four components served as the basis for comparing women who had children and women who were voluntarily childless. In addition, the respondents in each parental status category were contrasted with respect to overall marital adjustment.

Methods

Sample

A nonprobability, precision-matched sample of 50 currently-married women who were childless by choice and 50 married mothers was located by means of a modified network approach. In initial names were suggested by family planning clinics, hospitals, the National Organization for Nonparents, day care centers and various persons in administrative positions rather than by respondents. In those few cases in which a respondent did suggest someone, that person was contacted only if the respondent assured the interviewer that the person was an acquaintance and not a close friend.

Six criteria determined whether or not a childless woman was accepted for participation in the study. In addition to affirming that she had never borne a child nor adopted one, she also had to state clearly that her childlessness was due to choice, not biological reasons. She also had to have been married for a minimimum of five years if neither she nor her spouse had been sterilized for contraceptive purposes. An additional measure of commitment was an attitude-certainty measure. She had to answer "very certain" or "fairly certain" that no children were desired in the future. Finally, all of the respondents, including the mothers and the childless women, had to be between 25 and 40 years of age.

Each of the 50 voluntarily childless respondents were precision-matched on three variables—education, religion, and participation in the labor force—with a woman who had children. Choosing mothers who precisely matched the childless women on these three variables was an important aspect of this study for reasons that were previously mentioned.

Selected social characteristics of the samples are summarized in Table 1. It is important to note that the mothers had been married for an average of 12.5 years, whereas the childless women had been married only for an average of 7.3 years. However, a correlational analysis revealed that marital adjustment and number of years married were not related in either the childless sample ($r = .07$) or in the sample of mothers ($r = .08$).

Measurement of Marital Adjustment

During the course of an in-depth interview that was conducted with each respondent, Spanier's Dyadic Adjustment Scale (1976) was self-administered in its entirety (32 items) to measure overall marital adjustment. As measured by this scale, dyadic adjustment refers to a process, the outcome of which is determined by the degree of: (1) dyadic satisfaction; (2) consensus on matters of importance to dyadic functioning; (3) dyadic cohesion; and (4) affection expression. The scale was designed to be divided into four subscales—marital satisfaction, dyadic consensus, dyadic cohesion, and affectual expression—which permitted measurement of the four components of adjustment that Spanier (1976) had identified. Each respondent's score was obtained by summing the values for the individual items. *T*-tests were used in the analyses. Using

Table 1 Selected Social Characteristics by Parental Status

Characteristic	Childless Females	Mothers
Mean Age	29.9	33.6
Mean Years Married	7.3	12.5
Percent in Labor Force	98	98
Education:		
Percent High School	6	6
Percent 1-3 Years Beyond High School	16	16
Percent 4 Years Beyond High School	26	26
Percent 5-6 Years Beyond High School	48	48
Percent 7 or More Years Beyond High School	4	4
Religion:		
Percent Atheist, Agnostic, None	52	52
Percent Catholic	8	8
Percent Jewish	2	2
Percent Protestant	38	38

Cronbach's coefficient *alpha,* the total scale reliability for this sample is .90. The data indicate that the total scale as well as its components have sufficiently high reliability to justify their use.

It is important to note that marital adjustment in this study is defined as the individual's adjustment to the marriage (Burr, 1970; Spanier, 1972; Scanzoni and Scanzoni, 1976), since the results are based only on data obtained from wives.

Results

The findings, which are presented in Table 2, demonstrate that the scale used to measure dyadic adjustment did, in fact, uncover a significant difference between voluntarily childless women and mothers. The childless women scored higher in overall adjustment ($\bar{X}$ = 112.72) than did the mothers ($\bar{X}$ = 107.34; t = 2.16, 98 *df*, $p < .04$).

Looking at the scores on the various subscales, however, it becomes apparent that this difference was not uniform across all areas of adjustment. The component that possessed the greatest discriminatory power was "cohesion." The childless marriages were significantly more cohesive

Table 2   Scores[a] on the Dyadic Adjustment Scale and Its Subscales[b] by Parental Status

Dyadic Adjustment	Childless Females			Mothers			
	Mean	Standard Deviation	Standard Error	Mean	Standard Deviation	Standard Error	t-test
Dyadic Cohesion Subscale	17.32	2.853	.403	15.20	3.429	.485	3.36*
Dyadic Satisfaction Subscale	39.28	4.794	.678	37.36	5.256	.743	1.91
Dyadic Consensus Subscale	47.52	5.003	.708	46.14	5.827	.824	1.27
Affectional Expression Subscale	8.60	1.895	.268	8.64	1.925	.272	.10
Dyadic Adjustment Scale	112.72	11.803 (N = 50)	1.669	107.34	13.082 (N = 50)	1.850	2.16**

*$p < .04$.
**$p < .001$.
[a]Based on the Dyadic Adjustment Scale (Spanier, 1976).
[b]Range of possible scores: Total scale   0-161
                                          Cohesion subscale   0-24
                                          Satisfaction subscale   0-50
                                          Consensus subscale   0-65
                                          Affectual expression subscale 0-12

($\bar{X} = 17.32$) than the marriages with children ($\bar{X} = 15.20$; $t = 3.36$, 98 df, $p < .001$). They also tended to be higher with regard to level of marital satisfaction (childless $\bar{X} = 39.28$ and mother $\bar{X} = 37.36$; $t = 1.91$, 98 df, $p < .06$).

It is informative to see precisely which items intended to measure cohesiveness and/or satisfaction significantly distinguished between the childless women and the mothers. First, with regard to cohesiveness, the females who were childless by choice indicated that they engaged in outside interests with their spouses more frequently than did the mothers ($t = 2.48$, 98 df, $p < .02$). Those who were childless also reported a more frequent exchange of stimulating ideas with their spouses ($t = 3.00$, 98 df, $p < .01$). Calmly discussing something with one's partner was another measure of cohesiveness that occurred more frequently among the childless women than it did among the mothers ($t = 2.84$, 98 df, $p < .01$). Finally, working together with their spouses on a project was more common for the respondents who had decided not to have children than it was for those who had become mothers ($t = 2.04$, 98 df, $p < .05$).

Turning to another component of adjustment, marital satisfaction, there were two items on which the childless women and the women with children differed significantly. The childless women expressed a stronger desire and determination to continue the marital relationship ($t = 2.42$, 98 df, $p < .02$). They also reported a higher degree of happiness in their marital relationship relative to the happiness of most relationships than did the mothers ($t = 3.12$, 98 df, $p < .01$).

There were two other areas of dyadic adjustment that did not seem to be dependent on parental status. The women in both samples reported similar levels of consensus and affectual expression in their marriages. However, to say that there were no overall differences for each of these subscales does not necessarily mean that there were not significant differences between the samples with regard to specific items. In fact, three items in the consensus subscale disclosed disparities. The women who were childless by choice reported a greater extent of agreement between their husbands and themselves than did the mothers on the matters of household tasks ($t = 2.41$, 98 df, $p < .02$), leisure time interests and activities ($t = 2.16$, 98 df, $p < .04$), and career decisions ($t = 2.09$, 98 df, $p < .04$).

The items in the affection expression subscale did not reveal any significant differences between the two types of women. The majority of women in each parental status category indicated that sex relations and demonstrations of affection were not problematic in their relationships.

Discussion

It is important to note that although the research design did not require or even suggest it, the voluntarily childless women that participated in this study shared the characteristics that typified those in earlier studies. They were disproportionately highly educated (Gustavus and Henley, 1971; Veevers, 1973); disproportionately involved in the labor force (Gustavus and Henley, 1971; Veevers, 1974; Bram, 1974; Ory, 1976); and disproportionately unidentified with a formal religious denomination (Gustavus and Henley, 1971; Veevers, 1973; Houseknecht, 1974, 1977, 1978; Bram, 1974; Ory, 1976).

The mothers in this study were unusual with respect to education, employment and religion primarily because they have been selected to match the childless women in these areas. This research design served to reduce the differences between the two samples that might have resulted if there had been no control on these important demographic variables.

Because this study investigated voluntarily childless women exclusively and because it precision-matched childless women and mothers, it provides a more refined answer to the question of the impact of children on marital adjustment than earlier studies were able to do. Unfortunately, there is a paradox in that the more carefully researchers eliminate alternative explanations, the less certain they can be of the extent to which the findings can be generalized to broader social groups. In other words, external validity was reduced in the present study because of the emphasis that was placed on internal validity (*i.e.*, isolating the effect of the independent variable by eliminating alternative explanations). According to Stanley and Campbell (1963), however, external validity is a very important consideration only if it does not interfere with internal validity.

The detailed analysis with regard to the various components of marital adjustment adds to the understanding of the dynamics involved. Consensus, cohesion, satisfaction, and affection expression were the four components that served as the basis for comparing these women. The findings reveal that although the childless women scored higher than the mothers in overall adjustment, it was in terms of "cohesiveness" that they differed the most. They did not differ significantly on the three remaining components of adjustment.

It is interesting, however, that even though there was no overall difference between the childless women and the mothers on the spousal "consensus" component, they did differ significantly on three of the items intended to measure extent of spousal agreement—leisure time interests and activities, household tasks, and career decisions. The greater extent of spousal agreement reported by the childless women on household tasks and career decisions does not reveal who was doing what. It only indicates that the childless women were more satisfied with the ways in which these matters were being handled in their marriages. However, a recent longitudinal study concluded that education and employment are the most important variables for predicting women's sex-role attitudes (Mason et al., 1976). It was found that well-educated women and those with the most recent employment experiences held more egalitarian attitudes. In the present study, 90 percent of the women in each parental status category were working full-time and 52 percent of each type had five or more years of college. Therefore, it seems probable that the greater extent of interspousal agreement reported by the childless women implies that their husbands were not only more likely to be supportive of their careers but also more inclined to share the housekeeper role.

Some writers have shown associations between divorce proneness and childlessness (Cahen, 1932; Wilcox, 1940; Jacobson, 1950; Ory, 1976). In fact, Renne (1970) suggested, as an explanation of her finding of more dissatisfaction in marriages where there are children, that couples with children may continue in unsatisfactory marriages while childless couples would feel more free to separate. All but one (Ory, 1976) of the studies reporting an association between divorce and childlessness lumped the various types of childlessness together, a methodological shortcoming discussed earlier. All of the studies failed to control for wife's education, employment, and religious identification. As mentioned previously, voluntarily childless women are more likely to be highly educated, employed outside the home, and unidentified with a formal religious denomination—three variables that are associated with higher rates of marital disruption (Lenski, 1961; O'Neill, 1967; Bumpass and Sweet, 1972; Havens, 1973; Levinger, 1978; Houseknecht and Spanier, 1976; Mott et al., 1977). Therefore, it is conceivable that the higher rates of divorce among the voluntarily childless reported by Ory (1976) might well have been spurious.

The results of the present study do not lend support to the notion that voluntarily childless women are more divorce prone than women with children. Only 12 percent of the childless women and 4 percent of the mothers had been married before and divorced. The difference was not statistically significant.

Conclusions

The purpose of this study was: (1) to examine the relationship between voluntary childlessness and marital adjustment and (2) to eliminate the possibility of certain alternative explanations that could account for any difference that might be observed. To accomplish this aim, voluntarily childless wives were precision-matched with mothers on three variables —education, religion, and participation in the labor force. The results lend support to the notion that the relationship between childlessness and enhanced marital adjustment/satisfaction found by earlier investigators (Renne, 1970; Feldman, 1971; Ryder, 1973; Bram, 1974) is not spurious.

Nevertheless, even though these voluntarily childless women and mothers did differ significantly in their overall marital adjustment, it is important to note that the difference was small in magnitude and resulted mainly from a difference in "cohesion," one of four components of marital adjustment that were measured. The finding that the difference between childless women and mothers in overall marital adjustment was not very large may suggest that it is not the presence or absence of children per se but rather education, employment, or religion (or some combination of these variables) that has the major impact on marital adjustment.

Based on this study, it appears that there is a need for further research to more precisely define the effect of these demographic variables on marital adjustment, controlling for the presence of children. Also, it would be enlightening if future research would focus on the remaining two types of childlessness, the involuntarily childless and the postponers, to see if the relationship between childlessness and enhanced marital adjustment holds for people who are childless for reasons beyong their control and for people who are simply postponing childbearing.

References

Axelson, Leland
   1963 "Marital adjustment and marital role definitions of husbands of working and non-working wives." Marriage and Family Living 25 (May): 189–195.
Bogue, D. J.
   1969 Principles of Demography. New York: John Wiley and Sons.
Booth, Alan
   1977 "Wife's employment and husband's stress: A replication and refutation." Journal of Marriage and the Family 39 (November): 645–650.
Bram, Susan
   1974 "To have or have not: A social psychological study of voluntarily childless couples, parents-to-be, and parents." Unpublished doctoral dissertation, University of Michigan.
Bumpass, Larry L., and James A. Sweet
   1972 "Differentials in marital instability: 1970." American Sociological Review 37 (December): 754–766.
Burke, Ronald J., and Tamara Weir
   1976 "Relationship of wives' employment status to husband, wife pair satisfaction and performance." Journal of Marriage and the Family 38 (May): 279–287.
Burr, Wesley
   1970 "Satisfaction with various aspects of marriage over the life cycle: A random middle-class sample." Journal of Marriage and the Family 32 (February): 29–37.
Cahen, Alfred
   1932 Statistical Analysis of American Divorce. New York: Columbia University Press.
Campbell, Donald T., and Julian C. Stanley
   1963 Experimental and Quasi-Experimental Designs for Research. Chicago: Rand McNally and Co.
Feldman, Harold
   1971 "The effects of children on the family." Pp. 107–125 in Andrée Michel (Ed.), Family Issues of Employed Women in Europe and America. Lieden, The Netherlands: E. F. Brill.
Fogarty, Michael, Rhona Rapoport, and Robert N. Rapoport
   1971 Sex, Career and Family. Beverly Hills, California: Sage.
Gover, David A.
   1963 "Socio-economic differential in the relationship between marital adjustment and wife's employment status." Marriage and Family Living 25 (November): 452–456.
Gustavus, Susan O., and James R. Henley, Jr.
   1971 "Correlates of voluntary childlessness in a select population." Social Biology 18 (September): 277–284.
Havens, Elizabeth M.
   1973 "Women, work and wedlock: A note on female marital patterns in the U.S." Pp. 213–219 in Joan Huber (Ed.), Changing Women in a Changing Society. Chicago: The University of Chicago Press.
Houseknecht, Sharon K.
   1974 "Social psychological aspects of voluntary childlessness." Unpublished master's thesis, The Pennsylvania State University.
   1977 "Reference group support for voluntary childlessness: Evidence for conformity." Journal of Marriage and the Family 39 (May): 285–292.
   1978 "A social psychological model of voluntary childlessness." Alternative Lifestyles 1 (August): 379–402.
Houseknecht, Sharon K., and Graham B. Spanier
   1976 "Marital disruption among highly educated women: An exception to the rule."

Paper presented at the Conference on Women in Midlife Crises, Cornell University, Ithaca, New York, October.

Jacobson, Paul H.
1950   "Differentials in divorce by duration of marriage and size of family." American Sociological Review 15 (April): 235–244.

Lenski, Gerhard
1961   The Religious Factor: A Sociological Study of Religion's Impact on Politics, Economics, and Family Life. Garden City, New York: Doubleday.

Levinger, George
1978   Personal communication.

Mason, Karen Oppenheim, John L. Czajka, and Sara Arber
1976   "Changes in U.S. women's sex-role attitudes, 1964–1974." American Sociological Review 41 (August): 573–596.

Mott, Frank L., Steven H. Sandell, David Shapiro, Patricia K. Brito, Timothy J. Carr, Rex C. Johnson, Carol L. Jusenius, Peter J. Koenig, and Sylvia F. Moore
1977   "Years for decision: A longitudinal study of the education labor market and family experiences of young women, 1968 to 1973." Report prepared for the Employment and Training Administration. Washington, D.C.: U.S. Department of Labor.

O'Neill, William L.
1967   Divorce in the Progressive Era. New Haven, Connecticut: Yale University Press.

Ory, Marcia
1976   "The decision to parent or not: Normative and structural components." Unpublished doctoral dissertation, Purdue University.

Panko, Thomas
1972   "Zero parity: A demographic analysis of childlessness." Unpublished doctoral dissertation, Louisiana State University and Agricultural and Mechanical College.

Rao, S. L. N.
1974   "A comparative study of childlessness and never pregnant status." Journal of Marriage and the Family 36 (February): 149–157.

Renne, Karen S.
1970   "Correlates of dissatisfaction in marriage." Journal of Marriage and the Family 32 (February): 54–66.

Ryder, Robert G.
1973   "Longitudinal data relating marriage satisfaction and having a child." Journal of Marriage and the Family 35 (November): 604–606.

Scanzoni, Letha, and John Scanzoni
1976   Men, Women and Change: A Sociology of Marriage and Family. New York: McGraw-Hill Book Co.

Spanier, Graham B.
1972   "Further evidence on methodological weaknesses in the Locke-Wallace marital adjustment scale and other measures of adjustment." Journal of Marriage and the Family 34 (August): 403–404.
1976   "Measuring dyadic adjustment: New scales for assessing the quality of marriage and other dyads." Journal of Marriage and the Family 38 (February): 15–25.

U.S. Bureau of the Census
1974   "Prospects for American Fertility: June 1974." Current Population Reports, Series P–20, No. 269. Washington, D.C.: U.S. Government Printing Office.

Veevers, J. E.
1973   "Voluntarily childless wives: An exploratory study." Sociology and Social Research 57 (April): 356–366.
1974   "The life style of voluntarily childless couples." Pp. 359–411 in Lyle Larson (Ed.), The Canadian Family in Comparative Perspective. Toronto: Prentice-Hall.

Wilcox, Walter F.
1940   Studies in American Demography. Ithaca, New York: Cornell University Press.

Who Waits to Have Children? And Why?
Jane Price

■   The cover of a 1976 issue of *Ms.* magazine featured a woman close to nine months pregnant. Her hair was flecked with gray and her eyes framed by wrinkles. She clearly was not one of the "young mamas" cultivated by women's magazines and television commercials. In some circles, minus her distended belly, she could have been taken for a grandmother.

This picture of an expectant mother nearly forty years old highlighted the magazine's lead article, "Over 30? Over 35? Over 40? How Late Can You Wait to Have a Baby?" While the cover and story were intended to capture readers' attention, they also confirmed an established social fact: more and more women in this country are delaying childbirth until they are well into their thirties. And "How late can you wait to have a baby?" is a question that growing numbers seriously ask.

Recent statistics are documenting a trend toward older parenthood. Demographers in California have reported a surging birth rate for women twenty-five to thirty-four between 1966 and 1974. Many of these women are first-time mothers who put off having children until their thirties. In 1974 almost one third of all married women under thirty had not had children, compared to one fourth in 1970 and one fifth in 1960. "It is not likely that such large proportions of married women will remain childless," say demographers June Sklar and Beth Berkov. "Among childless married women age 30 in 1974, more than three-fourths expected to have two or more children by the end of their childbearing period."

What is happening in California is being reflected nationwide: products of the postwar baby boom who decided to become older parents are creating a mini baby boom of their own. The National Center for Health Statistics reported a 6 percent rise in first births during 1974 for women twenty-five to thirty-nine at a time when first births on the average were increasing by only 1 percent and the national birth rate continued to decline.

All indicators point to the fact that couples are marrying and starting their families later. Reversing a century-long trend, the age at which women marry and have children has risen since 1965. That year the median age for a woman bearing her first child was 21.9; by 1971 it had climbed to 22.1. While this rise isn't dramatic, it does reflect the beginning of a movement toward delaying childbearing in a society where one third of the women give birth to their first child by the time they're twenty years old.

Part of this trend can be attributed to young brides who put off having children for several years but still start their families in their twenties. But the number of women who don't have children until their thirties or forties continues to mount. In some areas the visibility of older parents is quite striking.

"I've seen a definite increase in patients over thirty having their first child during the past five years," says Dr. Sheldon H. Cherry, obstetrician-gynecologist at Mount Sinai Hospital in New York and assistant clinical professor of obstetrics and gynecology at the Mount Sinai School of Medicine. Manhattan obstetrician Theodore Tobias, who is also associated with Mount Sinai, has observed that the average age of his first-time maternity patient is now about thirty.

It's common to find couples in their thirties and early forties preparing for their first births in childbirth classes at Mount Sinai and New York Hospital. And the growing numbers of older mothers are beginning to revolutionize maternity fashions, too. Mater's Market, a Manhattan maternity boutique, is putting out designs for older women. "I noticed that women were becoming pregnant at an older age and had more money to spend, but they were having a difficult time finding elegant things to wear to business dinners and such," said co-owner Myrna Tarnower.

This movement toward delayed parenthood is, however, a minority trend—only about 5 percent of women having their first child in 1974 were thirty or over. But the trend will grow more pronounced in middle- and upper-income groups, especially in our large urban centers.

Dr. P. Theodore Watson, a prominent obstetrician-gynecologist in St. Paul-Minneapolis, has observed that his patients now produce their first children five years later than they used to. "Most of them marry when they are between twenty and twenty-four and deliver before they are thirty," he told me. "But they are still older than they were before." If New York and California are in the vanguard, one will see the number of older parents multiply in other American cities as well in the next few years. Perhaps five years from now the average age of Dr. Watson's first-time maternity patients will be over thirty. First-time mothers in their late thirties will never become a majority, but they are no longer an anomaly.

Why Some People Wait

What accounts for the rise in first-time mothers over thirty and the trend toward older parenthood? First of all, more Americans are delaying the age at which they marry. While most men and women still wed young, the average marriage age has climbed slowly since 1960. There are sufficient numbers of young people—especially women—delaying entry into matrimony to raise the average age of first marriages by one month every year. Over the past decade the median marriage age of American women has thus risen from twenty to twenty-one years.

Those who come late to married life may reflect the impersonal forces of demography. Some single women now in their thirties are products of the "marriage squeeze," an oversupply of marriageable women relative to the number of eligible males. Since women in this country tend to marry men older than themselves, those born while World War II was underway most often found their supply of mates from the males born during the lean childbearing years of the thirties. Although some victims of the "marriage squeeze" eventually find spouses from among younger males or formerly married men, many marry and start their families later.

Women are also remaining single longer out of conscious choice. The proliferation of apartment houses, bars, and consumer items geared to young unmarrieds testifies to the growing popularity of the solitary life-style. Women, as well as men, find the pursuit of a career and the freedom of living alone an attractive option. The number of marriages in the United States fell by nearly 3 percent in the year ending August 1974. Our country is now witnessing the first significant decline in its marriage rate since World War II, and as marriages are postponed, births are, too.

In a larger sense, the decision to forgo or postpone having children is an outgrowth of the transformation in the institution of marriage. In more traditional societies, such as our country one hundred years ago, marriage had several key functions: it provided a setting for procreation and an anchor for one's ties to community and job. Old-style marriages had clearly prescribed roles for husbands and wives: a good wife had many children and took care of the home; a good husband was the family provider. Marriage was synonymous with having children—one wed to "start a family." Love and emotional attachment were relegated to the background.

The permanent contractual relationship between husband and wife still carries certain financial advantages and is still associated with the rearing of children. However, most people today see marriage primarily as an interpersonal relationship that satisfies certain emotional needs. Children are no longer the economic asset they were when most families lived on farms or ran small businesses. Their labor cannot easily be translated into family income and they aren't as likely to support their parents in old age.

Reproduction has ceased to be an economic necessity and children have become a luxury option. "Children have . . . been viewed as consumer goods," states sociologist Jessie Bernard, one of this country's leading authorities on the family. "The young husband and working wife ask themselves when they can 'afford' to have children and how many they can 'afford.'"

Industrialization has speeded the transformation of family life, opening up a new range of jobs for women. They are now able to choose occupations other than wife and mother and have been given additional impetus from the women's liberation movement to change their traditional roles. "As recently as ten years ago, a woman had to defend her position if she wanted to work," observed Beatrice Buckler, former editor of *Working Woman* magazine. "Now you have only to go out and ask the nearest housewife what she does and she'll answer, 'I'm just a housewife.' There's been a tremendous change in attitude."

The number of women who work outside the home has been rising since 1947, but the most striking changes in their status have occurred since the mid-sixties. Record numbers of women of all ages have surged into the labor force. By 1976, 38.6 milion women, constituting two fifths of the entire labor force, were working or seeking work. This move outside the home reflects both the expansion of job opportunities for women and changes in women's conception of themselves. Columbia University economist Eli Ginzburg, chairman of the National Commission for Manpower Policy, calls this trend "the single most outstanding phenomenon of our century."

Today, two fifths of all married women are in the labor force, compared to one fourth in the mid-fifties. Forty-eight percent of American women sixteen and older are working women, in contrast to 23 percent in 1920. And the fastest rate of entrance into the work force has come from women between the ages of twenty and thirty-four.

The nature of jobs open to women has affected their attitudes toward work outside the home. While much of the expansion has been in traditionally "female" jobs—clerical work, waitressing, secretarial work, nursing, etc.—women have also been gaining access to high-level employment. Increased educational opportunities have enabled them to compete for interesting and lucrative positions. The number of women in professional and technical jobs is on the rise. In 1970 the Department of Labor classified 4.3 million women, 15 percent of the female labor force, as "professional and technical workers," compared to 2.7 million, or 13 percent of the female labor force, ten years earlier.

Women with a relatively high level of education and income are more likely to stick with their jobs than those who are ill-educated and poorly paid. They tend to delay marriage and childbearing much longer and generally wind up with smaller families. It is this privileged group that has supplied most of the older parents on the current scene. The greatest increase in labor-force participation among college graduates has come from women between twenty-five and thirty-four, the period when most would normally leave work to raise children.

Attractive jobs now require more years of training than they did twenty years ago. For both men and women, job-related educational requirements have put a brake on marriage and childbearing. Young people are reluctant to start families when costly training lies ahead of them. Many of those who complete their education want to enjoy the fruit of their careers before taking on the burden of additional dependents. As one M.A. candidate at the City University of New York put it, "Now I have a good job that pays $18,000 a year, a luxury apartment, a Porsche, and a fabulous stereo system and jazz collection. I'm not ready to get married and have children; why should I give all this up? If I do get married—which won't be for a long time—I'll expect my wife to work, too."

If young adults wish to postpone marriage or childbearing, recent advances in birth control have made that choice possible. Contraception in this country is not new, but genuinely effective forms of birth control have been available for only the past fifteen years. Before the Pill and the IUD most people obtained their contraceptives from the local drugstore. The diaphragm, which has been available to women through physicians since the turn of the century, is nearly foolproof if properly used, but it doesn't allow for spontaneous sex. Before the sixties successful practitioners of birth control were those who either resisted the sweep of passion or had a high degree of luck.

Today, those who use the Pill, an IUD, or abortion as a last resort need leave little to chance. Birth control is no longer a gamble, and people can, for the first time, actually control their fertility. While these developments have cut down illegitimacy and unwanted pregnancy among the poor, the chief beneficiaries have been members of the middle class, who, by virtue of their education and commitment to careers, are more likely to follow through on birth control correctly and conscientiously.

Inexpensive abortion on demand has been particularly useful to young couples seeking to delay parenthood. Before its legalization, most women seeking abortion were unmarried. Now many patients of abortion clinics are married women who wish to limit their families or postpone child rearing. It has been estimated that one third of the 900,000 legal abortions performed in 1974 were on women who would have completed their pregnancies if legal termination were not an option. A decade earlier, abortions were expensive, illegal and frequently dangerous; women who did not fear illegitimacy shied away from the risk and expense.

Economics now figure heavily in a couple's timing of childbearing, and improved methods of birth control, as well as legalized abortion, have lent more control to this conscious scheduling. People have children for a wide range of motives: they may believe reproduction a social or religious obligation; they may find children a source of novelty and stimulation; they may need children to bolster their sense of accomplishment or to confirm their sexual identity. Some couples with a weak interpersonal relationship find children their only source of marital happiness. But few parents in this country today expect to come out ahead financially.

Most couples cite finances as the primary reason for restricting family size: "We want to provide a better quality of life for our children and ourselves." And recent recessionary turns in the American economy have made having children even more financially burdensome. In 1975 the average number of children born to each family plummeted to 1.8, less than half of what it was in 1957. For the vast majority of Americans, a family of two children has become "ideal."

Some credit for the growing popularity of the small family should go to the environmental movement. Until very recently there was enormous cultural and social pressure to marry and have children. Couples who did not have offspring were often labeled "selfish" or "weird," and most families were encouraged to have as many children as they could afford. Our developing knowledge of the social and environmental problems linked to population pressures has become a counterforce to the pronatalists. We now have active organizations promoting a "zero population growth," the voluntary limitation of two children to a couple, and even a National Organization for Non-Parents. It has become increasingly common for couples to swear off reproduction. In some circles, having children meets with the same critical reception formerly reserved for the childless. It is doubtful that people who forgo or limit childbearing do so for the sake of the environment alone. But antinatalist sentiment can bolster other, more personal, reasons for starting a family later and limiting its size.

The large-scale changes in our society that have altered our conceptions of family and parenthood have also found expression in new conjugal styles. While larger numbers of Americans are remaining single, they are not necessarily living alone. Couples are living together as a form of single lifestyle or as an alternative to marriage. Some mutual living arrangements become "trial marriages," which eventually turn into the real thing. But whatever the reason, living together out of wedlock usually involves a moratorium on having children. Many who become older parents have experimented with this type of arrangement for a number of years before signing an official marriage contract.

Divorce, which has reached epidemic proportions, can also encourage older parenthood. Thirty-seven percent of all first marriages in this country end in divorce and one million people now file into the nation's divorce courts every year. Four out of five remarry, usually to another divorced person. Recoupling generally takes place about three years after the divorce, and the average age for second marriages is around thirty for women and thirty-five for men. Those with childless first marriages don't have another opportunity for childbearing until they reach their thirties.

Do our rising rate of divorce and falling rate of marriage, a smaller family size and changing conception of family life foreshadow an end to marriage and parenthood? The answer is clearly no. We may be marrying and reproducing less and divorcing more, but the interest in marriage and children is as high as ever. A nationwide poll conducted in 1974 showed that only 1 percent of men and women in this country wish to remain single or live alone. Most young people are still in favor of having children, even those with attractive single lifestyles.

A series of studies has shown that the vast majority of career-oriented women see their jobs as adjuncts to husband and family. According to Joseph Veroff and Sheila Feld, authors of *Marriage and Work in America,* "Motherhood still remains a role in which an educated woman can find the personal gratification she needs to justify her existence." "Parenthood is an important stage and child rearing is an important function in the life of an adult," says psychiatrist Henry Greenbaum. "To downgrade them is to ignore deep human psychological needs."

This perhaps explains why many couples who have full lives without children eventually decide to have them. Writer Gail Sheehy, who studied stages of adult development, feels that women in their thirties become sensitive to needs left unfulfilled when they were younger. If they devoted themselves to their careers, they are likely to focus more on their personal lives.

Sheehy believes that when such women near the age of thirty-five, they may develop an intense desire for children. "Thirty-five brings the biological boundary into sight," she says. "Probably for the first time a woman glimpses that vague, uncharted realm ahead leading to what demographers so aridly call the end of her 'fecund and bearing years.'" Ms. Sheehy and others have theorized that the approach of menopause triggers an urge to assert the reproductive function before it is taken away. Psychoanalyst Helene Deutsch refers to this last-minute desire for children as "closing the gates."

In having a child late in life, couples also have the chance to participate in an experience usually reserved for the young. Ours is a society that glorifies youthfulness; combating the aging process is something of a national preoccupation. This youth mystique may operate as a subliminal catalyst for late parenthood. Observes a Manhattan prepared-childbirth instructor: "I've seen older couples react to the experience of having a child as if they're young again. Going through childbirth together takes away their age."

A number of older parents have told me that having a child as they neared middle age made them feel younger. "It keeps me young," said the fifty-year-old father of a fourth-grader. President Jimmy Carter reacted the same way to the birth of his daughter when he was in his forties. "She made me feel young again," he wrote. I'm not suggesting that older parents have children for the same reasons they go to exercise classes or use face cream, but having a baby later on does keep them in an earlier stage of the life cycle. In our society, the power of children to revitalize and refresh is part of the host of forces encouraging men and women to become parents much later than they did in the past. . . .

The Case for Older Parenthood

Older parents are a growing social phenomenon. But is this trend good or bad? Should more people be encouraged to delay having children in the future? Can one make an actual case for older parenthood? Certainly from a financial point of view there are many advantages to postponing childbearing until one's thirties. A trained money manager or expert on family finances would probably nod vigorously with approval.

Daily living has become very costly and insecure, and there is little relief in sight for the future. An individual attempting to steer a course between inflation and unemployment will find supporting himself risky enough. The going is that much more rough if he has to provide for others as well.

Let's start with maternity costs. Babies aren't delivered by storks free of charge. The bill for the obstetrician, hospital room, delivery room, and nursery can run from mildly hefty to downright staggering figures. The most expensive place in the United States to have a baby is New York City. There, charges average about $2,000 per child. With complications, a private hospital room, or ultra-fancy obstetrician, the bill can run 50 percent higher. As one moves outside the New York metropolitan area, these expenses go down. The average cost of childbirth for most of the country is slightly less than half of that in the Big Apple. Still, that's a lot of cash to muster and most medical plans cover only a fraction of maternity expenses. One can mitigate the pinch to the pocketbook by using a maternity clinic, or—if one is a bit daring and in good health—by having the baby at home.

Aside from basics in food, clothing, and shelter, the cost of raising a child varies with parents' income level and tastes. But assuming one forgoes such popular "extras" as professional baby photographs and silver feeding spoons, the wallet will be lightened by about $1,500 during the infant's first year alone—for food, clothing, nursery furniture, diapers and laundry, visits to the pediatrician, and a few toys. That's a relatively conservative estimate for a middle-income family. Those who wish to maintain an active social life should add the cost of babysitters as well.

Child-rearing expenses climb as the child gets older: it costs 30 to 45 percent more to support an eighteen-year-old than a one-year-old—and that excludes college. *Esquire* magazine estimated in March 1974 that the price of one "good to superior-quality child" in a major city could run as high as $25,000 for the first five years; $55,000 for ages six through eleven; and $54,000 for ages twelve through seventeen. These amounts could be lowered about 50 percent by eliminating private school, braces, and summer camp. Nevertheless, that would still leave the average pre-college cost of each child a whopping $80,000. Then there's college: $5,000 to $7,000 a year for tuition, room, and board at most private institutions; about half that amount annually at state universities or publicly supported schools. The lucky few will be able to cut corners through scholarships or by having college-age children live at home.

An upper-middle-class urban family could thus run the cost of one child from conception through graduate or professional school to over $200,000. For most of us, this figure is high. But how much lower can we go? A recent study, "Costs of Children," by the Commission for Population Growth and the American Future, put the bill for raising two children, in a typical American family from birth through college, at between $80,000 and $150,000. In other words, the "direct cost" of rearing one child is still approximately 15 to 17 percent of family income.

What can push these figures toward the higher range is the "opportunity costs" of child rearing for women—the potential earnings a woman forfeits to stay at home with her family. Opportunity costs rise with the level of a woman's education and earning power. A mother who remains at home until her youngest child reaches fourteen will "lose" earnings totaling $58,904 if she completed high school, $82,467 if she had a college degree, and $103,023 if she had postgraduate training.

High opportunity costs help account for the large proportion of educated women who limit their family size and remain in the work force. Here the older woman has a distinct advantage. She is generally well established in her career and more likely to win from her employer time for a maternity leave or a flexible work schedule. Her salary may be high enough to afford child care. Seniority gives her a vested interest in continuing her job.

There are other forms of indirect cost that raise the bill for children even higher—increased rent on larger living quarters or the mortgage on a house; lawyer's fees to draw up a will; washing machine and dryer; a new life-insurance policy. Some of these expenses may be offset by tax deductions for additional dependents and high medical expenses (the first child is a bit more costly than the others), but under present conditions parenthood must be associated with heavy financial responsibilities.

In addition to dealing with the opportunity-cost factor for women, the older couple is in a much stronger position to meet child-related expenses all around. If one were able to save all the money needed to raise the child before its birth, it would be possible to reduce yearly child-rearing costs substantially. Interest would accrue on the original amount or portions of it while smaller amounts were being spent for the child on a yearly basis. Assuming an annual interest of 8 percent on the unspent portion of the money, the cost of raising a first child could be "discounted." The couple who has been working a number of years would be most capable of amassing the savings required.

It is also the case that salary levels for the older couple will generally be higher than those of their younger counterparts. Salaries for those aged thirty-five to forty-four tend to rise more rapidly than for those under thirty-four. Older parents should also prove more capable of managing what money they have. People now under thirty grew up during the most prosperous period in our nation's history, when their parents' incomes rose faster than prices for goods and services. They experienced gains in real income in the form of a rising standard of living—and rising expectations. Many in this generation anticipate the same level of material luxury they grew up with and are tempted to spend beyond their means when they set up their own households. The older couple has more time in which to learn how to budget—and how to do without—and are much more likely to anticipate and plan for the additional financial strains that children bring. . . .

Does everything fall on the plus side for the older parent? Finances and emotional maturity are but part of the complex web of concerns prospective parents should take into account. Deciding how long to wait involves other compelling issues—medical, psychological, and social. To raise the age of childbearing is to dramatically alter patterns of reproduction and family life that have been with us for thousands of years. . . .

Licensing Parents:
A New Age of Child-Rearing?
Jerry Bergman

One way to help solve some of society's most intractable problems would be to require that people have licenses before becoming parents. Already, some European countries have offered televised courses leading to a "parent certificate." In today's complex world, the responsibility that a person undertakes by becoming a parent can no longer be taken lightly.

■ Teachers, child psychologists, members of the clergy, and others have recently begun to talk about a system that would require a person to have a license before becoming a parent. They reason that "parenting" is such an important determinant of a child's development that society should make a much more concerted effort to minimize the damage done by incompetent parents.

Almost all the professions that deal with a person's physical or mental health require extensive training. A license to practice as a lawyer, doctor, registered nurse, social worker, or teacher is given only after at least four years of college. Yet to become a parent—the person most responsible for a child's development—presently requires no training, license, or experience. Society demands that a person obtain a license before pursuing such relatively simple tasks as driving a car, operating a ham radio, wiring a house, or prescribing a pair of glasses. Yet to do the job of a parent—one much more complex and crucial to the lives of so many —requires no license at all.

Those who work extensively with families have often noted that many parents are deficient in basic child-raising skills. An important reason for this is that most parents have virtually no training in general nutrition, developmental psychology, or the legal rights of children. Most people would never expect someone to perform a job as comparably complex as that of being a parent without substantial instruction. It would be like placing a third-grader in an atomic energy lab and expecting him to carry on research.

One example of the problems a lack of information can cause is seen in a case reported by pediatrician Margaret A. Ribble. She writes of a woman who came to a clinic complaining that her baby would rock violently back and forth with his arms tightly clasped around the end of a blanket. Observations showed that this behavior occurred regularly. During an interview, the baby's mother repeatedly stressed that she "had never played with him, that he had never been rocked or jiggled and had always been left in his own bed in the nursery to go to sleep by himself." She insisted that "the nursery was perfectly quiet and entirely isolated from the rest of the house." When it was suggested that she spend more time holding and playing with the child, she was horrified and said that she had been especially careful "not even to let the child's father see him late in the afternoon when he came home from business lest the baby become excited."

Treatment consisted primarily of helping the mother understand the need that children have for tactile, physical, and kinesthetic stimulation. When the mother applied what she was learning, her son showed marked improvement. The woman was concerned about the child's behavior, but the problem was really with her own. Applying the same concern with correct information would do much to help her properly raise her child.

Many studies of parents who abuse their children have found that the parents' behavior is often caused simply by their ignorance of proper child-rearing practices. The parents were abused themselves as children, so they assume that abuse is the correct way to discipline their own children.

In these cases, simple instructions often almost totally halt the child abuse. The parents realize what they are doing, usually appreciate the help, and, although it takes time for them to overcome their habits, most eventually do. But first the necessary help must be given to the parents —and some would add, even if the parents are resistant to outside help.

If the state is able to step in and try to stop the short-term abuse that results in battered children, why shouldn't it have the same control over long-term abuse? Most people would get upset if they saw a parent abusing a child to the point of serious physical damage. But is not psychologically abusing a child just as harmful? Whereas bruises, lacerations, and broken bones will usually completely heal, psychological abuse may last until the child dies. Granted, long-term abuse is harder to detect, but our concern should be focused on the end result just as much as on the paths taken to get there.

The Rights of Children

The social problems that swell from the ranks of the young are both obvious and growing fast. One out of every nine boys runs "afoul" of the law before his 18th birthday; from 10 to 30% of America's children clearly need some kind of psychological help. The problems are so rampant that people often pass them off as just "growing pains." But these growing pains cause suicides (the second leading cause of death among adolescents) and contribute to the rampant pessimism that marks society today.

Extensive research supports the contention that the way children cope with society is largely determined by the way their parents treat them during the first five years of their lives. Poor performance in school, mental retardation, crime, alcoholism, various sexual "deviations," and virtually all other social problems can be traced back, with varying degrees of evidence, to the family and the family structure.

All of society's efforts to ease these problems—spending billions for correctional institutions, prisons, mental hospitals, reformatories, Alcoholics Anonymous programs, etc.—are attempts to change the child *after the fact.* Even if these programs were effective, the present stream of maladjusted children that well-meaning but poorly trained parents continue to turn out is more than our system can handle.

We are not going to make serious inroads into the problems of crime, health, poverty, and poor school performance until we attack social problems directly at their source. By making sure that every parent at least knows the basics of child-rearing, we could do much to guarantee that many of the social problems that grip society today would diminish in years to come.

Any proposal to license parents would necessarily fall under attack by those proclaiming the "rights" of parents to have children. But what about the rights of children? Do not they also have a right to the pursuit of happiness? Unfortunately, a child's happiness depends largely upon his parents, a factor over which the child has no control.

The issue of licensing parents forms only part of a movement that is pressing for the recognition of children's rights. Books such as *Are Parents Bad For Children?* by Graham Blaine, *Birth Rights* by Richard Farson, *The Children's Rights Movement* edited by Beatrice and Ronald Gross, and *Children's Liberation* by David Gottlieb are leading the crusade. The fundamental argument of the many anti-abortion groups is that even fetuses have a right to life.

Children constitute probably one of the last groups against which American society still grossly discriminates. Most minority groups have fought for and won, at least on the law books, many of their rights. This is not so for children today.

However, the courts have recently begun to conclude that children do have some rights, including the right to receive an education and the right not to be sexually, physically, psychologically, or economically abused. Children's interests are starting to become sufficiently recognized for lawmakers and others to begin to enter the parental domain. And, although signs of resistance by parents have recently appeared, protection for children is being extended in more and more areas.

Controlling Conception

Licensing parents is actually just one more step in a process that for centuries has been giving human beings more and more control over conception. At one time people believed that conception depended on factors that today seem completely unrelated. But when people noticed that women have certain cycles of fertility, mankind gained some control over the process of birth. Later, mechanical and biochemical contraception further increased people's ability to control conception.

Today licensing parents has become feasible because of the increasing effectiveness of and knowledge about birth control methods, especially pill contraceptives, which have made it possible to decide who will be fertile and when. Of course, current contraceptives are not yet foolproof. Sterilization methods can't be used for licensing because such methods are generally irreversible. Scientists must develop the technology both to prevent conception before a license is obtained and then to restore fertility once a license is granted.

Such a technology now seems to lie only a few years away. The World Health Organization is experimenting in London with a "once a year pill" which has already been tested by 6,000 women in West Germany. Doctors claim that the pill is as safe as birth control pills taken daily. It consists of a 1 1/2-inch tube containing the hormone progesterone which is implanted in the womb.

Researchers led by Sheldon Segal at the Rockefeller University Bio-Medical Division have also developed a contraceptive capsule implant that has passed clinical tests. The capsule is inserted under a woman's skin by a hypodermic needle and leaks a steady supply of progestin, a female hormone that prevents pregnancy by simulating pregnancy. Researchers have already perfected a three-year capsule, and work is under way to fashion a fairly permanent capsule. Reversal would require only removing the capsule. Men, too, could someday choose infertility if researchers develop contraceptives which render a man's sperm largely inoperative.

But even though present methods of birth control are not yet totally effective, people now still have little excuse for conceiving an unwanted child (and thus little excuse for abortion, since abortion is merely a belated means of birth control). Thanks to the contraceptives now available, parents can choose if and when to have a child. As a result, parents often wait until they reach certain personal or economic goals before having a child. Each child is thus planned, expected, and desired, so each child receives adequate care. From the perspective of history, it is only one more step for the government to help prospective parents decide on the best time to have a child.

If science establishes a procedure that would render males or females reversibly sterile, the question would automatically arise, Under what conditions should fertility be restored? These conditions could range all the way from those of personal choice to those of a strict licensing program. But some standard will be adopted. Now is the time to be concerned about developing the criteria. When the technology is suddenly upon us, we may have to act without proper experience and research.

The institutions that prospective parents could use in the future to gain the information needed for any kind of license are already available and plentiful. As more and more high schools offer child-rearing courses, more and more students could probably meet the requirements for a license without additional training. Thus the majority of young people could easily be prepared for licensing requirements well before any plan was begun. Then it would simply be a matter of slowly increasing the requirements to a realistic, but high level.

Already three regional television networks in West Germany have broadcasted an instructional course leading to a "parent certificate." If people who participate in the course can answer 32 out of 46 questions correctly, they receive a document which acknowledges that they have understood the material presented. Although West Germany does not require this course for parenthood, its existence points out the need parents have for certain basic skills.

If a general course of study were made the requirement for obtaining a license to become a parent, all prospective parents would know some of the basic, accepted principles of raising children. Of course, differences of opinion enliven virtually any subject area, and the teaching of parenting would be no exception. But the parent-to-be would not necessarily have to accept everything taught, and the class could discuss and debate points of contention. Then parents would at least know both sides—clearly a better situation than knowing neither side.

If schools develop educational programs such as this, presumably very few people would not be able to eventually qualify for a license. And for those that cannot, most people would probably agree that they should not have children anyway. This pool would include the severely retarded, those with brain damage, and the very young or very old. Many of these people already cannot have children for physical reasons.

A few of the basic areas with which prospective parents should be familiar are nutrition, anatomy, physiology, hygiene, child development, first aid, physical fitness, learning, and the psychological concepts of modeling, imitation, reinforcement, and discipline. Skills in the areas of child care, tolerance, control, and concern would also be of value.

Aside from having up-to-date knowledge about feeding formulas, bathing, changing diapers, taking care of diaper rashes, and the other nuances of child care, parents must understand the importance of showing concern for the child by fondling, caressing, rocking, singing, and speaking to the baby. Pediatrician Ribble has stated that a mother must be taught "that the handling and fondling which she gives are by no means casual expressions of sentiment but are biologically necessary for the healthy mental development of the baby."

True, having the proper knowledge does not guarantee that a person will be a good parent, but it is a step in the right direction. If parents were at least taught the basics of child-rearing, then work on the next step—insuring that those basics were effectively applied—could begin. We cannot assume that adults have the necessary awareness just because they are of age to be legally married and have children.

To pass drivers' education, states require both book knowledge and road experience. Likewise it may become feasible to require that parents not only have "the book work," but "the road work" as well. This would entail a parents' training program designed to make sure that parents learn how to effectively work with children.

The Problems and Possibilities of Licensing

Becoming a parent now requires only finding a mate. This task demands qualifications such as appearance, sociability, and availability, which are largely irrelevant to parenting. The choice depends primarily on a person's fussiness in selection. Nowhere in the process is any concern given to the children likely to be born from the union.

Yet the very mention of licensing parents raises fears of "1984"—of a world where courtship and marriage are completely subjugated to procreation. Of course, such extreme abuse is unlikely, and just because something can be abused does not argue against that thing—it argues rather for controlling or preventing the abuse. The prohibition fiasco is a good example of how society should not try to completely outlaw something that potentially can be abused; in the case of alcohol, society is much better off just trying to prevent the abuse.

Any proposal to license parents will probably elicit a barrage of protests that such a system limits the individual's freedom of choice and equal opportunity. "If I want to have a child," some will argue, "I have a right to have one." But the U.S. Constitution gives citizens no such right. It does give Americans the right "to the pursuit of happiness," but this guarantee could be used to argue for almost any desire. Also, neither the Hebrew nor Greek scriptures, nor even the Koran, support the contention that the right to have children is "God's law."

Even now, not every parent has the "right" to have a child. If a couple, for example, wants to adopt a child, they must undergo a fairly complex procedure to do so. Also, the retarded, criminals, and people below a certain age are barred from adopting children.

Some of these screening procedures may be open to criticism, but few people would argue that there should not be any screening. If we feel a need to screen the second set of parents, is there not just as great a need to screen the original set? Perhaps if the original set were screened, a second set would not be needed so often.

It is possible that a licensing agency could become a tool for people with selfish political or social ends in mind. However, any licensing board would wield only a limited amount of power. Once guidelines were set up, the board would have to follow existing rules. True, the head of a licensing board could influence the procedure according to his own personality, desires, goals, or political feelings, but strict guidelines would minimize this possibility.

Discrimination on the basis of social class could be another problem. Those most able to afford the schooling needed for a license, and those most intellectually capable, will probably be from the higher socioeconomic classes, resulting in favorable discrimination towards this group. Thus some people could see a licensing program as a racist attempt to wipe out certain ethnic groups that often have a difficult time in school.

A licensing program *would* inevitably bring a bias against certain groups of people. But if the primary requirement were passing a valid test, the bias would fall only against those who did not have the information needed to pass the test, regardless of why they lacked the information. Furthermore, even though the lower classes often show more affection for their children than the middle and upper socioeconomic classes, the higher classes are often the most financially and intellectually capable of raising children. A licensing system could reverse the current situation, where reproduction rates are negatively related to education and income (i.e., the more income and education one has, the smaller the family one has).

Another argument against any licensing requirement stems from the common belief that child psychologists disagree among themselves on how to raise a child. But a survey of the leading books on child rearing finds the advice fairly consistent. The tone and stress may differ, but there are generally few major disagreements in the advice given.

The mandatory sterilization part of licensing would probably cause the most severe problems. Those with religious objections, including the Christian Scientists, some evangelical Christians, and most Catholics, would strongly object. This religious factor alone may cause a significant proportion of Americans to fight licensing. According to a recent Gallup poll, almost half of Americans consider themselves "evangelical Christians," and Catholics constitute 24% of the population.

Those with honest religious objections to a program of temporary sterilization must be considered separately. The program planners could easily isolate this group and not require them to submit to the program's regulations. As with the conscientious objectors, a few people would strongly oppose the program, and it will not be that difficult to determine the sincerity of their belief.

All of these problems facing the implementation of a licensing program must be considered before any steps are taken. With this careful examination, programs could be developed to insure that problems do not and cannot materialize. Obviously, the immediate imposition of a wholesale licensing program would be foolish; it must rather be phased in gradually, probably over several generations. Even if a full-scale program were effective, it might do more harm than good. We must be sure of the advantages before we intrude further on the lives of individuals.

Alternatives and Inevitabilities

Let us look at some alternatives to licensing parents. One is to improve the child guidance clinics, juvenile courts, family service clinics, and other agencies that try to deal with the problems of youth. Unfortunately, parents usually do not confront situations and use these agencies until the problem becomes severe, and then it is usually too late. Even if correction at this point is possible, it is extremely inefficient. Parents may be able to turn on to the correct road if they have clear directions well ahead of time, but once past their turn it is difficult to find their way back. Compared to curative programs, preventive programs are much more humane, cost less, and are undoubtedly much more effective.

Another method of giving a child high quality parents, which makes use of an institution called the kibbutz, has been tried in Israel. On a kibbutz, the responsibility for raising the children is invested in a few highly qualified people. Such a program is even more drastic than licensing parents. Taking children away from their natural parents and putting them in an institution staffed by highly qualified people may prove successful, but it is extremely expensive and clearly more radical than the alternative considered in this article.

The potential for improvement in the current system of child-rearing awaits our action. If society continues to muddle through without somehow beginning to influence the quality of parents a child has, the social problems that afflict the U.S. will undoubtedly prove very difficult to subdue.

The feeling held by the public that people have a "right" to have children, regardless of their financial or intellectual capacities, sanctions almost any parental behavior short of obvious bodily disfigurement. However, in American society, rights are generally abridged if exercising them harms someone else. And the child raised by inept parents has not only been harmed himself but will probably go on to harm society as a whole through the medical, criminal, or simply psychological burden he places upon it.

Thus, considering both the rights of the child and of society, governments have the authority to control parents if their actions transgress upon those rights. Even now, if parents are sufficiently incompetent, the government will step in. Therefore, society already has a limited right to screen potential parents. Licensing parents would simply be an extension of this right to more fully recognize the damage a bad parent can do.

Screening and selecting potential parents will by no means guarantee that a child will have ideal parents, but screening will weed out most of the more grossly unqualified individuals. Even if the procedure is only partly successful, the requirements will undoubtedly prove better than no standards. Furthermore, since licensing will help determine what factors make for good parents, a licensing system can later be improved.

This self-correcting aspect of a licensing system could be one of its greatest benefits. Because a licensing agency presumably would have the power to rescind as well as grant a license, the agency could both insure high standards of child care and carry on the extensive research needed to understand the variables of raising children. Even under the present system, children that are abused can be taken away from their parents. A licensing system would not be drastically different.

Just as there were strong objections to licensing doctors and lawyers nearly a generation ago, likewise people will have many objections to licensing parents. However, few would argue that a person's right to practice medicine is more important than society's right to be free of quacks, charlatans, and incompetent physicians. Today, the licensing of physicians is generally accepted, and the push is for stronger licensing in the field. Qualified physicians stand only to gain by licensing changes that upgrade their profession and eliminate physicians who not only harm patients but harm the reputation of medicine as a whole.

The present system of letting people produce children and rear them until the parents are proven incapable is no more sensible than letting a doctor practice for a while to see if he can cure anyone. When he mistakes a spleen for an appendix, he can no longer practice. Unfortunately, in the case of children, the damage done is often just as irreparable. Presently society cannot declare parents incompetent until the damage is clear and obvious. Only by identifying bad parents before they become so can irreversible damage be avoided. And this means looking at a couple *before* they become parents. By the time it shows up in the child, it is often too late.

The licensing of parents will probably arrive slowly through a series of court cases. As permanent birth control spreads, someone such as a convicted child abuser will most likely seek a court decision allowing his wife to become refertile. But the court will not want to grant permission without first insuring that the man will be able to raise a child without abuse. Once that step is taken, it is only one step further to control the reproduction of other groups not suited for parenthood—and then to gradually extend this control until everyone in society is included.

In time, the optimal ways of raising children, controlling for the many important variables often present, will be developed. An accurate knowledge of what works could then generate higher standards and more functional licensing requirements.

Probably the main benefit of licensing parents is that it will teach parents just how serious is the business of raising children by forcing them to think about the problems they will likely confront as parents. The tragedies caused by neglect, ignorance, and inability will not be eliminated, but they will undoubtedly be reduced. Even a small reduction would probably justify a licensing program, for even a small reduction, once achieved, would allow us to restructure future programs in an attempt to guarantee good parents for everyone.

Early Parenting

The Family as a Child-Care Environment
Alison Clarke-Stewart

■ The following set of policy propositions derived from our review of research on child development is most directly linked to the focus of that review—namely, *the family*. Before going into these propositions, a few words of caution or clarification are necessary. There is a danger that some readers will interpret the propositions as a conservative plea to save the nuclear family at all costs since this is the optimal environment for rearing children. That is *not* the intention of the proposition. In fact, we have not examined literature that could lead to that inference. The research that was reviewed merely identified some characteristics of the most adequate kinds of environment and care for young children. However, it does seem true that *at present in our society* these conditions are most *likely* to occur within families. The "families" may be biological, adoptive, or self-chosen, but are small groups of people committed to the long-term care of their children. We are not claiming anything magical about "the family," but merely noting that in our society it is the most likely environment in which people will be decent and committed to each other and thus provide adequate child care. Research does suggest, however, that when outside pressures and environmental stresses act on the family this has an effect not only on children directly but also on the quality of child care that is provided. Research also shows that the number of families affected by these stressful circumstances—divorce, illegitimacy, urbanization, isolation, fragmentation, working mothers—is increasing from year to year (cf. Bronfenbrenner, 1975). Consequently, our propositions about the family take as their general theme urging, suggesting, and justifying services to provide supports that will help parents raise their children and give them satisfactory care.

A Child Should Be Helped to Develop a Secure Attachment to His or Her Parents, and Then, Increasingly, Be Given Opportunities to Interact with Other Adults and Children

During the infant's first year of life forming a *secure* "attachment" relation with another person—usually the mother—is important for development. The child's need for such a relationship has several implications for policy. First, we know that a necessary condition for the development of such an attachment is adequate positive, active interaction with a caregiver. We cannot yet specify precisely the limits of what is "adequate"—this would vary from baby to baby and caregiver to caregiver—but within the limits observed in normal families, the relation seems to be that the *more* interaction engaged in with *more* affection and *more* responsiveness the better. This suggests that the person who has primary responsibility for the infant's care (typically the parent or foster parent) should be encouraged to interact with the infant warmly and frequently, particularly when the baby expresses a social or physical need.

There is also evidence that attachment develops more easily if there are *few* caregivers and if the same ones *continue* for a substantial period of time. This is a situation that in our society is most often provided by parents in a stable family. Children who have been observed by researchers developed attachments in the first year most successfully in the environment provided by a small family which had enough time for frequent, regular, consistent, and positive interaction among family members. If parents behaved negatively and unresponsively to the child or if they were seldom available for interaction, secure attachments did not develop. Under the latter circumstances, when family care in the first year is not adequate or available, other arrangements for child care should be made. When an alternative child-care arrangement is used at this age, however, parents should be especially sensitive to the quality of their—limited—interaction with the child and to the quality of the care provided by the substitute caregiver. Because the quality of interaction more than the quantity affects the attachment relation, it is possible that even brief, regular, interactions with parents, as long as they are positive and responsive, may be sufficient for the development of the infant's attachment to the parents. This issue requires further research.

Although it is true that having too many different caregivers is detrimental to the development of optimal attachment, this does not mean that a child is best raised by one person alone. In fact, after a primary attachment relation has been established, it is necessary for further development that the child separate from that person and form other social relations. This is best achieved when the child interacts often with a variety of people. Therefore, after the child has developed a primary attachment in the first year, parents should be encouraged to share the child's care with other adults, to offer the child opportunities to interact with other adults and, later, with other children. Supportive services for families that are socially isolated might well include supplementary part-time child care—babysitters, parents' helpers, family day care, center day care, nursery school, or play groups.

As we have noted, when a strong relationship with the mother or other caregiver has developed, children often react negatively to separations from that person or to strangers who approach the child intrusively or when alone. Whenever separation from the mother is necessary (for example, if she has to work or be hospitalized, or if the child needs to be hospitalized), measures should be taken to minimize the painful effect on the child. This is especially important from about seven months to three years, when effects of such separation are most pronounced. Such measures to alleviate separation distress might include providing adequate substitute care, preferably in the child's own home so he or she is in at least familiar surroundings; introducing separation gradually so the child learns that the mother will return; allowing the child to visit the mother in the hospital or vice versa; and not leaving the child alone with a stranger (i.e., the substitute caregiver or babysitter) but having mother stay with them until the child gets to know the other person.

Although most research on the development of attachment has focused on mothers, there is evidence that children also form attachments to their fathers in the first year. There are clear advantages for a child in having two strong social relationships—particularly when circumstances necessitate the mother's absence, as in the reasons listed above. To foster children's attachment to their fathers, therefore, fathers also should be encouraged to participate actively and frequently in positive interaction with their infants.

Policy Should Also Promote the Parents' Attachment to the Baby from the Beginning

Adults, as well as infants, develop strong emotional attachments—one of particular significance being that of a mother to her baby. It is this attachment that allows mothers to tolerate the burdens of child rearing and to provide the loving care essential to children's development.

Research suggests that the development of this attachment is associated with the birth, initial contact, and early care of the infant; the reciprocally interactive mother-child system clearly begins at the moment of birth, if not before. This has implications for at least three areas of policy: hospital maternity procedures, day-care arrangements, and employment practices.

To foster mutual mother-infant interaction and attachment, a "rooming-in" arrangement in the hospital, in which the newborn baby stays with the mother and is cared for by her rather than staying in a nursery, is supported by the data and is recommended as hospital policy unless there are prohibiting factors such as ill health or prematurity. The rooming-in arrangement should begin immediately after the birth. To facilitate a strong father-child relationship—and possibly to strengthen the mother-father tie at the same time—we might also propose that fathers "room-in" too. If rooming-in for fathers is unfeasible, hospital visiting hours could provide the father with free access to mother and infant at any time of day or night (family-centered maternity care), whereas visiting by others than those likely to be significantly involved in the child's life would be strictly limited. Not only should mother and father be given free access to the newborn, however, they should also—at least with their first infant—be given some guidance in infant care by the medical staff. Since having mothers care for their infants would relieve nurses of some of their nursery chores, the nursing staff might have more time in a family-centered ward to counsel parents who wanted it.

An alternative to the rooming-in scheme, and one which might have economic advantages for parents, would be to provide supportive services for having babies delivered at home. These deliveries could be performed by professional midwives associated with hospitals. In that way, emergency medical services would be available if needed. Another supportive service might be the provision of inexpensive but trained "mother's helpers" who would aid (but not supplant) mothers during the first few days or weeks postpartum, thus permitting an earlier return home from the hospital and an easier recovery for the mother.

Research on parental attachment has also clear and important implications for parents' use of nonparental day care for their infants. Although the quality and continuity of caregiving in the first three months is not as critical for the *infant's* psychological development as care from then on (i.e., the effects of early deprivation are often reversible), this period may be more critical for the development of the *parent's* attachment to the infant. Consequently, full-time day care in the first three months would not ordinarily be advisable.

Finally, the research on early parent-child attachment has implications for employment practices. In particular, it suggests the value for family relations of maternity and paternity leaves. Leaves from work for both mothers and fathers would, ideally, occur at the same time, following the infant's birth, and last for at least a month for both parents and for at least three months for the parent who was to be the primary caregiver. By this time, the parent would surely be "hooked," and the development of strong bonds between parents and infant well established.

Services Should Be Provided to Help Parents Plan Their Families and Raise Their Children

No one family structure is "ideal" for children's development. But it is possible to discuss the likely pros or cons for children in different family structures. The small, intact nuclear family of two parents and two to four children represents the present modal American family. This structure gives children the opportunity to develop an attachment to one or two adults; it gives parents the opportunity to interact often with each child; it allows each parent some help with child care from another adult; and it provides a buffer for unstable or deviant care from one parent, since there is another parent to take over or to provide a balancing influence. The larger extended family, however, has the advantage of providing parents with additional help and guidance with child care, and of providing children with ready access to a variety of different people. Since most families in the United States today are small and without the support of resident relatives, one policy suggestion is that these nuclear families be provided with the additional services ordinarily offered by larger extended families, for instance, supplementary care and social contacts, and, for poor families, "hand-me-down" toys, books, and clothes.

Another suggestion related to family size and structure is that information about and resources for family planning be made more readily accessible to parents and potential parents. Such information could include not only medical advice about birth control, but also information about the *costs* of having children—monetary, practical, and psychological—as well as about the rewards and joy that children can provide. Guidelines for counseling on family size and composition might be derived from research showing that a small family with spacing of at least 3 or 4 years between children may be most encouraging to children's development, because of possible withdrawal, lack of, or competition for parental attention in a large family of closely spaced siblings; or even from research suggesting the advantages of boy-girl sibling combinations for the development of both children's nonstereotyped sex roles. Such counseling naturally would be done on an individual basis, taking into account the clients' personal and cultural values and goals. It would include examination of the clients' motivation for having children, and provision of information that would let them realistically appraise the costs and benefits of having children, so they could make an intelligent and informed decision about having children, when, and how many. Such a counseling service could be particularly valuable for young adults.

There is also research on the *parental* structure of families, which seems to suggest that for children's development, family functioning and climate are more important than the number of parents *per se*. The *lack* of a father (or mother) is not as bad as *having* a father (or mother) is good. However, in our society, two-parent families generally have advantages over one-parent families in terms of status, monetary resources, and division of labor. Moreover, when a single parent has to be both caretaker and breadwinner, this presents great difficulties that can be alleviated only by services to assist him or her either financially or with child care. In line with the suggestion that we propose multiple solutions to such complex problems, here, we might suggest *both* strategies: income support for single parents in any income redistribution scheme, and "homemaker services" to assist single parents with cleaning, housekeeping, laundry, and cooking, thus relieving the physical burdens of parenting. Many single parents, especially those who are divorced or, until very recently at least, unmarried, also face problems of reduction in social status and activities. They must struggle against resentment of the opposite sex, the ex-spouse, or the child. They must overcome isolation, self-doubt, and overprotection or overpermissiveness toward the child. Supportive services for "parents without partners," therefore, might include: psychological or psychiatric counseling to counteract hurt or rejection, social activities (parties, discussions, group activities, etc.) to alleviate loneliness, consciousness-raising activities with other parents without partners, and counseling or help (parent aides) directly oriented toward child care. If the single parent can share the burden of child care with another adult—who is not necessarily a spouse or even of the opposite sex—it will benefit both parent and child. For the parent, it provides relief from the tedium of child care and consultation about child-related problems; for the child, it may break a too-intense bond with the parent, and it provides another role model—another adult to interact with.

As we have just suggested, there are difficulties for parents and children associated with the single parent family. Raising children is a difficult and consuming task—and more so for one person than for two. Problems are more common in one-parent families and more difficult to overcome; such families need extra support. As well as proposing services to assist single parents, therefore, we should also think of ways of preventing families from breaking up unnecesarily, of supporting families in crisis. More ready access for parents to marital counseling services may be one way. This could be accomplished by making marital counseling a tax-deductible expense, by including it in the coverage of insurance or health plans, or by giving or increasing government subsidies to marital therapy clinics (for example, in Community Mental Health Centers). Another preventive measure would be to revise or avoid welfare regulations that make it more profitable for a family to live apart—or to fake living apart. A third strategy would be to give priority to parents with young children or parents in conflict when measures to relieve environmental stresses are recommended or enacted. These measures might include job training and job satisfaction programs, guaranteed income programs, promotion systems, and housing programs. Finally, we might increase public awareness about birth control, abortion, and adoption options for married as well as unmarried parents.

The intention of the proposition and these suggestions about family counseling and family support, it must be stressed once more, is not to "preserve the institution of marriage" and "save the nuclear family," but rather to provide a variety of services to ease the stresses of parenting, prevent unnecessary family breakups, and allow parents of young children to *choose* whether to rear their children together or apart. Our primary goal, here, and elsewhere, is the provision of the best environments for the care of young children.

In the interests of that goal, other strategies for supporting families so they can better care for children can also be envisioned or devised. These, even more clearly than those already suggested, are beyond the domain of the research on child care that was reviewed. They are offered merely as some tentative suggestions of possible strategies for family support. We have no evidence for their relative effectiveness or feasibility—but would propose that all such possibilities be investigated, and then that those which are successful ultimately be made available to all parents who wish or need them.

Day care.   Although it is often viewed as a threat to family integrity, day care can also be seen as a support service for families. Specific suggestions for day-care policy and practice are discussed in a later section. Here, we would just point out that day care—of a variety of forms—can provide a valuable, indeed, often necessary, resource for families in which parents cannot or will not provide adequate and continuous child care.

Temporary (crisis) child care.   Such care often could be used even by normally well-functioning families; for example, when the mother is hospitalized. If adequate substitute care during this period is not available, children may suffer. Agencies might be established to provide trained substitute caregivers (like substitute school teachers) who would go into the child's home or, if necessary, take the child into their own home, on a temporary basis.

Child-family screening.   Especially for parents who are worried about the progress of their child or the adequacy of their child care, a diagnostic screening service could provide support as well as evaluation. In addition to assessing children's development, and pointing out any problems in their intellectual, physical, or psychological development, the screening could include assessment of the child's social and material environment and identification of any major deficiencies there. Such a service could be made available and encouraged on a regular basis from the time a woman became pregnant until the children were grown.

Child-development specialists or child-care counselors. These would be concerned and qualified adults who, at the request of the family or some other agency such as the school or a pediatrician, could observe family dynamics, provide a neutral setting for discussion of child-rearing problems among family members, and offer advice about solutions when asked. They would be neither social workers nor family therapists (although their training might be similar to those professionals), but a resource for normal families with difficulties or problems. Such problems might arise with the birth of a new baby, for example. A good way to introduce the service, therefore, would be in the hospital at the time of birth (or adoption) of the baby. Women suffering a depressive postpartum reaction might very well find the child-care counselor a valuable resource. Such counselors would not regard the family as "ill," would not be evaluating the family or controlling the welfare check; they would attempt to increase rather than undermine parents' confidence and competence.

Homemaker services. These services would include cleaning, cooking (e.g., "meals on wheels"), laundering, child care, and occasional babysitting to relieve parents of some of the *physical* burdens of parenting. Services now available only for the affluent could be subsidized for middle- and low-income families by providing inexpensive help with such activities. Teenagers and senior citizens might be available to work as such "house-helpers" or "family aides."

Family resource center. A particularly interesting, but untested proposal—the family resource center—could be a place in the neighborhood, a telephone "hotline," a series of special public programs, or all of these. Its aim would be to offer a centralized service for all families, not just poor ones. Such a resource center might provide:

—information about local schools and day-care facilities (costs, admission criteria, evaluative descriptions, locations)
—diagnostic screening and testing of children

—access to other community social services, including referrals for therapy or health care, counseling for divorce, marital conflict, child custody, or family-planning

—educational programs for parents or expectant parents in child-care skills, nutrition, homemaking, consumerism, home repairs, etc.

—help in organizing parent groups or cooperative child-care facilities (day care, playgroups, babysitting cooperatives, etc.)

—advice concerning legal rights of parents, children, and families

—adoption and foster care referrals

—information about income supplements, food stamps, housing, etc.

—a welcome service for new neighbors

—organization or provision of temporary crisis care or occasional day care for children

—toy/book/film/curriculum library, particularly for materials for and about children and child care

—a service for child abuse—reporting, treatment, preventive programs

—training programs for child-care workers (family helpers, parent aides, day-care workers)

—organization or provision of homemaker services (laundry, meals-on-wheels, etc.)

Support Services, Work Practices, and Income Maintenance Should Be Provided for Mothers to Choose Whether They Want to Work or to Stay Home

Mothers of young children, in larger and larger numbers, are going to work—and will probably continue to do so. One survey shows, however, that even when mothers are working they still spend about the same amount of time on child care as when they are not employed. The outcome of this practice is probably often less adequate care—as mothers are tired from working all day—and less adequate work—since mothers still have to worry about parental and household responsibilities while on the job. It has also been observed that mothers who work are less able than those who do not work to participate in educational programs with their children. Policies to alleviate mothers' double burden would seem to be in order. These might include (a) provision of adequate services for supplementary child care (day care, etc.); (b) shorter work hours for mothers *and* fathers; (c) more opportunities for part-time employment for those who want it; (d) creative work schedules that permit extended periods off for parenting in the first few years of a child's life—"work now, nurture later" or "nurture now, work later" schemes—and reentry and retraining opportunities for parents who take advantage of such schemes; and (e) income support for mothers who wish to stay at home but cannot afford to. Since empirical data suggest that a mother's satisfaction with her role, whether it be at home or in the work force, is related to her behavior toward her children, giving women the option of staying home or working may be one way of increasing the likelihood of positive parenting. It should be noted, however, that the data for this generalization are merely correlational, and therefore, although it makes intuitive sense, the assumption that maternal role satisfaction necessarily leads to more positive child care is not strictly empirically based.

Fathers Should Be Encouraged to Spend More Time Parenting and to Adopt a More Nurturant Role if They Choose to

The literature on families suggests that fathers are an underutilized resource for child care. When given the opportunity, many fathers are willing and able to interact with their infants and young children—but in "real life" apparently they seldom do. As women are entering the work force in greater numbers and, consequently, are less available as full-time caregivers, since children benefit from close relations with fathers who are accepting, nurturant, playful, and stimulating, and because a balance between the roles of mother and father (in which neither parent dominates the affection or discipline of the child) is beneficial for children's development, policies that allow and encourage fathers to take a more active role in caring for their children are indicated. Such policies need to be explored on a number of levels. First, we might explore ways of promoting a change in the attitude and values of American society so that such nurturing care would be perceived as appropriate for men to give as well as women. A public campaign might show how skilled men can be at caring for children in day-care centers, as babysitters, as "big brothers," as single parents, and in two-parent families in which the mothers work, for instance. Such a campaign could also stress the subjective experiences—of fun and frustration—for such male caregivers and the benefits of treating child care as a joint, cooperative venture between parents. A number of TV programs on the subject have already been aired, and some magazines now regularly include articles about fathers' experiences. These may reflect a promising trend toward increased participation of men in child care.

On a different level, classes in high school on child development, family life, or preparation for parenthood, should actively recruit and appeal to boys as well as girls. Similarly, prenatal classes for expectant parents, or postnatal programs for first-time parents, could include more information directed specifically to men—supporting, guiding, instructing, and preparing them for fatherhood. Hospital policies that allow the participation of fathers in the birth and early care of the infant could be encouraged more widely. This does seem to be a current trend, but there are still many hospitals that exclude fathers from the delivery room and impose restricted visiting hours. Finally, and perhaps most important, work schedules that allow fathers more time for their families could be explored (paternity leaves, etc.).

As well as generally spending less time with their children, fathers tend to behave differently from mothers when they do interact with their children. With preschool and school-aged children, mothers, traditionally, have been observed to be more expressive, warm, accepting, nurturant, and positive; fathers, more distant and controlling. To the extent that these different patterns of parental behavior are accurate and are the result of parents' behaving in sex-role stereotyped ways—because they think they're *supposed* to—programs or policies which would counteract such stereotypes and demonstrate increased role options would be valuable. Educational programs for parents might well include suggestions for fathers that encourage them to express their affection for their children and participate more in nondisciplinary caregiving. It is not necessary, or even desirable, however, that mothers and fathers behave identically toward their children. Observation of some variety in adult roles and behavior—if not vastly unbalanced or inconsistent in intention— is beneficial for children's development. Moreover, families, like small groups, may be more productive or harmonious when they have a "social leader" and a "task leader." What should perhaps be avoided, however, is the parents' assumption of markedly different responsibilities and rigid roles strictly on the basis of sex identity. It is perfectly reasonable that in some families the father might feel more comfortable with and therefore assume the relatively more nurturant role.

One of the critical ways in which mothers and fathers differ in their treatment of children is in the area of sex-role development. It has been observed that fathers tend to differentiate more sharply than mothers in their behavior toward girls and boys and in what they consider appropriate activities for each. If this means, as it often does, that fathers do not encourage boys to be expressive and nurturant or girls to be thoughtful and achieving, then any programs that promote the "liberation" of fathers' attitudes and behavior should be recommended.

Parent Education Programs Should Be Improved and Made Available to All Parents and Prospective Parents Who Want Them

Even if it were possible to relieve all environmental stresses, redistribute income equitably, and provide adequate wages, housing, health care, day care, legal care, consumer protection, schools or non-schools for all families, there would still be intrafamilial and interpersonal conflicts and inadequacies, and consequently a place for educational or therapeutic programs for parents. Here, we discuss various formats such programs might adopt.

Unfortunately, we do not yet know very effective ways of providing educational experiences to enhance parenting skills; we do know that some strategies are relatively less effective (cf. Bronfenbrenner, 1974; Horowitz & Paden, 1973). Group education programs for parents, such as lecture and group discussions—even if their children are involved, but especially if they are not—do not particularly attract parents, particularly less affluent, single, working parents with large families or personal problems. Nor are programs as likely to be attractive if parents are contacted by the school or agency rather than initiating that contact themselves. Moreover, programs which attempt to change parents' attitudes are typically not effective in producing that change. It is not surprising that any program, especially a discussion or lecture-type program, does not cause a radical shift in parents' feeling or attitude toward their children. Such profound changes are likely to evolve only gradually through experiencing repeated, rewarding interaction with the child. Similarly, simply *telling* a mother to change her attitude, feeling, or behavior does not produce marked change. At the very least, *demonstration* of the desired behavior, particularly of a more complex behavior, in *interaction* with a child is necessary.

The possibilities of preparental education courses in child development and family life as part of the high school curriculum have not been explored in depth. Particularly if accompanied by extensive practical experience with real children and real family problems, this would seem to be a promising way of reaching and educating prospective parents before the real burdens of parenting descend and before firm attitudes toward one's own children are established. Field experience could be gained in day-care or babysitting settings, with pupils' own families, or by simulated incidents in the classroom. Similar experiences could also be offered in adult education courses in child care and development, in prenatal programs for expectant parents, or at the "family resource center" described earlier. Another medium for parent education that deserves further exploration is television; creative programming here could effectively inform and advise parents about child-care skills.

Judging by results of past educational attempts to enhance the quality of parental child care, programs with the greatest probability of success in attracting parents and changing their behavior would likely involve:

—neighborhood or, better, home-based instruction
—parents' active involvement and participation in teaching or interacting with their own children

—specific, focused, interactional educational experiences for each child, presented individually, in a one-to-one situation

—goal-specific curricula (to date, curricula aimed specifically at children's cognitive or language skills have been most effectively communicated to parents. Curricula should be extended to include experiences that demonstrate to parents the need for being responsive to children's behavior as well as stimulating their senses)

—projects determined, planned, and carried out by parents themselves

—relatively long-term programs that continue instruction and maintain support

—small, intensive programs with a research/evaluation component

In general, it also seems likely that the optimal timing for such programs would be from the prenatal period through the first two or three years of the child's life. As well as being an important period in the child's development, this is a critical time for parents, a time in which they develop expectations about infants and parenting and find out if they were realistic, form initial attitudes toward the child, and evolve strategies and patterns of caregiving.

References

Bronfenbrenner, U. *Is early intervention effective? A report on longitudinal evaluations of preschool programs.* [DHEW Publication No. (OHD) 74–25]. Washington: Department of Health, Education and Welfare, 1974.

Bronfenbrenner, U. The challenge of social change to public policy and developmental research. Paper presented at biennial meetings of the Society for Research in Child Development, Denver, April, 1975.

Horowitz, F. D., & Paden, L. Y. The effectiveness of environmental intervention programs. In B. M. Caldwell & H. N. Ricciuti (Eds.), *Review of child development research.* Volume 3. Chicago: University of Chicago Press, 1973. Pp. 331–402.

The Differences Between Having One and Two Children*
David Knox and Kenneth Wilson

Young mothers of two children responded to a 49 item questionnaire designed to assess their motivations for and consequences (personal and marital) of having a second child. Results indicated that while the impact of the first child was greater than the second, the latter involved less time for self, more work, more noise, and decreased marital happiness. Implications of these findings are suggested.

◼ A re-examination of the myths associated with only children and concerns ranging from inflation to over-population have resulted in an increasing number of young married couples considering the one-child family as a desirable family size (Hawke & Knox, 1977). In 1972, 6% of a national probability sample of young Americans between the ages of fourteen and twenty-five expressed their desire to have an only child. By 1974, the percentage had risen to 10% (Youth, 1975). Among the issues considered by those evaluating the one-child alternative are the differences between having one child and having two. Folklore doesn't help much. They are told that "Two are as easy as one" and that "After you've adjusted to one, the next one is a breeze." But what do mothers with two children report about the differences between having one and two?

To obtain some empirical information about this question, we developed a 49 item questionnaire to measure the motivations for and consequences (both personal and marital) of having a second child. The questionnaire was given to a non-probability (snowball) sample of 144 mothers who met two criteria: (a) Each mother had only two children, and (b) the second child was under five years old. By restricting the sample to mothers who met these criteria, distortion by subsequent children was eliminated and distortion by time was minimized.

"The Differences Between Having One and Two Children" by David Knox and Kenneth Wilson from THE FAMILY COORDINATOR, January 1978. Copyright © 1978 by the National Council on Family Relations. Reprinted by permission.

*This research was supported through a grant from the Research Council of East Carolina University. The authors express their appreciation to Drs. Charles Garrison and Paul Tschetter and their wives, Maureen and Elaine, for their insights in developing the questionnaire and to Shelly Bencini for coding the questionnaires.

Mothers with Two Children

The respondents may best be described as white (96.6%), Protestant (72.0%), highly educated, middle class (72.7% had completed some college work), and traditional (83.3% had part-time jobs and 72.3% described themselves as doing 70% or more of the child care responsibilities).

Motivations for the Second Child

"I really enjoyed my first child and wanted another to repeat the experience," was the reason reported by exactly half of the mothers for having their second child. Not one of the 144 mothers reported that she had ever strongly wished she could return to the time when she had only one child (only 6.9% of the mothers had ever expressed the desire). "Children are a delight," expressed one mother. One fourth (27.9%) of the respondents had their second child because they "wanted a companion for the first." "We had our second child to save the first," recalled one mother. "It's not fair to the child to be reared without a brother or sister. Only children are lonely and don't have anyone their age to share life's experiences and problems," she continued.

Other reasons for having the second child included "my husband" (5.8%), "personal fulfillment" (4.8%), "our first child was a girl so we tried again for a boy" (4.8%), and "our first child was a boy so we tried again for a girl" (3.8%). But regardless of the motivation for having the second child, about half (45.4%) of the mothers reported that they had decided to have the second child before they had their first. Such timing reflects the cultural bias toward the two-child family and a desire to avoid having an only child. "It never occurred to me not to have at least two children."

Personal Consequences of One vs. Two Children

Magnitude of Difference

When asked, "Was the effect of the first child on you personally greater than the effect of the second child?", 48.9% of the mothers answered "yes" (31.2%—no; 19.9%—no difference). Common explanations for the greater adjustment necessitated by the first child were in reference to loss of freedom, loss of privacy, and the new experience of parenthood. Specific expressions follow (a) "I lost my freedom to truly enjoy life and do what I wanted with the first child. Once I began forgetting self, my second child had little effect;" (b) "Childbirth and responsibility for a baby were new experiences with the first child. I felt more confident with the second child;" (c) "I got used to never being alone after my first child was born." Some responses were unique. One woman said that her first child was a shock which resulted in her quitting her job and her husband dropping out of graduate school. Another said there wasn't any difference because "I stayed sick for nine months with both of them."

Less Time for Self

But while the mothers reported that their first child had a greater effect than the second, they noted that two children involve more time, work, and noise than one. Regarding time, 76.6% of the mothers reported that they had less time for themselves after the second child was born. One mother reflected, "There is less time to relax when you've got two. Everything I do is interrupted by one or the other wanting something. I can't read a book; I can only read at a book. Also, if one gets sick, the other gets sick too and I'm up all night running between beds."

More Work

When asked, "How would you describe the amount of work two children require (dressing, feeding, laundry) as opposed to the amount one child requires?", fewer than 4% reported that "two are as easy as one." But most mothers (68.3%) felt that the additional work was "a little more but not much." One mother said, "When I'm washing a load of clothes or fixing toast, it doesn't matter too much. It's when I need to get them dressed to go somewhere that it's a hassle."

More Noise

In addition to less time for one's self and more work, the mothers (75.7%) reported that the second child created "more noise" in the household. "They argue and fight and bicker at unpredictable times," expressed one mother. "Sibling rivalry is the biggest change I have noticed between having one and two children."

It's Worth It

But the additional noise, time, and work necessitated by the second child was regarded as inconsequential when compared to the benefits. Most of the mothers (93.1%) said that they had "never" wished that they could return to the one-child family. The primary benefits derived after the second child was born included, "they are company to each other," "my husband and I have one apiece," and "they are twice as much pleasure."

Career

Since the majority (83.3%) of these mothers had part-time jobs and were not currently pursuing a full-time career, they did not regard their careers as being hampered by their second child. When asked, "How did your second child affect your career?", common responses were: "I have always worked part-time so that I could be with my children when they needed me," "I don't want my children reared by another person," and "All mothers should be home in the afternoon when their children come home from school."

Some mothers (14.7%) reported that their second child had made their career "very difficult" in contrast to 11.8% who made this observation about their first child. One mother said, "Since my second child was born, I have to organize and plan a little better and be content to wait a few years to accomplish certain goals."

Marital Consequences of One vs. Two Children

To assess the effect of each child on marital satisfaction, the mothers responded to a Likert-type scale. The five point continuum was collapsed into three categories (improved, stayed the same, got worse). Table 1 suggests a progressive negative effect of children on the marital relationship as reported by these mothers. With the first child, 22% of their marriages improved compared to 15.6% of the marriages that got worse. But after the second child was born, fewer marriages improved (10.8%) and more got worse (17.3%).

Specific statements made by these mothers included: "The main difference I noticed with the second child was that I was more tired more of the time since I had to relate emotionally to two children throughout

Table 1   Reported Marital Satisfaction from Before First
Pregnancy to After Birth of First and Second Child

	After First %	After Second %
Improved	22.0	10.8
Stayed the Same	62.4	71.9
Got Worse	15.6	17.3

the day," expressed one wife. "After I had listened to incessant pleadings such as 'I need a fork,' 'Can I have some more grape juice?' and 'I don't like oatmeal,' there was litle left of me for my husband. And when the children were finally in bed, I needed to use the rest of the evening to catch up on the housework I was unable to do because of the constant interruptions." In addition to the wife feeling more emotionally and physically drained at the end of the day, looking into each other's eyes, holding hands, laughing together, having calm discussions, and working together on projects tend to decrease with children (Rollins & Feldman, 1970; Ryder, 1973; Rosenblatt, 1974).

When the mothers compared their marital happiness before any children and after the birth of the second child, more reported that their marriages improved (22.5%) than got worse (19.6%). But while the second child tended to have a negative effect (if it had any effect), the level of satisfaction in most of the marriages was unaffected (58%). Other researchers have reported the absence of any effect children have on the marital relationship (Russell, 1974; Knox & Gilman, 1974; Gilman & Knox, 1976). Additional research is needed to identify the ways in which spouses integrate each child into the marital and family unit. Whatever the mechanisms, this research suggests that parents are more effective with the first child than the second.

Summary and Implications

"There is more adjustment from none to one than from one to two" summarizes the difference between having one and two children. Although mothers report less time for themselves, more work, and more noise as consequences of having the second child, they are confident that they made the right decision to have provided a companion for their first child. Sacrifices for their careers and marriages are regarded as "worth it." One mother observed, "Two kids may increase your grief, but they will increase your joy."

In formulating decisions about family size, prospective parents and parents of one child who are considering having an only child can profit from the experiences of mothers who already have two children. These experiences suggest that "two are not as easy as one" but that "it's worth it."

References

Gilman, R. C., & Knox, D. Coping with fatherhood: The first year. *Child Psychiatry and Human Development,* 1976, 6, 134–148.

Hawke, S., & Knox, D. *One child by choice.* Englewood Cliffs, New Jersey: Prentice-Hall, 1977.

Knox, D., & Gilman, R. C. The first year of fatherhood. *Family Perspective,* 1974, 9, 31–34.

Rollins, B. C., & Feldman, H. Marital satisfaction over the family life cycle. *Journal of Marriage and the Family,* 1970, 32, 20–28.

Rosenblatt, P. C. Behavior in public places: Comparison of couples accompanied and unaccompanied by children. *Journal of Marriage and Family Living,* 1974, 36, 750–755.

Russell, C. S. Transition to parenthood: Problems and gratifications. *Journal of Marriage and the Family,* 1974, 36, 294–301.

Ryder, R. G. Longitudinal data relating marriage satisfaction and having a child. *Journal of Marriage and the Family,* 1973, 35, 604–606.

Youth-1974: A survey of Americans ages 14 through 25. New York: Institute of Life Insurance, 277 Park Avenue, New York, NY. 1975.

Single Parent Adoptions
William Feigelman and Arnold R. Silverman

■ Adoption by single individuals represents a relatively unprecedented phenomenon in the field of American social services. In the past such a policy would have been considered "unthinkable" by most agency workers. Earlier viewpoints assumed that only couples possessed the necessary role models and resources that could offer children psychologically supportive experiences. Today, however, child care professionals and social workers are increasingly aware of the large number of children who are permanently estranged from their families. These professionals are intimately acquainted with the fates of children whose early lives consist of passage through a series of foster and institutional residences. Ultimately, these children are likely to be disproportionally overrepresented in reformatories, prisons, and mental institutions. Agency personnel have become increasingly receptive to new alternatives that could offer children permanency in a familial context.

Child care professionals have also become aware of the changing nature of American family life; increasing divorce, and the large numbers of children growing up in the absence of close association with both parents. As American family lifestyles have become varied and as single parenting has become a relatively commonplace experience, agency personnel have begun to consider placing children in one parent homes, especially in cases where institutionalization or long-term foster care would be the only other likely alternative.

Perhaps the earliest relatively large scale effort at single parent placements was undertaken by the Los Angeles Department of Adoptions, when forty children were placed in single parent homes during 1966 and 1967.[1] More recently, the Los Angeles Department of Adoptions reports that 379 children have been placed in single parent homes.[2] Across the country the number of single parent placements slowly and steadily continues to mount. Single parent adoptions have been made in a number of American cities, including Washington, D.C., Chicago, New York City, Portland, Oregon, Minneapolis, Indianapolis, and Bridgeport, Connecticut.[3] Nationwide, approximately between 1,000 and 2,000 single parent adoptions have been effected.

Alfred Kadushin's research has been particularly influential in stimulating single parent placements. Reviewing the research evidence of children reared in "fatherless" families in the areas of mental health, emotional adjustments, suicide, delinquency, and sexual identification he found no compelling evidence that single parent family life is inherently or necessarily pathogenic. He states:

Research seems to indicate that children are able to surmount the lack of a father and some of the real shortcomings of a single parent home . . . the material suggests a greater appreciation of the variety of different kinds of contexts in which children can be reared in without damage.[4]

Yet, the philosophy governing single parent adoptions has viewed these placements as less desirable and the single prospective adopter is perceived as an adoptive parent of last resort. In most situations, single parents have been assigned older, minority, and handicapped children— the least preferred kinds of children, whose emotional, physical, and social needs are considerable, often exceeding those of most other children. Although consistent with the laws of supply and demand and the child welfare perspective these placements appear paradoxical: those who are felt to possess the least resources to parent have been assigned the children who would seem to require the most demanding kinds of care.

Questions arise regarding the success of these adoptions. How well do children adjust in single parent homes? How well do their adjustments compare with children reared in two parent adoptive homes? Moreover, what are the common social characteristics among single parent adopters? How do these characteristics compare with those of other adoptive couples? In selecting prospective single adoptive parents, agencies generally insist that applicants have close relationships with their extended families to aid with the many demanding tasks of child rearing. How essential are extended family involvements for facilitating children's adjustments? Are there other sources of support which single parents utilize to meet the demands of child rearing?

A Review of the Research

The limited research done to date indicates wholly positive results for the children adopted by single individuals. The earliest published study based upon eight adoptive placements, undertaken by the Los Angeles Department of Adoptions, came to the following conclusion:

Our experience with single-parent adoptive placements has, to date, been very promising. In no instance have we observed regression on the part of any of these children. There has been steady progress in the development of the child as a person in his adoptive home, and in several instances, the development has been truly dramatic.[5]

A later study, also conducted under the auspices of the Los Angeles Department of Adoptions, was based on thirty-six single parent placements.[6] This study found that of thirty-six single parent adopters, thirty-five were women. Blacks were overrepresented (almost 66 percent). Although the sample varied in its educational achievements, sample members tended to be more highly educated than most; half had completed at least some college. Most had close relationships with extended family members; 66 percent of the women were formerly married. Most sample members were employed and incomes ranged from $3,000 to $13,000. Although this research was primarily descriptive it was noted that, "these thirty-six case records strongly suggest that the children involved have found true 'familiness'."[7]

More recently, Joan Shireman and Penny Johnson[8] completed a study of thirty-one single parent adoptions of black infants in the Chicago area between 1970 and 1972. Eighteen of these families were reinterviewed three years later.

Like the Ethel Branham study most single parents were women; most were black; most had been married before. Although educational backgrounds, occupations, and incomes varied, comparable trends were noted with this sample: The Chicago group was somewhat high in occupational status, half of the sample were engaged in professional occupations, with low to moderate incomes; the median income was only $9,000. The group also appeared to be extended family oriented.

Although initial adjustments of the children tended to be somewhat negative, two months later, their adjustments were reported to be problem free by 81 percent of the parents. Trained interviewers substantially confirmed parental assessments. A followup study conducted three years later showed only two of the eighteen children in the reinterviewed families to have emotional adjustment problems.

Many questions, however, remain unanswered. Almost no information has been acquired on the smaller but growing number of male single adoptive parents.

Because these three studies have been completed with clients served by two agencies—the Los Angeles Department of Adoptions and the Chicago Child Care Society—it is unclear whether the social characteristics of these single parents accurately reflect the single parent population, whether they represent selection criteria of the agencies, local features, or some combination of all three factors. A survey drawing single parents from a diversity of sources and localities, would offer a better base to form a general picture of single adoptive parents.

Further, in discussing adjustments of adopted children in single parent homes, studies should be designed that offer some kind of control population, for example, comparisons with other children who were not placed in single parent homes. In the present survey the authors have attempted to address these matters.

Method and Sample

This study[9] was based upon a mailed questionnaire taken from a nationwide sample of adoptive parents. This work is part of a larger, now ongoing study of adoption. The data were collected between November 1974 and March 1976.

The sample was drawn from membership lists provided by adoptive parent organizations throughout the country. The single parent respondents had received their adopted children from a variety of sources domestically and abroad: private agencies, regional social service departments, and independent adoptions.

The sample of adoptive couples tended to overrepresent those who had adopted minority children. The typical adoptive couple in the sample consisted of white, native American parents who adopted a foreign-born child, most often from Asia. In selecting parent organizations to cooperate with the research, efforts were made to enlist the participation of parent groups whose memberships were acknowledged to include members who had completed transracial and transnational adoptions.

Attempts were also made to ensure the inclusion of at least several constituencies that represented in-country, in-race adopting families. Participating executive officers of the various organizations were asked to provide the names and addresses of any individuals they may have known who had adopted children but who did not belong to their organizations. Seven hundred thirteen questionnaires were returned in the samples of adoptive parents; a response rate of 60 percent.

A comparison of the characteristics of these respondents with those of other adoption studies reveals that the sub-samples of white native-born parents adopting domestically and abroad do not differ in any significant way from those respondents found in similar studies.[10]

Findings

Of the fifty-eight single adoptive parents in the sample, fifteen were males and forty-three were females. As a group they were much more likely to live in urban areas; couples, on the other hand, were much more likely to be suburbanites.[11] Only 16 percent of the couples lived in urban places, compared to 51 percent of single parents. Seventy percent of the couples lived in suburban areas, compared to 35 percent among single parents. These urban residence patterns of single adoptive parents probably reflect the residential patterns of single individuals, the higher levels of tolerance for unconventional lifestyles found in cities, and the wider availability of services such as clinics, day care centers, special schools, and medical facilities sought by single parents.

Single adoptive parents tended to be more highly educated than their adoptive couple counterparts. Seventy-five percent of the male and female single parents had completed some graduate study beyond the bachelor's degree level, compared with 47 percent of the married fathers and 33 percent of the married mothers. This relationship was statistically significant for the women, and approached significance for the men. Also, single parents generally held higher status occupations; yet, their incomes tended to trail behind those of couples. Only 22 percent of the single parents had annual incomes that exceeded $25,000, compared with 40 percent among the couples.

There are a number of reasons why the incomes of the single parents generally were below those of the couples. First, couples possess dual earning power. Second, women are overrepresented among the single parents, and it is widely known that women in nearly every occupational category earn less than men performing similar functions. Also, women are more likely to pursue their occupations on a part-time basis. Virtually all the single parent women in the sample were employed; 87 percent were working full time, 11 percent part time, and only one was unemployed.

Other minority members are similarly subject to discrimination. Minority members were far more common among the single parents of the sample. While only 2 percent of the married couples was nonwhite, 14 percent of the single parents was nonwhite.

Further, the single parents were concentrated primarily in two fields: education and social work. Typical occupations included a social worker, a professor of social work, a coordinator for a school based drug prevention program, an elementary school teacher, a special education teacher, a university professor, a teacher of Asian studies, and a school psychologist. It is probable that those choosing careers in human services initially are more likely to be receptive to single parent adoption. Moreover, occupational experiences with children and the needy tend to support and sustain motivations toward single parent adoption. Also, service professionals are more likely to be knowledgeable about children who might be available for adoption.

In terms of religious preferences no differences were noted between single parents and the married adoptive parents. Similarly, no differences were observed in the frequency of religious participation between the two groups. Single parents were somewhat more likely to describe their political viewpoints as liberal. Fifty-eight percent of the female single parents called themselves liberal compared with 45 percent among the wives of the sample; this finding was significant at the .05 level. A similar trend prevailed among the men. Fifty-four percent of the single parent men were self-described liberals and only 38 percent of the husbands; these differences approached, but did not achieve, statistical significance. The liberal perspectives of single parents may well reflect the occupational ideologies of educational and social service professionals.

While the literature would suggest that single parents are more likely to be closely affiliated with their extended families than married couples, the opposite trend was noted. Sixty-three percent of the adoptive couples saw their extended family members once a month or more often, compared with 55 percent among the single adoptive parents. Although the meaning of these findings is not certain, it is possible that the urban living patterns of the single parents may impose time and interest barriers against more frequent visiting with their usually suburban-based kin. Otherwise, in interaction with friends and organizational involvements, both groups showed similar patterns.

One other difference between the two groups was their relative ages. Although single fathers and husbands showed similarities in age, single mothers tended on the average to be older. Twenty-five percent were forty-five years of age or older, compared with only 11 percent of the wives. Fifty-six percent of the wives were less than thirty-four years of age, compared with only 38 percent of single mothers. These differences may reflect the greater period of time required to achieve sufficient resources, maturity, and the desire to adopt a child as a single parent. And in turn, may correspond to agency requirements for prospective single adoptive parents.

Adoptive Experiences of Single Parents and Couples

Fifty-seven percent of the single adoptive parents were first time adopters. Single parents tended to adopt children of the same sex; 80 percent of the fathers adopted boys and 75 percent of the mothers adopted girls.

As one might have expected, single parents tended to have more difficulties in completing their adoptions. Thirty-nine percent had made three or more previous attempts to adopt, compared with only 18 percent among the couples. Also, experiences with adoption professionals were more often reported by single parents to be negative. Eighteen percent found adoption agencies to be uncooperative, compared with only 6 percent among couples. Fifty-five percent found the Immigration and Naturalization Service to be uncooperative, compared with only 19 percent among couples. Recent changes in immigration laws should reduce frustrating experiences with the Immigration and Naturalization Service for single parents. There was a slight trend toward more single parents reporting uncooperative responses from regional social service departments, which fell short of statistical significance. Among each of the specified caretakers—adoption agencies and immigration social service departments—male single parent adopters tended to report more uncooperative responses. Also, the data revealed that courts are less likely to be helpful to single parents. While 59 percent of the couples found the courts helpful, only 36 percent of single parents described courts this way.

Single parents showed substantially greater willingness to adopt hard-to-place children and these attitudes were reflected in the kinds of children they actually adopted. Seventy-nine percent would accept an older child, compared with 60 percent among adopting couples; 82 percent were willing to adopt a black child, compared with 56 percent among couples; 51 percent were willing to adopt a slightly retarded child, compared with 32 percent of couples; 40 percent were willing to adopt a handicapped child, compared with only 35 percent among couples. Although substantially similar trends in attitude were noted for both single fathers and mothers, men showed a greater tendency to actually adopt various hard-to-place children. Approximately 60 percent of the men adopted children six years of age or older, compared with 23 percent of the single mothers and 9 percent of the couples. Men also were more likely to adopt black children. Forty-seven percent had actually adopted blacks, compared with 30 percent among single mothers and 10 percent among couples. These patterns probably reflect the unwillingness of agencies to place children with male single parents.

As a group, the single parent adopters tended to adopt children who were older. Thirty-three percent adopted children six years or older, 22 percent adopted children between the ages of three and five, and 45 percent adopted children under three years of age. Couples, on the other hand, were much more likely to adopt infants; only 9 percent adopted children over six and 74 percent adopted children under three years of age.

Several major areas where parents normally confront problems in raising children were also investigated. Three areas were surveyed: physical health; emotional adjustments; and growth or development problems. Parents were asked to evaluate whether their children had problems in these areas—often, sometimes, rarely, or never. Parents were also asked whether their adopted children had received any extensive medical care in the past year. The responses given by the single parents paralleled those given by adopting couples. No statistically significant differences were noted, except in one case where making adjustments was difficult.

Male and female single parents reported substantially similar responses in their appraisals of the four problem areas. Single parents reported significantly more emotional adjustment problems than were true for couples. Forty-three percent reported problems sometimes or often, compared with 33 percent among the couples. Many earlier studies of adoption[12] have noted that older child adoptions generally present more adjustment difficulties because the child's personality development is already well underway before joining his adoptive family. Therefore, the authors attempted to control the age factor.

When age was controlled they found that the relationship between single parenting and poorer emotional adjustments disappeared for younger children but still persisted among children six years or older. Among seventy-nine cases adopting children six years or older, 77 percent of single parents reported emotional adjustment problems sometimes or often, compared with only 52 percent among couples. This difference was statistically significant with chi square at the .02 level. It is the authors' belief that these trends reflect existing placement realities. Single parents, as the agencies' adoptive placements of last resort, are more often obliged to accept children whose earlier experiences of deprivation, instability, and abuse have led to substantially more emotional adjustment problems. In addition, the professional experiences of these parents may lead them to recognize such problems more readily than other parents.

The respondents were asked to offer a subjective evaluation of their child's overall adjustment. Approximately 68 percent reported excellent adjustments, 26 percent good, 4 percent fair, and 2 percent poor. Substantially similar responses were indicated by both single adoptive parents and couple respondents; no apparent differences were noted between male and female single parents.

Children's adjustments are salient for their parent's own sense of ego integrity and well-being. Therefore, the authors included two indirect measurements of adjustment. Parents were asked how long it took for the child to be considered "their own." Responses were divided into two groups; those taking place within a month or less, and those taking place within longer time periods. Single parents took longer to consider their children as their own. While 36 percent of the single parents required more than a month to feel that the child was their own, only 26 percent of the couples required this much time. This difference fell a fraction short of the .05 level of significance.

Again, the authors believed it advisable to control for the child's age at adoption. With age controlled, both groups required substantially similar time periods to fully accept their adopted children.

Examining gender differences among single parents on adjustment, it was found that males required more time to fully accept their adopted children than females. While only 32 percent of female single parents took more than a month for the child to be regarded as their own, 53 percent of the single fathers took this long. Yet, when the age of the child was adjusted for, these differences disappeared.

The other indirect measure of adjustment used was response to the following question. On the basis of your own experience would you encourage others to adopt as you have adopted? Yes; Yes, with some reservation; No. Eighty-six percent of the adoptive couples responded with unreserved affirmation, compared with only 72 percent among single mothers and 67 percent among single fathers. This difference was statistically significant. Yet, when the authors compared single adopting parents with other couples adopting children of similar ages the statistically significant association between these two variables again dissolved. Apparently, when the authors adjusted for differences in the ages of the child adopted, single parents and couples show substantially alike responses in recommending adoption to others. This factor would seem consistent with the interpretation that the older more problematic nature of the children adopted by single parents is the source of much of the difference between their experiences and that of the couples.

Agency workers frequently stress the importance of extended families in helping provide aid and support to the single adoptive parent with the many responsibilities of child rearing. In fact, most agencies engaged in single parent placements insist that prospective applicants possess extended family resources before they will be approved. An attempt was made to test this assumption that extended family affiliations are associated with children's adjustments. Seventy percent of the single adoptive respondents who saw kin at least monthly reported well-adjusted children compared with 63 percent among those seeing kin less often. Thus, the data show no significant association between the frequency of interaction with kin and adjustment of adopted children. On investigating the two indirect measures of adjustment—the time it takes to regard the child as a member of the family, and the willingness to recommend adoption to others—those who saw kin less often were no more likely to indicate adjustment difficulties than those seeing kin more frequently.

Yet, when the responses of extended families to the adoptions were investigated it was found that when parents reacted positively it correlated with better adjustments. Eighty percent of single parents whose parents responded positively to their adoptions, had children judged to have excellent adjustments, compared with only 40 percent among those whose parents responded with indifference, mixed reactions, or negatively. This difference was significant at the .02 level. Similar trends were also noted with our indirect measures of adjustment.

Those whose parents responded positively tended to feel that their child became their own sooner. This difference also was statistically significant. They were also more likely to urge others to adopt; this association approached but did not achieve statistical significance. The patterns which were observed among the single parents were also noted among the adoptive couples. Thus, positive extended family support facilitates adoptive adjustments not only among single parents but among all adoptive parents.

Apparently, friends also play an analogous supportive role in the adoptive process. Seventy-two percent of single parents whose close friends responded positively felt their children were well-adjusted compared with only 46 percent among those whose close friends responded with indifference, mixed feelings, or negatively. This difference fell a fraction short of significance at the .05 level among the single parents but was significant among the couples. Those whose close friends responded positively were also more likely to urge others to adopt; this difference was significant. The responses of close friends, however, is apparently unrelated to the time it takes for the child to become a member of the family.

Another area that was potentially important was society's response to the single adoptive parent. Does the community generally approve of or reject the single adoptive parent? The authors investigated what reactions adopting parents experienced from their parents, other extended kin, close friends, and neighbors. Respondents were asked whether reactions had been positive, mixed, indifferent, or negative. On the whole, the experiences of our single parents were comparable to those of the adopting couples. Single adoptive parents reported substantially similar responses from their parents, other relatives, and neighbors as was reported by the adoptive couples; no statistically significant differences were noted between the two groups. Positive responses ranged from a high of 74 percent among mothers' parents to a low of 64 percent among fathers' parents. Friends of single parents, however, were less likely to respond positively. While 89 percent of couples encountered positive responses by close friends, only 77 percent of the friends of single parents responded similarly. Male single parents were somewhat more likely to report their friends' disapproval, although this relationship fell short of statistical significance.

Summary

The data have documented some trends that are probably well-known to many single adoptive parents. Namely, that single parents are much more likely to encounter resistance from the various social agencies with whom they must deal in completing their adoptions; they are more likely to be turned away and discouraged in the adoptive process. Once they adopt, they are more likely to be subject to disapproval by their close friends than is true among other adopters. This uniformly discouraging response on the part of the community seems to be slightly more intense toward male single adoptive parents. Yet, these negative evaluations appear to be without foundation when one considers the outcomes of these adoptions. With few exceptions, both male and female single parents report substantially similar experiences to adoptive couples in raising adopted children.

The results obtained in this research offer positive support for the new and growing practice of single parent adoption. With the one exception of emotional adjustment problems, it was found that single adoptive parents report substantially similar information on the variety and severity of problems encountered in raising their children as is reported by other adoptive couples. When controlling for the age of the children adopted, both direct and indirect assessments of children's overall adjustments show fundamentally corresponding patterns among single parents and adoptive couples. These findings confirm earlier studies on the success of the overwhelming majority of single parent placements and suggest that single parents are as viable a resource for adoptive placements as couples. In fact, given the present discrimination against single parents in the adoption process, the absence of spouse supports and their more limited economic resources these positive findings suggest that single adoptive parents possess unusually high commitments to parenting.

Before being entirely confident that single parents offer similar benefits to waiting children as are found in two-parent homes, additional studies will be necessary. Future research should examine more objective indicators of adjustments such as school records, psychological adjustment test scores, and so forth, among comparable groups of children, in single-parent and in two-parent homes.

If future studies confirm the present results then there would be a need for reconceptualization of a great many theories of child development. Numerous viewpoints of child development maintain that two-parent families are indispensable to successfully resolve the Oedipus complex, to offer role modeling opportunities, and to insure the intergenerational transmission of cultural values and conforming behavior patterns. Most of the theories positing the inherent need for the two-parent family were conceived, however, during the early and mid-twentieth century, at a time when sex roles were far more differentiated and segregated than is true today.

Today, with married women participating in the labor force and pursuing careers in formerly male-dominated occupations in ever increasing numbers, with household and child-rearing tasks increasingly becoming shared by both men and women alike, with formal educational experiences of both sexes more nearly convergent there is considerable commingling of sex roles. No longer are men the exclusive task specialists and women the providers of nurturance they were in earlier times. With the increasing flexibility of contemporary sex roles, culturally appropriate role learning can be acquired from either parent as well as from both parents.

The findings outlined here also point to a need for reconsideration of the role of extended families in aiding and supporting the single adoptive parent. The mere availability of extended families, whether through living in the same community or frequent mutual visitations, has little to do with contributing to the success of single parent adoptions. A core of positively responding intimates, composed of kin or close friends—rather than availability of kin per se—would seem to offer a good prognosis for adoption success.

Notes

1. Ethel Branham, One Parent Adoptions, *Children,* 17:103–107 (May-June 1970).
2. Personal communication, September 21, 1976.
3. Alfred Kadushin, Single Parent Adoptions: An Overview and Some Relevant Research, *Social Service Review,* 44:263–74 (September 1970).
4. Ibid., p. 271.
5. Velma Jordan and William Little, Early Comments on Single Parent Adoptive Homes, *Child Welfare,* 45:536–38 (November 1966).
6. Branham, One Parent Adoptions, pp. 103–107.
7. Ibid.
8. Joan Shireman and Penny Johnson, Single Persons as Adoptive Parents, *Social Service Review,* 50:103–116 (March 1976).
9. This research was supported by the Research Foundation of the State University of New York (Grant Nos. 082–7105A and 082–7106A) and the National Institute of Mental Health (Grant No. MH 27 129–01).
10. Lawrence Falk, A Comparative Study of Transracial and Inracial Adoptions, *Child Welfare,* 49:82–88 (February 1970); Lucille J. Grow and Deborah Shapiro, *Black Children: White Parents* (New York: Child Welfare League of America, 1974); Elizabeth Lawder et al., *A Follow up Study of Adoptions: Postplacement Functioning of Adoptive Families* (New York: Child Welfare League of America, 1969); and Thomas Nutt and John Snyder, *Trans-racial Adoption,* February 1973, Department of Urban and Regional Planning, Massachusetts Institute of Technology, Cambridge, Massachusetts.
11. All tests of significance employed in this article were calculated from contingency tables employing chi square as a test of significance. Unless indicated otherwise, all associations mentioned in this section achieved statistical significance at the .05 level of significance or higher.
12. Alfred Kadushin, *Adopting Older Children* (New York: Columbia University Press, 1970).

Later Parenting

Parenting with Adolescent Children
Rhona Rapoport and Robert N. Rapoport

Issues in Parenting

■ The adolescent children have grown into young people, developing their own firm and specific identities, restlessly searching for stimulation and new experience, testing the limits that their parents and others will tolerate and the consequences of taking various risks. We wish to examine some of the specific issues in parenting, some of the dynamics in the relationships between parents and children that arise in this situation.

Parenting with adolescent children is decidedly *not* the relief it may have been assumed to be in earlier times when children took on adult roles earlier and norms favouring expressiveness of various kinds were less in evidence. Though children may not require detailed, day by day physical care in the same way as in infancy, there may be heavy demands for parental involvement of another kind. Different facets of this have been dealt with in research and clinical discussions, and different emphases have been adopted. Some psychoanalysts, for example, have not only taken the adolescent's turmoil to be akin to a psychiatric disturbance (the

From FATHERS, MOTHERS AND SOCIETY: TOWARDS NEW ALLIANCES by Rhona Rapoport and Robert N. Rapoport and Ziona Strelitz with Stephen Kew. Copyright © 1977 by Institute of Family and Environmental Research. Reprinted by permission of Basic Books, Inc. Excerpts from JOYS AND SORROWS OF PARENTHOOD by the Group for the Advancement of Psychiatry. Copyright © 1973 by the Group for the Advancement of Psychiatry. Reprinted by permission of Charles Scribner's Sons.

cure for which is the passage of time) but the correlative disturbance of the parents to be an expectable accompaniment, often also needing treatment.

It is only recently that there have been concerted efforts to analyse the *interlocking* nature of parents' and adolescents' needs at this stage, and to understand them in terms of normal psychodynamic development. The nature of the interlocking preoccupations is complex and is likely to vary with a number of factors, including the sex of the parent and of the child. The efflorescence of sexuality in the adolescent has repercussions on parents who may be on the wane in this respect, and more or less uncomfortable about it. Similarly, the fluctuations between exaggerated independence and child-like dependence in the child may have particularly acute repercussions for parents who, at mid-life, may be seeking new patterns of independence or dependence for themselves in relation to their families. The adolescent's wish to 'fly', to find adventure and new experience may repercuss particularly poignantly on the psychic equilibrium of parents who feel trapped in the ruts of their social roles and responsibilities. There is more to it than this. The accelerated rate of social and technological change creates a special set of problems in the parent-adolescent child relationship which may threaten parental authority when it is already being precariously stretched. Parents may feel it particularly difficult to be self-confident in their encounters with their children who seem so mature, so competent, so sexually precocious and independent-minded, with values of their own which may be sharply at variance with them. The GAP Committee observe (1973, p. 26):

The accelerated rate of change in our society has made the adjustments of teen-ager and parents even more difficult. . . . The generation gap, or generational differences, in cultural values, knowledge, and outlook tend to be magnified. If parents look only to their own experiences for guidance in understanding their teen-ager's needs, they are almost bound to encounter frustration, bewilderment, and disappointment. As a consequence of being exposed to the concerns of their adolescent children, many parents have undertaken an agonizing reappraisal of a number of their own attitudes and beliefs.

Parents who can open themselves to influence by their adolescent children in respect of some of their expectations may find the experience very rewarding. Those who do not find some of their adolescent's ideas compelling in themselves may still tolerate behaviour and attitudes from their children that conflict with parental expectations. This may be rationalized in terms of the child's individuality, or in terms of his or her identity formation. There are, however, many parents who find the expression of behaviour that conflicts with their expectations very distressing. It may be that they 'confuse the rebellion in manners for a rebellion in morals' (GAP, 1973, p. 43), or alternatively they may personalize their children's depreciation of parental standards and authority as attacks directed at them as individual parents and people.

A major element in parent-child relations in this phase is the requirement of parents to facilitate their adolescent children's launching. From the adolescent's point of view, it may be difficult to seek adequate guidance and direction without feeling it to indicate a lack of competence; to seek support and reassurance needed without feeling smothered; to seek one's own patterns, without feeling selfish.

Whilst many parents will themselves feel the need to do the best for their children in this critical period, there are often difficulties in doing so. Parents may feel themselves to be better placed than others to lead their children towards a valid assessment of options. But they may be rejected by their children as out of touch, and they may feel unable to influence their children and so may withdraw rather than risk conflict.

Some parents create difficulties by projecting their own particular ambitions onto their adolescent children. They may feel they have not accomplished their own goals and wish to help their children to make better use of their opportunities. Or they may feel that their accomplishments must be taken up and carried on by their children. Apart from the difficulties and pressures such projections create for the developing adolescent, parents themselves may be disappointed. The GAP Committee (1973, p. 43) observe:

Around the issue of going to college, some parents expect the adolescent vicariously to accomplish for them or successfully to compete for them. Rebellion against such pressures again causes some parents to expect the worst. It is helpful if parents do not lose faith in themselves or in the child's potential. They should expect the adolescent to behave consistently with society, to develop a reasonable degree of independence, to make educational and vocational choices within his competence and his interests, and to develop a healthy social and sexual identification. Optimistic expectations are often an expression of the parent's trust in himself, whereas pessimistic expectations may be feelings of distrust of one's self projected onto the child.

Another issue which may develop in parenting with adolescents relates to difficulties in undoing the past. There is an increasing amount of information now available to document the idea that many problems of adolescents are exacerbated by their earlier experiences in the home— separations, lack of love, lack of harmony, lack of communication, lack of organized control and so on. It may be painful for parents to learn when their children are adolescents and begin showing signs of difficulties caused by events in childhood, particularly if they are events over which there is no possibility of any corrective action being taken.

The study of adolescent problems—for example, juvenile delinquency, promiscuity, or psychiatric disorder—suggest that there are two types of background factor; one that may be dealt with by administrative intervention (given appropriate resources) and one that is less amenable to such intervention. Examples of the first are family size, poverty, poor material conditions of housing and deficiencies in parenting behaviour. Examples of the second are mental deficiency, history of family criminality or psychiatric disorder.

The type of situation most frequently found among parents of problematic adolescents centres on psychosocial deficiencies: in love from mother and/or father, in patterns of family communications, in training and role modelling, and in maintaining a reasonably happy and harmonious emotional atmosphere in the family (Glueck and Glueck, 1950; Andry, 1960; McCord and Thurber, 1962; Shields, 1962; West and Farrington, 1973; Wilson, 1975). One difficulty that is apparent on a widespread basis is that it is precisely in families which are deficient in these ways that there may be the greatest difficulty in taking countermeasures to correct the undesirable effects of earlier experience.

Recently, attention has been focused on another dimension of parenting that may be particularly difficult to undo, even for 'ordinary' parents. This is the background to over-permissiveness and overindulgence which Spock (1974) observes coming to fruition in rising cohorts of American adolescents. Maintaining a satisfactory balance of discipline with adolescent children emerging from this kind of early experience can be very difficult. The issues are complex and often paradoxical. The child who presses hard on his parents to allow him to do something he/she feels underneath he/she is not yet ready for is perhaps as relieved as the parents when the line is drawn and accepted. The parent who apologizes when he or she is 'wrong' may experience an increase in esteem from the child rather than, as he feared, a loss.

Many specific questions recur in parenting with adolescent children, and there is no clear-cut indication of the way these should be handled, or indeed, that they should always be handled in the same way. Sometimes there are clear divergences of parents' needs from children's needs. Where these cannot be reconciled, the resolution inevitably takes the interests of one party into account more than the interests of another. The felt needs of the adolescent need not always be the decisive element, even where the child's best interests are of paramount value.

The specific questions that recur in the caring experience may be focused quite differently for the parents and the adolescents. From our previous studies of parent-adolescent relations (Rapoport, 1975), the following consensus seems to prevail at present.

Setting limits is a key concern to parents. From their viewpoint, recurrent questions include: How permissive to be? In what way? Should there be phases of relaxation of limits? Are the different kinds of limits for hours? money? friends? use of stimulants? sex? etc. Where should one be adamant; where should one relax? From the adolescent's perspective, the focal questions regarding limits may be different. How far to press the boundaries set by parents? How daring to be about doing things *probably* disapproved of? What to battle over and what to bend with?

Confrontations over limits are perhaps the most frequent and problematic in the lives of parents of adolescent children. For the parent: how late to allow the young person to come in? What behaviour is tolerable in 'checking' the parent? What amount of travel, where and with whom is allowable on holidays? What degree of informality or peculiarity of dress to allow, and so on. The adolescent may be bigger, stronger, better-educated and even in some instances high-earning and more competent occupationally than the parent. Yet, in this phase when (s)he is still living at home (s)he is under parental authority. Whether justifiably or not, parents feel that their judgment ought to be applied for the protection of the child in many situations where the child considers that he or she knows better.

Characteristically, when disagreements are intense the tendency is toward conflict or withdrawal. Overt conflict generally means a family row. The consequences of a row can be disastrous or the air may be cleared and a new basis of relationships in the family evolved. Byng-Hall (1975) describes how a characteristic family row over issues of social control with an adolescent child may be managed constructively or become enmeshed in a recurrent and self-defeating pattern of neurotic interaction.

The limits issue may play itself out over a number of different topics: drugs, sex, friends, hours kept, participation in social movements or activities. In the USA, and perhaps increasingly in Europe as well, the explosive quality of the confrontation, when it occurs, is increased through the circumstances of social mobility. Families move residence a great deal more than they used to and this may pose special difficulties for the young people. They may have difficulty in making the adjustments necessary for a new school curriculum (this is more pronounced, obviously, for the less academic-minded); they may have problems about forming new friendships (this is more pronounced to the extent that they are lacking in social attractiveness, or in social skills including sport and other interests). Above all, there may be difficulties associated with achieving and sustaining a good interactive relationship with their parents. The latter may at this point be preoccupied with their own problems of adjustment—to new jobs, homes and social circumstances. Young people often, under these conditions, resort to extreme measures, including drugs, running away from home, associating with groups that seek excitement in delinquent ways (Seidenberg, 1973).

In Britain there is also a good deal of tension over the use of motorbikes, the choice of friends, the hours of returning home. Cyril Smith (1968, p. 70) describes the issues of social control which parents face, and notes:

Parents show an intense interest in their children's friends, especially of their daughter's boy friends. Chaperonage may have largely disappeared but parents still have their say about when their children are allowed out for courting and where. Such control is naturally greater with pubescent children than it is with young adults, and a recent survey of youth in a small Lancashire town showed that the majority of fourteen year old girls are made to stay in by their parents for some nights of the week, and most nights they are expected to be home before ten.

Fogelman (1976, p. 36), in a report of the National Children's Bureau follow-up of their 1958 cohort of children, now aged sixteen, indicates that the most frequent sources of disagreement between parents and children at this phase are 'Dress or hairstyle' ('Sometimes or often', 46 percent) and 'Time of coming in at night or going to bed' (34 percent). The latter in particular, is associated with setting limits to behaviour that parents feel puts their children at risk.

Lidz and other psychiatrists have noted that the issue of setting limits is very widely experienced but the form it takes varies. The question of how far parents should trust their children is an excruciatingly difficult one at this phase, because they feel acutely aware of the risks to which their children often seem oblivious: 'Their trust in the child they have raised and in their own capacities to raise a child undergoes its most severe test' (Lidz, 1968, p. 329). Lidz (p. 328) observes that the adolescent may press the limits very hard in other ways as well:

Typically, the youth begins to search out flaws in his parents. The process may start with a basic disillusionment in learning about their sexual life—their hypocrisy in practising what they have forbidden—but he seeks shortcomings that he can attack openly and resent rationally. The criticism of the parents' behaviour, and even more the attacks on their character constitute a serious blow to the parents' authority and self-esteem.

They may also *reject their parents*. This may be specially likely if they become involved in social mobility, as Jackson and Marsden (1962) noted in their study of education and social class. Sometimes there is a vicious cycle of rejection and counter-rejection in which the young person is ejected from the household, or takes himself off, drifting into urban areas in search of jobs.

Many rebellious adolescents who remain in the family 'suss out' their parents, searching with the unerring instinct of one who knows intimately the points of particular vulnerability. The channels and form through which this process occurs varies with the sub-culture and environmental setting. An action that may suffice in a highly norm-bound goldfish bowl may pass quite unnoticed in a metropolitan setting. However, hitting at aspects of the parents' own identity is widespread and may make for a hurtful experience for the parents. If the father is a policeman, for example, the rebellious son wields a specially potent weapon when he flirts with delinquent peer groups, because of the vulnerability of his father in the community. Young girls whose consciousness may have been aroused by the ideals of the women's movement may attack their fathers for male chauvinism (and their mothers for spineless acquiescence). The daughter of a clergyman who becomes pregnant or contracts venereal disease would be another case in point. Children of eminently reasonable and permissive, trusting parents have often to press the limits particularly vigorously to get a rise out of their parents. By then it may be too late to intervene effectively as many a shocked parent from a busy professional family has learned to his distress when the child has been picked up by the police, or is in a ward for drug addicts.

The GAP Committe (1973, pp. 51–2) describe the process whereby rejection of parents, and parents' values, may serve to let the adolescent grow:

Often his rebellion is against what he thought was taught him, not what he actually was taught. Sometimes he rebels because what he has been taught is different from what is practised. In general, he is basically rejecting not a mature religious belief, but his own childhood conceptions. Many years may pass before he realizes that his rebellion was not so much against parents, church, or culture as against his own immaturity. However, few things are so upsetting to parents as an adolescent, struggling with emancipation, who attacks their treasured value system. It may shake the parents' security and cause the child to be experienced as obnoxious.

They (GAP, 1973, pp. 52–3) explain in detail the process of parental rejection and personal development as it may work via the channel of *religion* in families where that channel is meaningful:

Particularly difficult for parents to weather with a sense of perspective is the adolescent stage of atheism. . . . Usually this involves the young person's relationship to his father and to the being he calls God. In the small child the religious experience is closely bound up with his experiences with his parents. God is thought of in essentially the same way as the father. . . . If development proceeds normally, the young person learns to separate the two; parents are seen as less divine and more human, and God becomes less identified with the father. This separation is one of the tasks of adolescence; in the process the adolescent may reject God or father or both. This is a normal phase and usually transient. Even when it is of relatively short duration it is trying and perplexing to the parents. As the child works through his rebellion and gains a firmer idea of his own identity, he arrives at a new relationship with both God and father.

In contemporary secular society, the reaction of the adolescent may be against parental agnosticism and in favour of a fundamentalist religion, perhaps one remote from anything the parent might have espoused.

Derek Miller (1974, p. 98) observes that late adolescents in particular often reject parental beliefs and attitudes if they feel these have been imposed for hypocritical reasons.

Clinical, anecdotal and qualitative accounts of confrontations be-tween adolescents and their parents provide a great deal of material documenting the difficulties of this period. The turbulence, conflict, discord and unhappiness that can come if confrontations are not well handled are legion. Adolescents accuse their parents of being authoritari-an, antiquated, chauvinistic, hypocritical or stupid, and the result may be unhappy for both—however 'functional' a breakaway element in the relationship may be at this point. Some degree of tension is important for both young person and parent to 'distance' themselves from their earlier modes of relationship—appropriate between parents and younger chil-dren. But if this exceeds the optimal point, the consequences may embitter the lives of each party, as well as the relationship.

One psychiatrist, writing about a positive outcome to a confrontation over one of the most difficult issues in contemporary American adoles-cent-parent relationships—drug use—describes her own experience, both professional and as a mother. In the introduction she writes as a parent to other parents:

Parents like you and me are frequently bewildered by the changing world. Our children are facing different problems than we did, in a world with a seeming breakdown of morals and values, without the familiar guideposts that helped us through our own adolescent years (Densen-Gerber and Bader, 1972, p. 12).

Her daughter, Trissa Austin Bader, writes in response to the mother's question about what parents should know about drugs:

Two different things. Young people my age need to know one thing, parents another. Parents need to know how to keep their children from taking drugs. First, they should pay attention to them as people instead of worrying about little things—for example, whether their little girl is in a white dress which might become spotted . . . [and] you'd have to give the facts of what drugs can do; such as, they will kill you eventually. Perhaps not kill you, but maybe cause you to jump off a bridge and be crippled for the rest of your life. . . . It's not enough to just hear parents say, 'Oh, no, they're terrible, don't get mixed up with them, and that's that.' Children want to know why (Densen-Gerber and Bader, 1972, pp. 20–1).

The mother adds, from her experience, that provision of information is not enough. Limits have to be set, and policies developed.

In general, research from a number of fields has re-enforced the idea that a satisfactory outcome to parent-adolescent confrontations is likely to emerge only through a satisfactory blending of the twin elements of *love* and *discipline* (Glueck and Glueck, 1950; West, 1967; Andry, 1962). But this is partly a matter of feeling and expression, partly a matter of technique: *how* to communicate?

There is often a feeling on both sides of the parent-child relationship at this phase of an impasse in *communications*. Key questions from the parents' viewpoint may include: How much to probe into the children's private lives? How much to discuss one's own personal problems with them? How to make one's own viewpoints understood without simply becoming dogmatic, which may lead to a foreclosure of communications? From the adolescent's viewpoint, the pressing question may be: How much to tell parents about what actually goes on (especially when it may be near or over the limits set)?

Another issue centres on the question of *participation*. Parental concerns may include: How much to allow children's participation in family decision-making? How much to expect their participation in the family chores? What to do together; what separately? The adolescents' questions may be: How much to participate? Do I have to? Will it be boring? What will I get out of it? What would I otherwise be doing? Will I miss anything? Will I be letting anyone down if I don't participate?

Another set of questions recur for parents around the issue of organizing the activities of, or *programming* their adolescents. How much to structure the child's activities? How much guidance to offer without being asked? When? How? From their children's perspective, the questions are: How to define and respond to parental organizing efforts: Is it controlling? fussing? protecting? caring? Is it belittling or insulting if a parent intervenes or is helpful? Does acceptance imply incompetence?

Parents of adolescents are often concerned about appropriate *distancing*. When to keep 'hands off'? How to stay clear without implying you do not care? Adolescents are often concerned to press for distance. How and when to opt out of family things? How to distinguish between 'their' (parental) concerns and 'my' concerns without too much guilt or anger? Once having opted for distance, is it a sign of weakness to want to come back into the fold? This is an era in which both parents' and adolescents' felt needs oscillate, and divergence and disappointment is likely. At the same time, the need to recuperate from strains or disappointments, to rehearse for new sallies into the world outside and to regroup one's resources is acknowledged to be an important element in the family enabling process (Rapoport et al., 1975).

Throughout the experience of parenting with adolescents, the two sets of lifelines intersect and reverberate most often in relation to *values*. We noted above the dynamics that often occur through the channel of religious values. Another major channel in which parents' values are tested in caring for adolescents is *sexuality*. This is an area in which parents often feel especially confused about their responsibilities in relation to their children. Whilst the wider society to which the adolescent is becoming orientated may focus attention on genital sexuality, parents may feel more comfortable to play this down. It is not only because contemporary parents were reared in an earlier era of more repressive sexual morality, or even because they feel their own sexuality to be on the wane and are therefore made envious and uncomfortable in the face of their children's. It is partly because contemporary youngsters link sexuality to the development of the person and of the capacity for interpersonal relationships in a way that is new and difficult for many parents to accept. It is at this phase of parenting that the most difficult dilemmas may arise in parenting, to reconcile general abstract values with specific values as parents in particular situations.

The GAP Committee's perspective on the role of the parent in relation to general life values, which we see as the core of the experience of parenting with adolescents, is well-rounded and compatible with our orientation. We quote their view at length (GAP, 1973, p. 63).

In the area of values, it is necessary for the parents to establish a working set of values for themselves—not 'super-modern' or 'loose-minded' but open-minded. Parents need not accept valuelessness as a way of life. They have a right and duty to advocate particular values and expectations; they have the right to attempt to pass these values on to their children. However, they must respect the child's right to go through a phase of living in which he contradicts parental or societal values or establishes different values. This is not a negative reflection upon parents. It is in the nature of the child-parent relationship and at times may reflect positively upon the parents' rearing of the child.

Communication, which is a positive value, can go a long way, but there may come a point when communication has to come to an end and action take place.

The problem of the relationship between actions and values often becomes acute, both for parents and their adolescent children at this stage. Parents may recognize that their earlier failures to act may be interpreted by their children to mean that they have not cared; and a new form of struggle may occur to reassert parental influence against forces in their children's lives which have gained in strength. The children are likely to have involved themselves in groups and activities which bolster specific values, which may or may not be compatible with their parents.

Condry and Siman (1974) in a study of forty-one adolescent peer groups in New York, distinguish three different types of activities, each reflecting a set of values; *socially constructive activities* (e.g. doing useful work for the community); *neutral activities* (e.g. listening to records); and *anti-social activities* (e.g. doing something illegal). They also obtained information on the young people's perception of their parental values in relation to these activities, and found that the gap increased in the order of divergence from socially valued activities. The researchers concluded, in the face of the fact that so many young people were participating in these sub-groups that the power of the peer-group influences were greater at this stage than the parents.

Bronfenbrenner, noting that the increase in delinquent activity in the past decade has been very steep among people in this age group, searches for factors in the social environment which alienate young people from socially valued activities, usually mediated by their parents. Citing the White House Conference on Children (1970), and particularly the report of the committee under his chairmanship, Bronfenbrenner

(1974, pp. 161–2) makes the following summary of elements in the contemporary situation which counteract any parental effort to be influential with their children:

In today's world parents find themselves at the mercy of a society which imposes pressures and priorities that allow neither time nor place for meaningful activities and relations between children and adults, which downgrade the role of parents and the functions of parenthood, and which prevent the parent from doing things he wants to do as a guide, friend and companion to his children. . . .

In our modern way of life, children are deprived not only of parents but of people in general. A host of factors conspires to isolate children from the rest of society. The fragmentation of the extended family, the separation of residential and business areas, the disappearance of neighbourhood, zoning ordinances, occupational mobility, child labor laws, the abolishment of the apprentice system, consolidated schools, television, separate patterns of social life for different age groups, the working mother, the delegation of child care to specialists—all these manifestations of progress operate to decrease opportunity and incentive for meaningful contact between children and persons older, or younger, than themselves. . . .

We are experiencing a breakdown in the process of making human beings human. By isolating our children from the rest of society, we abandon them to a world devoid of adults and ruled by the destructive impulses and compelling pressures both of the age-segregated peer group and the aggressive and exploitive television screen, we leave our children bereft of standards and support and our own lives impoverished and corrupted.

This reversal of priorities, which amounts to a betrayal of our children, underlies the growing disillusionment and alienation among young people in all segments of American society. Those who grew up in settings where children and families still counted are able to react to their frustration in positive ways— through constructive protest, participation, and public service. Those who come from circumstances in which the family could not function, be it in slum or suburb, can only strike out against an environment they have experienced as indifferent, callous, cruel, and unresponsive. This report does not condone the destruction and violence manifested by young people in widely disparate sections of our society; it merely points to the roots of a process which, if not reversed . . . can have only one result: the far more rapid and pervasive growth of alienation, apathy, drugs, delinquency, and violence among the young, and not so young, in all segments of our national life. We face the prospect of a society which resents its own children and fears its youth. . . . What is needed is a change in our patterns of living which will once again bring people back into the lives of children and children back into the lives of people.

While many of these 'roots of alienation' apply to the whole range of parenting phases, they have a particular relevance to parenting with adolescent children, as the problems come to a head at this point and parents feel particularly powerless. Many express the feeling that they have 'given up' on their children by this time, and may rely on the social services or the police to control their adolescents who are beyond their capacity. The literature increasingly indicates parental concern about the management of adolescent reactions of various kinds—from withdrawal to overt rebelliousness. This is a point at which professional supports are needed but are likely to have to take a variety of unorthodox forms to reach young people who have got into trouble (Tyler, 1976). There is relatively little information about how parents handle their problems at this stage. There are suggestions that siblings may play an important part as intermediaries (Rapoport, 1975), and there are indications that often the parents themselves experience a crisis at this point.

Changing Models: Today's Parents, Today's Adolescents, Tomorrow's Parents

The differing value systems of parents and their adolescent children pervades parent-child relations in this phase. A UNESCO-sponsored study of reciprocal images between parents and children in the family (Mahler, 1973) found that education drives a wedge between parents and their children (particularly in the 'developing' countries where parents are much more tradition-minded). But in all fast-changing societies, including 'developed' ones, the experiences of respective generations vary, and give rise to differences in prevailing values. Thus, for example, the present cohort of adolescent girls are likely to have many experiences that were unavailable to their mothers, as their mothers' experiences differed from their grandmothers'. These include the growth of the feminist movement, the public discussion of contraception and abortion, and public challenges to sexism in schools and in the workplace. These events provide social forces that affect the young (particularly girls) differently from their parents.

Models of acceptable social roles are altering quite rapidly and, on the whole, adolescents have many more family life options open to them than did their parents. Whereas conventional parents are more likely to be concerned with the family background and occupational prospects of the man their daughter wishes to marry, the young girl whose consciousness has been raised is more likely to be concerned with whether he is a relatively egalitarian-minded companion and shares personal interests. There are many young people at least as conventional-minded as their parents, and the adoption of modern attitudes and aspirations by the young does not necessarily put them into conflict with their parents. However, new styles of life, and new concerns for future family and work interaction, do mean that parents have to cope with changing models of right and wrong.

In families in which daughters aspire to an occupational career *and* marriage, the confrontations that parents find themselves involved in are more likely to have positive outcomes if they understand social trends and accept a value orientation which may allow for new patterns given appropriate supports. Many young couples wish to live together without getting married; others marry while both continue their education or while one supports the other. They may defer or even reject the idea of having children. This may be a source of considerable dismay to conventional parents who dream not only of church weddings but of grandchildren and a way of life in which they see their children 'settled' in a manner they understand.

Parents are faced with changing sex roles in society and so themselves go through changes in expectations of their sons and daughters. Until fairly recently, the way adolescent girls and boys channelled their identity concerns tended to be different and to result in different behaviour patterns. While many differences still exist—partly as a result of earlier and current socialization experiences and partly as a result of channels open to them—in many ways the *adolescent girls' and boys' patterns are becoming more similar.* For instance, there have been considerable changes in female sex mores in the past fifteen years or so; with increasing sex equality for males and females and the widespread use of effective contraceptives, 'the development of the female sex drive may become more and more similar to that of the male' (Chilman, 1968, p. 302). Divergence in interest patterns may also be decreasing. Strong (1931) described adolescent young men's (15–25) interests as characterized by multiple and shifting interests, enjoyment of risk-taking and active sports, gregariousness and restlessness. This research, undertaken over forty years ago, also reported that at age fifteen, the measured interests of boys and girls was further apart at that stage than at any other time during the life span; it also indicated the striking dissimilarity between the interests of fifteen-year-old boys and middle-aged women; such situations have implications for parent-adolescent relationships as well as general family dynamics within which they take place at mid-stage.

These interest patterns may well have altered with increasingly shared activities of male and female groups, and with the decreasing segregation of behaviour and options. Fewer and fewer females at adolescence, for instance, are likely to consider marriage and motherhood their exclusive option. Various patterns of combination are likely to be found, and there is likely to be an increase in non-marriage as a primary choice (rather than through force of circumstances, as in the cohort of women immediately after the Second World War). Jessie Bernard (1975a, p. 70) quotes the following excerpt from *Monthly Vital Statistics Report* in the USA (23 October 1974, p. 1):

During the 12 months ending with August 1974, 2,233,000 marriages were reported. This was 68,000 fewer than the number for the 12 months ending with August 1973, a 3.0 percent decline. The marriage rate for that period was 10.6 per thousand population, a decline of 3.6 percent. Cumulative data for the first 8 months of 1974 show a 2.9 percent decline in the number of marriages and a 3.6 percent decline in the marriage rate from the comparable figures for 1973.

Glick and Norton (1973) also suggest that demographic trends show a lessening of enthusiasm for marriage among women. More young women are seeking fulfilment in channels other than child-bearing and -rearing. In this way, the disjunction between early patterns of parent-child relations (in which the child's needs are paramount) and the expectations that when a girl child becomes an adult she will suddenly give this up and concentrate on her husband's and children's needs, are decreasing.

Jessie Bernard describes the current intergenerational issues (Bernard, 1975a, pp. 70ff). Previously the literature concentrated on the problems stimulated by adolescent boys. During the lifetime of the present generation of adolescents, new life styles have been adopted by mothers as well as the children. If the mothers are between 35–54, over half were in the labour force in 1972 in the USA. They may be more feminist in value orientation than their daughters. They may have cried as well as laughed when their young daughters had said they wanted babies of their own to play with. They are the first young women to be exposed to the feminist movement, to the rebellion against motherhood as it has been recently known, and to the idealization of parenthood more generally; they are attuned to a concept of motherhood which no longer takes up the whole of a woman's lifespace. Bernard (1975a, p. 72) has described how the mother's own socialization for motherhood was counter-productive in their view—and how the modern mother may seek to counteract this culturally pervasive force in which 'the young woman in marriage moved from one dependency to another, that of the parental family to that of her husband.'

This dependency model is felt increasingly to be inadequate for socializing young women for the world they inhabit today, whether as mothers (which also requires strength, cf. Newton, 1955) or as workers.

Another element in the contemporary situation centres on contraception. As a consequence of modern contraception a girl can defend herself against irresponsible motherhood without remaining a virgin. In addition, as Bernard points out, the girl may engage her young men in the responsibility for parenthood more actively. Exactly how this will work out is still unclear. But socialization for a new kind of adolescent—young man and young woman—in a new kind of world for a new kind of parenthood 'calls for a thoughtful new look'.

It also seems likely that the quality and content of parent-adolescent relationships will alter with these changes. It may be that after a transitional period it will be easier to incorporate a fully sexual being, who is also one's child, in the family. Some contemporary problems may thus decrease while others increase (Rapoport and Oakley, 1975).

The point about all this, for the parent-child relations at this phase of the family cycle, is that changes in the socialization of the adolescent generation and changes in the expectations of mothers and fathers in parenting are likely to affect the quality of all these relationships. What is striking about the literature is the lack of research on the parent-child relationship during this period. As Chilman points out, the bulk of research has been on the younger years and even it has great deficiencies, particularly on father-child relations.

Furthermore, Hoffman (1974) points out that the research on the effects of mothers working is mainly concerned with children under three. The little that does exist about adolescents and their parents, is rather superficial and does little to inform us about the quality of the experience of parents in relation to their adolescent children.

On changes in socialization that are being observed, we need to know more about relevant adult intentions and experiences. Through an analysis of these processes, we may begin to consider strategies which might facilitate specific experiences (Brim and Wheeler, 1966).

To end this chapter we reiterate the requirement for research on parent-adolescent relations and summarize some speculations about parent-child relations—that have been made for this period. The most useful publications available on this topic at present are those by Chilman (1968), the GAP report on the *Joys and Sorrows of Parenthood* (1973) and Jessie Bernard's papers in *Women, Wives, Mothers: Values and Options* (1975b).

In general, these deal more focally with mother-daughter relations than the other possibilities. The mother-daughter relationship is affected by the biological changes that take place in both generations about the same time. As the mother's reproductive capacity wanes, her daughter's reaches a peak; both mother and daughter are likely to be subject to mood swings and other psychosomatic phenomena related to hormonal and other changes at this phase of life. The situation has built-in conflicts and potential comforts. The ties between mother and daughter (which may or may not be stronger than those, say, between father and daughter) lead to difficulties and have potential strengths. The stronger the bond, the more difficult for the adolescent child to break away; on the other hand, perhaps there is potential in such a situation for a more satisfactory return at a different level after the break-away. To maintain a positive relationship at this stage seems to involve tight-rope walking: as Chilman puts it, both mother and daughter want to be understood by each other—but not too much. To really understand what goes on, new research must concentrate on experimental processes.

The turbulent processes that occur between mothers and daughters probably have an analogy in father-son relationships. Chilman (1968, pp. 306–7) feels that this

may be less intensely relational and sex-specific because the father-son identifica- tion is not likely to be so strong and personal in these days when fathers are out of the home so much of the time. Then, too, changes in the reproductive cycle are not so dramatic for males nor is a man's sense of sexual adequacy so closely tied to physical appearance, as it is in the case of a woman's. On the other hand, adequate virility is generally a source of extreme concern for father and son alike, and it is apt to be spread over a broader range of roles. Thus, both father and son, at mid-stage of family development, are likely to be caught up in similar anxieties over many areas, such as: physical strength and agility, economic adequacy and, of course, desirability and prowess with women, both within and outside the family circle.

The son, in his ascendancy to all these spheres of manhood, has not yet reached the plateau of the 'years of culmination' and the father has many intimations that he has begun a gradual descent to increasingly waning powers. Thus, father and son, like mother and daughter, are apt to find themselves coming full circle, simultaneously, to a similar, but different point in human development.

Mother-son and father-daughter relations are even less discussed in the literature, though we do know that close ties with mothers are found amongst sons as well as daughters (Hagestad and Fagan, 1974; Rapoport and Rapoport, 1971). We know from our own field studies, both among dual-career families and in families of adolescents, that mothers who feel they have no way of influencing their husbands—for example, to take a more active part in domestic life—feel they can, at least, influence their sons. We still have to rethink what the important dimensions are for looking at parent-child relationships at adolescence. With change in sex roles, in which men may spend more time at home and women more time out of the home, theories about identification processes between children and their same-sex parents may require revision. New patterns should contribute to improved theories.

Another aspect of changes in sex roles, is that far more of the socialization of children may be shared with people not in the immediate family. This too will alter not only identification processes of the young, but the needs of their parents at this phase, and the potentials available, if these new relationships are seen as alliances, for avoidance of some of the characteristic strains on the marital relationship. It may become less necessary than in the past to await the children's leaving home to create or discover the potential for an 'upswing' in marital satisfaction (Troll, 1975, pp. 88–9).

References

Andry, R. (1960), *Delinquency and Parental Pathology*, London, Methuen.

Andry, R. (1962), 'Paternal and maternal roles and delinquency', *Deprivation of Maternal Care*, Geneva, WHO Public Health Papers, no. 14.

Bernard, J. (1975a), *The Future of Motherhood*, Baltimore, Penguin.

Bernard, J. (1975b), *Women, Wives, Mothers: Values and Options*, Chicago, Aldine.

Brim, O. and Wheeler, S. (1966), *Socialization after Childhood: Two Essays*, New York, John Wiley.

Bronfenbrenner, U. (1974), 'Children, families and social policy: an American perspective', *The Family in Society, Dimensions of Parenthood,* 89–104, London, DHSS, HMSO.

Byng-Hall, J. and Miller, M. J. (1975), 'Adolescence and the family', in Meyerson, S. (ed.), *Adolescence,* London, Allen & Unwin.

Chilman, C. S. (1968), 'Families in development at mid-stage of the family life cycle', *Family Coordinator,* 17, 4, 306.

Condry, J. D. and Siman, M. A. (1974), 'Characteristics of poor- and adult-oriented children', *Journal of Marriage and the Family,* 36, 543–54.

Densen-Gerber, J. and Bader, T. (1972), *Drugs, Sex, Parents and You,* Philadelphia, Lippincott.

Fogelman, K. (1976), *Britain's Sixteen-year-olds,* London, National Children's Bureau.

Glick, P. C. and Norton, A. J. (1973), 'Perspectives on the recent upturn in divorce and remarriage', *Demography,* 10, 301–14.

Glueck, S. and Glueck, E. (1950), *Unravelling Juvenile Delinquency,* New York, Commonwealth.

Group for the Advancement of Psychiatry (1973), *Joys and Sorrows of Parenthood,* New York, Scribner.

Hagestad, G. O. and Fagan, M. A. (1974), 'Patterns of fathering in the middle years', paper presented at the Annual Meeting of the National Council on Family Relations, St. Louis, Missouri.

Hoffman, L. (1974), 'The effects of maternal employment on the child—a review of the research', *Developmental Psychology,* 10, 2, 204–28.

Jackson, B. and Marsden, D. (1962), *Education and the Working Class,* London, Routledge & Kegan Paul.

Lidz, T. (1968), *The Person,* New York, Basic Books.

McCord, J., McCord, W. and Thurber, E. (1962), 'Some effects of paternal absence on male children', *Journal of Abnormal and Social Psychology,* 64, 361–9.

Mahler, F. (1973), *L'Image réciproque des parents et enfants dans la famille,* Centre de recherches sur les problémes de la jeunesse, Bucarest.

Miller, D. (1974), *Adolescence,* New York, Jason Aronson.

Newton, N. (1955), *Maternal Emotions,* New York, Paul B. Hoeber.

Rapoport, R. and Oakley, A. (1975), 'Towards a review of parent-child relationships in social science', paper given at Ford Foundation Conference on *Sex Rules in Sociology,* Merrill-Palmer Institute, 10–12 November, convened by C. Safilios-Rothschild.

Rapoport, R. and Rapoport, R. N. (1976), *Dual Career Families Re-examined,* London, Martin Robertson; New York, Harper & Row (an earlier edition published by Penguin Books, 1971).

Rapoport, R. N. (1975), 'Home and school at the launch: some preliminary observations', *Oxford Review of Education,* 1, 3, 277–86.

Rapoport, R., Rapoport, R. N. with Strelitz, Z. (1975), *Leisure and the Family Life Cycle,* London, Routledge & Kegan Paul.

Seidenberg, R. (1973), *Marriage Between Equals,* New York, Anchor (Doubleday).

Shields, R. (1962), *A Cure of Delinquents,* London, Heinemann.

Smith, C. (1968), *Adolescence,* London, Longmans.

Spock, B. (1974), *Bringing Up Children in a Difficult Time,* London, Bodley Head.

Strong, E. K. (1931), *Changes of Interests with Age,* Stanford University Press.

Troll, L. E. (1975), *Early and Middle Adulthood* (part of the Life-Span Human Development Series), Monterey, Calif., Brooks/Cole.

Tyler, M. (1976), 'Advisory and counselling services for young people', unpublished report, London, DHSS.

West, D. (1967), *The Young Offender,* Harmondsworth, Penguin.

West, J. J. and Farrington, D. P. (1973), *Who Becomes Delinquent?* London, Heinemann.

Wilson, H. (1975), 'Juvenile delinquency, parental criminality and social handicap,' *British Journal of Criminology,* July, 241–50.

Runaway Adolescents' Perceptions of Parents and Self

Stephen Wolk and Janet Brandon

ABSTRACT

The purpose of the study was to investigate the relationship between runaway behavior in adolescence and an adolescent's self-concept and antecedent parental treatment. The Cornell Parent Behavior Questionnaire and the Adjective Check List were used to assess 47 runaways and a matched group of non-runaways. Analyses of the data indicated: (a) runaway adolescents report more punishment and less support from their parents; (b) runaway girls report the most and runaway boys the least degrees of parental control; (c) runaways hold a less favorable self-concept, specifically on the dimensions of anxiety, self-doubt, poor interpersonal relationships, and defensiveness; (d) runaways also manifest, as an aspect of the self, a readiness for counseling.

■ The purpose of the present paper was a verification of predicted familial interactions and self-perception correlates of the adolescent behavior of running away from home. The correlates selected for assessment are represented in the body of theory and research concerning child and adolescent development which has indicated the importance of parental treatment and the self-concept of a child and adolescent to behavior.

Research considering parental antecedents of emotional, social, and intellectual development of children, converges in suggesting that varying degrees of parental warmth, acceptance, and support are salient dimensions of influence (22). As a specific example Peterson (19) in a study of adolescents, found that adolescent perception of parents as more or less controlling and interested predicted the presence or absence of delinquency, happiness, school achievement, and peer friendship. Other investigators (16; 9; 6; 18) would also support the generalization that the nature of parent-child interaction plays a strong role in the psychological development and social responses of children and adolescents, both for socially desirable development (school achievement) as well as conventional anti-social behavior (delinquency).

In an effort to extend the relationship of parental antecedent behavior to the less conventional adolescent response of running away the following prediction was offered: relative to non-runaway adolescents, runaways will perceive and report their parents as less *supportive,*

"Runaway Adolescents' Perceptions of Parents and Self" by Stephen Wolk and Janet Brandon from ADOLESCENCE, vol. 12, no. 46, Summer 1977. Reprinted by permission of Libra Publishers, Inc., and the authors.

more *controlling,* and more *punishing.* This prediction assumes that the act of running away stems from a type of parental-adolescent relationship that can be characterized as restrictive and punitive. Medinnus (15) and Peterson (19) have found that adolescents who exhibit problem behavior tend to have parents who are extremely rejecting, punitive, and neglectful.

An additional and related question concerns whether the sex of the child and parent interact to influence differentially the perceptions of runaways and non-runaways. Bronfenbrenner (5) and Devereux (8) have argued that boys require high level of support and authority from fathers for satisfactory development to proceed. On the other hand girls may often suffer, developmentally, from too much paternal control and restrictiveness. This research, as well as that by Peterson (19) seems to suggest that the role of the father is crucial in socialization but of differing importance to males and females. In the context of the present study possible different perceptions of fathers and mothers were considered as a function of the sex of the child and the decision to run away from home.

The dimension of the individual's perception of self as playing a role in adjustment and development has been taken as an axiom by many psychologists. Self-perceptions have been related to studies of achievement, delinquency and vocational choice (7; 6; 17). Very little systematic research has covered possible self-concept conditions of runaway adolescents. Yet the self-concept and aspects of the self, such as ego control, anxiety, and self-esteem, have been identified in the causality or consequence of maladjustment. Thus, Scarpetti (20) found that adequacy of the self-concept clearly differentiated delinquents from non-delinquents. Levinson (13) in one of the few empirical studies of male runaways, found a lack of self-acceptance to be characteristic of this group, who reported themselves as dull, weak and sad. From this research it is tentatively hypothesized that runaway adolescents, relative to non-runaways, would manifest a more negative self-concept.

It is this latter prediction which hopefully reflects the importance of a systematic study of a fairly undefined clinical phenomenon, i. e., running away. While the phenomenon of running away from home apparently is increasing among adolescents, relatively little in the way of objective systematic information exists, suggesting causes, or at the minimum, correlated conditions. It is not uncommon to encounter popular discussions of the phenomenon in which the runaway adolescent is considered to be responding for mature and adaptive reasons, or out of desperation and in response to inadequate ego strength and/or punitive familial interaction. These alternative conceptualizations grow out of the vested interests of specific societal agencies and therapeutic approaches employed to rehabilitate the runaways. It would seem important that objective and unbiased data be brought to bear upon an intriguing and equally confusing behavioral response common to adolescence.

Method

Sample

Runaways.   Adolescent runaway male and female subjects were solicited for participation from runaway houses in the suburban Maryland Area. Six locations were identified and a total of 47 subjects from these locations (female = 26, male = 21) participated in the study. These runaway houses represented a non-directed, family oriented type assistance extended to runaways who voluntarily had placed themselves in the houses. The age distribution of the group was: 13 years (4), 14 years (10), 15 years (12), 16 years (16), 17 years (5). Only those subjects who had both parents present in the home during their childhood constituted the final data producing sample. The entire sample was Caucasian.

Non-runaways.   A control group of 47 non-runaway adolescents (female = 26, male = 21) were paired with the runaway subjects as a function of sex, age (maximum of 6-month age difference) and race. Additionally, the non-runaways were selected from the same neighborhoods from which the runaways had originated, neighborhoods fairly homogeneous with regard to socioeconomic status, and considered to be in the lower two-thirds of the middle class.

Procedure

Contact with runaway subjects was made by the counselors at the runaway houses, who arranged for participation of volunteers. Subjects responded anonymously to the questionnaires.

Non-runaway adolescents participating in after school activities were contacted for voluntary participation. These activities were not related to academic or sports achievement, but rather represented more informal club-type meetings.

Instrumentation

Cornell Parent Behavior Description (CPBD).   The CPBD was chosen to depict a subject's perception of parental treatment. The instrument consists of 30 items which are responded to for each parent. The CPBD yields six subscale scores for each parent. Those scores of relevance to the hypotheses of the study were:

Support (parent available for counseling, support, and assistance); *Punishment* (use of physical and non-physical punishment); *Control* (demanding, protecting, and intrusive).   The validity of the scale has been established in the research literature (1; 8), including correlations with direct observation of parent-child interaction. Additionally, cross cultural studies of parental behaviors have made ample use of the CPBD (10). Seigelman (21) and MacDonald (14) report reliability coefficients for the total scale that range from .70 to .81 and for individual subscales that range from .48 to .82. Additionally, reliability estimates were calculated for both groups in the present study (alpha coefficient) for each subscale by parent. These coefficients ranged from a high of .90 (Father-Support) to a low of .56 (Mother-Control).

Adjective Check List (ACL).   The ACL afforded an assessment of adolescents' perceptions of self. The instrument consists of 300 adjectives commonly used to describe personal attributes. Thirteen of the total 24 indices of self-concept were selected for study and are related to the hypotheses. These are (attributes in parentheses): *total number of adjectives checked* (relative presence of repressive tendencies); *defensiveness* (tendency to be anxious, apprehensive, and critical of self); *number of favorable adjectives checked* (anxiety, self-doubt); *self-confidence; personal adjustment; achievement* (dubious about the rewards coming from effort); *affiliation; exhibition* (lack of self-confidence); *number of unfavorable adjectives checked* (lack of control over hostile aspects of self); *lability* (impelled toward an endless flight from perplexities); *abasement* (self-punishing to ward off external criticism); *counseling readiness* (pessimism concerning ability to resolve problems). The subject was instructed to check the items which best describe him as he really is. The score for each index is determined by subtracting the number of contra-indicative (negative) from indicative (positive) items. Raw scores are converted to standard scores ($\bar{X} = 50.0$; $SD = 10.0$). Previous use of the ACL both for basic research and counseling has been extensive (3). Gough and Heilbrun (12) report reliability coefficients of from .61 to .75 between judges using the ACL to describe a group of subjects; the same authors report coefficients of correlation between each index and the total number of adjectives checked that argue for the discriminant validity of each index.

Statistical Treatment of Data

A three-way analysis of variance (Runaway/Non-runaway X Sex of Subject X Sex of Parent) with repeated measurements on the last factor assessed the effects upon adolescent perception of parents. The dependent variables were represented by total raw scores for Support, Punishment, and Control of the CPBD.

A one-way multivariate analysis of variance (Runaway/Non-runaway) was employed to assess overall differences between the two groups in regard to their self-perceptions. The dependent variables were represented by standard scores for the selected 13 indices of the ACL. As a follow-up procedure univariate F-tests were conducted on each of the thirteen scores, for which the alpha level was set at $p < .004$. This allowed rejection of the null hypothesis of no self-concept differences between groups to be made at $p < .05$, since this follow-up procedure involved 13 individual comparisons.

Results

It was predicted that runaway adolescents compared to non-runaways, would report their parents to be more punishing and controlling, and less supporting. For the variables of support ($F(1,90) = 26.69$, $p < .01$) and punishment ($F(1,90) = 19.00$, $p < .01$) such main effect differences were obtained and are reflected in the pattern of mean scores reported in Table 1. No difference existed between groups for the variable of control. The only interaction effect observed involved the sex of the child and the decision to run away. Runaway girls, relative to runaway boys, reported more control on the part of both parents; the difference between

Table 1   Mean Scores for the Variables of Support, Punishment, and Control by Classification of Subject and Parent

| | Runaway | | | Non-runaway | |
	Girls	Boys		Girls	Boys
Support					
Mother	22.31	21.95		28.03	29.38
Father	19.69	17.71		26.50	28.33
$\bar{X}t$		20.48		27.99	
Punishment					
Mother	23.81	17.71		18.23	18.31
Father	24.15	21.29		16.81	15.48
$\bar{X}t$		21.98		17.32	
Control					
Mother	28.42	23.38		27.54	27.05
Father	27.92	22.90		26.62	26.52
$\bar{X}t$		25.93		26.95	

non-runaway boys and girls was slight and non-significant (see Table 1). Additionally runaway boys perceived less control of both parents than any of the other groups of subjects. Two unpredicted main effects were also observed. For the variable of support, all subjects reported less support from father than mother (F (1,90) = 6.65, p < .05); in regard to punishment, girls reported more punishment by both parents than boys (F (1,90) = 9.44, p < .01).

A multivariate analysis of variance (least likelihood ratio) was conducted on the 13 measures of self-perception. This test resulted in an F value of 2.58 (p < .005), indicating that runaways held a distinctly different self-perception from non-runaways. In order to define this difference more fully, univariate F tests examined the variations between groups for each index of self-concept singly. The results of these tests, in addition to mean scores for each group are presented in Table 2.

Five of the 13 indices of self-concept significantly (p < .05) distinguished runaways from non-runaways: defensiveness, total favorable adjectives checked, personal adjustment, affiliation, and counseling readiness. Therefore, runaway adolescents, compared to non-runaways, manifest a self-concept that is more defensive, self-doubting and less trusting. It is a self-concept that also reflects a difficulty in maintaining interpersonal relationships and a preoccupation with and a pessimism for resolving personal problems.

Table 2 Summary of the Analyses of Variance of the Dependent Variables of Self-Perception and Mean Scores by Group

Variable	Runaway	Non-runaway	F
Total Checked[b]	50.34	47.36	1.09
Defensiveness[b]	41.13	47.34	8.94[a]
Favorable Checked[b]	40.81	48.87	13.54[a]
Unfavorable Checked[c]	56.72	52.70	1.41
Self-Confidence[b]	45.85	49.19	4.32
Self-Control[b]	39.89	42.85	2.56
Lability[c]	50.81	51.34	.08
Personal Adjustment[b]	39.53	46.70	11.48[a]
Achievement[b]	43.92	48.34	5.22
Affiliation[b]	42.49	48.71	9.07[a]
Exhibition[b]	54.60	56.75	1.86
Abasement[c]	49.64	48.26	.79
Counseling Readiness[c]	51.21	45.53	10.11[a]

[a] Represents a difference between means at p < .05 for 13 tests.
[b] Low score indicates negative self-concept.
[c] High score indicates negative self-concept.

Discussion

It appears that the runaway adolescents in the present sample report less favorable perceptions of parents on two of the three predicted variables: support and punishment. This finding is consistent with other research which has found that runaways experience frequent punishment and describe their parents as rejecting (2). Such perceived negative parental treatment might well influence the decision to run away as a reaction to family stress. Blood and D'Angelo (2) report that runaways identified more items as conflicts with parents and suggested that deficiencies in positive reinforcement accounted for this. The runaways did not differ from the non-runaways in regard to perceived parental control. Had the runaways perceived more parental control than non-runaways, it might have been reasonable to surmise that the runaway act is a reaction to over control by the parent, as some popular accounts do argue. Rather, some runaways have frequently stated that running away represents an effort to make the parents notice them, as several counselors have noted to the authors. Perhaps the finding of more reported punishment and less support, in conjunction with the absence of control differences, suggests the parent of the runaway, relative to the non-runaway, may be responding more punitively and arbitrarily.

For the variable of control, runaway girls did perceive significantly more parental control than any other group. Runaway boys, on the other hand, perceived less parental control than any other group. Thus, the predicted difference between runaways and non-runaways in regard to parental control was to some extent further contingent upon the sex of the child. It may be that for girls the presence of added punishment, reported by all runaways, in conjunction with excessive parental control, differentially directed toward females, makes the decision to run away a reaction to a punitive, restrictive family atmosphere.

A somewhat different explanation may be offered to explain why runaway boys report the lowest levels of parental control. Bronfenbrenner (4) found that relatively high amounts of discipline and authority were necessary to cultivate traits of responsibility and leadership in boys. To the extent that runaway behavior can be considered immature it may not be surprising that the runaway boys in the present study reported less control than the non-runaway boys. For boys, when a necessary degree of control and parental restriction is absent, behavior may proceed to develop immaturely and non-adaptively, resulting in a high incidence of running away. For girls, to whom control may be generally more often directed by parents, an excess of such parental action may lead to conflict and a sense of hopelessness.

The literature on adolescent development frequently has focused on the adolescent's struggle to achieve psychological autonomy from parental values and controls. Douvan and Adelson (11) have employed this concept in extensive research with adolescents. Furthermore, these authors and others have distinguished two dimensions to adolescent autonomy: associational autonomy (friendship, activities) and normative autonomy (ethics, attitudes). It has been established in this research that adolescents strive for and achieve more autonomy in the associational than the normative area, suggesting that both parents and peer groups exert influence in different areas of adolescent development. In considering the findings of the present study it could be argued that the report of more punishment and less support by runaways on the part of their parents suggests some deviation and conflict from the norm of adolescent-familial interaction. Parental punishment, for the runaway, may be impinging upon the adolescent's quest and success for associational autonomy; parents may be negatively reinforcing behavior related to the development of this type of autonomy. Similarly, the report of less parental support by adolescent runaways could imply that these parents do not supply the kind of guidance in the normative area that adolescents apparently do seek. The runaway act may then be interpreted as an extreme form of response to what is perceived by the adolescent as a lack of validation of the struggle for autonomy, when compared to the more typical adolescent experience. However, the findings concerning parental control might also suggest a further dimension to running away, concerning a motivation for the act, for males and females. To the adolescent girl, running away represents a desperate reaction to familial restrictiveness; to the adolescent boy, running away may be indicative of relative normlessness represented in the failure of parents to exert enough control over the more aggressive actions of males.

One of the strongest findings of the present study concerns the overall and specific differences in perceptions of self between runaways and non-runaways. It was the case that runaway adolescents held much less favorable perceptions.

The lower scores of the runaways on the defensiveness scale can be interpreted that they are anxious, critical of themselves and others and given to complaints about their circumstances. Such an individual not only has more problems than his peers, but tends to dwell on them and put them at the center of his attention. For the index of number of favorable adjectives checked, the lower scores of the runaways characterize them as experiencing anxiety, self-doubts, and perplexities, while often being headstrong, pleasure seeking, and original in thought and behavior. Personal adjustment defines a positive attitude toward life more than an absence of problems or worries. The relatively lower score of the runaway adolescent suggests he or she sees himself or herself at odds with other people and as dissatisfied. Others see the runaway as defensive, anxious, inhibited, worrying, and withdrawn. The difference between runaways and non-runaways on the scale of affiliation suggests that the former are less trusting of others and more restless and unsuccessful in interpersonal situations. The final scale which differentiated runaways from non-runaways was counseling readiness. Runaways scored significantly higher than non-runaways on this scale. The person who is "ready" for counseling must have a certain degree of motivation for change and improvement if counseling is to be effective. This scale functions as an aid in identifying counseling clients who are ready for help and who seem likely to profit from it. The runaway who goes to a runaway house may be more likely to profit from counseling techniques. The segment of runaway adolescents who seek out some type of counseling setting or interim residence, as in the present study, could be manifesting such a readiness for counseling.

In summary, the five indices of self-concept which significantly differentiated runaways from non-runaways are consistent with an interpretation of runaway behavior as stemming from negative self-development. Popular accounts describing or defining running away as behavior reflective of a well-adjusted adolescent fleeing intolerable, over-demanding social and familial environments, are not fully congruent with the present data. Although it was found that the present sample of adolescents reported less support and more punishment by parents, it was also found that runaway boys may be responding to the absence of sufficient control, while runaway girls are repelled by too much control.

Several areas of practical significance appear appropriate to explore toward the goal of improved and effective counseling for runaways. At least two dimensions of parent behavior in the lives of runaways who come to runaway houses for assistance appear substantiated. It would be useful for counselors to know on what dimensions to focus their attention when considering treatment for runaways. The possible role of a counselor as a parent surrogate would be enhanced should he/she be aware that it is quite likely the runaway is seeking support and encouragement. Additionally, recognition of the varying perceptions of parental control by male and female runaways would seem of value to the direction and techniques of counseling. The findings of the study also suggest that counseling for runaways should consider employing techniques which are effective in developing more positive perceptions of self. It might be worthwhile to consider that the finding concerning counseling readiness indicated that some runaways are motivated in such a way that they will benefit from the counseling experiences they encounter.

Of considerable importance to the results and interpretations of the present study, are apparent methodological limitations. The use of volunteers for both groups studied, and, in particular, the runaways, may restrict inferences and generalizations that can be drawn. It is conceivable that runaways who respond to personal inventories and questioning possess a personality and self-concept distinctly different from those who opt not to volunteer. While one can only speculate on such a notion, it would be methodologically positive if future research could survey a wider spectrum of runaways in halfway or runaway houses. It may also be accurate to acknowledge that a study of only those runaways who seek interim settings cannot generalize its findings to all groups of runaways. Perhaps these runaways represent a type more favorably disposed to a reestablishment of familial ties (as evidenced by a greater need or readiness for counseling). If this is so then the differences between runaways and non-runaways observed in the present study represent a conservative estimate of the self-concept and parental antecedent correlates of adolescents who choose to leave home. Finally the obvious limits of retrospective reports of family interactions need to be acknowledged. Perhaps it could be argued that the differing perceptions of parents, by runaways and non-runaways, represents the attempt of runaway adolescents to rationalize their behavior. Thus, what may be taken as antecedent conditions to the act of running away may, in fact, be a consequence of the need to justify an extreme act, i.e., establish some fault with parents. No correlational study, in the present case, can establish a cause-effect relationship. However, excluding a longitudinal approach that could develop data files early in childhood to which subsequent adolescent reactions, including acts of running away might be related, the adolescent phenomena of running away seems destined to be studied retrospectively. However, from a basic research point of view the understanding of the adolescent act of running away represents a small but important extension to a full definition of adolescent development. Adolescent running away is also a phenomenon that deserves continued delineation for counselors and mental health specialists who desire firm conceptual grounds upon which to develop a rehabilitative program.

References

1. **Barker, R. G., and L. S. Barker.** "Social Actions in the Behavior Streams of American and English Children," in *The Stream of Behavior* edited by R. G. Barker. New York: Appleton-Century-Crofts, 1963.
2. **Blood, L. and R. D'Angelo.** "A Progress Research Report on Value Issues in Conflict between Runaways and Their Parents," *Journal of Marriage and the Family* (August), 1974, 486–491.
3. **Buros, O. K.** (Ed.). *The Sixth Mental Measurements Yearbook.* Highland Park, N.J.: Gryphon Press, 1965.
4. **Bronfenbrenner, Urie.** "Some Familial Antecedents of Responsibility and Leadership in Adolescents," in L. Petrullo and B. M. Bass (Eds.), *Leadership and Interpersonal Behavior.* New York: Holt, Rinehart, and Winston, 1961a.
5. **Bronfenbrenner, Urie.** "Toward a Theoretical Model for Analysis of Parent-Child Relationships in a Social Context," in J. Glidewell (Ed.), *Parental Attitudes and Child Behavior.* Springfield: Charles C. Thomas, 1961b.
6. **Cervantes, L.** *The Drop Out: Causes and Cures.* Ann Arbor: University of Michigan Press, 1965.
7. **Coopersmith, S.** "A Method for Determining Types of Self-esteem," *Journal of Educational Psychology,* 1959, (59) 87–94.

8. **Devereux, E. C. and Urie Bronfenbrenner.** "Child-rearing in England and the United States," *Journal of Marriage and the Family,* 1969, (31) 257–270.

9. **Elder, Glen H.** "Parental Power Legitimation and Its Effect on the Adolescent," *Sociometry,* 1963, (26), 50–65.

10. **Devereux, E. C., Urie Bronfenbrenner, and G. S. Suci.** "Patterns of Parent Behavior in the United States of America and the Federal Republic of West Germany," *International Social Science Journal,* 1962, (14), 488–506.

11. **Douvan, Elizabeth and J. Adelson.** *The Adolescent Experience.* New York: John Wiley, 1966.

12. **Gough, H. G. and A. B. Heilbrun.** *The Adjective Check List Manual.* Palo Alto: Consulting Psychologist's Press, 1965.

13. **Levinson, B. M.** "Self-concept and Ideal Self-concept of Runaway Youths: Counseling Implications," *Psychological Reports,* 1970, 871–874.

14. **MacDonald, A. P.** "Internal-external Locus of Control and Parental Antecedents," *Journal of Consulting and Clinical Psychology,* 1971, (39), 141–147.

15. **Medinnus, Gene R.** "Delinquents' Perceptions of Their Parents," *Journal of Consulting Psychology,* 1965, (29), 592–593.

16. **Morrow, W. R. and R. C. Wilson.** "Family Relationships of Bright, High Achieving and Underachieving High School Boys," *Child Development,* 1961, (32), 501–510.

17. **Offer, Daniel.** *The Psychological World of the Teenager.* New York: Basic Books, 1969.

18. **Peck, R. and R. Havighurst.** *The Psychology of Character Development.* New York: John Wiley, 1960.

19. **Peterson, Evan T.** "The Adolescent Male and Parental Relations." Paper read at the National Council of Family Relations annual meeting, New Orleans, (October) 1968.

20. **Scarpetti, Frank R.** "Delinquency and Non-delinquency, Perception of Self, Values, and Opportunity," *Mental Hygiene,* 1965, (49), 399–404.

21. **Seigelman, M.** "Evaluation of Bronfenbrenner's Questionnaire for Children Concerning Parental Behavior," *Child Development,* 1965, (36), 163–174.

22. **Walters, J. and N. Stinnett.** "Parent-Child Relationships: A Decade Review of Research," *Journal of Marriage and the Family,* 1971, (2), 70–111.

The Kids Who Won't Leave Home
Audrey C. Foote

■   Along with all the other miseries of the modern woman's middle years there is a predicament which has been a favorite motif of syndicated psychologists in the last few years. They call it the Empty Nest Syndrome. Just in case there is anyone out there who hasn't heard about it, this quaintly labeled malady is the devastating depression of the mother whose children have all grown up and left home. But current sociology is now questioning this dilemma. Delia Ephron, in *Esquire,* writes that three national surveys have exposed the Empty Nest Syndrome as a pious fiction. And Patricia Williams, in the New York *Times,* asserts, "Women whose children have grown up and gone are found to be happier than women of the same age who are still mothering on a daily basis." "The Empty Nest syndrome," she says, "is for the birds."

While I read these findings with interest, I am suspicious of those neat categories "children who have grown up and left home" and "mothering on a daily basis." There is a universe of nuances between those two extremes. *Whose* empty nest? I thought with only a twinge of irony as I looked up from the *Times* to see two of my children playing Mastermind at the coffee table, another slouched by the stereo replacing Vivaldi with James Taylor, and the fourth bent over his math at the dining room table. A traditional heartwarming family vignette, except for the fact that apart from the youngest, age eleven, not one will ever again celebrate his or her twenty-first birthday. And yet for a considerable portion of this past year, as in the years before, they have all been, both *de jure* and *de facto,* resident at home.

Like parents of the past, my husband and I assumed when our children went off to college that it was an irrevocable break. It has turned out that entry into college was not the final flight from home but merely a four-year intermission.

Eight years ago, when our oldest left for Harvard, I produced an elaborate dinner at which I lachrymosely observed that this might well be the last time, at least as part of daily routine, that we six would dine together. We have had quite a number of such valedictory dinners since, but they have become mere pretexts for a party since we all now know that the youth leaving today may be back in a month and departing again the next, equally inconclusively. Had I foreseen this state of affairs, say ten years ago, I might well have assumed that it would brand me as a Philip Wylie-style Mom, and my children as emotional and social retards. Fortunately, in the intervening years I've had the benefit of the experience of friends with slightly older children. From observing them I've learned that to have grown children living at home is not necessarily a Freudian failing or an ethnic joke but rather a new "life-style" of the 1970s. As we stood with bulging grocery bags on the porch of Sewards Market in Menemsha this summer, a friend observed, "In the fifties the kids went to college and got married when they graduated or else took an apartment with a pal of the same sex; in the sixties they dropped out, made leather sandals, and lived in communes. But now, why, they aren't even *living together!*"

The first hint of this peculiar change in youthful mores came to me a few years ago when I had tea with a friend in the library of her five-story Washington town house. Sally had always been a kind of bellwether for me as she progressed through the maternal miseries and splendors of the 1960s. She had accepted her children's idealistic but often dangerous involvements with awesome equanimity. But that day she mentioned that her oldest son had come home for an apparently indefinite stay, and remarked, "I simply don't understand it. He has a lovely girl with a nice little apartment in Georgetown who I know would be delighted to share it with him." Not long afterward I learned that they had sold their handsome mansion and moved into a chic but minuscule apartment nearby. The big house kept being broken into and robbed when they were traveling, Sally first explained. This was indeed true, but she later confessed it was also to elude all their postgraduate children who simply *would* keep coming back to camp in their old bedrooms, appearing hopefully at mealtimes and helplessly with armloads of dirty shirts.

Now in Sally's case this congregation of the young may well have been a deserved personal tribute, but in the following years I saw this bizarre exception become a trend and then finally a whole new alternative life-style. My neighbor has a twenty-eight-year-old son living at home and commuting to New York to his job in public relations; a friend of a friend in Monsey has two post-college daughters at home, one going to law school, the other a cocktail waitress. (The other innovation now is, I think, the diversity of occupations. Our children are as likely to be mechanics, carpenters, butchers, and policemen as doctors or lawyers; often there are both extremes in a family. My friend in Croton has one son who is a newspaper writer, another who is a moving man. The latter's girlfriend is a doctor and her sister is going to clown school. Their friends have produced a geologist, a magazine editor, and a short-order cook. Of my own grown children, the oldest is a postal clerk, one sister is in publishing, and the other is studying to become a costume designer. This does make life interesting, for the parents as well. Former routine inquiries at large cocktail parties concerning the offspring of acquaintances are answered no longer with prideful accounts of progress at the Chase Manhattan but often with piquant incongruities. I encountered one the other night: the older boy was already a famous rock star—*really* famous; even I had heard him on the radio—while the younger son was a nurse.) But however original and various their *métiers,* a great many of the young people we know are living in the family home.

We mothers quite often ask ourselves how and why this has happened. Except in classic cliché cases of flagrant Oedipal attachment or literal incompetence, the primary motive appears to be quite simple—to save money. Nothing is ever quite that simple, however. The young have always needed to save money, but in the past they would have sold themselves piece by piece—in futurity—to medical schools rather than move back home. This phenomenon must be related to another trend, the tendency to postpone marriage or even the commitment of living together. Like the costume of dirty jeans and unisex haircuts, it may be one of Nature's sneaky ways of exerting population control. But in any case, it is made feasible surely by the fact that home is an easier place to return to now that mother and father aren't so punctilious about schedules, dress codes, and table manners. The children drift in and out with often maddening insouciance.

I hardly ever know just how many places to lay on the table, be it breakfast or dinner, or whose socks are whirling around in the dryer. The dog starts to wag her tail and grin at no matter what hour the front door creaks open. Nor have I figured out an appropriate answer to phone calls for the children, even the 3 A.M. ones, other than to mumble, "Well I don't know whether she's here, I suppose I might find her." A yet older generation might think this feckless, but one would feel just *silly*, I think, expressing concern for the safety or doubt about the resourcefulness of the son or daughter who has hitchhiked through Nigeria or backpacked in Nepal.

And as for the inconvenience, one brings that on oneself, of course, if one can't get the knack of being "laid back," of "hanging loose"; the kids don't care if they go without supper, miss phone calls and buses, have to wear the same shirt four days in a row. Other than employing the *force majeure* of "for *my* sake, then," which one needs to keep in reserve to forestall schemes like weekend parachute jumping, there is nothing a parent can say or do short of expulsion. Occasionally we sulk a little, but mostly we come to take it all in stride, with only a stumble now and then. Therefore it is obvious that the modern home offers a number of conveniences, even pleasures, and only a manageable number of "hassles." So it is after all no mystery that the children keep coming home. The real question is, Why do we let them in?

For the parents the situation can be a trying one. The first thing one notices is the matter of diminishing physical space. A house which once comfortably contained two adults and three to five children, with rooms and furniture adequate to their size, has to accommodate five to seven big people, all adults at least in physique. These new grown-ups need large beds in place of cots, cribs, or convertibles, large closets, extra showers, and cupboards for their curling irons. Moreover, returning from their colleges and apartments, they import the funky furnishings of those temporary digs. Our basement and attic, once repositories for tools, storm windows, Christmas decorations, and old love letters, now bulge and buckle with Coca-Cola cartons filled with books and records, electric hot plates, mini-fridges, toaster-ovens, fans, rolls of posters and remnant rugs, two guitars, four sets of skis, and a canoe. What a garage sale! I think wistfully; the proceeds could easily pay off the mortgage. But alas, not one item of this vast commercial cornucopia can be sold or even given away, since the time will come when it will all be shoehorned back into the weary station wagon or U-Haul and driven off many miles away to adorn yet another room.

Sometimes muttering "Om" and standing in that basement, which looks like a Green Stamp warehouse or backstage at a giveaway quiz show, I reflect that despite their jeans and rubber sandals, and their proudly proletarian occupations (my son was shocked when my husband once said to him, "Working in the post office isn't proletarian—it's petty bourgeois"), our children live in some ways on a more elevated economic scale than we do—at least in terms of material acquisition. Even as I type here I am tapping, gratefully, on Victoria's Smith-Corona electric with power return instead of on my $65 portable. I am wearing Valerie's Bulova Accutron, which she passed on to me when she got a watch she liked better. Beside me is our oldest's tape recorder, borrowed and not returned since he has a more elaborate model upstairs. In the next room is his Zenith color TV; our own Sears black and white portable with its wobbly rabbit ears now lives in the attic. Stereos, ten-speed bikes, Japanese cameras, calculators, hair-dryers, they have them all, often in duplicate.

But then I remind myself that 1) many of these baubles were given by us as Christmas or birthday presents or awards for academic achievements; 2) the rest, the kids bought for themselves with money earned at jobs we would not have endured at their age; 3) the children are generous in sharing them or even giving them away, hand-me-ups, as they replace them with newer models; and 4) there is nothing much really to keep me from going out and buying at least some of these gadgets for *myself*—except for the fact that like most of my generation I did not grow up with these electronic marvels. We went off to college on *trains*—with *suitcases*. So we don't quite regard these things as necessities, and sometimes we can hardly master the intricacies of their operation. No, I begrudge the children not their possession of these tools and playthings but rather the space that they monopolize. The house swells and sags as they are moved in, is stripped and stark as they are moved out; one must be constantly making room or filling cavities.

After space, the major problem is transportation. Grown children living at home either still haven't learned to drive and must be chauffeured about or entrusted to their peers; *do* know how to drive but have no cars of their own and are thus invariably cruising in the parents' vehicle; do have a car/cars of their own so the driveway looks like a used-car lot and it requires the skill and recklessness of a parking attendant to get out of the garage. Actually, all these combinations have their inherent compensations. The nondrivers can be marooned at home occasionally to answer phones, welcome plumbers, or make yogurt. The carless drivers can often be bribed into collecting cat food or dry cleaning on their way to *Star Wars*. Those with multiple cars can serve as the family's private Hertz company when the station wagon—hernia'd from all that moving—is in hospital. Our son, while not precisely forthcoming with his silver Mercedes or even his Volkswagen bug for petty chores like taking the golden retriever to the vet, carting costumes to our local amateur theater, or collecting his younger brother who, the school nurse says, feels he's about to throw up, rises to the occasion when it is a question of a big mission. He is good for about one major moving job a season, and positively saintly about delivering and collecting his sisters at the airport. (Money saved roughing it at home can be diverted into holidays.) This free limousine service is no small contribution to my own leisure time and peace of mind.

One last problem for the mother with resident grown children is the extra housework involved, most of which invariably falls upon her *if she is at home.* Many of us have discovered that proviso and have renounced gardening and gourmet dinners for two and begun stampeding offices, boutiques, and graduate schools, which in their mercy often let us in. All statistics show that more middle-aged women are entering the work force; it has been naively assumed that a large segment are trying to escape the doldrums of an empty nest. *Au contraire!* Lots I know have abandoned housewifery to make room in that nest for all the returnees and to help pay for the extra wheat germ and long-distance phone calls. (Characteristic episode: Phone rings. Our son, age twenty-six, picks it up. Operator asks, "Is this Mr. Foote?" Short pause. Judicious answer. "That depends.") But above all, the mother's flight from home is a means of decently ducking the dishes and the dusting, which somehow manage to get done by someone else in her absence but *never* in her presence. Or, if not, who notices after dark and a long day in the office?

In spite of the crowding, chauffeuring, and extra housework, there are rewards in having the children home again: they help with engine rattles, making rum cake, and pinning up hems, and they provide company for afternoon tea and Scrabble. What's more, one learns so much. After all those years of teaching them skills—shoelace tying, New Math, soufflé baking, and parallel parking—how satisfying to learn a few from them, like putting on mascara, raising a spinnaker, and basic yoga.

My husband, who relishes having all the children under our roof, cherishes illusions, which periodically soar into ambitions, of making this arrangement not merely a sometime pleasure but also an economic asset like the traditional farm family. He visualizes us turning our collective talents to some sort of cottage industry. The girls have always made ingenious family gifts from various *objets trouvés,* flotsam and jetsam of the Hudson River or our neighbors' curbside offerings to Goodwill. Valerie once got a citation "Worthy" at a county fair for her apple pie, her first try, too. And as an assistant den mother I have helped make medieval castles from milk cartons, egg boxes, and beer-can tabs. So the children's father dreams of us all clustered, chortling, in a revamped corner of our dank and crowded basement, turning out boudoir wastebaskets covered with flocked wallpaper, pickled picture frames, jars of jam from our dying quince tree, velvet-covered jewel cases created from cigar boxes, scissors-holders from sequined tennis-ball cans, and decoupage umbrella stands from transmogrified plastic Clorox bottles. Our attic groans under the weight of empty but promising coffee tins, wooden cheese cartons, oatmeal boxes, and samples of tweed suit materials received in the mail. We will sell our creations in the local boutiques or antique shops—on consignment, if necessary—or perhaps peddle them door-to-door. (Actually, our only entrepreneurial success is Andrew, who at age seven borrowed a pound of peat moss from our neighbors, put two level tablespoons in each of a stack of plastic Baggies, and sold them to the other neighbors for a quarter a shot.) Or better still, we will market them by mail order. My husband is quite prepared to leave his editorial job in the city to help Victoria, who has studied Chinese calligraphy, and Valerie, who does etchings, concoct a catalogue. When these fits come upon him, usually during snowstorms, torrential rains, or heat waves, and at breakfast just before train time, the children and I pat him fondly on the arm and hand him his briefcase. After all, he has all those mouths to feed.

5
AGING

Americans are rediscovering midlife, although many of them get intimidated by what they find. It once was possible, even fashionable, to ignore fears of impotence, menopause, and loss of social function. Though people are now more candid about these worries and many verbalize them more freely, they continue to fear the worst after they pass the mid-40s. All their verbalizing cannot compensate for the fact that many people are still woefully misinformed about midlife, its social contexts and relationships, and therefore feel threatened.

There continue to be two kinds of exaggeration which invariably surface when people begin talking about midlife. The first of these embellishes the theme of loss. It forecasts traumas of the empty nest when children grow up, and the empty bed when change of life saps people of their sexual vigor. In short, people currently associate middle age with loss of social and sexual function. As if this were not depressing enough, there is also a tendency to minimize or even to ignore social gains accruing at midlife. There is evidence that people's actual prestige at work and in the community are higher than ever during middle age; and it is known that the biological changes associated with menopause actually increase sexual appetite while liberating women from worry about pregnancy. Yet these aspects of midlife are usually glossed over by the American public. Instead there is a tendency to stress the negative aspects of middle age without giving personal and social satisfactions their due.

Midlife, like other transitions, is a social and psychological turning point, nothing more and nothing less. Like other turning points in life, such as adolescence or advanced old age, it is more a time for rethinking and regrouping social roles rather than a time for relinquishing them.

If people report that midlife is more stressful than adolescence or advanced old age, however, it is in keeping with the kinds of social roles they must evaluate at this time. Parenthood, career, even marriage are scrutinized. Middle-aged people must take a long hard look at their ongoing responsibilities. And unlike the elderly, who look back on their lives and evaluate previous actions, middle-aged people still have to plan ahead. All of this evaluating and planning goes by the name of *midlife review*.

Gillespie's "Meditation" is precisely such a midlife review. Her message is that middle age is a period when past experience and hopes for the future take on added significance. Gillespie's meditating parent expresses self-confidence and religious faith. It is worth considering that these are two feelings which may have been difficult to verbalize, let alone appreciate, at earlier periods in life.

Men are as susceptible to midlife crises as women are. They too must reevaluate the meaning of family and work. Orville Brim sketches some competing theories of the male midlife crisis, each with its particular interpretation of masculinity and social obligation. Brim concentrates on personal crisis and growth. But midlife occurs in a social context, and in the United States today this context is synonymous with social change.

A sure sign of social change is the Gerber company's recent decision to begin selling insurance policies. The decision to sell baby food as well as life insurance is significant for what it says about the demographics of the U.S. population. Increased longevity, along with declines in the birth rate, have made us an older society. For example, the number of people 75 or older swelled by more than 40 percent between 1960 and 1973; and since 1973 the growth of this group has continued to outstrip the growth rate for people between 65 and 74. One-and-a-half million people are currently 75 or older; and an estimated 16 million people will be that old in the year 2020. It is not surprising then that this pattern has been called "The Graying of America." The elderly, especially people in advanced old age, constitute an ever-growing segment of society.

These changes have already begun affecting relationships among family members. Beth Hess and Joan Waring speculate about "Changing Patterns of Aging and Family Bonds in Later Life." Their research focuses on demographic and historical change and on opportunities for realignment among generations of kin.

The future of relationships between elderly people and their families is still uncertain. But there are already some interesting developments which will lead to new reciprocities—and animosities—in years to come. Increments in longevity, for example, mean that more families will contain four generations rather than the familiar three. Apart from the responsibilities involved in caring for and interacting with great-grandparents, there are new life-styles developing for older Americans.

The retirement community and nursing home have gradually begun to exchange social functions; more nursing homes try to provide social activities and networks of peers for elderly people. Meanwhile, retirement communities increasingly anticipate the day when residents become too frail or incapacitated to care for themselves and many have added health-care components which offer long-term nursing care. Elsewhere I have argued that experiences on the ward and in the retirement village have had an effect on people's testamentary behavior. Older people who move to such locales are more likely than those in the population at large to name new beneficiaries in their wills.[1] Dorothy-Anne Flor provides other examples of how social roles and obligations of older people are changing. She describes them in an essay called "The Vanishing Grandmother."

---

1. Jeffrey P. Rosenfeld, "Old Age, New Beneficiaries: Kinship, Friendship, and (Dis)Inheritance," *Sociology & Social Research* (October 1979).

Midlife

Meditation of a Middle-Aged, (Upper) Middle-Class, White, Liberal, Protestant Parent

Joanna Bowen Gillespie

The lesson we taught our children was how to say No.

■ Recently on late-night television news, some vivid footage showed a college campus protest against current legislative attempts to reinstate the draft. The *New York Times* contends that today's students are apathetic about such issues, but apathy wasn't what I saw.

The students were screaming "Hell, no, we won't go" at Representative Pete McCloskey, effectively preventing themselves from hearing what he had to say. He had come to the campus at Berkeley, California, to defend his version of a national-service bill. It would require 17-year-old men *and* women to choose one of four options: active military duty for two years, with educational benefits; six months of active duty followed by extended reserve obligations; one year of civilian service in a Peace Corps-type domestic project; or placement in a draft lottery for a period of six years.

McCloskey had been an early opponent of the Vietnam war, and therefore something of a hero on liberal campuses in the '60s, but few in his Berkeley audience seemed aware of that history. In a televised interview after he left the platform in defeat, McCloskey said he had hoped these young Americans would support his proposal (by far the most lenient and reasonable of the draft bills introduced up to now) because it would make our military-defense system more equitable and representative; the present all-volunteer army is made up of more than 40 per cent minority youth. One might think that our white, upper-middle-class, nothing-but-the-best youngsters would respond positively to such concepts as "fairness" and "egalitarianism"—but apparently the best lesson we parents taught them was how to say No.

As I watched, I was struck with dismay that these healthy and beautiful young people felt they owed nothing to anybody or anything. One of their placards read, reasonably enough, "Draft the Politicians—Not Us." But their faces showed resistance to authority, not love of peace; they were screaming No in the same way they fight deadlines for term papers or rules against pot-smoking—to protect what they perceive as their autonomy. The speaker they cheered at that rally preached the gospel of privilege: no one can make you do anything you don't want to do. It is your right to decide whether or not you will register; your choice is what counts; there is no such thing as obligation.

Even as part of me agreed with him, I blanched. We good liberal parents have brought up a generation whose members think of them-selves as outside or beyond the social fabric. They have never had to worry about anyone other than themselves, and Voilà! they don't.

I

Child-rearing is always a blend of the parents' world view and that of the surrounding society. Along with what *we* didn't give this egocentric cohort of emerging adults, there was the influence of the postwar world into which we bore them. It confirmed for these blessed children of affluent, intelligent parents that very little was expected of them—no physical rites-of-passage, very few limitations on their self-expression, no hunger, no poverty. We produced children who had the luxury of saying what they would or would not do—from choice of college to choice of blue jeans. They had very little experience of belonging to something bigger than themselves; they did not learn the meaning of "esprit de corps" or camaraderie. The Boy Scouts or Girl Scouts may have been the last creedal experience many of them had.

Some of us are quite proud of our children's independence—we have worked so hard for it. We announce that our 19-year-old son has "taken his life into his own hands" (though we may still subsidize him) or that our 20-year-old daughter is now "living on her own." In some cultures this attitude would be perceived as gross neglect or apathy. An Asian diplomat confronted some fellow parents of children enrolled in a private "progressive" nursery school (where children were encouraged to "fulfill their own potential") with the accusation: "You Americans don't *care* what happens to your children." He spoke from a culture in which caring meant controlling, directing, making decisions for children of far older than nursery-school age. His listeners were horrified at such a medieval view of parenting. They also felt somewhat aggrieved, since caring, in our culture, has come to be equated with getting out of the child's way. It seemed more important to us to be passionate about our children rather than toward them; the prescribed stance was one of genteel noninvolvement.

What we neglected to give our young was a counterbalance to the emphasis on personal freedom and self-determination which they got from both us and the culture. We didn't talk much about giving anything back to the world that made them. Of course, it is hard to learn real responsibility when the most important job a child has is carrying out the garbage or cleaning his or her room. Suburbia may also have fostered the absorption of the monetary value-standard; the question most frequently asked by thousands of wide-eyed schoolchildren visiting the traveling King Tut exhibit was not anything about that fabulous era, or what those people believed as they prepared for afterlife, but rather, "How much does it cost?"

What could motivate a suburban adolescent to do volunteer work, when the understanding of the importance of work is based on how much one is paid for it? The best way to "sell" one's teenager on being a hospital volunteer or helping in a summer camp for the retarded is self-interest: "It will look good on your college application; it will teach you something you can use later on." If the young manage to catch a glimpse of selflessness in the process, fine; but we didn't direct them to value that part of the experience, nor did we expect that they would think of it in terms of "service" to others.

We "prepared" our children, as parents always do, for a world *we* wanted. We told ourselves that buying the best children's records and books, providing ballet, guitar or painting lessons, purchasing bicycles and ice skates, paying for summer camp and birthday parties would somehow convey to our children how much we loved them. We hoped they would catch on to the idea of parental authority—ours—without its being too uncomfortably visible.

We didn't want to "make an issue" of manners, even of minimal standards for human interaction. "Polite" became a useless word; an unsolicited gift from Great-Aunt Alice could be ignored. We had hated writing thank-you notes, so we let our children slide, effectively teaching them that their pleasure, their receiving, was all that mattered; they didn't have to take into account the feelings of the giver or participate in the basic human ritual of reciprocity if they didn't want to.

Current social history and psychology call narcissism the primary characteristic of this age (see Christopher Lasch's *The Culture of Narcissism* and Shirley Sugerman's *Sin and Madness: Studies in Narcissism*). The "me generation" child can't direct much interest or energy outside his or her individual boundaries. A psychiatrist describing a troubled 20-year-old recently said, in the vernacular: "This kid is hooked. He's addicted to doing what he wants to. Today's kids are addicts to doing their own thing; they can't seem to make that step to adulthood where they would find the ultimate legitimation of being able to do something for somebody else."

I discovered this lack of community when I taught in a fine small suburban liberal-arts college; my otherwise delightful, intelligent students were almost illiterate in group experience. They had participated little in any organization which might have demanded loyalty or submission of one's own agenda for the achievement of a whole greater than the sum of its parts. An amazing number of them had never been part of an orchestra or a band, a chorus or a theater group, a political campaign or even student government. A few had had some competitive team-sports background; even fewer had had a vital church youth group experience. Mostly their earlier lives had consisted of school, a few family rituals (Christmas, Easter, and birthdays), and television.

II

Of course, none of this parental disappointment is really new to America. It was clear from the first generation of white settlers that family authority—in the traditional patriarchal European sense—was in trouble. Bernard Bailyn and other historians of New England point out that as early as 1648 the Puritans had to pass stringent laws to help keep their children in line. Obviously children born here were at home in the wilderness in a way their parents could never be. That fact, plus the possibility of striking out for new territory when things got tight, and a religious attitude which emphasized the individual self in relationship with God, made it pretty hard for a father to maintain control over his children. Within several colonial generations, we were a youth-oriented culture; the child literally became "father," or guide, to the "man"—his elder. One interpretation of our War of Independence casts it in terms of an adolescent rebellion against Father/King and Mother England.

So the Puritans too found their children going their own way; even Cotton Mather bemoans "how little pleasure have I had in my children." The Puritans had to swallow some of their dreams in order to keep in touch with their young. They too had to see their children come up with their own version of religion, as that first youth movement, the Great Awakening of the 1730s, swept the young into revivalism.

A century later, frontier parents—those sturdy Protestant adventurers and land developers—carried with them their secret for success: method, system, organization. New worlds were being conquered not just geographically but in science and technology as well. No wonder the stories in the Sunday school "libraries" of early midwestern villages were full of a sense of indomitable progress and hope.

A typical story is that of a family moving from established Massachusetts in 1819 to the wilds of northern Ohio. Mother is pictured as pious and dutiful, an angel on a domestic hearth that is still being hacked from the forest. Father, in his zeal to finish the cabin before winter, fells a log on the Sabbath and—therefore—breaks his leg. In that world God was present, direct and inexorable; his messages to parents were everywhere: from flour spilled on the floor (that child needs more discipline) to the tragic death of an infant (confirmation that God had better things in store for them, in another world).

Along with this awesome domestic Presence, always divinely intervening, there was exuberance; a sense of power suffused the life of even the poorest and most powerless Christian. One knew beyond doubting that life was significant, that hideous circumstance—a broken leg miles from help—could be transcended through faith in Jesus and fierce moral purpose. Those parents had a method, a discipline for preparing their young for the world; they thought they knew how to transmit a system of meanings which would arm their children for a wonderful Christian American Protestant future.

III

This century's parents have lost that confidence in the future. We no longer trust our household gods—cleanliness, order, Dr. Spock, nutrition, routine, comfort—nor do we have any real belief in a divine immanence in our lives. Did we ever talk much with our children about loving our country, much less about loving God? Was offering thanks for the petunias in the window box or for a full refrigerator an automatic part of our household litany? Did we ever think the overflowing heart of the 23rd Psalm could be experienced in Pittsburgh as well as in rural Israel? We were afraid to speak of religious things or to make biblical references, lest we sound moralistic or preachy.

Today when an irate grandmother demands, "Why don't you just *make* them do it?" she is reflecting a nostalgic view of child-rearing. In our lifetime, the expectation that a child will conform to a pre-existing norm has continued to erode in the direction of more individual latitude. We have learned to change external factors rather than to change the child.

A recently retired executive of an eastern corporation recalls that, as a youth, he was bounced out of three different preparatory schools; he simply couldn't cut the mustard, as his autocratic old father had always said. No hint in that parental dictum that there might be anything wrong with the school. No such institution-questioning took place; it was simply taken for granted that the child would have to measure up. Such clarity was unthinkable for us.

With our lost sense of order and of a world in which God is involved in one's daily life, we lack that vigor and optimism which used to be called "strength of conviction." We are fearful of impinging too much on our children's lives, and they respond with both anger and hunger. Their anger is the No they scream at interference in their individual paths— military service, deadlines, legal or conventional restraints, not getting into medical school. This anger is expressed in tantrums—vandalism of college buildings—or in depression. Their hunger is often a Yes to the kind of idealism and structured community represented in Jonestown or by the Moonies. Or it is a Yes to a variety of psychologically intense experiences such as drug-euphoria, disco dancing or religious fundamentalism.

IV

Quite aside from the antidraft component of the student protest which I viewed on television, my parent-heart wanted to see some sense of belonging to the world, of caring or conviction. We don't want our children to be good Nazis obeying without question; we want them to hate war more than we did, somehow to face up to the overwhelming forces in this period of history. But we'd like them to understand the electrifying challenge our generation heard in John Kennedy's inaugural: "Ask not what your country can do for you; ask what you can do for your country." Did we ever express to them how that charge catapulted our better natures right into the enthusiasm of the '60s? Well, no, maybe we didn't talk much about it, what with the hippies and all that.

Of course the jury isn't in yet on this "rising seed," as the Puritans would have called them; we won't be able to add it all up until we see what values they pass along to their young. But we elders may well have to face the millennium on our knees, because we surely didn't teach our kids how to get down on theirs. "It is not possible to make good men and good women without an element of transcendence and grace," wrote Malcolm Muggeridge—British scholar, journalist and Christian. He was speaking to teachers about education, but his observation applies also to parenting—to parents who know they have an ideal for the concept of the "good" and a relation with a gracious God. Many of us middle-aged genteel Christians know we settled for considerably less.

Theories of the Male Mid-Life Crisis[1]
Orville G. Brim, Jr.

■ To have many middle-aged men in society is practically a modern phenomenon. In earlier times, 90 percent of the species were dead by age forty. Prehistoric man lived less than three decades. The lifespan of an ancient Greek or Roman was about four decades. Today more than a tenth of the population in this nation are males between the ages of forty and sixty, numbering nearly 25 million. These normbearers and decision makers, bill payers and power brokers have been the subjects of commentary and serious study for only a short time. In 1932 Walter B. Pitkin wrote *Life Begins at Forty,* and in the mid-thirties Charlotte Buhler (1935) and Elsa Frenkel-Brunswick (1968) had started their studies of personality changes during the middle years. But until a decade or so ago, most studies of adults were not developmental in perspective; most of the information we had about adults came from cross-sectional studies, as a by-product of other research interests. With few exceptions the dominant view was that nothing of significance takes place in the male personality during the mid-life period. People felt life ended at forty and there was nothing to do but wait around for retirement and death.

This is still the prevailing view, it seems. Robert R. Sears reports that in teaching his course at Stanford on human development through the life cycle, it comes as a surprise to many students to recognize that their parents may be having their own growth and adaptation crises. It is reminiscent of the story about Stalin's young son, before the revolution, who said to his mother. "Father should get out and do something; all he does is walk in the park with Lenin." Why this attribution of constancy of personality should occur for mid-life males, in the face of the experiences and evidence noted later, is a puzzle worth working on. We know that one attributes more trait consistency over time to others than to oneself, that lives seem more coherent from the outside than from the inside, but this should apply equally at all ages and to women as well as men, if it is a fundamental cognitive process in attribution. Could it be that society is heavily invested in this particular age-sex category; and must count on conformity and stability? Is it motivated also by matters not quite so

"Theories of the Male Mid-Life Crisis" by Orville G. Brim, Jr., from THE COUNSELING PSYCHOLOGIST, vol. 6, 1976. Reprinted by permission of The Counseling Psychologist and the author.

1. Invited address to Division 20, at the 82nd Annual Convention of the American Psychological Association, New Orleans, September, 1974. Preparation of this paper was partially supported by the National Institute of Mental Health under Research Grant 1 RO1 MH25547–01.

pragmatic, namely, that these men are fathers, and children, of all ages, desire a stable father figure? Or is it that they need to believe that somewhere, someone knows and can explain; but the fact that nobody knows, is one that nobody tells? Are middle-aged men rewarded for stoicism, and punished for expressions of uncertainty and suffering?

The body of scholarly work here under consideration challenges the premises that nothing happens to men in mid-life, and that middle-aged males need no help or attention. And, there is fiction (Bissell, 1965; Heller, 1974; Leggett, 1964; Stern, 1973); popular work (LeShan, 1973); self-help books (Bergler, 1967; Hills, 1973; O'Neill & O'Neill, 1974; Vorspan, 1974); mass media treatments (e.g. *True Story* magazine carried a lead article entitled "I Am the Wife of a Man in a Mid-Life Crisis"), and the next season in television will see the launching, I am told, of a series on males at mid-life called "A Second Chance."

Because the concept of male mid-life crisis implies personality change, this work is germane. Here too there is fiction—the genre of work dealing with personality change, the stories and great legends of metamorphosis, e.g., *Dr. Jekyll and Mr. Hyde* (Stevenson, 1922) and *Seconds* (Ely, 1963). The popular, self-help literature is really vast on this topic, as we all know, and there are notable, serious, scholarly works, say Jerome Frank's (1963) *Persuasion and Healing* and John Mann's (1965) *Changing Human Behavior.*

Comparative Analysis

In my analysis three authors and their colleagues receive most of my commentary: Daniel J. Levinson, Marjorie Fiske Lowenthal, and Bernice L. Neugarten. Levinson and his colleagues are completing their intensive study of forty males about age forty, from four different occupational groups.[2] The methods involve intensive case studies, within the context of a comprehensive psychosocial developmental theory. Levinson uses a naturalistic and biographic research approach in his interviews with the forty males, and also draws heavily on fiction and biographical protocols. Lowenthal, Thurnher, and Chiriboga (1975) report on a major interview survey of California men and women at four different ages. This first volume presents descriptive base-line data, against which changes will be measured in a second field study in the next several years. Neither of these two research programs are longitudinal studies; e.g., the four groups

---

2. This study will be published soon as a book. I have had the opportunity to read unpublished papers and parts of the book manuscript, and have had personal communications from Dr. Levinson, orally and by letter. The account presented here however is based on an early and partial version of his work. The final published version undoubtedly will differ in some respects.

delineated in the Lowenthal study represent an age span of some forty years, say between twenty and sixty, but cannot be viewed as points on an individual developmental process. Neugarten and her colleagues are represented by a large number of publications over the past two decades, some from the well known Kansas City research and some from other field studies (Coleman & Neugarten, 1971; Havighurst, Munnichs, Neugarten, & Thomae, 1969; Neugarten, 1968, 1973; Neugarten & Associates, 1964; Neugarten & Datan, 1973, 1974).

I have also drawn on Kenneth Soddy's (1967) *Men in Middle Life,* John Clausen's (1972) reports on the Berkeley growth study, and also several others observers and commentators with a less extensive data base than these, but with valuable thoughts about the male mid-life period. I should mention in particular David A. Hamburg (Note 1), Elliott Jaques (1965), Erik Erikson (1950), and Raymond Kuhlen (1964).[3]

The evidence shows and most agree that the individual as he moves through the adult years becomes transformed in appearance, social or life patterns, interests, relationships, and also with regard to inner qualities, for example, ways of experiencing and expressing emotions and motivations and preoccupations. There are hundreds of investigations which substantiate personality change in adulthood, in reactions to situations, in attitudes, in reference groups, in self-descriptive items, in sources of gratification, in dyadic relationships, in the objective descriptions by friends, and on psychological tests. The data come from self-reports, longitudinal studies, observational materials, individual protocols, personal descriptions attesting to the fact that "everybody is working on something," and significantly, the inability to predict adult personality from childhood, or even adolescence. As John Clausen observes, "the natural state of the organism (person) is to be in the process of becoming something different while remaining in many respects the same."

The classic criticism of this view of adult personality change is of course that of the psychoanalyst. (In contrast, Jung, 1933, and Erikson, 1950, both postulate changes, e.g., Jung commenting on the increase in introversion in middle and later life and the reorganization of value systems that characterizes adult change, and Erikson postulating a developmental task of stagnation vs. generativity.) But the psychoanalytic view is in opposition: the sense of identity is essentially established in adolescence and it produces consistency in behavior thereafter; character structure becomes fixed in early adulthood and the essential nature or personality remains unchanged (Neugarten, 1973). Previously I noted

---

3. There are some visible omissions. Some simply are not utilized extensively, such as Jung, Maslow, and Fromm. Some are omitted, such as the Grant Study at Harvard, because the reports and interpretations are not well documented by the work of the study. As for others, such as the work of Roger Gould, Douglas Heath, Jerome K. Meyers, George Pollock, and Klaus Reigel, I have not given the time needed for a careful appraisal.

some other causes of the view that adult male personality does not change, namely, the mistaken attribution of continuity, the anxiety from perceiving the primary male figure in society as in uncertain change, and the normative pressure for stoicism. For these reasons, the burden seems to have been on behavior scientists to demonstrate change, rather than what seems more difficult, to demonstrate continuity.

Scientific documentation of change is difficult. As Neugarten (1973) points out, it is not the conviction that personality change occurs in adulthood, but the methods for measuring these changes that psychologists are lacking. Behavioral change is the ultimate criterion, but it cannot be measured except inferentially because it expresses itself variably over different situations. Therefore one needs various observers, in different situations over time, to capture the change either as manifest in changes in their responses or their ratings. Thus, it is difficult to demonstrate personality change except by this kind of summary of evidence from a variety of times and places.

Even the best of research is criticized as showing only phenotypic changes, leaving the genotypic personality underneath these surface manifestations still the same. The answer can be made as a three-fold challenge to the psychoanalytic view. First it is impossible for psychoanalysts to be convincing in moving from phenotypic behavior at time 1 to an accurate conceptualization of the genotypic trait that underlies it, and then to a conceptualization and measurement of the different phenotypical behavior appropriate at time 2.

Second, even if one says that traits like "ego strength" change little over time in contrast to other personality traits (e.g., interpersonal relationships or attitudes or self-esteem or social roles), one might be prepared to yield to the clinician the territory of "ego strength" and its durability, and move on to work with what is left, which in my view, is effectively almost all of the adult personality.

Third, if one takes the position that it is the natural state of the male adult to be stable in personality, we must ask how much of the stability depends on an unchanging environment. In primitive, slow-changing environments there is likely to be continuity in personality, but in the United States, where both work and family situations are in rapid alteration, life span personality change may be increasing—coming to public attention compared to four decades ago—and continuity of personality increasingly difficult to demonstrate.

Theorists of mid-life male changes have focused on different aspects of the person. Thus, Lowenthal et al. (1975) are concerned with the individual's goal domain, past, present, and future; with their values; with aspects of psychological functioning such as morale and anxiety; with behavior trait changes and modes of adaptation.

Levinson and his colleagues use the concept of "life structure." It is meant to integrate traditional social structural perspectives with personality structure concepts. Levinson says it "requires first a clear distinction between role and personality and then a way of thinking about multiple roles in their patterning and their 'interpenetration' with personality" (Note 2). For the sociological component, one can think of life structure as containing a uniquely personal social system, with one's own set of unique statuses and roles, residences, the physical space one spends time in, his leisure, his travel, and the like. For the psychological component, one can think of it as consisting primarily of role behavior and related motives, attitudes, beliefs, both conscious and unconscious. Life structure can be viewed as separate from social organization, when one compares his specific unique arrangements with that of the larger order and contrasts his position with what he might become, wishes to be, or was.

Neugarten is the most eclectic in theory and variety of empirical problems studied. Her work over a twenty-year period has examined the lifespan development process with reference to many personality characteristics—values, preferences, attitudes toward death, definitions of and expectations for age grades, perspectives on time, to name a few.

These scholars and most others mentioned here use the term "transition." The transition concept clearly implies a change which moves the person from one position or stage to another. Hence, implicit in the word transition is the concept of stages or stable periods in personality. Lowenthal et al. (1975) use the concept of transition in connection with changes in statuses and roles, e.g., marriage, retirement; Levinson et al. use the term transition in connection with changes in stages of life structure, e.g., "getting into the adult world," "becoming one's own man." Even so the definition of transition for Levinson is difficult to pin down. Sometimes he says it is making something out of that which is new, but most often it is both death and rebirth, the best of the old along with the best of the new; in this way he speaks in allegory rather than using precise definition. Neugarten thinks of stages—whether social or psychological—much less formally, if at all, and hence speaks less often of "transitions."

As for "mid-life crisis," none of the three main theorists emphasizes crises in mid-life, although each recognizes that in some instances regular transitions can become crises. For example, Levinson says, "A transition may proceed relatively smoothly or with moderate or severe turmoil and disruption. In the latter case I speak of a developmental crisis" (Note 3). Other theorists agree. For instance, Clausen (1972) suggests that in the Berkeley growth study lowered aspirations and downward mobility are made with a smooth transition for a substantial number of the subjects. He goes on to add that those in transition often are not aware of it, that there are individual differences in how much and how often persons reflect on these matters—some subjects having undergone substantial change but thinking about it only when interviewed, while others seem to have mused about it almost every day.[4] The concept of "crisis," in mid-life and at other times, implies a rapid or substantial change in personality, and it is probably both rapid and substantial rather than either one alone, which is dislocating with respect to one's sense of identity—his usual reference groups, his role models, his principles, his values, his dyadic relationships, so that the whole framework of his earlier life is in question.

For some unknown number of men a mid-life crisis is a notable experience. An elusive concept to pin down, it reminds me of the story of the Southern mountain man who, when asked if he believed in baptism, said, "Believe in it, I've seen it." Elliot Jaques (1965) refers us to this theme in *The Divine Comedy*. This masterpiece of all time was begun by Dante following his banishment from Florence at the age of thirty-seven. In the opening stanza he created his setting in words of great power and tremendous psychological depth:

> Nel mezzo del cammin di nostra vita
> mi retrovai per una selva oscura
> che la diritta via era smarrita.
> Ah quanto a dir qual era e cosa dura
> esta selva selvaggia e aspra e forte
> che nel pensier rinova la paura!
> Tant' e amara che poco e piu morte:[5]

Causes and Content

As one person has summed up the mid-life period, "The hormone production levels are dropping, the head is balding, the sexual vigor is diminishing, the stress is unending, the children are leaving, the parents are dying, the job horizons are narrowing, the friends are having their first heart attacks; the past floats by in a fog of hopes not realized, opportunities not grasped, women not bedded, potentials not fulfilled, and the future is a confrontation with one's own mortality" (Lear, 1973).

The causes set forth for transitions—which may be crises—during the male mid-life period can be summarized in these concepts: (1) endocrine changes, (2) aspiration-achievement gap, (3) resurgence of "The Dream," (4) stagnation vs. growth ("generativity"), (5) confrontation with death,

---

4. We can also say that there are crises without transitions or personality changes, but this requires a different definition of crisis, namely, one of intense suffering, such as a temporary physical ailment, or extreme fear for an event that does not take place, neither of which need yield any significant durable change in personality.

5. Translation: In the middle of the journey of our life I came to myself within a dark wood where the straight way was lost. Ah, how hard a thing it is to tell of that wood, savage and harsh and dense, the thought of which renews my fear! So bitter is it that death is hardly more.

(6) relationships within the family, (7) social status and role changes. I have not tried to order these theoretically, a point I consider shortly, but they are arrayed from the biological to the social structural.

Endocrine Changes

From about age thirty on there is a gradual decline in testosterone and cortisol and from thirty through the remainder of life there is a gradual decline in secretion of androgens for the male. There are other steroids identified, many of which are produced in large amounts and with greater age trends than the foregoing, but they are not as yet linked theoretically to physiological processes. There is much to be examined on this psychobiology frontier—in this unknown area of hormonal changes during the male mid-life period. To what extent the changes themselves contribute to individual self-reappraisals or vulnerability to stress we simply do not know at this time.

Aspirations and Achievements

Work still takes the largest single percentage of one's waking hours and constitutes for most a fundamental influence on the development and change in the sense of self through the life cycle. The search for self-esteem—to be valued by others who matter, and to be valued by oneself; to feel in control of the world, one's life course, time, and self in its values and behavior; to believe one is distinctive, unique even, that one counts for something special in the common pilgrimage of man; to sense personal growth and development so that one is something more than as of a week ago—the pursuit of these and other elements in the summary sense of self-esteem pervades the work of most people. (Note 4.)

The aspirations in life that men set for themselves are primarily expressed through the institution of work. Over the course of the working life, from entry to the mid-life period, it is likely that although aspirations may be adjusted downward on occasion, one usually believes there is enough time left for the desired level of achievement to be reached in future years. But during mid-life most American males must adjust their career aspirations of earlier years downward to fit current reality. A man may be told that he has risen as high as he can go in his place of work; that his present position must be accepted by him as the achievement level for his lifetime. In one of our best known studies Chinoy (1955) reports that automobile workers, comparing their career dreams with what they have actually accomplished, solved the problem of discrepancies by considering their work to be temporary and by maintaining their hopes of becoming an entrepreneur or farmer. Eventually, though, the worker faces a day of reckoning when he must recognize that he is "trapped," that his American dream of becoming his own boss will not be fulfilled.

This causative factor has been in the explanatory theories of many commentators on the mid-life period who make use of the aspiration-achievement gap and its reconciliation as the source and content of personality change. While many men may make this adaptation, in small steps, in a gradual alteration of one's self image, so that a transition to a new sense of self is accomplished without a crisis, for others depression emerges as one realizes he can no longer count on seemingly limitless years ahead. We note that moving toward old age there is cross-cultural evidence showing a decline in expressions of competition and risk (Gutmann, 1969) and a concern in the older age period not with reducing the aspiration-achievement gap but simply in holding on to what one has achieved, in protecting what one has from others, usually younger insurgent groups.

Resurgence of "The Dream"

Levinson and his colleagues most clearly set forth the view that maturation requires one to go through a period of suppression of certain aspects of the self in order to develop and commit to a given life structure, involving an occupation and a family, and that during middle age the suppressed aspects of the self push toward the surface and demand that the man reappraise who he is and what he has been doing. They use the concept of "The Dream" as a youthful aspiration, as an early image of the future self which never dies.

It seems to me that the major component of "The Dream" for males involves their work. It makes a sharp contrast, though, to the aspiration-achievement problem just described, because the middle-aged malaise may arise even though one achieves what he set out to do. The man may feel that he has attempted too little, not stretched himself, not seized opportunities. He may feel it is meaningless and ask, is this what I really wanted? Was it worth all I had to give up? Do I want to go on doing these things for the years I have left? What of those parts of myself that I had to neglect—to suppress—to sacrifice? There is a pervading sense of great sadness in these mid-life men of unfulfilled dreams, and it is the resolution of this crisis that is crucial to Levinson's theory. The man must give up the early adulthood life structure, allowing resurgence and expression of "The Dream," and work through the mid-life transition to the restructuring for middle adulthood.

Stagnation vs. "Generativity"

Erikson (1950), in his work on stages of psychosocial development, sets one adult task as the resolution of the issue of stagnation vs. generativity. The essence of a successful transition is to shift one's life interests and concerns to the development and achievements of the younger generation and to accept and value one's responsibility to care for this next generation of man.

The concept of generativity may describe the possible resolution of a mid-life crisis rather than its cause, but I include it here because it seems to me to be closest to the idea that a desire for a sense of personal growth is a deepseated characteristic of the human organism and that a failure of a sense of growth generates depression and leads to attempts to avoid this stagnation. (It may be that this developmental process is most important for gifted and successful men such as Erikson has studied and also may be of significance for men of early climax stories—e.g. Irwin Shaw's (1941) "The 80 Yard Run"—where one fears that he never again will do as much or as well in his career.)

Recently Helen Vendler (1974) in reviewing Allen Ginsburg's book *The Fall of America* describes the despair of Ginsburg's middle age: "Everything is already known, and everything has stopped happening . . . Friends are now what they will be for good: no one would change. Everything has been encountered: sex, love, friendship, drugs, even fame, even the boundary dimensions of self."

Confrontation with Death

Elliott Jaques (1965) in his influential paper "Death and the Mid-Life Crisis" says:

Family and occupation have become established: parents have grown old, and children are at the threshold of adulthood. Youth and childhood are past and gone, and demand to be mourned. The achievement of mature and independent adulthood presents itself as the main psychological task. The paradox is that of entering the prime of life, the stage of fulfillment, but at the same time the prime and fulfillment are dated. Death lies beyond . . . I believe, and shall try to demonstrate, that it is this fact of the entry upon the psychological scene of the reality and inevitability of one's own eventual personal death that is the central and crucial feature of the mid-life phase—the feature which precipitates the critical nature of the period. Death—at the conscious level—instead of being a general conception, or an event experienced in terms of the loss of someone else, becomes a personal matter, one's own death, one's own real and actual mortality. (p. 506)

And then, referring to a particular case in his practice, he says, describing the man:

He began his adjustment to the fact that he would not be able to accomplish in the span of a single lifetime everything he had desired to do. He could achieve only a finite amount. Much would have to remain unfinished and unrealized . . .
This perspective on the finitude of life was accompanied by a greater solidity and robustness in his outlook and introduced a new quality of earthly resignation. It reflected a diminishing of his unconscious wish for immortality. Such ideas are commonly lived out in terms of denial of mourning and death, or in terms of ideas of immortality, from notions of reincarnation and life after death, to notions of longevity like those expressed by the successful twenty-eight year old novelist who writes in his diary, "I shall be the most serious of men, and I shall live longer than any man." (p. 507)

Signs to oneself that he is getting old—the hearing, the vision, the hair color, the body functions, the stamina, the teeth, the skin, the rate of healing wounds—are gradual in development and one recognizes that he has stopped growing up, and begun to grow old, that from here on out, everything is downhill. But these indices of aging are nothing compared to the vivid sudden confrontation with the fact of one's own mortality. One of Neugarten's (1968) several significant empirically-based observations about the personality change involves time orientation, and a change in mid-life when one stops counting "time since birth" and begins to think of one's life in reference to "time yet to live." Death represents to the middle-aged man the fact that he will not achieve what he thought he was going to achieve. He will not see those places he had planned to see, he will not explore those ideas he had on his future agenda.

One looks on with some pathos, and occasionally with a sense of tragedy, when the attempted mid-life solution to mortality is to intensify efforts and to engage in complicated attempts to master the use of time. It seems to me, as it must to you, that this is a clear expression of the actual or incipient confrontation with death in its fullest sense. Neugarten has suggested that the central task for middle age relates to the use of time and the essential polarities are between time mastery and capitulation; but this seems to me to pose the question or task too simply. We can say that one of the major psychological tasks for middle age is resignation to death and a permutation, a reordering, of life priorities. As Jaques shows in his many clinical cases, successful resolution liberates energy and leads one to self acceptance.

Relationships Within the Family

As Anne Boedecker (Note 5) has written regarding the family, middle age is generally the time when a man's children are leaving the home for work and families of their own, his wife is readjusting to the role of housewife without children and perhaps entering or reentering the job market, and his parents may be aging to the point of becoming dependent on him.

Some writers see this as a period of high tension and conflict within the family system and a period of high risk for the post-parental couple. On the other hand, there is a good bit of solid research reporting that couples rate the post-parental period as one of the best in their marriage, and have significant role changes only when family continuity is low. Lowenthal and colleagues are studying this empty-nest period as transition period, and we will know more later as a result.

In any event, two unusual points are noteworthy: Levinson and his colleagues point out that a man during his children's adolescence must inevitably compare a fantasy, his belief in his own power and influence to mold his child into some ideal being, with what is now becoming a reality, and accept the limited nature of his own influence. This reconciliation of aspirations to reality likely is taking place at the same time that his occupational aspiration-achievement gap is being worked through. We do not seem to have many facts about the expression of aspirations for children by parents at this older age level, although the work on earlier childhood aspirations with reference to certain character traits (e.g., Kohn, 1969) has been charted. The subtleties of the transference of the father's aspirations upon the children has been described, but not counted. Since blue collar and white collar workers "top out" at different ages, it might mean that the interaction with the adolescent would be different because the sons might differ in age as much as ten years. On the other hand, since blue collar workers marry earlier and have children earlier the age gap may not be as large. The actual facts here bear looking into because the problem may be more acute for the white collar worker with the older son.

As for husband-wife relations, I want to note the suggestion from Neugarten and the Committee on Human Development group, and specifically from David Gutmann's cross-cultural work (1969). It is that there are some concurrent age changes in the psychological stances of both men and women which bear on the male mid-life crisis. In essence, the older men are more diffusely sensual, more sensitive to the incidental pleasures and pains, less aggressive, more affiliative, more interested in love than conquest or power, more present than future oriented. At the same time, women are aging in the reverse direction, becoming more aggressive, less sentimental, and more domineering. While in the earlier years the husband tends to be dominant, during the aging process he comes to be more dependent. Apparently this comprehensive developmental event of middle and later life acts to reverse or at least equalize the domestic status of the partners, and tends to redistribute the so-called masculine and feminine traits among them, so that through these various sex-role changes there is ushered in the "normal unisex of later life."

What needs to be attended to here in regard to mid-life males—and Lowenthal and colleagues (Lowenthal et al., 1975; Lowenthal & Chiriboga, 1973) have made an excellent start—is that mid-life female personality changes and trajectories are outward, away from dependency on the husband, away from providing nurturance and support to him, so this source of his recognition, affection and sense of value becomes precarious, threatens to disappear.

Social Status and Role Changes

With this concept we move on to consider simply external events in male mid-life, where the theories of causation emphasize changes in position in social organization. It is the predictable sequence of changes in status and role through the lifespan that receives attention from Lowenthal and her colleagues (Lowenthal et al., 1975; Lowenthal & Chiriboga, 1973; Thurnher, 1974). Specifically, the volume reports on four populations facing imminent role gains or losses in transitions of adult life: high-school seniors before starting full-time work; newlyweds before the birth of their first child; parents whose youngest child will leave home within the year; and pre-retirement couples, leaving employment within a year or two. Now, Lowenthal, as noted, does not believe that such changes necessarily bring crises, but rather are occasions for both incremental and decremental changes, in which one stage is left behind, a phase of life over, but new growth and development ahead.

Neugarten also has considered the influence of status changes on mid-life personality and, although asserting personality does change, it is an inaccurate view that middle age constitutes a crisis period in the life-cycle any more than any other period of life. For most persons middle age brings with it the anticipated changes in family and work and health. Some of these changes are not necessarily interpreted as losses by the people who experience them. Whether perceived as losses or gains, the life events of middle age may produce new stresses for the individual, but they bring also occasions to demonstrate an enriched sense of self and new capacities for coping with complexity.

She says that since we have been socialized into a developmental view, the predictable on-time events when they arrive are not unsettling, "that the events are anticipated and rehearsed, the grief work completed, the reconciliation accomplished without shattering this sense of continuity of the life cycle" (Neugarten, 1970, p. 86). But, then she uses her concept of "on time—off-time" in a new hypothesis about status changes causing mid-life crises and contends that it is the unanticipated, not the anticipated, which is likely to represent the traumatic event. Major stresses are caused by events that upset the sequence and rhythm of the expected life cycle, as when death of a parent comes in adolescence rather than in middle age; when the birth of a child is too early or too late; when occupational achievement is delayed; when the empty nest, grandparenthood, retirement, major illness, or widowhood occur off-time. We should note that there is another class of unexpected traumatic events, which must be viewed as stress events inducing crises which are not necessarily related to chronological age or to passage through the social structure. Instead these are cohort experiences, such as wars, depressions—and historically, plagues and holocausts. We do not find any major sociological analysis of the impact of these stress events on adult males in the United States since the work on the Great Depression of the 1930s, e.g., Bakke (1940) on unemployment, and more recently Studs Terkel's (1970) *Hard Times*.

By way of comment on these seven "causes," we see at the one extreme physiological theories of personality change which might stress the importance of hormonal shifts, while the other anchoring point is a strict sociological perspective which views the life cycle as a succession of social roles with personality change viewed as a product of life-long socialization experiences. Arrayed somewhere in between are the other propositions briefly reviewed above: e.g., the mid-life confrontation with death seems virtually unavoidable simply as one gets older, while the crunch of aspiration-achievement discrepancies, or the surfacing of the set-aside "Dream," lack the same inexorability, for both are partly dependent on external happenings.

Experience has shown that the extreme positions are not acceptable, alone, and that the study of adult personality change requires the conceptual ability to deal with both inside and outside determinants in interaction. Indeed, our three major figures in this review are distinguished by rare interdisciplinary perspectives.

Nevertheless, as must be evident from previous comments, they do differ in their emphases. Lowenthal and her colleagues are examining status changes—increments and decrements—on one hand, while Levinson and his colleagues, in spite of their concept of life structure, in my judgement lean toward a preference for intrapsychic changes.[6] Neugarten describes the influence of external social status changes, where they are off-time and hence disruptive, and the transition to a "time yet to live" orientation. But, most often she and her colleagues

---

6. Levinson says, "For me the term 'Life Course' refers to the phenomenal stuff of life over time—the ongoing events, the raw materials out of which biographies are written. 'Socialization' is one theoretical perspective from which a life course can be examined and analyzed. It deals primarily with the shaping of the life course by social institutions and groups. It is the usual orientation of sociologists and is well exemplified by Lowenthal (who uses personal characteristics mainly to explain the residual variance). The paradigm of development ordinarily refers to an unfolding from within and is the primary orientation of psychologists, especially in the study of pre-adult development. Erikson and I are similar in our conception of development as an unfolding that depends on both internal and external social factors. This is only partly explicit in our work and is a source of much confusion. To put it most simply: I see development as the evolution of Life Structure, which has both internal and external aspects; and the determinants of development are also both internal and external." (Personal communication)

stress intrapsychic change from a developmental point of view. Her main theoretical position is that ego processes become increasingly important. In the first two-thirds of the lifespan the ego development is outward toward the environment, and for the last part of the lifespan inward toward the self.

She and Levinson are similar in viewing these changes as mainly internally paced, not triggered by outside events. She says (1973) that given the limitations of our methods and our variables, intrapsychic changes in middle and later life proceed in ways that not necessarily parallel social interaction or levels of psychological well-being. She says that the direction of change is from outer to inner preoccupation and sees a major reason for these changes as primarily inherent or developmental, in that they seem to occur well before the "losses" of aging can be said to begin. In other words, the fact that these personality changes appear by the mid-forties in a group of well-functioning adults seems congruent with a developmental, rather than a reactive view of personality.[7]

I must say that I find the various presentations by Levinson and Neugarten of their ontogenetic views incomplete. What still is missing is a clear specification of the causal process: we want to know both what are the mid-life changes, and also why they happen. If it is not mystical, beyond explanation, which it clearly is not in their views; and if it is not simply biochemically determined, which it also is not, in their views, then it would seem fair to ask them as behavior scientists to at least speculate about the causes. Contrast this to Lowenthal's approach, where the social-psychological meaning of the structural transitions and the role gains and losses can be made clear in clinical and learning theory terms. (In all fairness, though, this may be too facile. The concepts may be clear, but lack explanatory power. Lowenthal does not have a "developmental theory" in the usual sense.)

"Ages and Stages"

Does this bring reminiscences of the 1920s in developmental psychology? It may be that the field of adult development is similar to child development some fifty years ago in its exploration of age-linked developmental sequences. And, like child development then, it is in real danger from pop culture renderings of "life stages," from the public seizing on the idea of age-linked stages of development, such as the "male mid-life crisis," just

---

7. Neugarten says, "This isn't quite what I think. Changes *can* be triggered by outside events, but the outside event isn't a sufficient explanation of personality change. The problem is a semantic and conceptual one, since 'personality' is such a poorly-defined term. But in my view there are changes which result from accumulated life experiences—some of these experiences are role changes, some are not. And personality changes can't be said to be 'caused' by any one type of thing." (Personal communication)

as it seizes on astrology and tea-leaf reading. Certainly, the evidence does not justify linkage of crises either to stages, or to specific ages, during the mid-life period.

Considering "stages" first, in a succinct analysis Kohlberg (1973) states the distinction between three concepts of stages, namely, those consisting of age-linked social roles or developmental tasks; those consisting of biological maturational stages; and third, a structural concept which is more advanced and sophisticated. In regard to the latter he says, after Piaget, that:

1. Stages imply distinct or qualitative differences which still serve the same basic function at various points in this development (e.g., modes of thinking in relation to intelligence).
2. These different structures form an invariant sequence, order or succession in individual development. While cultural factors may speed up, slow down, or stop development, they may not change its sequence.
3. Each of these different and sequential modes form a "structured whole."
4. Stages are hierarchical integrations. Accordingly, higher stages displace (or, rather, reintegrate) the structures found at lower stages.

The characteristics of stages just mentioned, while defined by structural theory, are amenable to research examination. We can ask, "are they qualitative changes in adulthood forming an invariant sequence in any socio-cultural environment, which form a generalized structured whole and which hierarchically relate to earlier qualitative developmental changes." (p. 498)

Now, none of the major theorists under discussion advance a theory of stages in the true structural sense just described. Levinson's work deals with the psycho-social periods in the development of men from age 18 to 45, and these are: leaving the family; getting into the adult world; age 30 transition; settling down; mid-life transition; and restabilization—entry into middle adulthood. The important view of the developmental sequence is that it starts early, and one cannot understand the mid-life transition, or the advent of any crisis, as a stage in the developmental history without knowing the position one is in vis-a-vis the prior stages. He says one must remember that it has not all been smooth up to that point of age 40, from adolescence on, for there have been four intervening stages to work through with varying degrees of success. At this point it is too early to say more than that the stages that he postulates are intriguing, and that biographical analyses to be presented in the forthcoming volume will attempt to link the stages to each other, so that we can see if the theoretical case is convincing. Levinson writes, "Kohlberg's view of stages does not hold either for me or for Erikson. I explicitly do *not* present the psychosocial developmental periods in adulthood as forming a hierarchical progression. They are more in the metaphor of seasons in the year: they follow an invariant order and each can be seen as arising out of the previous one and leading to the next one, but they do not differ in value and all are necessary" (Note 6).

Considering "ages" now, three types of evidence do not support the existence of age-specific crises. The first is the epidemiological. Probably the fundamental symptom of a mid-life crisis is depression. As David Hamburg notes, the usual presenting symptoms or "depressive equivalents" are physical complaints, and verbal self-descriptions involving hopelessness, helplessness and worthlessness. He observes that these characteristics of depression set it off from the "ubiquitous sad moods" of day-to-day life which are not incapacitating, and from "grief experiences" which focus on a temporary loss—but do not necessarily correlate with any personality change or crisis. Studies of the incidence of depression find it high in adolescence and common again in mid-life, but with no age specificity.

As for the secondary symptoms themselves, such as the attempts by men at self-medication for depression, with alcohol—or chronic fatigue, loss of energy, impotence, agitation, social withdrawal—a recent review by Morton Kramer (Note 7) for the SSRC Committee on Work and Personality in the Middle Years summarizing mid-life epidemiological data does not show any specific ages of high incidence within the mid-life passage, e.g., the 8 million alcoholics and the 25 million heavy drinkers in the United States show no notable age clustering throughout the male middle years.

Secondly, clinical data and inferences from fiction or biography cannot document age links. While there certainly are many novels, many personal protocols, they are not admissible because of the missing cases. The data simply demonstrate that some males at the age of 40 report for others, or themselves, a mid-life crisis. Maybe most 40 year olds do not have this experience; maybe more 50 year olds do.

Nor do we have, thirdly, any set of major field studies linking personality crisis to chronological age. On the one hand, Neugarten and colleagues do not believe in age-specific changes, and moreover, report that when attempts were made to operationalize concepts of ego development or concepts of psychological crises, subject differences were not age related. In the near future though, this picture may change because of forthcoming publication of national survey data in which specific attention is given to relationships between age and the sense of loss of personal control over one's life. Two still unpublished studies by Gerald Gurin and Patricia Gurin at the Institute of Social Research (Ann Arbor, Michigan), and by Daniel Yankelovich, Inc. (New York City) show a decline in the sense of personal control beginning about age 50 to 55. More such studies will be valuable in our understanding of age-linked crises.

In Conclusion

Six statements seem to me to follow from this brief review:

First, the mid-life male is likely to be undergoing some profound personality changes.

Second, these changes will have more than one cause, along the lines delineated above.

Third, a "male mid-life crisis" will occur for some men if there are multiple, simultaneous demands for personality change; if, for instance, during the same month or year the man throws off his last illusions about great success; accepts his children for what they are; buries his father and his mother and yields to the truth of his mortality; recognizes that his sexual vigor and, indeed, interest, are declining, and even finds relief in the fact.

Fourth, these challenges may be stretched out over ten or twenty years. Some men are obsessed about their achievements, but not yet confronting the fact of death; other men are sharply disappointed in their children's personalities but not yet concerned about sexual potency. The events come early for some men, much later for others. There is no evidence that they are related to chronological age in any but the most general sense, e.g., "sometime during the forties."

Fifth, there is as yet no evidence either for developmental periods or "stages" in the mid-life period, in which one event must come after another, or one personality change brings another in its wake. The existence of "stages," if proved true, would be a powerful concept in studying mid-life; meanwhile there is a danger of our using this facile scheme as a cover for loose thinking about human development, without carrying forward the necessary hard-headed analyses of the evidence.

Sixth, the "growing pains" of mid-life, like those of youth and of old age, are transitions from one comparatively steady state to another, and these changes, even when they occur in crisis dimensions, bring for many men more happiness than they had found in younger days.

Notes

1. Hamburg, D. A., & Hamburg, B. Occupational stress, endocrine changes, and coping behavior in the middle years of adult life. Unpublished paper, 1974.
2. Levinson, D. J. Personal communication, July 2, 1975.
3. Levinson, D. J. Personal communication, July 2, 1975.
4. Social Science Research Council. Description of proposed activities, Committee on Work and Personality in the Middle Years. New York, June, 1973.
5. Boedecker, A. The impact of career success or failure on the male mid-life crisis: A proposal for research on adult development. Unpublished paper, Pennsylvania State University.

6. Levinson, D. J. Personal communication, July 2, 1975.
7. Kramer, M., & Redick, R. W. Epidemiological indices in the middle years. Unpublished paper.

References

Bakke, E. W. *The unemployed worker*. New Haven: Yale University Press, 1940.

Bergler, E. *The revolt of the middle aged man*. New York: Grosset & Dunlap, 1967.

Bissell, R. *Still circling Moose Jaw*. New York: McGraw-Hill, 1965.

Buhler, C. The curve of life as studied in biographies. *Journal of Applied Psychology*, 1935, 19, 405–409.

Chinoy, E. *Automobile workers and the American dream*. New York: Doubleday, 1955.

Clausen J. The life course of individuals. In M. W. Riley, M. Johnson, & A. Foner (Eds.), *Aging and society* (Vol. III). New York: Russell Sage Foundation, 1972.

Coleman, R., & Neugarten, B. L. *Social status in the city*. San Francisco: Jossey-Bass, 1971.

Ely, D. *Seconds*. New York: Signet Books, 1963.

Erikson, E. *Childhood and society*. New York: W. W. Norton, 1950.

Frank, J. *Persuasion and healing*. New York: Schocken Books, 1963.

Frenkel-Brunswik, E. Adjustments and reorientation in the course of the life-span. In B. Neugarten (Ed.), *Middle age and aging*. Chicago: University of Chicago Press, 1968.

Gutmann, D. The country of old men: Cross-cultural studies in the psychology of later life. In W. Donahue (Ed.), *Occasional papers in gerontology*. Ann Arbor: University of Michigan, 1969.

Havighurst, R., Munnichs, J. M., Neugarten, B., & Thomae, H. *Adjustment to retirement: A cross-national study*. Assen, Netherlands: Van Gorcum & Co., 1969.

Heller, J. Something happened. *New York Times Book Review*, October 6, 1974, p 1.

Hills, L. R. *How to retire at 41*. New York: Doubleday, 1973.

Jaques, E. Death and the mid-life crisis. *International Journal of Psychoanalysis*, 1965, 4, 502–514.

Jung, C. G. *Modern man in search of a soul*. New York: Harcourt, Brace, & World, 1933.

Kohlberg, L. Stages and aging in moral development: Some speculations. *Gerontologist*, 1973, 13, 497–502.

Kohn, M. L. *Class and conformity: A study in values*. Homewood, Illinois: Dorsey Press, 1969.

Kuhlen, R. G. Developmental changes in motivation during the adult years. In J. E. Birren (Ed.), *Relations of development and aging*. Springfield, Illinois: Charles C. Thomas, 1964, 209–264.

Lear, M. W. Is there a male menopause? *New York Times Magazine*, January 28, 1973.

Leggett, J. *The Gloucester branch*. New York: Harper & Row, 1964.

LeShan, E. *The wonderful crisis of middle age*. New York: David McKay, 1973.

Lowenthal, J. F., & Chiriboga, D. Social stress and adaptations: Toward a life-course perspective. In C. Eisdorfer & M. P. Lawton (Eds.), *Psychology of adult development and aging*. Washington, D.C.: American Psychological Association, 1973, 281–310.

Lowenthal, M. F., Thurnher, M., Chiriboga, D., & Associates. *Four stages of life: A comparative study of women and men facing transitions*. San Francisco: Jossey-Bass, 1975.

Mann, J. *Changing human behavior*. New York: Charles Scribner's Sons, 1965.

Neugarten, B. L. (Ed.). *Middle age and aging: A reader in social psychology*. Chicago: University of Chicago Press, 1968.

Neugarten, B. L. Dynamics of transition to old age. *Journal of Geriatric Psychiatry*, 1970, 4, 71–87.

Neugarten, B. L. Personality change in late life: A developmental perspective. In C. Eisdorfer & M. P. Lawton (eds.), *Psychology of adult development and aging.* Washington, D.C.: American Psychological Association, 1973, 311–335.

Neugarten, B. L., & Associates. *Personality in middle and late life.* New York: Atherton Press, 1964.

Neugarten, B. L., & Datan, N. Sociological perspectives on the life cycle. In P. B. Baltes & K. W. Schaie (Eds.), *Life-span developmental psychology: Personality and socialization.* New York: Academic Press, 1973, 53–69.

Neugarten, B. L. & Datan, N. The middle years. In S. Arieti (Ed.), *American handbook of psychiatry.* New York: Basic Books, 1974.

O'Neill, N., & O'Neill, G. *Shifting gears.* New York: E. M. Evans, 1974.

Pitkin, W. B. *Life begins at forty.* New York: Whittlesey House, McGraw-Hill, 1932.

Shaw, I. The eighty yard run. In C. Grayson (Ed.), *New stories for men.* New York: Doubleday, 1941.

Soddy, K. *Men in middle life.* New York: Lippincott, 1967.

Stern, R. *Other men's daughters.* New York: E. P. Dutton, 1973.

Stevenson, R. L. *The strange case of Dr. Jekyll and Mr. Hyde.* New York: J. H. Sears & Co., 1922.

Terkel, S. *Hard times.* New York: Pantheon, 1970.

Thurnher, M. Goals, values, and the life evaluations at the pre-retirement stage. *Journal of Gerontology,* 1974, 29, 85–96.

Vendler, H. Review of Allen Ginsburg's book, *The fall of America. New York Times Book Review,* February, 1974.

Vorspan, A. *Mazel Tov! You're middle-aged.* New York: Doubleday, 1974.

The Graying
of American Families

Changing Patterns of Aging
and Family Bonds in Later Life*
Beth B. Hess and Joan M. Waring

A critical review of demographic trends and the research literature suggests a transition from relationships based upon obligation to those voluntarily assumed and maintained by aged parents and their adult offspring.

■   Family sociology has gained in sophistication from developments in related disciplines. For example, research by historians of the family has put to rest, at last, the "classical family of Western nostalgia" (Goode, 1963). Unfortunately, this mythical family does not rest in peace, but inhabits the consciousness of the general public with a wondrous tenacity.

The use of the cohort analysis in the study of social change or continuity directs attention to the changing characteristics of specific age cohorts or generations not only as they move through their life course but

"Changing Patterns of Aging and Family Bonds in Later Life" by Beth B. Hess and Joan M. Waring from THE FAMILY COORDINATOR, vol. 27, October 1978. Copyright © 1978 by the National Council on Family Relations. Reprinted by permission.

*Adapted from a more extensive essay, Parent and child in later life: Rethinking the relationship. In R. M. Lerner & G. B. Spanier (Eds.), *Child influences on marital and family interaction: A life span perspective.* New York: Academic, 1978.

also among successive cohorts in a particular society. Both foci warn us against generalizations regarding parent-child relations as fixed. Intergenerational relationships must be studied in historical context, especially in terms of the linkages between family and other institutional spheres as these undergo continual change.

While we may never disabuse the general public of the notion that there once was a time in which the extended family reigned supreme—and, more importantly, that mutual respect and satisfaction governed adult child/aged parent interaction—we must, as family sociologists and practitioners, take an unromanticized view of intergenerational relations at the distal end of the life course. The question usually asked of this topic is "how can such bonds be strengthened?" The one we propose here is "why have any such bonds persisted?"

The modern family is characterized by choice: whom to marry, where to live, how to earn a living, how many children to bear, and, increasingly, how to conduct interpersonal relations and allocate tasks within the nuclear family. As we move from the family of obligatory ties to one of voluntary bonds, relationships outside the nuclear unit similarly lose whatever normative certainty or consistency governed them at earlier times. For example, sibling relationships today are almost completely voluntary, subject to disruption through occupational and geographic mobility, as, indeed, it might be said of marriage itself. Is this also to be the fate of parent-offspring ties in later life? There are many indicators of growing distance between generations, especially so in later life. There are also clues to enduring qualities of the parent/child bond. We shall examine the most important of these forces—centripetal and centrifugal—at both the societal and familial levels.

Societal Level Processes

Social-Historical Change

Family studies often have concentrated exclusively on the effects of world-wide social trends for young people. Goode's (1963) influential analysis of the "world revolution" in family systems is, for example, basically concerned with the freedom of younger generations, although he does make note of the potential dysfunctions for older family members. But a change in one part of a system has ramifications for other parts; thus, if respect for parents and the obligation to care for elders once was based upon their control of resources, reinforced by religious tradition and normative sanction, then the increasing ability of younger members to determine their own fates in marriage and in work must necessarily reduce the power of elders to demand filial piety. Nonetheless, filial responsibility is often mandated in the law, if not fully realized in practice (Schorr, Note 1; Brody, 1970, for a decade comparison).

The choices which we consider our birthright and that of our children, today, are at the expense of claims on care from our offspring many decades later. Recognition of this dilemma may be one of the compelling forces behind another trend in modern nation states—toward the public assumption of responsibility for income maintenance and primary health care of the aged. In many developed countries, transportation, housing and recreation have also been provided through allocation of societal rather than familial resources. The trade-off is evident: removing claims from the inter-personal system achieves the same aims which Weber (1958) suggests for bureaucracy over nepotism.

Considerations of kinship give way to impersonal but theoretically fairer mechanisms of allocation, "without fear or favor." Although the politically conservative might perceive a usurpation of family obligations, these trends in no way preclude high levels of kin caring for those families willing and able to do so. Yet public programs do ensure that all old people will be taken care of, albeit minimally in many cases, thus removing a financial (and often emotional) burden from both generations. Intergenerational hostility will most likely be muted by transposing this issue to the societal level, so that family ties are strengthened rather than attenuated: an extremely difficult concept to convey to members of a society which idealizes family life. To the extent that practitioners and educators share the public value orientation that families should take care of their own, the myth of the extended family will continue to generate unnecessary levels of guilt among middle-aged children, and resentment among their parent(s).

Cohort Differences

The model for cohort analysis follows the life course of successive birth aggregates, thus allowing us to distinguish (though never perfectly) historical from biographical from aging effects. Several points are immediately apparent: at any one historical moment, cohorts are of different ages. At the same ages, each is in a different historical epoch. And closer analysis will indicate that cohorts vary in their original composition, in fertility and mortality, in life course experiences such as educational and occupational opportunities, and ultimately in the needs and resources they bring to old age.

Before comparing today's oldest cohorts (those 65+) with those of their offspring, we should note the overriding significance of one *similarity:* aged parents and their children are both adults. This means, first, that they are to be considered status equals; and, second, that each is the product of decades of living outside the daily orbit of the other. Moreover, in our society, primary loyalties in adulthood are to the conjugal rather than the consanguine bond. Parent-child relationships in later life are, for the most part, negotiated from positions of independence vis-à-vis the other, and may, during adulthood, actually resemble those of friendship formation and maintenance, what Goode (1963) refers to as "ascriptive friendships," more than the family model of earlier stages with its imbalance in power and emotional dependencies. In extreme old age or illness, of course, the parent may be placed in a position of dependence upon a caretaking offspring, a "role reversal" often difficult for both parties to accept or enact appropriately (Blau, 1973; Simos, 1970). In this respect, Arling (1976) found that friendships are even more important than contacts with grown children for high morale in old age, and for precisely the reasons we suggest: cohort and life stage differences between generations, and intra-cohort similarities.

Age and Life Stage Differences

Differences in age mean differences in life stage concerns and exigencies, which, for example, are reflected in considerations of *life space.* The middle-aged male in our society is often portrayed as overburdened with commitments to family, work and community. Many are caught in a "life-cycle squeeze" when earnings have peaked while expenses continue to rise, especially if there are college-age children to be educated (Oppenheimer, 1974).

Goode (1960) has analyzed the "role strain" arising from simultaneous demands placed on status-incumbents by role partners, and Brim (1976) speaks of a male "mid-life crisis" as social, economic and biological stresses accumulate. At this point, to deal also with the needs of an aging parent for time, energy, care or financial assistance can only exacerbate the strain. Typically, the beleaguered male could delegate kinkeeping tasks to his wife, freed of her own child-rearing responsibilities, and considered to be the family specialist in interpersonal relations. But no more may she be thus taken for granted. College enrollment (U.S. Dept. of Labor, Note 2) and labor force participation rates of middle-aged women have risen dramatically in the past decade (U.S. Dept. of Labor, Note 3). It is possible that her plans remain somewhat tentative, however, inhibited by the knowledge that an ailing parent or adult child experiencing some setback may require her attention.

Conversely, the aged parents experience a constriction of life space— a spouse or friends die, work-place contacts are given up, neighborhoods are less hospitable than before, energies flag, the body becomes recalcitrant. Needs increase as resources decline. Schooled in independence and self-sufficiency, it is difficult for many old people to place demands upon adult children, especially if they are aware that such needs will conflict with those of grandchildren. Once again, intergenerational tensions are reduced by shifting the offspring's responsibility from the filial to the citizen role. By the same token, with the state rather than the family as caretaker, the recipient of retirement income and health care can define such entitlements as a right of citizenship. However, as one anonymous referee of this paper noted, we are assuming continuing expansion of the economy. Under conditions of contraction and scarcity, the maintenance of nucleated households becomes problematic, with what we would predict to be very stressful outcomes in many cases (including increased incidence of "parent abuse" [Steinmetz, Note 4]).

Differences in Cohorts as Populations

The two age groups of interest here also vary greatly in original composition. Among those who are older Americans today are large numbers of foreign-born, or individuals who grew up on farms and villages here as well as abroad, with less than high school education and a high probability of relatively low-skill employment. Many may have lingering expectations of intrafamily caretaking (Seelbach & Sauer, Note 5), while others are ill adapted to coping with urban life (Lopata, 1973). But most will have internalized the great American virtues of independence and self-reliance, and consider making a home with an adult child only as last resort (Riley & Foner, 1968; National Council on Aging, Note 6; Sussman, Vanderwyst & Williams, Note 7) yet would call for assistance upon a child rather than a friend or neighbor (Berghorn, Schaefer, Steere & Wisemen, 1977).

Their children, on the other hand, are primarily native-born, at least high school educated, beneficiaries of an expanding economy in the post-war era, and exemplars of urban or suburban family life. Where the older generation had experienced uprootedness, the Great Depression and other social instabilities of the 1930's, with a consequent low fertility rate, their offspring knew the Depression only as youngsters, and came to adulthood in time to participate in the Second World War, to enjoy the benefits of the GI Bill for further education, to marry and proceed to produce a bumper crop of infants, and to take advantage of the opportunities for geographic and occupational mobility which characterized their young adulthood.

When these mature adults reach old age in the coming decades they will have greater resources—personal and economic—than do their parents for coping with social change, the bureaucracy, and their own physical decrements. Further, they will have more children for whatever benefits can be derived from intergenerational contact. It would seem from the foregoing that a very large "generation gap" could exist between these cohorts today, potentially wider than that between these middle-aged parents and their own young adult children.

As demographic aggregates, birth cohorts not only vary in the characteristics just noted, but also in terms of original size, fertility and differential mortality. The size of any cohort is determined by three processes: fertility, mortality and migration, and all three of these have changed dramatically throughout this century. The experience of cohort members will vary accordingly—family size, dependency ratios, mobility opportunities, life expectancy and probability of institutionalization in old age are contingencies which ultimately affect individual lives (Waring, 1975).

The relative size of age cohorts exerts one of its most obvious effects on the ratios of wage earners to "dependents," namely children and the aged. As already mentioned, today's middle aged are small in number with many children and surviving parents. Cohorts differ in life expectancy at various ages, and in the sex ratio of these survivors, with female life expectancy continuing to diverge from that of males even as life styles are converging. The probability today is that the "dependent" older population as a whole will remain a constant 10–11% through the remainder of this century. But when the "baby boom" contingent reaches old age in the next century, proportions of old people will rise to 15–17% in the 2020's and 2030's (Seigel, Note 8). These shifting percentages place differential burdens on family members and on the society as a whole, but they also translate into political influence as well as the possibility of intergenerational conflict.

And lastly, the process of aging itself has changed over time—the ages at which roles are assumed or relinquished, health and income status, and self definitions. When is one "old," what is it to be old, how does one behave as an older person? Members of different cohorts will answer these questions differently, largely as a consequence of the cohort's experience and current situation. With respect to family interaction in later life, the primary question is "what are the appropriate modes of relating across generations?" Once the query is posed, the lack of a simple ready answer is striking. It is in this sense that we speak of a shift from obligatory to voluntary bonds, to a set of relationships which depend upon mutual initiative and persistence. The contact must be rewarding in some fashion for both parties to agree to its maintenance over time. Not only is the family context changed, but so are aging and old people. One might well reverse the theme of this volume and discuss "The Family in a Changing Context of Aging."

Family Level Processes

Factors Which Inhibit Generational Contacts

While residential and social mobility have not staunched the flow of help between generations, they have contributed to generating "distance" between adult children and their aged parents (Adams, 1970; but cf. Glasser & Glasser, 1962). It is noteworthy that four-fifths of all old parents live within easy visiting range of one child, but these researchers seldom tell us how many children live near their parents. Opportunities for helping may also decline because there is no need to call upon kin for *basic maintenance* (although socioemotional needs remain). That is, Social Security, Medicare and other programs free the older generation from potential dependency or even intimations of material need. Moreover, large numbers of old people value greatly their independence, preferring to live alone until they can no longer do so. There are no more grounds for assuming that older parents wish to live with their adult children than for believing that the middle aged regularly "dump" unwanted parents into institutions.

If parent-child interaction in later life resembles more the process of friendship than that of earlier intrafamily relations, relying upon similarities of values and attitudes leading to liking and the wish for more contact, i.e., homophily (Lazarsfeld & Merton, 1954; Hess, 1972), then the kinds of age and cohort differences discussed above should operate to reduce agreement and attraction between generations. Nonetheless, many similarities result from family socialization and stability of socioeconomic status within the lineage. Extent of value agreement might differentiate those children who maintain contact from those who do not, but much of our data is biased by not having measures from all family members.

Another source of intergenerational tension, rarely mentioned in the gerontological literature, are the residues of those earlier conflicts which dominate studies of childhood and adolescence. Can relationships originally founded on disparities of power easily evolve into those based upon mutual respect? What of the rivalries and hostilities engendered during the oedipal phase? And, as the aged parent experiences the inevitable decrements of old age, how graciously can the adult child assume the "parental" role of caretaking? Injunctions to "filial maturity" (Blenkner, 1965; Troll, 1971) notwithstanding, the barriers are considerable (Simos, 1970; Kent & Matson, 1972; Miller, Bernstein & Sharkey, 1975; Clark & Anderson, 1967). Contrary to public perception, most adult offspring make every effort to maintain a declining parent in the community (and often in the child's home) before seeking institutionalization (Riley &

Foner, 1968). Such efforts are at the expense of alternative investments of time and energy and finances, which cannot be entirely void of resentment, although ameliorated by a sense of sacrifice in having "honored thy father and mother,"[1] and, in many cases, thy mother-in-law as well.

These various sources of intergenerational distance probably "explain" the trend toward independent residence and the repeated assertions of old people that they prefer it that way. The percentage of aged parents making a home with an adult offspring has steadily declined, while the proportions living as one person households has risen commensurately (Kobrin, 1976; Siegel, Note 8). Thus, when an old person does move in with the child, she or he is apt to be quite ancient, frail or disoriented. There is, understandably, some ambivalence on the part of the adult offspring to undertake such a responsibility (Wake & Sporakowski, 1972; Fendetti & Gelfand, 1976; Sussman, Vanderwyst & Williams, Note 7).

A final consideration in this section has to do with transitions. Later life is characterized by a number of status passages, most of a decremental nature: post-parenthood, retirement, widowhood. While presenting opportunities for personal growth, these are also periods of difficult adjustment. Those undergoing transition often look to other family members for support in managing the strains of relinquishing an old role and learning a new one. But often family members are disappointing sources of support, absorbed as they are in their own problems. For example, both generations may be undergoing difficult transitions simultaneously, as when a parent reaches retirement at the same time the offspring faces an empty nest. Or both could be responding to the same loss in different ways, as when the death of a spouse for the parent is also the death of a parent for the child. In addition, an event may require of role partners a "counterpart transition," whereby family members must learn to relate to the other in terms of the new role, not always an easy task (Riley & Waring, 1976). Such complex demands may prevent meeting the needs of the other; but, on the other hand, becoming a source of strength to one another should help both in dealing with personal loss. This is illustrative of Erikson's (1959) discussion of "self-absorption" vs. "generativity," in which reaching out to help the other is defined as the "positive" outcome. It is characteristic of the later years that there are many such challenges and that some of these will strain the bonds between family members (Waring, Note 9). For example, remarriage of the parent often leads to generational strain—from fears of losing an inheritance, inability to perceive the parent as sexually active, or beliefs

---

1. We are indebted to Mildred Seltzer for pointing out that this injunction itself suggests that people needed to be reminded, under extreme sanction, of their duties—an ideal rather than a reflection of intergenerational relations in the earliest historical societies as well as contemporary ones.

that he or she is being exploited. Once the remarriage has taken place, however, the offspring typically appreciate its positive aspects (McKain, 1972; Treas & Van Hilst, Note 10).

We have discussed some of the more obvious elements tending to inhibit intergenerational contacts: mobility, declining opportunities for helping, age and cohort differences in attitudes and values, psychological barriers to closeness, desires for independence, and difficulties in coping with life-course transitions. In the absence of any pressing need to maintain the relationship, how are these impediments overcome by so many—and why?

Factors Which Enhance Intergenerational Bonds

It has been argued by anthropologists that the giving of a gift or favor obligates the recipient to return something of equal value, generating social ties among individuals and groups (Levi-Strauss, 1964). Gouldner (1960) speaks of the Norm of Reciprocity, and Sussman (1976) of an implicit bargain struck with parents during the years of the infant's dependency. The parental investment in the child's survival does create, at some level, a sense of obligation on the part of the child when grown to care for an ailing parent. Guilt and anxiety over one's performance as a dutiful offspring operate as a form of social control (Simos, 1970). The reactions of others—siblings, social work and medical personnel, neighbors, friends—reinforce the norms of filial piety.

Solidarity within lineages is supported by many aspects of socialization: the transmission of values across the generations, moral and religious upbringing, role modeling, and the continued flow of information among members of different age groups. There are powerful forces toward congruence, if not complete agreement, in value orientation within families (Troll, 1971; Bengtson, 1975; Jacobsen, Berry & Olsen, 1975; Hill, 1970; Kalish & Johnson, 1972; Bengtson & Acock, Note 11). However, some of this apparent harmony may be an artifact of selective perception or lack of data from offspring not in contact with parents. Bengtson and Kuypers (1971) suggest that some distortion arises from the "developmental stake" which old people have in minimizing value disagreement but which junior members of the family will emphasize in order to preserve their self-image as unique. Yet despite the many real and apparent potentials for value dissonance, most families appear to have developed a "tent of values" (Jacobsen, Berry & Olsen, 1975) under which members can meet, enjoy one another's company, share a consciousness of sameness and sense of responsibility for one another.

Socialization involves both direct transmission of expectations for behavior and the indirect learning which is conveyed through role modeling. For example, middle-aged parents caring for an aged relative can hope their own children will observe, record and repeat this behavior in due time, as protection against abandonment in their old age. As a socializing force, role modeling in later life cuts both ways. The aged parent is often coping with situations which will one day be the lot of the adult child, and the latter is attempting to demonstrate ways of gracious aging for the older parent to emulate (e.g., staying youthful). The role modeling efforts of both are complicated by the fact that there are few appropriate role models from previous generations regarding how to grow old or be old.

The exchange of visits and gifts across generations also serves to connect and reaffirm the viability of a lineage. The two- and three-way transfer of gifts, advice, help in emergencies, goods and services is amply documented (Sussman, 1976; Riley & Foner, 1968; Hill, 1970; Cantor, 1975; National Council on Aging, Note 6; Jackson, 1972). There is a "family network" if not precisely a "modified extended family," and it is based upon *voluntary* exchanges, with the amount and direction of flow affected by the relative resources at the disposal of generations. Among the inner city poor, for example, aged parents receive material support from adult children in return for services such as baby sitting or advice (Cantor, Note 12). In more affluent lineages, money and goods are distributed from the oldest generation downward through gifts and inheritance, while the younger members reciprocate with visits and services (Sussman, Cates & Smith, 1970). Two caveats are in order: (a) most adult children (a majority in a recent Social Security Administration survey [Murray, Note 13]) provide no material support to parents, and (b) there is no *necessary* relationship between these expressions of solidarity and positive affect (Arling, 1976; Brown, 1969; Berghorn et al., 1977), although some have found such a link (e.g., Adams, 1975; Medley, 1976). A respect for privacy and tactful assessment of the relationship may well govern visiting patterns (Aldous, 1967; Stinnett, Collins & Montgomery, 1970).

Nor can we assume that those who voluntarily establish multi-generation households do so without strain. To the contrary, when independent households are preferred by old and young (see above), sharing a home is a "last resort"—literally—and those who do so may not be in the best of health or spirits. On the other hand, when undertaken out of genuine affection as a freely chosen and well thought-out alternative, multi-generation living can be mutually beneficial (e.g., Lynn, 1976). We would expect that such arrangements in the future will be of this nature, given the characteristics of incoming cohorts of old people already noted. For this cohort, however, practitioners should be aware of the peculiar historical circumstances which have shaped the needs and resources of members of both adult generations.

While some of the tasks which traditionally linked generations have become attenuated or obsolete, Kreps (1977) and others in the volume by

Shanas and Sussman (1977) have noted the development of a new set of functions for family members: negotiating the bureaucracy and supervising the terminal phases of life. The adult offspring become the guides and interpretors of the administratively arcane, interceding on behalf of the aged parent, securing entitlements, and ultimately making judgments regarding institutionalization and heroic efforts at preserving life. The impersonal must ultimately be made personal. How ironic if this should be the source of a new-found closeness between parent and child in later life. Yet this may be precisely where educators and practitioners could also intercede effectively, offering support and proferring understanding.

Intergenerational Relations and Later Life Satisfaction

Given these varied sources of strain and solidarity at both the societal and interpersonal levels, our frank conclusion is that few conclusive statements can be made at this time. Not that we lack research but that there are no clear-cut patterns readily discernable yet. There are simply (or not so simply) too many vissicitudes to take into account. It would appear logical to state that elderly parents with many offspring should have greater resources for later life satisfaction than do those with a limited supply of family, but the data are equivocal. Some parents with larger families, often the foreign-born with "extended expectations," will be disappointed at the unwillingness or inability of children to meet such claims (Lopata, 1973, 1976). Even when such expectations are met some will remain resentful at having to feel like "guests" in the child's home (Cosneck, 1970).

What, then, do adult children contribute to parental well-being in later life? This whole question is clouded by methodological considerations: studies vary greatly in their sampling techniques, the questions asked, and the measurements utilized. Above all, the problem of selective survival intrudes (Spanier, Lewis & Cole, 1975); the only people able and willing to answer such questions are the survivors of a birth cohort whose poorer, less educated, less healthy and perhaps less happy members have already died off. Studies of life satisfaction among the aged may simply be measuring the qualities which have allowed certain subgroups to survive to answer the questionnaire.

Thus, we find Medley (1976, p. 448) declaring that "satisfaction with family was found to make the greatest single impact on life satisfaction" of old people, while finances had no direct impact. Edwards and Klemmack (1973), on the other hand, found that SES washed out other effects; similarly, Spreitzer and Snyder (1974) pinpoint perceived health status (as well as financial position). Sears and Barbee (1977), studying Terman's sample of gifted women in their middle years, find that children are related to one measure of life satisfaction for some women, but that childfree career women do very well on a variety of aspects of life satisfaction (see also Campbell, Converse & Rodgers, 1976). With incoming cohorts of older women being higher than those now old on *both* fertility and work experience, we might predict that life satisfaction of older females will be enhanced. Since males still typically define themselves in terms of occupation rather than family roles, their life satisfaction in old age should be minimally affected by intergenerational resources, which is the finding of Watson and Kivett (1976).

Whether or not children add much more to life satisfaction than does health or financial status, we do know that the absence of family can often have deleterious effects. Old men without family ties are prime candidates for suicide, accidental death, alcoholism and other socially generated diseases (Gove, 1973; Bock & Webber, 1972). There is evidence that older females are somewhat preserved by their ability to seek out and maintain close friends when family ties have disintegrated (Hess, Note 14).

Regarding the relationship between non-family networks—neighborhood, friendship and voluntary association participation—and family integration the evidence is conflicting and complex (Hess, 1972). Some find integration into community life more related to friendship than to family networks (Spakes, Note 15), and others note that respondents living alone, without strong family ties or opportunity to play traditional family roles, tend to compensate through community activity (Trela & Jackson, Note 16; see also Rutzen, Note 17). This pattern of dependency on family vs. friends or neighbors was also found among old people in Kansas City: where relatives were nearby, especially children, one depended upon these when necessary, but where no children lived in the area, old people were likely to depend upon friends and neighbors when in need (Berghorn et al., 1977). The researchers relate these patterns to a cultural level aversion to dependency of any sort in our society, but when it does become necessary, dependency on children carried the least stigma, and may even be justified by invoking the norms of reciprocity and filial piety which are also part of the value system.

Still other studies show that persons with high levels of kin interaction are also high interactors with non-kin, and those with low rates of contact with relatives have similarly depressed investments in other social networks (Booth, 1972; Biesty, DiComo & Hess, Note 18; Croog, Lipson & Levine, 1972). Clearly, there is no simple relationship between family and other social networks: some people will be high or low interactors with anybody; others compensate for losses in one area with enhanced involvement in different groups. Such substitutability, however, may be governed by considerations of functional alternatives; that is, various networks operate to meet certain kinds of needs, so that there are limits to how these can be mixed and matched (Weiss, 1969; Litwak & Szelenyi,

1969). In some cases, moreover, integration into non-family social systems—friendships, voluntary associations, neighborhood, even senior centers—is preferable to total dependence upon a spouse, for if that one person should die the survivor is, indeed, bereft (Bock & Webber, 1972; Rutzen, Note 17).

Much as children and non-family associations add to the life satisfaction of some old people, there is considerable evidence that for those elderly with surviving spouses the marital relationship not only remains paramount but is enhanced by the children's leaving after adolescence. Possibly, there was nowhere for scores of marital satisfaction to go except up since families with adolescent children do show signs of stress (Burr, 1970; Rollins & Feldman, 1970; Renne, 1970; Smart & Smart, 1975; Gilford & Bengtson, Note 19; Miller, 1976). If the presence of teen-age children strains the resources and emotional energies of mid-life parents, postparenthood offers relief which is reflected in satisfaction scores (e.g., Neugarten, 1976). But an additional benefit of the absence of children is the potential for an increase in couple-companionate activities (Miller, 1976; Rollins & Cannon, 1974). The literature on postparental marriages indicates a turning again toward one another for companionship and psychic satisfaction often described as comparable to that of the honeymoon period. However, it must be noted that selective processes have been operating. These are not static relationships—the marriage and the partners themselves have changed over time; efforts at enrichment have been made, experiences shared, tolerance deepened. Couples unable to adapt or develop in these directions drop out of the data base via divorce, desertion or separation. The very poor, whose marital satisfaction is highly problematic, have lower life expectancy as well, further reducing the probability of their experiencing long-term intact marriages (Spanier, Lewis & Cole, 1975).

Not only will selective survival of certain marriages bias the findings on later life satisfaction, perceptual processes may further distort the data. Spanier, Lewis and Cole (1975) note that the longer a couple has remained together, the greater their investment in believing that the commitment has been worthwhile, the less likely to acknowledge threats, and the more apt to reduce dissonance by denying unhappiness. Whatever the forces at work, the end result seems to be that many marriages are strengthened by the departure of offspring, and that the conjugal relationship is enhanced and deepened at this time. For the couples who jointly survive, through middle age and later, there is also evidence of a "coming together" of personality traits among postparental spouses (Livson, Note 20): i.e., a relaxing of rigid sex role expectations and behaviors, and a growing acceptance of previously inappropriate tendencies such as nurturance for men and dominance by women (see also Lowenthal, Thurnher & Chiriboga, 1975; Brim, 1976; Neugarten, 1968; Clausen, 1972). A "mellowing"—in every sense of the word—seems to infuse these relationships as the spouses relax from the rigors of rearing children and striving for occupational success. Of course, many couples grow further apart at this stage if a shared interest in the children has been the only bond, but there is no clear evidence of a surge of divorces (Schoen, 1975).

Unfortunately, the facts of later life are that many older women will not be members of a conjugal unit. While widows seem to cope with loss of a spouse less lethally than do widowers, they do not share the high morale of still-marrieds. As with measures of life satisfaction and morale applied to postparental couples, the widowed are also affected by non-family variables such as health, education and income (Lopata, 1973; Chevan & Korson, 1972; Morgan, 1976; Cosneck, 1970; Adams, 1968). The role of children in the life space of a widowed parent can be minimal or all embracing as in the case of sharing a home, and there will be happy and unhappy old people in both categories. However, the existence of adult children with whom one could make a home *is* a hedge against institutionalization (Soldo & Myers, Note 21). We might speculate, however, that in the future, women who limit fertility or choose to remain childfree will also have high educational attainment, retirement incomes from life-time work, and out-going relationships in a variety of non-family systems, and thus reduce the differences in old-age resources between women with many children and those with few or none. In other words, the preservative value of children may become less marked as the life course of women changes.

Conclusion

We began our exploration of intergenerational relations in later life by asking a basic, if impertinent, question, "why do they persist?" We think that the evidence suggests that the maintenance and sustenance of the parent-child bond will be increasingly based upon the willingness of both parties to engage in supportive behaviors, and that this willingness, in turn, hinges on the quality of the relationship over many preceding decades. While guilt and shame will remain powerful motivators of filial performance, and the injunction to "honor thy father and mother" continues to shape our socialization to obligations toward aged parents, the actual course of contacts and the satisfactions derived from them will be subject to the same type of role negotiation characterizing other interpersonal relationships. As a consequence, such variables as basic trust, respect, shared values and beliefs, and genuine affection—the foundations of homophily—will increasingly determine parent/child relations in later life.

The foundation of such a relationship can, of course, be laid in the early years of infancy and childhood dependency, or fostered by the skill with which the generations negotiate an ultimate release from these dependencies. But it is also possible that parents and offspring who were never deeply affectionate at earlier life stages can develop a mutual respect and liking when both are freed from relations of superordination/subordination. Although much of the literature deals with a "special relationship" between older women and their adult daughters (Neugarten, 1968), we would guess that the adult male child might also find his father easier to talk to and get along with after leaving the parental home and become a "man" in his own right, free of the need to compete with the father on the latter's own ground.

Trends at both the societal and familial level support our contention that parent and child relations in later life are moving toward the voluntaristic model. Demographically, compared with those now old, incoming cohorts of old people will be more independent financially, better educated, with higher probabilities of joint survival after completion of parental tasks. In terms of attitudes toward family responsibilities, there is evidence that extended expectations are being replaced by minimal anticipations of care from one's children (Espenshade, Note 22; Yankelovich, Skelly & White, 1977).

Family life educators and practitioners, looking ahead, might speculate on what such changes portend. Our guesses are that older women, especially, will be affected by the trends noted above, and although widowhood will remain the fate of most, those qualities that enhance independent living and adaptation to loss will increasingly characterize their lives: education, work experience, financial security and lifelong involvement in non-family associations. As for older men, there is some evidence that family roles and leisure activities are encroaching on the time and energies previously expended in the occupational sphere. In old age, these men will have alternative sources of satisfaction, and, possibly, more companionate relationships with their wives than do men currently retired. Aging parents will not have to make demands upon the material or social resources of offspring, although many may do so. Adult children will be spared excruciating choices between the needs of their own children, themselves, and their parents. And those bonds which do persist will do so because they have been willingly sought and nurtured by adults who are authentically concerned with the well-being of one another. Far from disintegrating, the future of parent-child relations in later life may be characterized by the strongest ties of all: mutual respect.

Notes

1. Schorr, A. Filial responsibility in the modern American family. Social Security Administration, DHEW, USGPO, Washington, D.C. 20402, 1960.
2. U.S. Department of Labor. *Marital and family characteristics of the labor force, March,*

1975. Special Labor Force Report 183, Bureau of Labor Statistics, Washington, D.C., 1975.

3. U.S. Department of Labor. *Going back to school at 35 and over.* Special Labor Force Report 184, Bureau of Labor Statistics, Washington, D.C., 1975.

4. Steinmetz, S. *The politics of selective inattention: The case of parent abuse.* Unpublished working paper, University of Delaware, 1978.

5. Seelbach, W., & Sauer, W. *Filial responsibility expectations and morale among aged parents.* Paper presented at the annual meeting of the Gerontological Society, New York City, October, 1976.

6. National Council on the Aging. *The myth and reality of aging in America.* 1974.

7. Sussman, M. B., Vanderwyst, D., & Williams, G. K. *Will you still need me, will you still feed me when I'm 64?* Paper presented at the annual meeting of the Gerontological Society, New York City, October, 1976.

8. Siegel, J. S. *Demographic aspects of aging and the older population in the United States.* Current Population Reports, Special Studies, Series P–23, No. 59, USGPO, Washington, D.C. 20402: U.S. Department of Commerce, Bureau of the Census, May, 1976.

9. Waring, J. M. *Conflict between the middle aged and old: Why not?* Paper presented at the annual meeting of the American Sociological Association, San Francisco, August, 1975.

10. Treas, J., & Van Hilst, A. *Marriage and remarriage among the older population.* Paper presented at the annual meeting of the Gerontological Society, Louisville, 1975.

11. Bengtson, V. L. & Acock, A. C. *On the influence of mothers and fathers: A covariance analysis of political and religious socialization.* Paper presented at the annual meeting of the American Sociological Society, New York, August, 1976.

12. Cantor, M. *The configuration and intensity of the informal support system in a New York City elderly population.* Paper presented at the annual meeting of the Gerontological Society, New York, October, 1976.

13. Murray, J. *Family structure in the pre-retirement years.* (Retirement History Study Report #4.) U.S. Dept. HEW, Social Security Administration, Publication No. (SSA) 74–11700 USGPO, Washington, D.C. 20402, 1973.

14. Hess, B. B. *Age, gender role and friendship.* Paper presented at annual meeting of the Gerontological Society, New York, October, 1976.

15. Spakes, P. *Social integration, age, and family participation.* Paper presented at the annual meeting of the Gerontological Society, New York, October, 1976.

16. Trela, J. E., & Jackson, D. *Family life and substitutes in old age.* Paper presented at the annual meeting of the Gerontological Society, New York, 1976.

17. Rutzen, R. *Varieties of social disengagement among the aged: A research report on correlates of primary socialization.* Paper presented at the annual meeting of the Eastern Sociological Society, New York City, March, 1977.

18. Biesty, P., DiComo, W., & Hess, B. B. *The elderly of Morris County, New Jersey: Findings of a senior citizens assessment of needs (SCAN) survey.* Mimeo. Morristown, N.J., Area Agency on Aging, 1977.

19. Gilford, R., & Bengtson, V. L. *Measuring marital satisfaction in three generations: Positive and negative dimensions.* Paper presented at the Gerontological Society, New York, October, 1976.

20. Livson, F. B. *Coming together in the middle years: A longitudinal study of sex role convergence.* Paper presented at the annual meeting of the Gerontological Society, New York, October, 1976.

21. Soldo, B. J., & Myers, G. C. *The effects of total fertility on living arrangements among elderly women.* Paper presented at the annual meeting of the Gerontological Society, New York, October, 1976.

22. Espanshade, T. J. *The value and cost of children.* Bulletin of the Population Reference Bureau, Inc. Washington, D.C., **32,** 1977.

References

Adams, B. N. The middle-class adult and his widowed or still-married mother. *Social Problems,* 1968, 16, 50–59.

Adams, B. N. *The family: A sociological interpretation* (2nd ed.). Chicago: Rand McNally, 1975.

Adams, B. N. Isolation, function and beyond: American kinship in the 1960's. *Journal of Marriage and the Family,* 1970, 32, 575–597.

Aldous, J. Intergenerational visiting patterns: Variations in boundary maintenance as an explanation. *Family process,* 1967, 6, 235–251.

Arling, G. The elderly widow and her family, neighbors and friends. *Journal of Marriage and the Family,* 1976, 38, 757–768.

Bengtson, V. L., & Kuypers, J. A. Generational differences and the developmental stake. *Aging and Human Development,* 1971, 2, 249–260.

Bengtson, V. L. Generation and family effects in value socialization. *American Sociological Review,* 1975, 40, 358–371.

Berghorn, F. L., Schafer, D. E., Steere, G. H., & Wiseman, R. F. *The urban elderly: A study of life satisfaction.* Montclair, N.J.: Allenheld Osman, 1977.

Blau, Z. S. *Old age in a changing society.* New York: New Viewpoints, 1973.

Blenkner, M. Social work and family relationships in later life, with some thought on filial maturity. In E. Shanas & G. Streib (Eds.), *Social structure and the family: Generational relations.* Englewood Cliffs, N.J.: Prentice-Hall, 1965.

Bock, E. W., & Webber, I. L. Suicide among the elderly: Isolating widowhood and migrating alternatives. *Journal of Marriage and the Family,* 1972, 34, 24–31.

Booth, A. Sex and social participation. *American Sociological Review,* 1972, 37, 183–192.

Brim, O. G., Jr. Male mid-life crisis: A comparative analysis. In B. B. Hess (Ed.), *Growing old in America.* New Brunswick, N.J.: Transaction, 1976.

Brody, E. M. Congregate care facilities and mental health of the elderly. *Aging and Human Development,* 1970, 1, 279–321.

Brown, R. Family structure and social isolation of older persons. *Journal of Gerontology,* 1969, 15, 170–174.

Burr, W. R. Satisfaction with various aspects of marriage over the life cycle: A random middle class sample. *Journal of Marriage and the Family,* 1970, 32, 29–37.

Campbell, A., Converse, P. E., & Rodgers, W. L. *The quality of American life: Perceptions, evaluations and satisfactions.* New York: Russell Sage, 1976.

Cantor, M. Life space and the social support system of the inner city elderly of New York. *The Gerontologist,* 1975, 15, 23–27.

Chevan, A., & Korson, J. H. The widowed who live alone: An examination of social and demographic factors. *Social Forces,* 1972, 51, 45–52.

Clark, M., & Anderson, B. G. *Culture and aging.* Springfield, Ill.: Thomas, 1967.

Clausen, J. The life course of individuals. In M. W. Riley, M. Johnson, & A. Foner (Eds.), *Aging and society* (Vol. 3): *A sociology of age stratification.* New York: Russell Sage, 1972.

Cosneck, B. J. Family patterns of older widowed Jewish people. *The Family Coordinator,* 1970, 19, 368–373.

Croog, S. H., Lipson, A., & Levine, S. Help patterns in severe illness: the roles of kin network, non-family resources and institutions. *Journal of Marriage and the Family,* 1972, 34, 32–41.

Edwards, J. N., & Klemmack, D. L. Correlates of life satisfaction: A re-examination. *Journal of Gerontology,* 1973, 28, 497–502.

Erikson, E. Identity and the life cycle. In G. Klein (Ed.), *Psychological issues.* New York: International, 1959.

Fendetti, D. V., & Gelfand, D. E. Care of the aged: Attitudes of white ethnic families. *The Gerontologist,* 1976, 16, 545–549.

Glasser, P. H., & Glasser, L. N. Role reversal and conflict between aged parents and their children. *Marriage and Family Living,* 1962, 24, 46–51.

Goode, W. J. A theory of role strain. *American Sociological Review,* 1960, 25, 46–51.

Goode, W. J. *World revolution and family patterns.* New York: Free Press, 1963.

Gouldner, A. The norm of reciprocity: A preliminary statement. *American Sociological Review,* 1960, 25, 161–178.

Gove, W. Sex, marital status and mortality. *American Journal of Sociology.* 1973, 79, 45–67.

Hess, B. B. Friendship. In M. W. Riley, M. Johnson, & A. Foner (Eds.), *Aging and society* (Vol. 3): *A sociology of age stratification.* New York: Russell Sage, 1972.

Hill, R. *Family development in three generations.* Cambridge, Mass.: Schenkman, 1970.

Jackson, J. J. Marital life among aging blacks. *The Family Coordinator,* 1972, 21, 21–27.

Jacobsen, R. B., Berry, K. J., & Olsen, K. F. An empirical test of the generation gap: A comparative intrafamily study. *Journal of Marriage and the Family,* 1975, 37, 841–852.

Kalish, R. A., & Johnson, A. I. Value similarities and differences in three generations of women. *Journal of Marriage and the Family,* 1972, 34, 49–53.

Kent, D. P., & Matson, M. B. The impact of health on the aged family. *The Family Coordinator,* 1972, 21, 29–36.

Kobrin, F. E. The primary individual and the family: changes in living arrangements in the United States since 1940. *Journal of Marriage and the Family,* 1976, 38, 233–239.

Kreps, J. M. Intergenerational transfers and the bureaucracy. In E. Shanas & M. B. Sussman (Eds.), *Family, bureaucracy and the elderly.* Durham, N.C.: Duke, 1977.

Lazarsfeld, P. F., & Merton, R. K. Friendship as social process: A substantive and methodological inquiry. In M. Berger, T. Abel & C. H. Page (Eds.), *Freedom and control in modern society.* Princeton, N.J.: Van Nostrand, 1954.

Levi-Strauss, C. Reciprocity, the essence of social life. In R. L. Coser (Ed.), *The family: Its structure and functions.* New York: St. Martin's, 1964.

Litwak, E., & Szelenyi, I. Primary group structures and their functions: Kin, neighbors and friends. *American Sociological Review,* 1969, 34, 64–78.

Lopata, H. Z. *Widowhood in an American city.* Cambridge, Mass.: Schenkman, 1973.

Lopata, H. Z. *Polish Americans.* Englewood Cliffs, N.J.: Prentice-Hall, 1976.

Lowenthal, M. F., Thurnher, M., & Chiriboga, D. *Four stages of life.* San Francisco: Jossey-Bass, 1975.

Lynn, I. Three-generation household in the middle-class. In B. B. Hess (Ed.), *Growing old in America.* New Brunswick, N.J.; Transaction, 1976.

McKain, W. C. A new look at older marriages. *The Family Coordinator,* 1972, 21, 61–69.

Medley, M. L. Satisfaction with life among persons sixty-five and over. *Journal of Gerontology,* 1976, 31, 448–455.

Miller, B. C. A multivariate developmental model of marital satisfaction. *Journal of Marriage and the Family,* 1976, 38, 643–657.

Miller, M. B., Bernstein, H., & Sharkey, H. Family extrusion of the aged patient. *The Gerontoloqist,* 1975, 15, 291–296.

Morgan, L. A. A re-examination of widowhood and morale. *Journal of Gerontology,* 1976, 31, 687–695.

Neugarten, B. L. The awareness of middle age. In B. L. Neugarten (Ed.), *Middle age and aging.* Chicago, Ill.: University of Chicago, 1968.

Neugarten, B. L. Middle age and aging. In B. B. Hess (Ed.), *Growing Old in America.* New Brunswick, N.J.: Transaction, 1976.

Oppenheimer, V. K. Life cycle squeeze: The interaction of men's occupational and family life cycles. *Demography,* 1974, 11, 227–245.

Renne, K. S. Correlates of dissatisfaction in marriage. *Journal of Marriage and the Family,* 1970, 32, 54–67.

Riley, M. W., & Foner, A. *Aging and society* (Vol. 1): *An inventory of research findings.* New York: Russell Sage, 1968.

Riley, M. W., Johnson, M., & Foner, A. *Aging and society* (Vol. 3): *A sociology of age stratification.* New York: Russell Sage, 1972.

Riley, M. W., & Waring, J. J. Age and aging. In R. K. Merton & R. Nisbet (Eds.), *Contemporary social problems* (4th ed.). New York: Harcourt, 1976.

Rollins, B. C., & Feldman, H. Marital satisfaction over the family life cycle. *Journal of Marriage and the Family,* 1970, 32, 20–28.

Rollins, B. C., & Cannon, K. L. Marital satisfaction over the family life cycle: A re-evaluation. *Journal of Marriage and the Family,* 1974, 36, 271–282.

Schoen, B. California divorce rates by age at first marriage and duration of first marriage. *Journal of Marriage and the Family,* 1975, 37, 548–555.

Sears, P., & Barbee, A. H. Career and life satisfaction among Terman's gifted women. In J. Stanley, W. George & C. Solano (Eds.), *The gifted and the creative: Fifty year perspective.* Baltimore: Johns Hopkins, 1977.

Shanas, E., & Sussman, M. B. (Eds.) *Family, bureaucracy and the elderly.* Durham, N.C.: Duke, 1977.

Simos, B. G. Relations of adults with aging parents. *The Gerontologist,* 1970, 10, 135–139.

Smart, M. S., & Smart, R. C. Recalled, present and predicted satisfaction in stages of the family life cycle in New Zealand. *Journal of Marriage and the Family,* 1975, 37, 408–415.

Spanier, G. B., Lewis, R. A., & Cole, C. L. Marital adjustment over the family life cycle: The issue of curvilinearity. *Journal of Marriage and the Family,* 1975, 37, 263–275.

Spreitzer, E., & Snyder, E. Correlates of life satisfaction among the aged. *The Gerontologist,* 1974, 29, 454–458.

Stinnett, N., Collins, J., & Montgomery, J. E. Marital need satisfaction of husbands and wives. *Journal of Marriage and the Family,* 1970, 32, 428–434.

Sussman, M. B., Cates, J. N., & Smith, D. T. *The family and inheritance.* New York: Russell Sage, 1970.

Sussman, M. B. The family life of old people. In R. Binstock & E. Shanas (Eds.), *Handbook of aging and the social sciences.* New York: Van Nostrand, 1976.

Troll, L. E. The family of later life: A decade review. *Journal of Marriage and the Family,* 1971, 33, 263–290.

Wake, S. B., & Sporakowski, M. J. An intergenerational comparison of attitudes toward supporting aged parents. *Journal of Marriage and the Family,* 1972, 34, 42–48.

Waring, J. M. Social replenishment and social change: The problem of disordered cohort flow. *American Behavioral Scientist,* 1975, 19, 237–256.

Watson, J. A., & Kivett, V. R. Influences on the life satisfaction of older fathers. *The Family Coordinator,* 1976, 25, 482–488.

Weber, M. Bureaucracy. In H. H. Gerth & C. W. Mills, *From Max Weber.* New York: Oxford, 1958.

Weiss, R. S. The fund of sociability. *Transaction,* 1969, 6, 36–43.

Yankelovich, Skelly, & White, Inc. *Raising children in a changing society.* Minneapolis, Minn.: General Mills, 1977.

The Vanishing Grandmother
Dorothy-Anne Flor

Once, it was assumed that after grandfather died, grandmother would come to live with her offspring, pampering them, or harassing them, or both. The family tolerated her, but they never asked how she liked the arrangement . . .

■ In the early '30s my grandfather died and my grandmother came to live with us. This was a natural arrangement in middle class life, then. There were few alternatives; those available required more money than most people had before social security and during the Depression.

She was old when she moved in. She knew it and we knew it. She was 62.

Grandmother joined a household which included my mother, four pre-teen children and a live-in housekeeper.

She brought with her two rooms of furniture and other not-to-be-parted-with possessions, including Caruso and Chaliapin records which she played on a large mahogany cabinet victrola in her room; when displeased she played them while mother was playing the piano. She brought with her also a conviction that children should be seen and not heard and that their prime function was to grow up to be a comfort to their parents.

The move wasn't easy on anyone. It took time for waves to subside and territory to be readjusted.

She made constructive contributions. She made us clothes. If she preferred brown when all our friends were wearing blue, no matter; it was not necessary to be a sheep. She took us to concerts and cultural events "for our own good." She crocheted endless afghans and at Christmas made fruitcake which she wrapped in damp cloths and hid in a dark place, bringing it out when the occasion was right and slicing it thin in a kind of seasonal ceremony.

From Memorial Day to Labor Day she wore pongee and other lightweight material; in winter dark colors, often a bit of lace somewhere, and amber beads. She stood straight, her hair piled high with ends turned under in a kind of puff on top, held in place with large bone hairpins. She liked to have it brushed and allowed us to do this as a reward for good behavior.

"The Vanishing Grandmother" by Dorothy-Anne Flor from TROPIC, The Miami Herald Sunday Magazine, December 14, 1975, vol. 9, no. 50. Copyright © 1975 by The Miami Herald Publishing Co., a division of Knight-Ridder Newspapers, Inc. Reprinted by permission.

Most children on our street had a grandparent in residence and while these varied in personality and interests, they shared things in common. All were considered old; all had white hair; all buffed their nails; none danced; they sang only in church, or nursery rhymes to children; their arms were covered and they wore sensible shoes. They had no noticeable social life apart from the family. They believed life progressed in stages with appropriate dress and conduct for each stage. All probably died in their own beds with a family member sitting by them.

There are still many people who see themselves as old at 62 and spend their remaining years absorbed into their children's family, playing the grandmother or grandfather role. The greater percentage now are from blue-collar families where, largely unsubjected to the transcience which has marked white-collar life since World War II, family members are still in frequent contact, and relatives are considered best friends and the nucleus of social life. Here, life still consists of the same few standard transitions from cradle to grave, with appropriate conduct and dress for each stage.

Almost 21 million people who live in the U.S. are 65 and over. Most are women. Because mortality rates for females are lower and their life expectancy longer, there are 138 women for every 100 men aged over 65. In 1972 80 per cent of men over 64 were married, less than 40 per cent of women over 64 were married.

Today many white-collar working women share homes with widowed or divorced mothers and fathers. Married daughters are more likely than sons to share the family home with an aging parent. In U.S. culture, sons frequently leave the care of parents to a sister, particularly if she is single, divorced or widowed, while they may assume care of their wives' parents.

The largest proportion of people over 65, whether or not they own their own homes and even with raises in social security income, live at borderline poverty or at poverty level.

Even if they come forward to help the old person, the family situation may provide a miserable existence. Many family relationships fall short of even basic decency. Max Friedson, President of the Congress of Senior Citizens Organization, has been quoted in a newspaper story as saying, "To the elderly person, the world is full of legal papers in fine print he can't read, financial pitfalls he can't avoid and bunco artists—often his own children—he can't outwit." Some parents are abandoned by children as punishment for what the children consider neglect or bad care during childhood. Many no longer follow the commandment "honor thy father and thy mother" unless they judge the honor deserved.

However, on a more cheerful note, there are hundreds of thousands of people, aside from the rich, who emerged from the '50s and '60s with some degree of affluence. These read the beautiful color advertisements of developers and builders which tell them that retirement can be the beginning of a new life; that there are choices as to what style of life this could be; that they have only to make a decision and sign the paper.

The new life is not rooted in family; instead it's part of what Alvin Toffler in *Future Shock* calls the emerging age of transcience; the shift toward the death of permanence in relationships and things.

With severely decreased emotional and other reliance on family, old friends and old work habits, as well as those which resulted from geography, it is rooted instead in newly cultivated, more temporary relationships, in building and furnishing a new nest, in enjoyment of interests not pursued to any significant degree in the old life, in considering yourself a person first with a responsibility to live fully.

Some people decide to remain where they are, with familiar things in the old house in the old neighborhood. Others find this a disadvantage. As one man said, "Why stay? Thirty years there means at least two sets of new children with parents following interests we have put aside—the lawn, the dancing lessons, the schools, the projects to improve the house. Sometime the old street is going downhill; get the mortgage paid up and suddenly there's a gas station on the corner."

However, the house in the old neighborhood, or any neighborhood, may be the last bastion of personal freedom from rules and regulations governing your conduct in your own home, short of making yourself a frequent public nuisance or absorbing the glare of the neighbor who combs his lawn every day and thinks your not doing the same decreases his property value, no one is sending you bulletins about new rules, or fining you if you don't conform.

There is a fourth life also, but unlike the third life, it isn't advertised. The key word is ambulatory. As long as you have enough money and are ambulatory, you have options and choices.

You may rent an apartment and try out a new area; buy a small home in a traditional neighborhood and blend in; buy in a retirement village; purchase a mobile home; give your property to a religious home for the aged and be guaranteed care for the rest of your life.

Or you can join the people, retired or otherwise, who are picking up an option which has emerged only in the last 10 to 12 years, but which some say heralds the way of the future: the condominium.

Condominium life differs from other lifestyles in that it is a package structured by a developer who will, even after he has departed to build another building, have a profound effect on owners as a result of what he designed for them. For some, fighting what he has done may be a vital part of the new life. One developer calls his complex "Your World Away From the World." This is what it's all about. It's largely about shutting some things in and shutting others out.

Many deplore society becoming layered and sterile where blocks of people communicate with other groups only in a temporary situation for practical purposes. The child doesn't get to bury his face in the aproned lap of the pink-cheeked woman in glasses and confide his secret thoughts. In fact, he may not be able to distinguish his grandmother from his mother from behind. The isolated aging person shrivels without feeling needed, fighting, loving, contributing to the family, they say.

Do retired people feel that they are deprived in their new life? What do they think now of the life they bought? How adaptable are they?

In his book deploring rootlessness, *A Nation of Strangers,* Vance Packard cites the Robert Weiss study published by the Harvard Medical School Department of Psychiatry about the lives of uprooted or loosely-rooted people. Weiss' conclusion was that five relationships were required for mental health and stability. These are family; knowing people who share our concerns; knowing people we can depend upon in a pinch; having one or more really close friends; and knowing people who respect our competence.

When you buy your new life in a condominium, how many of these stabilizers are available to you?

David Herman is a retired attorney from Chicago who, with Mrs. Herman, left a lovely home on a lovely street and a son and grandchildren nearby to come to Florida and live in a condominium. The Hermans bought one of the first units sold in Winston Towers 100, 22 stories high with 409 units. When the Hermans bought in Winston Towers 100, they purchased "The World Apart From the Outside World." They bought all the beautiful things in the ads: the pools; the health clubs with saunas; the hobby rooms, the game and social rooms; the bank and shops; the security guards in the lobby.

While Centrex Corporation, the builder, doesn't consider Winston Towers a retirement community, residents of the 100 building are in their 60s or over with 50 as a base age. About 95 per cent are Jewish. Residents are predominantly from Chicago and New York. About 65 per cent live there all year long. A large number are on fixed income.

Herman, now president of the Owners' Association, Inc., likes condominium life in general. "When I close my door, I am in my own home," he says. The family in Chicago is only as far away as the nearest telephone and the Hermans exchange visits several times a year. Visits with grandchildren are great, but short visits are best, Herman and his friends agree.

Herman and others think Weiss' criteria are met at Towers 100. They retain a deep family interest and certainly there are people around to share mutual concerns, many centering around problems of living together. Finding solutions to these problems may have taken a lot of people's minds off the difficulties inherent in a transition to the new life.

Centrex retains management of individual towers for one year, after which owners may hire a manager or manage themselves. Towers 100 tried a paid manager, then dismissed him, determined to manage themselves. A nine-member board was elected, including a president and chairman, presently Herman. The board names committees to deal with particular areas of management.

Monthly meetings to make plans and discuss building problems are well attended—around 150 owners. Actually the auditorium wasn't built large enough to hold all the people who live in 100, an unsolvable problem that brings a flush of anger to Herman's face. At the meetings building leaders and experts emerge to solve problems.

"We've got more talent in this building than you could afford to go out and buy," says David Abranowitz, who serves on the board as part of the management committee. "There are retired attorneys, accountants, business people, doctors, construction people, electrical manufacturers, among others. Some are still active in businesses run by families."

"Yes, we've got some difficult people," one owner says. "Every place does. Some just don't appreciate what they've got. We've got one lady who calls down to the office. 'I'm sick,' she says. So we call an ambulance. The ambulance men come. They go upstairs with the stretcher. They knock on her door. She won't let them in. They leave. After they've gone, she calls down to the office. 'There are some men trying to knock down my door,' she says.

"This isn't good," he said. "We use the ambulance service. You cry wolf and when you need them, maybe they won't come."

When Mrs. Mathield Cleaver, a childless widow, came five years ago to Cresthaven Villas in West Palm Beach to buy developer David Yorra's version of "Happiness Under the Sun," it was because her 84-year-old mother could no longer take Chicago winters.

She made a decision for Florida because she had spent winter vacations here and knew the area. She shopped the various lifestyles offered with the help of a cousin in Fort Lauderdale.

She bought a ground level "golden" condominium which will eventually be one of 5,000. Cresthaven Villas is built as a series of neighborhoods, each one limited to approximately 500 villas. The neighborhoods are laid out in a horseshoe and at the center of each is the clubhouse, with meeting room, cardroom, sewing room, billiard room, hobby room, library, woodworking shop, saunas and showers and a large auditorium for entertainment and social programs.

Unlike Winston Towers, the developer retains management and makes all decisions. Owners participate to the extent that each section has a representative who attends a monthly presidents' council where owner's gripes and/or suggestions are heard, if they are placed on the agenda in time.

Mrs. Cleaver is a comfortable, friendly woman. She came down more than willing to follow the brochure's suggestion and "lead an active life under the sun." She joined things and served on committees. Then, two years ago, her mother died; now she is considering her own future.

The daytime is fine but nighttime is a problem. "I'll be at the clubhouse—I'll walk over there just to sit around the pool and gab with some people, you know, just to have some human contact, and there's always somebody there. But, then there's the time when you walk down the street alone and you go into your house alone and this I don't like. I am moving," she says. "I am staying in my section—you get attached to your section—but in my new house I'll be able to see people walk by. Now you only see people through the kitchen window. I watched my mother sit there with nothing to look at but me and the boob tube and I said to myself, if I am going to grow old in Florida, I want to be where I can see some life."

Does she miss a variety in age groups? Yes. "I pick up a friend on Sunday and after church we eat dinner out. Last Sunday we went to a chicken barbecue at Forest Hill High School; the band came in and played. We had a good time. When we came away we talked about missing the excitement of these young people. However, whether we'd be up to that on a steady basis, I don't know. You know these apartment buildings where the kids tromp up and down stairs and jitterbug above you . . . you kind of miss this, but I don't know."

Sidney and Gertrude Reich chose to make a total change—to seek the new life—and they began shopping for it five years before he retired in 1969 as a Judgment Clerk for the City of New York. They traveled an estimated 3,000 miles in Florida alone, spending six weeks here, considering all options, with the exception of one—the high rise. She feared being lost in the shuffle in a high-rise; that she might find that friendships would be limited mostly to neighbors on one floor.

They found what they were looking for in Cresthaven Villas and moved in four years ago, bringing furniture for the living room and dining room. "Ours is not the traditional Florida home," she says, "but when we come in, it looks very nice."

While their son, his wife and their grandson live in California and they must resort to the weekly phone call for contact, they have a daughter in Miami who they see every Monday.

Do they miss being involved with growing children and family life? "We used to think it was terrible when a mother or father moved away from their children," she says, "but when a son or daughter finds another job, they just pull up stakes and go and this is the way it should be."

Yes, the transition was difficult, leaving friends was hard, but they have gone north three winters in a row, so it hasn't been too bad. We must know hundreds of people here, they say. Each cluster is a small town with someone always around to give you a bright smile.

It's a wonderful way to live, they say, with neighbors ready to help you in time of stress and ready to help you enjoy the good things, too. You have your privacy but someone is always there. You have to get out and do for yourself, and for others. The people who don't, probably never have.

They had belonged to a square dance club in New York. One evening in the clubhouse they taught a few people some steps. Now they run a Friday evening dance session for over 200 people with a friend, and every other week they hold a workshop on the dances they will do the next Friday. It takes a lot of time, but it's very gratifying.

Would they like to live with one of their children?

No, they said. "The young and the old shouldn't live together. Travel and the telephone are the answer."

6
REARRANGING

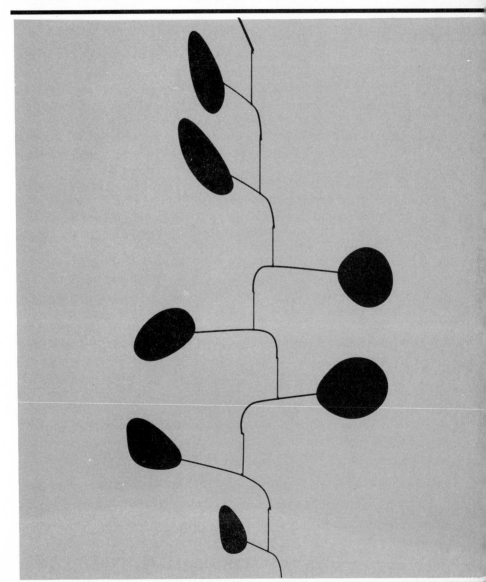

As recently as ten years ago, it was fashionable to predict that the American family was on the verge of extinction. Forecasts appeared everywhere, from newspapers to college texts, that the future of the family looked bleak, that new life-styles and alternative forms of intimacy were challenging the structures and functions of marriage and parenting.

In retrospect, nearly all of these predictions were inaccurate. Reports heralding a new age of communes, alternative life-styles, and experimental systems for raising children all tended to underestimate existing family systems. Among other lessons, the 1970s taught that the family is among the most adaptive and resilient of all social institutions. The family has endured; it is, to quote a recent essay in *U.S. News & World Report*, "bent—but not broken."[1]

Of course there have been and will continue to be changes in the social meaning of marriage and the family. Parenthood, for example, is in the process of being redefined. Basic questions such as "Who should be parents?" "When?" and "How many children to have?" are more open-ended than ever before. Between 1970 and 1980, to cite national statistics on the subject, the number of children living with two parents was down by 18 percent, and the number of children living with only one parent had increased by 40 percent. The continuing rise in divorces (which climbed 65 percent between 1970 and 1980) and remarriages will also have impact on how people define their marriages—and themselves—in the years to come. Part 6 of this book has been called "Rearranging" and attempts to deal with emerging styles and interpretations of marriage and the family. In addition, this section of readings tries to pinpoint some of the aspects of family living which will generate problems during the 1980s and beyond. In a sense, the treatment of new life-styles and the discussion of new or unforeseen problems are reciprocals of one another. New life-styles or living arrangements can never be problem-free; and social problems have historically been agents of change.

The opening section concentrates on violence and unemployment as disruptive elements that prompt rearranging within families. It is unfortunate but true, as Gelles and Straus remark, that apart from police stations and army camps, the family home is the most violent spot on our social landscape. Gelles and Straus, in "Violence in the American Family," elaborate on the extent of family violence—and the disruptions associated with a violent home.

Unemployment is yet another disruption that can be debilitating for members of a family. Louis Ferman was principal investigator of a study on unemployment for the National Institute of Mental Health. In "Family

---

1. "The American Family: Bent—But Not Broken," *U.S News & World Report,* 16 June 1980, p. 48.

Adjustment to Unemployment," Ferman's research reveals the experiences of seven types of unemployed men, ranging from the continuously unemployed to the career changers. In this current period of high unemployment and spiraling inflation, Ferman's research highlights the vulnerability of families to social and emotional disruptions when the principal wage earner is out of work.

The last section in Part 6 deals with divorce and remarriage as events that prompt rearranging, both within and among families. In "The Single Parent and Public Policy," Schorr and Moen consider the current status of public policy directed at single parents and also speculate about new directions that these policies could take. It is already known that there is a disproportionately high percentage of single-parent families composed of mothers with low levels of education and income (refer back to the work of Paul Glick in Part 1 and Kathleen Rudd Scharf in Part 2). It is less known that much of the existing policy directed at single-parent families does not encourage these mothers to increase either their educational or occupational levels. The time for an overhaul of such policies may be at hand.

Along with single-parent families, there has been a rise in mergers between divorced or widowed adults and their two sets of children. The new unit is called a *reconstituted family*. Westoff, in an excerpt from *The Second Time Around*, describes some differences in attitudes toward parenting and toward being married when the remnants of previous marriages become reconstituted.

Do reconstituted families live happily ever after? Probably not, or so says the U.S. Census. There is, in fact, a higher divorce rate for remarriages than for first marriages. No wonder some officials in Washington, D.C., have begun speaking half-humorously about adding a new category —called *redivorced*—to the U.S. Census. Andrew Cherlin refers to the structure of American society for clues to explain "Remarriage as an Incomplete Institution." He blames ambiguities in status and contradictory expectations which prevent any chance of a smooth merger between two previously distinct family units. Given current definitions of marriage and the family, Cherlin predicts the reconstituted family will remain an "incomplete institution" for years to come.

Disruptions

Violence in the American Family
Richard J. Gelles and Murray A. Straus

The paper reviews current knowledge on violence between family members in the United States, including how and why family violence became a topic of interest after years of being masked by a public and professional perceptual blackout. It presents data from a nationally representative sample of 2,143 American families that measured the extent of child abuse, wife abuse, husband abuse, and violence between siblings. The paper then reports differences in child abuse rates according to factors such as the age and sex of the child, family income, occupation, stress, unemployment, social isolation, and previous exposure or experience with violence. It is suggested that the roots of family violence lie in the organization of the family and in the implicit cultural norms tolerating or approving violence as a means for social control.

■   With the exception of the police and the military, the family is perhaps the most violent social group, and the home the most violent social setting, in our society. A person is more likely to be hit or killed in his or her home by another family member than anywhere else or by anyone else. Nearly one out of every four murder victims in the United States is a family member. Similarly, in Africa, Great Britain, and Denmark the

"Violence in the American Family" by Richard J. Gelles and Murray A. Straus from THE JOURNAL OF SOCIAL ISSUES, vol. 35, no. 2, 1979. Copyright © 1979 by The Society for the Psychological Study of Social Issues. Reprinted by permission.

This paper is one of a series of publications of the Family Violence Research Program at the University of New Hampshire. The program is supported by the University of New Hampshire and by NIMH grants MH 27557 and T 32 MH15161. A program bibliography and list of available publications will be sent on request.

greatest proportion of murders are intrafamilial (Bohannan, 1960; Curtis, 1974).

Although increased public attention to the problem of family violence would suggest that there has been a rapid increase in the level of family violence, most historical evidence suggests that the family has always been one of society's more violent institutions (see, for example, Bakan, 1971; DeMause, 1974, 1975; Newberger, Reed, Daniel, Hyde & Kotelchuch, 1977; Radbill, 1974). But despite the family's long history as a violent social setting, for many years the issue of violence in the home was subjected to "selective inattention" (Dexter, 1958). Battered children, women, husbands, and parents were the missing persons of the social problems literature until the late 1960's and early 1970's. While there were occasional articles on the "pathology" of child battering and rare articles on wife-beating, there was no systematic social-scientific study of the issue of family violence.

By contrast, the decade of the 1970's has produced a proliferation of books, articles, and monographs on the subjects of child abuse, wife abuse, and family violence. However, the available research evidence is clouded by problems of conceptualization and operationalization of key terms, (for example, the term "child abuse"). Moreover, the state of knowledge about child abuse is limited by a number of methodological problems involved in most past studies. This paper reviews some of these problems. It also draws heavily on data collected from a major national survey of violence in the American family (e.g., Gelles, 1976; Straus, Gelles & Steinmetz, 1979). That study, the first to employ a nationally representative sample of families, explored the extent of family violence and attempted to identify which families were more likely to be violent.

Family Violence as a Social Issue

Decades of overlooking family violence as a social problem were followed by one decade of intense public and professional interest. What accounted for the change in public and scientific attitudes toward family violence, and what accounted for family violence being discovered as a social issue? Straus (1974a) proposes that numerous streams of thought and action converged in the United States in the late 1960's and early 1970's to help uncover this hidden side of family life. First, the 1960's was a decade of public or visible violence. Race riots, political assassinations, rising rates of interpersonal violence, and an unpopular war that produced tens of thousands of casualties, all drew public attention to the problem of violence. The National Commission on the Causes and Prevention of Violence was formed as a response to the assassinations of Martin Luther

King and Robert Kennedy. The Commission produced the first comprehensive national study of attitudes and experiences with violent behavior.
The questions which dealt with family violence opened the eyes of many
people, who previously had thought that family violence was uncommon
as well as deviant. The evidence indicated otherwise. For example, Stark
and McEvoy's (1970) analysis of the Commission data showed that one in
four men and one in six women approved of a husband slapping a wife
under certain conditions.

A second force which brought family violence into public attention
was the women's movement. The struggle to gain liberation and equality
for women brought women of all ages and backgrounds together for
"consciousness raising sessions." One latent function of these sessions
was to help many participants discover that they shared similar dark
secrets: they had been battered by their husbands. These collective
sessions served to inform battered wives that being beaten and battered
by their husbands was neither their own fault nor their own unique
experience. There has been a children's rights movement somewhat
paralleled to the women's movement. Much of that effort has focussed
on maltreatment or abuse of children. This, too, has heightened public
awareness of violence in the family.

Finally, while such social movements gathered steam, some American
social scientists began to use a "conflict model" of human behavior,
rather than the long dominant "consensus-equilibrium model." Sprey
(1969) argues that a conflict model of family relations is much better
suited for the study of family violence than the previously dominant
model, which had been designed for studies of mate selection and similar
issues.

Other social scientists have postulated that family violence and child
abuse were "created" as social problems as a result of the entrepreneurial
efforts of certain professional groups. Pfohl (1977), for example, argues
that the "discovery" of child abuse as a social problem was due to the
efforts of diagnostic radiologists, who at that time constituted a marginal
speciality within the field of medicine, but who used the issue of battered
children to create a mandate for this professional speciality.

Major Questions in the Study of Family Violence

The social issue of family violence and violence toward children has
typically focused on three major questions. First, there has been considerable concern over exactly how widespread the phenomenon actually is.
Concern with measuring the incidence of family violence is perhaps best
viewed as a reaction to the general belief that family violence is really

quite rare and is confined to a few mentally disturbed people (Steinmetz & Straus, 1974).

The second question deals with the demographic distribution of family violence. Work on this particular problem has ranged all the way from some early studies arguing that, since child abuse was found in all social groups, social factors (such as socio-economic status) could not be used to account for such violence (e.g., Steele & Pollock, 1974), to later studies arguing that violence is either confined to or more prevalent in certain social groups (e.g., poor; certain racial or ethnic minorities, etc.). (See Pelton, 1978; Steinmetz & Straus, 1974).

The third major question concerns what causes people to be violent. Early investigators of child abuse and wife beating employed a psycho-dynamic model of abuse and violence. Consequently, they directed their efforts toward "discovering" the personality traits and disorders that were associated with, and that "therefore" caused, people to abuse family members. Other investigators have developed models emphasizing sociological, social psychological, or ecological factors, or various combi-nations of these. (For a review of 17 theories of violence, see Gelles & Straus, 1979).

Conceptual and Methodological Problems in the Study of Family Violence

The development of a knowledge base in the area of family violence, and especially in the study of violence toward children, has been hampered by two major difficulties, one conceptual and the other methodological. The conceptual problem is that the study of violence toward children is almost always subsumed within investigations of child "abuse." There are some studies of physical punishment of children (see, for example, Sears, Maccoby & Levin, 1957; Eron, Walder, & Lefkowitz, 1971). One notable exception is the analysis of the data collected by the National Commission on the Causes and Prevention of Violence (Owens & Straus, 1975; Stark & McEvoy, 1970). But by and large, there have been few studies of violence toward children which were conducted outside of the rubric of child abuse research.

This poses a major problem for investigators who want to determine how widespread violence is and what causes parents and caretakers to use violence toward their children. Usually, "child abuse" is defined to include behaviors beyond the use of physical force: malnourishment, failure to care for and protect a child, sexual assault, failure to clothe a child, and psychological abuse. The wide and varied definitions of the concept "child abuse" makes it nearly impossible to compare the findings of various investigators or even separate out of the data the part that pertains to the use of physical violence. It is therefore difficult to develop cumulative knowledge about violence toward children.

At the heart of the problem is the fact that the term "child abuse" is intended to draw attention to acts which are believed to deviate from appropriate standards of behavior for caretakers. Such standards vary over time (e.g., stubborn child laws in the seventeenth and eighteenth centuries allowed parents to put unruly children to death, although there is no evidence that such deaths occurred), across cultures (e.g., some cultures allow infanticide), and between social or cultural strata (e.g., physicians who physically injure their children are much less likely to be labeled "child abusers" than unemployed fathers who injure their children).

A second important problem in the study of violence in the family is that the issue is, at the very least, sensitive. There are taboos against talking about the subject with either friends or strangers. The private and intimate nature of the family makes it very difficult to use traditional research strategies to measure the extent and patterns of physical violence (Gelles, 1978).

Because violence in the family is a sensitive topic, it is difficult to study in terms of securing access to subjects, establishing rapport with them, and getting reliable and valid self report data from them. Researchers often try to design their studies to aid these problems. In doing so, they create other problems. One way to try to deal with these problems is to operationally define "child abuse" as those cases or families that have been officially labeled as "child abuse." This often insures that cases will be available for study. But it confounds the measurement of abuse with factors which lead a family to be publicly labeled a "child abuser" (for example, is poverty a correlate of high rates of child abuse, or are poor people simply more likely to be labeled child abusers?).

Other critics of past child abuse studies (and by inference, of research on violence toward children) have noted that these studies typically employ at-hand clinical cases, that they do not test hypotheses or build theory, and that they fail to employ adequate control or comparison groups (Spinetta & Rigler, 1972; Gelles, 1973).

The result of these conceptual and methodological limitations is that we have little valid and generalizable information about how extensive violence toward children actually is, and about how it is distributed in the population. In order to overcome some of these problems, Straus et al. (1979) designed and carried out a national survey of a representative sample of American couples. That study investigated the extent of violence in the American home and tried to learn more about which families are the most likely to engage in violent behavior within the family settings. Most of this paper will present results of that study and discuss the implications of those results. (The study is presented in more detail in Gelles, 1978; Straus, 1979a; and Straus et al., 1979).

A National Survey of Family Violence

The national survey of family violence defined violence as "an act carried out with the intention or perceived intention of physically hurting another person" (Gelles & Straus, 1979). The "physical hurt" can range from slight pain, as in a slap, to murder.

There were a number of important issues which had to be dealt with when we developed this definition. First, the definition includes acts which are not normally considered violent (and certainly not abusive), such as spanking a child. Our definition viewed spankings as violent for two reasons. First, a spanking is an act intended to cause physical pain. Second, a spanking, if administered to someone who is not a family member, would be viewed as assault in the eyes of the law.

A second problem was that our definition of violence did not take into account whether an injury is produced by the violent act. Many definitions of child abuse view an act as abuse only if it produces some harm or injury. However, harm or injury often depends on events or contingencies which are external to the behavior (e.g., aim, size and strength of actor and intended victim, luck, availability of weapons, etc.). We chose to focus only on acts rather than on outcomes.

Study Methods

The data are based on interviews with a nationally representative sample of 2,143 American couples, of whom 1,146 had one or more children aged 3 to 17 years old living at home at the time of the interview. Interviews were conducted with the husband in a randomly selected half of the families and with the wife in the other half. A more complete discussion of the methodology is given in Straus et al. (1979).

We measured violence and incidence of violence in American families using a series of questions called the "Conflict Tactics Scales" (CTS). The CTS were first developed at the University of New Hampshire in 1971. They have been used and modified in numerous studies of family violence in various countries (United States, Canada, Israel, Japan, Finland, Great Britain, and British Honduras). Data on validity and reliability of the scales are given in Straus (1979b).

Each person was asked to consider two time frames: (1) conflicts that took place in the preceding 12 months; and (2) conflicts during the duration of the marriage or the lifetime of his or her children. The first time frame is used to compute annual incidence rates; since we interviewed our subjects from January to April, 1976, these can be thought of as rates for 1975. The second provides more limited information about violence that had occurred during the duration of the relationship.

In our national survey, we interviewed each respondent with respect to *one* of his or her children (randomly chosen). To interview each parent with respect to all their children would have been too time consuming. Furthermore, it would have introduced some additional methodological problems involving order effects. The interviews covered a wide range of acts, from the "normal violence" of physical punishment such as spanking to more extreme forms of violence (hitting, biting, beating, threatening with a knife or gun, etc.).

Proportion of Families in Which Violence Toward Children Occurs

Estimates of the extent of child abuse and violence toward children vary widely. In any case, most of them are estimates of overall incidence with no breakdown by age, sex, or demographic characteristics of the children or parents. Since much of the research on child abuse relies on officially compiled statistics, they are probably underestimates of the true level of abuse. David Gil's 1968 survey of officially reported and validated cases of child abuse yielded 6,000 cases (Gil, 1970), but this data was collected before all fifty states had enacted mandatory child abuse reporting laws. The American Humane Association documented 26,438 reports of child abuse in 1976, but this number represents only reported child abuse and for only the 31 states that participated in the American Humane Association's national child abuse clearinghouse (American Humane Association, Note 1).

A national household survey in 1965 produced an estimate of between 2.53 and 4.07 million individuals who knew of a case of child abuse (Gil, 1970). Richard Light (1973) corrected for instances where the same case could be known to a number of people and estimated that there are 500,000 children abused each year.

Nagi's (1977) survey of community agencies produced an estimate that there are 167,000 annual reports of child abuse plus 91,000 unreported cases. Other investigators have projected an annual rate of child abuse as low as 30,000 abused children (DeFrancis, 1973) to as high as 1.5 million cases (Fontana, 1973). The estimates of how many children are killed each year as a result of abuse are also varied, from a low estimate of 365 (One child dies daily, 1975) to a high estimate of 5,000 deaths per year (United States Senate, 1973).

The limitations of the data on incidence of child abuse are compounded when it comes to determining if violence toward children is actually increasing. Certainly, if one goes by officially reported cases of child abuse, the evidence supports the claim that violence is increasing. However, official statistics cannot be relied upon to answer this question. They reflect public media campaigns aimed at increasing public knowledge about and concern with child abuse and child abuse reporting. Furthermore, they are based on varying definitions of child abuse. Since 1968, by which time all 50 states had enacted child abuse and neglect laws, there has been a tendency to *broaden* legal definitions of "child abuse." Thus, more behaviors are now defined as under the legal definition of child abuse.

The matter is further complicated when we attempt to study physical violence toward children as different from, though overlapping with, "child abuse." Past research indicated that the use of physical punishment in childrearing is nearly universal in the United States. Between 84% and 97% of all parents use some form(s) of physical punishment of their children at some time(s) during the childrearing relationship. (Erlanger, 1974; Newson & Newson, 1963; Stark & McEvoy, 1970). Drawing the line between "normal" physical violence used as a routine part of child training, and physical violence which results in a "recognized" case of "child abuse" involves social, political, legal, and moral, as well as scientific, issues.

In our national survey, the milder forms of violence were, of course, the most common. Of our respondents, 58% had used some form of violence toward their child during the current year; 71% had done so at some time. Since other studies have shown that 90% or more of all American children have been hit at least once by their parents, these figures must be regarded as underestimates of actual violence in families.

Of greater interest are age differences. Among 3 and 4 year olds, and also among 5 to 9 year olds, 82% had been hit during the year of the survey. Two thirds (66%) of the pre-teens and early teenage children (10 to 14 year olds) had been hit that year. "Only" one third (34%) of the 15 to 17 year olds had been hit by their parents during the year. These are likely to be substantial underestimates; but the differences may be accurate.

The more dangerous types of violence occurred less often. But even for these extreme forms of violence, and even for these underestimates, there are an astoundingly high number of American children who were kicked, punched, bit, threatened with a gun or knife, or had guns or knives used on them. Approximately three children in 100 were kicked, bitten or punched by their parents in that year; many more (8 in 100) had it happen at one time or another in their lives. Slightly more than one of 100 children were beaten by a parent in that year; 4 in 100 were beaten at least once while growing up.

One child in 1,000 faced a parent who threatened to use a gun or knife during the survey year. Nearly 3 children in 100 have been threatened with a gun or knife by a parent at least once in their lifetimes. The same proportions hold for children whose parents actually *used* a gun or a knife. These data are truly astonishing when we remember that these numbers are based on parents' *own* testimony.

Frequency of Violence in Families Where It Does Occur

We were surprised, although perhaps we should not have been, to find that the extreme forms of parental violence are not likely to be one shot events. These extreme forms of parental violence occur periodically and even regularly, in the families where they occur at all. For example, if a beating is considered an element of "child abuse," then our findings show that child abuse is a chronic condition for many children, not a once in a lifetime experience for them.

With the exception of being threatened with a knife or gun, or having a knife or gun used on them, children whose parents were violent to them generally experienced such violence more than once. Children who had something thrown at them had that happen an average of 4.5 times during the reported year. Children who were pushed, grabbed or shoved experienced that an average of 6.6 times over the prior 12 month period. As expected, spankings and slappings were the most frequent. They occurred an average of 9.6 times the previous year. The average for kicks, bites, and punches was 8.9 times that year, while children who were hit with objects had it happen an average of 8.6 times. For those who were beaten, it was repeated almost once every two months, on the average 5.9 times over the year. Where a gun or knife was used, though, it happened "only" once in the survey year.

Child Abuse Index

To estimate how many American children were "at risk" of being physically injured, we developed a Child Abuse Index that combines the items which imply a high probability of injury or damage to the child (kicks, bites, punches; beatings; threats with a gun or knife; use of a gun or knife). More than three out of every hundred children (3.6%) are at risk of serious injury each year from their parents using at least one of these dangerous forms of violence. Assuming that each of these acts has a high probability of causing harm to a child victim, then *between 1.4 and 1.9 million children in the United States were vulnerable to physical injury from their parents during the year of our study.* Moreover, as shown by the frequency data on individual violent acts, when such assaults occur, they tend to reoccur. In fact, "single incident" cases make up only 6% of all child abuse cases. The average number of serious assaults per year experienced by those children whose parents committed at least one abusive act was 10.5. The median, probably a better estimate for such data, was 4.5.

Being at risk of injury from parental violence is not the same thing as being a victim of child abuse. Many a child has been slammed against a wall or punched and kicked by his or her parents, who did not end up with a concussion or broken bones. Nevertheless, these figures probably are the best available ones for estimating how many children might be abused each year in the United States, because they are the only estimates ever generated from a nationally representative sample using consistent measurement procedures. If they represent a reasonable estimate of *potential* child abuse, then they offer some new and surprising information:

First, the estimates are *at least 1.2 million children higher than previous estimates of the incidence of physical abuse* (which are 150,000 to 250,000).

Second, even these figures probably *underestimate* the true level of abuse for five important reasons. First, they are based on self-reports of the parents. Underreporting is quite likely when sensitive questions about socially disapproved behavior are asked. Second, the survey deals with only seven specific forms of violence. There are others (e.g., burning). Third, the data on violence toward a given child refers to violent acts by only one of his or her parents. Fourth, the children we studied were between the ages of 3 and 17. Previous research suggests that much violence and abuse is directed toward children between three months and three years of age, who are not covered in our survey. Had they been included, our figures would necessarily have been higher. Fifth, we studied only "intact" families (husbands and wives who were living together). The literature on child abuse suggests that violence may be even more common in families where only one parent lives with the child. Had we studied single parent families, we might have found a higher rate of violence toward children. All of these suggest that the actual violence that children experience is probably much more frequent than even the astonishing figures we report here.

Factors Related to Variations in Rate of Child Abuse

Most studies of child abuse show the rate to be greatest among infants and very young children. Our Child Abuse Index revealed a slightly different pattern with regard to age of the child. The rates peaked at two ages: the youngest in our sample (3 and 4 year olds) and the oldest (15 to 17 year olds.) One reason for the difference in results may be that previous studies measured abuse on the basis of injuries sustained by a child, whereas this study measured abuse by the severity of the violent act. The predominance of infants and young children among the abused in previous research is probably in part because such children are more likely to require medical attention when subjected to violence, compared to an older child subjected to the same degree of force. However, that does not explain why our data show a peak at these two ages (3 to 4 and 15 to 17). Part of the explanation might be that infancy and adolescence are both ages at which many parents find verbal controls, such as reasoning, explaining, or ordering ineffective. But these unexpected findings deserve further exploration.

We found a small, but significant, difference between mothers and fathers in the use of physical violence on their children. Mothers were slightly more likely to use violence on their children than were fathers. Mothers were also more likely to use abusive violence, as defined by our Child Abuse Index.

Boys were slightly more likely than girls to be the targets of parental violence, and for all age groups, were also more likely to be abused.

Other Forms of Violence in the Family

We can perhaps get a better understanding about violence toward children by examining, briefly, the violence in other aspects of intra-family relationships which form part of the context of violence toward children.

One out of every six couples in our study (16% of the 2,143 surveyed) reported that they had engaged in at least one of the eight violent acts, toward the *spouse*, at least once during the survey year. These data are presented and analyzed in detail in Straus (1977) and in Straus et al. (1979).

As with violence toward children, the least dangerous acts of marital violence were the most common, but dangerous violence was also very common. We compiled an index of abusive violence toward spouse, paralleling our Child Abuse Index. It contained the five violence items which are the most likely to cause physical injury (the same four items used in the Child Abuse Index—kicking, biting, punching; beating up; threatening with knife or gun; using knife or gun; plus one additional item—hit with something). By this criterion, almost 1.8 million wives are physically abused by their husbands each year (3.8 percent), while nearly two million husbands are physically abused by their wives (4.6 percent).

We were particularly intrigued by the latter finding, especially in light of the traditional view that men are more violent than women. When we compared husbands and wives in terms of each of the eight violence items, we found that husbands and wives had similar rates of violence. Although most research suggests that females are less aggressive than males (Maccoby & Jacklin, 1974), research on aggression *within families*, either verbal or physical, has consistently shown very similar rates for husbands and wives, and for boys and girls (Gelles, 1974; Lefkowitz, Eron, Walder, & Huesmann, 1977, Table 2.8; Steinmetz, 1977; Straus, 1974b). We interpret this as reflecting the complex social rules that govern aggressive behavior. The standard rules and expectations concerning aggression toward men and toward women apply very stongly outside the family, but apply minimally if at all inside.

A note of caution should be added. Just because husbands and wives engage in violent and abusively violent behavior in equal numbers, this does not mean that as many husbands as wives are "abused." We measured *acts* of violence, *not outcomes*. Given that a husband is typically larger and stronger than his wife, he may well do more damage than his wife would do using the same form of violence. Second, it is important to take into account the context of marital violence. Although roughly as many wives kill husbands as husbands kill wives, studies of homicide show that wives are seven times more likely to murder in self defense (Wolfgang, 1957). Lastly, "abuse" is more than being hit. The economic, social and legal constraints that bind a wife to a violent marriage are greater than the ties that bind a husband (Gelles, 1979), thus putting women in a position of having to tolerate their own victimization much more often than men.

Although most media, public, and professional attention has been directed at violence toward children and violence between spouses, these are not the only forms of violence within families. Seven hundred and thirty-three of our 2,143 respondents had two or more children aged 3 to 17 living at home. On the basis of the behavior of these 733 children (as reported by a parent) we estimate that during the course of one year, four out of five American children use one of the eight forms of violence on a sibling. More than half of the children were reported as kicking, biting, punching, hitting with an object, or beating up a brother or sister. When the rate is projected to the 36.3 million children in the U.S., aged 3 to 17, who live with siblings in the same age range, it gives an estimate of 19 million attacks on siblings. If these were committed against a stranger, they would be considered assault and battery.

If violence in the home begets violence, as many students of child abuse and family violence assume, then we should expect to find that no family relationship is free of violent behavior. We were not surprised, therefore, to find that the level of child to parent violence is also quite high. Nearly one in five children between the ages of 3 and 17 (17%) used at least one of the eight forms of violence against their parents during the survey year (as reported by the parent). Almost one in ten children (9.4%) engaged in one of the five more dangerous forms of attack. Moreover, the rate of such attacks went up in direct proportion to the frequency of attacks by parents on the child (Straus et al., 1979).

Summary

As high as our figures may seem, they are probably substantial underestimates of the true level of family violence. Using parent self-reports, studying violence only toward and by children from 3 to 17 years old, and relying on parents to report child to parent and sibling violence, probably have all tended to make our data underestimates of the true level of family violence. And yet, even such underestimates are startling. If we were discussing the rate of a deadly communicable disease, or if we were reporting on violence outside of the home (for instance, school violence or violent street crime) many people would regard the rates given here as indicative of an "epidemic" of violence. Yet when we are discussing slaps, spankings and even beatings in the home, there often seems to be a tendency to downplay just how widespread, and how significant, the occurrence of family violence, including violence toward children, actually is.

Discussion of Factors Associated with Violence Toward Children

It is difficult to assess the current literature on the factors associated with violence toward children for three reasons. First, acts of severe violence are combined with non-physical acts of maltreatment in many definitions of child abuse. Second, data gathered from samples of cases publicly labeled as "abuse" can be generalized only to populations of cases publicly labeled as "abuse," not to incidence of violence toward children. Third, some factor may seem to be associated with violence toward children, when in fact it is a spurious relationship produced by selective labeling of cases as "abuse."

The early investigations of child abuse concluded that, since child abuse occurred in all social groups, social factors were not related to parent abuse of their children. (See, for example, Kempe, Silverman, Steele, Droegemueller, & Silver, 1962; Steele & Pollock, 1974). Ironically, the actual data presented by those who argued that social factors were unrelated to child abuse were reanalyzed to show that some social variables were, in fact, associated with abuse (Gelles, 1973). More recent research on abused children consistently finds social variables related to child abuse. (Newberger et al., 1977; Pelton 1978). The medical-psychiatric model which dominated both the early data analyses and the early theoretical formulations of the causes of child abuse has been replaced by much more multivariate theories which try to explain child abuse on the basis of a complex of social and psychological factors.

Child Rearing Histories of Abusive Parents

So many investigators have found or have proposed that abused children grow up to be abusive parents that this proposition has become commonly accepted among professionals and the public alike. The proposition has also taken on a "deterministic" flavor. Much of the public, and some professionals, interpret it to mean that all abused children *will* grow up to be abusive parents, and that anyone who is not abused as a child will grow up to be a non-abuser.

Our national survey of family violence supports a probabilistic interpretation of the proposition that violence begets violence. We asked each of our respondents to report on how often they were physically punished when they were 13 years of age and older. Those who reported that their mothers used physical punishment more than twice a year had a rate of severe violence toward their own children far greater than the rate for respondents who reported being hit less than twice a year (18.5% vs. 11.8%). Physical punishment by fathers showed less of a difference, but was still related to abusive violence toward their own children. Respondents whose fathers hit them more than twice a year at age 13 or older had a rate of abusive violence to their children of 16.7%. The rate for those hit by father less often than twice a year was 13.2% (Straus et al., 1979).

We also found that abusive violence toward children was related to whether or not a respondent saw his or her parents engage in physical violence toward one another. Men who saw their fathers strike their mothers grew up to have a rate of abusive violence toward their own children much higher than the rate for men who reported never having seen their fathers hit their mothers (13.3% vs. 9.7%). Women who saw their mothers being hit had a rate of abusive violence toward their own children which was slightly higher than the rate for women who reported no marital violence in their families of orientation (19.7% vs. 17.4%).

Finally, there was a greater chance that, in homes where there was conjugal violence, the parents would also use severe violence toward the children (Straus et al., 1979).

Clearly it is not unreasonable to suppose that people learn to be violent by observing and experiencing violence while growing up. In many cases, there seems to be an almost undiluted "transfer," with violence learned as a child being practiced as an adult (Gelles, 1974; Gil, 1970; Palmer, 1962; Steinmetz & Straus, 1974; Lefkowitz et al., 1977; Owens & Straus, 1975).

Social Class

Early research on child abuse suggested that abuse occurred in all levels of the socioeconomic system and, therefore, that social class was not to be considered a cause of child abuse (Steele & Pollock, 1974). Pelton (1978) has called this the "myth of classlessness." He presents data from a number of investigations that demonstrate that abuse is more likely to occur in families of low socioeconomic status. Nevertheless, it could be argued that this occurs because poor people are more likely to be "caught" abusing their children, while persons from higher socioeconomic groups are insulated from the stigma of being labeled abusers.

Our national survey avoided the biases inherent in studying officially labeled cases of child abuse. We found that social status does indeed make a difference in probability of violence toward children.

There is an inverse relationship between parental income and parental violence. Those with incomes below the poverty line (less than $6,000) have the highest rates of violence (22%), while families with incomes exceeding $20,000 have the lowest rate (11%) of violence toward their children (Straus et al., Chapter 6, 1979).

Our examination of occupational status also found that parental violence is related to father's occupation. The rate of severe violence in homes where the father is a blue collar worker is 16%, while the rate in homes where the father is a white collar worker is 11%. Although this is a substantial and statistically significant difference, it is smaller than the difference typically found in examinations of official reports of child abuse (Straus, 1979a). A reasonable interpretation is that low socioeconomic status is related to the actual incidence of child abuse, but that this difference is magnified in the data by many studies because socioeconomic status is also related to being identified as a child abuser.

Unemployment

Some researchers have postulated that unemployment contributes to child abuse (Galdston, 1965; Gil, 1970; Young, 1964). Many discussions of child abuse in the mass media argue that since the rate of child abuse has increased during times of high unemployment, unemployment must be one of the causes of child abuse. While this position is not unreasonable, it is a logical non sequitur. Furthermore, it is also reasonable to suppose that the rise in the officially recorded rate of child abuse may be due to increased media publicity, increased public awareness, and changes in reporting laws, rather than an actual increase in the occurrence of child abuse.

We found that in families where the husband was unemployed at the time of the interview, the rate of physical violence toward children was 22%, while in families where the husband was employed full-time the rate was 14%. In homes where the husband was employed part-time, the rate was nearly double the rate of parental violence in homes where the husband was employed full-time (27% vs. 14%). The interpretation of these results is not completely apparent. Perhaps these findings can be better understood in the broader context to be discussed below.

Stress

There are a number of reasons why low socioeconomic status and unemployment may be related to severe violence toward children. One concept which may help account for the relationship is stress. Stress is probably unequally distributed within the social structure with lower socioeconomic groups probably experiencing more, or at least different kinds of, stress. Unemployment, for example, is typically experienced as severely stressful on the family.

There are, of course, many problems, many "stressors," that a family can encounter. To get a more comprehensive measure of family stress, we asked questions about which of a list of 18 problems each family had encountered in the previous twelve months. Some of these 18 problems, or stressful life events, were taken from Holmes and Rahe's "Social Readjustment Rating Scale" (1967). The items were:

1. Troubles with boss
2. Troubles with other people at work
3. Laid off or fired from job
4. Arrested or convicted for something serious
5. Death of someone I felt close to
6. Foreclosure of mortgage or loan
7. Pregnant or having a child born
8. Serious sickness or injury
9. Serious problem with health or behavior of family member
10. Sexual difficulties
11. In-law troubles
12. Much worse off financially
13. Separated or divorced
14. Big increase in the number of arguments with husband/wife/partner
15. Big increase in hours worked or responsibility on the job
16. Moved to a different neighborhood or town
17. Child expelled from school or suspended
18. Child caught doing something illegal

We found that, among the very poor and the very well-to-do, level of stress had no relationship to chances of child abuse within their families. But for middle income families (those with earnings between $6,000 and $20,000) higher levels of stress are associated with higher rates of child abuse.

We do not have a totally compelling explanation for why higher levels of stress are not associated with higher levels of child abuse for either the very low or the very high income families, but are associated with higher levels of abuse for middle income families; but we can suggest some possibilities. Perhaps being poor is itself a strong stressor condition, one not included in our index, so that, in a sense, *all* low income families are under a high level of stress. Low income families have a relatively high child abuse rate, whether they are high or low on our stress index.

The well-to-do, on the other hand, may be in somewhat the obverse situation. While they may be experiencing certain stressor conditions (i.e., conditions listed for our stress index), they are not necessarily experiencing high levels of stress because they can use their financial and other resources to avoid the stressing consequences of those stressor conditions. Just as poverty itself may be regarded as a powerful stressor condition, so relative wealth may be regarded as a powerful resource for warding off or coping with stressor conditions. So, the well-to-do may never really be very highly stressed; hence always have low abuse rates regardless of "score" on our stress index; while the poor may always really be very highly stressed hence always have high abuse rates regardless of their "score" on our stress index.

The middle income families may be well enough off to be under low-stress if other conditions (such as those on our stress index) are favorable; but not be well enough off to "ward off" the stressing effects of unfavorable conditions (such as those on our stress index). Hence, their "real" level of stress, and their consequent rate of child abuse, may vary directly with changes in circumstances such as those reflected in our stress index.

Such an explanation for the complex relationship between stress level as measured by our stress index, abuse level as measured by our Child Abuse Index, and family income level is, admittedly, speculative, and goes far beyond the evidence now at hand. But it does jibe with evidence about effects of stress in other areas; and certainly seems worthy of further investigation.

Family Size

It has often been suggested that larger families are more likely to have abused children (Elmer, 1967; Gil, 1970; Johnson & Morse, 1968; Steinmetz & Straus, 1974:146; Young, 1964), presumably because of the difficulties of coping with many children. Our results do show that violence toward children varies by size of family, but not as we expected. Parents with two children have a higher rate of violence than parents with one child. The rate does *not* increase with further increases in family size.

Social Isolation

Past studies suggest that social isolation is a major correlate of child abuse (Helfer & Kempe, 1972; Maden & Wrench, 1977; Smith, 1973). Families without continuing relationships outside the home (Young, 1964), families with few memberships in organizations (Merrill, 1962), families high in anomie (Elmer, 1967) and families without telephone (Newberger et al., 1977) have been found to have higher rates of abuse.

We found that parents who lived in the same neighborhood for less than three years had higher rates of abusive violence (18.5% vs. 11.6%) than parents who have lived in the same neighborhood for three years or more (Straus, 1979a). Participation in organizations outside the home made an even greater difference. Those who did not belong to or attend meetings of any organization (clubs, lodges, unions, church groups, etc.) had violence rates much higher than parents who belonged to or attended meetings of at least one community organization (19.9% vs. 11.6%) (Straus, 1979a).

Cultural Norms and Violence Toward Children

Edward Zigler, former head of the Children's Bureau in the Department of Health, Education, and Welfare, has compared current knowledge about child abuse to the state of knowledge about mental illness in 1948 (Zigler, Note 2). That our study and some other studies have documented the extent of violence toward children, and analyzed some of the social factors associated with what we have called abusive violence, does not contradict Zigler's assessment.

The theoretical understanding of these diverse materials is at a very preliminary stage. Gelles & Straus (1979) present an inventory of theories of violence, and offer an integrated theory of violence in the family. Our research to date, however, has convinced us that an adequate theory of violence toward children will have to take into account the structure of the society and of the family and the norms or rules of the culture.

When "violence in the family" is mentioned, it evokes the picture of a child with broken bones or a husband beating up his wife for no good reason. Such instances make up only a small part of the violence that occurs in families. Most family violence does not become a matter of public concern because it is "normal violence," in the sense that it follows the implicit rules of our culture concerning violence. Any theory purporting to explain human violence must take into account such cultural rules or norms, that specify the conditions under which violence is and is not appropriate, and the nature of the violent acts which are legitimate (i.e., which are tolerated, permitted, or required.)

What are the "rules" governing the occurrence of violence within the family, and which forms are "legitimate" or acceptable? In many families the norm seems to be that if someone is doing wrong, and "won't listen to reason" it is all right to hit. In the case of parents in relation to children, it is more than just all right; many American parents see physical punishment to "teach" the child as their obligation. As we have tried to show elsewhere (Gelles, 1974; Straus, 1976; Straus & Hotaling, 1979) this norm often carries over to the relationship between husbands and wives.

In identifying a husband who beats up his wife as violent, we used the phrase "for no good reason." The implication of this phrase is that there can be situations in which there *is* "a good reason" for a husband to hit his wife, or vice versa. In fact, about one out of four Americans explicitly take that view (Stark & McEvoy, 1970.)

What is a "good reason" varies from couple to couple, and from subculture to subculture. But in our culture in general, the marriage license is also a license to hit. To be sure, there are certain normative restrictions. One cannot inflict "excessive" injury even with a marriage partner.

Just how much violence is "excessive," in marriage or to discipline children, also varies with the individual couple and their subculture. Usually, there is a distinction (again, seldom made explicit) between "ordinary" spanking, pushing, and slapping, and "real" violence. At one extreme are some couples for whom even one slap is taken in the same way as it would be if one of us were to slap a department colleague. Such couples are rare. Even rarer, almost non-existent, are parents who never hit their children.

At the other extreme are couples for whom physical punishment, spanking or slapping a child, are a common occurrence. That end of the continuum is also illustrated by the so-called "stitch rule." It used to be (and still may be) an informal understanding among the police in many cities that, in cases of family fights, no arrests would be made unless there was a wound that needed stitches. The same principle, of tolerating violence, unless there is an injury, is a norm that is very widely applied to violence by parents toward children.

Family Organization and Violence

Many aspects of the way American families are organized tend to produce conflict, even though that is an unintended effect. Such conflict often— not always—leads to violence. Many such characteristics of the family are discussed in detail elsewhere (Straus & Hotaling, 1979; Gelles & Straus, 1979). A few of them are noted here.

First, the most fundamental aspect of family organization is that the family includes persons of diverse ages and both sexes. This makes the family, automatically, the locus of the "generation gap" and the site of "the battle of the sexes." Furthermore, unlike special purpose groups such as academic departments, universities, or factories, the activities and interests of a family cover just about everything. There are simply more "events" over which a dispute can develop than is true for other groups.

There is also a greater intensity of involvement in family conflict. Love, paradoxically, gives the power to hurt. So, the degree of distress felt in conflicts with other family members is likely to be much greater than if the same issue were to arise in relation to someone outside the family.

Membership in a family also carries with it both a concern for other members and a presumed right to try to influence their behavior. Consequently, dissatisfaction over undesirable activities or behavior that impinges on one's own activities is further heightened when attempts are made to change the behavior of the other.

Finally, the rules of our society make what goes on in the family strictly a private affair. This aspect of the family system insulates the family both from social controls and from assistance in coping with conflicts. Moreover, even after violence occurs, the rule of family privacy is often so strong that it prevents the victims from seeking outside help. Pizzey's well-titled book on wife-beating is called *Scream Quietly or the Neighbors Will Hear* (1974).

Few would say that these aspects of family organization should change, that, for example, the family should not consist of people of mixed age and sexes; or that it should not encompass the whole of life; or that family members should not be intensely involved with one another and committed to the family; or that family members should not have an obligation to care about and a right to try to influence other family members; or that there should be no family privacy. These are all highly desirable aspects of family organization within the context of our culture. But they are also aspects of family organization that generate a high level of conflict. And a high level of conflict increases the probability of violence, especially when much violence is supported by cultural norms.

But it is not just the high level of conflict inherent in the organization of families which produces violence. There is also a high level of conflict in other groups, for example in academic departments. Yet instances of physical violence are extremely rare in most types of groups. The most violent event that either of us can remember from 30 years in six different academic departments is a department meeting during which someone threw an eraser *at the wall*. Obviously, something in addition to a high level of conflict is involved. The high frequency of physical violence in American families is produced by the combined effects of the high level of conflict in families with two other things: (1) training (or "modeling") in violence (Straus, 1977; Straus et al., 1979); and (2) the implicit cultural norm that gives family members the "right" to hit if someone is "doing wrong" and "won't listen to reason." That combination sets the stage for a high level of violence that is endemic to American families. Such violence is, in a sense, a product of the very nature of the family itself. In our culture, the family is the locus of a relatively high level of stress and conflict. It is isolated from outside aid and intervention. Certain cultural rules make physical force permissible within it. Violence toward youth in families can be understood only in the context of the forces leading to the violence that tends to occur in all family relationships for a very large proportion of families in our society.

Notes

1. American Humane Association. National analysis of official child neglect and abuse reporting. *American Humane Association.* Denver. Mimeographed, 1978.
2. Zigler, Edward. Controlling child abuse in America: An effort doomed to failure. Paper presented at the First National Conference on Child Abuse and Neglect. Atlanta, 1976.

References

Bakan, D. *Slaughter of the innocents: A study of the battered child phenomenon.* Boston: Beacon Press, 1971.
Bohannan, P. *African homicide and suicide.* New York: Athenium, 1960.
Curtis, L. *Criminal violence: National patterns and behavior.* Lexington, Mass.: Lexington Books, 1974.
DeFrancis, V. Testimony before the subcommittee on children and youth of the committee on labor and public welfare. United States Senate 93rd Congress, 1st Session. On S. 1191 *Child Abuse Prevention Act.* Washington, DC: Government Printing Office, 1973.
DeMause, L. (Ed.) *The history of childhood.* New York: The Psychohistory Press, 1974.
DeMause, L. Our forebearers made childhood a nightmare. *Psychology Today,* 1975, *8,* 85–87.
Dexter, L. A. A note on selective inattention in social science. *Social Problems,* 1958, *6,* 176–182.
Elmer, E. *Children in jeopardy: A study of abused minors and their families.* Pittsburgh: University of Pittsburgh Press, 1967.
Erlanger, H. B. Social class and corporal punishment in childrearing: A reassessment. *American Sociological Review,* 1974, *39,* 68–85.
Eron, L. D., Walder, L. O., & Lefkowitz, M. M. *Learning of aggression in children.* Boston: Little, Brown and Company, 1971.
Fontana, V. J. *Somewhere a child is crying: Maltreatment—causes and prevention.* New York: MacMillan, 1973.
Galdston, R. Observations of children who have been physically abused by their parents. *American Journal of Psychiatry,* 1965, *122,* 440–443.
Gelles, R. J. Child abuse as psychopathology: A sociological critique and reformulation. *American Journal of Orthopsychiatry,* 1973, *43,* 611–621. Also reprinted in Steinmetz and Straus, 1974.
Gelles, R. J. *The violent home: A study of physical aggression between husbands and wives.* Beverly Hills: Sage, 1974.
Gelles, R. J. Violence towards children in the United States. *American Journal of Orthopsychiatry,* 1978, *48,* 580–592.
Gelles, R. J. The Truth About Husband Abuse. *Ms. Magazine,* 1979, (in press).
Gelles, R. J. & Straus, M. A. Determinants of violence in the family: Toward a theoretical integration. In W. Burr, R. Hill, F. I. Nye, & I. Reiss, (Eds.), *Contemporary Theories About the Family,* New York: Free Press, 1979.
Gil, D. G. *Violence against children: Physical child abuse in the United States.* Cambridge, MA: Harvard University Press, 1970.

Helfer, R. E. & Kempe, C. H. *Helping the battered child and his family.* Philadelphia: Lippincott, 1972.

Holmes, T. H. & Rahe, R. H. The social readjustment rating scale. *Journal of Psychosomatic Research,* 1967, *11,* 213–218.

Johnson, B. & Morse, H. A. Injured children and their parents. *Children,* 1968, *15,* 147–152.

Kempe, C. H., Silverman, F. N., Steele, B. F., Droegmueller, W., & Silver, H. K. The battered child syndrome. *Journal of the American Medical Association,* 1962, *181,* 17–24.

Lefkowitz, M. M., Eron, L. D., Walder, L. O. & Huesmann, L. R. *Growing up to be violent: A longitudinal study of the development of aggression.* New York: Pergamon Press, 1977.

Light, R. J. Abused and neglected children in America: A study of alternative policies. *Harvard Educational Review,* 1973, *43,* 556–598.

Maccoby, E. E. & Jacklin, C. N. *The psychology of sex differences.* Stanford, California: Stanford University Press, 1974.

Maden, M. F. & Wrench, D. F. Significant findings in child abuse research. *Victimology,* 1977, *2,* 196–224.

Merrill, E. J. Protecting the battered child. Denver: Children's Division, *American Humane Association,* 1962.

Nagi, S. Z. *Child Maltreatment in the United States.* New York: Columbia University Press, 1977.

Newberger, E. H., Reed, R. B., Daniel, J. H., Hyde, J. N. Jr., & Kotglchuck, M. Pediatric social illness: Toward an etiologic classification. *Pediatrics,* 1977, *60,* 178–185.

Newson, J. & Newson, E. *Infant care in an urban community.* London: Allen and Unwin, 1963.

One child dies daily from abuse: Parent probably was abused. *Pediatric News,* 1975, *9,* 3ff.

Pelton, L. H. Child abuse and neglect: The myth of classlessness. *American Journal of Orthopsychiatry,* 1978, *48,* 608–617.

Pizzey, E. *Scream quietly or the neighbors will hear.* Baltimore, Maryland: Penguin Books, 1974.

Pfohl, S. J. The "discovery" of child abuse. *Social Problems,* 1977, *24*(3), 310–323.

Radbill, S. X. A history of child abuse and infanticide. In R. E. Helfer & C. H. Kempe, (Eds.), *The battered child.* (2nd Ed.), University of Chicago Press, 1974.

Sears, R. R., Maccoby, E. & Levin, H. *Patterns of child rearing.* Evanston, IL: Row Peterson, 1957.

Smith, S. M. *The battered child syndrome.* London: Butterworths, 1973.

Spinetta, J. J. & Rigler, D. The child-abusing parent: A psychological review. Psychological Bulletin, 1972, *77,* 296–304.

Stark, R. & McEvoy, J. Middle class violence. *Psychology Today,* 1970, *4,* 52–65.

Steele, B. F. & Pollock, C. B. A psychiatric study of parents who abuse infants and small children. In R. E. Helfer, & C. H. Kempe, (Eds.), *The battered child.* (2nd Ed.) Chicago: University of Chicago Press, 1974.

Steinmetz, S. K. *Cycle of violence: Assertive, aggressive, and abusive family interaction.* New York: Praeger Publishers, 1977.

Steinmetz, S. K. & Straus, M. A. *Violence in the family.* New York: Harper and Row (originally published by Dodd, Mead, and Co.), 1974.

Straus, M. A. Foreword. In Gelles, R. J., *The violent home: A study of physical aggression between husbands and wives.* Beverly Hills: Sage, 1974. (a)

Straus, M. A. Leveling, civility and violence in the family. *Journal of Marriage and the Family,* 1974, *36,* 13–29. Plus addendum August, 1974. (b)

Straus, M. A. Sexual inequality, cultural norms and wife-beating. *Victimology,* 1976, *1,* 54–76. Also reprinted in E. C. Viano, (Ed.), *Victims and society.* Washington, D.C.:

Visage Press, 1976: and in J. R. Chapman & M. Gates, (Eds.), *Women into wives: The legal and economic impact of marriage.* Sage Yearbooks in Women Policy Studies, Vol. 2. Beverly Hills, CA: Sage, 1977.

Straus, M. A. Wife-beating: How common and why? *Victimology,* 1977, *2,* 443–458. Also reprinted in Straus and Hotaling, 1979.

Straus, M. A. Family patterns and child abuse in a nationally representative American sample. *Child Abuse and Neglect,* 1979. (In press). (a)

Straus, M. A. Measuring intrafamily conflict and violence: The Conflict Tactics (CT) scales. *Journal of Marriage and the Family,* 1979, *41,* (b).

Straus, M. A., Gelles, R. J. & Steinmetz, S. K. *Behind closed doors: Violence in the American family.* Garden City, N.Y.: Doubleday/Anchor, 1979.

Straus, M. A. & Hotaling, G. T. (Eds.), *The social causes of husband-wife violence.* Minneapolis: University of Minnesota Press, 1979 (In press).

United States Senate Hearing before the subcommittee on Children and Youth, of the Committee on Labor and Public Welfare. United States Senate, 93rd Congress First Session. On S. 1191 *Child Abuse Prevention and Treatment Act.* Washington, DC: U.S. Government Printing Office, 1973.

Wolfgang, M. E. Husband-wife homicides. *Corrective psychiatry and Journal of Social Therapy,* 1956, *2,* 263–271. Also reprinted in C. D. Bryant & J. G. Wells, (Eds.), *Deviancy and the Family.* Philadelphia: F. A. Davis, 1973.

Young, L. R. *Wednesday's children: A study of child neglect and abuse.* New York: McGraw-Hill, 1964.

Family Adjustment to Unemployment

Principal Investigator: Louis A. Ferman

Author: Mary C. Blehar

■   Almost any week even a casual reader of the financial section of the daily newspaper can find articles that note the closing of this or that business. Some of the "obituaries" are so brief that they are barely noticed amid the scanning of stock quotes and economic indicators. In bolder print, headlines peg the unemployment rate for the 1970s at around 6 percent for the foreseeable future. But what the articles and statistics fail to convey is the human reality of economic upheaval. For many Americans, job loss is much, much more than a single event in time. Rather it is an occurrence of monumental import. It starts them down a long road, the end of which promises nothing.

Louis A. Ferman and Mary C. Blehar. "Family Adjustment to Unemployment" from FAMILIES TODAY, vol. 1, DHEW Publication No. (ADM)79–815.

While American society is such that unemployment can knock at any door, some people are more at risk than others: minorities, women, and youths among them. Tradition, however, has given special attention to the problem of job loss for male heads of household, on the assumption that they are responsible not just for themselves, but also for dependents. Unemployment for a married man is not usually just a personal crisis. It is a family crisis as well.

Dr. Louis Ferman, Research Director of the Institute of Labor and Industrial Relations, at The University of Michigan in Ann Arbor and Wayne State University, has been focusing his research on the plight of the unemployed family man. He is asking what happens when a man loses his job. Just what are his experiences and his reactions to them?

Ferman notes that the Recession of the mid-1970s touched many Americans, directly or indirectly. Because of its pervasive impact, large numbers of the Nation's adults became familiar with the institutional machinery that is called into play when a person ceases to be a member of the work force. Unemployment Insurance provides at least a temporary buffer against major economic setbacks. Employment agencies offer channels through which re-employment can be sought. Unions may provide assistance through special programs for members. Welfare offers relief for the truly destitute.

Psychological reactions to job loss are less clearly understood. In the case of a working man who is accustomed to defining himself in terms of his role as a "breadwinner," loss of this role can lead to profound depression, feelings of isolation from his fellows, and lack of hope for tomorrow.

Differences in reactions to job loss do exist. Some of these probably stem from fundamental differences in personality. Certain individuals are by nature optimists; others are pessimists. However influential they may be, personality variables are very difficult to measure, particularly on a large scale, whereas differences in sheer availability and quality of social supports can be documented more readily by the industrial sociologist. In general, the more institutional aids available, the better the outlook for the worker following unemployment and during readjustment to a new job.

Ferman points out that *informal social systems* can play a supportive role in a man's adjustment to unemployment, a role that is as yet poorly understood but more important than one might suspect. Factors such as the amount of sympathy and help received from family and friends can probably mediate between impersonal institutions and the jobless person and have a considerable influence on personal well-being.

Currently, Ferman, recipient of an NIMH grant, is studying career patterns among unemployed blue-collar workers in metropolitan Detroit. He is no novice in the field of industrial sociology. Describing himself as a psychological child of the Great Depression and its economic turmoil, he has been researching the area of unemployment for several years.

Over this period his focus has shifted. His earlier work demonstrated the impact of formal institutional supports on personal morale. Like other workers in the field at that time, he attributed importance to the actual loss of a job as a prime stressor in a person's life. Now his perspective has shifted, and he is more interested in scientific investigations into the informal supports a person receives. He is no longer convinced that the initial loss of work is the greatest trauma of the unemployment period. Events occurring during "recovery" may be more difficult for many people to cope with.

Sociological and economic research, he notes, mirrors the spirit of the times. Writings based on the Great Depression of the 1930s gave prominence to the informal kinds of assistance that were available to a man who had lost his job. In that era governmental props in the form of large-scale programs were nonexistent. Job loss usually meant real and immediate financial crisis. There was no Workman's Compensation, little welfare. Labor unions were in their infancy. Job programs weren't initiated until the Roosevelt era and even then were not brought into being without some popular resistance. A man typically had only his immediate family, kin, and friends to fall back on. The work ethic was so strong and the aversion to anything that could be construed as "charity" so firmly ingrained in most Americans that unemployment carried with it a stigma probably not appreciated today by people under age 50.

Sociology in the 1950s and 1960s eventually followed the zeitgeist. Institutions, it was thought, could save the American worker from distress. Problems associated with unemployment could be legislated away. Research trends followed correspondingly.

The 1970s have witnessed perhaps an inevitable pendulum swing away from faith in the efficacy of large-scale programs to solve all human woes back toward a renewed appreciation of the role of community- and family-based structures in helping the individual cope with crisis. . . .

The Detroit Unemployment Study

The present NIMH-funded study Ferman and his colleagues are working on is both an informal hypothesis-testing and an hypothesis-generating one. By means of survey-interview techniques a substantial amount of data has been gathered on a large and heterogeneous group of recently unemployed persons in Detroit, Mich., during the mid-1970s. Preliminary hypotheses concerning the role of economic deprivation and various kinds of social support were foremost in the minds of Ferman and his associates when they planned the design; therefore, survey respondents were polled repeatedly over a 2-year period about their economic position and about the state of their health. What economic setbacks, if any, had they suffered? How far were they from their "ideal" economic status? How did they feel physically? (Blood pressure readings were taken on two occasions.) How much had they been sick since becoming unemployed? Were they taking any medicines? Did they have mood swings or periods of depression? How were families and friends responding to their plight? What specific things were they doing to help or hinder the respondents?

The longitudinal feature of the design permits Ferman to look at changes in behavior and feelings over time. Do people optimistically start out seeking re-employment only to become demoralized if time passes and they haven't found a job or the "right" job? Do they hit emotional peaks and troughs? Is there any predictability to these? Are they related systematically to events happening to the person in the social environment?

The sample is not a random one. Because of protection-of-privacy constraints imposed during the period of data collection, Ferman and his research colleagues could not obtain a master list of Unemployment Insurance recipients from which to draw names of potential participants. With much ingenuity and leg work, they solicited the recently unemployed by various means. They went door to door; they distributed flyers about their project in front of Detroit's Unemployment Office. The resultant group of approximately 500 participants consisted of former wage earners, both black and white, and included married men, women, and secondary wage earners (those living with families and not fulfilling a primary support role). All the participants have been interviewed in person and over the telephone a total of five times in a 24-month period commencing shortly after their job loss. Eventually, data analysis will provide information about each of the subgroups in the larger sample. At present, Ferman's initial analytical efforts have concentrated mainly on the large subgroup of white married men who are primary wage earners for their families. Because the sample is not a random one, it may not be generalizable to national samples of unemployed. However, it provides the opportunity for intensive studies of individuals who have evolved different adaptations to their unemployed status. . . .

The Seven Types of Unemployed Men

Type 1. Those Who Remain Unemployed After Job Loss

The first of the seven groups contained those who had remained unemployed since losing their last job. The men interviewed by Dow had been unemployed for 3 years at least. Who were they? Contrary to popular stereotype, they were not the very young and very unskilled. It would be unusual, Ferman stated, to find such young men, if able-bodied, out of work for so long. Even though joblessness among the latter group is high, the statistics are probably a bit inflated. Many young men may actually be working in the irregular economy, but because their earnings go unrecorded, they remain formally on the lists of those seeking jobs.

In Dow's case, it was the middle-aged and sick who didn't go back to work again. All three men Dow interviewed had developed disabilities that prevented them from working efficiently or at least diminished them in their employer's eyes.

The similarities between the three male heads of household who fit career pattern type 1 were striking. One of them, fictitiously called Michael Ronan, had worked for a corporation for 33 years and had planned to continue until the age of 60. Early in 1975, at the age of 56, however, he was laid off with 30-minute notice. He felt that the reasons for his layoff—which was really the equivalent of a permanent firing—were his status as a salaried person instead of a union member, a personality conflict with the plant manager, and most importantly, continuing ill health resulting from a severe ulcer condition. The latter problem was costing the company money since Ronan received pay despite frequent week-long stays in the hospital. Ronan was only briefly entitled to Unemployment Insurance benefits but was able to prove his ulcer condition to be work related. Thus, he has lived on Workman's Compensation and a small pension since 1975.

The other two ex-workers interviewed also suffered from illnesses. One had developed cancer of the larynx and has, since the operation, lived on disability benefits and his wife's salary from a full-time job. The third man suffered a heart attack. After his recovery, he had found it impossible to be rehired either by his former employer or any other.

All the other data available in the study suggest that these three men and the lives they lead are typical of elderly, skilled workers whose poor health conditions rob them of their last several years of potentially productive employment. The pattern indicates that a worker's health record, once questionable, becomes anathema to potential employers. Even those who recover completely from a disabling disease seem dogged by it. Old age or illness, taken singly, are not usually sufficient to cause sustained unemployment; but in combination, they are almost insurmountable.

The men all felt keenly the frustration of having to lose years of income and most or all of their pensions because of events beyond their control. Even worse, each felt that his work situation had contributed to the health problem. They were bitter toward their former employers and toward the "system"—a bitterness fueled continually by shrinking incomes in the face of inflation. Even though the men had suffered illnesses that most people would consider catastrophic, Dow got the impression that sickness paled in comparison to the suffering caused by losing their jobs. The men expressed ultimate resignation to their plight, but their voices were filled with bitterness about the blind unfairness of life.

Type 2. Those Who Return to Work for Their Former Employers and Remain on the Job

The second pattern consisted of unemployment followed by return to work at the former job. The three individuals in the case study who fit this pattern were unemployed in 1975. In a 1976 questionnaire, Ferman and Dow learned that they had been subsequently rehired by their former employers. By the time of the interviews in the summer and fall of 1977, all three had been working steadily for more than a year. In each case, the men had done a lot of thinking about the impact of the unemployment period and were eager to communicate their thoughts to someone.

One man, Brian Canter, began working for Ford Motor Company in December 1973 and was laid off in November 1974. A college graduate, he has held a highly skilled job both before and after an 11-month period of unemployment. He worked as an experimental parts director, inspecting parts put into engines used in the development of automotive designs. Since he was relatively new in his job at the time when the layoff came, Canter was not eligible for SUB (Supplemental Unemployment Benefits) and was forced to subsist primarily on Unemployment Compensation and his wife's income.

Like other men in the second group, Canter is a skilled worker, but his skills are not widely marketable. When unemployed, he had little hope of finding a job as good as the one he had had with Ford, so he spent only a nominal amount of time exploring avenues of formal employment. Instead, he and a friend started a very modest and off-the-record janitorial service and thus avoided payment of taxes, while they continued to collect Unemployment Insurance. Despite this small supplemental income, Canter still found it difficult to make payments on all the debts he had incurred while with Ford. He watched his savings disappear and his Unemployment Compensation end. He became increasingly depressed and despondent.

To Canter, being unemployed was without a doubt the worst experience of his life. He felt agony when he realized that his family could not maintain its former lifestyle, in spite of his efforts. Toward the end of the 11-month layoff, the strain on his marriage was, in his opinion, critical. Canter asserted that his health was also affected because of emotional and psychological strains. Since his return to work, however, both his ability to meet financial obligations and his personal life have improved dramatically.

The two other men interviewed experienced many of the same emotions as Canter. One, an older, skilled tool-and-die worker was also worried about finances. While his physical health was not affected, his marriage was dealt a "mortal blow" by his job loss, and he and his wife divorced. The third man received SUB payments while out of work. With 95 percent of his pay not affected by his unemployed status, he was never subject to severe financial pressures. At first he even found his free time enjoyable, but after 2 months he became restless. His drinking increased, and the amount he spent on alcohol ate into the family's budget. Even though he has returned to work, his alcoholism continues unabated, and his wife is suing for a divorce.

Ferman puts forward some generalizations about this group. First, regardless of how stable income was, the men's personal security was affected by unemployment. Two of the men attributed most of their problems to lack of money but a third had money and still suffered. Personal relationships within the family seemed to deteriorate. In all three cases, there was an increase in marital strife. But, however difficult their situation may have been, the men in this group were better off by far than the men in group 3.

Type 3. Those Who Found a New Job and Remained Working at It.

Of all the distinctive career patterns observed in the case histories, the third one has proven to be most fraught with peril for the men who follow it. Without exception, these workers believe that the layoff period has been the most difficult challenge of their lives. Also, without exception, each has adjusted to new employment with a determination never again to suffer the humiliation and defeat of losing both job and income.

The men in type 3 never had hopes of being re-employed at their former jobs. They were victims of firms or businesses that had gone bankrupt or companies whose increased automation made their skills obsolete. Accustomed as they were to steady employment, they found job loss extremely devastating to themselves and to their families.

The experience of Miguel Sanchez is a prototype of other men in the group. Sanchez had worked as a security guard until December 1974, when he began a period of unemployment that continued for 14 months. After searching for work throughout his layoff period, he was hired in February 1976 as a patcher in the heating department of the Great Lakes Steel Company, a job he had maintained for 1 1/2 years at the time of the case interview.

Sanchez, his wife, and their three children lived through a series of crises during those 14 months between jobs. The family's only income was a small support payment Mrs. Sanchez received and the Unemployment Insurance benefits Sanchez was entitled to. After a year, however, these latter benefits expired, leaving the family without means to pay even modest bills. Shortly thereafter, they were "kicked out on the street" when their rent fell overdue. Their car was impounded. Prospects for the future seemed bleak indeed.

In the weeks that followed, Sanchez describes nightmares beyond comprehension as he searched for food and shelter for his family. When he finally was hired at his present position, he was a much relieved man. He still considers himself fortunate to have escaped even greater catastrophes while unemployed.

The second man, a middle-aged carpenter, lost his job "out of the clear blue sky." Because of his wife's new job as a secretary and his own unemployment insurance, however, he suffered relatively little economic deprivation. Nonetheless, he remembers the period out of work as one of profound problems. He drank more, ate more, slept more, and watched more TV, meanwhile enjoying all these activities less than before. He contemplated suicide more than once during his layoff period.

The third worker had experiences closely parallel to those of Miguel Sanchez. Because his wife worked and because they had no children, financial difficulties never were as insurmountable. Nonetheless, he did not escape emotional trauma. Particularly unsettling to him were loss of the "provider" role and having to take "handouts."

With all the men what was most disturbing was the increasing doubt that they would ever work again and the nagging realization that financial security might permanently elude them. Because they knew they would not be rehired by their former employers, they were pessimistic about ever being hired by any employer. This sense of hopelessness distinguished type-3 workers most readily from their type-2 counterparts. Uncertainty about the future for the men took perhaps as great a toll of human misery as did reduced income. Depression and anxiety were common experiences.

The men now report themselves as having recovered markedly from their symptoms, but each agrees that he is less optimistic, more cynical, and more thankful than ever that he is working.

Type 4. Those Who Have Been Periodically In and Out of Work With Their Former Employers

The fourth group of men were those who had been periodically in and out of work with their former employers. For each of the type-4 individuals interviewed, periods of work and joblessness were fairly predictable. They were also accompanied by SUB payments and rarely lasted for more than a few months. Economic deprivation was minimal. Under such conditions, unemployment came to resemble something closer to a vacation than a life crisis. Not every one of the type-4 men interviewed acknowledged unmitigated pleasure in being unemployed, but their reactions were so mild as to present an important alternative view to a usually dark picture.

Steve Zaiglin, a typical type 4, is a 29-year-old employee of Massy-Ferguson, a large Detroit producer of tractors and tractor accessories. His specific job involves spray-painting parts before assembly, labor he described as semiskilled. Since starting work there in 1974, he has been laid off intermittently, an average of 2 1/2 months during each year. For every year the layoffs have been spread over several 3-week intervals, each of which Zaiglin was able to anticipate by 2 months.

During a layoff, he received 95 percent of his normal pay plus the virtual guarantee that he would be called back to work. Not surprisingly, he referred to these periods as "the best of times." Far from presenting a threat to his security, unemployment offered him the opportunity to travel, relax, and spend time with his family, all luxuries that are unavailable to most holders of full-time jobs. The other two type-4 men didn't deviate much from Zaiglin in their patterns. One, when pressed to find an unpleasant aspect of his time out of work, mentioned jealousy directed toward him by friends of his who were working 40-hour weeks, yet earning comparable wages. At times he admitted to feelings of guilt that he was, in essence, "cheating the company," though for the most part these sentiments were overridden by his enthusiasm for his lifestyle, with its consequent reduced responsibilities and increased leisure time. The third worker didn't actually enjoy his periods of unemployment but admitted that economic penalties were few. What he disliked was having to spend so much time at home, since he believed that a man should spend only evenings and weekends with wife and children. However, he suffered no severe traumas in contrast to workers of types 1, 2, and 3.

It was after Dow's interview with the men of type 4 that he and Ferman became quite convinced that the unemployed were not homogeneous. The experiences of these men were very different from the others. Unemployment could be a pleasant interlude, a planned-for respite from the drudgery of 9-to-5 work, if a man was sure that he could work again, at will. It became a harrowing experience for the fellow who found his skills suddenly obsolete in the work force and who wasn't sure that he would meet with success in trying to get back in.

Type 5. Those Who Have Been Periodically In and Out of Work With One New Employer

The career pattern of type-5 workers was superficially similar to those in the fourth category in one way. Both types of men established patterns of employment, unemployment, and re-employment. In the case of type 5s, however, this pattern was established only after initial job loss from a first employer and subsequent re-employment with a new one, and type 5s rarely received SUB. Hence, it was unlikely that they had the financial flexibility necessary to pick and choose their next job.

This basic difference between the two types is illustrated by contrasting reactions to unemployment. Type 4s tended to view it as a slight bother at worst, a welcome vacation at best. Type 5s shared little of this attitude, since they had to struggle to supplement their Unemployment Insurance with some other form of income. While it is true that periods of unemployment for the type-5 worker might have been just as temporary and just as short as those experienced by type 4, the former's lack of SUB created an economic crisis seldom endured by the latter. Hence, unemployment was not a welcome respite. However, neither was it the agony of uncertainty faced by workers in the first three career patterns.

It is interesting to note that all three type-5 men interviewed by Dow were mechanics. This occupational similarity allowed them to engage in activities in the "irregular economy" which eased financial difficulties during periods of formal employment.

Jesse Wiley's career pattern exemplifies that of type-5 workers. Since losing his first job as a tool grinder over 15 years ago, Wiley has worked steadily with only temporary layoffs for a small Detroit tool-and-die company. During three layoffs he received no SUB and is entitled only to hospital insurance in addition to UI benefits.

Because he possesses skills as a mechanic, during periods of unemployment he works in the irregular economy and earns an income approaching 50 percent of his normal wages. This income, coupled with monthly unemployment checks, allows him and his family to continue in a lifestyle not radically different from the one they are used to. In short, adjustment made by the Wileys to unemployment is not as considerable as it would be were it not for the irregular economy. Not surprisingly, Wiley's overall response to his periods out of work is free of the trauma which appears virtually always to accompany a dramatic reduction in income.

Type 6. Those Who Have Been Periodically In and Out of Work With More Than One New Employer

The sixth career pattern illuminated in the larger survey study and examined more intensively in the case study was the most chaotic of all. Workers with this type of career history have not only experienced repeated layoffs, but each layoff followed a job with a different employer. Dow's three type-6 men revealed through their histories a variety of reasons for chronic unemployment, so that he and Ferman were left with little basis for generalization about the type. The following brief portraits of type-6 careers illustrate the extreme variability that exists.

Alan Ali, age 33, has worked for six different employers in a 14-year career. The jobs he has held range from stockman at a grocery store to mine worker in Arizona. In between jobs, Ali has worked sporadically as a handyman in the irregular economy, but with little success. He shows no signs of upward or downward job mobility, but remarkably he professes to be undiscouraged by his consistent failure to find work adequate to provide for his family. Not even qualified for Unemployment Insurance, Ali survives through the help of a welfare check. Although he expresses some concern over the emotional adjustment of his 9-year-old child to his father's unemployment and laments the debilitating effects of unemployment on his physical strength (an asset in many jobs he finds), his own adjustment has not been characterized by personal trauma. He remains hopeful and patient.

Keith Laren, another type-6 worker, has a work history quite similar to Ali's. Laren has been through seven jobs in 7 years. Unlike Ali, he shows little inclination to change this career pattern for one more stable or permanent. Throughout the interviews, Laren repeated his motto that "Responsibility isn't worth the heartache." He has long ago exhausted UI benefits and is content with an income well below the poverty line. A job as a mechanic in the irregular economy and a part-time job held by his wife are the only sources of income the family has. Despite this, Laren boasts of great enjoyment of his lifestyle.

The third type-6 worker, a 61-year-old bricklayer, offers an example of why it is difficult to make any generalizations about this career group. James Sullivan is a specialized laborer who throughout the years chose to move from job to job in order to go after "big money." Consequently, he has often found himself out of work and, lacking entry into the irregular economy, has depended on UI and savings to tide his family over during these periods.

Unlike Ali and Laren, Sullivan has experienced shame and bitterness over his failure to provide for his family as he would have liked. Not only a loser of his gamble for higher earnings, he has also sacrificed the benefits of a company pension, insurance, health care, and perhaps, most importantly, has given up the greater steadiness and security of a more conventional career. Though economic security is apparently unimportant to Ali and Laren it is crucial to Sullivan's sense of his own worth.

Because workers in the sixth career pattern are so different, Dow and Ferman have little in the way of generalization to offer. Perhaps the most that can be said is that such a work pattern should itself be divided into several subtypes, each of which warrants further observation. Indeed, in recognizing the oversimplification inherent in establishing any limited set of career patterns, they return to their original proposition: that unemployment is a multifaceted phenomenon and that each of its forms must be understood separately and independently before researchers will ever be able to grasp what it means to an individual when he loses his job.

Type 7. Those Whose Career Patterns Conform to None of the Above

A minority of the larger survey sample, 9.5 percent, had experienced work patterns so idiosyncratic as to defy attempts at classification. In selecting three individuals to interview in this catchall grouping, Ferman and Dow wanted to determine if career histories were really as distinctive as they seemed. The emergent data show that the cases are of importance precisely because they demonstrate the great variety of forms that unemployment and its consequence may take.

To give brief examples, the first type-7 worker, George Sampson, age 35, lost a position as a high school history teacher in 1975. The holder of an M.A. degree, he had hoped to remain employed permanently in teaching. During an otherwise arid year of unemployment, he taught as a substitute. Recently however, he became so disillusioned about ever teaching again that he has taken up painting in the irregular economy. Currently he is planning to leave Detroit altogether and seek a teaching position with the Peace Corps in Algeria. Sampson's disappointments are not primarily financial, since his wife has worked steadily at a full-time job which has provided enough money for them and their two children. What bothers him the most is the "humiliation of unemployment." He attributes several physical and emotional disorders he suffers from—overweight, insomnia, depression, and cynicism—to frustration and uncertainty.

Joseph Wininski illustrates another variety of unemployment. Wininski, now 59 and retired, quit his former job of 31 years with Chrysler Corporation because it was becoming increasingly onerous to him. He did so realizing that he was entitled to a modest pension which, together with a veteran's disability allowance, his wife's income, and their savings, allowed him to live comfortably even if he should never find another job. He never did. During the first interviews, Wininski professed to be seeking employment, but it soon became apparent that these efforts were at best halfhearted. At present, he says that he is wholly contented with his situation. Because he has a comfortable income available to him approximately 10 years before a more conventional retirement age of 63, Wininski opted for a work status that conforms officially to the category of unemployed but might more correctly be labeled voluntary early retirement.

The final case history of a worker whose career pattern was difficult to classify is that of Randy Jacobs. Jacobs' career has to some degree followed the type-2 pattern since he now has returned to work with a former employer and has remained on the job. What is unusual about his history is that he has worked for other employers in between. First employed as a machine repairman in 1970 by American Can, he continued there until he was laid off in 1974. Before returning to that company for work in 1977, Jacobs worked variously as a Dairy Queen manager and later as a retail salesman in a discount department store. The later two jobs were not sought merely as interim positions. Jacobs reports thinking about not returning to American Can, and he only took his present job because the offer included a pay raise. Unlike other type-2 workers, he had neither the desire to be rehired by his former employer nor the expectation that he ever would be.

As might be inferred from his attitude toward his former job, being unemployed was never a crisis for Jacobs. Dow found him to be one of those rare workers who genuinely enjoyed unemployment, even when it was accompanied by considerable economic sacrifice. His success in finding new jobs, coupled with savings and his wife's jobs, has enabled him to enjoy his time off as a pleasant, extended vacation. Throughout the interviews with Dow, he exulted that life had never treated him better than when he was unemployed, and he lamented his return to American Can. Like the other workers classified under type 7, Jacobs' case history reaffirms the broad range of responses to unemployment and suggests the need for analyzing other factors which mediate the individual's response to the loss of a job.

In generalizing about the findings of the case studies, Ferman noted that the individual's adjustment to unemployment is mediated in a most critical fashion by the postunemployment career pattern. Career pattern sets the background for being laid off and helps translate that event as quite stressful, relatively benign, or even welcome. This fact may be the study's single most important conclusion, for far too often unemployment is envisioned as a uniform, unicausal experience. On the contrary, from the case histories, it emerges clearly that unemployment's surest constant is its variation.

Within that variation, however, patterns of career histories hold much value for their ability to predict likely responses to unemployment. Where SUB is available, the worker is under little if any increased economic burden during his layoff and stands an excellent chance of weathering unemployment quite easily. Not surprisingly, the converse of the above is also true: The worker without SUB who suffers significant financial losses is most likely to succumb to the more destructive personal consequences of unemployment. Yet the picture is also complicated by the degree of certainty with which the worker is able to view the future. Those former employees who felt assured of re-employment were less prone to negative sentiments than those whose future remained uncertain. The analyses of career patterns suggest avoiding overly simplistic arguments regarding the obvious advantages of a stable income and propose an awareness of the vital influence of the worker's outlook toward his chances of finding another job.

As shown by the few case histories that offered exceptions to generalizations, no particular career pattern by itself was a sufficient indicator of adjustment to unemployment. For this reason, the case studies were also designed to determine the extent to which personal attributes influenced adjustments to the loss of a job. Dow and Ferman reasoned that such factors would aid interpretation of reactions to job loss that might not fit the "normal" patterns. Accordingly, in interviews, individual workers were asked questions specifically designed to reveal whether or not the informant felt that his age, education, or number of dependents played a significant role in his adjustment. Similarly, his opinion as to how much his ability to cope with unemployment was helped or hindered by people within his social milieu was sought. . . .

Summing Up

When asked about the project's broad implications, Ferman began by making some generalizations: Today's unemployed are an extremely heterogeneous group to whom unemployment can mean different things. For some people, it is the start of a difficult and tenuous course of readjustment, for others a temporary pause, perhaps frustrating, even pleasurable, but one that is more or less defined as time limited. Those who have to live with uncertainty about tomorrow are those who suffer. Not knowing about the future invariably takes a major toll on the individual and his family.

Especially for workers with good prospects of future employment and those whose economic deprivation is minimal, unemployment is not equivalent in psychological impact to that suffered by millions of Americans during the Great Depression. Where economic deprivation is great, however, it is still at the root of many problems, such as psychological depression, loss of hope, alcoholism, and family disruption.

Compounding the effects of economic deprivation, loss of status as a breadwinner adds to personal shame and humiliation. Such emotions are felt most forcefully by older workers who attach a stigma to the unemployed status.

Despite the availability of transfer payment supports such as SUB and UI and opportunities for work in the irregular economy, the majority of unemployed workers appear to remain attached to the world of steady work. A good job is certainly one that pays well, but other facets are important. Chief among these is predictability of employment with its implicit certainty for the future. Dollars and cents so often appear to dominate economic discussions that we are apt to forget that money may be a means to an end of achieving a lifestyle buffered against economic downturns. Other aspects of regular work that make it appealing are overtime, fringe benefits, and personal challenges. Thus, even when supplemental payments from institutional sources and informal work opportunities are available, regular work is sought for its psychological benefits.

Of all the informal social supports studied by Ferman and his colleagues, the only one to emerge as having real significance is kin support. Blood relationships seem to convey a responsibility to give aid that neighboring and worker relationships do not. While sociologists have been wont to speak glowingly of the importance of neighborhood social networks in assisting the individual, they may have been overly zealous in their estimations, at least as far as the unemployed person is concerned.

If the family system is indeed the most critical informal one in mediating the effects of unemployment, it may also be the most difficult one to influence. Congressional fiat and Presidential orders alone cannot strengthen the quality of family bonds. The forces affecting family cohesiveness are difficult to isolate. At times they are idiosyncratic, often so general as to be intertwined with broad economic and social forces. Notions of what is "good" or "right" for the family are open to interpretation and are, at any rate, difficult to implement through systematic action.

When asked where his research fits in the larger scheme of things, Ferman refers to a book, *Mental Illness and the Economy*, which has served as an intellectual inspiration for much of his work. In it, author M. Harvey Brenner argued that a major source of increased mental disorders and serious diseases in the twentieth century was economic recession and depression. Ferman aspires to fill in Brenner's more general sketch with details. "I hope that my study will provide a picture of the impact of job loss on mental health and some idea of the family's role in influencing economically conditioned outcomes."

References

Aiken, M. T.; Ferman, L. A; and Sheppard, H. *Economic Failure, Alienation and Extremism*. Ann Arbor, Mich.: The University of Michigan Press, 1968.

Angell, R. C. *The Family Encounters the Depression*. New York: Charles Scribner's Sons, 1936.

Bakke, E. W. *Citizens Without Work*. New Haven, Conn.: Yale University Press, 1940.

Brenner, M. H. *Mental Illness and the Economy*. Cambridge, Mass.: Harvard University Press, 1973.

Ferman, L. A., and Ferman, P. The underpinnings of the irregular economy. *Poverty and Human Resources Abstracts*. Beverly Hills: Sage Publications, March 1973.

Ferman, L. A. Sociological perspectives in unemployment research. In: Shostak, A. B., and Gomberg, W., eds. *Blue Collar World*. Englewood Cliffs, N.J.: Prentice-Hall, Inc., 1964. p. 512.

Ferman, L. A., and Aiken, M. T. The adjustment of older workers to job displacement. In: Shostak, A. B., and Gomberg, W., eds. *Blue Collar World*. Englewood Cliffs, N.J.: Prentice-Hall, Inc. 1964. pp. 493–498.

Ferman, L. A.; Berndt, L.; and Selo, E. "Analysis of the Irregular Economy: Cash Flow in the Informal Sector." A report to the Bureau of Employment and Training, Michigan Department of Labor. March 1978.

Gore, S. L. "The Influence of Social Support and Related Variables in Ameliorating the Consequences of Job Loss." Ph.D. Dissertation, Department of Sociology, University of Michigan, 1973.

Komarovsky, M. *The Unemployed Man and His Family.* New York: Holt, Rinehart and Winston, Inc. 1940.

Warren, Donald I. *Neighborhood and Community Contexts in Help Seeking, Problem Coping and Mental Health: Data Analysis Monograph.* Final unpublished report, U.S. Public Health Service, National Institute of Mental Health, Rockville, Md., August 31, 1976.

Divorce and Remarriage

The Single Parent and Public Policy
Alvin L. Schorr and Phyllis Moen

■ The divorce rate in the United States is at an all time high; we are commonly said to have the highest divorce rate in the world. One result of this has been a striking increase in female-headed families; the number of divorced women heading families nearly tripled between 1960 and 1975 alone.[1] As a result, the number of children living in one-parent families increased by 60 percent in the last decade.[2] A number of quite different forces have contributed to these changes—the increased propensity of mothers without husbands to form separate families, women's increased labor force participation, and the spread of no-fault divorce.

Despite these changes, somewhere in their minds Americans still tend to hold a conventional view of the family as having two parents and two or three children. This conventional version of the family is so powerful that scholars, like citizens, label other family forms pejoratively—as "deviant," "broken," or "unstable."[3] Indeed, single parents label themselves as unique and "abnormal."[4] Nor are conventional views quite repudiated by minorities and the poor. On the contrary, while in some neighborhoods or subcultures half or more of all children live in single-parent families, their parents regard their single status as demonstrably normal on one hand and as evidence of failure and delinquency on the other.

Meanwhile, the traditional family—husband, wife, and children from the first marriage of the spouses—accounts for only 45 percent of American families.[5] The next most frequent types are the single-parent family (15 percent) and the nuclear-dyad—husband and wife alone without children (15 percent).

By the age of eighteen, nearly one out of two children will have lived a period of time with a single parent.[6] Meanwhile, the number of husband-wife families has begun to decline. At any moment in time, 25 to 30 percent of all children are in one-parent families.[7] The gap between the public image of the single-parent family and reality cannot be laid to a new situation we have not had time to recognize. It may be stipulated that conditions are changing, but they have been changing for a long time, and there was extensive foreshadowing of current patterns. There have, for hundreds of years, been single-parent families and considerable variation in family form, including the three-generation family, the commune, and the nuclear family. Early death of the father combined with an extended span of child-bearing has made the single-parent family fairly common in the twentieth century.[8]

The view that the single-parent family is unique and deviant has other elements bound up in it. Single parenthood is seen as a transitional state. For example, four out of five divorced and widowed persons remarry. Nevertheless, past the age of 30, a greater proportion remain single,[9] and the tendency to remarry appears now to be declining.[10] A recent longitudinal study of unmarried women who headed households found that fewer than one-fifth had married in a five-year period.[11] Single-parent families may live "as if" in a permanent state, whatever their futures may hold, though policy-makers may see their status as transitional.

Pathology is a prominent element of the public view of single parenthood. Although the term has come to be associated with the "Moynihan controversy" of 1965, in truth professionals and social agencies have long regarded single parenthood as pathological for reasons arising from their own backgrounds.[12] "Trained in the clinical model, [they] are conditioned to recognize pathology. While some attention in professional education may be given to preventive care and normal growth and development, the overriding emphasis is on the successful treatment and reversal of problems."[13] Against the background of this public image of single parenthood, policy has been couched in terms of improving the stability of existing intact families and services have been designed to facilitate the reconstitution of families.

Public discussion of the single-parent family in the last decade or two has come to overlap considerably with a discussion of Black family life and welfare. Consequently, the mainstream reality of single-parent families is hidden. A larger proportion of Black families than white families have single parents, 35 percent compared with 11 percent. For reasons that are all but obvious—single parent families are usually headed by one wage-earner who is usually a woman and likely to earn less than a man—single-parent families are likely to rely on welfare. Still, a third of the women-headed, single-parent families never receive welfare.[14] The stereotype that recipients have simply resigned themselves to welfare has no relation to fact. Of seven million mothers who received welfare over a ten-year period, the typical woman was assisted for two years, left welfare, and eventually received it for two years more. Only 770,000 received welfare for nine or ten years.[15]

Generalizing inevitably leaves an impression of uniformity but the situation of single-parent families varies considerably. For example, single fathers may be in a markedly different position from single mothers. Though still a small minority, single fatherhood is increasing at a faster rate than families headed by women.[16] In part, this reflects changes in courtroom attitude toward custody, but also changing conceptions of the roles of men and women. As women have sought to define identities apart from that of wife and mother, so too have more men seen themselves in roles other than wage-earner.[17]

The most prominent difference is that single fathers command higher incomes. The average income of single mothers in 1973 was $6,000, compared to $12,000 for single fathers.[18] Though a single father's income may more easily permit him to buy housekeeping services, recent studies show that he too usually performs housekeeping duties—helped by his children.[19] Still, many of the stereotypes that constrain women also confine men. Since child care is not seen as their role, it is difficult for fathers to adjust their working hours to meet the needs of their children.[20] Although they report a need for services—child care in the evening, transportation to day care, and so forth, single fathers express feelings of success and satisfaction about parenting; in this they are like single mothers.[21]

Widows with children are a significantly different group from the divorced and separated. Less than a fifth are under 35 (compared with 55 percent of divorced and separated women with children). Possibly for that reason and because they usually receive Social Security benefits, their total income is substantially higher.[22] On the average, Black single-parent families are different from white. Black single mothers are twice as likely to have three children or more—30 out of 100 compared with 15 out of 100 for white single mothers. Black single parents are less likely than white to be working; they have higher unemployment rates, lower educational levels, and higher rates of poverty.[23]

One may attempt to classify single parents logically—as widowed, divorced, separated, and unmarried.[24] Such a distinction directs attention to the rather different causes and feelings that may be at play for the families. For example, death may be a more sudden and final blow. Separation may be a stage on the road to divorce. The unmarried mother faces more stigma, though possibly this is changing a little. She is likely to be younger than the others, and her financial difficulties even more serious. Unmarried mothers are becoming increasingly consequential, as one birth in seven in the United States is now illegitimate.[25]

In whatever ways they differ, however, all single parents suffer from public images of the ideal family.

Parenthood, Work, and Income

Closely linked to the image of the traditional two-parent family is an ideological stance concerning the proper division of labor within the family. Specifically, the male is thought of as the head of the household— the "breadwinner" of the family. Weitzman speaks of the "hidden contract" of marriage: 1) that the husband is the head of the household and responsible for economic support and 2) that the wife is responsible for child care.[26] Consequences of this role differentiation by sex are profound for women in general and especially painful for single mothers. Because women are viewed as marginal workers, they are given marginal jobs—low paying, low status, and insecure.[27]

Most of the wage differentials between men and women arise either from the smaller amount of labor market experience attained by women or from discrimination against women. The former arises directly from the hidden contract or the sexist assignment of roles. Discrimination arises indirectly and directly from the image of the male as provider.[28]

Because women earn 40 percent less than men, on the average, in every occupational category,[29] it is not surprising that in general the most important single determinant of a change in family economic well-being appears to be a change in family composition.[30] With divorce, the economic status of women relative to need goes down while that of men apparently goes up.[31] Three out of five poor children are in single-parent families.

One cannot explore single parenthood and work for women without becoming aware that work affects marital status and vice versa. More divorced than married women work and more work full time at every educational level.[32] Most divorced and separated mothers work a full year; others work less than a full year only because they have been laid off.[33] Conversely, the better a husband provides, the less likely is divorce.[34] Separation rates are twice as high among families where the husband experiences serious unemployment, suggesting that it is not the amount of income alone but its stability that is part of a decision to remain married or separate.[35] Studies of women's earnings produce quite consistent findings. As more women work, some postpone marriage and fewer get married in total.[36] Other things being equal, the higher a wife's earnings, the more likely that a couple will separate.[37] In short, a man's income tends to cement a marriage and a woman's tends to make dissolution possible.

It is important to remember that the amount of income alone does not equal financial security. For example, a study of women who had been divorced for up to two years found every woman saying that despite reduced income the family was better off financially. The researcher suggests that stability and control may have been more important than amount. Respondents said such things as, "I don't have much money to spend, but at least it's regular," and "Now I can buy things for the children."[38]

In any event, the problems concerning work for women are general and rooted in social arrangements broader than single parenthood. They have special impact for single parents but cannot be dealt with within that framework, nor avoided simply if single parenthood could be avoided.

Structured for time and commitment, jobs leave no more time for domestic activities to the mother than to the father. Hours are inflexible and long; few part-time jobs pay enough to support a family. Unless informal care is at hand, adequate, reliable, and inexpensive child care is rarely available. And institutions and businesses operate on the assumption that there are two parents, one of them free to carry on transactions during the day. As we noted the combined effect of working and mothering at once upon the income of single mothers, we now note the strain working creates for housekeeping and parenting. (The problem is felt by married mothers as well; half of them are employed.) If the parenting of single parents may suffer, part of the reason is that, like many mothers with husbands, they work outside the home.

A critical aspect for single parent and dual-worker families is that children are likely to be cared for by persons other than their parents. Implicit in the public image of poor parenting is the belief that small children spend their time in over-crowded institutional settings.[39] The fact is otherwise: Nine out of ten preschool children with working mothers spend their time in informal settings—with relatives, neighbors, or friends. Nor is that because congregate care is scarce, though to be sure it is. Single parents, poor parents, and welfare parents, like middle-class parents who live together, prefer informal care both because it appears to be better and is more practical.[40] As to congregate care, research reveals no effect on intellectual development but possible difficulty in emotional and social development. Studies have generally failed to distinguish between good and poor congregate care though and it is possible that studies of good care would produce different findings.[41] There is no body of research on the effects of informal care.

A modern view regards substitute care as a supplement to maternal care rather than as a substitute for it.[42] A considerable argument can be made for such a development as moderating the "hothouse" aspect of the mother and child bond and "shifting back towards a more natural [i.e., less confined and intense] way of life for both women and children."[43] Seen in this light, conflict is no longer so sharply drawn between maternal and substitute care. The questions about substitute care are no longer categorical: Is substitute care intrinsically a good or bad idea? What qualities are required in substitute care? What duration optimum? And so forth.

Single parents do, of course, face special circumstances. An asset in the two-parent home is the presence of another adult to provide consultation and support with respect to children.[44] "Parents . . . need to have other voices joined with theirs in transmitting values and maturity demands to their children."[45] Single parents may have no one to provide emotional support. The sense of failure which separation may have provoked may readily lead—without adult company and support—to feelings of isolation.[46] A British study reports these feelings as the main personal problem of single parents.[47] Conversely, children with single parents have access to fewer adults and tend to emphasize peer relationships.[48]

The presence or absence of both parents *per se* makes little difference in the adequacy of child-rearing[49] or the socialization of children.[50] There is no evidence that the absence of a father from the home has an effect on the child's sense of sex identity.[51] Single mothers hold the same values for their children as mothers with husbands.[52] A series of studies over the years has found more delinquency in unhappy intact homes than in single-parent ones.[53] In their famous study, Glueck and Glueck found the quality of maternal supervision more important for delinquency than the presence or absence of a man.[54] "What scientific evidence there is suggests that divorce is often better (or at least less harmful) for children than an unhappy conflict-ridden marriage."[55]

What can one make of all this? Do strain and the absence of one parent or another not alter child-rearing noticeably and adversely? Perhaps the key point with respect to parenting is that the choice of the parents and children does not lie between a sound marriage and single parenthood. Happy couples rarely separate. The choice for many children lies between an unhappy home and a single parent. Parents themselves—though they commonly worry about the effects of a divorce on their children[56]—with experience come to think they have done well by them.[57]

To be sure, some children from single-parent homes pay a penalty, and curiously they may suffer more from maternal than paternal absence, since a single mother without family, friends or the money to purchase help often must deprive a child of her company and attention; that is the deprivation the child feels most keenly.[58] This is consistent with the British finding that damage to school attainment and social adjustment, when they are observed, result from poverty rather than single parenthood itself.[59]

One final effect of single parenthood is relevant. Today, a higher proportion of children under five are living with only their mothers than ever before.[60] The number of children in institutions and in substitute families is declining. One reason is that children are remaining with single parents.[61] For children, single parenthood is an alternative not only to a two-parent family but to no family at all.

Of a sample of single mothers with preschool children, 72 percent had "a moderate or severe distress problem compared to 46 percent of 'married' mothers."[62] While this study shows the disadvantage of single-parent families, it is surely more important that half of the intact families has the same problem. If one starts with that as the basic issue, one can understand the reason why young mothers may feel exhaustion and depression and how single parenthood may add to the problem.[63] But the problem becomes general and not solely one of single parenthood. It is within that context that one must ask how society is to help single parent families.

Public Image and Public Policy

The core of the argument here is that single-parent families are misrepresented to the public and to themselves. They have special problems and they may benefit from special institutional supports, but that is true of any number of groups otherwise regarded as normal and acceptable. The unemployed, veterans, and widows are examples at one end of the alphabet while single-parent families are statistically and historically in the American mainstream.

Yet the image is itself a powerful policy. The most moving effect of misrepresentation is that many single parents believe what is said of them and add that belief to the problems they face. Separation and divorce are a troubled if not stormy period and so the people involved are vulnerable. While separation is part of every married person's at least occasional speculation, and the actual event a crystal around which fantasies cling, the people involved usually blame themselves, adding normality to their worries about financial responsibility, judgment, concern about children, sexual responsibility, and self-worth. The stereotypes involved are about as legitimate as most that are involved in discriminatory behavior—and as destructive.

It is apparent that changing the image would imply broad changes in government, employment, and other policies. Conversely, such policies are potent in maintaining or altering the image. Each set of policy issues requires extensive exploration not possible here. An examination of these issues indicates the powerful and pervasive influence of the current image in our social arrangements.

If one sees women as normal and regular wage-earners, issues of sex discrimination in wages and occupational opportunity must be faced. Both work at home with children and at outside occupations must permit more flexibility. On one hand are questions of aids for child-care and homemaking, and also the operating assumption that shopping and transactions with physicians and utilities can be carried on in the middle of the day. The spread of single parenthood creates a demand that has moved some businesses to expanded hours, but professions and public utilities seem less sensitive. On the other hand are questions of the structuring of work and careers, the scheduling of employment, the feasibility of shared work, and the growth of part-time work.

Issues in income maintenance policy are similarly complex. The financial problem of the working poor, much debated in the last few years, is from another perspective an issue of single parenthood and minimum wages. That is, a single year-round minimum wage does not provide enough income to keep four people (a couple and two children, a single parent and three children, a grandmother, her daughter, and two children) out of poverty. Most industrial countries have tried to meet this problem by relatively small payments for all children. Americans have preferred to regard the issue as a welfare policy problem, seeing low-paid working people pitted against separated or unmarried women—though often enough they are the same people. If we see these two groups as sharing a problem rather than competing, the solution of a small subsidy for children to which other Western countries have come may seem appealing. The Earned Income Credit, recently introduced into the federal income tax, would, if improved in level and expanded to all children, serve quite well.

In implementation, policies that favor two-parent families are likely to operate to the disadvantage of single-parent families. For example, a woman with children might receive a higher payment from welfare compared with the family's entitlement if the husband were present. Obviously, the family needs more if the husband is not there. On the other hand, making equivalent payments to two-parent families would present costs that are impossible in the real world of limited resources. The result is commonly a smaller payment to the single-parent family than even the amount thought minimally necessary. Regarding this issue, Isabel Sawhill has proposed an attempt to "define a neutral policy—that is one which would neither encourage [nor] discourage various kinds of family behavior such as marriage or childbearing." She concludes that considerations such as equity and need make a quite neutral system unlikely.[64] Nevertheless, seeking a system that neither rewards nor penalizes family structure would open negotiation about program design in a way that might portend progress.* But it would be difficult to work at designing neutral programs while talking the language of a policy partisan to intact families.

Another direction to go in income maintenance, more special to single parenthood, is to recognize separation and divorce as social risks similar to the risk of being widowed. There have been proposals to establish a program of "fatherless child insurance"—or "single parent insurance"—along lines well understood in Social Security. As single parenthood is voluntary, when compared with being widowed, careful design is required but appears to be feasible.[65] In one conception, such programs may be taken as supplementing income that would otherwise be inadequate. In another conception, one may argue that it is sound and constructive for one of the single parents to remain in the traditional role of homemaker, and not to work. The same programs providing "income by right," with possibly larger payments, would enable them to do this.[66] More conservatively and more limited, it has been argued that even if income is not provided, at least the government should provide credit towards Social Security for the work implicit in homemaking.[67]

The issue of parental support of children when there is marital separation is not, by any means, simply a welfare issue. "The primary purpose of child support laws is the protection of the public purse,"[68] but with respect to non-welfare families, the primary issue is one of family law. Courts and administrative agencies are likely to be more lenient in securing support than the law might seem to require. Each state has a welfare standard, a non-welfare standard or understanding, the understanding that will really be enforced, and the agreements that result from the pressures and evasive tactics that husband and wife can bring to bear. There is no general social contract to which courts, agencies, or couples (if they wish to avoid dispute or exploitation of one another) can refer. In this absence of public agreement, as always, the weakest and poorest suffer most.

A Change in Outlook

In this field, the development of a reasonable set of ideas that might lead to consensus would be a giant step for single "mankind." It is a difficult problem, for it involves reconciling concepts as old as common law with twentieth century reality; and balancing the rights and needs of a wage earner and, chances are, the wage earner's new family against those of

---

*As an example of recent confusion, in pressing their welfare reforms Presidents Nixon and Carter both said that welfare encourages family breakup. If the observation is accurate, which is doubtful despite the chorus to the contrary, both sets of proposals would still have provided an incentive to separation. That is, they would have allowed more income in total to a separated husband and mother with children than to the intact family.

the family that is being left; all in a context in which everyone's standard of living is at risk of declining.

The delivery of social services contains its own complex set of issues. Counsellors, for example, need to approach giving help in terms of managing the transition from a marital to a post-marital way of life.[69] Underlying this is professional acceptance that marital separation is a normal transition, a statement that may sound disarmingly simple but requires a profound change in professional point of view. Similarly, if single parenthood is regarded as a normal way of life, practical aids and supports must assume a degree of importance they have possibly not been accorded by social agencies. Day care for children has received a good deal of public attention; we have noted that the single-parent family seems to prefer and have good practical reasons for using informal and neighborhood arrangements rather than the congregate care that has been extensively discussed. Beyond this, service organizations attentive to their clients should help them to secure reasonable aid or arrangements from employers, public schools, hospitals, and other institutions. Once again, a more profound change in posture is implied than may have been indicated at first.

With or without the aid of established organizations, it would be constructive to see self-generated groups of single parents organize. In the nature of single parenthood, individuals tend to move in and out of such groups. Nevertheless, they provide a means for sharing experience, moderating the sense of loneliness from which single parents may suffer, and reinforcing their sense of self-esteem. Under certain circumstances such groups can exercise broad influence in securing the social changes that may be important.[70]

Employment, income maintenance, child support, and social services, present relatively self-evident issues, but when we grasp the broad changes that have swept over us, other issues will also appear. For example, it seems possible that single parents are living in housing designed for other times. That is, the basic design of apartments and houses was long since established for large families and other two-parent families. While the basic design has been modified to suit smaller families and new construction methods and to meet exigencies of cost and financing, those modifications have been mechanical, not functional—that is, fewer bedrooms, room sizes scaled down, and rooms devoted to certain functions (the dining room, the kitchen) in some cases made rudimentary. However, housing is not designed for one-parent family living. Preparing food and dining may be a unitary activity and more significant for single parents than for others; it may be that a single larger room would serve them better than the conventional kitchen and dining room. Again, it may be that two combination bedroom-work (or play) rooms would serve a parent and child better than the conventional two bedrooms and a living room.[71] Such issues will not be raised until we think of single parenthood as normal rather than marginal. Then designs may be worked out, money ventured, and the judgment of the market cast.

A good deal more thought is required about the issues related to single parents. This discussion is simply intended to indicate how issues change focus if one views single parenthood as a normal and permanent feature of our social landscale.

Notes

1. Allyson Sherman Grossman, "The Labor Force Patterns of Divorced and Separated Women," *Monthly Labor Review* 16 (1977), p. 50.
2. Isabel Sawhill, Gerald E. Peabody, Carol Jones, and Steven Caldwell, *Income Transfers and Family Structure* (Washington, D.C.: The Urban Institute, 1975).
3. Ruth Brandwein, Carol Brown, and Elizabeth Maury Fox, "Women and Children Last: The Social Situation of Divorced Mothers and Their Families," *Journal of Marriage and the Family* 36 (1974), pp. 488–489.
4. William J. Goode, "Economic Factors and Marital Stability," *American Sociological Review* 16 (1951); Robert S. Weiss, *Marital Separation* (New York: Basic Books, 1975).
5. Marvin B. Sussman, "Family Systems in the 1970s: Analysis, Policies and Programs," *The Annals of the American Academy* 396 (July 1971), p. 38.
6. Martin Rein and Lee Rainwater, *The Welfare Class and Welfare* (Cambridge, Mass.: Joint Center for Urban Studies, 1977); Mary Jo Bane, "Marital Disruption and the Lives of Children," *Journal of Social Issues* 32, no. 1 (1976), pp. 103–109.
7. Bane, *ibid.*
8. Tamara Hareven, "Family Time and Historical Time," *Daedalus* (Spring 1977), pp. 57–70.
9. Hugh Carter and Paul C. Glick, *Marriage and Divorce: A Social and Economic Study* (Cambridge: Harvard University Press, 1970); Paul C. Glick, "A Demographer Looks at American Families," *Journal of Marriage and the Family* 15 (1975), p. 26.
10. A. J. Norton and P. C. Glick, "Marital Instability: Past, Present and Future," *Journal of Social Issues* 32, no. 1 (1976), pp. 5–19.
11. Greg J. Duncan, "Unmarried Heads of Households and Marriage," in Greg J. Duncan and James N. Morgan (eds.) *Five Thousand American Families—Patterns of Economic Progress* (Ann Arbor, Mich.: Institute for Social Research, 1977).
12. Daniel P. Moynihan, *The Negro Family: The Case for National Action* (Washington, D.C.: U.S. Department of Labor, 1965).
13. Robert Moroney, *The Family and the State: Considerations for Social Play* (London: Longman, 1976).
14. Lee Rainwater, *Welfare and Working Mothers* (Cambridge, Mass.: Joint Center for Urban Studies, 1977).
15. Rein and Rainwater, *op. cit.*
16. Dennis K. Orthner, Terry Brown, and Dennis Ferguson, "Single-Parent Fatherhood: An Emerging Family Life Style," *The Family Coordinator* (October 1976), pp. 429–437.
17. Daniel D. Molinoff, "Life With Father," *New York Times Magazine* (May 22, 1977), p. 13.
18. Isabel V. Sawhill, "Discrimination and Poverty Among Women Who Head Families," *Signs* no. 1–3 (1976), pp. 201–221.
19. Brandwein, *op. cit.;* Orthner et al., *op. cit.;* Gasser and Taylor, *op. cit.*
20. James Levine, *Who Will Raise the Children? New Options for Fathers (and Mothers)* (Philadelphia: J. B. Lippincott, 1976).
21. Orthner, *op. cit.;* Gasser and Taylor, *op. cit.*

22. Lucy B. Mallan, "Young Widows and Their Children: A Comparative Report," *Social Security Bulletin* (May 1975).

23. J. Brubacher and W. Rudy, *Higher Education in Transition: A History of American Colleges and Universities, 1636–1968* (New York: Harper and Row, 1968), pp. 13–14.

24. Benjamin Schlesinger, *The One-Parent Family: Perspectives and Annotated Bibliography* (Toronto: University of Toronto, 1975).

25. Reynolds Farley and Suzanne Bianchi, "Demographic Aspects of Family Structure Among Blacks: A Look at Data a Decade After the Moynihan Report." Paper presented at the American Sociological Association; Chicago, Illinois; 1971.

26. L. J. Weitzman, "To Love, Honor, and Obey: Traditional Legal Marriage and Alternative Family Forms," *The Family Coordinator* 24 (1975).

27. Edward Gross, "Plus Ca Change?: The Sexual Structure of Occupations Over Time," *Social Problems* 16 (1968), pp. 198–208.

28. Erik Gronseth, "The Breadwinner Trap," in *The Future of the Family* (New York: Simon and Schuster, 1972), pp. 175–191; Erik Gronseth, "The Husband-Provider Role: A Critical Appraisal," in Andree Michel (ed.), *Family Issues of Employed Women in Europe and America* (Leiden: E. J. Brill, 1971).

29. U. S. Department of Labor, *The Earnings Gap Between Women and Men* (Washington, D.C.: U.S. Government Printing Office, 1976).

30. Greg J. Duncan and James W. Morgan, *Five Thousand American Families—Patterns of Economic Progress,* vol. V (Ann Arbor: Institute of Social Research, 1977).

31. Saul Hoffman and John Holmes, "Husbands, Wives and Divorce," in Greg J. Duncan and James N. Morgan (eds.), *Five Thousand American Families—Patterns of Economic Progress,* vol. IV (Ann Arbor: Institute for Social Research, 1976).

32. Grossman, *op. cit.*

33. *Ibid* and Beverly Johnson McEaddy, "Women Who Head Families: A Socioeconomic Analysis," *Monthly Labor Review* (June 1976).

34. Carter and Glick, *op. cit.;* Goode, *op. cit.*

35. Heather Ross and Isabel Sawhill, *Time of Transition: The Growth of Families Headed by Women* (Washington, D.C.: The Urban Institute, 1975).

36. S. G. Johnson, "The Impact of Women's Liberation on Marriage, Divorce, and Family Life-Style," in C. B. Lloyd (ed.), *Sex Discrimination and the Division of Labor* (New York: Columbia University Press); F. B. Santos, "The Economics of Marital Status," in C. Lloyd (ed.), *Sex Discrimination and Division of Labor* (New York: Columbia University Press).

37. Sawhill, *op. cit.*

38. Goode, *op. cit.*

39. Alice S. Rossi, "A Biosocial Perspective on Parenting," *Daedalus* (Spring 1977).

40. Suzanne H. Woolsey, "Pied Piper Politics and the Child Care Debate," *Daedalus* (Spring 1977), pp. 127–146; Arthur C. Emlen and Joseph B. Perry, "Child-Care Arrangements," in Hoffman and Nye (eds.), *Working Mothers* (San Francisco: Jossey-Bass, 1974).

41. Urie Bronfenbrenner, "Research on the Effects of Daycare on Child Development," in *Toward a National Policy for Children and Families* (Washington, D.C.: National Academy of Sciences, 1976).

42. B. Caldwell, "Infant Day Care—The Outcasts Gain Respectability," in P. Roby (ed.). *Child Care—Who Cares? Foreign and Domestic Infant and Early Childhood Development Policies* (New York: Basic Books, 1973).

43. Alice S. Rossi, "A Biosocial Perspective on Parenting," *Daedalus* (Spring 1977).

44. Ruth Brandwein, Carol Brown, and Elizabeth Maury Fox, "Women and Children Last: The Social Situation of Divorced Mothers and Their Families," *Journal of Marriage and the Family* 36 (1974), pp. 488–489.

45. Eleanor E. Maccoby, "Current Changes in the Family and Their Impact Upon the Socialization of Children." Paper presented at the American Sociological Association Meeting, 1977.

46. Maccoby, *op. cit.;* Weiss, *op. cit.*

47. Benjamin Schlesinger, "One-Parent Families in Great Britain," *The Family Coordinator* 26 (1977), pp. 139–141.
48. John C. Condry and M. A. Simon, "Characteristics of Peer and Adult-Oriented Children," *Journal of Marriage and the Family* 36 (1974), pp. 543–554.
49. Reuben Hill, "Social Stress on the Family," in Marvin Sussman (ed.), *Sourcebook in Marriage and the Family* (Boston: Houghton Mifflin, 1968).
50. Jane K. Burgess, "The Single-Parent Family: A Social and Sociological Problem," *The Family Coordinator* 9 (1970), pp. 137–144.
51. Maccoby, *op. cit.*
52. Louis Kriesberg, *Mothers in Poverty* (Chicago: Aldine, 1970).
53. Lee Burchinal, "Characteristics of Adolescents from Unbroken Homes and Reconstituted Families," *Journal of Marriage and the Family* 26 (1964), pp. 44–51; Judson Landis, "The Trauma of Children When Parents Divorce," *Marriage and Family Living* 22 (1960), pp. 7–13; F. Ivan Nye, "Child Adjustment in Broken and in Unhappy Unbroken Homes," *Marriage and Family Living* 19 (1957), pp. 356–361.
54. Sheldon Glueck and Eleanor Glueck, *Family Environment and Delinquency* (Boston: Houghton Mifflin, 1962).
55. Kenneth Kenniston, *All Our Children* (Carnegie Council on Children, 1977); and *Toward a National Policy for Children and Families* (Washington, D.C.: National Academy of Sciences, 1976).
56. William J. Goode, *Women in Divorce* (New York: Free Press, 1956); Dennis Marsden, *Mothers Alone: Poverty and the Fatherless Family* (London: Penguin, 1969).
57. C. A. Brown, R. Feldberg, E. M. Fox, and J. Kohen, "Divorce: Chance of a New Lifetime," *Journal of Social Issues* 32 (1976), pp. 119–132.
58. Brandwein *et al., op. cit.*
59. Elsa Ferri, "Growing-Up in a One-Parent Family," *Concern* 20 (1976), pp. 7–10; Schlesinger, *op. cit.*
60. Farley and Bianchi, *op. cit.*
61. Ross and Sawhill, *op. cit.*
62. Peter Moss and Ian Plewis, "Mental Distress in Mothers of Pre-School Children in Inner London." Undated paper from the Tomas Coram Research Unit, University of London.
63. Alison Clarke-Stewart, *Child Care in the Family: A Review of Research and Some Propositions for Policy* (New York: Academic Press, 1977); J. A. Clausen and S. R. Clausen, "The Effect of Family Size on Parents and Children," in J. T. Fawcett (ed.), *Psychological Perspectives on Population* (New York: Key Book Services, 1972); N. Richman, "Depression in Mothers of Pre-School Children," *Journal of Child Psychology and Psychiatry* 17 (1976); Rossi, *op. cit.*
64. Sawhill, 1977, *op. cit.*
65. Irvin Garfinkel, "Testimony on Welfare Reform to State Senate Human Services Committee," in Madison, Wisconsin; August 15 and 16, 1978.
66. Heather Ross, "Poverty: Women and Children Last," in Jane Roberts Chapman and Margaret Gates (eds), *Economic Independence for Women: The Foundation for Equal Rights* (Beverly Hills: Russell Sage, 1976).
67. "Working America." A report of a special task force to the Secretary of Health, Education, and Welfare (Cambridge: MIT Press, 1973).
68. James Kent, *Commentaries on American Law*, vol. 2 (New York: Da Capo, 1826).
69. Weiss, *op. cit.*
70. Michael J. Smith and Beth Moses, "Social Welfare Agencies and Social Reform Movements: The Case of the Single-Parent Family" (Community Service Society of New York, 1976).
71. Thelma Stackhouse, "Housing for One-Parent Families—Faddism or Favorable Options" (Community Service Society of New York, August 1975).

The Second Time Around: Remarriage in America
Leslie Aldridge Westoff

Facts and Myths

■   Old-fashioned, once-in-a-lifetime, till-death-do-us-part marriage may be going on the rocks these days, but remarriage has been booming. Divorce rates are soaring. Couples are breaking up like icebergs in a summer sea. Demographers report that more than a million people get divorced every year. This means that one out of every three couples decides to divorce sooner or later. Although our marriage rate appeared to be rising to counteract this destruction of existing marriages, until a few years ago, when it suddenly dropped, this rising rate was no more than a mirage. Our first-marriage rate has actually been *falling* for the last thirty years and what has buoyed up the figures has been remarriage. Every year, four out of five people who split up will remarry. As far as marriages are concerned, one out of every four is now usually a second, sometimes a third marriage, occasionally even a fourth. Only a small proportion of these involve widowed persons.

These second marriages are known as "blended families," or "reconstituted families," and with their complicated cross-currents of relationships, they are quite different from the nuclear families produced by first marriages. Unfortunately, little is known about second marriages—despite the sociologists, psychologists, and popular media waiting to pounce on anything new. There was a flurry of investigation in the 1950s, but no significant research has been done on the subject. It is shocking to find that there is almost nothing current, nothing in the journals or popular press to guide the average person or his psychiatrist or marriage counselor.

In a recent conversation with Mrs. Belle Parmet, a psychiatric social worker from New Jersey, she remarked on this astounding culture lag. She told me that she had attended a regional meeting of family therapists at which many counselors were gathered for several days of discussion. She said, "I sat there during the whole time listening to talks about THE family, studies of THE family, arguments about THE family, until I couldn't stand it any longer. I got up and said, 'What on earth do you mean . . . THE family? There is no such thing. There are two-parent families, one-parent families, no-parent families, three- or four-parent families, families without children.' There was a burst of applause when I finished."

This experience illustrates the incredible fact that many psychiatrists and counselors have been slow in recognizing the vital changes that have taken place in the family, in doing research on these changes, and in writing about them. The family can no longer be thought of as a neat, encapsulated entity, simple and easily definable. Mrs. Parmet said, "We have been taught to think of family as the biological family (parents and children related by blood ties). Well, that's not *the* family any longer. That's only *one* kind of family." She went on to lament that "there's very little written in the field. We have no guidelines. The culture hasn't institutionalized these new forms of the family yet."

Sociologists have concentrated on more flamboyant developments, such as cohabitation on the nation's campuses, and have largely ignored the growing phenomenon of remarriage. Marriage counselors say they have been so busy counseling that they simply have not taken time to study their cases. There has been an endless stream of articles and books on marriage and divorce, mainly divorce, and there the story stops. No one has adequately followed people who survive divorce, as most do, and tracked them on into their second marriages. Remarriage has always been sketchily dealt with. If the victims of divorce can be shown the tricks of how to grow strong and rebuild their lives, most writers then leave them drifting off into the sunset in this newfound state. What really happens to them afterward has never been properly pursued.

The U.S. Census Bureau has provided some of the basic facts: 75 percent of all marriages are first marriages, 20 per cent are second marriages, and 6 per cent are third marriages. Most divorced people tend to marry other divorced people. Most remarry soon, within an average of three years. And most choose August rather than June for the wedding. The average age at first marriage is twenty-one for women and twenty-four for men; the averages at second marriages are twenty-five for women, and thirty for men. Women wait (or are kept waiting) longer than men before remarrying. Up to age twenty-four, divorced men and women have the same chance of remarrying. But from age twenty-five to forty-four, the number of divorced men remarrying is almost double that of divorced women. And from forty-five to sixty-four, men remarry two and a half times more than do women—all of which would argue for a woman's leaving a bad marriage as soon as possible! More men remarry because their pool of potential wives covers an age range from young girls up to their own age level; but for most women, the choice is limited to the small number of available men in their own age bracket or older. For some reason, probably related to the egocentric male and his image of machismo, younger men rarely marry older women—they usually prefer to be sought after by younger women, those who represent the symbols of glamourous youth, more like nymphs than aging mothers.

Except for the woman with a graduate degree, the more education the individual has and the higher the income, the greater the chance of remarriage. Women with higher degrees have probably become more interested in careers than marriage and don't choose it so often. Some of the elements that were expected by the experts to have lowered the divorce rate, but obviously didn't, are rising ages for marriage (more stable marriages occur later), less poverty, and an increasing proportion of adults with a college education. (Are better-educated people really supposed to be better able to live with each other?) That has come to be one of the myths connected with remarriage, for the divorce rate has not yet dipped. Marriage later in life and more education and money have only served to help people feel more independent.

And this leads to the next myth of remarriage, one that has been around so long it has been set to music. Love is supposed to be better the second time around and second marriages must therefore be better than first marriages. All this may be true. Love may be lovier, the marriage may be better, but couples are still vulnerable to the problems of living with another person, the unbelievable complexities of trying to make two families into one, as well as the problems inherent in the institution of marriage itself. It is not a foolproof relationship—neither the first nor the second time. Remarriage is obviously not *all* good or *all* bad. It is some of each, though one might, and I will later, compare the *quality* of the "good" and the *quality* of the "bad" and find the "good" better the second time and the "bad" not so bad. However, the myth that second marriages are better and more successful must be qualified: they *may* be better, but, nevertheless, a higher proportion of second marriages fail than first marriages. They are statistically no more successful than first marriages. They are, in fact, slightly less so. Dr. Paul Glick, senior demographer at the U.S. Census Bureau, predicted in June 1975 that if things continue as they have, in addition to the 36 per cent of first marriages that end in divorce (a little over one in three), 40 per cent of second marriages will also dissolve.

Dr. Glick conjectures that one reason why many second marriages also fail is that remarrying couples have already been through one divorce and, consequently, will not hesitate to divorce again, if necessary—a kind of practice effect or learning experience. Second divorces, he believes, screen out the spoiled, the immature, and the less disciplined, some of whom are unable to live continuously with another person and perhaps should not be married at all. As each marriage becomes successful for those who made an earlier mistake, the proportion still failing will include more and more of the problem people. It's a sort of reverse panning-for-gold effect. By the third or fourth panning, those who are left are the chronically discontent and those people who may even find it difficult to live with themselves. As might be expected, second marriages ending in divorce do not last as long as first ones. The average duration of those that can't make it the second time is five years compared to the well-known seven-year itch of first marriages.

Why So Many Divorces?

Never before in history have there been so many divorces or remarriages. Something very profound seems to be shaking our traditional concepts of what a marriage is, or is supposed to be. Always frowned upon in the past, divorce has only recently become an accepted part of American life. As Jane Spock, the seventy-year-old wife of Dr. Benjamin Spock, put it in an interview in *The New York Times* on the occasion of the breakup of their forty-eight-year-old marriage: "I would have spoken up before but women just didn't do those things then. Instead of getting good and angry, you went into the other room and cried. . . . I wasn't able to come out and say what I thought because I thought it was wiser not to. In those days you got into trouble with your marriage if you did." Today she could and did speak up.

One reason why there are so many remarriages in our society is that it is now so easy for first marriages to break up. Liberal, no-fault divorce laws have lightened some of the economic burden on the man in a divorce, so that remarriage is becoming more financially feasible—though it's still a tough struggle supporting two families instead of one. Second, because of increasing education and the declining importance of older religious and traditional values, divorce has simply become more socially acceptable, and, in some circles, even fashionable. The advent of the women's rights movement and consciousness-raising (sitting on the floor with a group of friends and telling each other what's really bothering you) have undoubtedly influenced the woman's view of marriage. Today she is no longer satisfied by the children and security which her mother settled for. The feminist movement has been so vocal that it has resulted in legitimizing women's hitherto unrecognized, or at least unexpressed, emotional and intellectual needs. With the opening up of the job market to give women greater opportunity and independence, with an increased emphasis on the individual and on encountering the inner self—of saying, feeling, doing what one wishes—women's expectations in marriage have risen. Both partners, in fact, demand something positive and worthwhile out of a relationship, a more compatible and intimate bond than the strange, impersonal, nagging marriage that many of our parents accepted. A woman who might have hung on to marriage with desperation is now much more willing to split a relationship that isn't working or a marriage that falls short of some ideal.

Even the formerly conservative worlds of business, with corporation manners, and politics, with voter-consciousness, now sanction matrimonial switches, which not so long ago meant the instant demise of a once-promising career. Vice-President Rockefeller barely made it under the wire when he divorced and remarried at the time when the moral climate began to change. In the 1970s, a breath of fresh air swept in new attitudes toward behavior which have affected many areas of our lives. There has been a loosening of religious strictures, and of rigid social and moralistic judgments. People are more relaxed, less uptight, more apt to tell each other what they really think. Children have become more independent of their parents. Women have become more independent of men. Formality is vanishing, and the social rules are being modified. Instead of doing what they think they *ought* to do, people are doing what they *want* to do, or, as they like to call it, their own thing. There is a strong sense of equality in the family, where everyone is beginning to carry the same weight. Now men and women are telling each other for the first time, as honestly as they can, what they want out of life. They are sharing dreams that see through and go beyond the romantic illusions (nurtured for so long by Hollywood and popular fiction) with which we blindly plunged into our often superficial and flimsy first marriages.

But most marriages in this country were not made during these last few expressive years and do not benefit from current attitudes. Imposing the new freedoms on an old marriage has in many instances led to a great deal of friction. The once sought-after traditional marriage, which still exists and which has shaped American society for ages—the picket fences and silver patterns and for better or worse, is now beginning to look more like the result of an outmoded idea which never really worked as well as it was supposed to—although everyone pretended it did.

On the other hand, now that divorce can be obtained more easily and men and women have more opportunity to live alone, remarry, or choose careers, they have more reason to re-evaluate their lives and ask themselves, "Am I really happy?" There is an increasing self-consciousness about happiness, though. For every freedom there is a price to pay. The freedom we have won is the chance for a more diverse and interesting life. The price is an increased dissatisfaction with what we have, a restlessness spawned by the many options open to us. We are the victims of what one well-known sociologist, who happens to be my third husband, calls "marital hypochondria." We are becoming more concerned with the health of our marriages. As in the past, for example, the field of medicine had few cures, and people expected to be sick and die young. Today, with all the possibilities of prevention, cure, treatment, and transplant, we have developed an obsession about health and longevity— and it may be the same with marriage. There is a lot of similar public and private soul-searching going on, and all kinds of alternatives for every marital sickness. . . .

If it is a myth that most people marry because they are "in love" with one another, when mainly they are attracted to each other's appearance, it is no myth that divorces following first marriages are usually bitter. Complaints by men and women about the cruelties and vindictiveness of their former husbands and wives are universal. Men become violent and kick doors in when they come to visit their children; women make unmeetable demands. The destruction of a once-working relationship is felt by both partners and by the children who get caught in the middle when the parents they love wreak incredible havoc on each other's lives.

A woman told me that she could not believe that someone she used to love, someone who loved her, someone she used to take care of and do absolutely everything for, could suddenly turn on her and become so horrible. "Our love, if that's what it was, had developed into a wicked hate. Everything we had meant to each other suddenly was ground into nothing."

One man implored his wife to be "civilized" after their divorce, suggesting that as two mature people they could handle the breakup without resorting to accusations and dirty tricks. She agreed, and they then proceeded to have the usual troubles of his doing things behind her back, he not sending the checks every month, she writing nasty letters. Divorce American style simply isn't a "civilized" affair for the most part.

Another woman told me: "Our divorce was bitter. I had to change the locks. He threw chairs, pots, pans. He was a very angry person. But I'm not disillusioned about people being able to have a commitment to each other."

Whatever form the bitterness takes, divorce always leaves two people who have grown used to the routines and protection of marriage abruptly single again. They have to backtrack and start from the beginning. Depressed, miserable, at the lowest point in their lives, they must first survive, then learn to cope.

Between Marriages

I think of the pause between marriages as a period of stumbling blindly through a dark, boulder-strewn, humid valley which at times is frightening beyond endurance, until at last, through luck and the will not to give up, one staggers in the right direction—whether toward a new marriage or a fulfilling independent life—and there is light again. It is hard enough, under the best of circumstances, to rearrange one's life—but to have to do it in a state of shock, with continuing assaults from one's former mate, makes survival almost impossible for some. People must have an incredible resilience and strength to be able to take such psychic insult and still hold on. One certainly begins again at the bottom, rejected, defenses stripped to raw nerve, ego splintered beyond recognition, biologically alive, but psychologically a mess.

As one woman explained: "I was unhappily married and miserable, but I didn't want the divorce. I had the idea marriage is forever. I thought you just go on being miserable. I never had the nerve to speak up and say 'I want out.' My ego was totally shattered when he left. I even thought of suicide, but couldn't do it because of the two kids."

Another person still appeared agitated when he said: "I had to get out of that marriage. It was a choice between either divorce or suicide. I just picked the wrong person. I knew it was wrong, but I ignored the warning signals."

"I was really shaken up," a woman remembered. "It was like being kicked in the teeth. I couldn't sleep. I didn't want to take sleeping pills. You see, I hadn't wanted the divorce. Now I knew that I had to get my head together, and to do that I had to get my body together, get in physical shape. I joined the Y and swam every evening with the kids. Then I was able to sleep."

Divorce leaves men and women with a terrible sense of personal failure. One is always sure it is he who is at fault, "I am so imperfect that no one can live with me." But usually it is the woman who is made to feel this, believing she is not worthy. "After my first breakup," a woman said, "I felt a failure. I thought, Anyone who can't make a marriage succeed is not any good. Lots of people admire *him*. I must be crazy."

Another woman had a similar feeling: "I had been seeing a psychiatrist for several years. I thought something must be wrong with *me*, since my husband thought he was perfectly fine. I needed someone to tell me I was okay. I was always assuming if something was wrong, it was my fault. Now I know not only *I* could have caused the problems."

Yet things gradually begin to come together, whether because of a refusal to give up, because the children can't be left, or whatever. One doesn't commit suicide, although the thought may seem attractive at times. Finding the way back to complete sanity and usefulness is a tentative process, much like a child trying to fit a jigsaw puzzle together. If one piece doesn't go into the space, one hesitantly tries something else. One usually needs more money and so one looks for a job. Money, in fact, can be the most immediate headache, both for the man who has to support two households and for the woman who probably receives less than half of what she had when she was married. In addition, if the woman has not been working in any place other than her own kitchen, finding an employer who will be able to make use of her stale and limited talents, which have been out of the job market for five, ten, or fifteen years, may be difficult. She is likely to have to take an inferior job and earn less money than she needs. In fact, if she was a liberal-arts major in college, as so many are, she probably doesn't have many marketable talents. It can be demoralizing for her to have to compete with younger women, start somewhere at the bottom and work up, and at the same time keep a home going for the children. A woman remembered: "I had to take care of my son, live in a suitable place for him to grow up, try to find a job after not working for ten years. I was using up my money and not finding a job, and it was frightening."

Women usually keep the apartment or house for the sake of the children, men have to find a bachelor pad, and both will discard friends who are embarrassed by the divorce and don't know what to say. She will visit the hairdresser for a new coiffure; he will buy a new suit; and slowly and separately both will begin to do things, find life interesting or amusing once more. She learns to live with loneliness, finding advantages in not having to make the bed or prepare a large dinner because she is not committed and can do what she pleases when she feels like it. They both learn what it's like to sleep alone again (though, statistically, he is more likely than she to have found someone else before he leaves) and, finally, when quite far advanced, she gives dinner parties alone and they both enjoy dating. It's not only the emotional puzzle that needs solving but the mechanical ones. A man told me that the adjustments in the first three years after his divorce had been considerable (she may not be practiced in earning money, but he's not practiced in keeping house). He said: "I had been left one daybed, one kitchen table and chair, and a set of china and wedding silverware, and it took a lot of arranging and time to refurnish my house. For more than a year I slept in the front room on the daybed until friends gave me bedroom furniture."

The Learning Surprise

Almost everyone I interviewed told me of the surprising and unexpected learning process that had occurred between divorce and remarriage. They felt they were not the same people they had been in their first marriages. There is another myth stating that people don't change. But divorce is obviously a catalyst which causes people to change themselves, some with the aid of counselors and psychiatrists, who have only recently acknowledged that people are a lot more flexible and capable of learning than they previously supposed. The period between marriages, however painful, is an extremely important time of life. It is then, when left to lick the wounds that will never fully heal, that one can look back and analyze what went wrong, do the exploring and changing that make one strong, develop the best of one's potential, understand who one really is. And often it is a time of admitting the truth, since no one else is listening, that however much one tried to keep from letting go of the marriage, it is a tremendous relief to be out of it and free.

A young man described this period of change in his life: "I was not thinking of remarriage during this time. I tried to learn more about my first marriage, what had happened, why it had gone on for so long, why I had gotten married to begin with. It led to a new self-awareness, years overdue. It made me much less fearful of marriage as an institution. Seeing myself in new ways for the first time gave me an unprecedented self-confidence. I came into close touch with my feelings, feelings that had been trained out of me. I suddenly discovered I could relate to people in new ways that were exciting and not threatening. If I read about myself in a novel, I wouldn't think it was the same person."

Another man suggested that "the whole experience of being married and then being single again gives you a greater insight into who you are. In my second marriage, I am very clear about what I want out of life."

People report making very definite efforts at rehabilitating themselves. They zero in on something positive, and dive after it. "After divorce comes a need for self-definition. You have to be creative and learn to solve problems." Whether it is learning to fix sinks or exercising to keep fit or working hard to get a job promotion, people begin to do what makes them feel good and important again. They begin to develop personalities in their own right. They become more interesting. But recuperation from such a serious trauma is never a simple process. There are steps forward, but there is also slipping backward. And there is the recognition that part of one's past, one's permanent memories, will always include a first marriage and a divorce. . . .

Why People Try Again

One does wonder, however, how so many people, after surviving the disastrous experience of an unsuccessful first marriage and hitting the depths of despondency after divorce, can pick themselves up, put themselves back together at no small cost, and decide to try again. What makes them believe in the possibility that next time it can be different? With the bitterness of the first-marriage experience still fresh upon one, with memories of the hurt refusing to go away, with one's self-esteem painfully reconstructed, with good new feelings about the self and the future and a hard-won pride in independence, why does a man or a woman who has been through hell decide he or she wants to remarry? Why open oneself to a second failure and risk being hurt again? There are some people, of course, like Taylor, Burton, Mailer, Balanchine, and Ingmar Bergman, who remarry constantly. Five times is probably their average. For one reason or another—perhaps the instability of their lives, the capacity for being easily bored, or the drives that make it possible for them to be creative—they seem to find it impossible to live with the same person for very long. To put a sharper light on such marital fickleness, as Bertrand Russell chose to do in explaining his many marriages, "The more civilized people become, the less capable they seem of lifelong happiness with one partner." The world, it seems, is rapidly filling up with some very civilized people indeed.

It seems to be true for most people that in spite of all the devastation they have been through with one marriage, they don't hate marriage at the end of the recuperation period. They firmly say they believe in it, and they mean the traditional kind. Considering the labyrinthine complications looming in a second marriage, it is remarkable that so many people are willing to try again. Obviously, those who remarry consider marriage an essential commitment to someone they love. And there are other reasons: community pressure opposes living together for very long; divorced people want their children to have legal parents; they are lonely and find security in this symbolic gesture of permanence. People do not flounder around in the move toward remarriage. They enter second marriages the way lemmings head for the sea, with unswerving direction. Having learned and changed, they believe they can make it the second time. But they don't rush.

A man told me: "It was not marriage I was disillusioned with, but my former partner. After the initial depression, the necessary turnabout time, I wanted to remarry." Dr. Paul Bohannan of the Western Behavioral Science Institute says: "You remarry primarily because you are lonesome. You want someone to share the burdens." One of the many men I interviewed told me he always felt he wanted to be married: "I prefer living with someone else. It wasn't a fear that I couldn't survive by myself. Marriage just seems warm and nice and appropriate and correct." A minister who has been divorced said: "One of the main reasons people marry is the need for warmth, companionship, and intimacy. . . . It may look and feel like the need for legal sex . . . but sex is almost the only avenue of expression our society has offered for the communication of warmth and intimacy, especially to men. So it is a major surprise and disillusionment in many marriages to find that sex, in itself, does not produce warmth and intimacy . . . but that sex is a by-product, an end result. Warmth and intimacy come from talking, paying attention, sharing, caring, touching, spending time together."

There is a basic need for love in all people, which is probably the reason why most people marry the first time—although they may be confusing it with mere attraction. And the search for love is the reason why people marry the second time. How essential this need for love is has been demonstrated by Dr. Harry Harlow's well-known experiment with monkeys and surrogate mothers.* A cuddly terry-cloth mother and a bare-bodied welded-wire mother were both attached to eight cages

---

*Harry F. Harlow, Learning to Love (San Francisco: Albion Publishing Co., 1971).

containing baby monkeys. For four infants, the cloth mother was made to lactate and the wire mother was not. For the four other monkeys the situation was reversed, and they could get milk only from the wire mother. Both groups of infants were observed for a period of time and it turned out that *both* groups spent the most time with the soft, cuddly mother, even though some of the infants had to give up their milk to do so. Like all creatures, they felt the need for physical touch. If love is more important than food, it must also be more important than the less crucial basics of clothing and shelter, which would make it about the most important need we have. Many people told me they remarried because they fell in love again. A woman explained that she was desperate to remarry "because I assumed there were people somewhere that I could love and who would be good for me. I thought I had simply made a bad choice the first time. And I regretted that I hadn't left sooner, that it had taken me five years to realize that the marriage was no longer any good. During this time I had just sat back and watched everything deteriorate. I think I wasted five years of my life. I remarried because I was lonely, starved for love and sex with someone I loved, and I desperately wanted a father for my son. I had the feeling that life was in limbo, just a temporary thing until we replaced one divorced husband and one lost father."

The men and women I spoke to were optimistic about their new marriages. They didn't fall into remarriage the way they had tripped into marriage number one. They deliberated and sometimes they compromised. A prospective spouse for someone who has children may be able to make a good husband or wife but not a good parent, and this concern has to be included in the decision. As one woman said: "Every time I met a man I asked myself, 'Is this possible?' I wanted to remarry. I wanted a man for me. But also a father for my kids. I rejected one man I liked because he would have made a poor father."

Living Together vs. Remarriage

The problem of raising children is one of the reasons many women give for wanting to marry, rather than just living with someone. If there are children involved, they do not think that simple cohabitation can work. "I didn't like the total responsibility of two small kids and no father. I wanted very much to have someone fill the enormous gap in my life. I felt the pressure from my kids and the community to marry again." It is too awkward for children to explain new relationships to their friends when the parents live with but do not marry new partners. It's embarrassing to them and can cause great resentment.

Marriage is also considered more practical. "We lived together for a year before marriage. But we decided to marry because it's an extra commitment. When you're not married, it's always easier just to walk out if you're tired of working things out. Also, the man or woman might feel, I'm not married to you, I can't discipline your children."

There are also mundane advantages to remarriage, such as credit ratings, mortgages, charge accounts, and similar necessities which are still awarded much more easily to married people. "We lived together for a year and a half before remarrying. We didn't really care if we married. It would not have affected our friendship. But he said if we married I would have economic protection, retirement benefits, inheritance rights, and so on. So we did."

Almost all the people I interviewed tried test-living together for at least several months to verify their judgment, and to see if things would work in practice as well as theory. They also wanted to see it work on a full-time basis and not just in a dating situation. They wanted to see if they could handle the problems, do the dishes together, fill the long weekends with close companionship. But sooner or later most wanted to take the marriage step, whether they had children or not, simply because they consider marriage an extra measure of recognition. Just living together for these people was not enough. A young mother and theater critic explained: "When you marry you have to believe in your own choice, be in touch with your own responses, tell yourself that a person makes sense. Marriage stamps the union. You relax into the better parts of what a marriage can be." The legal paper is a signal of intention to the public, and gives both partners a sense of security. It is a gesture that assures both people that each intends to invest in the union. Each has, in a sense, bought legal stock in it. It may be that some people relax too much after acquiring this piece of paper. Nevertheless, it does mean that both partners will have to think twice before they walk out, because to nullify the paper requires an extraordinary amount of time and energy and recrimination.

Many times people prefer marriage because they want to reproduce the situation in which they grew up, and they feel nervous about living alone. "I didn't feel self-sufficient enough or secure," a woman told me. "I had always lived with people: first my family, then a husband. Living alone was frightening to me. But it was better than staying in a bad marriage. Women, though, are braver now. They don't feel so self-conscious."

There are, however, those who decide not to marry again, at least for a while. One woman said she could not afford remarriage because she would lose so much alimony if she changed her status. Marriage for her and her boy friend would be financially impossible. Another woman worried about remarrying because of "the tremendous amount of baggage you bring with you, not just the kids, but the scars, some raw." She thought she would marry when her children were older. Jane Spock, in her *Times* interview, said she thought about getting married again but decided not to. "What I might like to do, though, is just live with a man.

Now, that's very new for me to say that. Two years ago I would have said, 'Marriage and security.' But I don't think I want the hurt of a man leaving again." Some women, of course, would like to remarry but simply can't find a suitable man, a matter made more difficult because there are not many available in her age range—her own age or slightly older—to choose from.

What's Important the Second Time

As people themselves change when they come through a divorce, the things they expect out of a marriage change as well. Remarried people have a sharp awareness of each other's needs and weaknesses. They minister to the needs and avoid the rough spots. They don't just blunder along; they pick their way more consciously and carefully. Different things are important to them in the second marriage, just as different qualities are important to them in the new spouse. "I was dominated by my former husband. In my first marriage we did things for effect. In my second marriage, warmth and friendship are more important. There's a relaxed attitude, an informal life-style. I don't want sophistication any more. Money and success are less important."

Another woman pointed out that "the second time you are more practical. Now I know marriage isn't going to be perfect." In remarriage, the expectations are more realistic. People have a greater understanding of what is possible to ask of another person and what is too much. They are no longer looking for perfection. The quality of life is far more crucial than materialistic concerns. Closeness and companionship are more important, and by this I mean true friendship. People told me they were not only *in love,* but actually *liked* their new husbands and wives. They were great friends as well as lovers, and they were not competitors.

Perhaps because the quality of one's marriage becomes more important, because one does not feel trapped, because one knows what one wants and can express it more easily, people the second time are more willing, in many cases, to break up a marriage they don't like. There are other options to consider, a greater variety of accepted life-styles to try. The changing values of society have made the traditional institution of marriage less important. Attitudes toward marriage and the family have become more fluid, more understanding. There is a single society for those who divorce and don't remarry; there are a growing number of one-parent families; there are more career women who support them- selves and live the way they choose—all of which make divorce less frightening. And there are many people to talk to now—marriage counselors, singles groups, encounter groups, and consciousness-raising sessions. There are even neighborhood groups of women who just get together to talk about what they want out of life, or whether their husbands know how to satisfy them sexually. Second marriages may be better or worse than first marriages, but one thing is certain: they are quite different. There are often more difficult problems than were at first imagined, but no one I interviewed regretted having taken the step a second time. For most of them, the benefits far outweighed any problems. In retrospect, many of the couples saw their first marriages as a kind of training school, somewhat similar to the college they had left with academic degrees but little knowledge of themselves. Divorces were their diplomas. All agreed that a second marriage was the "real thing" at last. They had entered it with much clearer ideas regarding the things that really mattered, whether those things were love, friendship, understanding, or sex.

Remarriage as an Incomplete Institution[1]
Andrew Cherlin

The higher divorce rate for remarriages after divorce than for first marriages, it is argued, is due to the incomplete institutionalization of remarriage after divorce in the United States. Persons who are remarried after a divorce and have children from previous marriages face problems unlike those encountered in first marriages. The institution of the family provides no standard solutions to many of these problems, with the result that the unity of families of remarriages after divorce often becomes precarious. The incomplete institutionalization of remarriage shows us, by way of contrast, that family unity in first marriages is still supported by effective institutional controls, despite claims that the institutional nature of family life has eroded in the 20th century. Some suggestions for future research on remarriage and on the institutionalization of married life are presented.

■   Sociologists believe that social institutions shape people's behavior in important ways. Gerth and Mills (1953, p. 173) wrote that institutions are organizations of social roles which "imprint their stamps upon the individual, modifying his external conduct as well as his inner life." More recently, Berger and Luckmann (1966) argued that institutions define not only acceptable behavior, as Gerth and Mills believed, but also objective

Reprinted from "Remarriage as an Incomplete Institution" by Andrew Cherlin from AMERICAN JOURNAL OF SOCIOLOGY, vol. 84, no. 3, November 1978 by permission of The University of Chicago Press. Copyright © 1978 by The University of Chicago.

reality itself. Social institutions range from political and economic systems to religion and language. And displayed prominently in any sociologist's catalogue of institutions is a fundamental form of social organization, the family.

The institution of the family provides social control of reproduction and child rearing. It also provides family members with guidelines for proper behavior in everyday family life, and, presumably, these guidelines contribute to the unity and stability of families. But in recent years, sociologists have de-emphasized the institutional basis of family unity in the United States. According to many scholars, contemporary families are held together more by consensus and mutual affection than by formal, institutional controls.

The main source of this viewpoint is an influential text by Ernest Burgess and Harvey Locke which appeared in 1945. They wrote:

The central thesis of this volume is that the family in historical times has been, and at present is, in transition from an institution to a companionship. In the past, the important factors unifying the family have been external, formal, and authoritarian, as the law, the mores, public opinion, tradition, the authority of the family head, rigid discipline, and elaborate ritual. At present, in the new emerging form of the companionship family, its unity inheres less and less in community pressures and more and more in such interpersonal relationships as the mutual affection, the sympathetic understanding, and the comradeship of its members. [P. vii]

In the institutional family, Burgess and Locke stated, unity derived from the unchallenged authority of the patriarch, who was supported by strong social pressure. But, they argued, with urbanization and the decline of patriarchal authority, a democratic family has emerged which creates its own unity from interpersonal relations.

Many subsequent studies have retained the idea of the companionship family in some form, such as the equalitarian family of Blood and Wolfe (1960) or the symmetrical family of Young and Wilmott (1973). Common to all is the notion that patriarchal authority has declined and sex roles have become less segregated. Historical studies of family life demonstrate that the authority of the husband was indeed stronger in the preindustrial West than it is now (see, e.g., Ariès 1962; Shorter 1975). As for today, numerous studies of "family power" have attempted to show that authority and power are shared more equally between spouses (see Blood and Wolfe 1960). Although these studies have been criticized (Safilios-Rothschild 1970), no one has claimed that patriarchal authority is as strong now as the historical record indicates it once was. Even if we believe that husbands still have more authority than wives, we can nevertheless agree that patriarchal authority seems to have declined in the United States in this century.

But it does not follow that institutional sources of family unity have declined also. Burgess and Locke reached this conclusion in part because of their assumption that the patriarch was the transmitter of social norms and values to his family. With the decline of the patriarch, so they believed, a vital institutional link between family and society was broken. This argument is similar to the perspective of Gerth and Mills, who wrote that a set of social roles becomes an institution when it is stabilized by a "head" who wields authority over the members. It follows from this premise that if the head loses his authority, the institutional nature of family life will become problematic.

Yet institutionalized patterns of behavior clearly persist in family life, despite the trend away from patriarchy and segregated sex roles. As others have noted (Dyer and Urban 1958; Nye and Berardo 1973), the equalitarian pattern may be as firmly institutionalized now as the traditional pattern was in the past. In the terms of Berger and Luckmann, most family behavior today is habitualized action which is accepted as typical by all members—that is, it is institutionalized behavior. In most everyday situations, parents and children base their behavior on social norms: parents know how harshly to discipline their children, and children learn from parents and friends which parental rules are fair and which to protest. These sources of institutionalization in the contemporary American family have received little attention from students of family unity, just as family members themselves pay little attention to them.

The presence of these habitualized patterns directly affects family unity. "Habitualization," Berger and Luckmann wrote, "carries with it the important psychological gain that choices are narrowed" (1966, p. 53). With choices narrowed, family members face fewer decisions which will cause disagreements and, correspondingly, have less difficulty maintaining family unity. Thus, institutional support for family unity exists through the routinization of everyday behavior even though the husband is no longer the unchallenged agent of social control.

Nowhere in contemporary family life is the psychological gain from habitualization more evident than in the families of remarried spouses and their children, where, paradoxically, habitualized behavior is often absent. We know that the unity of families of remarriages which follow a divorce is often precarious—as evidenced by the higher divorce rate for these families than for families of first marriages (U.S. Bureau of the Census 1976). And in the last few decades, remarriage after divorce—as opposed to remarriage after widowhood—has become the predominant form of remarriage. In this paper, I will argue that the higher divorce rate for remarriages after divorce is a consequence of the incomplete institutionalization of remarriage after divorce in our society. The institution of the family in the United States has developed in response to the needs of families of first marriages and families of remarriages after widowhood. But because of their complex structure, families of remarriages after divorce that include children from previous marriages must solve problems unknown to other types of families. For many of these problems, such as proper kinship terms, authority to discipline stepchildren, and legal relationships, no institutionalized solutions have emerged. As a result, there is more opportunity for disagreements and divisions among family members and more strain in many remarriages after divorce.

The incomplete institutionalization of remarriage after divorce reveals, by way of contrast, the high degree of institutionalization still present in first marriages. Family members, especially those in first marriages, rely on a wide range of habitualized behaviors to assist them in solving the common problems of family life. We take these behavioral patterns for granted until their absence forces us to create solutions on our own. Only then do we see the continuing importance of institutionalized patterns of family behavior for maintaining family unity.

I cannot provide definitive proof of the hypothesis linking the higher divorce rate for remarriages after divorce to incomplete institutionalization. There is very little quantitative information concerning remarriages. In fact, we do not even know how many stepparents and stepchildren there are in the United States. Nor has there ever been a large, random-sample survey designed with families of remarriages in mind. (Bernard's 1956 book on remarriage, for example, was based on information supplied nonrandomly by third parties.) There are, nevertheless, several studies which do provide valuable information, and there is much indirect evidence bearing on the plausibility of this hypothesis and of alternative explanations. I will review this evidence, and I will also refer occasionally to information I collected through personal interviews with a small, nonrandom sample of remarried couples and family counselors in the northeast. Despite the lack of data, I believe that the problems of families of remarriages are worth examining, especially given the recent increases in divorce and remarriage rates. In the hope that this article will stimulate further investigations, I will also present suggestions for future research.

The Problem of Family Unity

Remarriages have been common in the United States since its beginnings, but until this century almost all remarriages followed widowhood. In the Plymouth Colony, for instance, about one-third of all men and one-quarter of all women who lived full lifetimes remarried after the death of a spouse, but there was little divorce (Demos 1970). Even as late as the 1920s, more brides and grooms were remarrying after widowhood than after divorce, according to estimates by Jacobson (1959). Since then, however, a continued increase in divorce (Norton and Glick 1976) has altered this pattern. By 1975, 84% of all brides who were remarrying were previously divorced, and 16% were widowed. For grooms who were remarrying in 1975, 86% were previously divorced (U.S. National Center for Health Statistics 1977). Thus, it is only recently that remarriage after divorce has become the predominant form of remarriage.

And since the turn of the century, remarriages after divorce have increased as a proportion of all marriages. In 1900 only 3% of all brides—including both the single and previously married—were divorced (Jacobson 1959). In 1930, 9% of all brides were divorced (Jacobson 1959), and in 1975, 25% of all brides were divorced (U.S. National Center for Health Statistics 1977). As a result, in 7 million families in 1970 one or both spouses had remarried after a divorce (U.S. Bureau of the Census 1973). Most of this increase is due to the rise in the divorce rate, but some part is due to the greater tendency of divorced and widowed adults to remarry. The remarriage rate for divorced and widowed women was about 50% higher in the mid-1970s than in 1940 (Norton and Glick 1976).

At the same time, the percentage of divorces which involved at least one child increased from 46% in 1950 to 60% in 1974 (U.S. National Center for Health Statistics 1953, 1977). The increase in the percentage of divorces which involve children means that more families of remarriages after divorce now have stepchildren. Although it is not possible with available data to calculate the exact number of families with stepchildren, we do know that in 1970 8.9 million children lived in two-parent families where one or both parents had been previously divorced (U.S. Bureau of the Census 1973). Some of these children—who constituted 15% of all children living in two-parent families—were from previous marriages, and others were from the remarriages.

Can these families of remarriages after divorce, many of which include children from previous marriages, maintain unity as well as do families of first marriages? Not according to the divorce rate. A number of studies have shown a greater risk of separation and divorce for remarriages after divorce (Becker, Landes, and Michael 1976; Bumpass and Sweet 1972; Cherlin 1977; Monahan 1958). Remarriages after widowhood appear, in contrast, to have a lower divorce rate than first marriages (Monahan 1958). A recent Bureau of the Census report (U.S. Bureau of the Census 1976) estimated that about 33% of all first marriages among people 25–35 may end in divorce, while about 40% of remarriages after divorce among people this age may end in divorce. The estimates are based on current rates of divorce, which could, of course, change greatly in the future.[2]

Conventional wisdom, however, seems to be that remarriages are more successful than first marriages. In a small, nonrandom sample of family counselors and remarried couples, I found most to be surprised at the news that divorce was more prevalent in remarriages. There are some plausible reasons for this popular misconception. Those who remarry are older, on the average, than those marrying for the first time and are presumably more mature. They have had more time to search the marriage market and to determine their own needs and preferences. In addition, divorced men may be in a better financial position and command greater work skills than younger, never-married men. (Divorced women who are supporting children, however, are often in a worse financial position—see Hoffman [1977].)

But despite these advantages, the divorce rate is higher in remarriages after divorce. The reported differences are often modest, but they appear consistently throughout 20 years of research. And the meaning of marital dissolution for family unity is clear: when a marriage dissolves, unity ends. The converse, though, is not necessarily true: a family may have a low degree of unity but remain nominally intact. Even with this limitation, I submit that the divorce rate is the best objective indicator of differences in family unity between remarriages and first marriages.

There are indicators of family unity other than divorce, but their meaning is less clear and their measurement is more difficult. There is the survey research tradition, for example, of asking people how happy or satisfied they are with their marriages. The invariable result is that almost everyone reports that they are very happy. (See, e.g., Bradburn and Caplovitz 1965; Glenn 1975; Campbell, Converse, and Rodgers 1976.) It may be that our high rate of divorce increases the general level of marital satisfaction by dissolving unsatisfactory marriages. But it is also possible that the satisfaction ratings are inflated by the reluctance of some respondents to admit that their marriages are less than fully satisfying. Marriage is an important part of life for most adults—the respondents in the Campbell et al. (1976) national sample rated it second only to health as the most important aspect of their lives—and people may be reluctant to admit publicly that their marriage is troubled.

Several recent studies, nevertheless, have shown that levels of satisfaction and happiness are lower among the remarried, although the differences typically are small. Besides the Campbell et al. study, these include Glenn and Weaver (1977), who found modest differences in marital happiness in the 1973, 1974, and 1975 General Social Surveys conducted by the National Opinion Research Center. They reported that for women, the difference between those who were remarried and those who were in a first marriage was statistically significant, while for men the difference was smaller and not significant. In addition, Renne (1971) reported that remarried, previously divorced persons were less happy with their marriages than those in first marriages in a probability sample of 4,452 Alameda County, California, households. Again, the differences were modest, but they were consistent within categories of age, sex, and race. No tests of significance were reported.

The higher divorce rate suggests that maintaining family unity is more difficult for families of remarriages after divorce. And the lower levels of marital satisfaction, which must be interpreted cautiously, also support this hypothesis. It is true, nevertheless, that many remarriages work well, and that the majority of remarriages will not end in divorce. And we must remember that the divorce rate is also at an all-time high for first marriages. But there is a difference of degree between remarriages and first marriages which appears consistently in research. We must ask why families of remarriages after divorce seem to have more difficulty maintaining family unity than do families of first marriages. Several explanations have been proposed, and we will now assess the available evidence for each.

Previous Explanations

One explanation, favored until recently by many psychiatrists, is that the problems of remarried people arise from personality disorders which preceded their marriages (see Bergler 1948). People in troubled marriages, according to this view, have unresolved personal conflicts which must be treated before a successful marriage can be achieved. Their problems lead them to marry second spouses who may be superficially quite different from their first spouse but are characterologically quite similar. As a result, this theory states, remarried people repeat the problems of their first marriages.

If this explanation were correct, one would expect that people in remarriages would show higher levels of psychiatric symptomatology than people in first marriages. But there is little evidence of this. On the contrary, Overall (1971) reported that in a sample of 2,000 clients seeking help for psychiatric problems, currently remarried people showed lower levels of psychopathology on a general rating scale than persons in first marriages and currently divorced persons. These findings, of course, apply only to people who sought psychiatric help. And it may be, as Overall noted, that the differences emerged because remarried people are more likely to seek help for less serious problems. The findings, nevertheless, weaken the psychoanalytic interpretation of the problems of remarried life.

On the other hand, Monahan (1958) and Cherlin (1977) reported that the divorce rate was considerably higher for people in their third marriages who had divorced twice than for people in their second marriages. Perhaps personality disorders among some of those who marry several times prevent them from achieving a successful marriage. But even with the currently high rates of divorce and remarriage, only a small proportion of all adults marry more than twice. About 10% of all adults in 1975 had married twice, but less than 2% had married three or more times (U.S. Bureau of the Census 1976).

Most remarried people, then, are in a second marriage. And the large number of people now divorcing and entering a second marriage also undercuts the psychoanalytic interpretation. If current rates hold, about one-third of all young married people will become divorced, and about four-fifths of these will remarry. It is hard to believe that the recent increases in divorce and remarriage are due to the sudden spread of marriage-threatening personality disorders to a large part of the young adult population. I conclude, instead, that the psychoanalytic explanation for the rise in divorce and the difficulties of remarried spouses and their children is at best incomplete.[3]

A second possible explanation is that once a person has divorced he or she is less hesitant to do so again. Having divorced once, a person knows how to get divorced and what to expect from family members, friends, and the courts. This explanation is plausible and probably accounts for some of the difference in divorce rates. But it does not account for all of the research findings on remarriage, such as the finding of Becker et al. (1976) that the presence of children from a previous marriage increased the probability of divorce for women in remarriages, while the presence of children from the new marriage reduced the probability of divorce. I will discuss the implications of this study below, but let me note here that a general decrease in the reluctance of remarried persons to divorce would not explain this finding. Moreover, the previously divorced may be more hesitant to divorce again because of the stigma attached to divorcing twice. Several remarried people I interviewed expressed great reluctance to divorce a second time. They reasoned that friends and relatives excused one divorce but would judge them incompetent at marriage after two divorces.

Yet another explanation for the higher divorce rate is the belief that many remarried men are deficient at fulfilling their economic responsibilities. We know that divorce is more likely in families where the husband has low earnings (Goode 1956). Some remarried men, therefore, may be unable to earn a sufficient amount of money to support a family. It is conceivable that this inability to be a successful breadwinner could account for all of the divorce rate differential, but statistical studies of divorce suggest otherwise. Three recent multivariate analyses of survey data on divorce have shown that remarried persons still had a higher probability of divorce or separation, independent of controls for such socioeconomic variables as husband's earnings (Becker et al. 1976), husband's educational attainment (Bumpass and Sweet 1972), and husband's and wife's earnings, employment status, and savings (Cherlin 1977). These analyses show that controlling for low earnings can reduce the difference in divorce probabilities, but they also show that low earnings cannot fully explain the difference. It is possible, nevertheless, that a given amount of income must be spread thinner in many remarriages, because of child-support or alimony payments (although the remarried couple also may be receiving these payments). But this type of financial strain must be distinguished from the questionable notion that many remarried husbands are inherently unable to provide for a wife and children.

Institutional Support

The unsatisfactory nature of all these explanations leads us to consider one more interpretation. I hypothesize that the difficulties of couples in remarriages after divorce stem from a lack of institutionalized guidelines for solving many common problems of their remarried life. The lack of institutional support is less serious when neither spouse has a child from a previous marriage. In this case, the family of remarriage closely resembles families of first marriages, and most of the norms for first marriages apply. But when at least one spouse has children from a previous marriage, family life often differs sharply from first marriages. Frequently, as I will show, family members face problems quite unlike those in first marriages—problems for which institutionalized solutions do not exist. And without accepted solutions to their problems, families of remarriages must resolve difficult issues by themselves. As a result, solving everyday problems is sometimes impossible without engendering conflict and confusion among family members.

The complex structure of families of remarriages after divorce which include children from a previous marriage has been noted by others (Bernard 1956; Bohannan 1970; Duberman 1975). These families are expanded in the number of social roles and relationships they possess and also are expanded in space over more than one household. The additional social roles include stepparents, stepchildren, stepsiblings, and the new spouses of noncustodial parents, among others. And the links between the households are the children of previous marriages. These children are commonly in the custody of one parent—usually the mother—but they normally visit the noncustodial parent regularly. Thus they promote communication among the divorced parents, the new stepparent, and the noncustodial parent's new spouse.

Family relationships can be quite complex, because the new kin in a remarriage after divorce do not, in general, replace the kin from the first marriage as they do in a remarriage after widowhood. Rather, they add to the existing kin (Fast and Cain 1966). But this complexity alone does not necessarily imply that problems of family unity will develop. While families of remarriages may appear complicated to Americans, there are many societies in which complicated kinship rules and family patterns coexist with a functioning, stable family system (Bohannan 1963; Fox 1967).

In most of these societies, however, familial roles and relationships are well defined. Family life may seem complex to Westerners, but activity is regulated by established patterns of behavior. The central difference, then, between families of remarriages in the United States and complicated family situations in other societies is the lack of institutionalized social regulation of remarried life in this country. Our society, oriented toward first marriages, provides little guidance on problems peculiar to remarriages, especially remarriages after divorce.

In order to illustrate the incomplete institutionalization of remarriage and its consequences for family life, let us examine two of the major institutions in society: language and the law. "Language," Gerth and Mills (1953, p. 305) wrote, "is necessary to the operations of institutions. For the symbols used in institutions coordinate the roles that compose them, and justify the enactment of these roles by the members of the institution." Where no adequate terms exist for an important social role, the institutional support for this role is deficient, and general acceptance of the role as a legitimate pattern of activity is questionable.

Consider English terms for the roles peculiar to remarriage after divorce. The term "stepparent," Bohannan (1970) has observed, originally meant a person who replaced a dead parent, not a person who was an additional parent. And the negative connotations of the "stepparent," especially the "stepmother," are well known (Bernard 1956: Smith 1953). Yet there are no other terms in use. In some situations, no term exists for a child to use in addressing a stepparent. If the child calls her mother "mom," for example, what should she call her stepmother? This lack of appropriate terms for parents in remarriages after divorce can have negative consequences for family functioning. In one family I interviewed, the wife's children wanted to call their stepfather "dad," but the stepfather's own children who also lived in the household, refused to allow this usage. To them, sharing the term "dad" represented a threat to their claim on their father's attention and affection. The dispute caused bad feelings, and it impaired the father's ability to act as a parent to all the children in the household.

For more extended relationships, the lack of appropriate terms is even more acute. At least the word "stepparent," however inadequate, has a widely accepted meaning. But there is no term a child living with his mother can use to describe his relationship to the woman his father remarried after he divorced the child's mother. And, not surprisingly, the rights and duties of the child and this woman toward each other are unclear. Nor is the problem limited to kinship terms. Suppose a child's parents both remarry and he alternates between their households under a joint custody arrangement. Where, then, is his "home"? And who are the members of his "family"? These linguistic inadequacies correspond to the absence of widely accepted definitions for many of the roles and relationships in families of remarriage. The absence of proper terms is both a symptom and a cause of some of the problems of remarried life.

As for the law, it is both a means of social control and an indicator of accepted patterns of behavior. It was to the law, for instance, that Durkheim turned for evidence on the forms of social solidarity. When we examine family law, we find a set of traditional guidelines, based on precedent, which define the rights and duties of family members. But as Weitzman (1974) has shown, implicit in the precedents is the assumption that the marriage in question is a first marriage. For example, Weitzman found no provisions for several problems of remarriage, such as balancing the financial obligations of husbands to their spouses and children from current and previous marriages, defining the wife's obligations to husbands and children from the new and the old marriages, and reconciling the competing claims of current and ex-spouses for shares of the estate of a deceased spouse.

Legal regulations concerning incest and consanguineal marriage are also inadequate for families of remarriages. In all states marriage and sexual relations are prohibited between persons closely related by blood, but in many states these restrictions do not cover sexual relations or marriage between other family members in a remarriage—between a stepmother and a stepson, for example, or between two stepchildren (Goldstein and Katz 1965). Mead (1970), among others, has argued that incest taboos serve the important function of allowing children to develop affection for and identification with other family members without the risk of sexual exploitation. She suggested that current beliefs about incest—as embodied in law and social norms—fail to provide adequate security and protection for children in households of remarriage.[4]

The law, then, ignores the special problems of families of remarriages after divorce. It assumes, for the most part, that remarriages are similar to first marriages. Families of remarriages after divorce, consequently, often must deal with problems such as financial obligations or sexual relations without legal regulations or clear legal precedent. The law, like the language, offers incomplete institutional support to families of remarriages.

In addition, other customs and conventions of family life are deficient when applied to remarriages after divorce. Stepparents, for example, have difficulty determining their proper disciplinary relationship to stepchildren. One woman I interviewed, determined not to show favoritism toward her own children, disciplined them more harshly than her stepchildren. Other couples who had children from the wife's previous marriage reported that the stepfather had difficulty establishing himself as a disciplinarian in the household. Fast and Cain (1966), in a study of about 50 case records from child-guidance settings, noted many uncertainties among stepparents about appropriate role behavior. They theorized that the uncertainties derived from the sharing of the role of parent between the stepparent and the non-custodial, biological parent. Years ago, when most remarriages took place after widowhood, this sharing did not exist. Now, even though most remarriages follow divorce, generally accepted guidelines for sharing parenthood still have not emerged.

There is other evidence consistent with the idea that the incomplete institutionalization of remarriage after divorce may underlie the difficulties of families of remarriages. Becker et al. (1976) analyzed the Survey of Economic Opportunity, a nationwide study of approximately 30,000 households. As I mentioned above, they found that the presence of children from a previous marriage increased the probability of divorce for women in remarriages, while the presence of children from the new marriage reduced the probability of divorce. This is as we would expect, since children from a previous marriage expand the family across households and complicate the structure of family roles and relationships. But children born into the new marriage bring none of these complications. Consequently, only children from a previous marriage should add to the special problems of families of remarriages.[5]

In addition, Goetting (1978a, 1978b) studied the attitudes of remarried people toward relationships among adults who are associated by broken marital ties, such as ex-spouses and the people ex-spouses remarry. Bohannan (1970) has called these people "quasi-kin." Geotting presented hypothetical situations involving the behavior of quasi-kin to 90 remarried men and 90 remarried women who were white, previously divorced, and who had children from previous marriages. The subjects were asked to approve, disapprove, or express indifference about the behavior in each situation. Goetting then arbitrarily decided that the respondents reached "consensus" on a given situation if any of the three possible response categories received more than half of all responses. But even by this lenient definition, consensus was not reached on the proper behavior in most of the hypothetical situations. For example, in situations involving conversations between a person's present spouse and his or her ex-spouse, the only consensus of the respondents was that the pair should say "hello." Beyond that, there was no consensus on whether they should engage in polite conversation in public places or on the telephone or whether the ex-spouse should be invited into the new spouse's home while waiting to pick up his or her children. Since meetings of various quasi-kin must occur regularly in the lives of most respondents, their disagreement is indicative of their own confusion about how to act in common family situations.

Still, there are many aspects of remarried life which are similar to life in first marriages, and these are subject to established rules of behavior. Even some of the unique aspects of remarriage may be regulated by social norms—such as the norms concerning the size and nature of wedding ceremonies in remarriages (Hollingshead 1952). Furthermore, as Goode (1956) noted, remarriage is itself an institutional solution to the ambiguous status of the divorced (and not remarried) parent. But the day-to-day life of remarried adults and their children also includes many problems for which there are no institutionalized solutions. And since members of a household of remarriage often have competing or conflicting interests (Bernard 1956), the lack of consensual solutions can make these problems more serious than they otherwise would be. One anthropologist, noting the lack of relevant social norms, wrote, "the present situation approaches chaos, with each individual set of families having to work out its own destiny without any realistic guidelines" (Bohannan 1970, p. 137).

Discussion and Suggestions for Research

The lack of institutionalized support for remarriage after divorce from language, the law, and custom is apparent. But when institutional support for family life exists, we take it for granted. People in first marriages rarely stop to notice that a full set of kinship terms exists, that the law regulates their relationships, or that custom dictates much of their behavior toward spouses and children. Because they pay little attention to it, the institutional nature of everyday life in first marriages can be easily underestimated. But such support contributes to the unity of first marriages despite the decline of the patriarch, who was the agent of social control in past time. Institutional guidelines become manifest not only through the transmission of social pressure by a family head but also through the general acceptance of certain habitual behavior patterns as typical of family life. Since this latter process is an ongoing characteristic of social life, the pure "companionship" family—which, in fairness, Burgess and Locke defined only as an ideal type—will never emerge. We have seen this by examining the contrasting case of remarriage after divorce. In this type of marriage, institutional support is noticeably lacking in several respects, and this deficiency has direct consequences for proper family functioning. I have tried to show how the incomplete institutionalization of remarriage after divorce makes the maintenance of family unity more difficult.

Notes

1. I wish to thank Doris Entwisle, George Levinger, Valerie Oppenheimer, and Richard Rubinson for comments on earlier drafts.
2. A study by McCarthy (1977), however, suggests that remarriages may be more stable than first marriages for blacks. Using life-table techniques on data from 10,000 women under age 45 collected in the 1973 Survey of Family Growth, McCarthy reported that the probability of separation and divorce during the first 15 years of marriage is lower for blacks in remarriages than in first marriages, but is about 50% higher for whites in remarriages than for whites in first marriages.
3. Despite the lack of convincing evidence, I am reluctant to discount this explanation completely. Clinical psychologists and psychiatrists with whom I have talked insist that

many troubled married persons they have treated had made the same mistakes twice and were in need of therapy to resolve long-standing problems. Their clinical experience should not be ignored, but this "divorce-proneness" syndrome seems inadequate as a complete explanation for the greater problems of remarried people.

4. Bernard (1956) noted this problem in the preface to the reprinted edition of her book on remarriage. "Institutional patterns," she wrote, "are needed to help remarried parents establish relationships with one another conducive to the protection of their children."

5. In an earlier paper (Cherlin 1977), I found that children affected the probability that a woman in a first marriage or remarriage would divorce only when the children were of preschool age. But the National Longitudinal Surveys of Mature Women, from which this analysis was drawn, contained no information about whether the children of remarried wives were from the woman's previous or current marriage. Since the Becker et al. (1976) results showed that this distinction is crucial, we cannot draw any relevant inferences about children and remarriage from my earlier study.

References

Ariès, Phillippe. 1962. *Centuries of Childhood.* New York: Knopf.

Becker, G., E. Landes, and R. Michael. 1976. "Economics of Marital Instability." Working Paper no. 153. Stanford, Calif.: National Bureau of Economic Research.

Berger, Peter L., and Thomas Luckmann. 1966. *The Social Construction of Reality.* New York: Doubleday.

Bergler, Edmund. 1948. *Divorce Won't Help.* New York: Harper & Bros.

Bernard, Jessie. 1956. *Remarriage.* New York: Dryden.

Blood, Robert O., and Donald M. Wolfe. 1960. *Husbands and Wives.* New York: Free Press.

Bohannan, Paul. 1963. *Social Anthropology.* New York: Holt, Rinehart & Winston.

———. 1970. "Divorce Chains, Households of Remarriage, and Multiple Divorces." Pp. 127–39 in *Divorce and After,* edited by Paul Bohannan. New York: Doubleday.

Bradburn, Norman, and David Caplovitz. 1965. *Reports on Happiness.* Chicago: Aldine.

Bumpass, L. L., and A. Sweet. 1972. "Differentials in Marital Instability: 1970." *American Sociological Review* 37 (December): 754–66.

Burgess, Ernest W., and Harvey J. Locke. 1945. *The Family: From Institution to Companionship.* New York: American.

Campbell, Angus, Phillip E. Converse, and Willard L. Rodgers. 1976. *The Quality of American Life.* New York: Russell Sage.

Cherlin, A. 1977. "The Effects of Children on Marital Dissolution." *Demography* 14 (August): 265–72.

Demos, John. 1970. *A Little Commonwealth: Family Life in Plymouth Colony.* New York: Oxford University Press.

Duberman, Lucile. 1975. *The Reconstituted Family.* Chicago; Nelson-Hall.

Dyer, W. G., and D. Urban. 1958. "The Institutionalization of Equalitarian Family Norms." *Journal of Marriage and Family Living* 20 (February): 53–58.

Fast, I., and A. C. Cain. 1966. "The Stepparent Role: Potential for Disturbances in Family Functioning." *American Journal of Orthopsychiatry* 36 (April): 485–91.

Fox, Robin. 1967. *Kinship and Marriage.* Baltimore: Penguin.

Gerth, Hans, and C. Wright Mills. 1953. *Character and Social Structure.* New York: Harcourt, Brace & Co.

Glenn, N. 1975. "The Contribution of Marriage to the Psychological Well-Being of Males and Females." *Journal of Marriage and the Family* 37 (August): 594–601.

Glenn, N., and C. Weaver. 1977. "The Marital Happiness of Remarried Divorced Persons." *Journal of Marriage and the Family* 39 (May) 331–37.

Goetting, Ann. 1978a. "The Normative Integration of the Former Spouse Relationship."
    Paper presented at the annual meeting of the American Sociological Association, San
    Francisco, September 4–8.

———. 1978b. "The Normative Integration of Two Divorce Chain Relationships." Paper
    presented at the annual meeting of the Southwestern Sociological Association,
    Houston, April 12–15.

Goldstein, Joseph, and Jay Katz. 1965. *The Family and the Law.* New York: Free Press.

Goode, William J. 1956. *Women in Divorce.* New York: Free Press.

Hoffman, S. 1977. "Marital Instability and the Economic Status of Women." *Demography*
    14 (February): 67–76.

Hollingshead, A. B. 1952. "Marital Status and Wedding Behavior." *Marriage and Family
    Living* (November), pp. 308–11.

Jacobson, Paul H. 1959. *American Marriage and Divorce.* New York: Rinehart.

McCarthy, J. F. 1977. "A Comparison of Dissolution of First and Second Marriages." Paper
    presented at the 1977 annual meeting of the Population Association of America, St.
    Louis, April 21–23.

Mead, M. 1970. "Anomalies in American Postdivorce Relationships." Pp. 107–25 in *Divorce
    and After,* edited by Paul Bohannan. New York: Doubleday.

Monahan, T. P. 1958. "The Changing Nature and Instability of Remarriages." *Eugenics
    Quarterly* 5: 73–85.

Norton, A. J., and P. C. Glick. 1976. "Marital Instability: Past, Present, and Future." *Journal
    of Social Issues* 32 (Winter): 5–20.

Nye, F. Ivan, and Felix M. Berardo. 1973. *The Family: Its Structure and Interaction.* New
    York: Macmillan.

Overall, J. E. 1971. "Associations between Marital History and the Nature of Manifest
    Psychopathology." *Journal of Abnormal Psychology* 78 (2): 213–21.

Renne, K. S. 1971. "Health and Marital Experience in an Urban Population." *Journal of
    Marriage and the Family* 33 (May): 338–50.

Safilios-Rothschild, Constantina. 1970. "The Study of Family Power Structure: A Review
    1960–1969." *Journal of Marriage and the Family* 32 (November): 539–52.

Shorter, Edward. 1975. *The Making of the Modern Family.* New York: Basic.

Smith, William C. 1953. *The Stepchild.* Chicago: University of Chicago Press.

U.S. Bureau of the Census. 1973. *U.S Census of the Population: 1970. Persons by Family
    Characteristics.* Final Report PC(2)–4B. Washington, D.C.: Government Printing Office.

———. 1976. *Number, Timing, and Duration of Marriages and Divorces in the United
    States: June 1975.* Current Population Reports, Series P–20, No. 297. Washington,
    D.C.; Government Printing Office.

U.S. National Center for Health Statistics. 1953. *Vital Statistics of the United States,
    1950.* Vol. 2. *Marriage, Divorce, Natality, Fetal Mortality, and Infant Mortality Data.*
    Washington, D.C.: Government Printing Office.

———. 1977. *Vital Statistics Report. Advance Report. Final Marriage Statistics, 1975.*
    Washington, D.C.: Government Printing Office.

Weitzman, L. J. 1974. "Legal Regulation of Marriage: Tradition and Change." *California
    Law Review* 62:1169–1288.

Young, Michael, and Peter Wilmott. 1973. *The Symmetrical Family.* New York: Pantheon.

CORRELATION CHART

CORRELATION CHART

This chart is provided as a guide for using *Relationships: The Marriage and Family Reader* in conjunction with the marriage and family textbooks listed below. The left-hand column lists the parts of *Relationships: The Marriage and Family Reader*. The numbers in the other columns indicate the chapter numbers that relate to these parts.

Clayton, Richard R. *The Family, Marriage and Social Change.* 2nd ed. New York: D. C. Heath, 1979.

Gagnon, John H., and Cathy S. Greenblat. *Life Designs: Individuals, Marriages, and Families.* Glenview, Ill.: Scott, Foresman, 1978.

Kelley, Robert. *Courtship, Marriage and the Family.* 3rd ed. New York: Harcourt Brace Jovanovich, 1979.

Knox, David. *Exploring Marriage and the Family.* Glenview, Ill.: Scott, Foresman, 1979.

Leslie, Gerald R. *The Family in Social Context.* 4th ed. New York: Oxford University Press, 1979.

Melville, Keith. *Marriage and Family Today.* 2nd ed. New York: Random House, 1980.

Orthner, Dennis K. *Intimate Relationships: An Introduction to Marriage and the Family.* Reading, Mass.: Addison-Wesley, 1981.

Saxton, Lloyd. *The Individual, Marriage and the Family.* 4th ed. Belmont, Calif.: Wadsworth, 1980.

Skolnick, Arlene. *The Intimate Environment: Exploring Marriage and the Family.* 2nd ed. Boston: Little, Brown, 1978.

Part	Clayton	Gagnon & Greenblat	Kelley	Knox	Leslie	Melville	Orthner	Saxton	Skolnick
1 Families in Social Perspective									
Precedents	1, 2	1	6	1	6	1	1	1	2, 3, 5
Prospects	4, 21	epilogue	2, 3	6	7	15	5	11	4, 13
Social Structure	3, 4	14	5, 6, 9	1, 2	1–5, 8	1	1	1, 7	5, 6
2 Courtship									
The Sexes	10	2, 3	4, 5	2, 4, 5	11, 12	2, 7	7	2, 3, 4	7
Attraction	9, 13	4, 5	3, 7	3, 7	12, 13	3	2, 6	4, 5	7
Involvements	10, 11, 12	6, 7	2, 8, 10	8, 9	13	4, 5	3, 4	5, 6, 8	8
3 Marriage									
Coping	14, 16	8, 9, 10, 15	11, 14	10, 12, 14	14	6, 9, 10	8, 9	1, 4, 9	9
Working	15, 18	12, 13	16, 13	11, 13	14	8	10, 11	9	
Belonging	5, 6, 7, 8	14	15	1	14	13	----	11	
4 Parenthood									
Parenting as a Social Issue	17	11	17, 18	15	15	12	12	12	
Early Parenting	17	----	19	16	15	12	13	13	
Later Parenting	17	----	20	17	16	12	15	----	
5 Aging									
Midlife	19	----	22	18	16, 19	11	15	----	
The Graying of American Families	19	----	22	18	19	1	16	----	
6 Rearranging									
Disruptions	20	17, 18	12	19	17	15	14, 16	----	
Divorce and Remarriage	20	16, 17, 18	21	19	17, 18	14	14	8, 10	